Praise for *An Illustrated Guide to AI Agents*

The authors are exceptional builders, and this book is a testament to the depth of their knowledge. The generous illustrations and hands-on TinyAgent exercise make the concepts approachable, intuitive, and fun to learn.

—*Chip Huyen, author of* AI Engineering *and* Designing Machine Learning Systems

I have thought a lot about how to teach AI systems, and this book still surprised me with how much of the domain of modern AI agents it could make clear through illustrations. Maarten and Jay do an impressive job identifying and explaining the timeless ideas in this fast-moving field, and I expect this to become the first book I recommend to anyone who wants to understand how modern agents work and how to build them.

—*Omar Khattab, assistant professor, MIT EECS*

Grootendorst and Alammar explain the entire AI agent stack, from tokenization to multi-agent systems, in an engaging visual style. As the field evolves, this book will continue to serve as a useful reference because it covers the subject matter so thoroughly.

—*Ofir Press, research scientist at Meta FAIR, coauthor of SWE-bench and SWE-agent*

Agents have become mainstream and are even approaching ubiquity over a very short period. They are poised to have a major impact on the global economy and the nature of future work. Who better to explain this new paradigm than the veteran duo of Maarten Grootendorst and Jay Alammar? This book has all the ingredients, bolstered by easy-to-understand illustrations and code, to help readers understand both the conceptual principles and practical know-how about one of the most consequential technologies of this decade.

—*Suhas Pai, cofounder and CTO of Hudson Labs, author of* Designing Large Language Model Applications

This book offers one of the clearest and most comprehensive explanations of the components that go into building AI agents, bridging cutting-edge research with practical system design in a way that is both rigorous, deeply usable, and accessible to practitioners.

—Sheldon Rodrigues, senior applied scientist, Microsoft

A beautifully crafted visual guide that makes the working of complex AI agents and the concepts around it intuitive, memorable, and genuinely enjoyable to explore.

—Lipi Deepaakshi Patnaik, software development engineer, Uber

An Illustrated Guide to AI Agents

Concepts and Code for Building Agents with LLMs, Tools, and Memory

Maarten Grootendorst and Jay Alammar

O'REILLY®

An Illustrated Guide to AI Agents
by Maarten Grootendorst and Jay Alammar

Published by O'Reilly Media, Inc., 141 Stony Circle, Suite 195, Santa Rosa, CA 95401.

O'Reilly books may be purchased for educational, business, or sales promotional use. Online editions are also available for most titles (*https://oreilly.com*). For more information, contact our corporate/institutional sales department: 800-998-9938 or *corporate@oreilly.com*.

Acquisitions Editor: Nicole Butterfield
Development Editor: Michele Cronin
Production Editor: Katherine Tozer
Copyeditor: Stephanie English
Proofreader: Emily Wydeven
Indexer: Krsta Technology Solutions
Cover Designer: Susan Brown
Cover Illustrator: José Marzan Jr.
Interior Designer: David Futato
Interior Illustrator: Kate Dullea
Flamingo designer: Ilse Grootendorst-Schellekens

September 2026: First Edition

Revision History for the First Edition
2026-09-02: First Release

See *https://oreilly.com/catalog/errata.csp?isbn=9798341662698* for release details.

979-8-341-66269-8

[LSI]

Table of Contents

Preface xi

Part I. The Anatomy of an AI Agent

1. Introduction **3**
- What Is an AI Agent? 4
  - Large Language Models 6
  - Reasoning Large Language Models 7
  - Augmenting the Large Language Model 10
  - An Agentic System 16
- Specializations 20
  - Multi-Agent Collaboration 21
  - The Multi-Modal Agent 22
  - The Coding Agent 24
- The TinyAgent 24
- Summary 29

2. Large Language Models **31**
- Part 1: What You Should Know About Large Language Models 33
  - Input and Output Tokens 33
  - From Language Modeling to Powering Agents 34
  - The TinyAgent 36
  - Training a Large Language Model 45
  - The Transformer Architecture 51
- Part 2: A Deeper Dive Into Large Language Models 64
  - How Self-Attention Works 64
  - KV-Caching Revisited 68

More Efficient Self-Attention 70
Mixture of Experts 73
Summary 80

3. Reasoning Large Language Models.... 83
The Paradigm Shift from Train-Time Compute to Test-Time Compute 86
Train-Time Compute Versus Test-Time Compute 86
Scaling Laws 89
Categories of Test-Time Compute 94
Reward Models 96
Prompt Engineering 98
Search Against Verifiers 102
Self-Consistency 104
Best-of-N Samples 106
Modifying Proposal Distribution 109
Supervised Fine-Tuning 111
Reinforcement Learning 114
Native Reasoning 120
Emerging Directions in Reasoning Research 122
Reasoning in Multi-Modal LLMs 122
Efficient Reasoning 125
Reasoning in Latent Space 127
Summary 130

4. Memory.... 131
Types of Memory 133
Short-Term Memory 135
Conversation Memory 135
Trimming 140
Summarization 142
Long-Term Memory 145
Retrieval-Augmented Generation 145
Agentic Retrieval-Augmented Generation 154
Context Engineering 161
Context Engineering for Multi-Agent Systems 166
Optimizing the Context 166
Context As the Specification 172
Summary 173

5. Tool Usage, Learning, and Protocols.... 175
Tool Usage 177
Tool Creation 179

Tool Definition 180
Tool Selection 185
Tool Calling 186
Tool Output Processing 188
TinyAgent with Tools 191
Tool Learning 195
In-Context Learning 196
Supervised Fine-tuning 197
Reinforcement Learning 201
TinyAgent with Native Tool-Calling Capabilities 206
Model Context Protocol 212
Core Components 215
The MCP Flow 216
Skills 218
The SKILL.md 219
The Bundled Resources 220
Summary 222

6. Planning and Reflection. 223
Planning 224
Task Decomposition 225
Action Sequencing 232
Agents That Continuously Improve 250
Reflection 250
Self-Improvement 254
Summary 260

7. Evaluating Agents. 261
Public Benchmarks and Leaderboards 262
Coding and Software Engineering 263
Tool Use 264
Software and Computer-Use Environments 264
Real-World Task Completion 264
Reasoning and Knowledge 265
Other Groups of Benchmarks 265
Reading Benchmark Scores Critically 266
Outcome Evaluation: Did the Agent Get the Right Output? 268
Human Evaluation 268
Automated Evaluation 270
Trajectory Evaluation: Did It Get There the Right Way? 282
Reliability: Does It Succeed Every Time? 283
Measuring Capability with pass@k 284

Measuring Reliability with pass^k 286
Safety: Does It Avoid Harm? 288
Building Your Own Evals 288
Summary 289

Part II. Specialized Agents

8. **Multi-Agent Systems** 293
The Multi-Agent System 294
Orchestrating Agents 297
Patterns 297
General-Purpose Frameworks for Collaborative Task-Solving Patterns 303
Communication Protocols 307
Agent Society 312
Emotional Intelligence 312
Simulations 315
Interactive Simulacra of Human Behavior 316
Deep Research Agents 321
Toward an AI Co-Scientist 322
Agent Laboratory 323
Summary 327

9. **Multi-Modal Understanding** 329
What Are Multi-Modal LLMs? 330
Encoding Modalities 333
Text 334
Images 337
Audio 340
Video 346
Many-Modality 356
Connecting Modalities 359
Projection-Based Connector 362
Query-Based Connector 365
Fusion-Based Connector 368
Advantages and Disadvantages 371
TinyAgent 371
Summary 375

10. **Code Agents and Code LLMs** 377
Users and Builders of Code Agents and Large Language Models 377
Building Code Agents 380

Code Agents to Serve Non-Coders 380
Code Tools 381
Context Management 391
Code Agents for Software Engineering 397
Task-Specific Workflows 400
Building Code LLMs 410
Summary 414

Afterword.... 417

Index.... 419

Preface

Something remarkable happened in the years following the broad public usage of large language models (LLMs): they stopped just talking and started doing. Given a goal, a set of tools, and a bit of memory, an LLM can now search the web, write and run code, revise its own plans, and work through problems over many steps with little hand-holding. We call these systems AI agents, and they represent one of the most consequential shifts in how work gets done and how software gets built.

This book provides a comprehensive and highly visual introduction to the world of AI agents, covering both the conceptual foundations and practical applications. We start with the "brain" of today's most powerful agents, the reasoning LLM, and then build the agent up piece by piece: memory, tools, planning, and reflection. From there we look at how agents behave as systems, how to evaluate them, and how they specialize, whether that means multiple agents collaborating, agents that can see and hear, or the coding agents that have become a staple of modern software development.

An Intuition-First Philosophy

The main goal of this book is to build intuition. The pace of development in AI agents is even more dizzying than that of the LLMs that power them. New frameworks, protocols, and architectures appear weekly, and keeping up can feel like a losing battle. Instead of chasing the latest releases, we focus on the fundamentals of agents, the components and principles that remain strikingly consistent underneath the churn, so that whatever comes next, you will have the mental models to understand it.

To achieve this, we return to the intuition-first philosophy of our previous book, *Hands-On Large Language Models*. The response to that book, from readers across industries, backgrounds, and languages, convinced us that visual, intuition-driven explanations are not a simplification of technical material but often the most direct path into it. So once again, we use visual language liberally. Hundreds of original illustrations give a visual identity to the major concepts and processes of agentic systems. One figure in particular, introduced in Chapter 1, serves as the foundation of the entire book. It shows the anatomy of an agent, and every subsequent chapter zooms into one of its components, so that by the end you will have assembled the complete picture piece by piece.

This book is about agents backed by LLMs. Other kinds of AI agents exist in practice, but rather than writing "LLM-backed AI agents" at every mention, we simply say AI agents and trust you to recall which kind we mean.

One more thing before we begin. The figures in this book are all custom made, and each went through more rounds of sketching, argument, and redrawing than we care to count before it earned its page. We worked this way because we were not assembling information for sale; we were making something for you, as carefully as we knew how. What we hope you do with it is a question we have saved for the afterword, on the very last page.

Building As You Read: The TinyAgent

Although "illustrated" is in the name of this book, understanding agents benefits greatly from building one. Alongside the visual journey, you will build a working agent in Python, one component at a time, which we call the `TinyAgent`. By the end of the book, it will reason, remember, use tools, plan, and reflect. The result is essentially a package you developed yourself, with a genuine understanding of every line in it.

The code printed in this book is here to teach; the code in the book's repository is here to run (*https://github.com/HandsOnLLM/An-Illustrated-Guide-To-AI-Agents*). While the pages of a book are fixed once printed, the repository is a living companion that we actively maintain with bug fixes, dependency updates, and adjustments as the libraries and APIs the examples rely on evolve. When you are ready to lean in and build, work from the repository rather than typing code from the page: you will get the current, tested version of every example, along with additional tutorials and material that did not fit in the book.

Audience

We wrote this book for several audiences at once, and we structured it so that each gets value from it:

- If you are a developer building agentic systems, the hands-on code and the `TinyAgent` you assemble across the chapters will give you a working foundation you understand down to the last line.

- If you come from a research or machine learning background, the deeper sections on model internals, training techniques, and evaluation methodology connect agent behavior back to how these models are actually made.
- If you are a technical leader, product builder, or curious reader who wants a rigorous mental model of agents without writing code, the illustrations and intuition-first explanations carry the full conceptual story on their own. The code can be skipped without losing the plot, or, fittingly, handed to your coding agent.

Where a chapter serves these audiences differently, we say so up front and tell you which parts you can skim. Whether you are encountering agents for the first time or already deploying them in production, we invite you to join us on this journey.

Prerequisites

What you need depends on how you plan to read this book. To follow the conceptual thread, the illustrations and intuition-first explanations, you need nothing beyond curiosity: no programming, no mathematics, and no prior exposure to agent frameworks. Familiarity with LLMs helps, but Chapters 2 and 3 cover everything about them that the rest of the book relies on.

To follow the hands-on thread and build the `TinyAgent` yourself, you will want some experience programming in Python. The deeper sections on model internals and training assume familiarity with the fundamentals of machine learning, though even there the focus is on building intuition rather than deriving equations.

If you are not familiar with Python, LearnPython.org, where you will find many tutorials on the basics of the language, is a great place to start. And to further ease the learning process, every example in this book can be run in the browser for free, without installing anything locally; see "Hardware and Software Requirements" on page xiv.

Book Structure

The book is divided into two parts:

Part 1: The Anatomy of an AI Agent
: In Part 1, we build a single agent from the ground up. Chapter 1 introduces the field and the core question, "What is an AI agent?," and presents the figure that anchors the rest of the book. Chapters 2 and 3 cover the agent's brain: how LLMs work (Chapter 2) and how reasoning LLMs extend them with the ability to think through problems before acting (Chapter 3). We then augment that brain with memory (Chapter 4) and with tools, including how tool use is standardized across models through the Model Context Protocol (Chapter 5). Chapter 6 adds the final ingredient, planning and reflection, which turns an augmented LLM

into a full agent. Part 1 closes with Chapter 7 on evaluation: how to judge agents by their outcomes and their trajectories, and how to think about reliability and safety, because evaluating an agent means evaluating an entire system, not just a model.

Part 2: Specialized Agents
: In Part 2, we explore how agents specialize. Chapter 8 covers multi-agent systems, where several specialized agents collaborate, and the architectures that orchestrate them. Chapter 9 covers multi-modal agents, which perceive and generate more than text, letting them see images, watch video, and speak. We end the book with Chapter 10 on coding agents and the code LLMs that power them, arguably the most impactful agent use case at the time of this writing, and the one reshaping the craft of software engineering itself.

Note that each chapter can be read independently, so feel free to skim chapters you are already familiar with. We have also provided a bibliography and a glossary as online-only resources in the book repository (*https://github.com/HandsOnLLM/An-Illustrated-Guide-To-AI-Agents/tree/main/appendix*).

Hardware and Software Requirements

Running LLM-backed agents can be a compute-intensive task, but a strong local machine is not required for this book. All examples are made to run in Google Colaboratory (*https://colab.research.google.com*), or "Google Colab" for short, which at the time of writing provides free access to an NVIDIA T4 GPU. Every chapter has a companion notebook in the book's repository that opens directly in Colab, and you have the option of running everything either locally or in the cloud without any additional costs involved.

All code, notebooks, and additional material are available in this book's repository. There you will also find the `TinyAgent` source as the illustrated-agents package, along with a quick-start guide in the setup folder for installing everything locally if you prefer to run the examples on your own machine.

API Keys

The code examples in this book run on open source models by default. A few examples are demonstrated using proprietary models instead; for those, you will need to create an account and an API key with the relevant provider. We have strived to include only proprietary examples that can run on free tiers. Note that these free tiers often have rate limits which may change over time.

Conventions Used in This Book

The following typographical conventions are used in this book:

Italic
: Indicates new terms, URLs, email addresses, filenames, and file extensions.

`Constant width`
: Used for program listings, as well as within paragraphs to refer to program elements such as variable or function names, databases, data types, environment variables, statements, and keywords.

`Constant width bold`
: Shows commands or other text that should be typed literally by the user.

`Constant width italic`
: Shows text that should be replaced with user-supplied values or by values determined by context.

> This element signifies a general note.

Using Code Examples

Supplemental material (code examples, exercises, etc.) is available for download at *https://github.com/HandsOnLLM/An-Illustrated-Guide-To-AI-Agents*.

If you have a technical question or a problem using the code examples, please send email to *support@oreilly.com*.

This book is here to help you get your job done. In general, if example code is offered with this book, you may use it in your programs and documentation. You do not need to contact us for permission unless you're reproducing a significant portion of the code. For example, writing a program that uses several chunks of code from this book does not require permission. Selling or distributing examples from O'Reilly books does require permission. Answering a question by citing this book and quoting example code does not require permission. Incorporating a significant amount of example code from this book into your product's documentation does require permission.

We appreciate, but generally do not require, attribution. An attribution usually includes the title, author, publisher, and ISBN. For example: "*An Illustrated Guide to AI Agents* by Maarten Grootendorst and Jay Alammar (O'Reilly). Copyright 2026 Arpeggio Inc. and Maarten Pieter Grootendorst, 979-8-341-66269-8."

If you feel your use of code examples falls outside fair use or the permission given above, feel free to contact us at *permissions@oreilly.com*.

O'Reilly Online Learning

O'REILLY®

For more than 40 years, O'Reilly Media has provided technology and business training, knowledge, and insight to help companies succeed.

Our unique network of experts and innovators share their knowledge and expertise through books, articles, and our online learning platform. O'Reilly's online learning platform gives you on-demand access to live training courses, in-depth learning paths, interactive coding environments, and a vast collection of text and video from O'Reilly and 200+ other publishers. For more information, visit *https://oreilly.com*.

How to Contact Us

Please address comments and questions concerning this book to the publisher:

O'Reilly Media, Inc.
141 Stony Circle, Suite 195
Santa Rosa, CA 95401
800-889-8969 (in the United States or Canada)
707-827-7019 (international or local)
707-829-0104 (fax)
support@oreilly.com
https://oreilly.com/about/contact.html

We have a web page for this book, where we list errata and any additional information. You can access this page at *https://oreil.ly/an-illustrated-guide*.

For news and information about our books and courses, visit *https://oreilly.com*.

Find us on LinkedIn: *https://linkedin.com/company/oreilly*.

Watch us on YouTube: *https://youtube.com/oreillymedia*.

Acknowledgments

Writing a second book is a different animal (about as different as a dolphin from a kangaroo). The first time, we were finding out whether the two of us could write a book at all. This time we knew we could, which meant the only acceptable reason to do it again was to make something better: more ambitious in scope, more demanding in its illustrations, and about a subject that was reinventing itself under our feet as we wrote. Agents went from research demos to daily infrastructure within the lifetime of this manuscript. Chasing a moving target like that is only possible with a lot of help.

That help started with our O'Reilly team. Michele Cronin edited both of our books now, and her fingerprints are on every chapter of this one; thank you for trusting us twice. Thank you Nicole Butterfield for once again getting this project off the ground, and Katherine Tozer for steering it through production. Kate Dullea took hundreds of our rough figures through round after round of refinement without ever losing patience.

Our technical reviewers saved you from more of our mistakes than we would like to admit: Girish Ahankari, Susan Chang, Chris Devers, Rafid Khalid, Suhas Pai, Lipi Deepaakshi Patnaik, Sheldon Rodrigues, Alexander Zdorovets.

Finally, thank you to the readers of our first book. Your messages, translations, study groups, and corrections are the reason a second book exists at all.

Maarten

A major thank you to my coauthor, Jay. Continuing our wonderful collaboration with yet another book has been an absolute joy. Writing about agents while the field itself moves at a frankly unreasonable pace has certainly kept things interesting. I still don't understand how you manage to stay on top of it all in such frightening detail, but I'm very glad one of us does.

My gratitude goes to my family for their unwavering support while I disappeared into yet another book. Mam and Pap, despite everything going on in your own lives (and there has been a lot), you have always found a way to be there when I needed you.

A heartfelt thank you to a friend without equal, Chris. Despite my habit of disappearing for months at a time to write, whenever I resurface, you're always there as though no time has passed. A friendship like that is truly a rare thing.

The final stretch of this book coincided with my move to Google DeepMind. In those six months, I can honestly say that I have seldom received such a warm welcome. I'm grateful for the encouragement you gave me, even as I was just beginning a new chapter with all of you.

With the last book, I was at a loss for words to adequately express my gratitude to my wife, Ilse. That has become rather inconvenient, because your support since then has only grown. You even took the time to create all these flamingo images throughout the book! Lieverd, you are my greatest source of encouragement. Through all the late nights, long weekends, and sentences beginning with "I'm almost done with this one last thing…" you somehow continued to believe in me.

One day I'll stop pursuing all these ridiculous projects and live a quiet, sensible life.

Probably.

Sarah, my sweet, perceptive daughter. Through no fault of your own, you have been cursed with a father who will happily drone on about the latest in AI whenever given the slightest opportunity. I can only apologize for the years ahead.

More importantly, everything in my life becomes brighter when I think of you. Of all the things I have written, built, or will ever create, nothing will make me prouder than being your father.

Sarah, all these flamingos are for you.

Jay

I owe a great deal to the colleagues, mentors, and friends who have been generous with me over the years, in this project and well beyond it. Thank you to Ahmet Üstün, Aidan Gomez, Alexander Zdorovets, Andrew Ng, Chris McCormick, Edward Grefenstette, Graham Neubig, Ivan Zhang, Josh Starmer, Luis Serrano, Mohammed Almeshekah, Nick Frosst, Patrick Lewis, Phil Blunsom, Rohan Alexander, Sarah Alsaleh, Sophia Althammer, Suhas Pai, and Tom Sherborne.

To the cafes and libraries in Toronto that hosted much of this book's writing: Dark Horse, Morning Parade, NEO Coffee Bar, The Sydney Grind, and the glorious Toronto Public Library system.

To Maarten. Two books, a shelf of open source, and a steady stream of writing, and I have yet to see you ship something that wasn't your best work. I don't know how you do it and I've now had two books to find out. Thank you for a second one I couldn't have written alone.

And to my family, again and always. The work often takes me away from you. What it costs us is time together. What it builds belongs to you as much as to me.

PART I

The Anatomy of an AI Agent

CHAPTER 1

Introduction

In the mid-2020s, AI agents began reshaping the AI landscape as we knew it. When ChatGPT, at the end of 2022, revolutionized the field of large language models (LLMs), AI agents started taking a major step further and were designed to act with autonomy, pursue goals, and even interact with the world. Rather than just generating text, these agents are capable of solving much more challenging problems using advanced reasoning, memorizing complex interactions, and creating entire codebases.

This shift is monumental and not just an incremental improvement. It redefines how we interact with AI. Where LLMs require significant handholding, AI agents are capable of autonomously deciding which actions to take, when to take them, and even how. It's this agency that makes them such interesting entities and will be a core focus throughout this book.

This book covers AI agents that rely on LLMs. It's important to note that there are other types of AI agents in practice that do not utilize LLMs. But instead of saying LLM-backed AI agents every time we mention agents in this book, we'll just use AI agents and wish the reader recalls the type we're addressing throughout the book.

With coding agents becoming a staple in every software developer's toolkit, we have just begun to understand the potential this technology has. AI agents, in various forms, are beginning to integrate into all manner of fields, from finance to healthcare, and marketing to scientific research. This pace of improvements in AI, and AI agents in particular, has been daunting.

That is where this book, and particularly this chapter, comes in. This chapter serves as the scaffolding for the rest of the book and will introduce concepts and terms that we'll use throughout all chapters. Mostly, we'll give a brief answer to the question "What is an AI agent?" This answer will be your guide throughout all of the upcoming chapters, where each subsequent chapter will uncover an important component of an AI agent. You can expect an intuitive, but in-depth journey, of what makes AI agents so special.

What Is an AI Agent?

The definition of an AI agent is ever-changing as the field progresses and as these entities grow in complexity. Fortunately, as with most technologies, the fundamentals of AI agents are static and a great way to build up to more state-of-the-art techniques. As such, we consider the following definition of AI agents meaningful through both the fundamentals and new advances in this field:

> An agent is anything that can be viewed as perceiving its environment through sensors and acting upon that environment through actuators.
>
> —Russell & Norvig, *Artificial Intelligence: A Modern Approach*[1]

This definition boils down agents to entities that perceive and interact with their environment. It's broad enough to consider entities other than LLMs, but at the same time, it gives us something structured to work with.

We can deconstruct this definition into the following components that lie at the heart of agents:

Environment
: The world the agent interacts with

Sensors
: Components of the agent used to observe the environment

Actuators
: Tools the agent uses to interact with the environment

Agent program
: The "brain" or rules the agent uses to decide how to go from observations to actions

The interaction of all these components is shown in Figure 1-1.

1 Russell, Stuart and Peter Norvig, *Artificial Intelligence: A Modern Approach*, 4th ed. (Pearson, 2020).

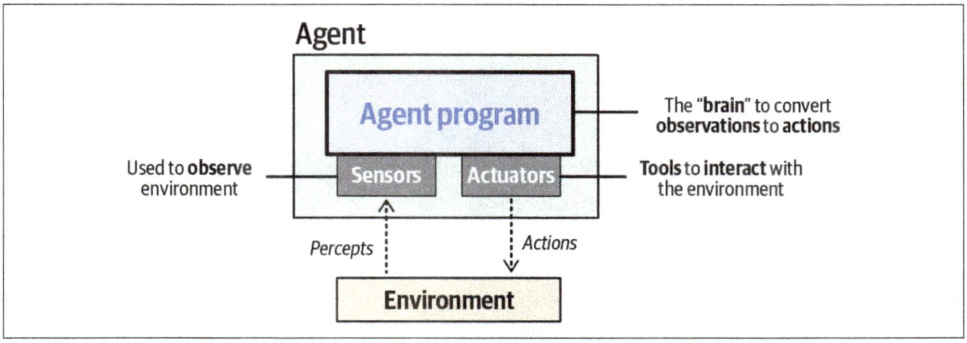

Figure 1-1. An agent perceives its environment through sensors and acts on it via tools or actuators

Let's clarify this terminology by relating it to LLMs.

In practice, the *agent program* or brain of an LLM-backed agent is a "reasoning" LLM, a model that is capable of complex thinking. Through additional modules (memory, tools, and planning), this LLM is capable of interacting with its environment. Here, the *actuators* are the tools of the LLM. Some LLMs can interpret more than text, such as images or sound, and can be considered as the *sensors* in this system. The last piece missing from this system is the user, who can be part of the *environment*. Users often initiate the interaction by stating a request for the agent to fulfill.

Together, these aspects are what we believe to be truly fundamental to AI agents as we see them in practice. Figure 1-2 illustrates how all these components are connected. More importantly, this figure does not just elucidate the principles of agents but also tells a story: a story of what agents truly are, how they're created, and how they behave. The figure serves as the foundation of this book and will be used throughout to build up the agent.

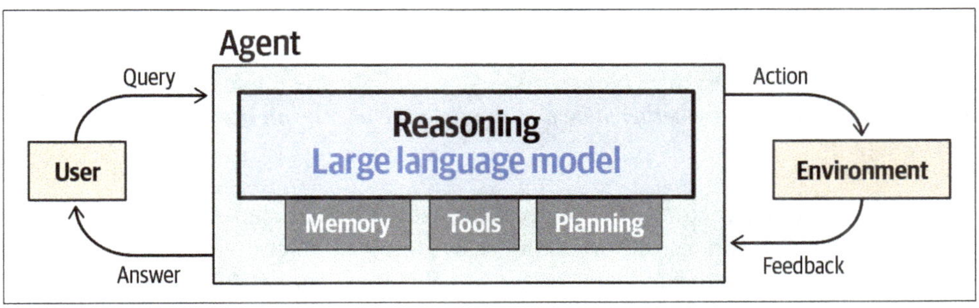

Figure 1-2. Agents operate in regular contact with a user and environment, and use reasoning models, memory, tools, and planning to decide their actions

Let's go through each component in more detail and clarify how they relate to the book structure.

Large Language Models

To understand what AI agents are, we first need to explore the basic capabilities of an LLM, as the LLM is typically considered to be the "brain" of an agent. Traditionally, an LLM is a model that does nothing more than predict the next word based on a given input text. As shown in Figure 1-3, the LLM first breaks down a given input query into tokens, which are subcomponents of words that allow the model to generalize to words it has not seen before. The LLM processes these tokens, and a prediction is made on what the next token could be.

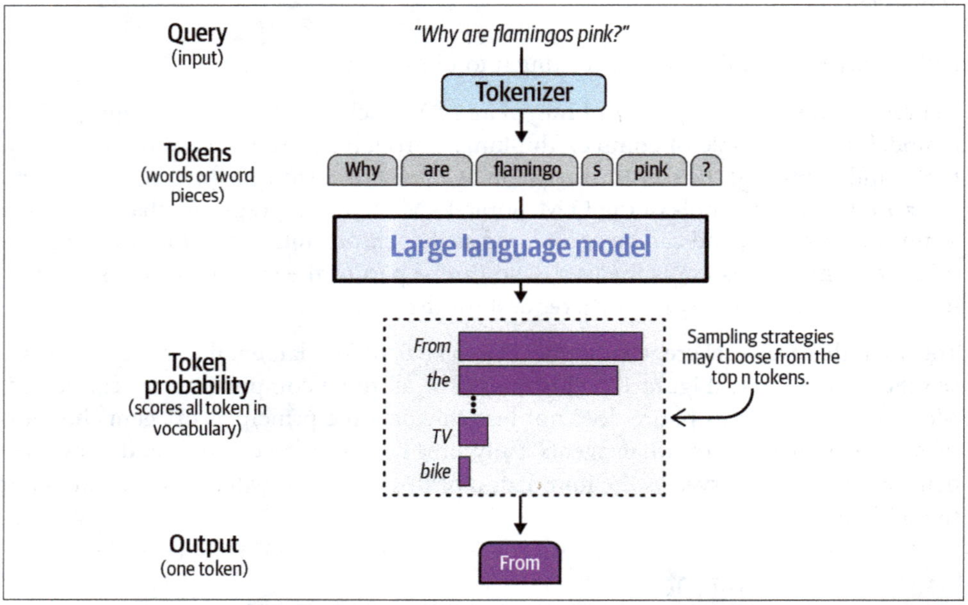

Figure 1-3. LLMs process their input messages by breaking them into tokens and produce their output as tokens—whether it be a message to the user or an action enacted on the environment

The LLM therefore predicts the next token, uses the predicted token to update its input, and then continues the predictions. By doing this iteratively (which is called autoregression), it can create entire answers to the user's query (shown in Figure 1-4).

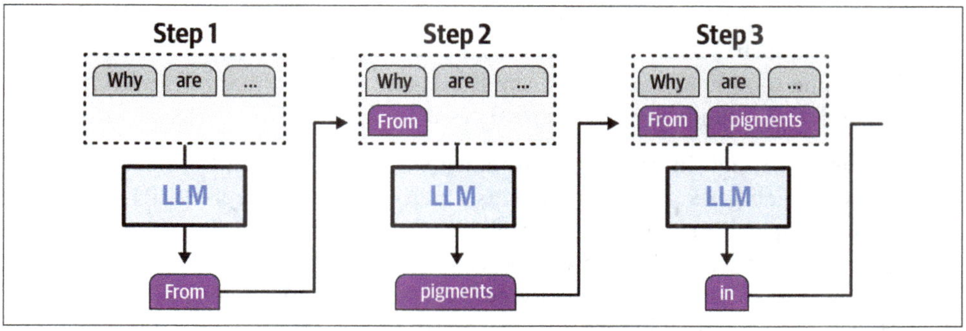

Figure 1-4. LLMs operate in an autoregressive loop, outputting one token at a time

In Chapter 2, we'll explore in detail how this system, the LLM, works. The common architecture of LLMs, attention, and its many variants, will be explored to give you an understanding of its internal mechanisms.

Reasoning Large Language Models

Arguably, one of the most impactful LLMs is GPT-3.5, which powered the original ChatGPT released in November 2022. As a chat model, GPT-3.5 could hold entire conversations, making it eerily similar to how humans would interact. It's safe to say that this model changed the world as we know it. Over the years since, OpenAI and many other LLM providers have focused on scaling GPT-3.5-like models to new heights by throwing more data, compute, and parameters at them. This is called train-time scaling (shown in Figure 1-5), where training on more data and making models larger led to reliable, predictable improvements in performance. The idea was that pre-training, the first and most expensive stage of training an LLM, was where the gains came from: the larger your pre-training budget, the better the resulting model.

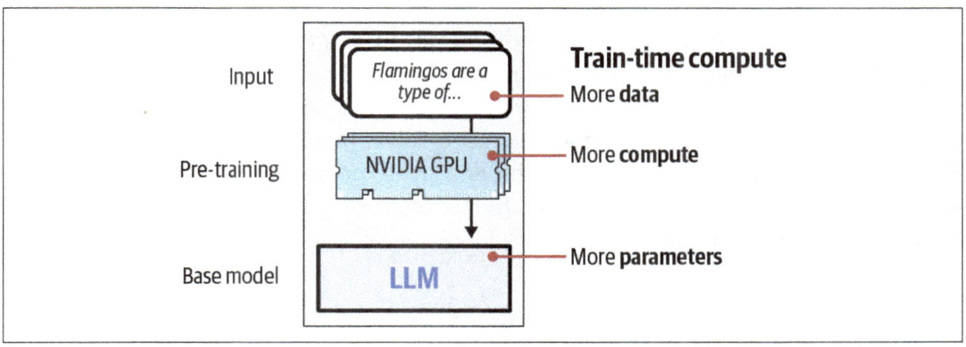

Figure 1-5. A lot of major LLM progress has been due to train-time compute: scaling data, compute, and model size

Although this improved the performance of these models, it uncovered a ceiling effect. Continuously scaling the model's size is not cost-effective, and soon, training simply became too expensive for the small increase in performance. As it turns out, scaling your model can be done in more ways than one.

A major breakthrough in model performance was achieved with the introduction of LLM reasoning abilities in models such as OpenAI o1 and DeepSeek-R1. Instead of having the model "think" quietly (or implicitly through the model's parameters) for a fixed amount of time, models were now trained to "think" out loud and spend more time to arrive at a correct answer (by generating reasoning tokens before deriving the answer). As shown in Figure 1-6, reasoning LLMs first generate "thoughts" and leverage that to generate the final answer.

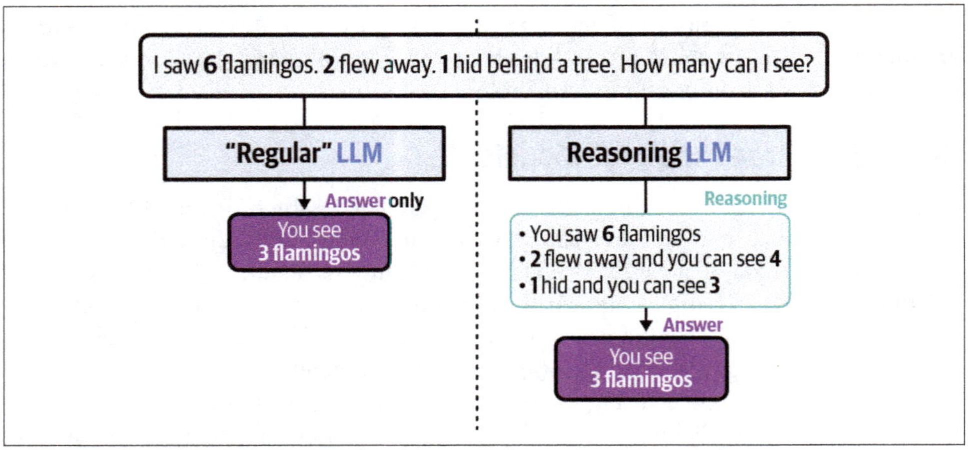

Figure 1-6. Reasoning improves the behavior of LLMs by allowing them to explicitly state and keep track of subproblems of the task at hand

The main idea is that it allows LLMs to write down their thoughts first through their autoregressive behavior before coming to an answer. Instead of spending all of its compute to generate only the answer, the LLM spends additional compute to first generate its "thoughts." By structuring its thoughts, more complex queries that require multi-step reasoning are easier to solve. In some LLM playgrounds, like ChatGPT, these thoughts are typically hidden from the user or summarized, whereas the answer to the user's query generally represents a conclusion building on the model's "thoughts" (Figure 1-7).

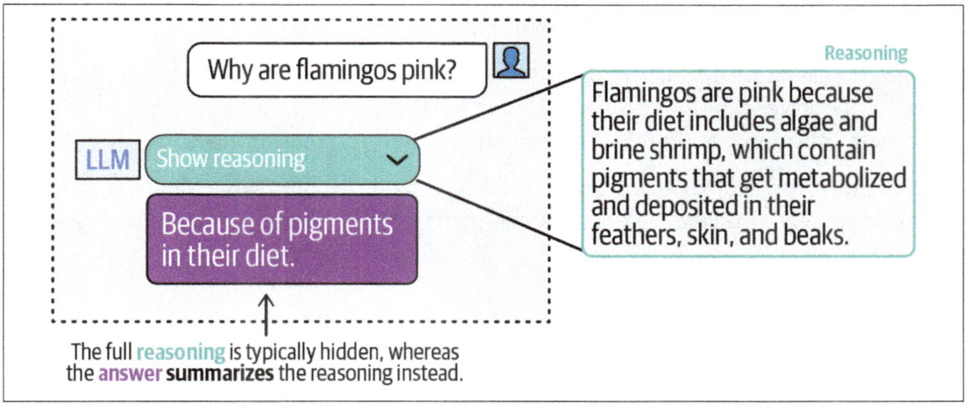

Figure 1-7. The final answers displayed in reasoning-LLM applications and playgrounds are aided by a reasoning trace that may be hidden or summarized

Part of what makes AI agents more capable is their ability to make extensive plans, select the appropriate tools, reflect on their mistakes, and even dynamically revise and update these plans. All of these require advanced reasoning behavior in LLMs. Reasoning LLMs are particularly capable at complex decision-making tasks, breaking down multi-step problems, and generalizing to novel problems. However, if you want fast and cheap responses, "regular" LLMs are preferred.

As such, reasoning LLMs will take a central role throughout most of this book, as reasoning is a key capability enabling these complex behaviors. In Chapter 3, you'll learn about various ways to create reasoning LLMs. We look at the fundamentals of reasoning LLMs, explore the famous reasoning LLM, DeepSeek-R1, and look beyond at what the future might hold in this field. Chapters 2 and 3 will therefore focus on the "brain" of the agent (Figure 1-8).

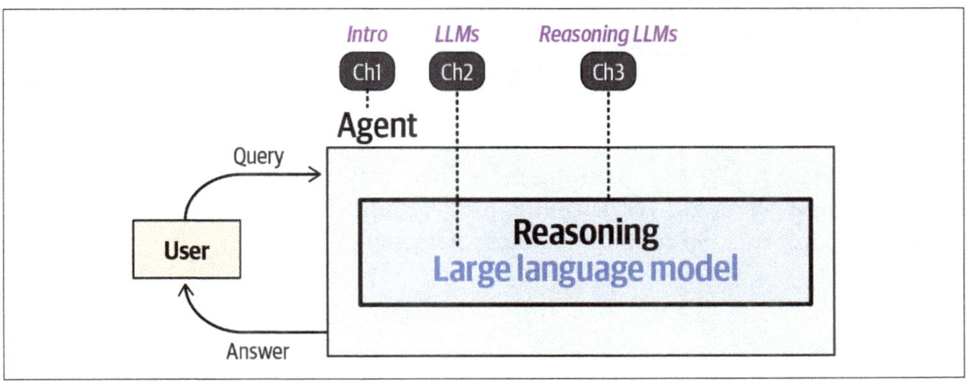

Figure 1-8. The first three chapters of the book focus on introducing agents, LLMs, and reasoning because these are foundational ideas for AI agents

Augmenting the Large Language Model

Although reasoning LLMs are vital to AI agents, they're still incomplete and miss certain functionalities. As static text-to-text entities, text-based LLMs have no control over their environment, nor do they remember their interactions or learn from them.

Let's explore how to go from an incredibly capable LLM to one that can remember interactions, interact with its environment, and demonstrate various degrees of autonomy.

Memory

Notice how, so far, we have shown only "single-turn" conversations. These conversations contain a single question and answer pair in the interaction with the LLM. If we were to continue this conversation and ask another question, we would turn it into a "multi-turn" conversation. Multi-turn conversations expose a vital flaw of LLMs, namely that they're forgetful entities and do not remember past conversations (Figure 1-9). They are stateless, which means that information is not persisted across calls.

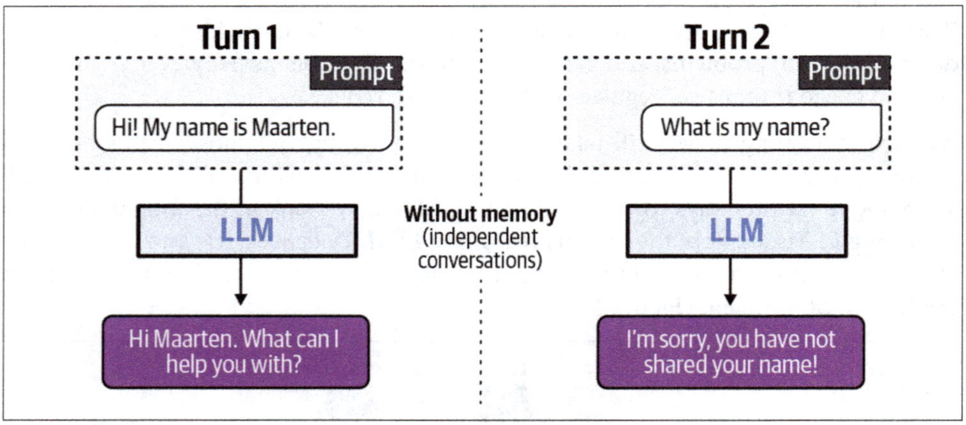

Figure 1-9. An LLM without a memory system to keep track of longer user conversations

Without memory, LLMs are nothing more than answering machines. Ask an LLM a question and get an answer. However, follow it up with another question, and the LLM has no information about the former interaction.

Fortunately, there are many ways we can add memory modules to LLMs to mimic memory. As shown in Figure 1-10, a common way to approach this is by simply adding the previous conversation to the current prompt.

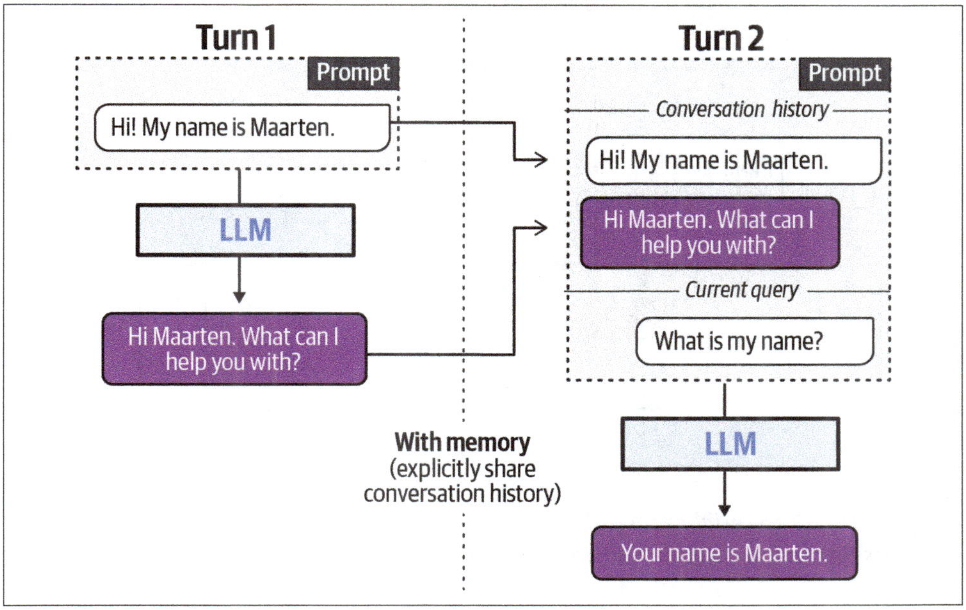

Figure 1-10. Adding conversation history to the LLM input is one of the first ways used to allow the model to glance at previous turns in the chat

In practice, however, memory modules can be quite complex. They share many similarities with human memory systems, such as short-term and long-term memory, but also how we process information. If we receive too much information, it becomes difficult to process, which can lead to poor decision-making. This is called information overload and can be a real problem even for LLMs. As such, memorizing every little detail might hurt the performance of an LLM, so a balance is needed between the amount and quality of the information in the prompt. This is called *context engineering* and, as shown in Figure 1-11, it attempts to balance the information available and what we give the LLM.

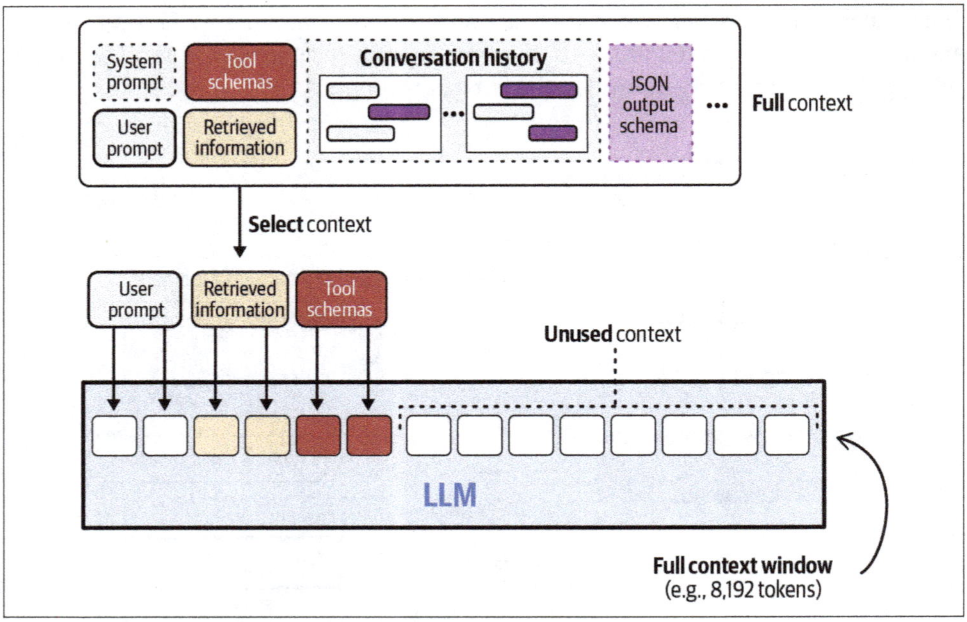

Figure 1-11. It's essential to carefully design the input we pass to the LLM to help it tackle its present task, called context engineering

Tools

With memory, LLMs remember the conversations they previously had, but they're not yet capable of interacting with their environment. LLMs can interact with their digital environment through external tools that may enhance their capabilities (like web search, for example). These tools vary in complexity and can range from straightforward calculators and search engines to more advanced tools with access to your command shell and coding environment.

However, LLMs are not capable of using tools by themselves. Fundamentally, LLMs can be seen as software or functions that, upon receiving input text, process it and then output some text. As text-in/text-out functions, LLMs can only describe or show the intent of taking the action when outputting text. This is shown in Figure 1-12, where the LLM, upon receiving the query "What is 5.1 times 7.3?" generates the string "multiply(5.1, 7.3)". This string merely represents the LLM's intention to take an action, but the action itself is not taken without outside intervention.

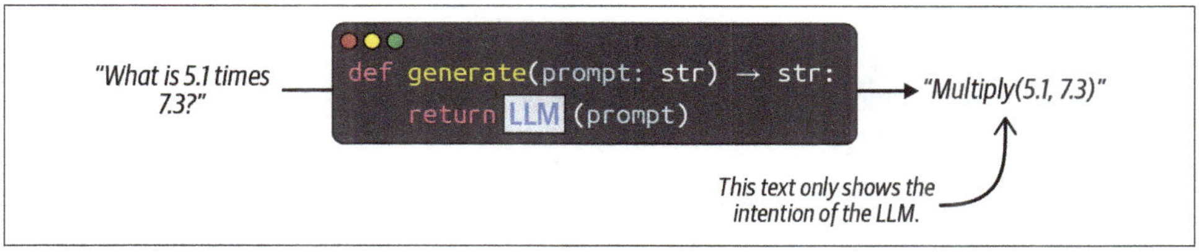

Figure 1-12. LLMs are able to invoke tools by outputting text in a specific format that other software systems parse and execute

The LLM can express the intent to use a tool, but it relies on us to turn that intent into an actual tool call. The user will need to write software to convert that text into an action. For instance, if the LLM's output were JSON, we would use that to choose the correct tool and fill in its parameters. Those actions would need to be programmed separately (optionally by using existing agent frameworks). Figure 1-13 illustrates these steps, showing a possible representation of the overall flow.

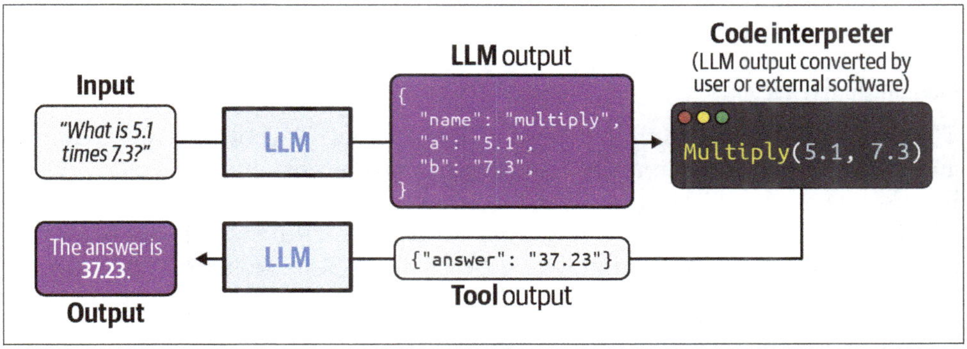

Figure 1-13. The workflow of an LLM calling a tool

There are many ways an LLM can use and learn tools, which we'll cover in Chapter 5, along with how using the same tools by different LLMs can be standardized with the Model Context Protocol.

Chapters 2 through 5 give us what LLM company Anthropic calls (*https://oreil.ly/ZdHIw*): "the augmented LLM" (Figure 1-14). This LLM is capable of deciding which tools to use, how to use them, and what kind of information to retain. These augmentations (memory and tools) allow for interaction with the environment in meaningful ways.

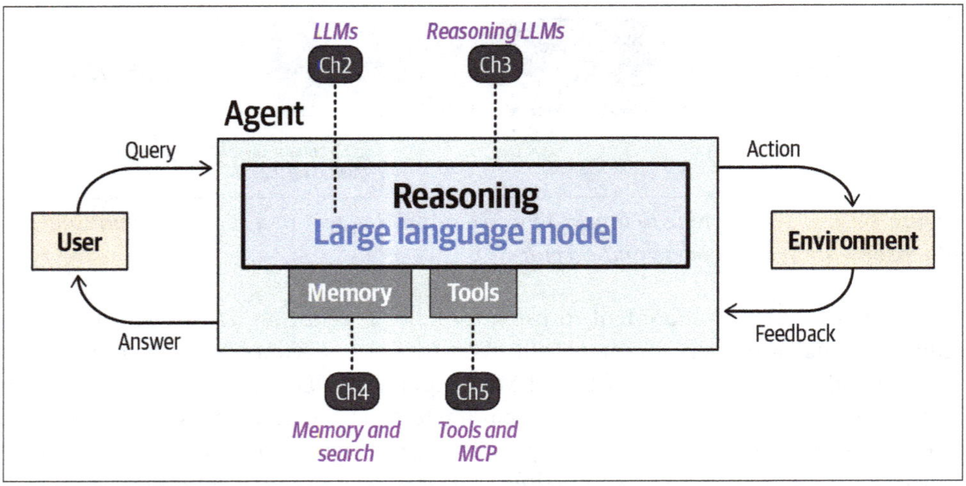

Figure 1-14. Augmenting a reasoning LLM with memory and tools: the "augmented LLM" that serves as the building block we turn into an agent

Planning and reflection

The final ingredient to go from a "regular" LLM to an AI agent is its ability to plan and reflect. These capabilities are important throughout much of an agentic system because the agent will need to decide which steps to take, how to take them, and when. For instance, if the LLM has access to dozens of GitHub API tools, such as looking at pull requests or commits, how does it decide which to use?

This is where planning comes in, which involves breaking down a large task into smaller, actionable steps, referred to as task decomposition. The first step is to typically create a plan to execute when presented with a query (Figure 1-15).

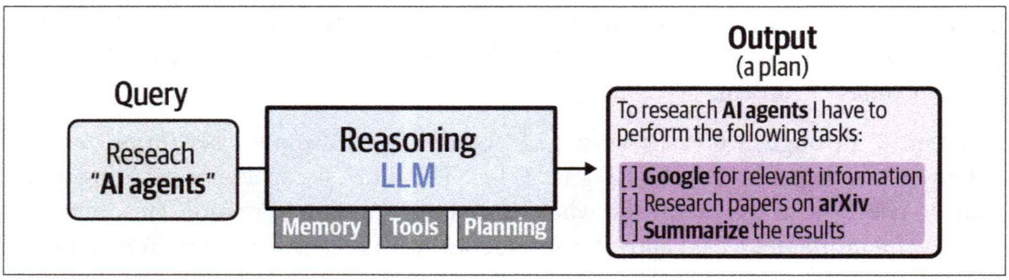

Figure 1-15. Plans enable agents to tackle larger tasks by breaking them down into smaller steps and updating that plan as it's executed to keep track of progress

By continuously referring back to this plan, the LLM is capable of executing each of these tasks one at a time. Performing them all at once is seldom efficient, and each task might influence another. As shown in Figure 1-16, after completing a specific task, the LLM might still reason about which steps to take next. As such, reasoning is fundamental and often a necessity for your agent to plan out complex behavior.

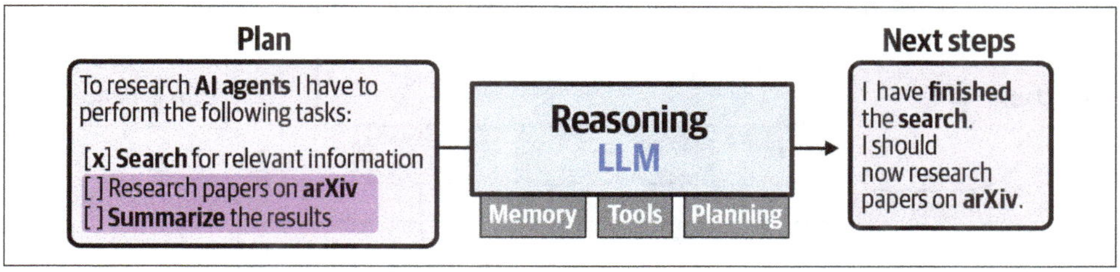

Figure 1-16. After finishing a task, the agent reasons over its current plan to choose the next step, here marking the Google search complete and moving on to research papers on arXiv

But creating a plan is not sufficient. The LLM might discover halfway through its plan that some of its steps might not be appropriate. In our previous example, the LLM would discover that Google and arXiv are insufficient as resources and instead add a task to add Semantic Scholar and PubMed as resources to search.[2]

By reflecting on past behavior, agents can attempt to uncover their faults and make attempts to fix them. Therefore, the initial plan can be continuously improved. Illustrated in Figure 1-17, planning and reflection create an iterative loop of planning out tasks, taking actions, and reflecting on the output.

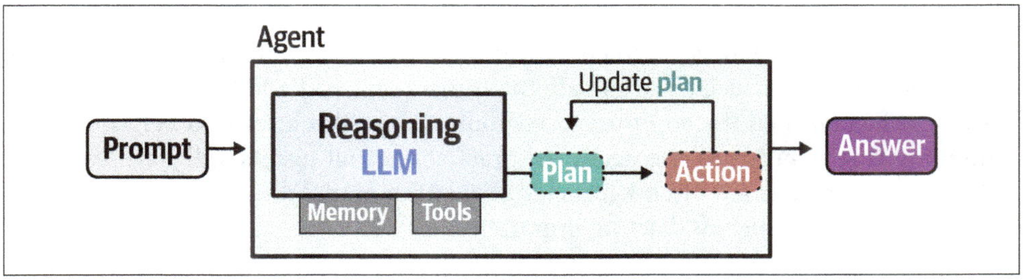

Figure 1-17. Reflection enables the agent to update a plan, often enabling it to adapt to new information uncovered during execution

Together, reasoning LLMs augmented with memory, tools, planning, and reflection are what we consider to be an AI agent. In Chapter 6, we will explore planning and reflection and how they connect all augmentations of the LLM to create the AI agent (Figure 1-18).

2 arXiv (*https://arxiv.org*) is an open access archive hosting millions of research papers on computer science and other topics.

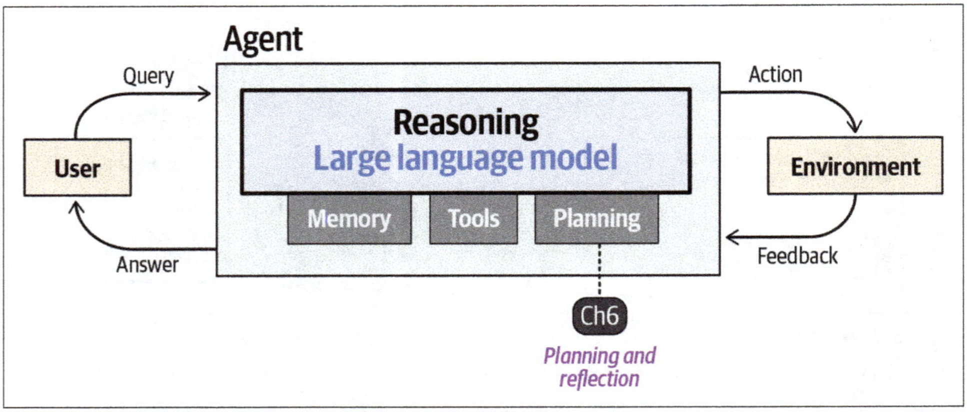

Figure 1-18. Planning and reflection to update plans are key capabilities for agents tackling more difficult problems

An Agentic System

With all these components, a reasoning LLM augmented with memory, tools, and planning, we arrive at the next stage of the agent: the way it behaves inside a system. This covers common use cases, degree of autonomy, ethical considerations, and how these agents and systems can be evaluated.

Autonomy

The AI agent, as we have defined it thus far, has a fair bit of freedom. It can choose between tools, decide to update the initial plan, add additional steps, or stop because it has reached the appropriate response. All of this advanced behavior is the autonomy that is given to the agent. In practice, not all agents will have complete autonomy; guardrails are often necessary so that the model does not take potentially destructive actions (such as deleting important files).

Depending on the AI agent and the system in which it's integrated, agents can have varying degrees of autonomy. As shown in Figure 1-19, this autonomy can be partial, where the model can execute only a single step but has the freedom to choose from tools, or it can be complete freedom without any guardrails.

Depending on who you ask, a system is more "agentic" the more the LLM has full control over its actions. However, we believe that as long as the agent exhibits goal-directed behavior and makes decisions, we can call it an agent. Autonomy exists on a spectrum, and partial autonomy in orchestrated workflows can still qualify as agency if the agent acts with some degree of independence. Across all chapters, we'll cover both autonomous systems as well as orchestrated workflows.

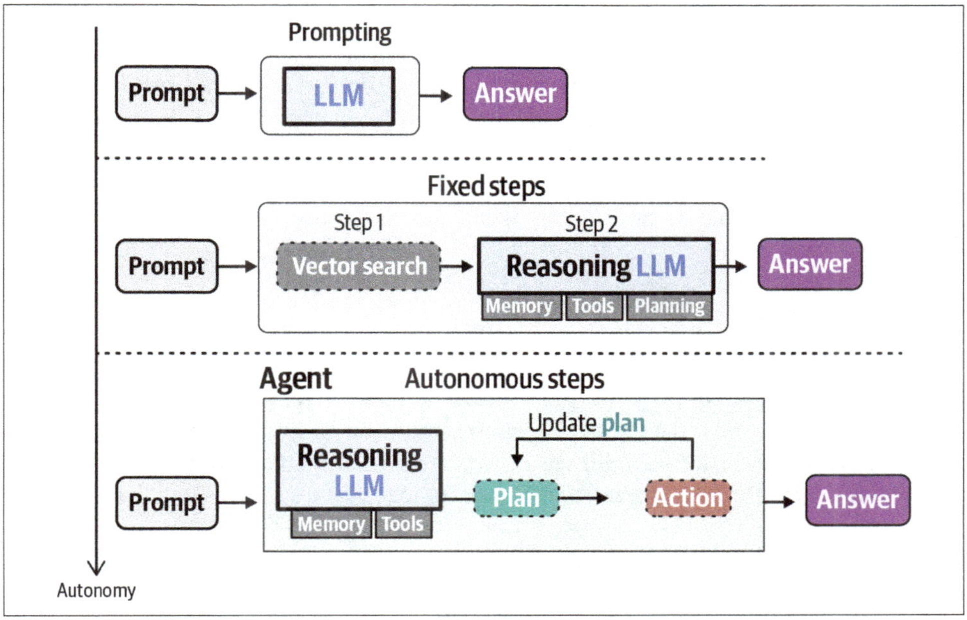

Figure 1-19. AI agents have more autonomy or agency than a single LLM generation or a fixed pipeline

Agentic applications: What makes them so useful?

Agents' abilities for autonomous behavior make them especially useful for open-ended problems where the exact steps required are not known beforehand. The LLM can reason on how to approach a problem and the number of turns to complete it. This autonomy and self-driving behavior thrives in environments where the goal might be clear, but the path to reach it is not.

As such, agents are often used for the following:

Coding
: Coding assistants (such as Antigravity (*https://antigravity.google*), Claude Code (*https://claude.com/product/claude-code*), and Codex (*https://chatgpt.com/codex*)) are arguably the most common use case at the time of writing, with companies like Cursor (*https://cursor.com*) being valued at tens of billions of dollars. With so much knowledge about code, agents are capable of writing it themselves and going through the steps of writing new code but also validating it. This is a use case where the agent truly shines because the goal is quite clear (a specific feature) and often with pre-defined requirements (language, frameworks, etc.) to work toward with some degree of freedom. Problems in the code domain also often benefit from the ability to be automatically verified, which is a useful property at both training and inference time.

Deep research

This is a field where agents are used to perform in-depth analyses on various topics without much intervention by the user. You can ask an agent to research a given topic, and it will, autonomously, search for everything related to that topic on sources such as arXiv, PubMed, and Google Scholar. These agents are not without flaws, but they're a great starting point whenever you want to dive into a new topic, and they're gaining popularity across platforms.

Automation

Although you wouldn't use an agent to diagnose patients or handle claims automatically without any human interaction, there are many useful places where an agent would have a large impact if designed thoughtfully. Standardization and automation of processes are great examples. For instance, hospitals across the world differ in how data is stored (both structured and unstructured). Agents are capable of searching through various data sources to structure the wide array of patient data, allowing for easier research in healthcare.

Responsible agent development and usage

As we explore the incredible capabilities of LLMs, it's important to keep their societal and ethical implications in mind. This is especially true for agents, which can have a degree of autonomy that might directly impact the digital or physical world. While many think the future of agents is fully autonomous systems, others state that fully autonomous agents should not be developed at all due to the risk of giving away control.[3] The field is currently somewhere in the middle. Agents can be amazing entities and help optimize many processes, such as coding agents. However, having an agent diagnose patients without any human intervention is, with the current state of technology, harmful behavior. As with most things, it's all about the context in which agents are used.[4]

As such, here are key points to consider:

Human in the loop

As agents become more autonomous, there is a greater need for humans in the loop to authorize, check, and audit the decisions that agents make. This can take many forms, as will be discussed throughout the book, but typically involves a human checking either the output or intermediate steps before continuing.

Guardrails

It's essential to be careful with the level of autonomy we grant agents. Not only can full autonomy be overkill for the task at hand, but it can often be harmful.

3 Mitchell, Margaret et al. 2025. "Fully Autonomous AI Agents Should Not Be Developed." *arXiv,* 2502.02649.

4 Gabriel, Iason et al. 2024. "The Ethics of Advanced AI Assistants." *arXiv,*2404.16244.

A system with many guardrails is often more effective, as it allows steering the agent toward expected behaviors and away from undesired ones.

Misinformation
: AI agents are still LLMs, which are prone to confidently generating incorrect information, called hallucinations. Although LLMs are becoming much more capable, additional checks and balances are needed in systems where correct information is critical.

Evaluating agents

Responsible agent development brings us to an important component of building any agent: evaluation. LLMs are already hard to evaluate, usually using benchmarks and scored text outputs, and agents raise the bar further. They reason over multiple steps, call tools, and sequences of actions, so a single quality score for the final text rarely captures whether the agent did its job.

Because an agent acts on its environment instead of producing only text, evaluation has to look at more than the words the agent generates. One lens is the outcome: did the task actually get done, such as the message sent or the record updated? The other is the trajectory: the steps and tool calls the agent took to get there, which can be judged on efficiency and soundness even when the outcome is correct. Chapter 7 treats these as its two main lenses, outcome evaluation and trajectory evaluation.

Two additional properties get dedicated treatment because they don't surface in a single run. Reliability asks whether an agent succeeds every time, not just once, since its outputs are stochastic. Safety asks whether it avoids harm, whether the risk comes from a malicious user, from manipulated data the agent reads, or from its own mistakes on an ordinary task. Taken together, this is why evaluating an agent is much more than evaluating a model: you are evaluating an entire system.

In Chapter 7 we go deeper on all of this, from reading public benchmarks critically to building an evaluation suite of your own.

The book is organized in two parts: the first covers a single agent on its own, and the second covers what happens when agents work with each other and with the wider world. Together with Chapter 7, Part I will primarily focus on the fundamentals of a single agent, how it's built, and how it can be evaluated. Part I is visualized in Figure 1-20 and will serve as the common thread throughout Chapter 1 to Chapter 7.

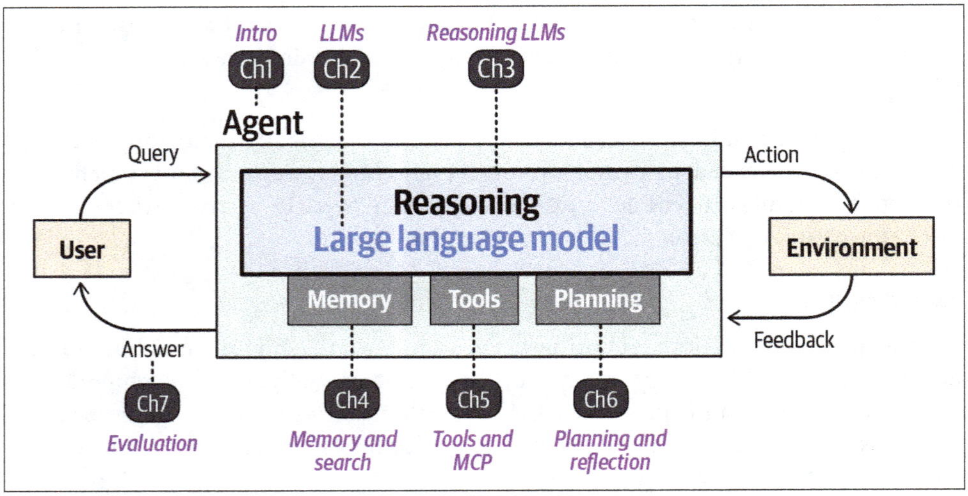

Figure 1-20. Part I covers the major components of a single AI agent

Specializations

The single agent covered in Part I gives you an assistant that, to a certain degree, can autonomously decide how to tackle a given problem. Although it's already an entity on its own that can achieve amazing results, there are many variants of agents that can take results a step further. Specializations such as multi-modal agents can see the world through more lenses than just text, whereas others, such as coding agents, are created for specific use cases.

In the second part of the book, we'll explore these specialized agents and their use cases, starting with how systems can be created where multiple agents work together (see Figure 1-21).

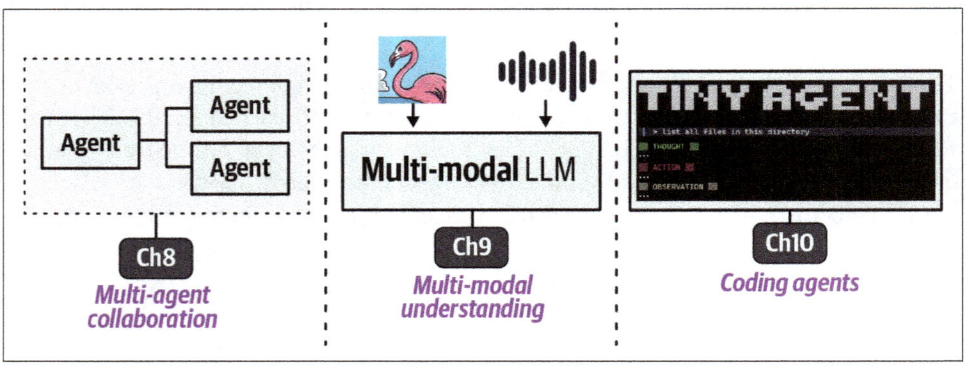

Figure 1-21. Part II of the book covers multi-agent collaboration, multi-modal understanding, and coding agents

Multi-Agent Collaboration

When systems grow larger and tasks are more specialized, we start looking toward multi-agent collaborations. These are systems where multiple different agents are deployed that are each responsible for different tasks. Compared to single-agent systems, multi-agent systems interact with one another and might consult each other's specialties. The main differences lie in how many agents are deployed and their interactions with one another (Figure 1-22).

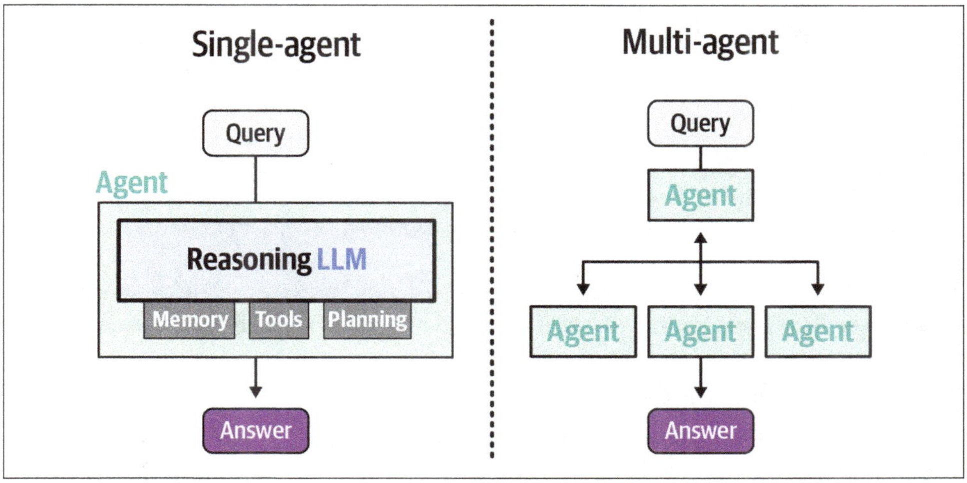

Figure 1-22. Multiple agents can collaborate to solve certain tasks and could achieve better results than those possible by a single agent

These multi-agent systems often contain specialized agents, each equipped with different toolsets. Although workflows may differ, there is often a supervisor agent that manages communication among, and sometimes within, agents. In practice, the supervisor agent tends to have the most capable LLM because the supervisor is in charge of advanced behavior such as planning, decomposing, and assigning tasks (Figure 1-23).

Although the supervisor agent is common, this does not always have to be the case. In practice, there are dozens of multi-agent architectures to explore, some with structured orchestration (like the supervisor) and some with unstructured orchestration.

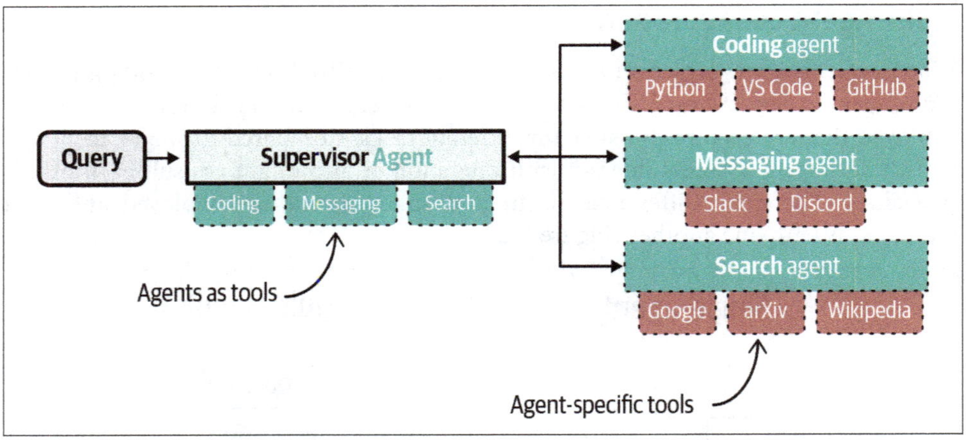

Figure 1-23. One way to design multi-agent collaboration is with a capable supervisor agent delegating tasks to specialized agents each with their own set of relevant tools

In Chapter 8, we explore these multi-agent architectures with concrete examples. You'll learn how these architectures are created and when they should be used.

The Multi-Modal Agent

Understanding of its environment and the interactions the agent has with it are fundamental to an agent's behavior. An agent relying on a text-only LLM will do so only through text. The digital world, however, is much more than a place filled with text. An agent might need to optimize the color schemes of your website and will need to "see" it. It can only go so far by reading through the hexadecimal values in your code. Likewise, a traditional agent can reply only in text, but what if the situation requires it to have a voice instead? If your vision deteriorates, or you can't type because of a repetitive strain injury, being able to talk to your agent through voice becomes necessary. This is where multi-modal agents are gaining traction. The digital world is not composed of a single modality, so interaction with it should not be done only through text.

Whether agents are multi-modal is primarily decided by the nature of their "brains," namely the LLM. We can consider an agent to be multi-modal if the LLM it uses is capable of processing and/or generating different modalities. This also points us toward the two most important components of what makes an LLM multi-modal—their capabilities for the following:

- *Understand* multiple modalities
- *Generate* multiple modalities

When the LLM can reason about several modalities simultaneously, such as text, images, audio, and video, we refer to this multi-modal LLM as being capable of understanding multiple modalities. This can be quite helpful in various situations, such as optimizing a website design, where the LLM needs to be able to "see" what is actually happening. Chapter 9 will explore multi-modal understanding in LLMs through two important components: an encoder for converting modalities into numeric information and a connector to connect those representations to the LLM (Figure 1-24).

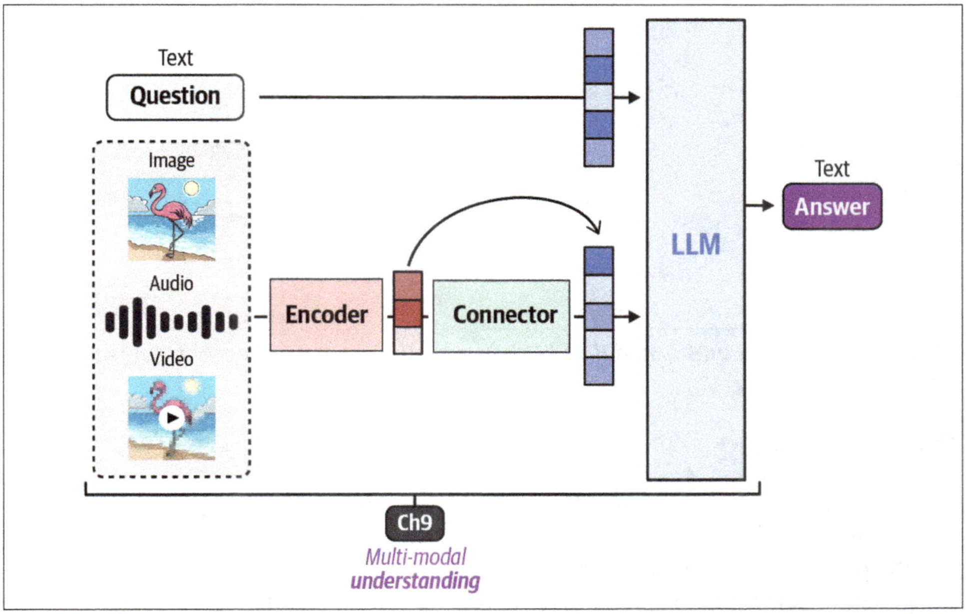

Figure 1-24. AI agents can have better representation of their environments if they can process additional data modalities, such as images, video, and/or audio

For an LLM to generate output in a modality other than text requires a vastly different process than simply understanding multiple modalities. Shown in Figure 1-25, the other side of the process is where a generator is used to generate modalities other than text.

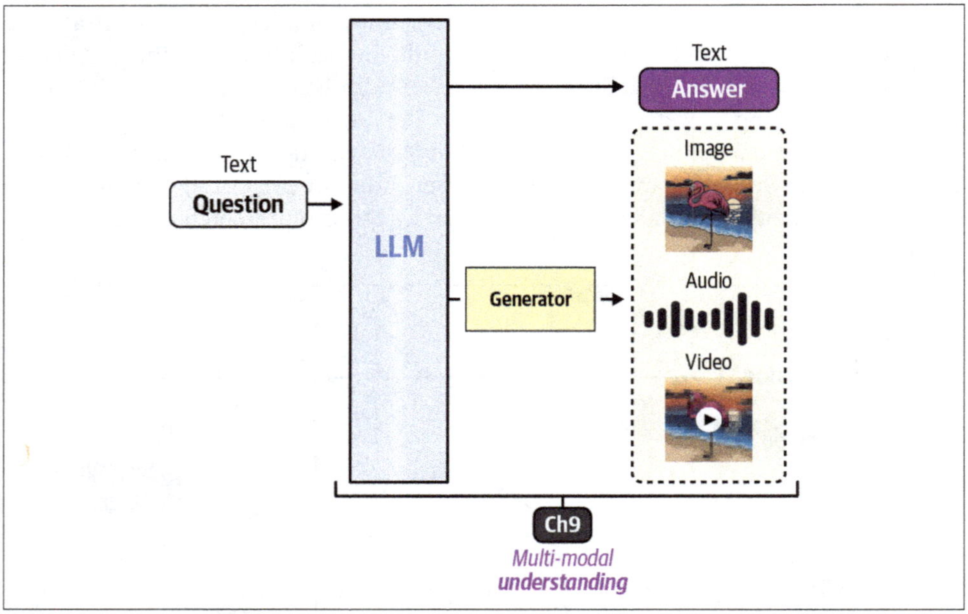

Figure 1-25. Certain multi-modal LLMs can have the capability of generating modalities other than text

The Coding Agent

Another popular variant of agents is the coding agent. Unlike traditional AI assistants, where you have a back-and-forth discussing code, a coding agent can actually run the program in a dedicated environment. Even more, it can read existing codebases, generate new functions, fix bugs, and test what it has created. Increasingly, coding agents are reshaping the nature of software engineering while granting non-software engineers capabilities that would be beyond their reach had they not had access to such agents. This has led to the concept of "vibe coding," where agents are relied on to build software for non-developers.

Building and using coding agents effectively is the subject of Chapter 10, along with how the underlying code LLMs are trained to power them. Coding benchmarks such as SWE-bench, and how agents are scored on them, are covered in Chapter 7.

The TinyAgent

Although "illustrated" is in the name of this book, wouldn't it be nice to put some of the principles covered into practice? As you explore various components of AI agents and slowly build up the theoretical foundation of an agent through visuals, you'll do the same in code.

Specifically, you'll build up a `TinyAgent` one step at a time. Using the foundations learned in this book, we'll explore how to convert them into actual Python code. You can follow along with the notebooks provided in our GitHub repository (*https://github.com/HandsOnLLM/An-Illustrated-Guide-To-AI-Agents*). There, you'll find all code along with bonus content that's not covered in this book. To be able to run this code anywhere, we provided several options to install it as a package (*https://pypi.org/project/illustrated-agents*), through pip (*https://github.com/pypa/pip*), or uv (*https://docs.astral.sh/uv*). This code is what implements the behavior of the `TinyAgent` and is typically called the *agent harness*. There are many different types of harnesses that you might come across:

Terminal-based
: Agents that run directly in the terminal, such as Claude Code (*https://oreil.ly/Ye1at*), Gemini CLI (*https://oreil.ly/wPk9Q*), OpenAI Codex CLI (*https://oreil.ly/LiBmc*), OpenCode (*https://oreil.ly/wOpw5*), etc.

Code-based
: Libraries you write code against to build your own agent, such as LangGraph (*https://oreil.ly/UzECb*), Smolagents (*https://oreil.ly/Y455Q*), Pydantic AI (*https://oreil.ly/OwHUp*), etc.

Personal assistant
: Persistent agents that retain memory and skills across sessions, such as OpenClaw (*https://oreil.ly/9hsmr*), Hermes Agent (*https://oreil.ly/8KK-H*), etc.

Hosted
: Agents that run in the cloud as a hosted product, such as Replit (*https://replit.com*), v0 (*https://v0.app*), Manus (*https://manus.im*), etc.

UI-based
: Agents embedded inside a user-friendly interface, such as Antigravity, Cursor, Windsurf (*https://devin.ai/desktop*), GitHub Copilot (*https://github.com/features/copilot*), etc.

> Interestingly, while writing this overview of agentic harnesses, it feels like this list is already becoming outdated. That's how fast things can move in this field! So how do you keep up? We believe that as long as you learn the foundations well, it will be easier to navigate new releases, frameworks, and models. After all, all of these harnesses essentially use the same type of agent scaffolding (LLM, memory, tools, etc.). They just flavor them a bit differently.

Note that these harnesses are starting to evolve more into personal assistants. These harnesses focus on making agents persistent and always on. You can chat with your agent via any messaging system (such as WhatsApp, Discord, Slack, or even email) and they can autonomously solve tasks for you. These harnesses tend to give agents the most autonomy, such as checking your email, calendar, personal files, etc.

Arguably, the most famous example is OpenClaw, which gained an astonishing 300,000 stars on GitHub in only a couple of months after its release. OpenClaw is one of the first harnesses that allows users to easily create a persistent personal assistant. Since then, there have been many different alternatives, such as Hermes Agent (*https://oreil.ly/pNR_M*), that gained popularity (Figure 1-26).

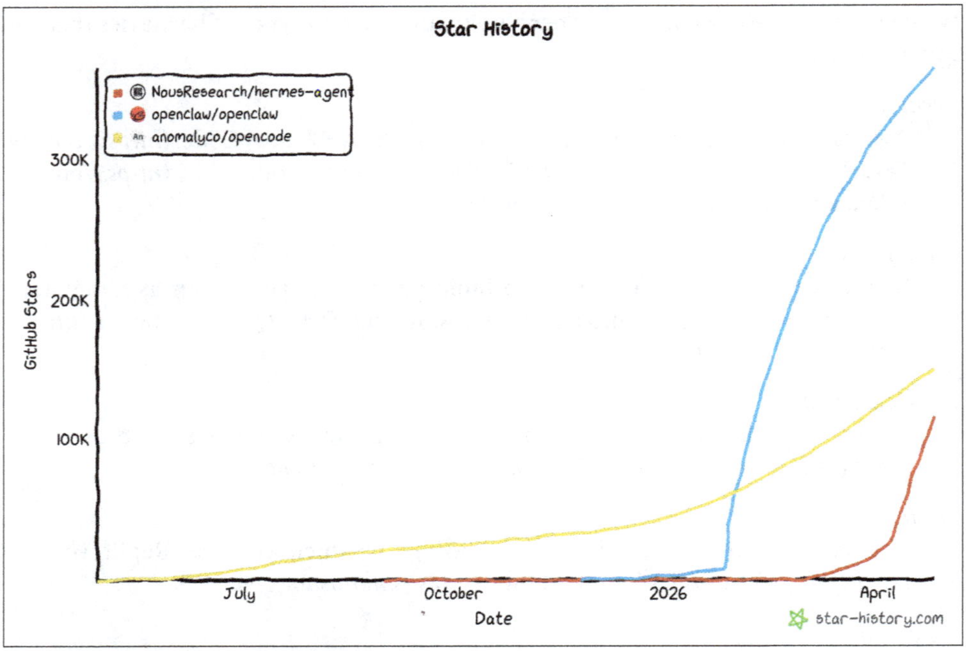

Figure 1-26. The number of stars on GitHub for open source personal assistant harnesses since their release

The harness of the `TinyAgent` that you're going to build is mostly code-based and will have a terminal implementation. We focus on the educational nature of this harness and decided that the best way to learn is to *build an agent from scratch*!

We're not going to use packages that abstract away the complexities but instead dive deep into them. The `TinyAgent` will be built with minimal dependencies and we'll explain everything you implement along the way. To do so, we make use of a highly modular and educational structure that focuses on understanding the vital components of an agent. Figure 1-27 shows some of the components that will be added to the `TinyAgent`.

Figure 1-27. A sneak peek into the different modules that we're going to explore and you're going to build

In this chapter, you'll take your first step!

We start with building the `TinyAgent` class, which is used as the skeleton on which we slowly add components in each chapter. This class is meant to remain small and showcase only the fundamental principles:

```
class TinyAgent:
    """A minimal, modular, and educational agent framework."""

    def __init__(self):
        self.llm = None  # Chapter 2 & 3: Add LLM
        self.memory = None  # Chapter 4: Add Memory
        self.tools = None  # Chapter 5: Add Tools
        self.planner = None  # Chapter 6: Add Planning

    def run(self, task: str) -> str:
        """Run the agent on a task."""
        return self._step(task)

    def _step(self, task: str) -> str:
        """Perform a single step."""
        # Placeholder - will be implemented in later chapters
        return f"Received: {task}"

    def _execute_action(self, action: str) -> str:
        """Execute a tool action."""
        # Placeholder - will be implemented in later chapters
        return f"Executed action: {action}"
```

This scaffolding of the agent does not do anything at the moment other than parroting what you say. The components are as follows:

`run`
: Run the agent on a given task

`_step`
: Perform a single step, which might include an answer or a tool call (Chapter 2)

`_execute_action`
: Execute a single action using a tool (Chapter 5)

Throughout this chapter, you will be able to run your `TinyAgent` with the following:

```
agent = TinyAgent()
agent.run("What is 2 + 2?")
```

Because this (the LLM) is merely a skeleton without a brain, the agent simply returns our question:

```
'Received: What is 2 + 2?'
```

The code we explore in this book revolves around a single core entity: building your `TinyAgent`. Although each chapter is designed to be self-contained, all code across chapters can be run out of order. However, each chapter builds on your `TinyAgent` and evolves it as you progress through the chapter. The result is essentially a package that you have developed yourself. To track this evolution, at the end of all code in a chapter, we conclude with a summary of what we built. Reviewing this small overview will give you a sense of the changes that were made to your `TinyAgent`.

What We Built

```
TinyAgent/
 └── agent.py ← New (`TinyAgent` skeleton)
```

Likewise, as you go through each chapter, your `TinyAgent` might need some small updates, such as tracking the state of the agent. We have provided various tools that allow you to easily view these differences (or "diffs") in the illustrated-agents package (*https://github.com/HandsOnLLM/An-Illustrated-Guide-To-AI-Agents*). We will first explore that in Chapter 2, along with arguably the most important component of an agent, its brain!

Summary

This first chapter serves as the scaffolding of this book. Consider it an overview of what an agent is and how it relates to every upcoming chapter, split up into two main parts.

In Part I, we'll cover the "brain" of the agent, namely, reasoning LLMs and how they can be augmented with memory, tools, and planning to interact with their environment. They show a degree of autonomy that requires a thorough understanding of the use case to decide when to implement additional guardrails and limit its autonomy or give it full control. This makes evaluation even more important and potentially complex.

In Part II, we will cover various specializations, starting with how agents might interact with each other as specialized entities. Then, we explore how LLMs understand the world through lenses other than text. A special focus will be on images, sound, and video because these are common other modalities the agent might interact with. We end this book with a chapter on coding agents as one of the most common use cases of agentic systems.

In the next two chapters, we'll cover the fundamentals of LLMs and reasoning LLMs, the "brain" of AI agents.

CHAPTER 2
Large Language Models

As we saw in Chapter 1, the LLM powers agents to go from observations to actions. In Figure 2-1, we can see this general workflow. Here, we color-code the areas where the agent interacts with the user (on the left) and where the agent interacts with the environment (on the right).

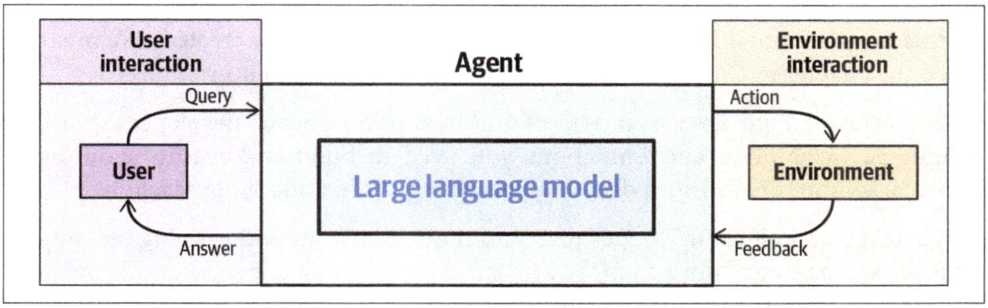

Figure 2-1. The agent acts as a bridge between user and environment

Let's take a simple example to unroll the loop we see in the figure. The example is a simple information-seeking agent trying to answer a question for a user using a web search tool.

In Figure 2-2, we can see that interaction:

1. The user asks the agent a question.
2. The agent uses a web search tool, effectively pulling in information from the environment.
3. The retrieved information is presented to the agent, which decides that it now has enough information to answer the user's question.

4. The agent prints out its answer to the user.

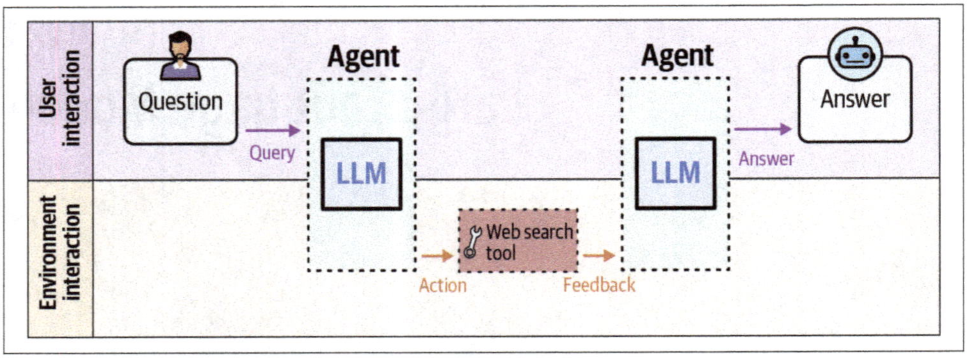

Figure 2-2. The agent receives a user's question (left), calls a web search tool to retrieve information from the environment, then uses the retrieved information to generate and return an answer (right)

In LLM-backed agents, the LLM is tasked with processing the user query, choosing the right action, processing the feedback or observation resulting from the action, and communicating back to the user.

In this chapter, you'll learn how LLMs work and how they're created. We've structured the chapter in two parts with intentionally different audiences in mind.

Part 1 offers a high-level overview of LLMs aimed at agent developers: the core intuitions, capabilities, and limitations you need to build and reason about agent systems—without requiring a deep understanding of the underlying machinery.

Part 2 takes a significantly deeper dive into model internals and training techniques. This section assumes more comfort with machine learning concepts and is intended for readers who want to understand why LLMs behave the way they do, not just how to use them. This understanding can be valuable when diagnosing agent failures, selecting models, or pushing the boundaries of what agents can do.

If you're primarily focused on building agents, feel free to proceed to the next chapter after reading Part 1—you'll have everything you need. You can return to Part 2 when you're ready to go deeper.

Part 1: What You Should Know About Large Language Models

Language models are systems trained to predict and generate text sequences. Their inputs and outputs are best understood initially as sequences of words, or more precisely, tokens—which can be words, parts of words, numbers, or punctuation.

Input and Output Tokens

We can see the perspective of an LLM's inputs and outputs in Figure 2-3. The input text (which can be a query from the user or feedback from the environment) is first broken down into tokens, then presented to the language model. The language model generates the first token, then the next one, then the next, until its response is completed.

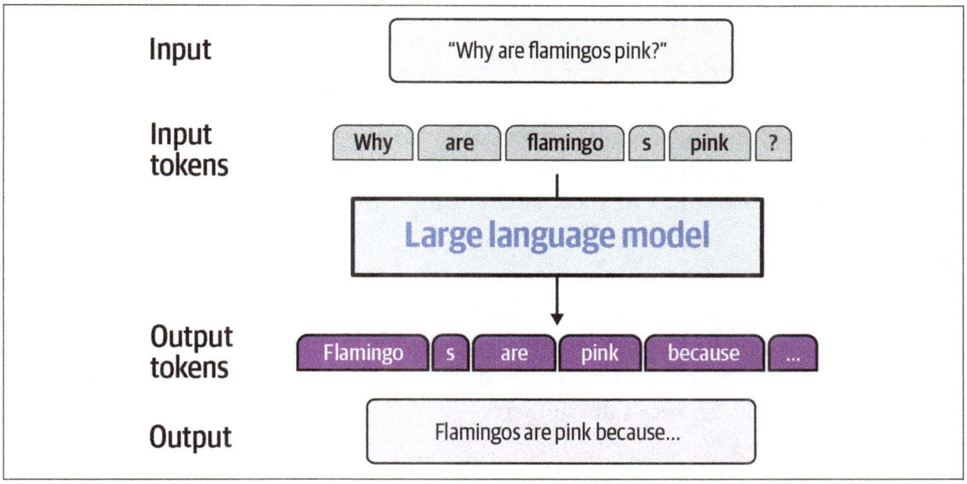

Figure 2-3. Input text is split into tokens—"flamingos" becomes two tokens ("flamingo" and "s")—passed to the LLM, which generates output tokens sequentially to form the final response

This one step of generating this output text is actually a loop where the model generates a token, adds it to the input, and then processes this new input again to generate the next token. We can see the first of these steps in Figure 2-4. Models that operate like this, consuming their own output from one step as inputs in a following step, are called *autoregressive models*.

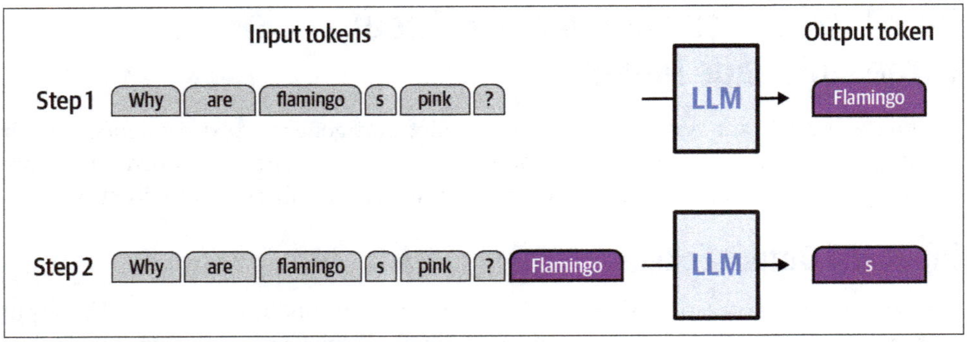

Figure 2-4. The model generates "Flamingo" from the input tokens (step 1); that output token is appended to the input and the model generates the next token, "s" (step 2)

From Language Modeling to Powering Agents

The LLMs that power agents start out as general language models, as previously discussed. This is done in the first training phase of a language model and creates what's called a base language model. But for an LLM to be able to power an agent, it needs an additional set of capabilities to fit the expected role. LLM creators train LLMs in the subsequent phase of training, called post-training, to be able to parse inputs and generate outputs in a format that supports these expected capabilities.

System prompt

Language models are most often deployed by one entity, say a company, to serve a set of users, say the employees of the company. The party that deploys the model needs a way to describe the expected behavior of the model in a way that takes precedence over what the end users ask of the model.

This is the role of the *system prompt*: a privileged input that shapes model behavior before the model sees a single token from the user. Because it's baked into how the model is used rather than how it's trained, system prompts let deployers customize behavior without touching the underlying model.

In Figure 2-5, we see how a system prompt is added to the beginning of a user message. We also see a simple example of a formatting style that identifies the various parts of the input and output. Shown here is a simplified format that looks like the OpenAI Harmony format (*https://oreil.ly/T-966*) used for models such as OpenAI's GPT-OSS (*https://oreil.ly/jGgkO*), released in 2025.

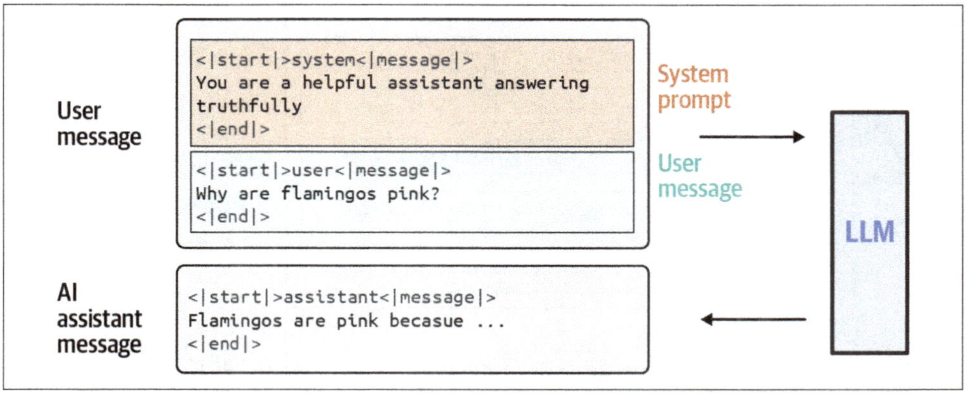

Figure 2-5. A system prompt prepended to the user message shapes how the model will respond—here instructing it to "answer truthfully"—before the full input is passed to the LLM

Multi-turn conversations

Popular LLM systems like ChatGPT are modeled as a conversation between a user and an AI chatbot. This way, the LLM can keep track of a longer conversation and identify who said what in the history of the conversation. In Chapter 4, we'll touch on this as being one way we give an LLM some form of memory to be able to recollect earlier messages in the conversation.

Tool use

The conversation formats define a specific way for a language model to take an action. The LLM outputs a specific format, choosing a software function to invoke. The agentic software wrapper around the language model looks for these patterns and calls the functions that the LLM is trying to invoke. These functions are usually listed in the system prompt telling the LLM what actions are available to it.

Chapter 5 is dedicated to tools, their definitions, invocations, and processing their outputs. We touch on them here for an early example of the types of text that flow into and out of language models, enabling them to power agents.

In Figure 2-6, we can see an example message passed to an LLM. It has a system prompt, multiple turns in the chat history, and a final question asked by the user. The LLM responds by choosing to call a web search tool to retrieve the information required to answer the question.

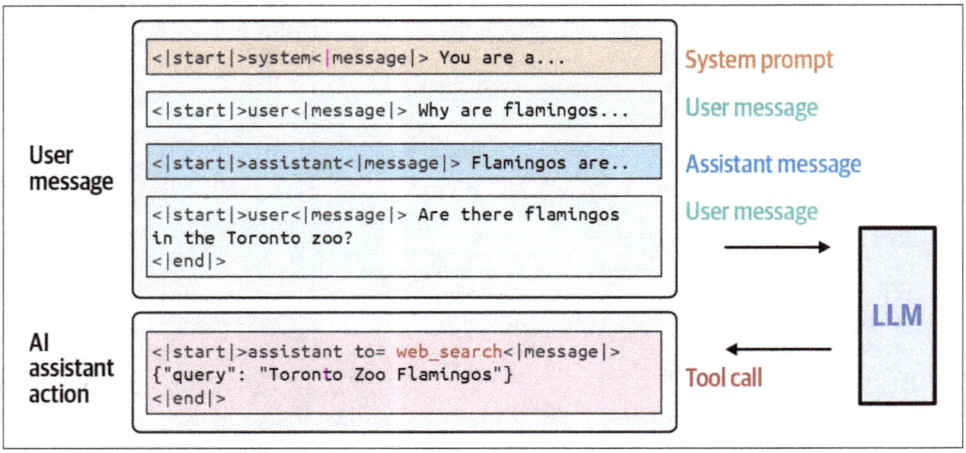

Figure 2-6. The LLM responds to a user question by emitting a tool call (`web_search` with a structured query) and executing it before the conversation continues

All of the input text we see in this figure is an example of the text that gets tokenized and sent to the LLM. And the output text is what the LLM generates one token at a time.

The TinyAgent

The LLM is the agent's brain, and it's the first thing we want to implement in your `TinyAgent`. To do so, we will need to consider which LLM to use, as there are hundreds of options depending on your hardware, use case, and the LLM's capabilities. Newer models such as Gemma 4 have been trained to perform native reasoning and tool calling and have various options for different hardware. However, rather than only showing an LLM that "just does" reasoning and tool calling, we also want to show you what it's like to build the tool calling and reasoning behavior yourself.

We decided to show you both! Throughout the book, we will demonstrate these capabilities both from a prompt-driven and model-driven perspective. By doing it yourself through various prompting techniques, you'll gain insight into how these newer models have learned to perform reasoning and tool calling natively.

As such, we choose two models to use throughout this book: one that cannot natively perform any reasoning or tool calling whatsoever (Gemma 3) and one that has been trained specifically to perform agentic tasks through reasoning and tool calling (Gemma 4). They both have various sizes, where bigger models tend to be stronger than smaller models. For Gemma 3, we opt for the 12-billion-parameter model (Gemma 3 12B (*https://oreil.ly/GTvvJ*)), and for Gemma 4, we opt for the smaller model that has effectively 4 billion parameters (Gemma 4 E4B (*https://oreil.ly/zhw45*)).

The large language model

Before we start creating the main class for the brain, the LLM, we first explore a common way of interacting with LLMs, namely through the OpenAI-endpoint. It is a standardization of LLM inference that includes set fields, parameters, and responses so that you always get the same standardized format back. OpenAI, with the release of GPT 3.5 in 2022, set this standard for parsing an LLM's response.

This endpoint generally contains the following pieces of information:

`base_url`
: The URL of your hosted LLM

`api_key`
: The key for accessing your hosted LLM

`model`
: The name of your LLM

`messages`
: The query to send to your LLM

Before you can use the LLM, you will first have to spin up a server that hosts your LLM. Don't worry, this is much easier than it sounds. There are many different ways to download and host your LLM on your device. Popular options include Ollama (*https://ollama.com*), LMStudio (*https://lmstudio.ai*), and llama.cpp (*https://oreil.ly/XYUKj*). Ollama and LMStudio work well for both developers and non-developers, whereas llama.cpp is ideal for developers. Throughout this book, we'll assume you use Ollama, which hosts its LLMs locally on *http://localhost:11434/v1/*. However, you can use any inference engine, both locally and hosted, as long as it is OpenAI-compatible (which most are).

After installing Ollama (*https://ollama.com/download*), you can download the models like so:

```
ollama pull gemma4:e4b
ollama pull gemma3:12b
```

As we covered previously, all LLMs have a specific prompt template that decides how to format the text that passes through the LLM. Instead of having to look up what this template is for each model, most inference engines (like Ollama) do this for you with the `messages` structure. These `messages` are a common format for structuring multiple turns of questions and responses between you (`user`) and the LLM (`assistant`). You can then use the `messages` structure to talk to the LLM, which will automatically convert it to the prompt template of the LLM.

We'll use this structure to call the OpenAI-endpoint, which, in turn, will return a response. This response can contain multiple answers in parallel but is generally a single answer. As such, we focus on inspecting its one answer, namely `result["choices"][0]`:

```
import json
import urllib.request

# Prepare request
data = json.dumps(
    {
        "model": "gemma4:e4b",
        "messages": [{"role": "user", "content": "Hi! How's life?"}]
    }
).encode("utf-8")

# Post request
req = urllib.request.Request(
    url="http://localhost:11434/v1/chat/completions",
    data=data,
    headers={"Content-Type": "application/json"}
)

# Parse response
with urllib.request.urlopen(req) as response:
    result = json.loads(response.read())

# Print response
print(result["choices"][0])
```

This will give the following output:

```
{
    'index': 0,
    'message': {
        'role': 'assistant',
        'content': "I\'m doing really well, thank you for asking! 😊\n\n
        How about you? What\'s going on with you today?",
        'reasoning': 'Thinking Process:\n\n1.
        **Analyze the Request:** The user said, "Hi! How\'s life?" This is a
        casual, conversational greeting seeking an update or general positive
        interaction.\n2.
        **Determine the Persona/Role:**  I am an AI assistant...'
    },
    'finish_reason': 'stop'
}
```

Note that we truncated the reasoning a bit to prevent it from being too long for this book. As we cover in Chapter 3, reasoning significantly improves the response of an LLM.

Depending on the capabilities of the underlying LLM, it might output more fields than just the content and reasoning. Some models are capable of returning tool calls, which get a field of their own. As discussed before, we are not going to use the tool and reasoning fields immediately. The reason is two-fold and is important for the philosophy behind understanding what is happening under the hood:

1. Using the `reasoning` and `tool_calls` fields is a bit "magical" and does not teach you how these are actually created and used. Instead, we're going to show you how to do this explicitly through prompting techniques.
2. Some models actually do not support `reasoning` and `tool_calls`, but with proper prompting, can still be used as agents. So instead of blindly relying on these fields, we want to show you how to nudge the model to do explicit reasoning and tool calling with prompting.

In Chapter 3 (reasoning) and Chapter 5 (tool calling), we will show you first how to use these capabilities by leveraging prompting techniques before exploring how a model does this natively.

After we get the output, we are going to create a `Response` dataclass where we will track the `content`, `reasoning`, `tool_call`, and other `metadata` the model may provide:

```
from dataclasses import dataclass

@dataclass
class Response:
    """Structured response from LLM calls."""

    content: str = ""
    reasoning: str | None = None
    tool_call: dict | None = None
    metadata: dict | None = None
```

For now, we are only interested in using the `content` of the model, as we want to show you how to have a non-reasoning model that still shows reasoning behavior. To do that, we are adding a parameter to the `LLM` class we'll be building that can disable thinking. Lastly, we also track metadata that the backend might provide, such as the model's name (`"model"`), the number of tokens in the prompt (`"prompt_tokens"`), and the number of tokens that were generated (`"completion_tokens"`).

In this `LLM` class, we're going to query the OpenAI-compatible endpoint directly as we did before. However, we add a few functionalities to prepare you for later chapters, such as adding tools/reasoning and extracting them:

```
import json
import urllib.request

class LLM:
    def __init__(
        self,
        model: str,
```

```
        base_url: str = "http://localhost:11434/v1",
        api_key: str = "no_key",
        think: bool = False,
    ):
        """Initialize the LLM with the given model."""
        self.model = model
        self.base_url = base_url
        self.api_key = api_key
        self.think = think

    def generate(
        self, messages: list[dict], tools: list | None = None
    ) -> Response:
        """Generate a response from the LLM given a list of messages."""
        # Build the request body
        body = {
            "model": self.model,
            "messages": messages,
        }

        # Tools and Reasoning
        if tools:
            body["tools"] = tools
        if not self.think:
            body["reasoning_effort"] = "none"

        # POST to the OpenAI-compatible /chat/completions endpoint
        request = urllib.request.Request(
            f"{self.base_url}/chat/completions",
            data=json.dumps(body).encode(),
            headers={
                "Content-Type": "application/json",
                "Authorization": f"Bearer {self.api_key}",
            },
        )
        with urllib.request.urlopen(request) as response:
            data = json.loads(response.read())

        # Extract message, tool_call, and metadata
        message = data["choices"][0]["message"]
        tool_calls = message.get("tool_calls")
        tool_call = tool_calls[0] if tool_calls else None
        metadata = {
            "model": data["model"],
            "prompt_tokens": data["usage"]["prompt_tokens"],
            "completion_tokens": data["usage"]["completion_tokens"],
        }

        # Format as Response dataclass
        return Response(
            content=message.get("content"),
            reasoning=message.get("reasoning"),
```

```
            tool_call=tool_call,
            metadata=metadata,
        )
```

We also added the option to add tools to your LLM and extract a tool call if it exists. These options are explored in more detail in Chapter 5. We make sure to have this now so we do not need to update this class later.

Finally, you can call the LLM with our updated class and extract the response only:

```
# Re-initialize the LLM with the updated class
llm = LLM(model="gemma4:e4b")

# Generate a `Response` dataclass
response = llm.generate([{"role": "user", "content": "Hi! How's life?"}])
print(response)
```

This gives you:

```
Response(
    content="Life is going well, thank you for asking!
    I'm busy processing information and helping users like you, which is always
    interesting. How about I ask you? How's life on your end? 😊",
        reasoning=None,
        tool_call=None,
        metadata={
            "model": "gemma4:e4b",
            "prompt_tokens": 16,
            "completion_tokens": 43,
        },
    )
```

The `Response` object is going to be used throughout the `TinyAgent` so that we can easily access the output of the LLM. Before integrating it into the agent, let's first explore how we can track the state of an agent.

A step and trajectory

Remember that we are creating an agentic harness and a vital component of any harness, is that you can easily debug what is happening during inference. An agent might run for several turns at a time and run into an incorrect tool usage. To easily debug that, we want to keep track of everything the model has done so far. To do so, we track each `Step` the agent has taken (including observation from the output of a tool):

```
from dataclasses import dataclass

@dataclass
class Step:
    """A single step in an agent's trajectory."""

    thought: str = ""
```

```python
    action: dict | None = None
    observation: str | None = None
    answer: str | None = None
    metadata: dict | None = None
```

The `Step` is very much like the `Response` object with one major difference, the `answer` and `observation` fields. The answer is the final answer of the model and represents that the agent has reached the end of its turn. The observation is the output of tool usage. They are consequences of any processing or results we get from the `TinyAgent`. Finally, we use the term *action* to describe a tool call because in Chapter 6 we will explore loops of thought → action → observation that allow for autonomous behavior.

To reach its final answer, an agent might need various steps and use different actions. This sequence of steps is called the agent's *trajectory*. We likewise track this information as it allows for easily debugging this sequence of steps to identify where and why an agent might have failed.

The `Trajectory` that you are going to create is where each `Step` will be created and filled with information related to the `TinyAgent`:

```python
class Trajectory:
    """Records agent execution as a sequence of runs."""
    def __init__(self) -> None:
        self.runs: list[dict] = []

    def initialize(self, query: str) -> None:
        """Register a new run with the given query."""
        self.runs.append({"query": query, "steps": []})

    def add(self, response: Response, observation: str | None = None) -> None:
        """Record a step from a Response, optionally with an observation."""
        # Add THOUGHT
        step = Step(
            thought=response.reasoning or "",
            metadata=response.metadata,
        )

        # Add ACTION/OBSERVATION or ANSWER
        if observation is not None:
            step.action = response.tool_call
            step.observation = observation
        else:
            step.answer = response.content

        self.runs[-1]["steps"].append(step)
```

Updating your TinyAgent

Finally, you need to update the TinyAgent with only a few lines of code to add this brain (the LLM) to your agent. Note that we focus on only single-step agents for now, without any autonomy. This is behavior that will be added and explored in-depth in Chapter 6:

```
class TinyAgent:
    """A minimal, modular, and educational agent framework."""

    def __init__(self, llm: LLM):
        self.llm = llm
        self.memory = None  # Chapter 4: Add Memory
        self.tools = None  # Chapter 5: Add Tools
        self.planner = None  # Chapter 6: Add Planning

        self.trajectory = Trajectory()

    def run(self, task: str) -> str:
        """Run the agent on a task."""
        self.trajectory.initialize(task)
        return self._step(task)

    def _step(self, task: str) -> str:
        """Perform a single step."""
        messages = [{"role": "user", "content": task}]
        response = self.llm.generate(messages)
        self.trajectory.add(response)
        return response.content

    def _execute_action(self, action: str) -> str | None:
        """Execute a tool action."""
        # Placeholder - will be implemented in later chapters
        return f"Executed action: {action}"
```

Helper Functions

As you progress through the chapters, you might add just a single line of code to TinyAgent. That becomes difficult to spot as the number of lines of code in TinyAgent grows. We prepared a number of helper functions in the illustrated-agents package (*https://github.com/HandsOnLLM/An-Illustrated-Guide-To-AI-Agents*) that will help you quickly see what (small) changes were made between two versions of, for example, TinyAgent. These are all added to the notebooks in the associated GitHub repository and are generally used like so:

```
from illustrated_agents.chapters.ch2 import tinyagents_diff
tinyagents_diff
```

Or you can use them to inspect how a given class has changed between two chapters, even if the chapters are far apart:

```
from illustrated_agents.chapters import ch1, ch6
from illustrated_agents.utils import DiffViewer

tinyagents_diff = DiffViewer(
    ch1.TinyAgent, ch6.TinyAgent,
    "Chapter 1 - TinyAgent", "Chapter 6 - TinyAgent"
)
```

To test if it works, initialize the `TinyAgent` again with the updated LLM and ask it a question:

```
agent = TinyAgent(llm=llm)
response = agent.run("What is 2 + 2?")
print(response)
```

This gives you:

```
"2 + 2 is 4."
```

A straightforward answer—great!

Throughout these chapters we also will be looking at the trajectory quite often to debug and see if the `TinyAgent` performed as expected. You can access the full trajectory with:

```
print(agent.trajectory.runs)
```

This gives:

```
[
  {
    'query': 'What is 2 + 2?',
    'steps': [
      Step(
        thought='',
        action=None,
        observation=None,
        answer='2 + 2 is 4.',
        metadata={
          'model': 'gemma4:e4b', 'prompt_tokens': 17, 'completion_tokens': 9
        }
      )
    ]
  }
]
```

Your "Agent" is still nothing more than the LLM and has no additional behavior/capabilities that we can showcase yet. For that, we need to add more modules, such as reasoning (Chapter 3), memory (Chapter 4), tools (Chapter 5), and planning (Chapter 6).

> Trajectories can get unwieldy quickly when you have dozens of steps, tool calls, long reasoning, and more. We created a small helper utility that visualizes these components without seeming unwieldy. As always, these can be found in the notebook on the associated GitHub repository (*https://github.com/HandsOnLLM/An-Illustrated-Guide-To-AI-Agents*). The utility is called the `TrajectoryViewer` and is used at the end of each notebook:
>
> ```
> from illustrated_agents.utils import TrajectoryViewer
> TrajectoryViewer(agent.trajectory)
> ```

There was a lot of code to explore but it was vital for creating this foundation of `LLM`, `Response`, `Step`, and `Trajectory`. These are things that are going to be used quite often to standardize behavior in your `TinyAgent`.

What We Built

```
TinyAgent/
├── agent.py ← Updated (Integrated the `LLM` into your `TinyAgent`)
├── llm.py  ← New (An LLM wrapper for local or cloud models)
└── trajectory.py  ← New (Step and Trajectory tracking)
```

Now that you have a working LLM and added it to your `TinyAgent`, let's explore how these models are actually trained!

Training a Large Language Model

LLMs go through two major phases of training: pre-training and post-training (Figure 2-7). Pre-training is where they get their name from, because they are trained on a language processing task called *language modeling*.

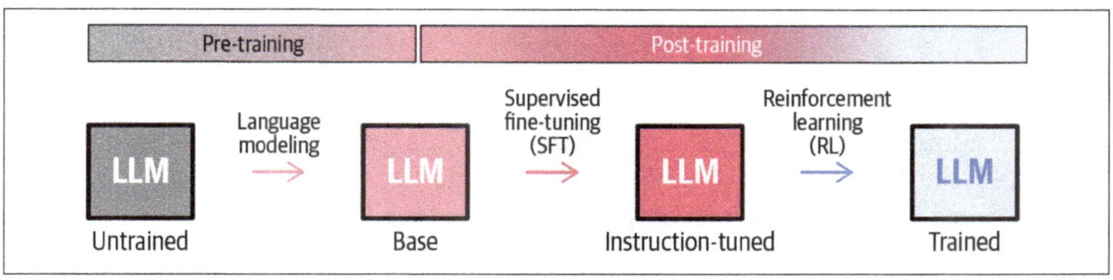

Figure 2-7. The two phases of LLM training: pre-training produces a base model, and post-training applies supervised fine-tuning (SFT) and reinforcement learning (RL) to produce the final model

Pre-training: language modeling

Language modeling is the task of presenting a model with a sequence of words (or more precisely, tokens) and asking it to predict the next word that is most likely to appear. This phase requires vast amounts of data and it takes a major part of the computing done during the training process.

Pre-training data is drawn from curated mixtures of sources including web text, books, and code, each filtered to satisfy quality criteria. From this text data, we can extract different spans of text and use each one as a training example. Say, for example, we handsomely pay O'Reilly Media to license the data on its website describing our earlier book, *Hands-On Large Language Models*. As we can see in Figure 2-8, we can take one span of that text and present it to the model. We hide the last token, give the model all the previous tokens, and ask it to predict the next word in the sequence.

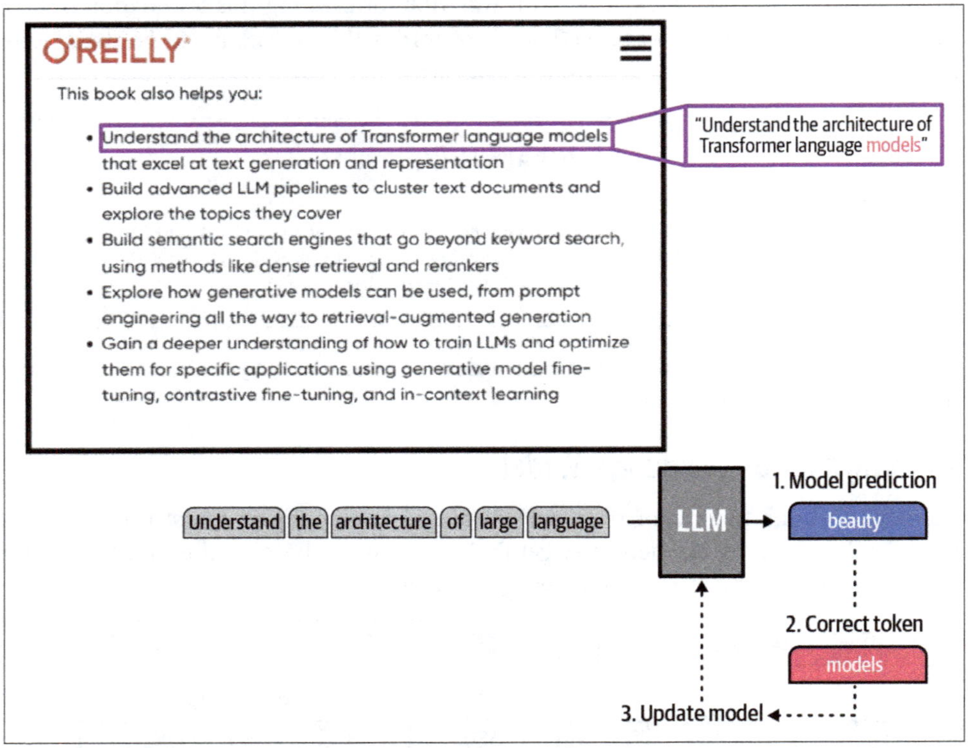

Figure 2-8. Pre-training as next-token prediction, where the model attempts to predict the next word in a sentence and updates its weights based on errors

At the start, the model under training would almost always guess incorrectly, which is part of the process. Now that we have its wrong prediction and the correct word, we plug them both in our loss calculation and update the weights of the model so that next time it has a better chance of making the right prediction. This is done billions of times and in the end results in a *base model*. The most famous and transformational of these is OpenAI's GPT3, released in 2020. Since then, the later steps in the training process were widely adopted to lead to a model that requires less prompt engineering and behaves more in line with how people (and agent scaffolds) expect it to behave.

Post-training: supervised fine-tuning

Base models have strong latent capabilities, including reasoning, summarization, translation, and code generation, that often require heavy prompt engineering to unlock. Post-training helps polish these model behaviors using a much smaller set of training examples.

The first step of post-training is called supervised fine-tuning (SFT). It is also sometimes referred to as instruction-tuning because it's where a model is trained to follow instructions we give it in prompts.

As we can see in Figure 2-9, an SFT training example is composed of a prompt and a completion that shows how we want the model to behave if it sees such a prompt. The update rule is almost identical to that of pre-training. The key difference is that while prompt tokens are included in the input context, they are excluded from the loss computation so the model is trained on only the response tokens. This is why we've assigned these tokens different colors and borders in the figure.

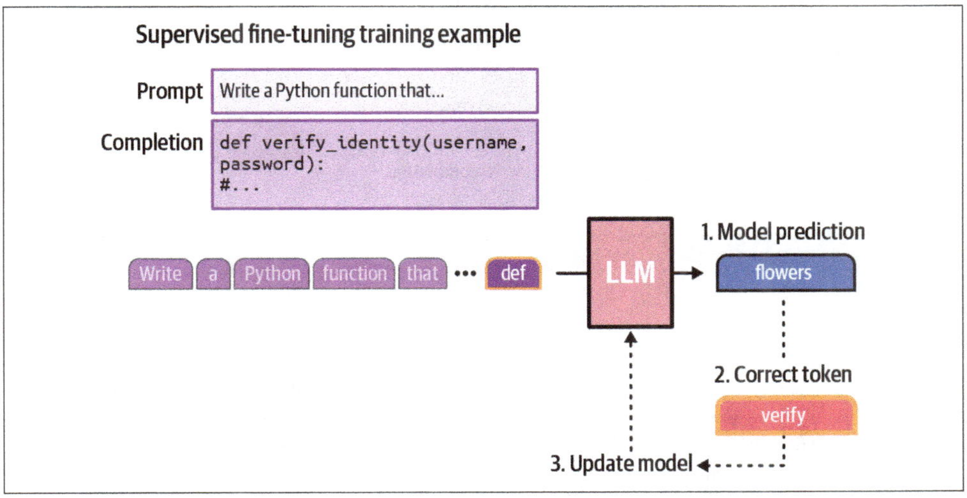

Figure 2-9. SFT trains the model on prompt-completion pairs. The prompt tokens (light purple) are fed as context but excluded from the loss; only the completion tokens (dark purple) are trained on—here, the model predicts "flowers" where "verify" is correct, and the weights are updated accordingly.

The SFT training phase is essential, yet not enough to produce a cutting-edge model. It teaches the model to follow instructions, but it cannot fully capture human preferences about what makes a response genuinely helpful, accurate, or well-reasoned. The reinforcement learning step that follows is what pushes the model in that direction.

Post-training: reinforcement learning

Notice how in SFT, we show the model what the desired output looks like. Reinforcement learning (RL) is a different training methodology that doesn't require having a complete targeted response. Instead, we use methods that evaluate the quality of a model-generated response and update the model's weights based on that quality score, called a *reward*.

One of the most commonly used RL methods in training LLMs is *Reinforcement Learning from Human Feedback* (RLHF), which relies on preference scores collected from humans or specialized models called *reward models*, themselves often being LLMs as well.

A single training example in an RLHF step, as shown in Figure 2-10, can be a prompt and two completions for it: one that is preferred, and another that is rejected.

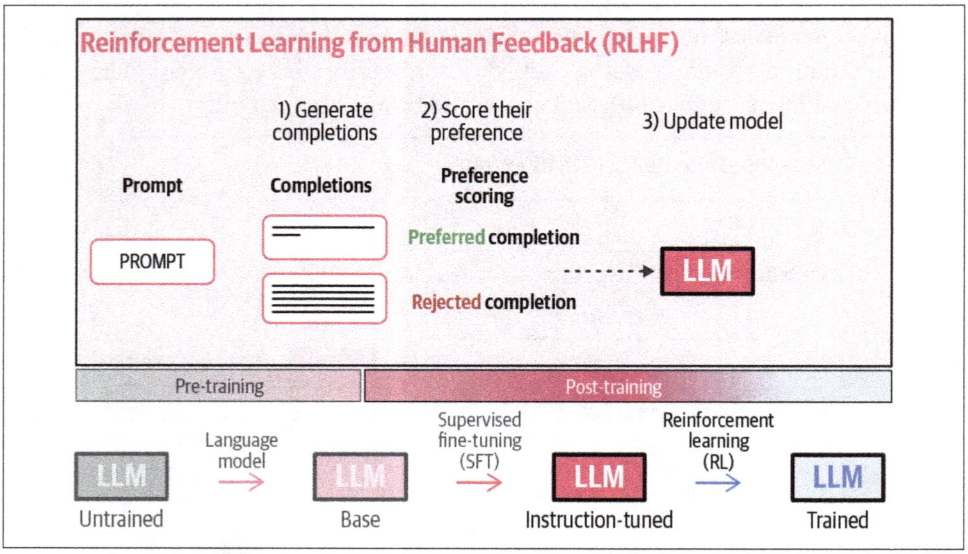

Figure 2-10. The model generates multiple completions, which are scored by human raters or a reward model trained on human preferences, and the model is updated toward producing higher-scoring responses

The RLHF training objective is to update the model to increase the likelihood of generating output like the preferred response and decrease the likelihood of generating output like the rejected response. This can be used to polish model behaviors such as response length, type of language the model uses, safe type of completions to generate or to avoid, and many other types of behaviors.

The other major RL method widely used in post-training today's leading LLMs is Reinforcement Learning with Verifiable Rewards (RLVR). Similar to RLHF, it updates the model based on a reward score. The difference here is that the rewards can be obtained from automated ways of verifying the output; for example, if it follows a certain format, or the final answer it results in is equal to the correct answer (that we knew beforehand, in the case of math problems, for example). We see a couple of very basic verifiers in Figure 2-11 that hint at the actual verifiers used in RLVR methods.

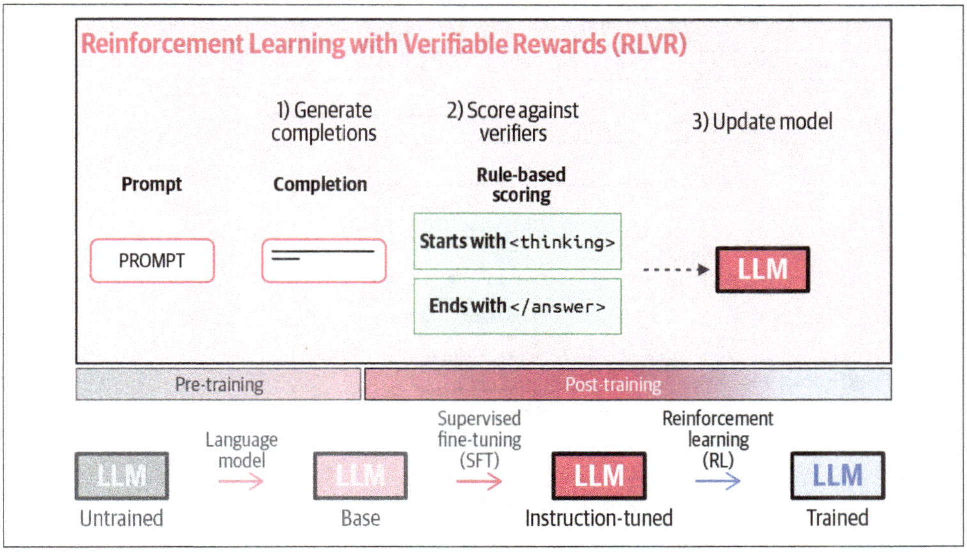

Figure 2-11. With RLVR, correctness is determined automatically by verifiers rather than relying on human preference

We'll dig deeper into RLVR and various types of verifiers at multiple points in the book.

The Group Relative Policy Optimization reinforcement learning algorithm

To better grasp the intuitions behind RLVR, we can look at a more specific example for a model that solves math problems. Let's say we have a set of math problems and the final correct answer for each of them. We want to train the model to solve them correctly and to print the answer in the format `<answer>42</answer>`, if 42 was the answer to a specific problem, for example.

In Figure 2-12, we can see an example showing an RL training dataset made up of math word problems and their answers. In an RLVR training step, we take one of the problems and pass it to the model with instructions about the format that we want.

Once the model generates its output, we can automatically verify whether it followed the requested format and if it arrived at the correct solution of the problem. The model's response is then scored on two verifiable dimensions: format (did it use the correct tags?) and accuracy (was the answer right?). The combined reward signal is used to update the model weights.

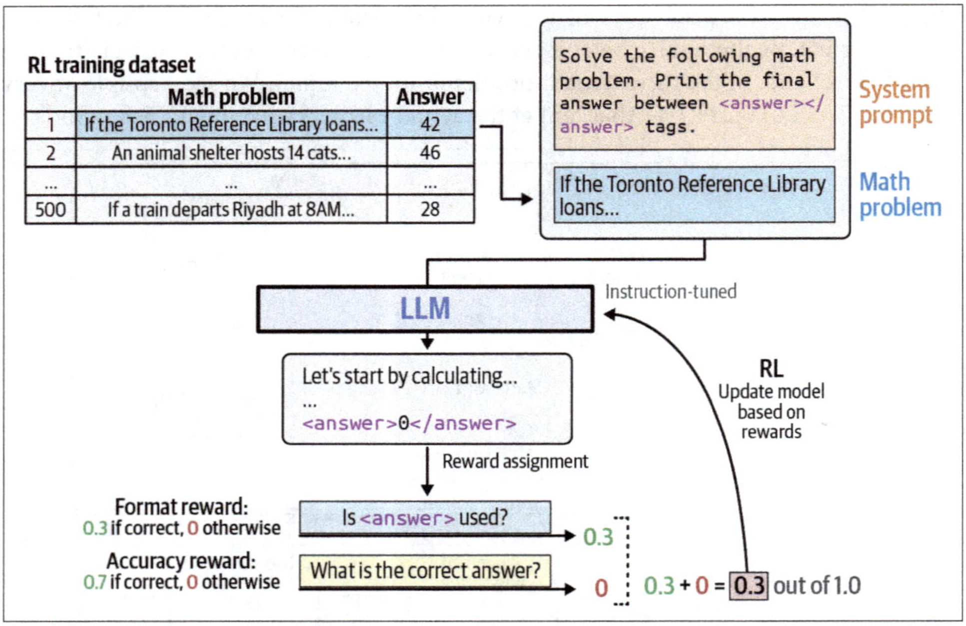

Figure 2-12. RLVR training on math problems

In this example we had two kinds of rewards, a format reward scoring whether the model uses the correct format for the output and assigning a reward of 0.3 if correct or 0 if incorrect. Then there's an accuracy reward that compares the final result to the actual result and assigns a reward of 0.7 if correct and 0 if incorrect. In Chapter 3, we'll see how this method was used to train DeepSeek-R1, one of the first open-weight reasoning LLMs.

The Group Relative Policy Optimization (GRPO) algorithm has another key ingredient beyond reward assignment. Rather than scoring a single response, at each training step GRPO generates a group of responses for the same prompt using a temperature setting that ensures diversity among them. Rewards are then computed relative to this group, reinforcing responses that score higher than the others. This comparative approach is what the word "group" in the name refers to.

In Figure 2-13, we can see this intuition for a group size of five. We generate five answers from the model, assign a reward to each one, and use those scores to update the model.

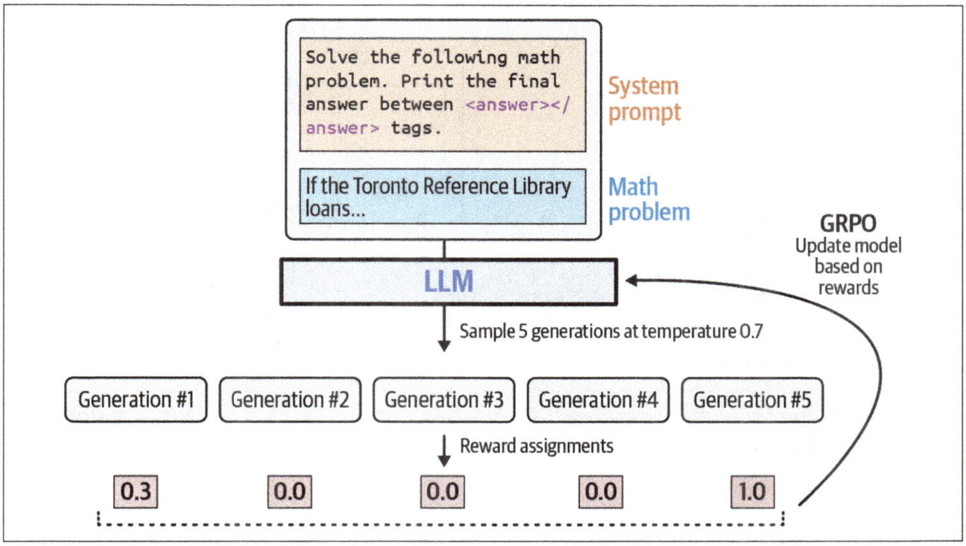

Figure 2-13. GRPO generates multiple responses to a single prompt, assigns rewards, and updates the model based on relative scores

This concludes the main intuitions for model training we think are useful for builders of AI agents to know about how LLMs are trained. Next, we'll take a closer look at the architecture of the neural network that this process trains.

The Transformer Architecture

Now that we've seen the inputs and outputs of the model and covered how the model gets trained, it's time to look inside the trained model and get a sense of the inner workings. LLMs have predominantly been neural networks built in the Transformer decoder architecture since around 2020.

The tokenizer, Transformer blocks, and language modeling head

A Transformer decoder has three major components: a tokenizer, a stack of Transformer blocks, and a language modeling head (LM head). We see these components in Figure 2-14.

The tokenizer is the piece of software responsible for breaking the text input into tokens. It is carefully optimized earlier in the training process of the LLM to help bring out the capabilities we need in the trained LLM. The vast majority of agent developers will work with a ready-made tokenizer prepared by the model provider.

For an LLM intended to power agents, careful tuning for a tokenizer includes support for generating software code, the various languages intended for use, and adding special tokens (like `<|start|>`) that are used in the specified data format.

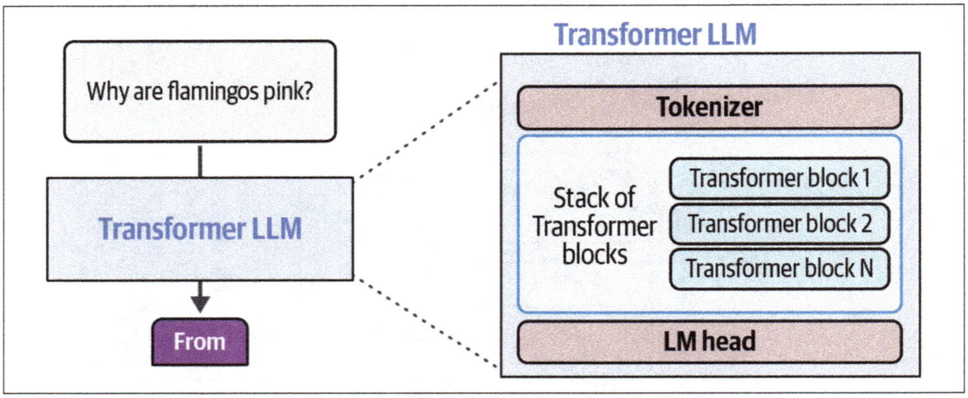

Figure 2-14. The three main components of a Transformer LLM: a tokenizer, a stack of Transformer blocks, and an LM head

A tokenizer has a set number of tokens in its *vocabulary*, say 50,000. We see an example of these in Figure 2-15.

We can also see in the figure that the model has an equal number of vector embeddings—one per token in our vocabulary. These embeddings vectors are numeric representations of each token and they are what the model uses to calculate language and how it processes its inputs.

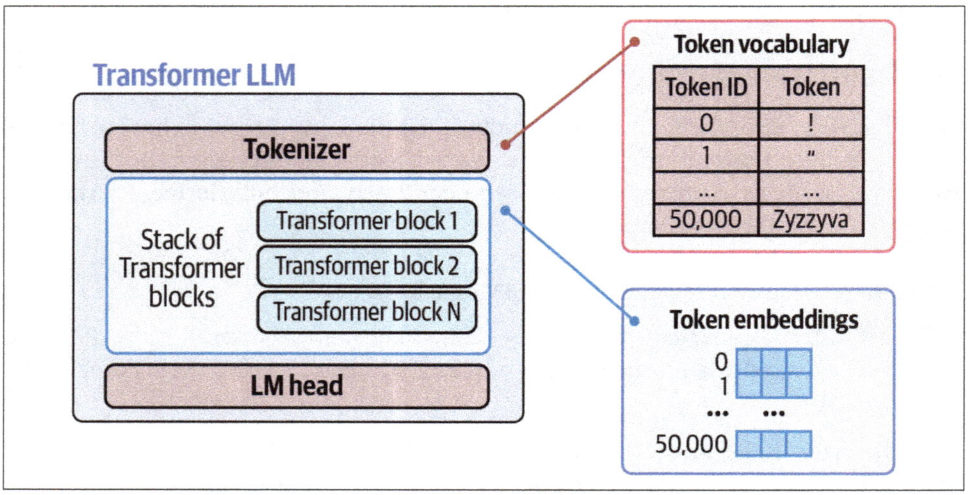

Figure 2-15. The tokenizer maps input text to token IDs drawn from a fixed vocabulary (here, 50,000 tokens), each of which is then looked up in an embeddings table to retrieve a numeric vector before being passed to the Transformer blocks

Almost the entirety of the processing done inside a language model is conducted inside the stack of Transformer blocks, which we cover in more detail in the next section. But what results from that process is a single vector containing information on what the next token should be.

That vector is passed to the LM head to interpret. It makes a simple calculation, which results in a probability score for each token in its vocabulary. That score is informed by everything the model learned in its training phases, and tokens with high probabilities are the ones most likely to appear as a completion in response to the input tokens. In Figure 2-16, we can see an example of such a scoring of probabilities.

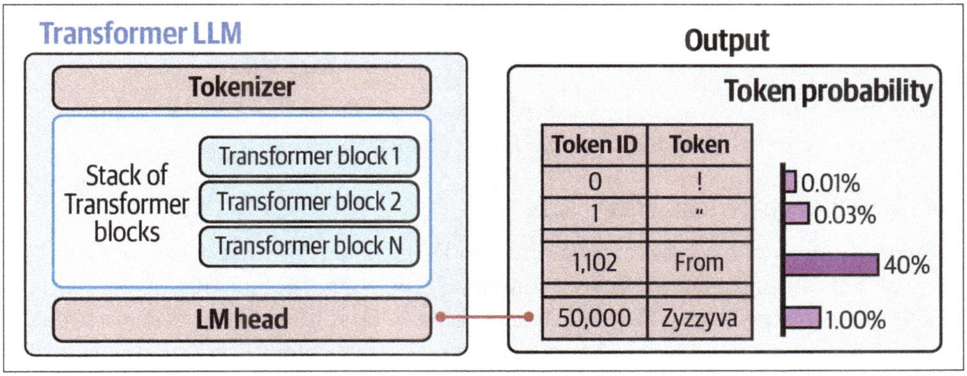

Figure 2-16. The LM head converts final representations into a probability distribution over the entire vocabulary

The next natural step would be to actually pick the output token as informed by these probabilities. We may choose the highest probability token, but there are often good reasons for picking other tokens. The method to pick tokens from the probability distribution is called a decoding strategy.

If you've played with the temperature setting of an LLM, then you have interacted with these probabilities. A temperature value of zero leads to always choosing the single token with the highest probability. Increasing that temperature allows *sampling*, which means choosing from the distribution in a way where higher-probability tokens have a higher chance of being picked (Figure 2-17).

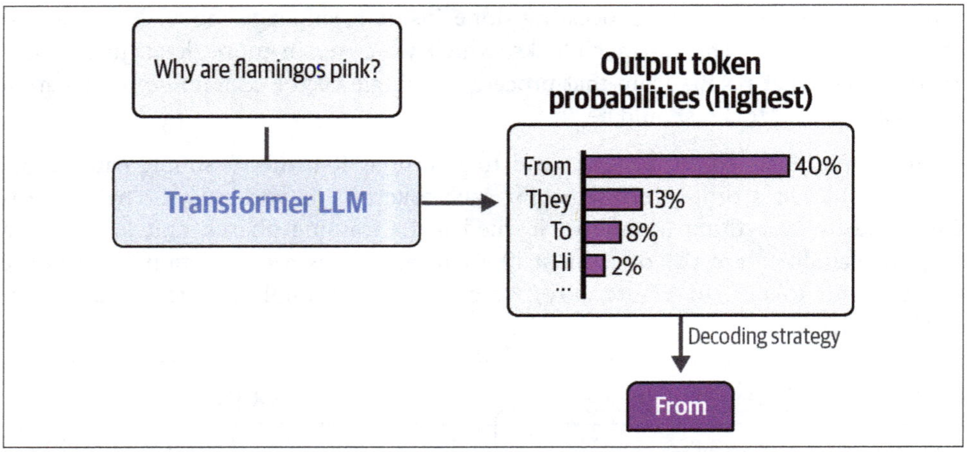

Figure 2-17. The decoding strategy selects a token from the probability distribution, where higher temperatures increase the chance of lower-probability tokens

Processing through the Transformer blocks

A neural network processes inputs and produces an output in a *forward pass*. This means that the calculation flows sequentially through the various layers. This is exactly what happens with the Transformer blocks. First the first block starts processing, then it passes its results of processing to the next block, and so on. The final block passes its result to the LM head, and we proceed to decoding as we saw in the previous section.

Figure 2-18 shows this flow through the stack of Transformer blocks. It also shows how each token can be seen flowing through its own track.

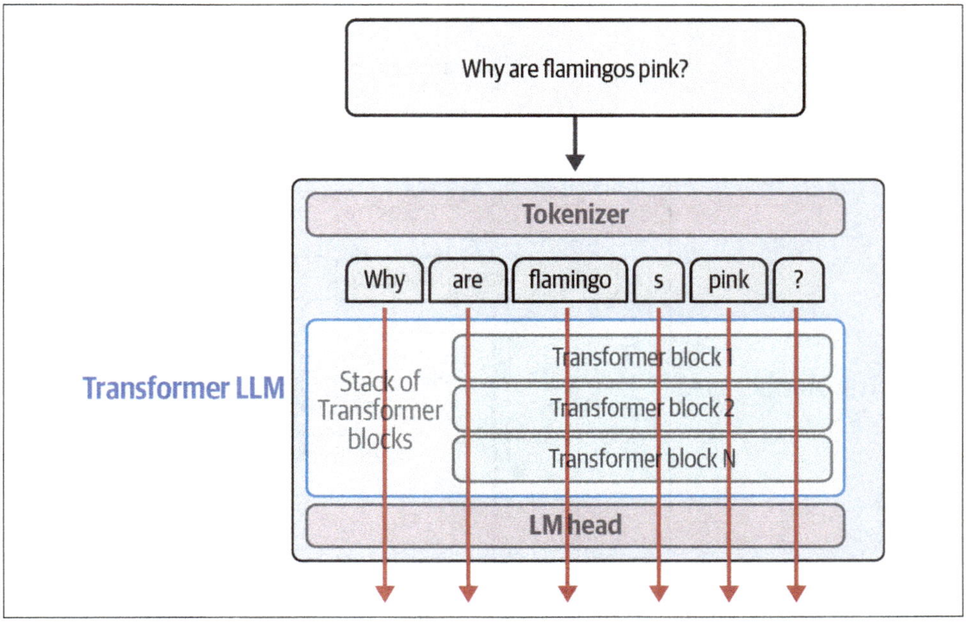

Figure 2-18. Each input token is processed through the full stack of Transformer blocks in parallel, with every token position producing its own output vector passed to the LM head—though only the final token's output is used to predict the next token

The number of tracks that a model supports is commonly known as its context size. So, a model that has a context length of 100,000 can have only that number of tokens flowing through it simultaneously, which generally limits its input and output capacity to text of that size.

For text generation, the processing flow of the last token is what's used to generate the next token, as we can see in Figure 2-19. That calculation is informed, however, by all the processing conducted on the previous tokens, as we'll see next when looking closer at the insides of a Transformer block.

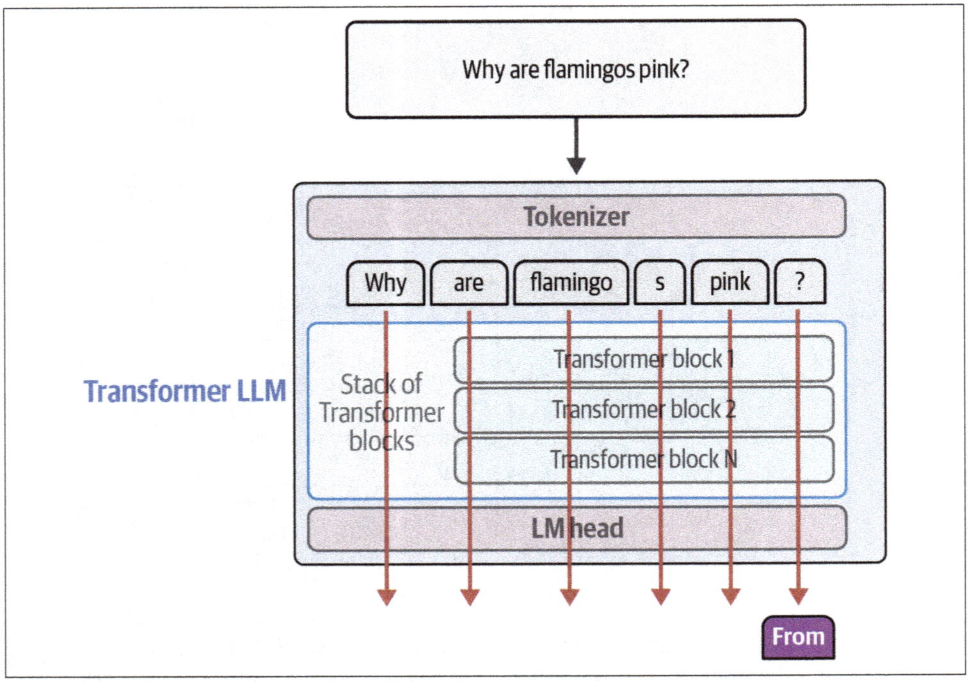

Figure 2-19. Each token flows through its own track in the stack, with only the final token's track passed to the LM head to predict the next token

For agent developers, context length is a key property for selecting the best model to build an agent around. It sets a limit on how much information we can pack in the input of the model. This limitation gives rise to a whole discipline of *context engineering* that we'll revisit repeatedly in this book. This is the discipline of choosing the most relevant information for the model to fit within this architectural limitation of the Transformer model.

Another key concept for agent developers is to realize that after that first pass where all the input tokens are processed, it's common to cache the results so that in the next forward pass, we process the information along only the one track associated with the new token we're generating. This is referred to as prompt-caching, prefix-caching, or more technically, kv-caching.

In Figure 2-20, we can see how only one track is active and information from previous tracks is cached and used for that one active calculation. This leads to dramatically increased speed and reduces the amount of processing required.

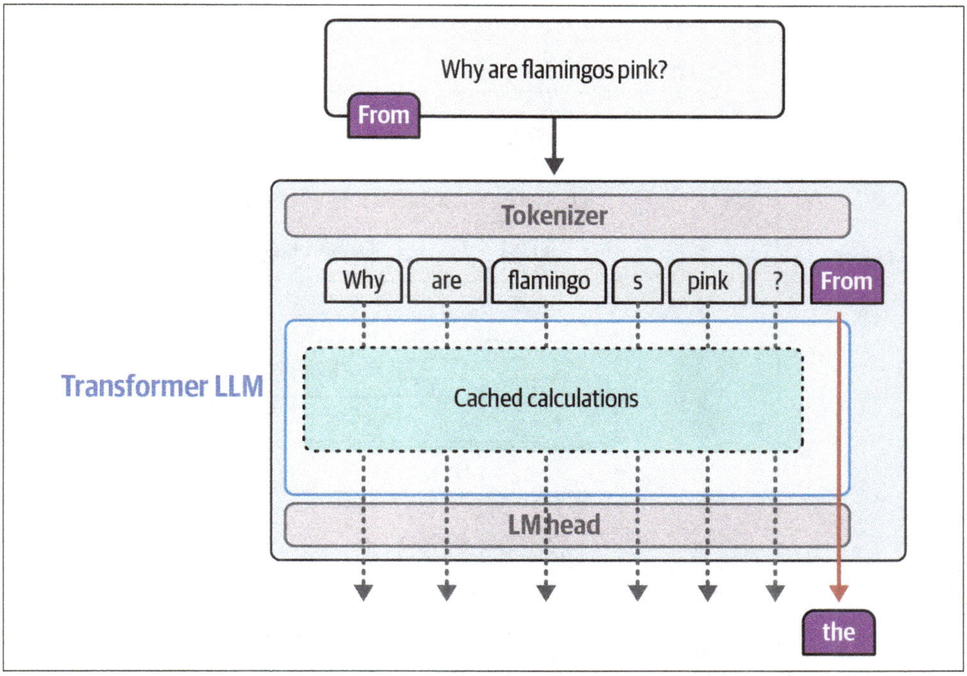

Figure 2-20. Previous token calculations are cached so each subsequent generation step processes only the single new token's track

Optimizing for the kv-cache is a key responsibility for agent developers to increase the speed and reduce the cost of the agents they build. In Chapter 10, we cover some strategies used by developers of software engineering agents to optimize for this cache, reducing the latency and improving the economics of their agents.

Inside the Transformer block

We've seen how the input text is broken down into tokens. And we've also seen that each token has an associated static embedding vector in the model. The Transformer operates on these embedding vectors. The first Transformer block is presented with the embedding vectors associated with the tokens in the input text.

As we can see in Figure 2-21, the first block does a bit of processing on these input vectors and hands off the results of its processing (as the same number and size of vectors) to the next Transformer block. This goes on block by block until the last block in the stack.

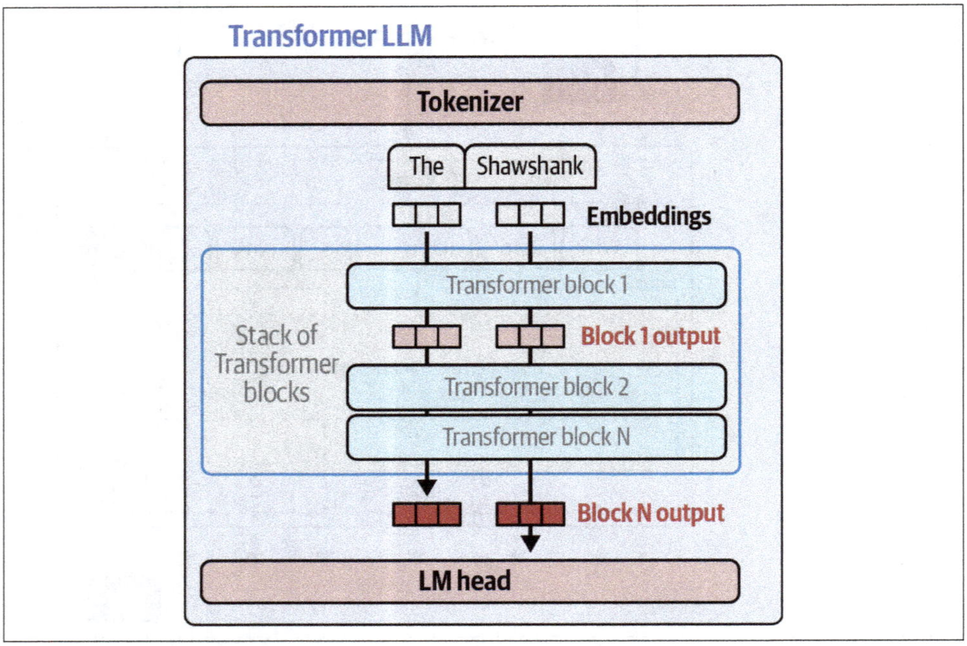

Figure 2-21. Token embeddings flow through the stack as fixed-size vectors, with each Transformer block progressively refining representations while keeping size constant

But what processing actually happens inside a Transformer block?

There are two major components inside a Transformer block: a self-attention layer and a feed-forward neural network layer (Figure 2-22). Without going into too much detail, in the next section we explain the intuition for each of these two components, starting with feed-forward neural networks and then coming back to self-attention.

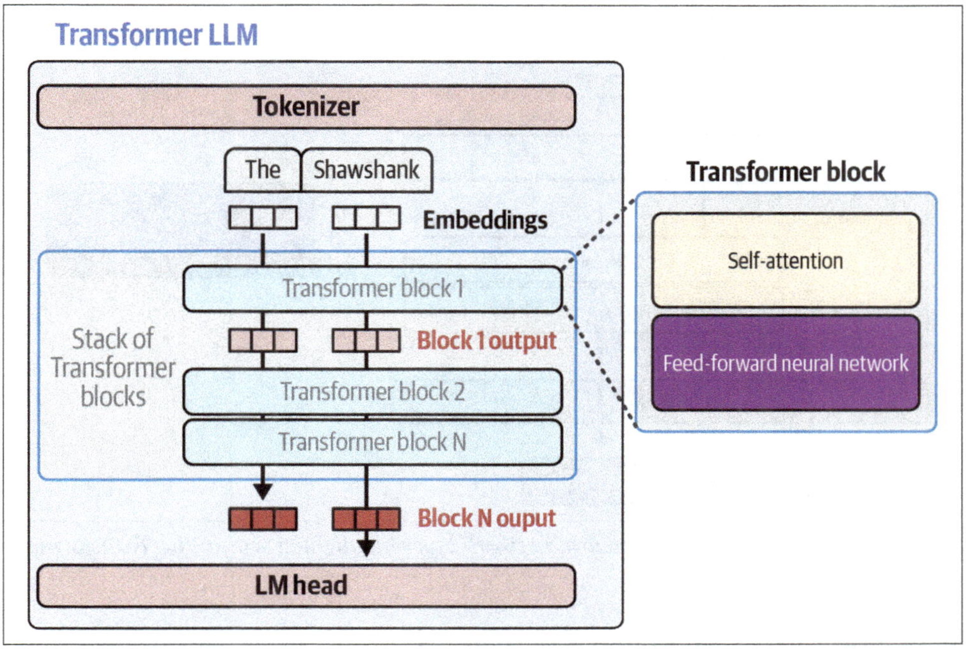

Figure 2-22. Inside each Transformer block are a self-attention layer for gathering context and a feed-forward neural network for processing representations

The Transformer block: the feed-forward neural network

Let's first talk about the feed-forward neural network because it's simpler, even though in the architecture it comes after self-attention. This layer does the heavy lifting in predicting the next token because the training process shapes its ability to predict the patterns encoded in the training dataset.

If we train a feed-forward neural network on vast amounts of web data, when we give it the words "The Shawshank," it would be able to predict that the next word would be "Redemption," because the 1994 film with that name is the most common occurrence of this sequence of tokens. Figure 2-23 shows this oversimplified example, which suggests the feed-forward layers store factual associations learned during training.

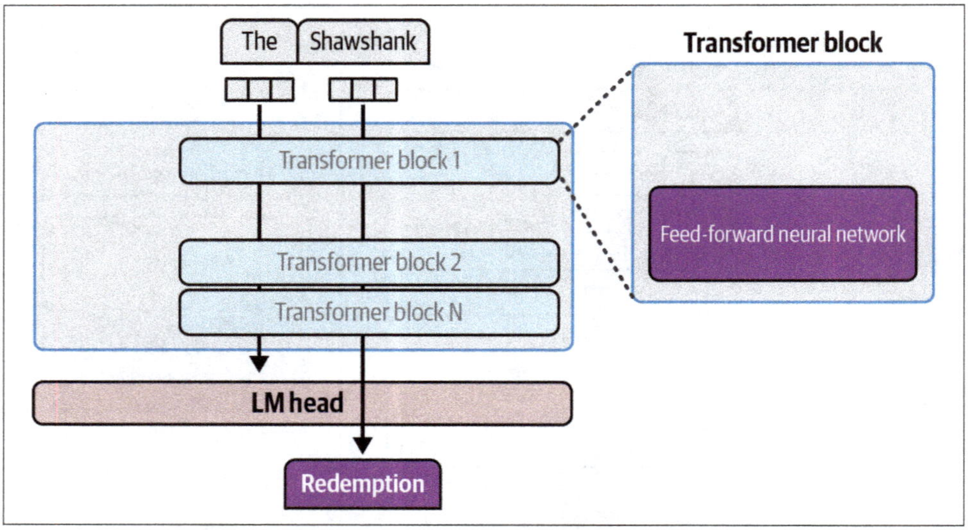

Figure 2-23. The feed-forward neural network layer highlighted within the Transformer block

In the original Transformer as well as in the majority of LLMs at the time of writing, the feed-forward neural network layer is one big neural network, as we can see in Figure 2-24. The training process prunes and adapts its connections in a way that encodes the patterns in *language*. Recall that by now, we're no longer talking about a specific human language, we're talking about a model that supports multiple human languages, multiple programming languages, as well as the patterns we need to define tool calling, multi-turn conversations, and, as we'll see in Chapter 3, reasoning patterns.

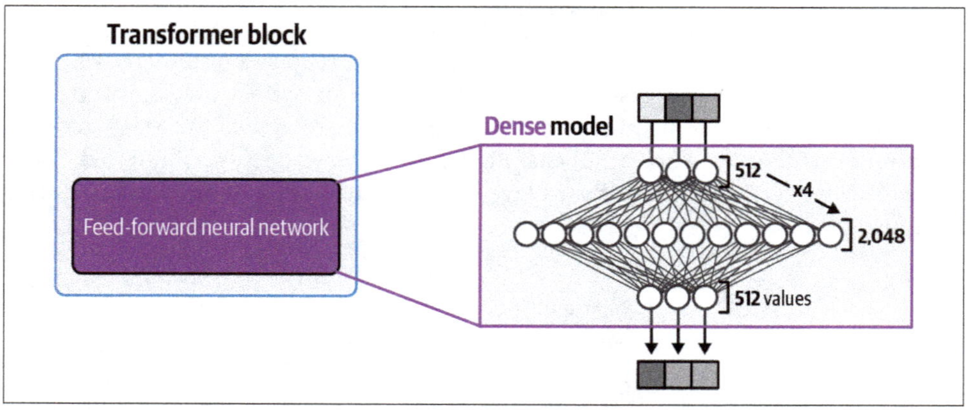

Figure 2-24. The feed-forward neural network in a dense model expands the token representation to a larger hidden dimension before compressing it back down

In recent years, there has been a trend away from having a single large network, and replacing it with a large number of smaller, more specialized networks. This architecture is called a mixture-of-experts (MoE), and we talk about it more in the second part of this chapter. We mention this here because as you select a model to power your agent, you may come across a choice of a dense model and an MoE model, especially if you're looking at open source models.

In Figure 2-25, we see a basic MoE feed-forward layer that contains four sublayers; each is called an *expert*. These are preceded by a router that looks at the input token and decides which expert (or set of experts) is best suited to process this particular token.

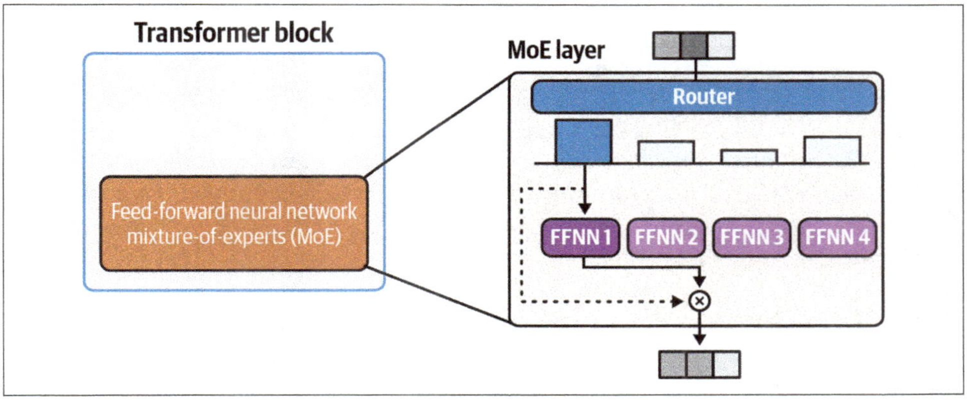

Figure 2-25. A mixture-of-experts feed-forward layer replaces a single large neural network with multiple smaller expert neural networks, routed per token to save capacity

Let's now turn to the other major component of the Transformer block.

The Transformer block: an overview of self-attention

Language encodes a lot of information in the order of words in a sequence and the context that a word is used in. A word such as *bank* can mean a financial institution or can mean a riverbank. We would only know which is meant by looking at the context where the word is used. The self-attention layer allows the Transformer to make these distinctions.

As we can see in Figure 2-26, a model is presented with an input sentence that is, "The dog chased the llama because it." When processing the word *it* in its own processing track, the model needs to know whether *it* refers to the dog or the llama. Self-attention is tuned to resolve this kind of problem.

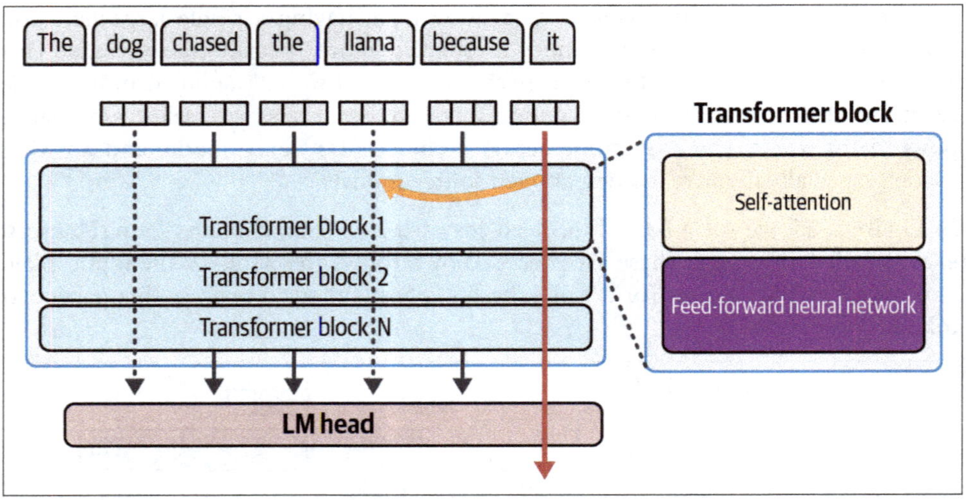

Figure 2-26. Self-attention allows each token to draw on context from other positions in the sequence. Here, when processing "it" (red track), the model attends back to "lama" (orange arc) to resolve the ambiguity of what "it" refers to—a distinction the feed-forward layer alone could not make.

Part 2 of this chapter goes into how self-attention is calculated, but the high-level intuition is that it *attends* to the most relevant previous tokens in the sequence. It learns that relevance from the training process. Figure 2-27 shows this function in its most basic form: we have the token we're currently processing (in red), and four previous tokens. Self-attention enriches the information encoded in the input vector with information from the most relevant previous tokens in the sequence.

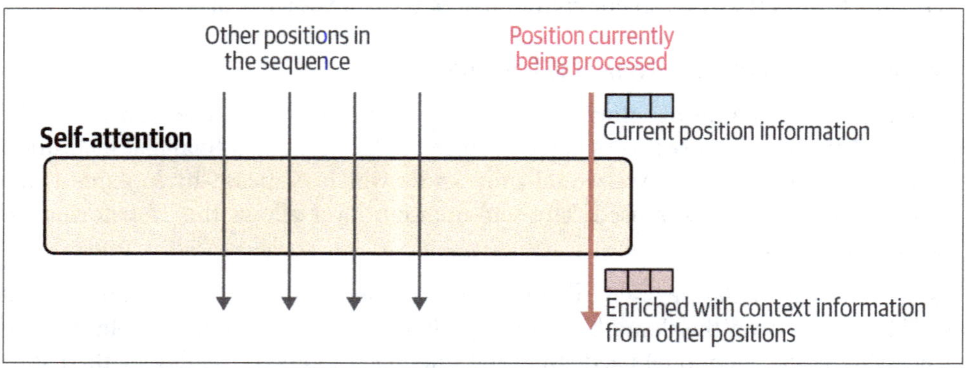

Figure 2-27. Self-attention enriches the current token's representation by drawing in information from the most relevant preceding positions

Self-attention does this by taking two steps: first, it scores the relevance of the previous tokens and then proceeds to a step of combining the relevant information into the token we're processing, as we can see in Figure 2-28.

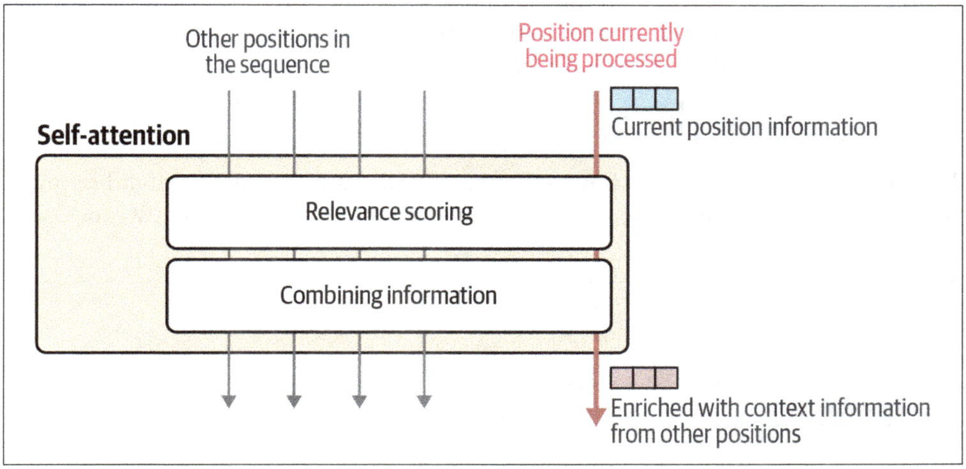

Figure 2-28. Self-attention operates in two steps: relevance scoring determines how much attention to pay to each preceding position, and combining information blends those positions' representations into the current token's output vector in proportion to their relevance scores

Self-attention is one of the most resource-intensive operations in the Transformer. That's why it's commonly one of the areas most targeted for improvement. Now we'll turn to the second half of this chapter, where we look at how self-attention is calculated and newer and more efficient forms of self-attention.

Part 2: A Deeper Dive Into Large Language Models

We'll now switch gears and move into a collection of LLM-related concepts in more depth. Namely, we'll build on what we've learned in the first half of the chapter on LLM architectures and training and take a closer look at self-attention, some of its more efficient variants, and MoE models.

How Self-Attention Works

Earlier in the chapter, we saw how self-attention allows the model to attend to previous tokens, thus enriching the representation of the token we're currently processing, as shown in Figure 2-29.

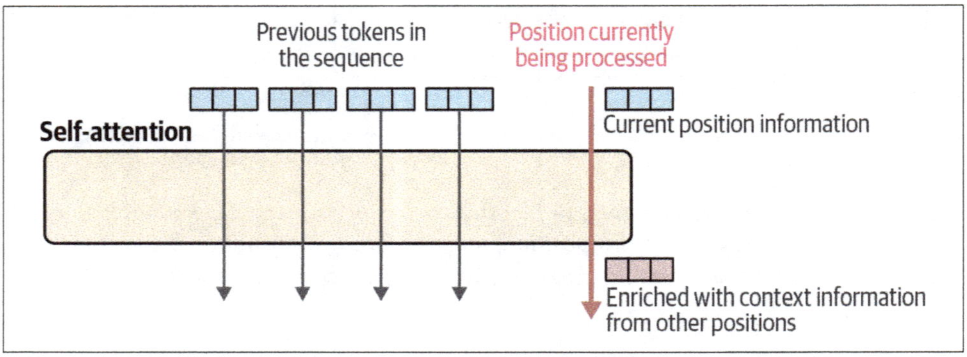

Figure 2-29. Self-attention takes the current token's vector (pink) along with those of preceding tokens and produces an enriched output vector for the current position that incorporates context from the rest of the sequence

Going into the attention calculation are a collection of vectors: the vector for the current position and the vectors for the previous positions.

A trained model is able to attend properly by utilizing three projection matrices that resulted from the training process. We multiply the input vectors by each of these projection matrices, resulting in matrices we call the queries, keys, and values matrices (Figure 2-30).

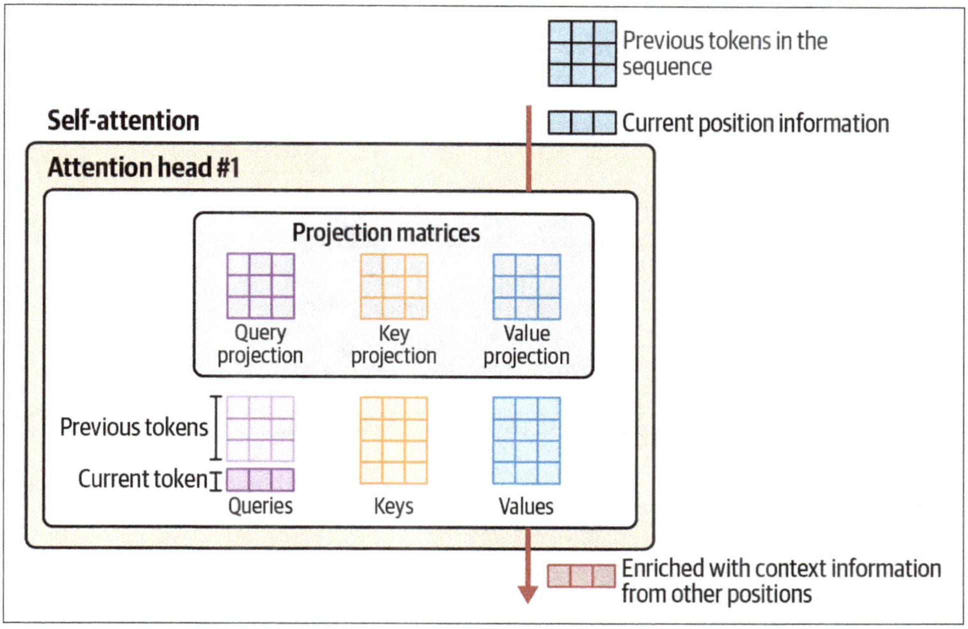

Figure 2-30. Inside an attention head, the input vectors for the current and preceding positions are multiplied by three learned projection matrices to produce the queries, keys, and values used in the attention calculation

The first step of self-attention, relevance scoring, involves multiplying the query for the token we're currently processing by the key vectors associated with all the input tokens. This results in a relevance score for each vector, as Figure 2-31 shows.

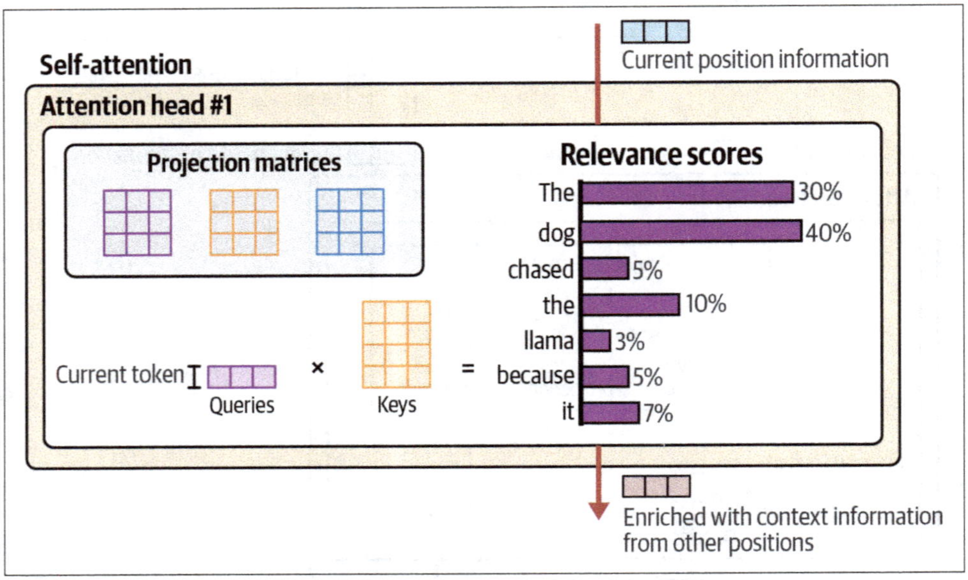

Figure 2-31. Relevance scoring multiplies the current token's query vector by key vectors of all input tokens to produce relevance scores

After deciding the relevance values, self-attention then proceeds to combine information from these tokens, weighted by how relevant they are, and merge them into the vector of the current token we're processing. We see that weighted summation calculation in Figure 2-32.

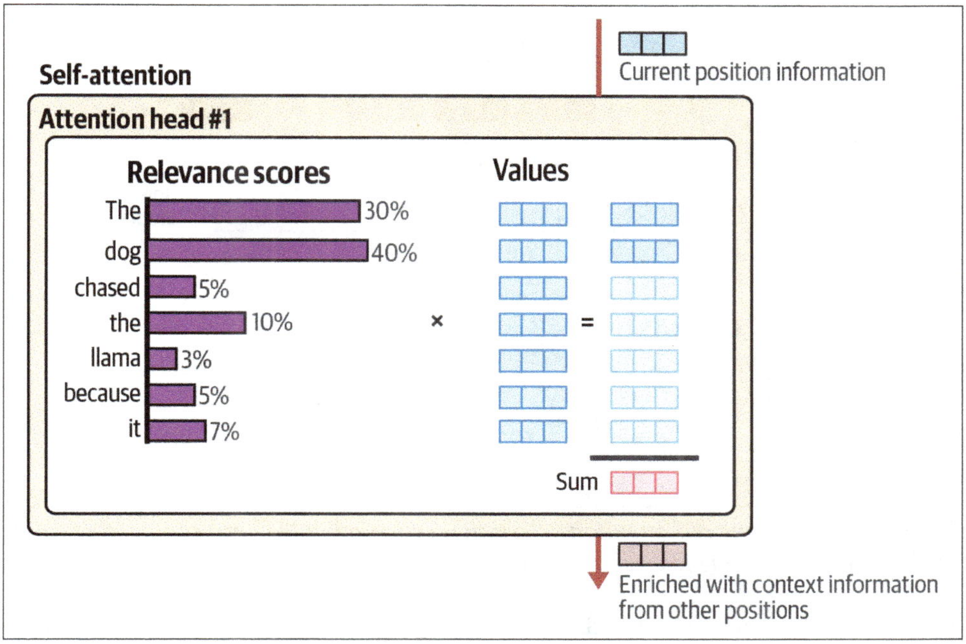

Figure 2-32. Information-combining multiplies each token's value vector by its relevance score and sums the results, producing the enriched output vector for the current position

This vector becomes the output of the self-attention layer. Figure 2-33 presents this in another way, closer to the mathematical formula you'll often see in LLM literature. The current and previous tokens are projected into queries, keys, and values; the query-key product (scaled by $\sqrt{d_k}$ and passed through softmax) produces the relevance scores, which are then multiplied by the values to produce the attention output for the current position.

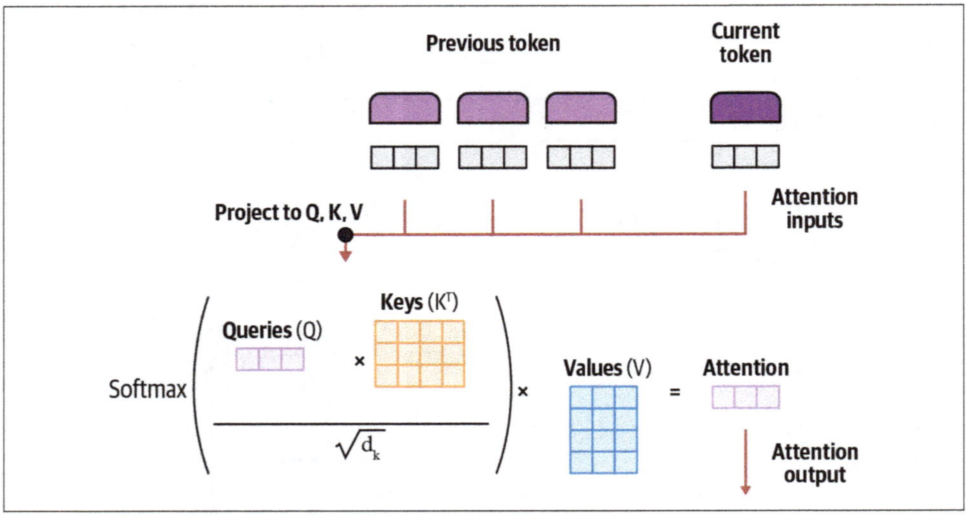

Figure 2-33. The same self-attention calculation expressed in the form commonly seen in the literature: projecting tokens into queries, keys, and values to calculate attention

As we'll see in the next section, there is one final operation after calculating attention this way.

KV-Caching Revisited

What we've described so far are major components of self-attention as described in the Transformer paper (*https://arxiv.org/abs/1706.03762*), which is often called "vanilla attention." This early form of self-attention, however, does a lot of redundant calculations of the K and V weights for each generated attention score if we apply it naively to text generation. Specifically, at each step, attention is recalculated for the entire sequence despite having calculated the K and V vectors of the previously seen tokens before. Imagine that a model is processing the attention scores for the tokens "My" and "name." As shown in Figure 2-34, regular attention would recalculate the K and V vectors at each subsequent step despite having calculated them before.

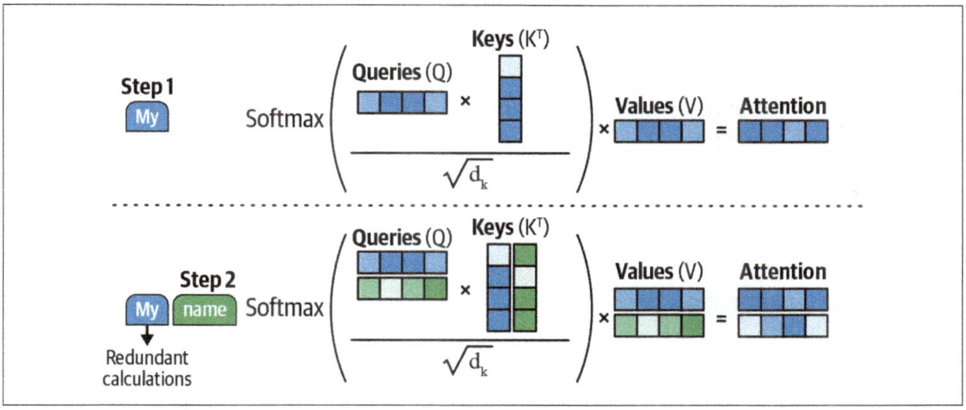

Figure 2-34. Vanilla attention recomputes the keys and values for every previous token at each generation step, causing redundant calculations

This is where the KV cache comes in. Instead of having to recalculate those vectors, we can simply cache and reuse them for subsequent decoding steps. This makes inference much faster by reducing the redundant computation. A basic KV cache is shown in Figure 2-35 and demonstrates how the K and V vectors are reused from previous steps instead. Also note that the query (Q) vectors do not need to be cached because they become unnecessary in subsequent iterations. Specifically, we need only the query vector of the latest token to compute the self-attention.

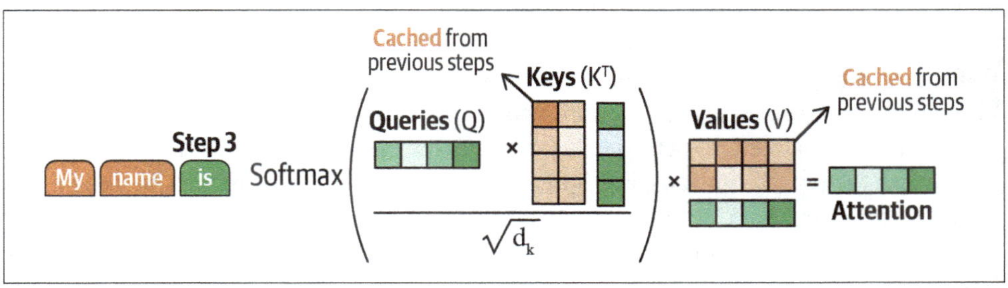

Figure 2-35. The KV cache stores keys and values from previous steps to avoid recomputation, processing only the new token's query

Although such a KV cache can make inference much faster, it does require significantly more memory if all KV values are cached. For that, there are many different forms of attention created that attempt to reduce the calculations needed, which should therefore also reduce the KV cache that needs to be maintained.

More Efficient Self-Attention

Variants of attention mechanisms have since been developed to alleviate the memory issue of the KV cache and optimize the attention calculations. Popular techniques include Grouped-Query Attention and FlashAttention.[1] More recently, however, DeepSeek introduced two attention mechanisms that showed tremendous improvements in the efficiency of attention calculations, namely Multi-head Latent Attention (MLA) and DeepSeek Sparse Attention (DSA).

Multi-head Latent Attention

A major step in making the KV-cache more memory efficient is through MLA, first used in DeepSeek-V2 and popularized by DeepSeek-R1.[2,3] MLA is a variant of Multi-head Attention, which maintains separate Q, K, and V projection matrices for each attention head, producing a different Q, K, and V matrix per head. MLA uses low-rank joint compression of the keys and values to reduce the KV cache during inference. At its core, it compresses the keys and values into a smaller latent representation that is cached in place of the full K and V. In practice, this compressed cache is often combined with quantization (reducing the numerical precision of stored values) for additional memory savings.

MLA first compresses the input embeddings into lower-dimensional representations called the latent Q and latent KV. These representations are significantly smaller than the full Q and KV, which allows us to cache the latent KV instead of the full K and V. Positional information via Rotary Position Embedding (RoPE) is applied to a decoupled component of the latent Q, since the latent Q is recomputed at every step. RoPE is not applied to the latent K itself, because the cached K would then need to be recomputed at every step, breaking the benefit of caching. Therefore, positional information is carried by a separate small key instead. Note that at this step, the Q, K, and V representations are split across multiple attention heads, much like standard Multi-head Attention. Finally, the content and positional components are concatenated and passed through standard Multi-head Attention. The full procedure is shown in Figure 2-36.

1 Dao, Tri et al. 2022. "FlashAttention: Fast and Memory-efficient Exact Attention with IO-Awareness," *NIPS'22: Proceedings of the 36th International Conference on Neural Information Processing Systems,* 1189: 16344-16359.

2 Shao, Zhihong et al. 2024. "DeepSeek-V2: A Strong, Economical, and Efficient Mixture-of-Experts Language Model." *arXiv*, 2405.04434.

3 Guo, Daya et al. 2025. "DeepSeek-R1 Incentivizes Reasoning in LLMs Through Reinforcement Learning." *Nature* 645: 633–638. *https://doi.org/10.1038/s41586-025-09422-z.*

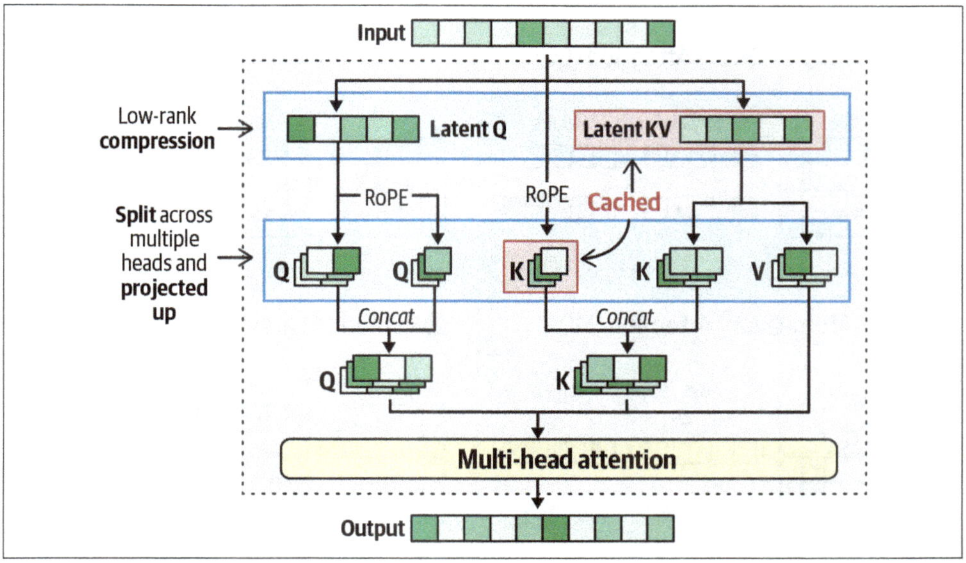

Figure 2-36. Multi-head Latent Attention compresses input into low-rank representations and caches the smaller latent KV to save memory

As such, MLA is essentially Multi-head Attention but with a compressed KV cache containing the previously mentioned Latent KV representation. This compression reduces the KV cache quite a bit and allows for much faster inference. It's also more efficient than previous methods, such as Grouped-Query Attention. An overview of MLA versus other common attention mechanisms can be found in Figure 2-37. Note that Grouped-Query Attention and Multi-Query Attention share K and V across query heads to reduce the memory necessary for the KV cache but tend to be less accurate.

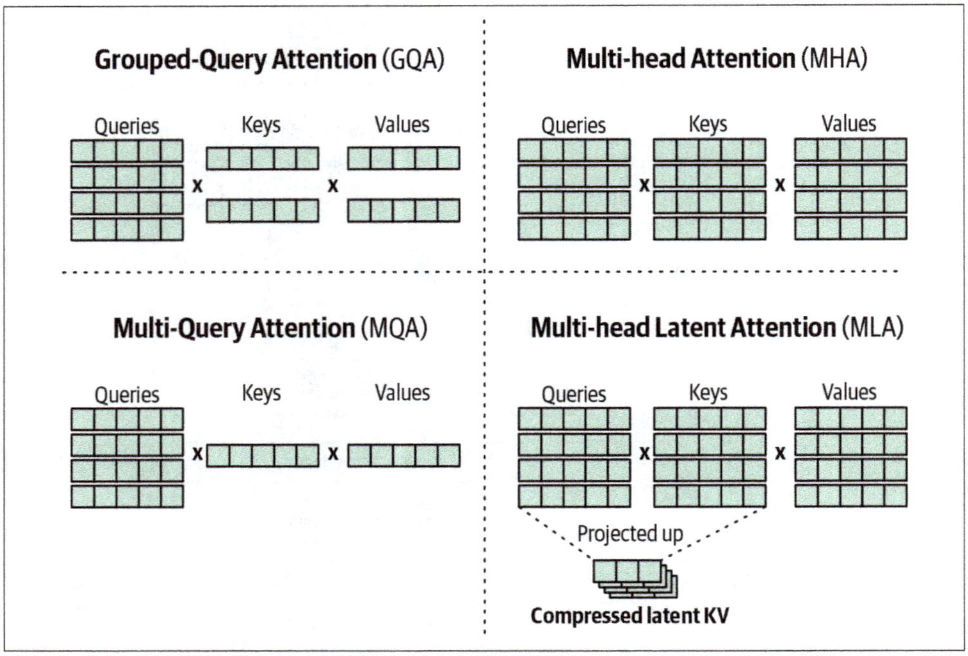

Figure 2-37. Four approaches to attention: MHA uses full K and V; GQA and MQA reduce K and V directly; MLA caches compressed latent KV

DeepSeek Sparse Attention

The next step in making MLA more efficient was first introduced in DeepSeek-V3.2. This new attention mechanism, called DeepSeek Sparse Attention (DSA), is instantiated under MLA and is an additional module to more efficiently select the tokens to attend to.[4] It has two main components, a lightning indexer and a Top-K Selector. The lightning indexer determines how relevant each preceding token is to the current query. For that, it uses the Q/K values that both have RoPE applied to them. Likewise, it takes in a scalar weight parameter *w* that helps the lightning indexer make better decisions about which tokens to select for the full attention mechanism. The output of the lightning indexer is scores fed to the Top-K Selector, which in turn retrieves only the KV entries that correspond to the Top-K index scores. As a result, the attention output is computed through the query token and a subset of KV entries. This full procedure is shown in Figure 2-38.

4 Liu, Aixin et al. 2025. "DeepSeek-V3. 2: Pushing the Frontier of Open Large Language Models," *arXiv*, 2512.02556.

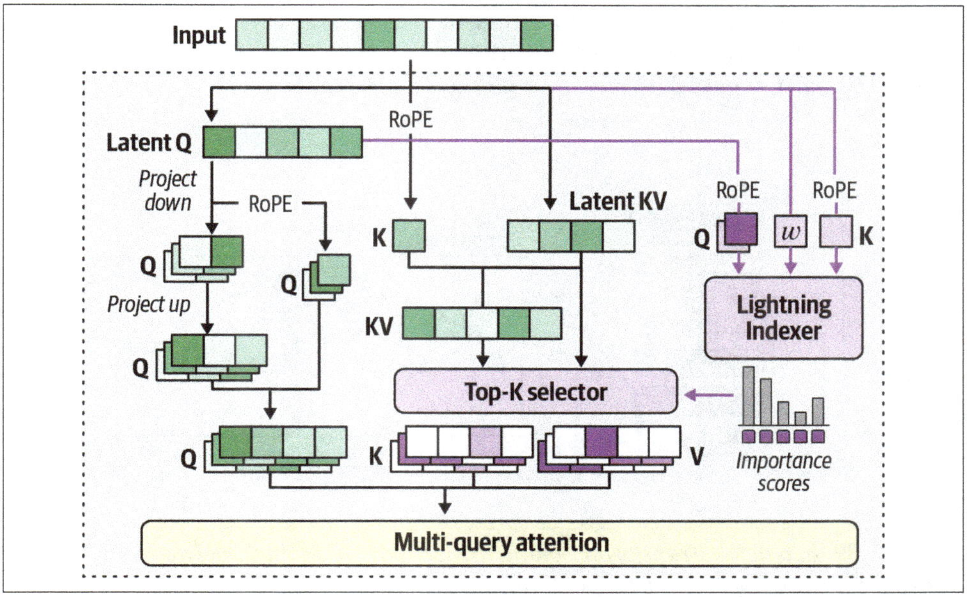

Figure 2-38. DeepSeek Sparse Attention (DSA) adds a Lightning Indexer and a Top-K Selector to compute attention over a sparse subset

Together, the Lightning Indexer and Top-K Selector reduce the number of tokens to attend to K. In the paper referenced, the authors selected 2,048 tokens to attend to, which drastically reduces the computation necessary for the attention computations.

Note that since MLA is used, there is already a significant memory benefit due to the compression of the KV-cache. In their construction of MLA, instead of using MHA as the core attention mechanism, MQA was used. The authors mentioned optimizing for computational efficiency, which is true for MQA, considering it uses fewer keys and values than MHA.

Mixture of Experts

MoE is a technique that is becoming more mainstream to create more efficient LLMs. MoE uses several submodels or "experts" to improve the quality and efficiency of LLMs. There are two main components of an MoE:

Experts
: Each feed-forward neural network in an LLM is replaced by a set of "experts."

Router or gate network
: Determines which tokens are sent to which experts.

Let's first explore *experts*. Remember that a typical Transformer-based LLM uses self-attention followed by a feed-forward neural network. As shown in Figure 2-39, we call this a dense model because everything is activated.

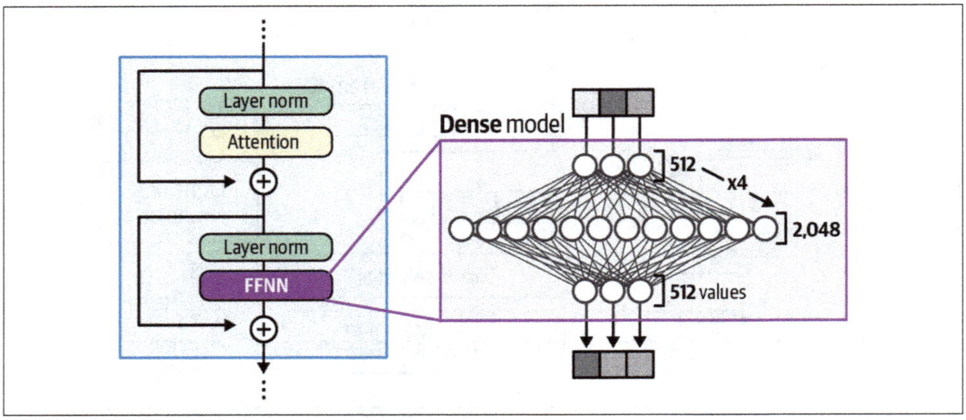

Figure 2-39. In a dense Transformer block, the feed-forward neural network (FFNN) is active for every single token passing through

A sparse model, in contrast, may deploy several feed-forward neural networks instead. These are typically smaller than a regular network, but together they tend to be bigger. Each feed-forward neural network in a sparse model is typically referred to as an "expert" because, during training, each "expert" learns different information and may specialize in the processing of certain tokens (Figure 2-40). For instance, one expert might be used for processing numbers, whereas another processes verbs. It's still a bit unclear what these experts actually learn, but there has been some research suggesting that they specialize in fine-grained information such as verbs versus numbers rather than each learning an entirely different domain.[5]

Note that in this example, all experts are used, which does not allow for any efficiency gains. To choose a subset of experts during inference, we make use of the *router* (also called a gate network). This is a small feed-forward neural network that is trained to choose an expert for a given token. The router, together with the experts, makes up the MoE layer as shown in Figure 2-41.

5 Zoph, Barret et al. 2022. "ST-MoE: Designing Stable and Transferable Sparse Expert Models." *arXiv*, 2202.08906.

The router is arguably the most important component because the experts are nothing more than just small feed-forward neural networks. So, how exactly does the router then choose which expert to use for each token? Let's go through a minimal example step-by-step.

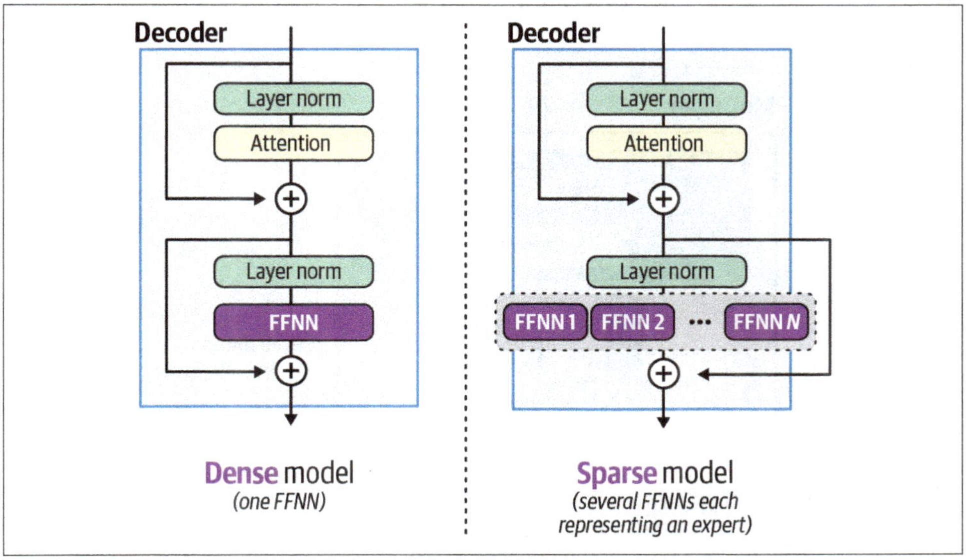

Figure 2-40. A dense block (left) applies a single network to all tokens, while a sparse block (right) routes different tokens to different experts

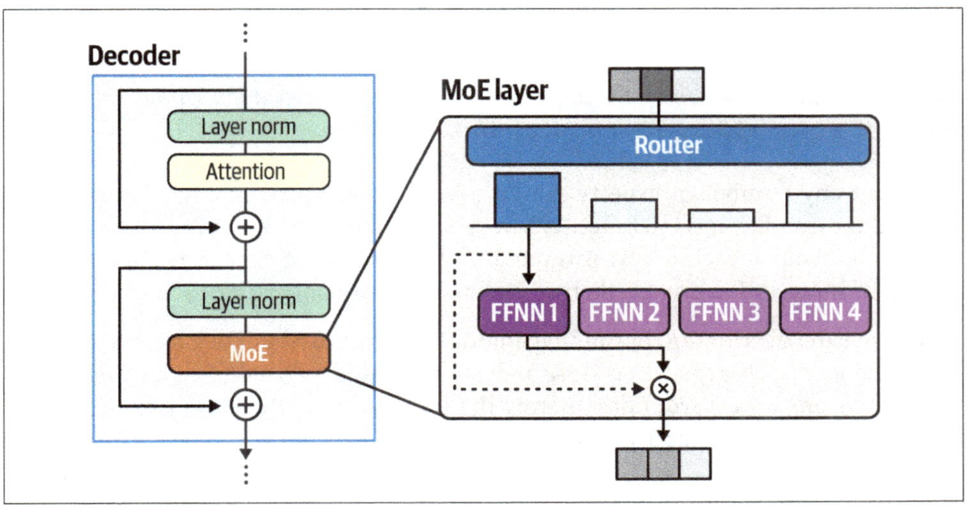

Figure 2-41. An MoE layer uses a router to score experts and direct each token to a small active subset, leaving others inactive

The router, as a neural network, will have its own weight matrix, which is used to multiply the input token embeddings. Applying a softmax on the output will result in a probability distribution per expert. This probability distribution provides the likelihood that an expert will be chosen given an input token. Figure 2-42 shows everything put together, demonstrating how the input flows through the router and experts.

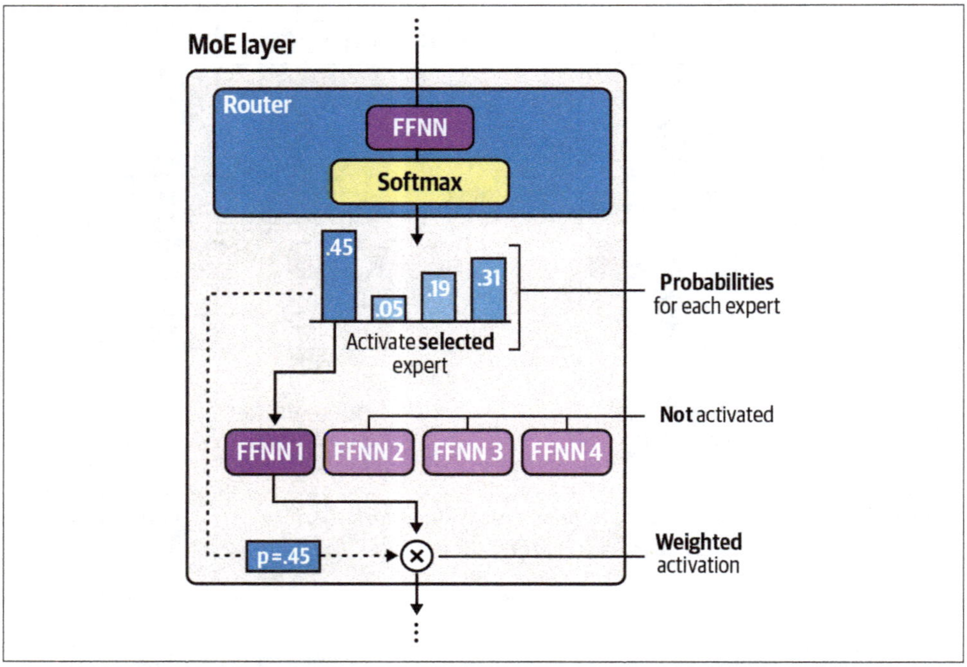

Figure 2-42. Inside the router, the token representation is mapped to a probability distribution over experts using a small network and softmax

Note that any number of experts can be selected, but generally a fixed number are selected for training and inference. When selecting multiple experts, there is a need to balance how much each expert is trained. If the same set of experts is always chosen during training and inference, then all other experts are undertrained.

To balance the distribution of training among experts, the router will have to dynamically balance which expert to choose and when. This is referred to as *load balancing*. To prevent one expert from dominating the training time, there are two main techniques that are often employed in one way or another, namely expert capacity and auxiliary loss.

Expert capacity gives each expert in the MoE layer a limit to how many tokens it can process.[6] Instead of having a single expert do all the work, the tokens are somewhat more equally distributed. For instance, by the time an expert has reached capacity, each subsequent token routed to it will be sent to the next-highest scoring expert, as shown in Figure 2-43.

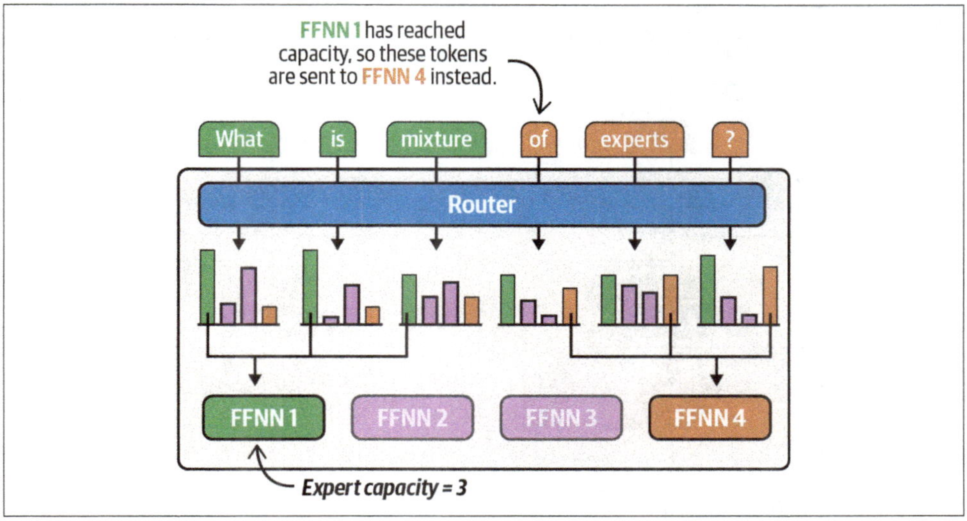

Figure 2-43. Expert capacity caps how many tokens each expert can process per batch, routing excess tokens to the next-highest expert

In contrast, instead of limiting the experts, the router can also be adjusted to account for this probability imbalance. A straightforward technique is to add Gaussian noise just before the router produces its probabilities. By introducing noise, the distributions will slightly change, and by (slight) chance, sometimes choose different experts to use. A more advanced technique to balance how the router selects experts is called *auxiliary loss*.[7] These are loss functions that can be added to the router to reward it for equally distributing the experts during training or punish it when the same expert is chosen.

6 Lepikhin, Dmitry et al. 2020. "Gshard: Scaling Giant Models with Conditional Computation and Automatic Sharding," *International Conference on Learning Representations*, poster.

7 Shazeer, Noam et al. 2017. "Outrageously Large Neural Networks: The Sparsely-Gated Mixture-of-Experts Layer," *International Conference on Learning Representations*, poster.

The main benefit of MoE is its computational requirements. Although using MoE does not make the resulting model smaller, it runs much faster because only a few experts are activated at a given time. As Figure 2-44 shows, all parameters that a MoE model has need to be loaded into memory and are called *sparse parameters*. The *active parameters*, in contrast, are those that are activated only during inference.

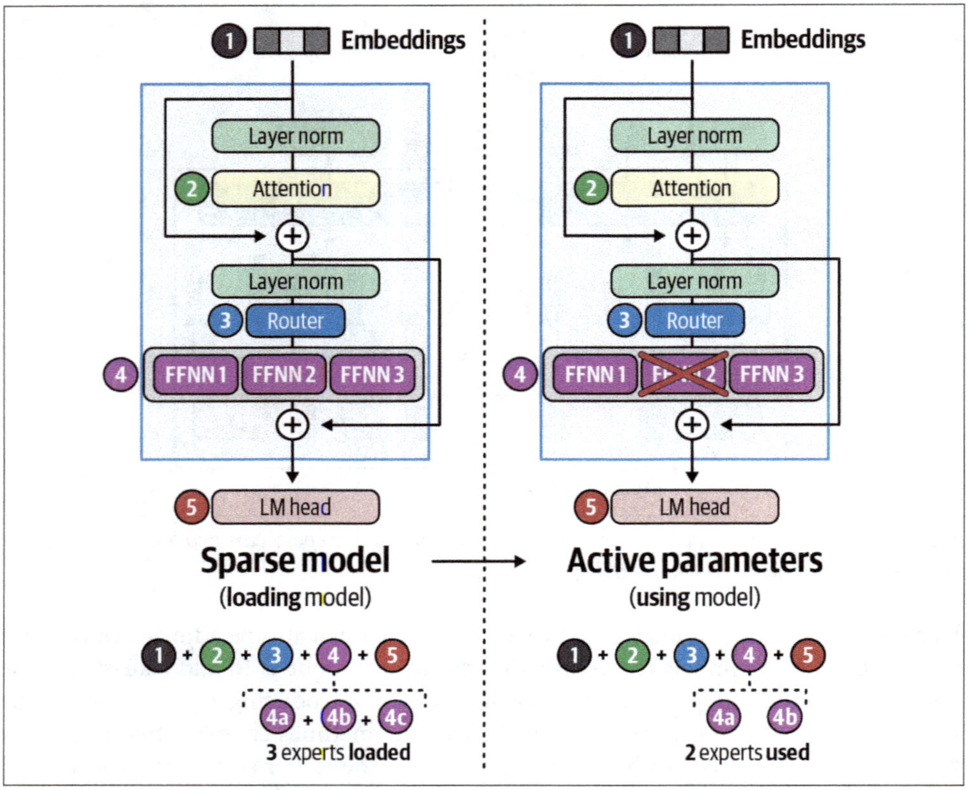

Figure 2-44. In an MoE model, all experts must be loaded into memory, but only an active subset is used per forward pass

Most recent models tend to use MoE layers, such as OpenAI's GPT-OSS (*https://oreil.ly/IVWoy*) and NVIDIA's Nemotron 3 (*https://oreil.ly/tRnEn*). Often, you'll see models like Qwen3-30B-A3B that put the number of sparse parameters (30 billion) and active parameters (3 billion) in their name.[8] As such, even though 30 billion parameters need to be loaded in memory, only 3 billion are used, which makes it much faster for inference.

8 Yang, An et al. 2025. "Qwen3 Technical Report," *arXiv*, 2505.09388.

Another example of MoE is the previously discussed DeepSeek-R1. As Figure 2-45 shows, DeepSeek-R1 has 256 experts, of which 8 are always chosen. Note that there is also a shared expert bypassing the router. This expert is always chosen, which often helps the model divert all general knowledge to that expert and more specialized knowledge to all others.

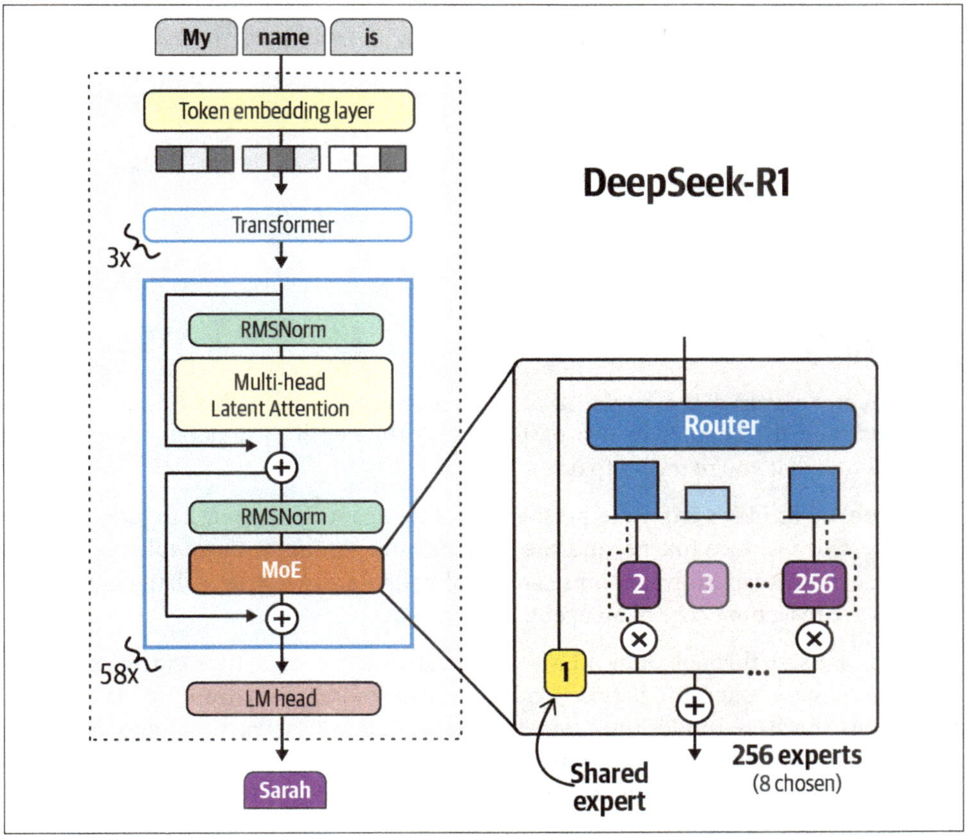

Figure 2-45. DeepSeek-R1 uses MoE layers with 256 experts per layer, of which 8 are selected by the router for each token. A shared expert bypasses the router and is always active

In practice, there are many different choices for the number of experts chosen for a given LLM and the sizes of each expert compared to the overall size of the LLM. Table 2-1 demonstrates various open-weight LLMs and their implementations of MoE.

Table 2-1. Open-weight LLMs and their MoE

Model	Sparse parameters (billion)	Active parameters (billion)	Number of experts	Experts activated	Shared experts
Mistral 7x8B	46.7	12.8	8	4	0
DeepSeek-R1	671	37	256	8	1
Llama 4 Maverick	400	17	128	1	1
Qwen3 235B-A22B	235	22	128	8	0
Kimi-K2	1,000	32	384	8	1
GPT-OSS 120B	120	5.1	128	4	0
GPT-OSS 20B	20	3.6	32	4	0
GLM 4.5	335	12	160	8	1
Qwen3 Next	80	3	512	10	1
Mistral Large 3	671	41	128	4	1
Nemotron-3-Nano-30B-A3B	31.6	3.6	128	6	2

Summary

This chapter covered the engine that powers every agent in this book: the LLM. We structured the chapter in two parts because the depth of understanding needed depends on what you're trying to do.

Part 1 looked at LLMs from the perspective of an agent developer. Language models consume and produce tokens, and the formats built on top of those tokens—system prompts, multi-turn conversations, and tool calls—are what let a language model serve as the reasoning core of an agent.

We then walked through how LLMs are created across two training phases. Pre-training via next-token prediction produces a base model. Post-training via SFT and RL shapes the base model into something that follows instructions and generates responses aligned with human preferences. We looked at how RLVR and the GRPO algorithm use verifiable signals such as format and correctness to push models toward reliable behavior.

We also opened up the Transformer itself, tracing how tokens flow through a stack of blocks, each containing a self-attention layer and a feed-forward neural network, before the LM head converts the final representation into a next-token probability distribution. For agent developers, the two architectural properties worth carrying into later chapters are context length, which limits how much information we can pack into a model's input, and the KV cache, which shapes the economics and latency of every agent we build.

Part 2 went deeper into the internals. We saw how self-attention is actually computed through the queries, keys, and values produced by three projection matrices and how relevance scoring and information combining make up the two steps of the attention operation.

We then looked at how self-attention has evolved to address its memory and compute costs. The KV cache itself avoids redundant recomputation. Grouped-Query and Multi-query Attention shrink the cache by sharing K and V across heads. DeepSeek's Multi-head Latent Attention takes a different approach, caching a low-rank compressed representation that gets projected back up when needed. DeepSeek Sparse Attention adds a Lightning Indexer and Top-K Selector to attend to only the most relevant tokens instead of the entire sequence.

We closed with MoE architectures, which replaced the dense feed-forward layer with a router and a set of smaller expert networks. This produces models where the total and active parameter counts can differ by an order of magnitude, a distinction that matters when selecting a model to deploy.

In the next chapter, we turn to reasoning LLMs, the class of models that has reshaped what agents can do by producing long chains of thought before committing to an answer.

CHAPTER 3

Reasoning Large Language Models

LLMs such as DeepSeek-R1 (*https://oreil.ly/7kt3A*), OpenAI GPT-5 (*https://openai.com/gpt-5*), and Google Gemini (*https://oreil.ly/jVUbU*) are prime examples of how LLMs can be scaled to new heights through reasoning frameworks. Reasoning in LLMs attempts to mimic human thinking by generating thoughts through tokens before giving a final answer. As shown in Figure 3-1, these tokens explain LLMs' chain-of-thought and allow reasoning LLMs to break down a problem into smaller steps (often called *reasoning steps* or *thought processes*).

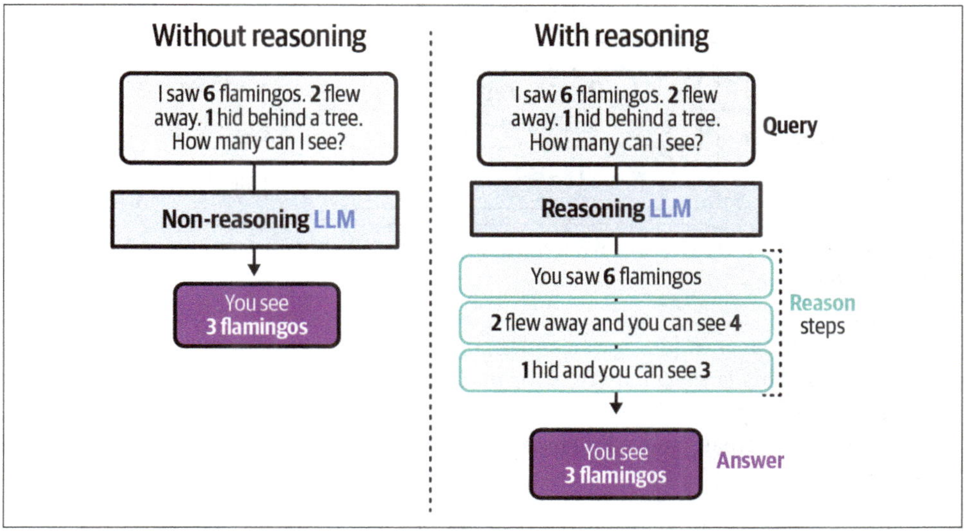

Figure 3-1. The differences between a non-reasoning and reasoning LLM

Reasoning LLMs first "think" and generate intermediate information before finally answering the query.

Interestingly, the differences between *non-reasoning* and *reasoning* LLMs can be viewed through the lens of human cognition, specifically System 1 and System 2 thinking from Daniel Kahneman's dual-process theory,[1] which describes two modes of human cognition.

System 1, in human cognition, operates automatically and quickly, relying on intuition and learned associations to make snap judgments. Non-reasoning LLMs operate much like System 1 thinking and generate responses quickly based on patterns they learned during training. They produce immediate answers without step-by-step (explicit) thinking.

System 2, in human cognition, engages in slower, more deliberate reasoning that requires conscious effort and attention. Reasoning LLMs operate much like System 2 thinking and generate more deliberate step-by-step analyses before reaching conclusions. They explicitly work through problems and catch errors that a non-reasoning LLM might miss.

System 1 is efficient for routine tasks but is prone to cognitive biases, whereas System 2 relies on logical reasoning and tends to result in more accurate decisions. Reasoning is critical in AI agents because it allows them to plan out behavior, decide which actions to take, and reflect on the actions they have taken (see Figure 3-2). This involves enabling them to actively seek information, utilize diverse tools, and dynamically refine their reasoning.

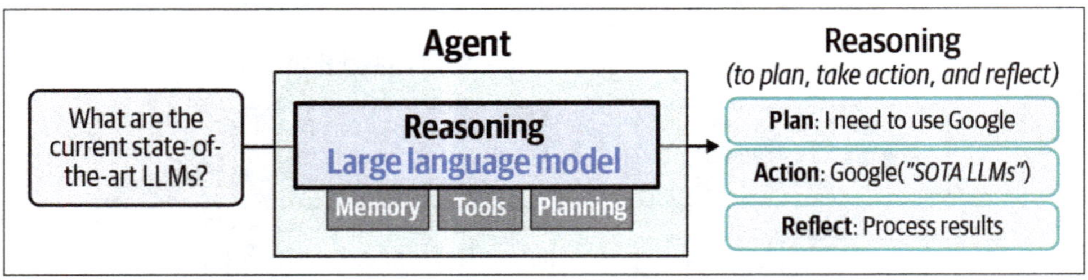

Figure 3-2. Agents use extended reasoning to plan their behavior, act out each step, and reflect on the results

AI agents need reasoning to devise a plan, decide on the actions they take, and reflect on the results. This is especially true for planning out actions and reflecting on them. For instance, in typical AI-assisted coding environments, such as Cursor and Cline, the agents might create special Markdown files to track their plan and revise when necessary.

1 Kahneman, Daniel. *Thinking, Fast and Slow*. (Macmillan, 2011).

As shown in Figure 3-3, before we go into how AI agents showcase autonomous behavior, we first explore how LLMs can demonstrate advanced thinking processes. In Chapters 5 and 6, we explore how reasoning enables tool selection and enables planning and reflection.

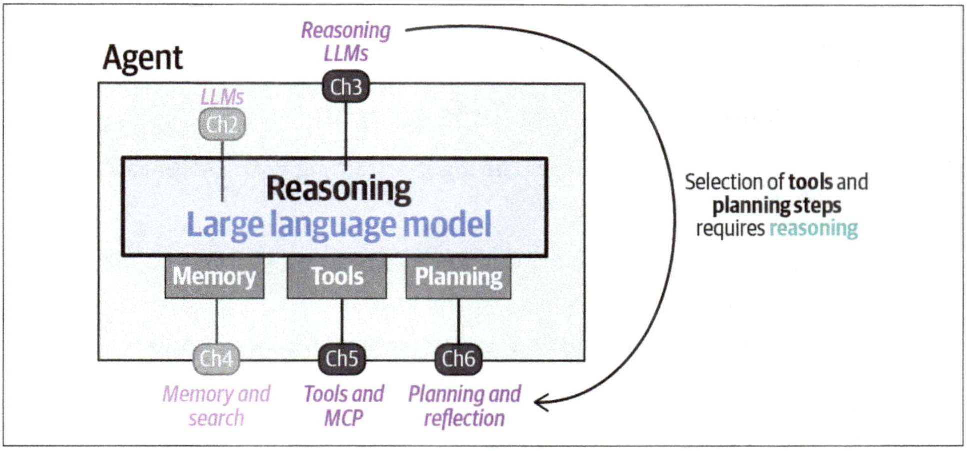

Figure 3-3. Reasoning LLMs are a vital component for enabling advanced planning and tool use. Without reasoning, methodologies such as reflection will be less accurate.

In this chapter, we uncover the history of reasoning LLMs through an important paradigm shift from training to inference and explore various methods for creating reasoning LLMs. We will also introduce coding examples for enabling and improving reasoning behavior for the section "Search Against Verifiers" on page 102. Note that there will be no changes to the `TinyAgent` because this chapter demonstrates reasoning behavior.

> Many terms in this chapter normally appear in abbreviated form. To prevent confusion, we have spelled them out in this chapter, with the acronyms included in parentheses in the first instance. We have also included a glossary of key terms and acronyms in the book's repository (*https://github.com/HandsOnLLM/An-Illustrated-Guide-To-AI-Agents*).

The Paradigm Shift from Train-Time Compute to Test-Time Compute

Before we explore reasoning LLMs in more detail, it's important to discover why there is such a big focus on them currently. This relates to a fundamental shift that has changed our focus from scaling train-time compute to test-time compute.

Train-Time Compute Versus Test-Time Compute

To improve the performance of LLMs during pre-training, developers used to focus on three main factors (see Figure 3-4):

- Increasing the *model size* (number of parameters)
- Increasing the *dataset size* (number of tokens)
- Increasing *compute* (number of floating point operations per second [FLOPs])

This combination of factors, called *train-time compute*, has been a key strategy. The basic principle is that more pre-training resources lead to a better, more powerful model.

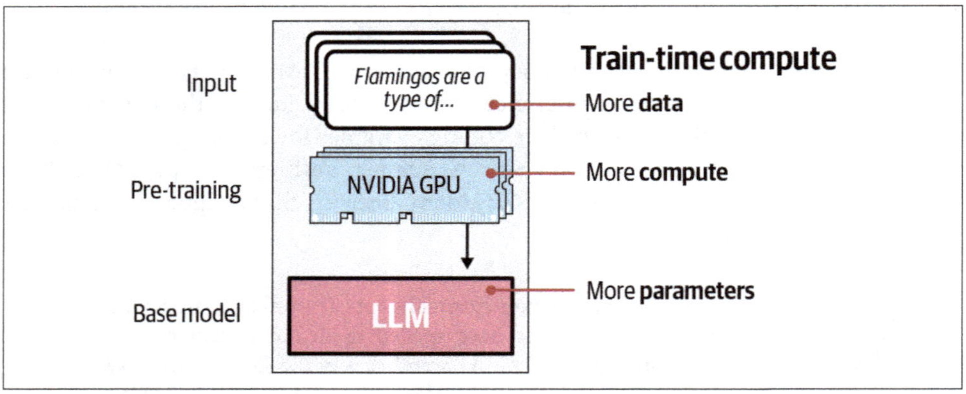

Figure 3-4. Train-time compute relates to the entire training process of LLMs

When we explore train-time compute, it does not only relate to pre-training but also what you can tweak during post-training. In Figure 3-5, you can see how both data and compute can also be increased to improve its performance. When you fine-tune a model, you can often decide how many of its parameters you would like to update. In a way, even during post-training, you can increase the "model size."

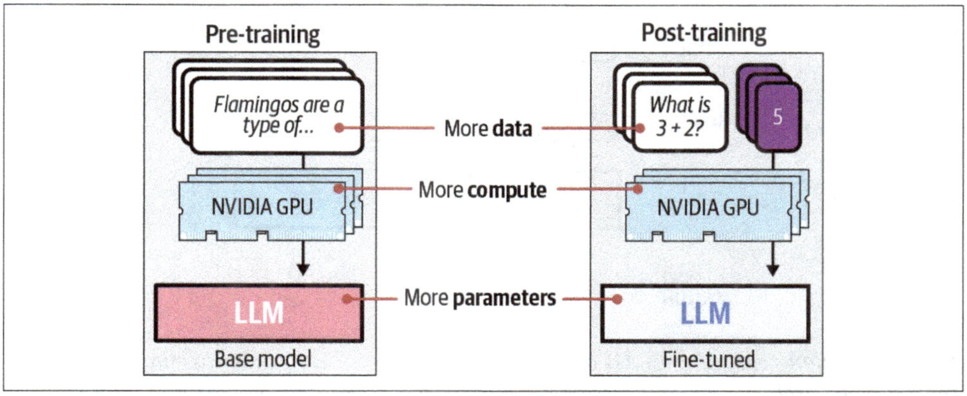

Figure 3-5. Train-time compute relates to both pre-training and post-training LLMs

Shown in Figure 3-6, train-time compute means a focus on increasing pre-training and post-training resources, and little attention is spent on inference. This generally applies to non-reasoning LLMs.

Figure 3-6. The distribution of train-time compute when training non-reasoning LLMs

In contrast, *test-time compute* focuses more on scaling inference instead of pre-training and post-training. Scaling inference generally applies to reasoning LLMs and allows them to "think longer" during inference.

Let's illustrate this with an example. Figure 3-7 shows how non-reasoning LLMs directly generate an answer without any intermediate generated tokens. To the question, "What is 3 + 2?," it answers "5." All of its compute is used to generate this one token.

In this example, scaling inference means generating more tokens in the output so that the model has spent more resources getting to the final answers. Simplified, if one token is one "compute," then dozens of tokens would mean dozens of "compute." "Compute" can mean several things, but it generally refers to how much computational work the model performs during inference.

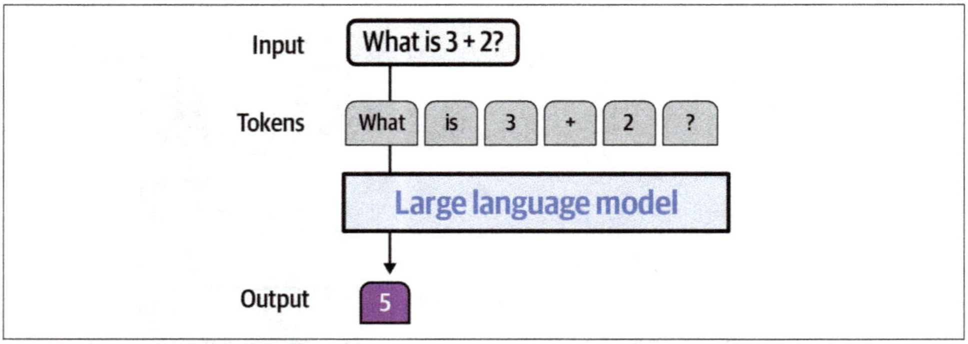

Figure 3-7. Non-reasoning LLMs output only the answer. Although this may include reasoning or prefixes such as "The answer is...", the reasoning is not a separate stage.

This is especially true for reasoning models, as they would use more tokens (which we can think of as "thinking" tokens) to derive their answer (Figure 3-8).

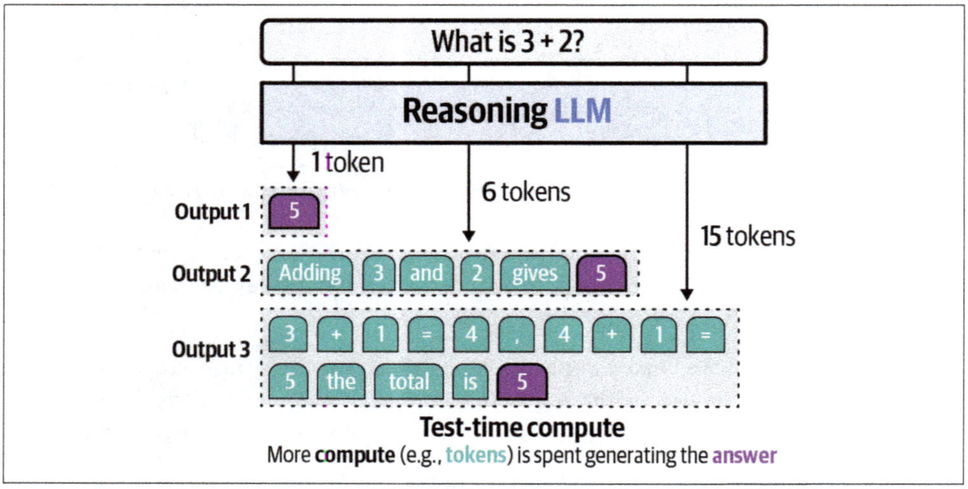

Figure 3-8. Each token requires computational resources to generate, which adds up the more tokens that are generated

The underlying idea is that the more tokens you generate, the better the resulting performance will be. However, you cannot just produce many random tokens to get a better output. Instead, tokens need to be generated that, for instance, contain additional relationships and new thoughts about the original problem.

In other words, it is giving the reasoning LLM more time to "think" (see Figure 3-9).

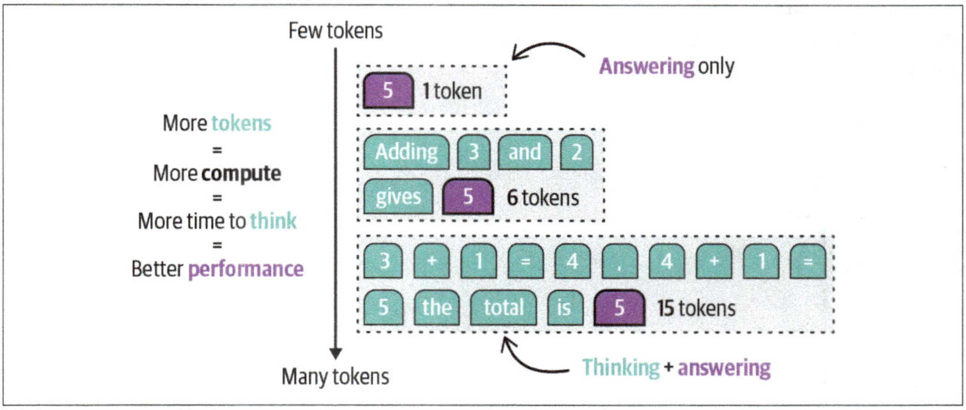

Figure 3-9. Generally, the more computational resources are spent generating the answer, the better the performance

To sum up, train-time compute focuses on scaling resources (e.g., data and compute) spent during pre-training and post-training, while test-time compute focuses on scaling resources (e.g., compute) spent during inference (Figure 3-10).

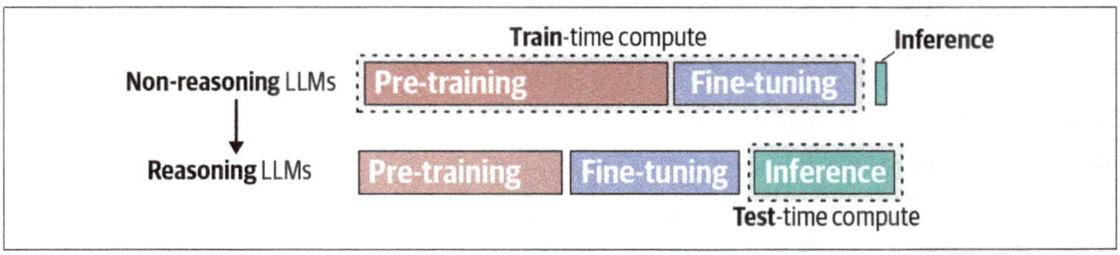

Figure 3-10. The switch from train-time compute to test-time is a focus toward inference instead of primarily focusing on the pre-training and fine-tuning stages

The question remains: "Why has there been a paradigm shift from scaling train-time compute to test-time compute?" Let's look at scaling laws to answer this question.

Scaling Laws

The relationship between a model's scale (e.g., compute, dataset size, and parameter counts) and its performance is described by scaling laws. They often take the form of power laws, where increasing one variable (e.g., compute) leads to a proportional change in another (e.g., performance).

In these power laws, these relationships tend to follow diminishing returns: each doubling of compute gives smaller gains than the previous doubling.

When plotted on regular axes, this creates a curve that flattens out. But when both axes are put on a *log-log scale*, the power-law relationship becomes a straight line, making trends easier to see and compare across many orders of magnitude (see Figure 3-11).

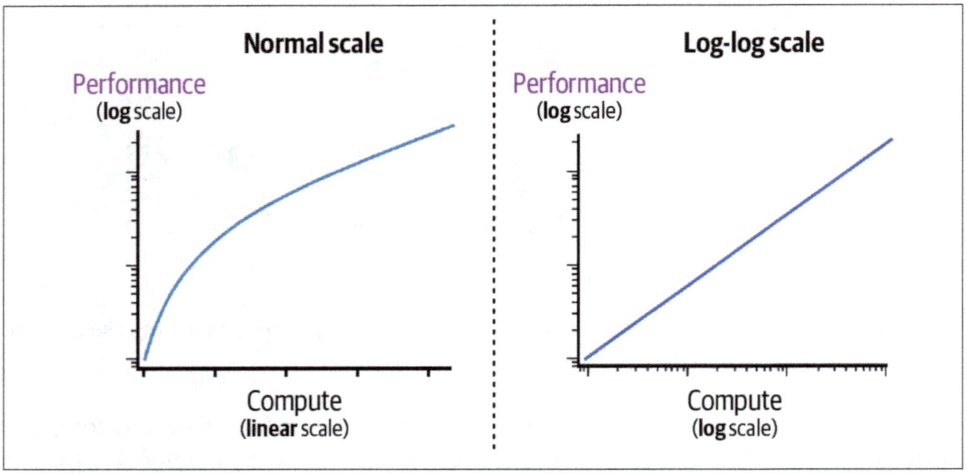

Figure 3-11. A normal scale, shown on the left, has difficulty demonstrating the relationship between compute and performance at larger values compared to the log-log scale on the right

The most influential scaling laws in train-time compute are the Kaplan and Chinchilla scaling laws.[2,3]

Jared Kaplan found that a model's performance improves predictably as you increase compute, dataset size, and parameters, but with diminishing returns. It follows the same power-law form just described. For a fixed compute budget, the best strategy was to keep increasing the model size and train on as much data as possible without overfitting. Figure 3-12 is an annotated image from Kaplan's paper detailing this relationship. Note that a balance is important between data, parameters, and compute.

Following Kaplan's finding, the Chinchilla scaling law demonstrated similar findings and reinforced these power-law relationships. However, they showed that models were often undertrained and that for a fixed compute budget, it's better to use a smaller model and train it on much more data.

---

2 Kaplan, Jared et al. 2020. "Scaling Laws for Neural Language Models," *arXiv*, 2001.08361.

3 Hoffmann, Jordan et al. 2022. "Training Compute-Optimal Large Language Models." *arXiv*, 2203.15556.

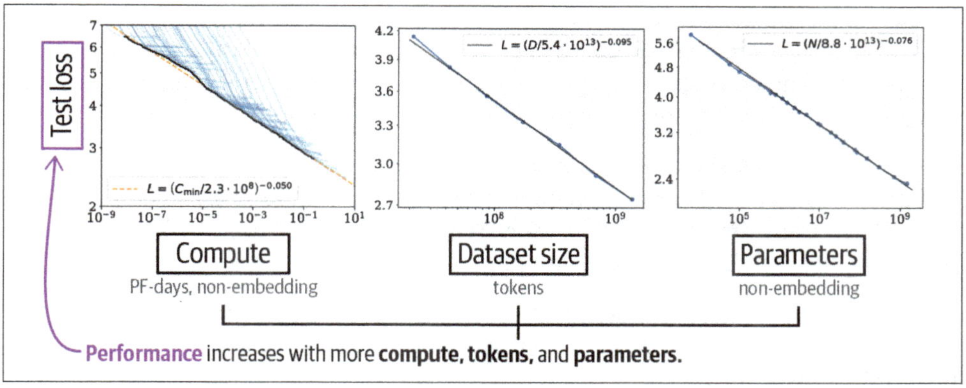

Figure 3-12. A balance between the used compute, number of tokens, and parameters tends to give the best performance according to Kaplan's scaling laws

Both laws suggest that all three factors (compute, data, and model size) should be scaled up in tandem for optimal performance.

However, these power laws state that at some point there will be diminishing returns, which is what the field of LLM research started to see throughout 2024. Although compute, data, and model sizes have steadily grown, the gains have not grown linearly with them. As shown in Figure 3-13, we had likely reached a limit. Note that this assumes that there are no major architectural improvements to the models. Performance of models can be improved with things other than compute, data, and model sizes.

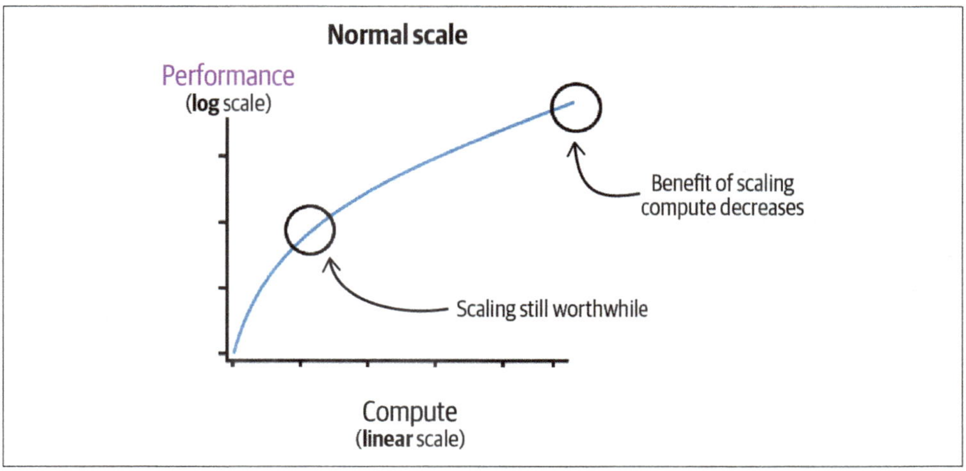

Figure 3-13. The normal scale demonstrates how there continuously needs to be more computing to get the same rise in performance

This meant that researchers had to look elsewhere. Unsurprisingly, test-time compute turned out to be a prime candidate to continue scaling LLMs. Although scaling laws for test-time compute are relatively unexplored, there are several interesting sources comparing scaling train-time compute with test-time compute.

First, a post by OpenAI (*https://oreil.ly/NCPeQ*) detailed that increasing test-time compute might affect performance the same as increasing train-time compute. They defined the train-time compute as more reinforcement learning (RL), and the test-time compute as more time spent thinking.

Figure 3-14 is an annotated image from the OpenAI post showcasing similar relationships. Note how OpenAI suggests that test-time compute might scale even further than train-time compute.

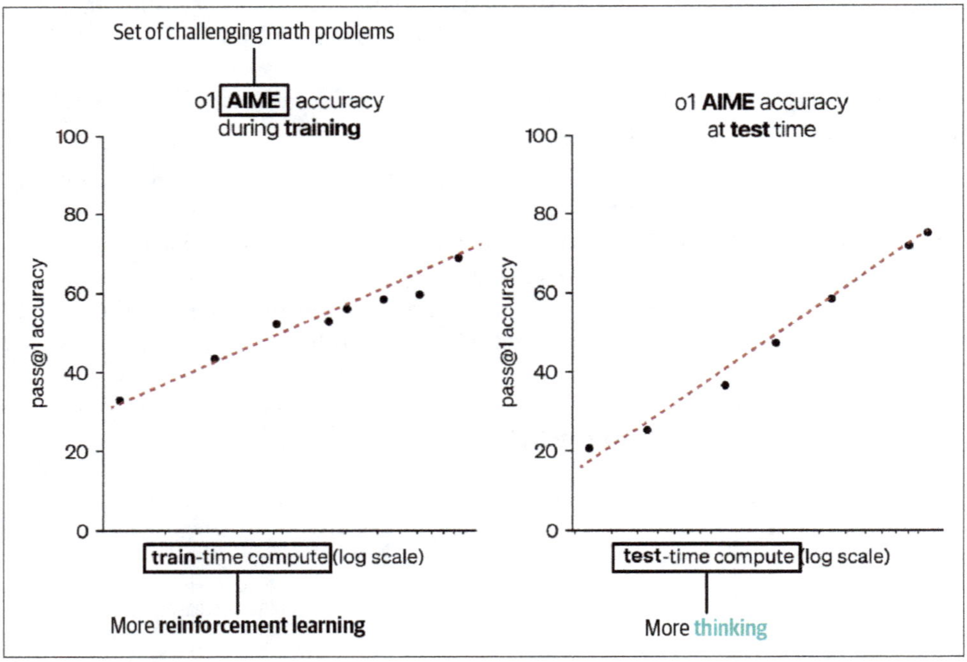

Figure 3-14. The left graph demonstrates increasing train-time compute, and the right graph demonstrates increasing test-time compute, suggesting that test-time compute might scale similarly to train-time compute (from OpenAI)

Second, "Scaling Scaling Laws with Board Games" an interesting paper by Andy L. Jones,[4] explores *AlphaZero* and trains it to various degrees of compute to play a board game called Hex.[5] Hex is a two-player board game in which players take turns placing stones on a hexagonal grid to form a path between opposite sides of the board before the opponent does. AlphaZero is a deep neural network that uses a tree-based search method to consider the moves it can take in this game of Hex.

In Jones' research, train-time compute was identified as increasing the number of parameters in their model and training for more epochs. In contrast, test-time compute was defined as considering more solutions by scaling the depth of their tree search. An overview of both is given in Figure 3-15.

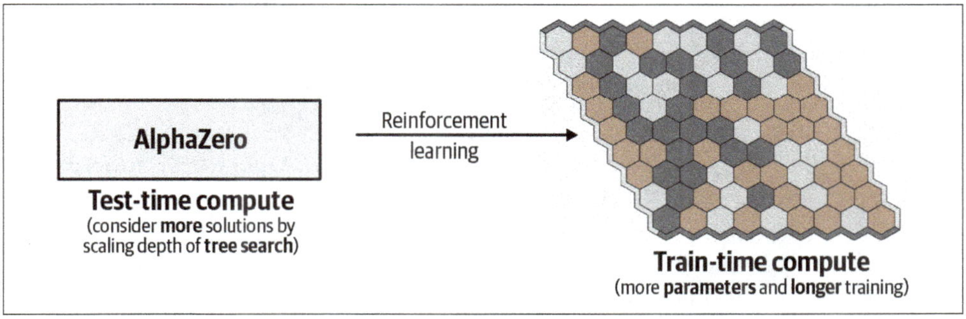

Figure 3-15. AlphaZero was trained to play Hex through reinforcement learning that allowed for scaling both train-time compute and test-time compute

Their results showed that both forms of compute are tightly related. As shown in the annotated Figure 3-16, each dotted line represents the minimum compute needed to reach a given Elo score. Elo is a rating system commonly used in chess that estimates a player's strength based on their past results. The figure suggests that, for a target Elo score, train-time compute and test-time compute should be kept in balance. To maintain the same score, a decrease in one form of compute should be offset by an increase in the other. Likewise, for the best performance, both forms of compute should be increased together.

Research in scaling laws for test-time compute all point to the significant benefit of scaling test-time compute. As a result, a paradigm shift happened in 2024 and 2025 toward reasoning models that focus on using more test-time compute. Through this paradigm shift, instead of focusing purely on train-time compute (pre-training and fine-tuning), these reasoning models instead balance training with inference.

4 Jones, Andy L. 2021. "Scaling Scaling Laws with Board Games," *arXiv*, 2104.03113.

5 Silver, David et al. 2018. "A General Reinforcement Learning Algorithm That Masters Chess, Shogi, and Go Through Self-play," *Science*, 362.6419:1140-1144.

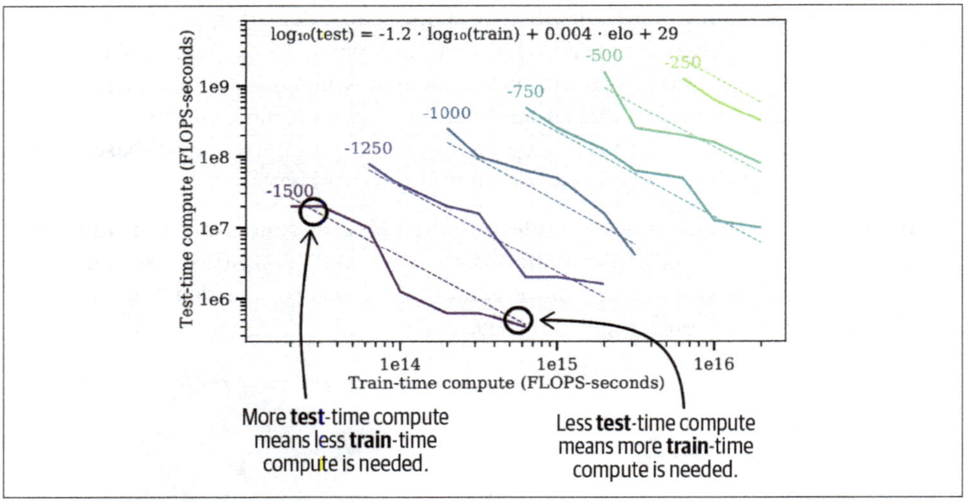

Figure 3-16. Each diagonal line represents a fixed performance that can be achieved by balancing train-time and test-time compute

> Test-time compute doesn't necessarily mean scaling-only thinking; it refers to scaling time and compute spent on inference. Instead of thinking longer, we could also generate many different answers and vote on the best one. By creating more answers, we could likewise scale time to run inference, and stabilize and improve on the output.

Categories of Test-Time Compute

Throughout this chapter, we'll explore methodologies in scaling test-time compute with a focus on extending and improving the thinking processes of LLMs. There are many methods for scaling test-time compute, such as search-based techniques, reward modeling, self-improvement, and more.[6]

To keep things manageable, these can also be put into the following two categories that we will use throughout this chapter:[7]

Search against verifiers
: Sampling generations and selecting the best answer

6 Qu, Xiaoye et al. 2025. "A Survey of Efficient Reasoning for Large Reasoning Models: Language, Multimodality, and Beyond," *arXiv*, 2503.21614.

7 Snell, Charlie et al. 2024. "Scaling LLM Test-Time Compute Optimally Can Be More Effective Than Scaling Model Parameters," *arXiv*, 2408.03314.

Modifying proposal distribution
  Trained "thinking" process

Search against verifiers is a set of techniques that revolve around sampling many answers and/or reasoning traces. Selecting the best answer is done through some form of reward model (RM; or verifier), a model that scores the quality of the given answer and/or reasoning trace.

Modifying proposal distribution involves tuning or prompting the model in such a way that it outputs improved reasoning steps. The proposal distribution is commonly referred to the token probabilities, which propose the tokens to generate next. This distribution from which tokens are sampled is modified to show more advanced reasoning traces. Compared to search against verifiers, it may also use RMs during training to score more promising reasoning traces.

An overview of both methods is shown in Figure 3-17.

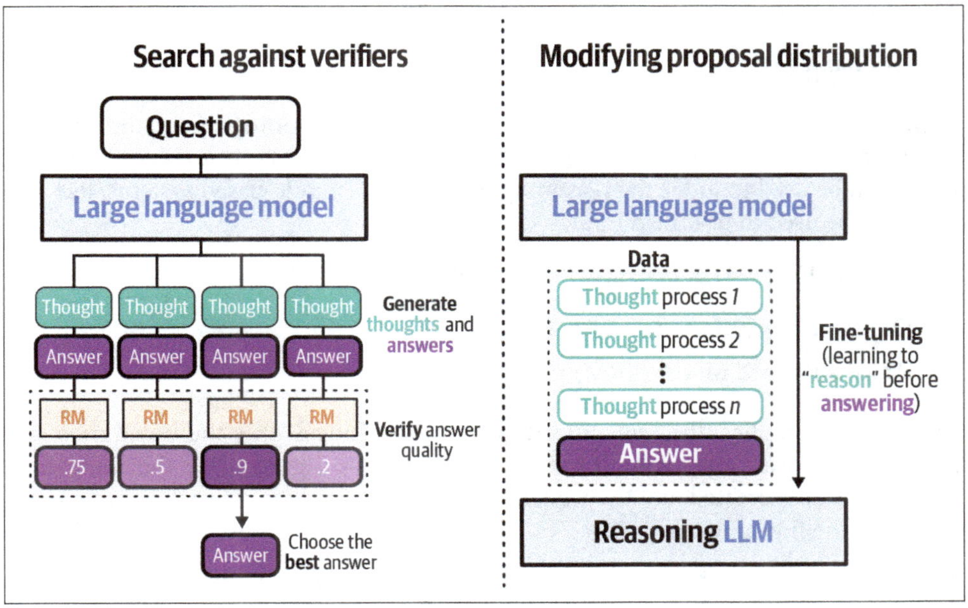

Figure 3-17. Search against verifiers (left) generates multiple traces and from them chooses the best answer by often using reward models. Modifying proposal distribution (right) typically fine-tunes the model.

Due to its focus on sampling generations, search against verifiers is *output*-focused, whereas modifying the proposal distribution is *input*-focused since it focuses on either training or prompting the model. Figure 3-18 shows how these techniques relate to one another.

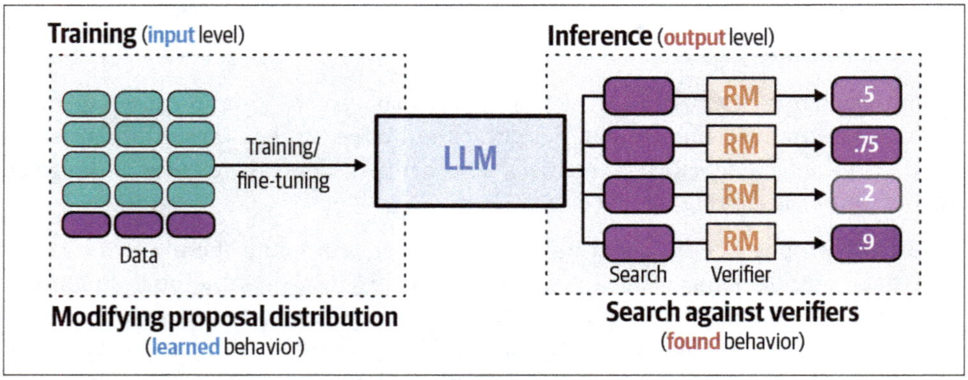

Figure 3-18. Modifying proposal distribution (left) is typically achieved by training the model, which represents learned behavior. Search against verifiers (right) is typically achieved by generating many outputs, scoring using a reward model (verifier), and choosing the best output.

Reward Models

Reward models are used to score the LLM-generated reasoning traces and answers. They can be many things but are generally (fine-tuned) LLMs or rule-based systems. LLMs can be used to judge the reasoning traces, whereas rule-based systems, like unit tests, can be used to test the output.

We will explore two types of verifiers for both methods of test-time compute:

- Outcome Reward Model (ORM)
- Process Reward Model (PRM)

As the name implies, the Outcome Reward Model judges only the outcome of the LLM and ignores any reasoning steps. As shown in Figure 3-19, the number of reasoning traces created and their quality is not taken into account when judging the quality of the final answer.

The Process Reward Model tends to focus on the processes that lead to a given outcome. In the context of reasoning models, those processes are the reasoning steps leading to the final answer. Figure 3-20 demonstrates how one or more PRMs can judge the quality of the reasoning steps. Note that the final answer is not always taken into account, and that often a mix between a Process Reward Model and Outcome Reward Model might be preferred.

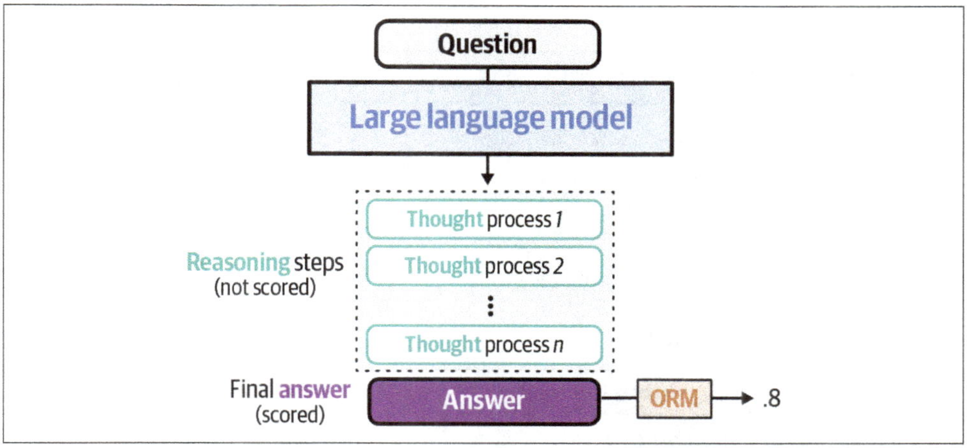

Figure 3-19. An ORM judges only the output and not intermediate reasoning steps

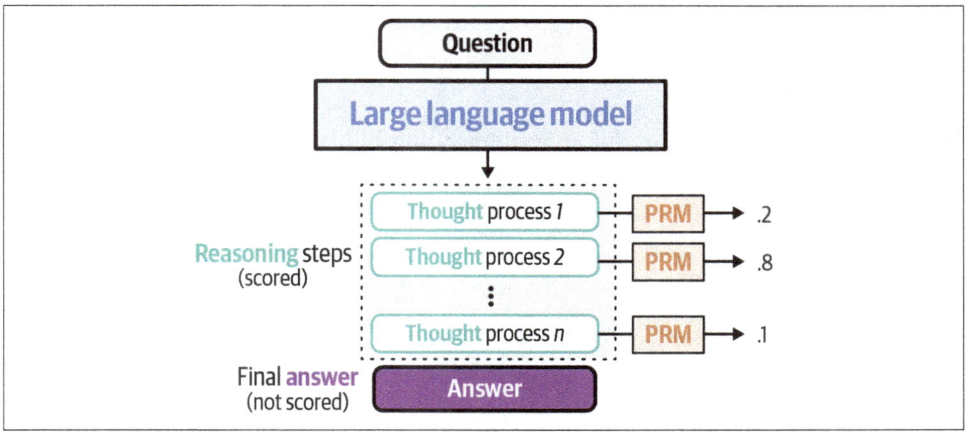

Figure 3-20. A PRM judges only the intermediate reasoning steps and not the output

To make these reasoning steps a bit more explicit, let's use the example we saw at the beginning of this chapter. The question we ask the reasoning LLM is: "I saw 6 flamingos. 2 flew away. 1 hid behind a tree. How many can I see?" As shown in Figure 3-21, reasoning steps are the intermediate thinking steps of the reasoning LLM. How many reasoning steps it has will depend on the specific model because some are more verbose than others.

Note how each Process Reward Model scores a specific part of these reasoning steps and aggregates the scores. Although it starts out strong, reasoning step 2 makes a mistake and is scored low by the PRM. However, the very next reasoning step corrects its mistakes, which is scored highly by the PRM.

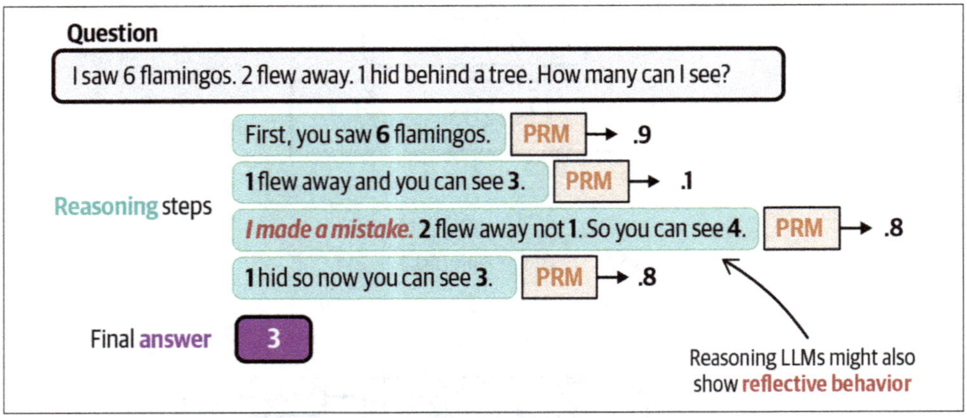

Figure 3-21. Reasoning steps can each be judged by a reward model

How these scores are then used to judge the quality of the answer or select the best answer depends on the specific category of test-time compute.

Prompt Engineering

In some of our previous examples, non-reasoning LLMs were assumed to be able to output reasoning traces (thoughts). This was especially true of techniques in search against verifiers that sample many reasoning traces and answers before selecting the best one.

So, how are these non-reasoning LLMs able to output reasoning traces?

Prompt engineering plays a vital role in this process, with a technique called Chain-of-Thought (CoT).[8] This is one of the first techniques to elicit reasoning in LLMs that were not trained for reasoning tasks.

Chain-of-Thought prompting requires the model to explain its reasoning process by specifying that in the prompt. LLMs are quite adept at following examples. By demonstrating the desired reasoning style, it increases the likelihood that the LLM will replicate it, as illustrated in Figure 3-22. Such demonstrations in a prompt are typically referred to as one-shot prompting or few-shot prompting. One-shot prompting uses a single example to demonstrate a task or targeted behavior while few-shot prompting uses two or more examples, which tends to result in higher accuracy as it helps the model recognize patterns.

8 Wei, Jason et al. 2022. "Chain-of-Thought Prompting Elicits Reasoning in Large Language Models," *NIPS '22: Proceedings of the 36th International Conference on Neural Information Processing Systems*, 24824-24837.

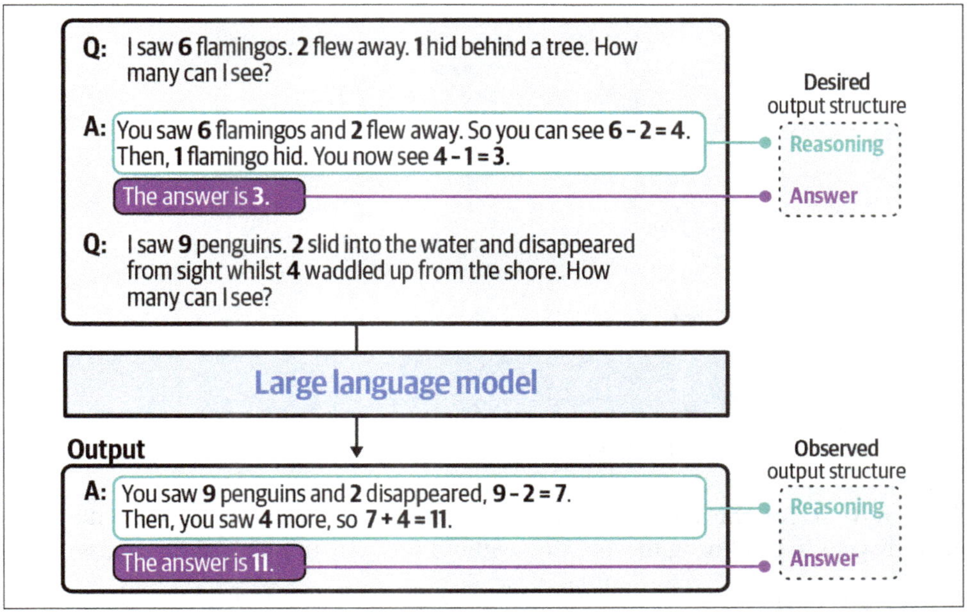

Figure 3-22. An example of one-shot learning where a single example is given to the LLM that describes how it should reason

We can use the LLM we created in Chapter 2 to demonstrate the behavior. Let's first load in the LLM:

```
from illustrated_agents.chapters.ch2 import LLM

# Gemma 3 12B (no native thinking or tool calling)
llm = LLM(model="gemma3:12b", temperature=1)
```

Note that we set the `temperature` to 1 as that will allow us to generate different answers that we can use later for sampling. If we were to set it to 0, then the output would always be the same regardless of how many times we run it.

After doing so, let's give the LLM a riddle and ask it to be concise in its answer as an example. As discussed, this is a form of few-shot learning where you give examples of what you want the answer to the interaction to be:

```
# Example of one-shot prompting
prompt_example = "I saw 6 flamingos. 2 flew away. 1 hid behind a tree. How many
can I see? Be concise."
prompt_answer = "3"

# The query we want to ask the model
query = "I saw 9 penguins. 2 slid in the water and disappeared from sight
while 4 waddled up from the shore. How many can I see?"
```

```
# Messages
messages = [
    {"role": "user", "content": prompt_example},
    {"role": "assistant", "content": prompt_answer},
    {"role": "user", "content": query},
]

# Generate response
response = llm.generate(messages)
print(response)
```

This gives us:

```
Response(
    content='7\n',
    reasoning=None,
    tool_call=None,
    metadata={'model': 'gemma3:12b', 'prompt_tokens': 82, 'completion_tokens': 3}
)
```

Note how it got the answer wrong! Without any extensive reasoning, the LLM directly goes to answering the question without properly thinking of this puzzle.

Instead of using a concise answer, let's give the LLM a more thorough one that mimics the type of reasoning we would like to see:

```
pprompt_example = "I saw 6 flamingos. 2 flew away. 1 hid behind a tree.
How many can I see?"
prompt_answer = "You saw 6 flamingos 2 flew away. 6 - 2 = 4.
Then, 1 flamingo hid. You see now 4 - 1 = 3."

# Messages
messages = [
    {"role": "user", "content": prompt_example},
    {"role": "assistant", "content": prompt_answer},
    {"role": "user", "content": query},
]

# Generate response
response = llm.generate(messages)
print(response)
```

This gives us:

```
Response(
  content="Okay, let's break it down:\n\n
*   You started with 9 penguins.\n
*   2 slid into the water and disappeared: 9 - 2 = 7\n
*   4 waddled up from the shore: 7 + 4 = 11\n\nYou can see **11** penguins!",
  reasoning=None,
  tool_call=None,
  metadata={'model': 'gemma3:12b', 'prompt_tokens': 117, 'completion_tokens': 70}
)
```

This is the correct answer! Just by giving the model a couple of examples on how to reason, it follows that behavior and allows for a reasoning process.

This process can be further simplified by foregoing any examples of reasoning steps and instead simply stating: "Let's think step-by-step."[9] This is a form of zero-shot prompting where no examples are used that has a chance of working with some models.

> Zero-shot prompting tends to perform worse than one-shot prompting, which tends to perform worse than few-shot prompting. Although providing examples helps guide the model, it can still achieve similar behavior without them.

What makes prompting special in the context of non-reasoning LLMs is that non-reasoning LLMs do have reasoning capabilities hidden somewhere in their parameters. It's a matter of prompting it in an elegant way to extract those capabilities.

Let's see if we can reproduce the behavior we explored before by simply adding, "Let's think step-by-step" to the prompt:

```
# Messages with zero-shot Chain-of-Thought prompting
messages = [{"role": "user", "content": query + " Let's think step by step."}]

# Generate response
response = llm.generate(messages)
print(response)
```

This gives us:

```
Response(
  content="Okay, let's break this down step by step:\n\n
1. **Start:** You initially see 9 penguins.\n\n
2. **Penguins disappear:** 2 penguins slid into the water and
are no longer visible. So, 9 - 2 = 7 penguins.\n\n
3. **Penguins appear:**
4 penguins waddled up from the shore, and you can now see them.
So, 7 + 4 = 11 penguins.\n\n**Answer:** You can now see 11 penguins.\n",
  reasoning=None,
  tool_call=None,
  metadata=
  {
    'model': 'gemma3:12b', 'prompt_tokens': 51, 'completion_tokens': 112
  }
)
```

9 Kojima, Takeshi et al. 2022. "Large Language Models Are Zero-Shot Reasoners," *NIPS '22: Proceedings of the 36th International Conference on Neural Information Processing Systems*: 22199-22213.

Also the correct answer! Now instead of having to create a bunch of examples, you can just append "Let's think step-by-step" to the prompt. To enable the `TinyAgent`'s reasoning, all we have to do is add that "thinking" prompt to the task like we did before:

```
from illustrated_agents.chapters.ch2 import TinyAgent

agent = TinyAgent(llm=llm)
response = agent.run(query + " Let's think step by step.")
```

We'll use this idea of zero-shot Chain-of-Thought more in Chapter 6, where we will enable reasoning by telling the model to use separate THOUGHT and ANSWER fields for the reasoning and the answer, respectively.

A test-time compute category that relies heavily on Chain-of-Thought-like prompting is search against verifiers. By sampling many reasoning traces through Chain-of-Thought, much of its instability can be prevented.

Search Against Verifiers

Search against verifiers refers to a family of techniques that involve generating multiple candidate answers or reasoning traces and then evaluating them to choose the best answer. The scorer is typically referred to as the *reward model* (RM), also called the *verifier*. However, as we will explore in the first example, not all of these techniques have to use a reward model.

Search against verifiers does not necessarily enable reasoning but is more akin to what we expect of non-human behavior. It programmatically goes through many answers and scores the best ones. As such, the techniques that we will explore might remind you of traditional methods, like majority voting or tree-search techniques.

As shown in Figure 3-23, search against verifiers typically consists of three steps:

1. Sampling multiple reasoning processes and/or answers.
2. A reward model (verifier) scores the generated output.
3. The best answer based on the generated scores is chosen.

The verifier is typically an LLM, fine-tuned for either judging the outcome (ORM) or the process (PRM). This fine-tuning can be through actual training or by creating a specialized prompt with few-shot examples, as we explored before.

To sample many different thoughts and answers to a given question, LLMs can use different temperature values. The temperature parameter in LLMs controls the randomness of the model's output by changing the distribution of the model's next token probabilities. Shown in Figure 3-24, low temperatures focus on high-probability tokens and tend to generate similar texts, while high temperatures allow for more creative and different texts to be generated.

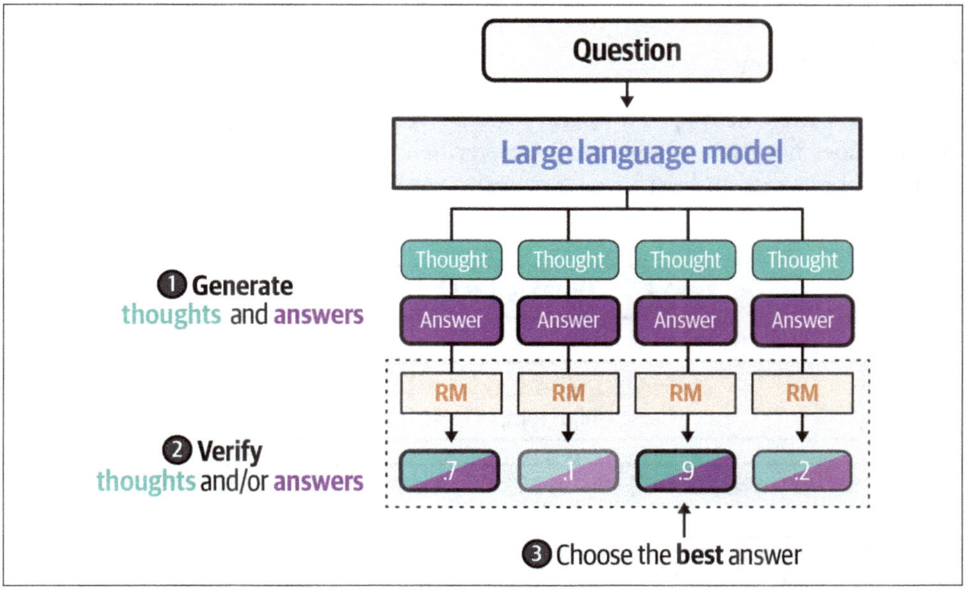

Figure 3-23. The three steps of search against verifiers

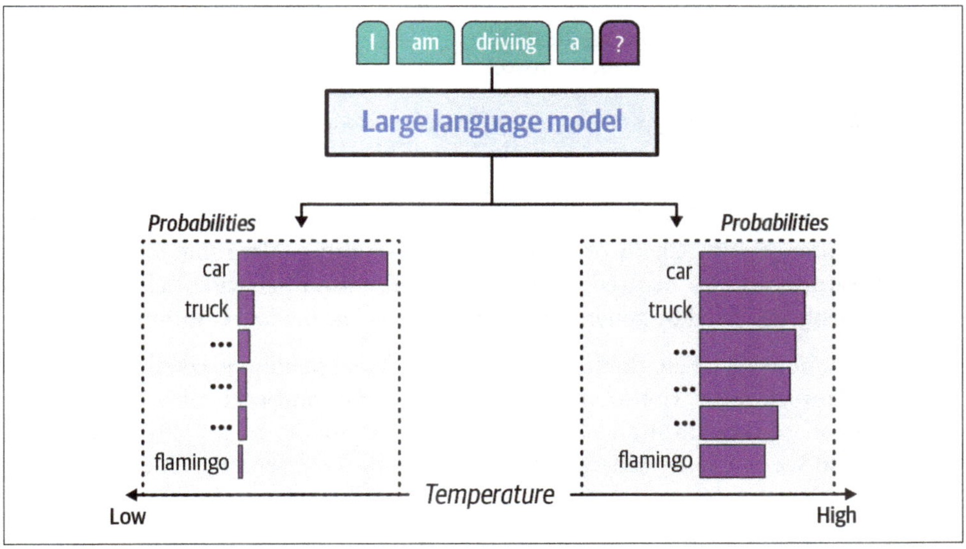

Figure 3-24. A higher temperature has a higher likelihood of the LLM generating different outputs, whereas a lower temperature typically results in similar outputs

A major advantage of using verifiers is that there is no need to retrain or fine-tune the LLM that you use for answering the question. Likewise, you can easily scale the test-time compute up by sampling more answers or restricting it by sampling fewer.

Self-Consistency

One of the first methods for search against verifiers is called *self-consistency* and actually does not use a reward model or verifier.[10] Instead, it samples a user-defined number of answers and performs a majority vote to select the most frequent answer (Figure 3-25).

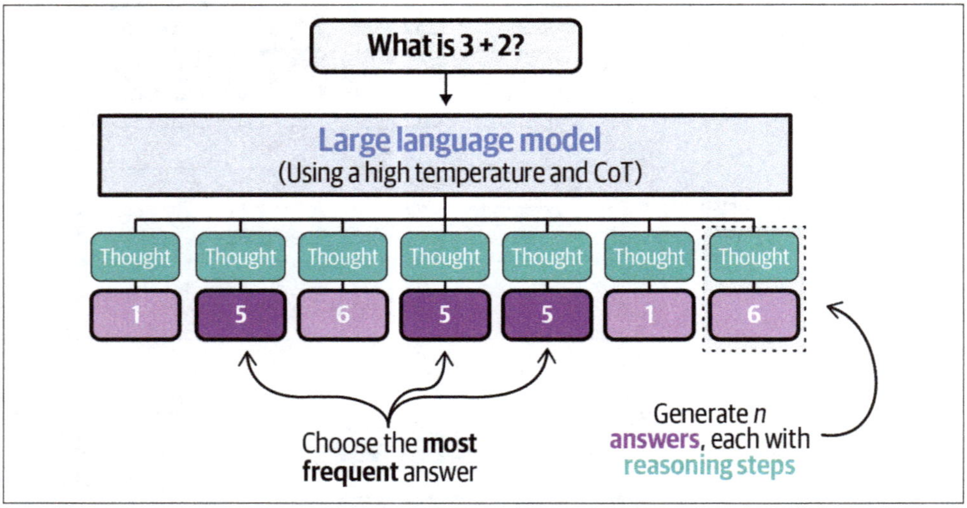

Figure 3-25. Self-consistency samples many thoughts and answers and will choose the most frequent answer

To generate many different reasoning traces and answers, a high temperature is usually combined with Chain-of-Thought-like prompting. Note that varying values of temperature can also be used to get more randomized behavior. Self-consistency can then easily be scaled by generating more answers, each with reasoning steps.

Let's explore how we would do this in practice. We use a seating puzzle that the model has to reason through. The model is queried 10 times and each time can generate a different reasoning trace and answer. We ask the model to put its answer after "Answer:" so we can easily separate the answer from the reasoning. The answers are then counted:

10 Wang, Xuezhi et al. 2022. "Self-Consistency Improves Chain of Thought Reasoning in Language Models," *arXiv*, 2203.11171.

```
from collections import Counter

answers = []
for _ in range(10):
    query = """Six friends (Maarten, Ilse, Sarah, Jor, Irene, and Chris)
    are sitting in a row.

- Sarah is in seat 3.
- Chris is sitting at one of the ends of the row.
- Jor is sitting immediately to the right of Chris.
- Ilse is sitting exactly in the middle of Sarah and Maarten.
- Irene is not sitting next to Sarah.
- Maarten is sitting somewhere to the left of Irene.

In which seat is Maarten sitting?
Let's think step by step and give back your answer only after 'Answer:'.
"""

    # Generate response
    messages = [{"role": "user", "content": query},]
    response = llm.generate(messages)
    answer = response.content.split("Answer:")[-1].replace("\n", "").strip()
    answers.append(answer)

Counter(answers)
```

This gives us:

```
Counter({'5': 4, '1': 3, '4': 1, '2': 2})
```

The most common answer is 5 (which is correct). However, in some runs the model has produced the incorrect answer. By rerunning the model several times, we increase the likelihood that the model gets the answer correct.

> Self-consistency works surprisingly well, considering that it selects the most frequent answer and not necessarily the best answer. As it turns out, sampling over many answers reduces the chance of selecting an infrequent and potentially incorrect answer. However, for very complex tasks that the LLM seldom gets correct, self-consistency is unlikely to improve the output.
>
> The previous code example illustrates this nicely because it is right on the edge of what the model knows. In our experiments, the model tends to lean toward the correct answer (5) but sometimes might produce too many incorrect answers. Since we have a temperature of 1, the results will be different each time you run the model.

Best-of-N Samples

A common and straightforward method for using a verifier is called Best-of-N samples.[11] In this method, the LLM generates N candidate answers, typically using a high or varying temperature to encourage diversity. Then, a verifier evaluates each answer and selects the highest-scoring one.

There are two main forms of Best-of-N samples, using:

Outcome Reward Models (ORM)
: Only the answers are scored using a verifier (e.g., LLM, unit tests, compiler) and the highest scoring answer is chosen.

Process Reward Models (PRM)
: Only the processes (thoughts) are scored using verifiers. When there are multiple reasoning traces for a given question, each trace is scored and averaged. The answer that has traces with the highest scores is selected.

An overview of these two techniques is shown in Figure 3-26. For more information on how to create and train reward models, we highly suggest reading Cameron R. Wolfe's post on reward models (*https://oreil.ly/qtXRw*).

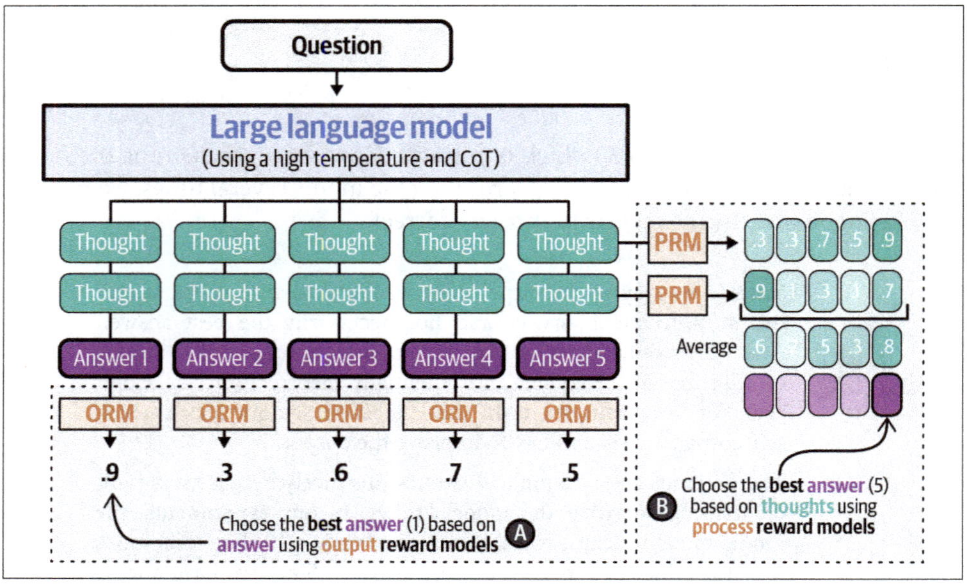

Figure 3-26. Best-of-N samples can use Outcome Reward Models (ORMs; left) and/or Process Reward Models (PRMs; right)

11 Lightman, Hunter et al. 2023. "Let's Verify Step by Step," *The Twelfth International Conference on Learning Representations*.

Let's go through an example on how we could verify the output of an LLM and choose the best one through sampling. We will ask the model to generate a function that converts Roman numerals (e.g., IV) to integers (e.g., 4). There are many different ways you can verify this output, such as using another LLM, creating tests, or checking whether the code compiles. The choice depends on what you have available. Checking if the code compiles is a great first step but does not check the correctness of the output. Let's assume that we have a couple of test cases. With those, we can create a simple verification function that checks how many test cases pass:

```
test_cases = [
    ("III", 3),
    ("IV", 4),
    ("IX", 9),
    ("LVIII", 58),
    ("MCMXCIV", 1994),
    ("MMMCMXCIX", 3999),
    ("", 0),
    ("IIII", 0),        # invalid: four in a row
    ("VV", 0),          # invalid: V can't repeat
    ("IC", 0),          # invalid: I can only subtract from V or X
    ("ABC", 0),         # invalid: non-Roman characters
    ("MMMM", 0),        # invalid: exceeds 3999
]


def verify(answer):
    try:
        # Extract the function
        namespace = {}
        exec(answer, namespace)
        fn = namespace["roman_to_int"]

        # Evaluate the function on test cases
        score = sum(fn(inp) == expected for inp, expected in test_cases) / len
        (test_cases)
        return score
    except Exception:
        # Return 0 if the code is not valid Python
        return 0.0
```

Using those test cases, we can run a similar loop as we did with the self-consistency example:

```
responses = []
for _ in range(10):
    # The query we want to ask the model
    query = """Write a Python function `roman_to_int(s)` that converts a Roman
    numeral
string to an integer. The function should:
- Handle standard Roman numerals from 1 to 3999.
- Correctly handle subtractive notation (e.g., IV=4, IX=9, XL=40, XC=90, CD=400,
```

```
CM=900).
- Return 0 for invalid inputs (empty string, non-Roman characters, or invalid
patterns
  like "IIII" or "VV").

Give only the function definition, no explanation or markdown formatting."""

    # Generate response
    response = llm.generate([{"role": "user", "content": query}])

    # Verify the response and compute a score
    score = verify(response.content)

    # Store the response and its score
    responses.append((response.content, score))

# Get highest score and the corresponding answer
best_answer, best_score = max(responses, key=lambda x: x[1])

# Show all scores
[response[1] for response in responses]
```

When you run this, the model creates 10 answers, each of which is judged with the verify function. In our case, this gives the following range of scores:

```
[0.6666666666666666,
 0.5833333333333334,
 0.9166666666666666,
 0.9166666666666666,
 0.8333333333333334,
 0.75,
 0.9166666666666666,
 0.9166666666666666,
 1.0,
 0.25]
```

Note that we have found only one answer that is correct. Without having a verify function and without sampling, it's unlikely the model would have gotten the correct answer.

The great thing about the Best-of-N samples method is that it allows for a wide degree of creativity and flexibility in how you structure the application of these verifiers. For instance, we can also weigh each answer candidate by the Process Reward Model and use that to create an aggregate score for answers that appear multiple times. An example is given in Figure 3-27 of this weighted Best-of-N samples.

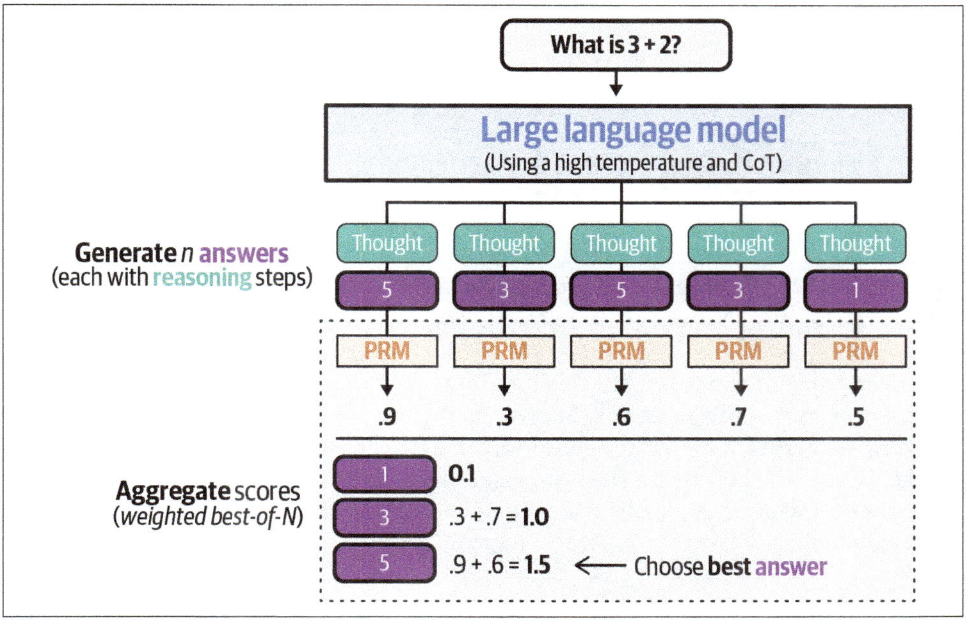

Figure 3-27. Weighted Best-of-N samples add a Process Reward Model (PRM) to judge each output

Modifying Proposal Distribution

The second category of scaling test-time compute is called modifying proposal distribution and is a popular method of creating reasoning LLMs. Instead of searching for the correct reasoning steps with verifiers (*output*-focused), the model is trained to demonstrate advanced reasoning steps (*input*-focused). Remember that both the Process Reward Model and the Outcome Reward Model focus on the output generated by the LLM, the reasoning traces, and the final answer, respectively.

The term "modifying proposal distribution" refers to the distribution from which tokens are sampled. Imagine that we have a question that we pass to the LLM. As shown in Figure 3-28, it creates a distribution of token probabilities from which we can sample. A common strategy would be to select the token with the highest probability.

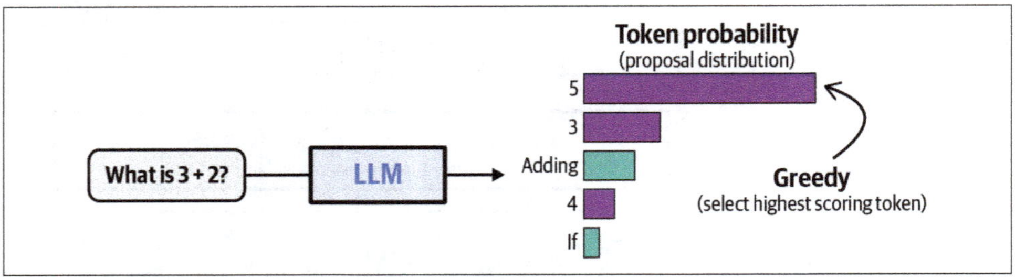

Figure 3-28. Each LLM generates token probabilities, and by looking a bit closer at each token, we can consider them either related to output or to reasoning

However, some of the tokens in this distribution are not a direct answer but instead the start of reasoning behavior. Shown in Figure 3-29, if we choose a token that answers the question directly, then it immediately generates a stop token. However, if a token is chosen that is the start of reasoning, then it completes its reasoning until it reaches an answer. As such, you can view them as "answer" and "reason" tokens, respectively.

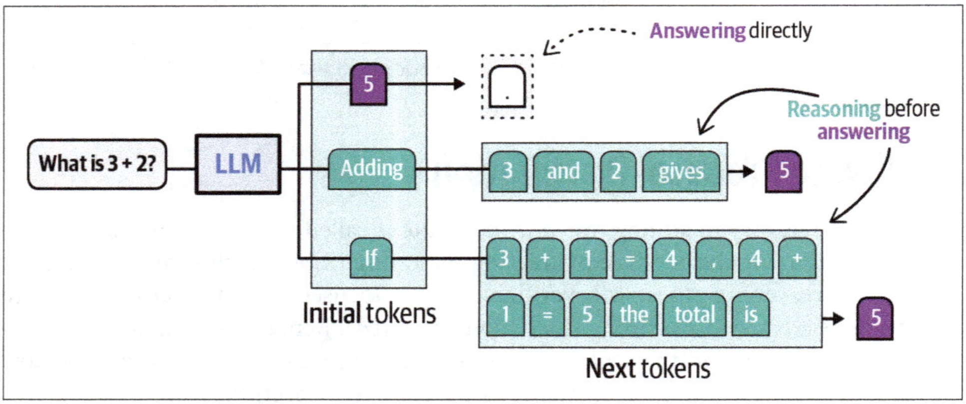

Figure 3-29. Forcing the LLM to choose tokens that are the start of a sentence rather than the immediate answer tends to generate simple forms of reasoning

When we modify the proposal distribution (the token probability distribution), we are essentially making it so that the model re-ranks the distribution such that "reasoning" tokens are selected more frequently (Figure 3-30).

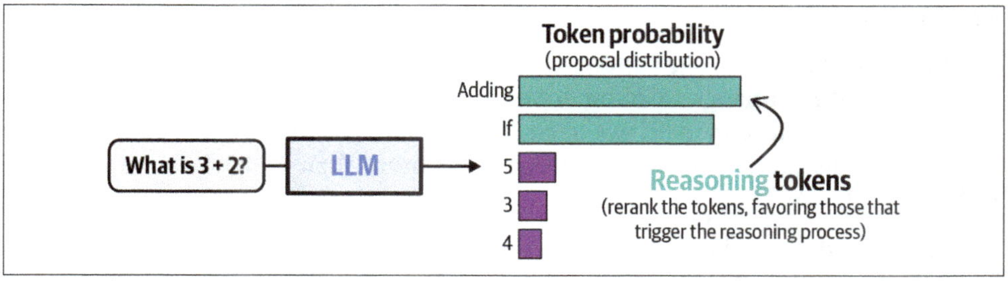

Figure 3-30. Modifying the proposal distribution is essentially reranking the tokens such that it is much more common for the LLM to choose tokens that allow for a degree of reasoning

We can achieve modifying or reranking this distribution by training the LLM. Two common methods of training are:

Supervised fine-tuning (SFT)
: Reasoning behavior is mimicked through supervised fine-tuning, where the LLM is asked to reproduce pre-defined reasoning traces. The model learns to approximate the reasoning patterns present in the training data.

Reinforcement learning (RL)
: The LLM discovers reasoning itself through a reward system. During training, the LLM discovers good reasoning strategies by being rewarded for generating high-quality responses.

In other words, supervised fine-tuning stabilizes the model outputs by serving as a memory process to uncover learned reasoning behavior, while reinforcement learning enables self-learning and generalization.

Supervised Fine-Tuning

The most straightforward method for enabling reasoning behavior in LLMs is to apply supervised fine-tuning. Similar to what we saw in Chapter 2, the model is exposed to triplet-like data, which contains the user's query, a reasoning trace, and an answer.

Although using supervised fine-tuning is quite straightforward, collecting these large amounts of reasoning traces is quite difficult, as they generally have to be manually created by potentially labeling hundreds of thousands of samples.

Flan-PaLM

An early example of using supervised fine-tuning on Chain-of-Thought-like data was the Flan-PaLM paper.[12] Chung et al.'s main method of fine-tuning is called Flan (Fine-tuning language models; not to be confused with the FLAN models),[13] in which a variety of instruction templates are used on more than 1,800 tasks to fine-tune LLMs.

In several of these tasks, examples were added that included annotated Chain-of-Thought traces that the model could train on. They include arithmetic reasoning, multi-hop reasoning, and natural language inference (determining the truthfulness of a given statement).

As shown in Figure 3-31, the training data contained both reasoning and non-reasoning examples, both without (zero-shot) and with (few-shot) examples. Chung et al. fine-tuned various LLMs, including PaLM, which has 540 billion parameters, and prefixed the fine-tuned models with "Flan."

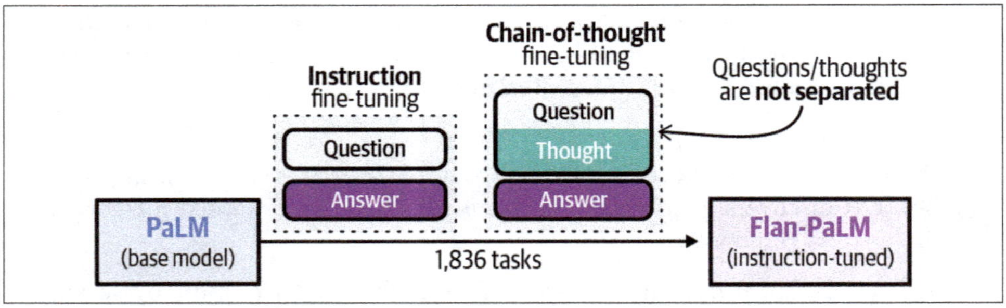

Figure 3-31. Flan-PaLM is created through supervised fine-tuning on various data

By mixing in Chain-of-Thought data in their pool of training data, the resulting models could be more easily prompted to demonstrate reasoning (e.g., through prompting "let's think step-by-step").

This is an early example of enforcing reasoning in LLMs through supervised fine-tuning. However, the researchers' data mostly contained non-reasoning examples mixed in with reasoning traces to improve the model's performance, such as straightforward queries and answers combined with more extensive queries that include examples of thoughts. Although this model can demonstrate Chain-of-Thought through proper prompting, it's still a bit premature to call this a reasoning model.

12 Chung, Hyung Won et al. 2024. "Scaling Instruction-Finetuned Language Models," *Journal of Machine Learning Research*, 25(70): 1-53.

13 Wei, Jason et al. 2021. "Finetuned Language Models Are Zero-Shot Learners," *arXiv*, 2109.01652.

Instead, let us explore supervised fine-tuning variants that purely focus on instilling reasoning.

s1: Simple test-time scaling

Since Flan-PaLM, reasoning in LLMs has gained more traction. However, creating reasoning data is quite difficult as it typically requires human annotators for large amounts of query/answer pairs. Training data can easily reach hundreds of thousands of examples, and adding reasoning traces to each can become costly.

The authors of "s1: Simple test-time scaling" demonstrate that you could get a reasoning LLM using only small data.[14] Using only 1,000 questions paired with reasoning traces, they successfully fine-tuned the Qwen2.5 32B-Instruct LLM to demonstrate stable reasoning.

Compared to Flan-PaLM, they used special tokens to separate the thinking stage from the answering stage. To do so, the thinking stage was enclosed with `<|im_start|>think` while the following answer was enclosed with `<|im_start|>answer` (see Figure 3-32).

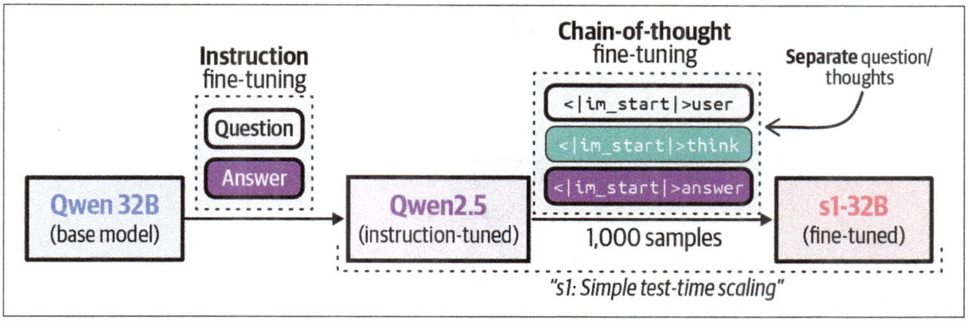

Figure 3-32. A reasoning model could be created by using a dataset as small as 1,000 samples

Using special types of tokens to separate thinking from the final answer is a common method you will see employed by recent LLMs, such as Qwen3 and GPT-OSS (*https://oreil.ly/7jGhk*).[15]

14 Muennighoff, Niklas et al. 2025. "s1: Simple Test-Time Scaling," *Proceedings of the 2025 Conference on Empirical Methods in Natural Language Processing*.

15 Yang, An et al. 2025. "Qwen3 Technical Report," *arXiv*, 2505.09388.

Additionally, the authors applied test-time scaling explorations by controlling test-time compute in two ways:

- Forcefully terminating the model's thinking process
- Lengthening the thinking process by spending "Wait" multiple times to the generation when it tries to end

Doing so allowed them to explore test-time scaling and the impact it has on performance on various tasks. Figure 3-33 is an annotated figure from their paper illustrating this idea of limiting and lengthening the thinking process to explore test-time scaling.

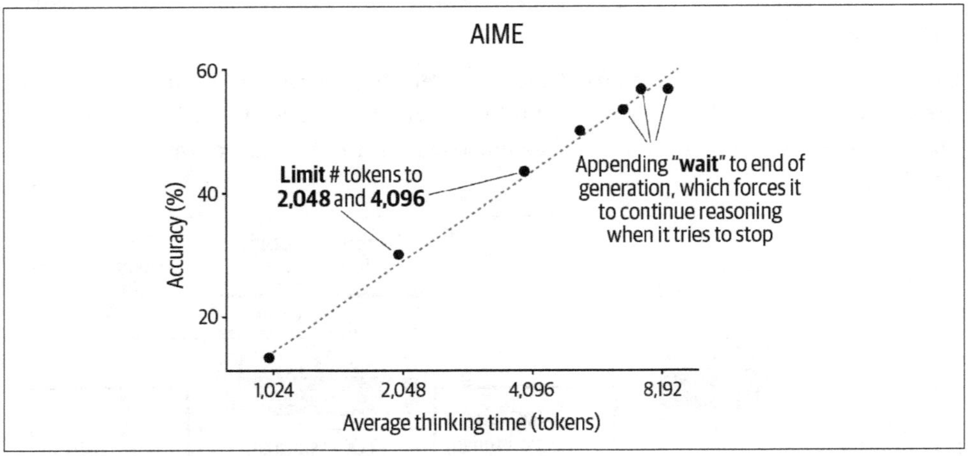

Figure 3-33. Continuing the generation allows for more reasoning, which in turn tends to increase performance

Going back to OpenAI's experiment, the s1 paper showed similar results in scaling test-time compute; more test-time compute resulted in a better performance.

Reinforcement Learning

In Chapter 2, we saw how RLVR uses verifiable rewards to update model weights and met GRPO as the algorithm DeepSeek used. Here we'll see what that looks like in practice and how it produces reasoning behavior as an emergent property.

Reasoning with DeepSeek-R1 Zero

A key stepping stone to DeepSeek-R1 was an experimental variant called *DeepSeek-R1-Zero*. It began with the *DeepSeek-V3-Base* model, but instead of applying supervised fine-tuning on large reasoning datasets, the authors relied solely on reinforcement learning to enable reasoning behavior.

In their training procedure, they used a custom system prompt that outlined how the LLM should respond. To do so, the thinking stage was enclosed with `<think>` and `</think>` while the following answer was enclosed with `<answer>` and `</answer>` (see Figure 3-34). Note that the tags are mentioned but not what the reasoning process itself should look like. That's for the LLM to figure out during training.

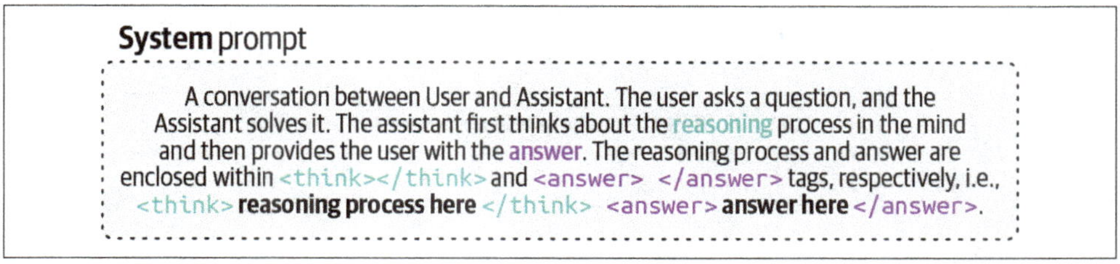

Figure 3-34. The system prompt used to steer DeepSeek-V3-Base during training

DeepSeek used the same two rule-based rewards we saw in Chapter 2: an accuracy reward for arriving at the correct answer, and a format reward for using the `<think>` and `<answer>` tags correctly.

You can see these rewards and the general training process in Figure 3-35. The algorithm is GRPO, which we covered in Chapter 2.

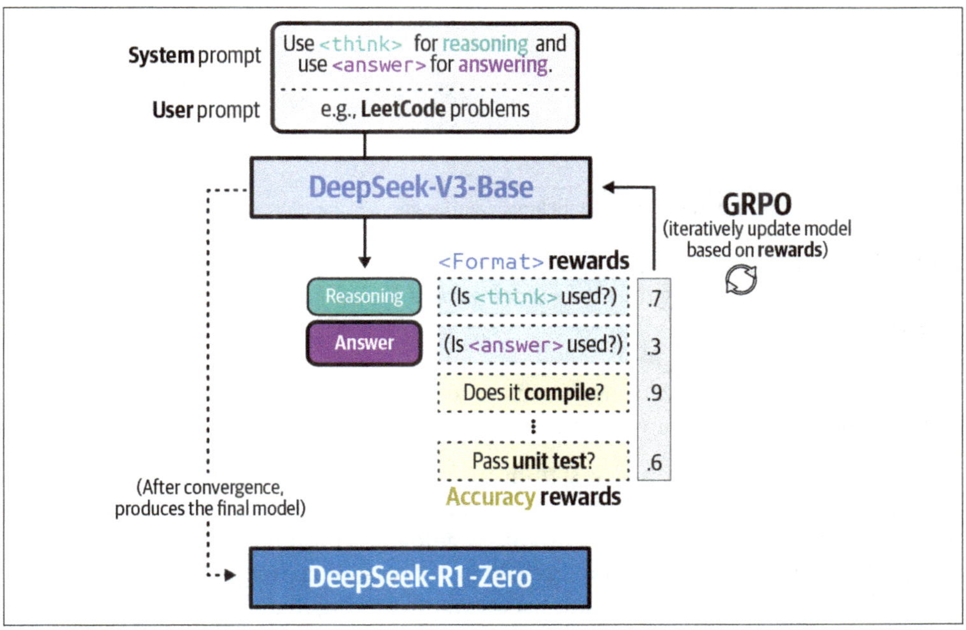

Figure 3-35. The training process of DeepSeek-R1-Zero

Again, note how the rewards state only whether the correct format is used and whether the output is correct. How it gets there (through reasoning) is something for the model to figure out.

By providing these indirect rewards related to Chain-of-Thought-like behavior, the model found that longer and more complex reasoning processes would often lead to better answers. These results are shown in Figure 3-36, which is an annotated figure of the paper indicating how the model started to create longer reasoning traces.

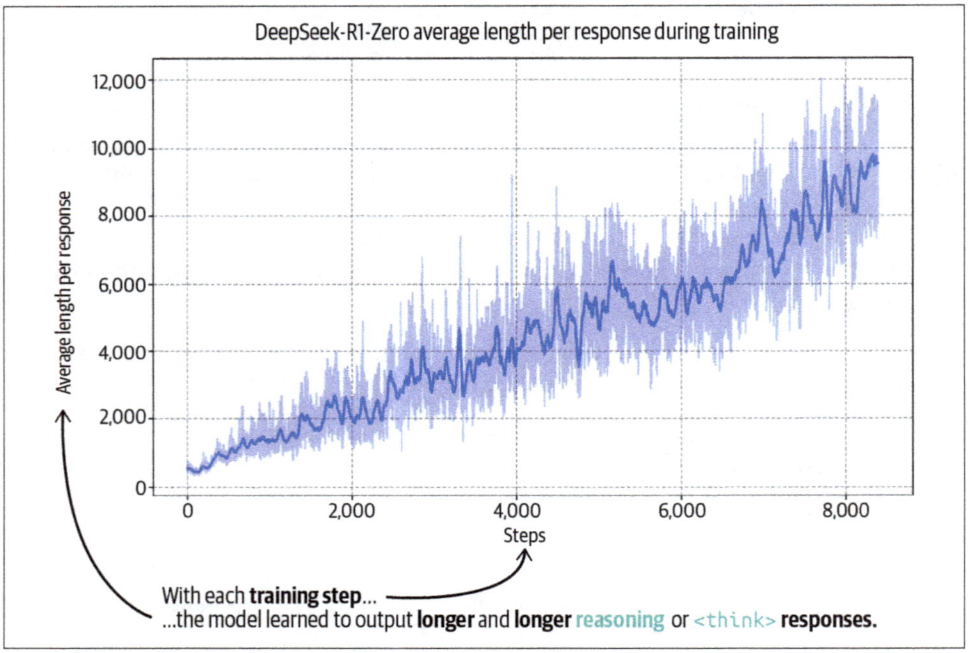

Figure 3-36. An annotated figure from the DeepSeek-R1 paper (https://arxiv.org/pdf/2501.12948) demonstrating that the model learned by itself that longer responses tend to be more accurate

Interestingly, this graph can also be used to reinforce test-time scaling, where the model scales test-time compute itself through lengthening its response.

The model, however, still had a significant drawback. By skipping over supervised fine-tuning and going directly to reinforcement learning, the model suffered from a "cold start" problem. Without any initial guidance, the model started to mix languages (e.g., mixing English and French in its reasoning traces) and showed poor readability because it lacked Markdown formatting to highlight answers for users.

This is an interesting perspective because they assumed that any reasoning trace should also be readable by users and not merely used to improve its own output.

There is something to say for reasoning that is not comprehensible by users, such as reasoning in latent space, but we'll get to this later in this chapter.

DeepSeek-R1

Using the lessons learned from DeepSeek-R1-Zero, the authors come up with the following five training steps to create DeepSeek-R1:[16]

1. Cold start prevention
2. Reasoning-oriented reinforcement learning
3. Rejection sampling
4. Supervised fine-tuning
5. Reinforcement learning for all scenarios

In step 1, to prevent the cold start problem, DeepSeek-V3-Base was fine-tuned with a small but high-quality reasoning dataset containing about 5,000 samples with long Chain-of-Thought traces (Figure 3-37). This supervised fine-tuning initialization acts as a reliable starting point to improve readability and monolingual consistency before the model enters the reinforcement learning training. Let's call this resulting model DeepSeek-V3-1 as the intermediate model.

Figure 3-37. A small supervised fine-tuning step was taken to prevent the cold start problem

In step 2, DeepSeek-V3-1 was further fine-tuned using GRPO, much like was done in DeepSeek-R1-Zero. To further prevent mixing languages in the reasoning traces, a reward was added to ensure the target language remains consistent (see Figure 3-38). The resulting model (DeepSeek-V3-2) is a model trained purely for reasoning, much like DeepSeek-R1-Zero. Like DeepSeek-R1-Zero, this has its pros and cons. Although the model excels at advanced reasoning tasks, it does not do well on tasks that do not require extensive reasoning, such as translation or writing tasks. It did, however, outperform DeepSeek-R1-Zero in most instances that required extensive reasoning and had similar performance on all others.

16 Guo, Daya et al. 2025. "DeepSeek-R1: Incentivizing Reasoning Capability in LLMs via Reinforcement Learning," *arXiv*, 2501.12948.

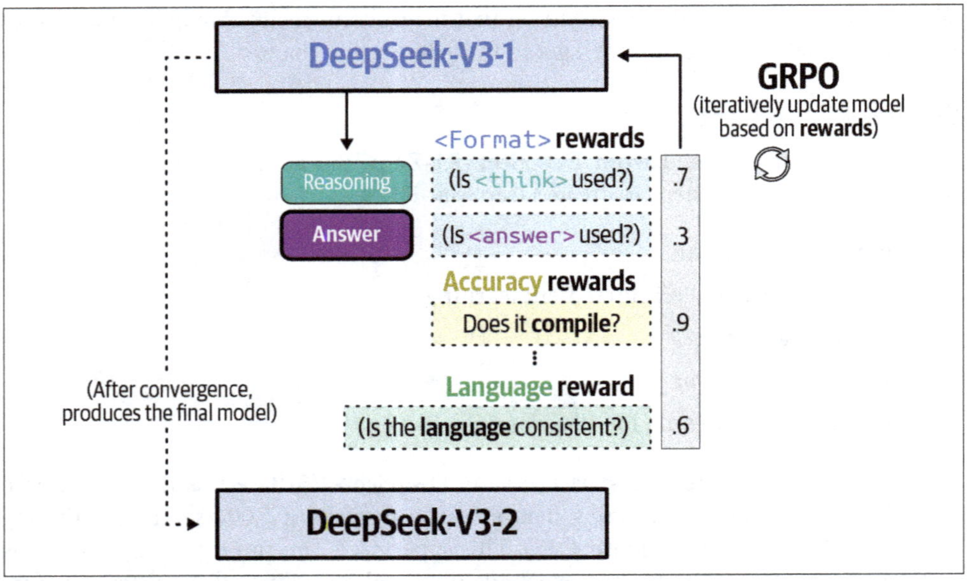

Figure 3-38. The training process to create a first version of the reasoning model

In step 3, the reasoning DeepSeek-V3-2 model was used to generate synthetic reasoning data because it excelled at reasoning tasks. A reward model (DeepSeek-V3-Base) was used to select the high-quality reasoning traces.

To make the model more adept at non-reasoning tasks, such as writing and translation, DeepSeek-V3-Base was used to sample mostly non-reasoning data that could be trained on.

The result was 800,000 samples that contained both reasoning and non-reasoning data (see Figure 3-39).

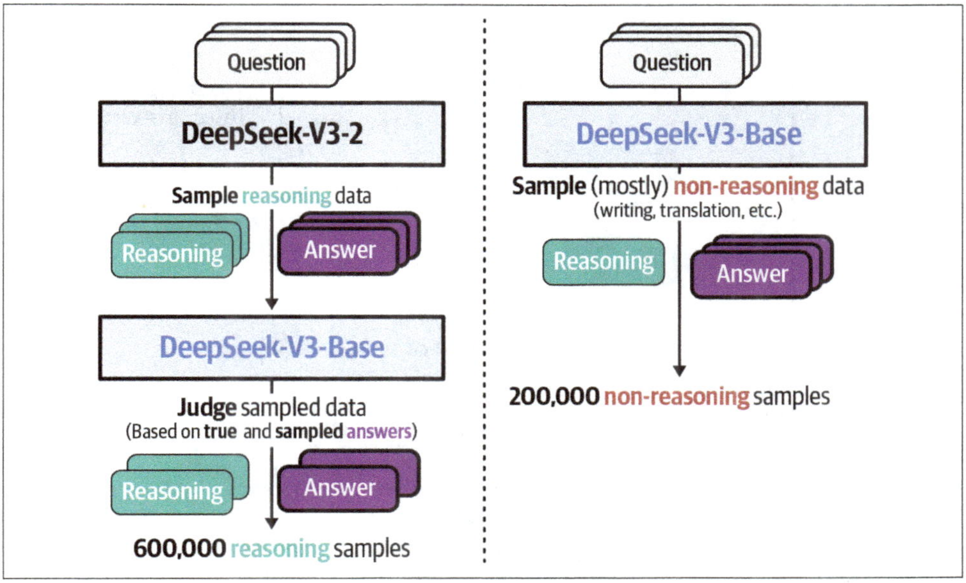

Figure 3-39. Reasoning and non-reasoning traces were sampled to create 800,000 high-quality samples

In step 4, this dataset of 800,000 samples was used to perform supervised fine-tuning of the DeepSeek-V3-Base model. This was done, in part, to resolve the cold start problem and to expose the model to these kinds of reasoning traces (Figure 3-40). The resulting model was the first version of DeepSeek-R1.

Figure 3-40. The first version of DeepSeek-R1 was created through a supervised fine-tuning step

Finally, in step 5, reinforcement learning was done on the first version of DeepSeek-R1 so it could develop its own reasoning traces instead of mimicking them from the data. However, to align with human preferences, additional reward signals were added that focused on helpfulness and harmlessness (Figure 3-41). The model was also asked to summarize the reasoning process to prevent readability issues.

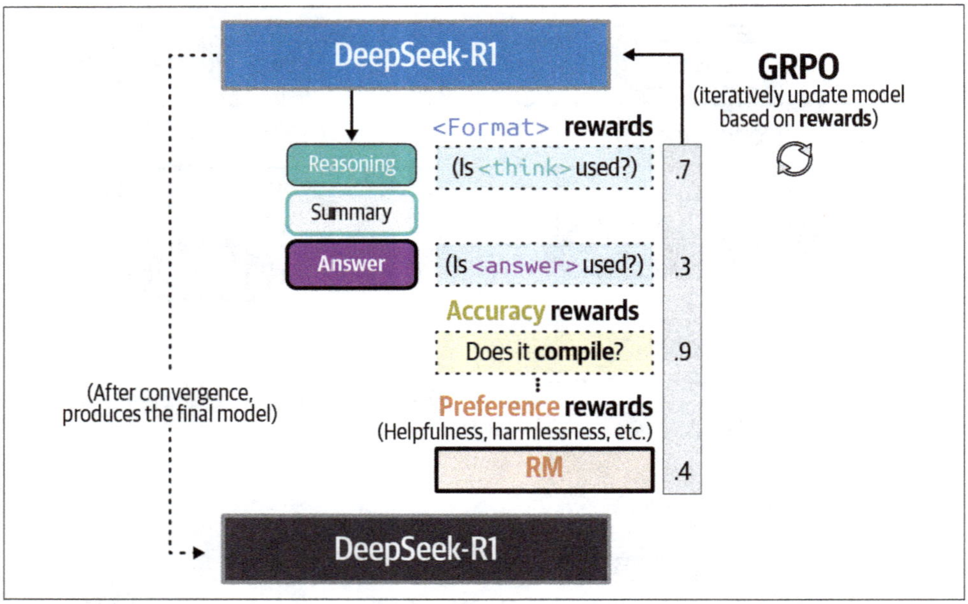

Figure 3-41. The final version of DeepSeek-R1 was trained using reinforcement learning and various rewards

This resulted in the final DeepSeek-R1 model. Interestingly, the first three steps of the training pipeline were purely done to create the synthetic data to eventually fine-tune DeepSeek-V3.

In sum, DeepSeek-R1 is created through first using supervised fine-tuning on DeepSeek-V3-Base and then applying GRPO with format, accuracy, and preference rewards.

Native Reasoning

We have explored various techniques in supervised fine-tuning and reinforcement learning. However, after the model has learned to reason, how do you then actually use it? We covered an important part of that during the fine-tuning examples and in Chapter 2, namely the chat template.

Let's illustrate this with the Gemma 4 E4B model. Its chat template (when you don't consider any tool usage) uses, among others, the following special tokens:

`<bos>`
: Signals the beginning of the sequence.

`<|turn>system`
: The start of a system prompt.

<|turn>user
: The start of the user turn.

<|turn>model
: The start of the model's turn.

<turn|>
: Signals the end of a turn.

<|think|>
: Adding this token in the system turn enables reasoning. Removing this token in the system turn disables reasoning.

Like DeepSeek-R1, Gemma 4 was trained with these special tokens to make sure it understands when it's your turn and when it's the model's turn. Ollama has been parsing our queries automatically based on this chat template, but let's explore what it would look like if it did not automatically parse the queries.

The Gemma 4 E4B model expects the following chat template to differentiate between roles and to enable thinking:

```
<bos><|turn>system
<|think|>
SYSTEM PROMPT<turn|>
<|turn>user
USER PROMPT<turn|>
<|turn>model
```

Note how there are separate turns for the system, user, and model. The thinking can be enabled by adding the <|think|> token to the system turn. If you want to disable thinking, you would only have to remove that token.

If we want to query the model, then we would need to send the following prompt to the model:

```
<bos><|turn>system
<|think|>
You are a helpful assistant<turn|>
<|turn>user
I saw 6 flamingos. 2 flew away. 1 hid behind a tree. How many can I see?
<turn|>
<|turn>model
```

The model would then respond with a structure like so:

```
<|channel>thought
You started with 6, but 2 flew away, leaving 4 behind. Out of those 4,
1 is hiding behind a tree, so you can only actually see 3.
<channel|>
You can see **3** flamingos
```

As such, any training and fine-tuning that we saw before can now be enabled by the prompt template of that specific model. Instead of needing to use "tricks" like Chain-of-Thought, the model was trained on Chain-of-Thought examples instead.

Emerging Directions in Reasoning Research

Reasoning in LLMs has started to advance beyond text-only reasoning, now using new modalities, improved architectures, and more abstract ways of representing information.

In this section, we look at three key areas pushing LLM reasoning forward:

Reasoning in multi-modal LLMs
: Reasoning LLMs learn to reason with modalities other than text, like images, audio, and video

Efficient reasoning
: Focuses on improving reasoning while using less computation

Reasoning in latent space
: Models think in compressed, abstract forms and often non-textual forms to reach deeper insights

Reasoning in Multi-Modal LLMs

The LLMs serving as the main brains of agentic systems do not only need to reason about text. They may need to think about the best way to design a website or interpret what is happening in a given picture. This requires reasoning in ways that differ from textual inputs as more modalities might be processed. As we will discuss in Chapter 9, there are many methods for making LLMs multi-modal, which often naturally extend them to include reasoning behavior. However, without any reasoning grounding, performance on multi-modal reasoning tasks is usually worse.

As with mono-modal LLMs, reasoning is often enhanced through methods like those we discussed before, such as prompting, search against verifiers, or modifying the proposal distribution with supervised fine-tuning and/or reinforcement learning.

A common method for multi-modal prompting is called Multi-modal Chain-of-Thought (MCoT). Multi-modal Chain-of-Thought, compared to traditional Chain-of-Thought, attempts to incorporate text and vision into a two-stage framework. As shown in Figure 3-42, Multi-modal Chain-of-Thought contains a two-step approach where the first step creates reasoning by combining the original language and visual input to produce an explicit reasoning process. In the second step, this rationale is appended to the original language input and, together with the same visual input, is used to infer the final answer. Both stages use models with the same architecture, trained separately on annotated rationale and answer data using supervised fine-tuning.

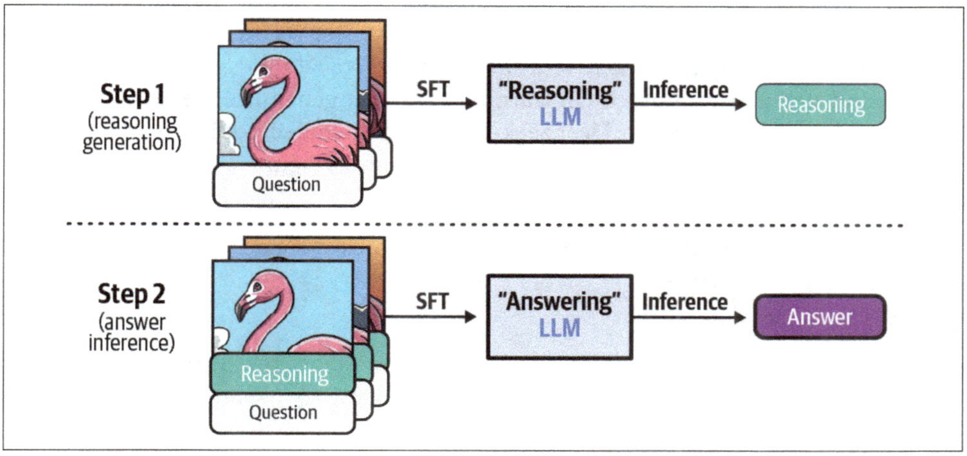

Figure 3-42. A two-step approach to sample reasoning data using supervised fine-tuning

Making vision language models reason step-by-step through supervised fine-tuning was further covered in Llava-Chain-of-Thought. Here, the authors used GPT-4o to create synthetic data based on input images through four reasoning stages: summary, caption, reasoning, and answer. These four structured reasoning stages allow for the separation of thinking types and help the model to prevent errors in thinking. As shown in Figure 3-43, this annotated dataset of 100,000 records is then used to fine-tune Llama 3.2v, a vision LLM.

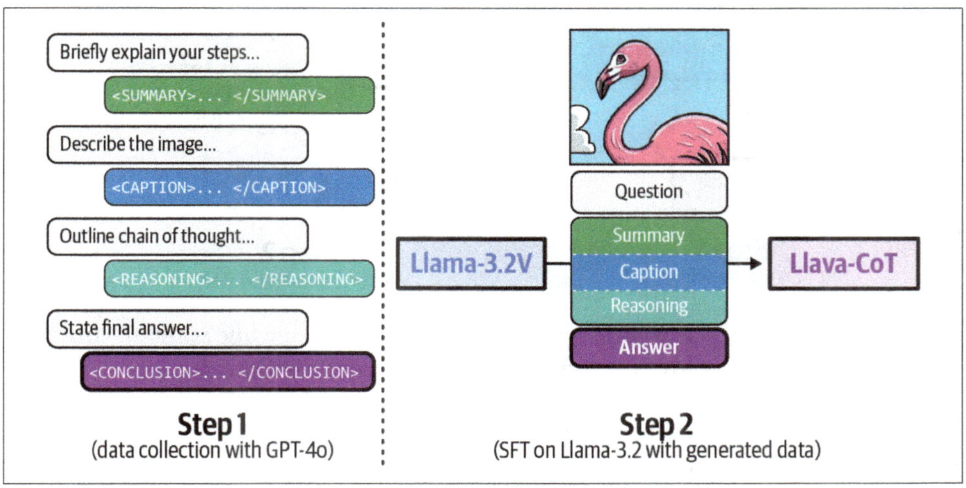

Figure 3-43. Llava-Chain-of-Thought was trained using generated data

Following this two-step supervised fine-tuning approach is Reason-RFT, a reinforcement fine-tuning approach for visual reasoning that follows the two-step approach of DeepSeek-R1 quite closely. Its two-step approach is meant to go from a base vision LLM to a reasoning vision LLM. The first step is supervised fine-tuning with Chain-of-Thought that activates the reasoning capabilities of the vision LLM. The second step uses reinforcement learning to further generalize the learned reasoning capabilities. Compared to DeepSeek-R1, which included coding-based accuracy rewards, Reason-RFT focuses on three types of rewards (Figure 3-44):

Mathematical
: Scores numerical answers and gives larger scores for exact matches and lower scores for small errors

Function-based
: Compares predicted and target transformation steps, rewarding exact, partial, and function-only matches with different weights, e.g., *rotate(cube, 90°)* versus *rotate(cube, 45°)*

Discrete-valued
: Uses binary scoring for categorical or integer answers, giving credit only for exact matches

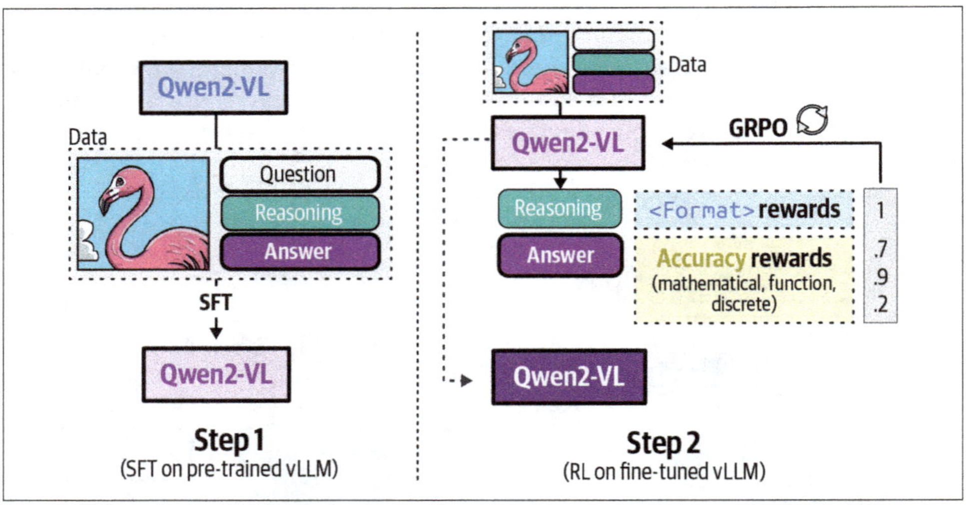

Figure 3-44. A two-step approach of supervised fine-tuning using the reasoning traces (left) and reinforcement learning using format and accuracy rewards (right)

As such, enabling reasoning in multi-modal LLMs is much like in text-only LLMs, but the types of Chain-of-Thought data need to be adapted for the multi-modal use cases. Often, existing Chain-of-Thought data is for text-only inputs and not multi-modal inputs.

Efficient Reasoning

Scaling test-time compute can significantly improve performance and has been a main focus of scaling LLMs. However, it can be quite expensive to calculate these additional thousands of tokens or to explore multiple solutions and reasoning paths. Consequently, there has been a growing interest in strategies that achieve similar gains but through more select reasoning and adaptive computation. Typically, this involves reducing the length of the reasoning trace. A nice example is the ever-increasing length of reasoning we explored in DeepSeek-R1. If left without any additional constraints, reasoning LLMs might learn to create unnecessarily large reasoning traces during reinforcement learning.

The most straightforward method to reduce the reasoning length is through prompting. Traditionally, Chain-of-Thought-like prompting techniques emphasize verbose, step-by-step reasoning, which can create long and expensive reasoning traces that contain redundant information. Chain-of-Draft (CoD), inspired by human cognitive processes, instead employs a more efficient strategy by drafting concise intermediate thoughts.[17]

In Figure 3-45, you can see the system prompts used for Chain-of-Draft compared to regular prompting and Chain-of-Thought. Note how similar it is to Chain-of-Thought, but it adds that each reasoning step should be kept to a draft and use five words at most. Other values are possible, but the authors of Chain-of-Draft used five words as a general guideline to create short prompts rather than strictly enforcing it.

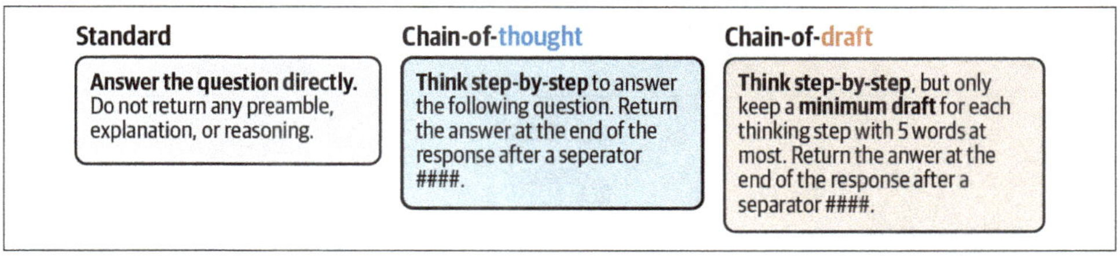

Figure 3-45. Comparing a standard prompt with Chain-of-Thought and Chain-of-Draft

Compared to Chain-of-Thought, Chain-of-Draft generates shorter reasoning traces with less verbosity while having similar performance (shown in Figure 3-46).

The balance between minimizing verbosity and keeping the accuracy of reasoning traces is difficult to maintain in Chain-of-Draft. Moreover, it is more difficult to read for users compared to the verbose reasoning traces of traditional Chain-of-Thought.

The length of reasoning traces can also be controlled more directly during training. These are often referred to as token-budget-aware LLMs that have been trained to

17 Xu, Silei et al. 2025. "Chain of Draft: Thinking Faster by Writing Less," *arXiv*, 2502.18600.

adaptively change the length of the reasoning trace they create based on the complexity of the initial problem. Likewise, they may be trained to prefer shorter reasoning traces through specific length rewards.

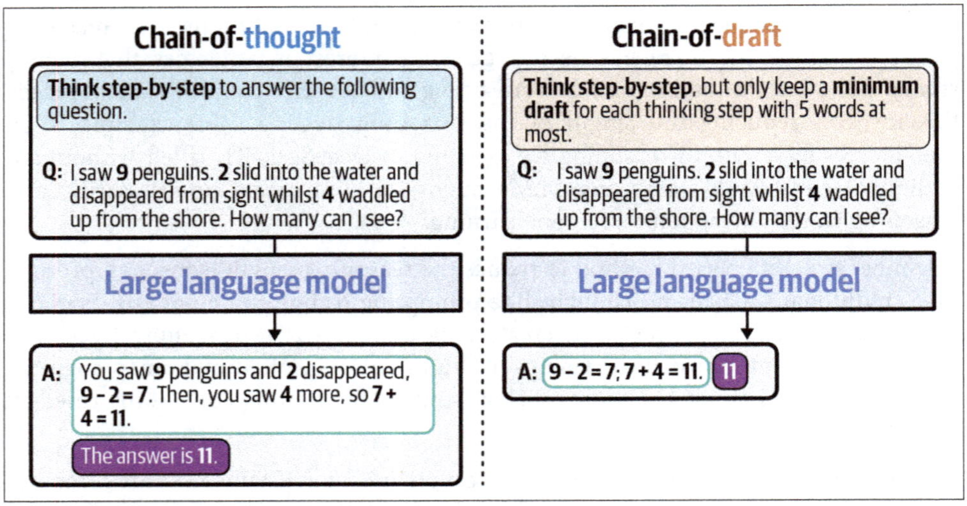

Figure 3-46. Comparing the processes of Chain-of-Thought and Chain-of-Draft

As shown in Figure 3-47, the idea of reinforcement learning with length reward designs generally rewards short, correct answers while penalizing lengthy or wrong answers to achieve efficient reasoning. Often, short, correct answers are given greater rewards than long, correct answers.

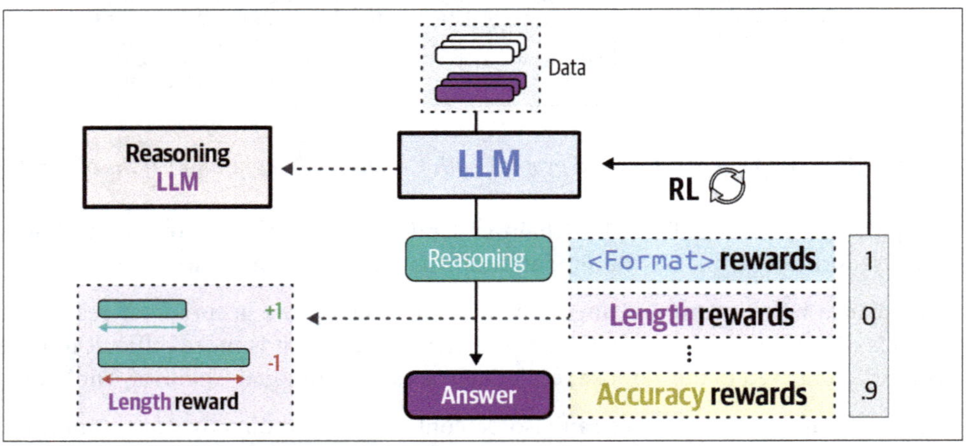

Figure 3-47. An example of length rewards that may punish reasoning traces that are too long and reward those that are short and succinct

Many such methods include a length reward. Kimi k1.5, a closed-sourced multimodal LLM, was trained using reinforcement learning to give extra rewards to correct, short answers while penalizing wrong, long answers the most.[18] Interestingly, this length reward slowed down early learning, so they gradually warmed up the length penalty during training, which alleviated this problem. Similarly, the O1-Pruner technique compares the length of the model's answer to what a reference model typically produces and rewards based on the difference between them.[19] Longer answers get a penalty while same lengths get no change in rewards and shorter answers get a high reward. They balance this with a dynamic accuracy reward so that not only short, correct answers get high rewards but also long, correct answers when it is needed for hard problems. Finally, L1 is a reasoning LLM that is trained by telling it up front how long, in terms of tokens, it should think (e.g., "Think for 30 tokens").[20] The model gets rewarded for both being correct and matching the requested length.

Some models attempt to go in a different direction to control the length of reasoning and implement an *on/off switch* for reasoning that can either fully disable or enable reasoning. A great example is the Qwen3 family of models, which, during their release in April 2025 (*https://oreil.ly/7csxg*), were known to be state-of-the-art for their sizes.[21] They introduced special tokens for thinking mode (`/think`) and non-thinking mode (`/no_think`), where each is trained respectively with and without Chain-of-Thought data. This is also called *hybrid reasoning*, where thinking mode uses additional reasoning, whereas no reasoning is used for the non-thinking mode, which will only provide the answer, as was the case with traditional LLMs. Think of it as essentially turning thinking off and on.

Reasoning in Latent Space

Chain-of-Thought, as we explored thus far, has been explicit. It's like we are listening to someone work through a problem out loud. The reasoning LLM "talks to itself" in tokens so we can trace its logic. However, it's not like we are always making our thoughts explicit; we often internalize our thinking processes. An upcoming and interesting take on reasoning is to make the explicit Chain-of-Thought of LLMs internal via latent space reasoning. Here, the explicit Chain-of-Thought steps are replaced by hidden representations. Instead of producing visible reasoning steps, the model thinks entirely in its "mind's eye," its latent space. So instead of producing

18 Kimi Team et al. 2025. "Kimi k1. 5: Scaling Reinforcement Learning with LLMs," *arXiv*, 2501.12599.

19 Luo, Haotian et al. 2025. "O1-Pruner: Length-Harmonizing Fine-Tuning for O1-Like Reasoning Pruning," *arXiv*, 2501.12570.

20 Aggarwal, Pranjal, and Sean Welleck. 2025. "L1: Controlling How Long a eReasoning Model Thinks With Reinforcement Learning," *arXiv*, 2503.04697.

21 Yang, An et al. 2025. "Qwen3 Technical Report," *arXiv*, 2505.09388.

these long reasoning traces, the model will skip straight from the question to the answer and perform all of its reasoning without us being able to see it.

To explore latent space reasoning, let's first recap Chain-of-Thought reasoning. As shown in Figure 3-48, Chain-of-Thought reasoning starts from a given query and autoregressively generates a token at a time by continuously appending the output to the updated input. After processing an input, the model produces an output by sampling from its last hidden state. The output, a token, is then embedded together with the rest of the input. In other words, the last hidden state is only used to generate the next token.

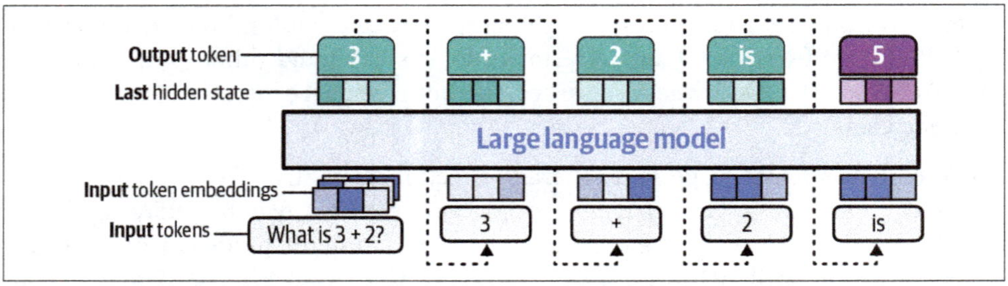

Figure 3-48. A recap of Chain-of-Thought reasoning and how data flows through the model

One of the first methods of latent space reasoning is Chain-of-Continuous-Thought, a method that skips over the decoding of the embeddings and instead directly operates on the last hidden state.[22] As shown in Figure 3-49, instead of embedding new output tokens and adding them to the input, it generates the last hidden state and uses it directly as the input. To differentiate between thoughts and answers, special tokens are used (<bot> for beginning of thought and <eot> for end of thought). By using the last hidden state as the input, the model does not produce any tokens until it reaches the <eot>. After that, it can still generate intermediate reasoning steps if necessary or directly give back the output.

22 Hao, Shibo et al. 2024. "Training Large Language Models to Reason in a Continuous Latent Space," *arXiv*, 2412.06769.

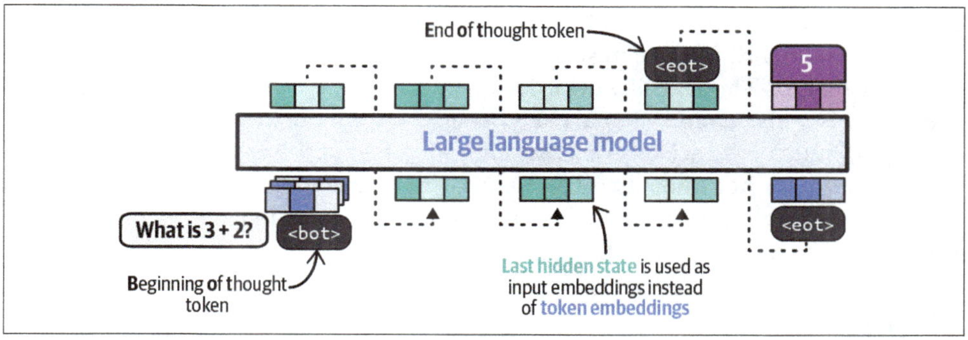

Figure 3-49. Chain-of-Continuous-Thought reasons in latent space by not producing reasoning tokens but by using the last hidden state instead

This methodology was further extended by Continuous Chain-of-Thought via Self-Distillation (CODI).[23] CODI simultaneously trains a teacher and student LLM. The teacher LLM is trained on explicit Chain-of-Thought data and sees the reasoning during training. The teacher LLM learns from this annotated Chain-of-Thought data using cross-entropy loss and has to produce a correct answer with a reasoning trace. In contrast, the student follows a Chain-of-Continuous-Thought-like process and does not produce any explicit Chain-of-Thought but does so instead on the last hidden states. Then, the answers of the teacher LLM and student LLM are compared, and an additional loss is factored in during training. In other words, the explicit Chain-of-Thought that the teacher learns is implicitly being taught to the student LLM (Figure 3-50).

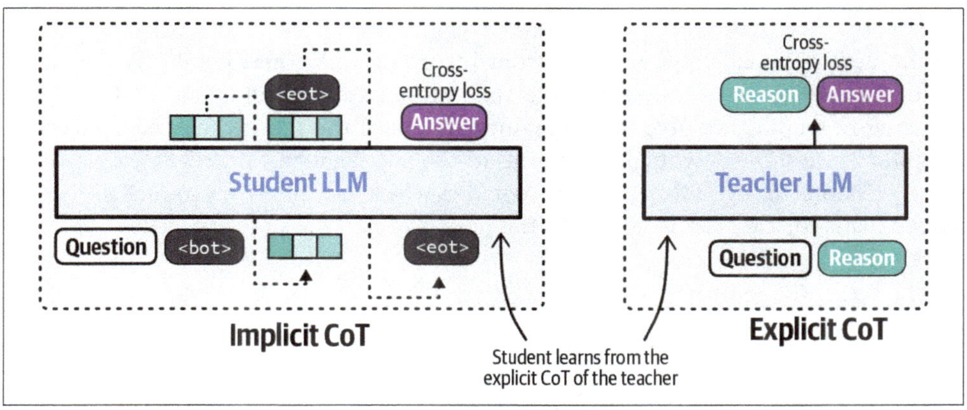

Figure 3-50. CODI's process of training a teacher and student LLM for implicit and explicit Chain-of-Thought

23 Shen, Zhenyi 2025. "CODI: Compressing Chain-of-Thought into Continuous Space via Self-Distillation," *arXiv*, 2502.21074.

Latent space reasoning is a relatively new field, and new technologies are seemingly being released daily. One interesting perspective is how to balance the implicit and explicit Chain-of-Thought-like behavior of an LLM, given what users might want to see. There is a big advantage to actually seeing how a model reasons, as it will make debugging much easier. However, reasoning in latent space can be a more efficient process and does not limit the LLM to text-based reasoning. Imagine the LLM not reasoning in text but in symbolic language instead, or perhaps purely in latent space through mathematical equations.

Summary

In this chapter, we explored how LLMs could develop advanced reasoning. We first covered the paradigm from a focus on train-time compute to test-time compute, of which scaling reasoning is an important component. Reasoning is often shown as either short or long Chain-of-Thought traces. We covered two broad categories for scaling test-time compute. The first, search against verifiers, involved expanding the output of LLMs dynamically through methods such as self-consistency (*https://oreil.ly/BJB2Z*) and Best-of-N samples (*https://oreil.ly/V0qiw*). The second, modifying the proposal distribution, typically involves training or fine-tuning an LLM to demonstrate advanced reasoning traces. We covered two categories of modifying the proposal distribution, namely supervised fine-tuning (e.g., Flan-PaLM, s1) and reinforcement learning (e.g., DeepSeek-R1 Zero, DeepSeek-R1).

We ended the chapter by exploring upcoming fields in reasoning LLMs, including reasoning in latent space, making reasoning more efficient, and methods for multimodal reasoning.

In the next three chapters, we start from reasoning LLMs and iteratively give them more capabilities until they reach the state of being called an agent. In Chapter 4, we explore methods to give them memory and track the actions they have taken. In Chapter 5, we show how to give the tools to use and what best practices are for doing so. In Chapter 6, everything comes together where advanced reasoning is used to create plans for agents and reflect to them; reasoning LLMs are especially important here.

CHAPTER 4
Memory

Among all the added modules to the augmented LLM, memory is a key component needed to go from an LLM to an agent. By themselves, LLMs are forgetful entities; they do not remember past conversations, nor do they have access to all actions they have taken. If you were to locally load up an LLM and ask it to remember your name, it can't—not without explicitly giving it memory. In contrast, the interactions that you might have with hosted LLMs, like ChatGPT and Claude, are not regular LLMs. Rather, they are LLMs augmented with modules like memory and tools. Figure 4-1 illustrates this forgetfulness well, as it demonstrates the interaction you might have with a regular LLM. As such, LLMs are stateless, and information is not persisted across calls.

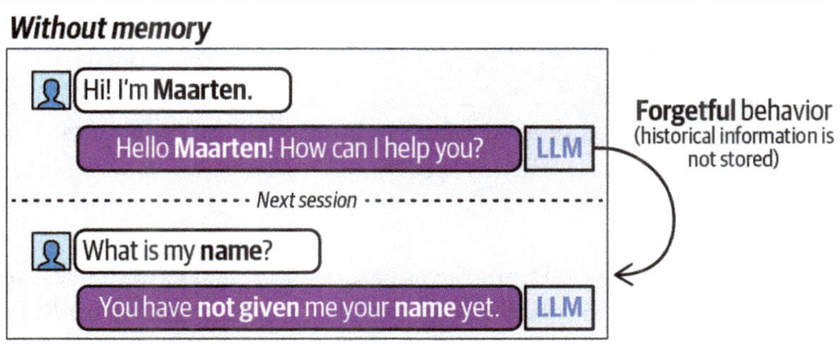

Figure 4-1. LLMs without any additional processing are forgetful and will not remember information between sessions

Over the years, significant attention has been paid to aspects of agents like tool usage, reasoning LLMs, and multi-agent collaboration. Each is quite important by itself, but don't underestimate the importance of memory. Without memory, a personal assistant agent wouldn't be able to remember past conversations. Without memory, a coding agent wouldn't understand your entire codebase. Without memory, an agent would forget that it has already taken an action and keep on repeating it.

Memory can be quite difficult to define. From a narrow view, it may relate to all historical information during the execution of an agent. In this chapter, however, we take a broader perspective. Memory relates not only to all past actions of an agent, but also external information beyond the agent-environment interactions. A coding agent's memory would not only consist of the actions it has taken to fix your bugs, but also your hosted documentation and issues pages.

Memory is not only the act of remembering information but also storing newly generated information. Likewise, often a choice has to be made on which information to store and how, which information to remember and which parts of the memory to forget or delete. All these methodologies and choices have important implications on the agent's behavior. As shown in Figure 4-2, updating and using memory is an iterative process that requires careful handling of intermediate information.

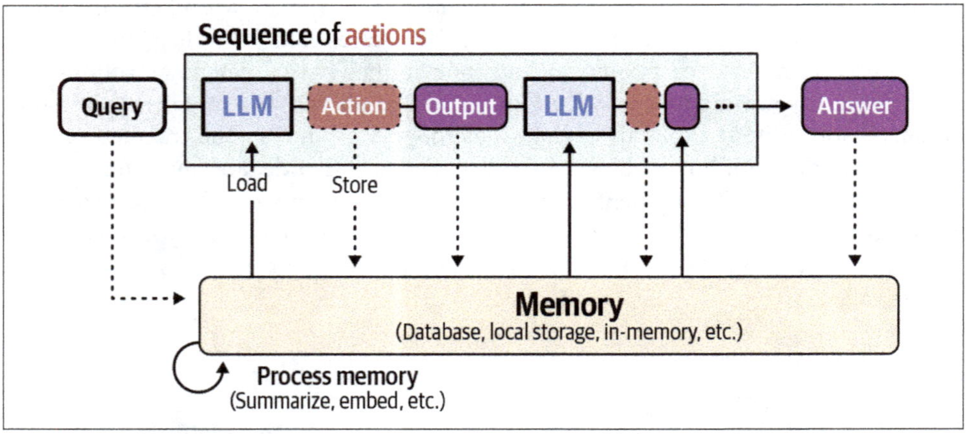

Figure 4-2. Memory in agentic systems relates to more than the conversation and may include the query, answer, and intermediate steps that were taken and the outputs of those steps

Memory allows the agent to remember past errors and failed experiences, so it can be more effective for handling similar tasks in the future. Although the underlying LLMs might still be the same entities, memory enables agents to learn and evolve as they have more information through experiences that guide their behavior. By interacting with the environment and storing the feedback, agents learn from their previous experiences. Memory is, therefore, application-specific, and implementations may not only decide *what* to remember but also *how* it is remembered.

Throughout this chapter, we'll explore many types of memory modules, ranging from short-term and long-term memory to external memory modules, through methods like (agentic) Retrieval-Augmented Generation. Shown in Figure 4-3, it forms the foundation of the agent. After all, how would an agent be able to use tools or create plans if it keeps forgetting them?

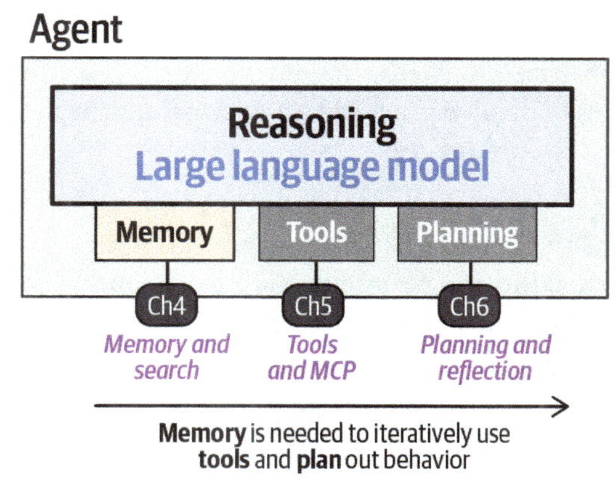

Figure 4-3. Without memory, tool usage and planning would not be possible. Both require memory modules to track behavior over long traces.

Types of Memory

Memory for LLMs tends to follow human memory types, as the agents that we attempt to create are often modeled after human behavior. Instead of going through all forms of human memory types, of which there are many, the "Cognitive Architectures for Language Agents" paper describes four types of external memory that we often see in agents, working memory for short-term use, and three variants of long-term memory: episodic, semantic, and procedural memory.[1]

Working memory is a type of *short-term memory* that is typically defined as a system with limited capacity that temporarily holds information that we need for things like decision-making and reasoning. For LLMs, it's typically data that persists across LLM calls. More specifically, it's the chat history of the LLM that is continuously fed back to the LLM.

1 Sumers, Theodore et al. 2023. "Cognitive Architectures for Language Agents," *Transactions on Machine Learning Research.*

For *long-term memory*, there are three forms described:

Episodic memory
: Involves remembering specific events and experiences from one's past (e.g., your last birthday party). For agents, this typically involves specific actions the agent has taken thus far and their outcomes.

Semantic memory
: Involves remembering knowledge about the world (e.g., the capital of France). For agents, this may involve querying an external database like Wikipedia or the codebase that you're working on.

Procedural memory
: Involves remembering patterns of how to do things (e.g., writing code in Python). For agents, this can be information hidden in its parameters (also called parametric memory) or the system prompt, which persists across calls.

Figure 4-4 shows an example of how these different forms of memory can be used and interpreted during a single agent's session.

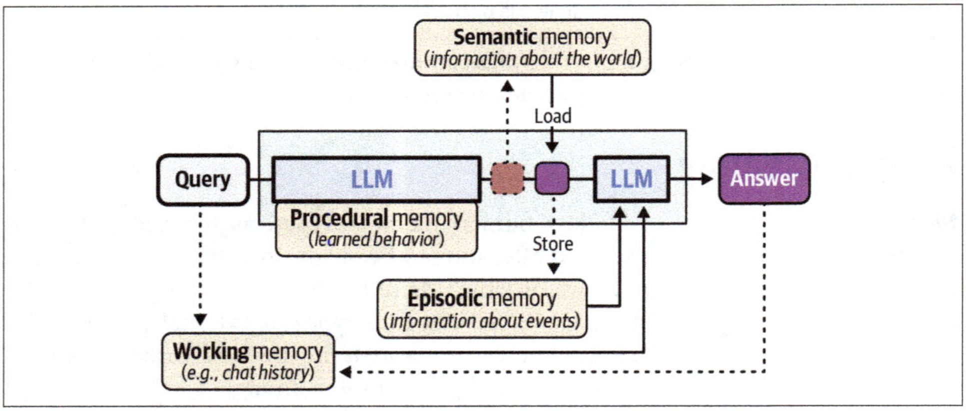

Figure 4-4. Memory can be divided into four different types when interacting with LLMs, namely working, procedural, episodic, and semantic memory

As mentioned previously, we can also consider the type of memory that the model already has, *parametric memory*.[2] Without any memory modules, LLMs are trained to a certain extent to retain information. If you ask an LLM what the capital of France is, most LLMs will correctly remember that it is Paris. The answer is therefore contained within the parameters of the model and the model attempts to retrieve it. Although a relatively new field, it's technically possible to instill information into

2 Zhang, Zeyu et al. 2024. "A Survey on the Memory Mechanism of Large Language Model based Agents," *ACM Transactions on Information Systems*, 43(6):1-47.

an LLM through SFT. Note that this is not a stable method, as we are not entirely sure beforehand which information gets retained explicitly and which is incorrectly reconstructed.

Although these memory types may differ, they may not always be stored as such. Depending on the specific implementation, they could be seen as one big pile of information or separated into different databases to be remembered for specific tasks and actions.

Short-Term Memory

Short-term memory in agents is the information it has about recent interactions, typically the ongoing conversations with the user or the behavior of the LLM. Without short-term memory, the LLM or agent does not know what was said before and therefore does not retain any information.

Let's illustrate with an example. We can start by querying the agent we made in Chapter 2 with a basic question:

```
from illustrated_agents.chapters.ch2 import LLM, TinyAgent

# Gemma 3 12B (no native thinking or tool calling)
llm = LLM(model="gemma3:12b")

# Run a query
ch_2_agent = TinyAgent(llm=llm)
response = ch_2_agent.run("Hi! We are Maarten and Jay, authors of
'An Illustrated Guide to AI Agents'.")
```

We then give it a follow-up question to see if the agent knows the interaction we had before:

```
response = ch_2_agent.run("Hi! What are our names?")
print(response)
```

This gives us:

```
"I do not know what your name is, as you have not told me!"
```

The agent doesn't seem to know our names. Every time you query an LLM directly with only the query you have, it starts from a blank slate. You'll have to fill this in yourself through the message structure that we explored in previous chapters.

Let's start with the most fundamental way of adding memory to the messages, namely tracking the conversation history.

Conversation Memory

The conversation history of the LLM serves as the context for generating responses. Illustrated in Figure 4-5, they are generally formatted as messages demonstrating the differences between system prompts, the user's query, and the LLM's answer. It's a conversation where the user tells something about themselves, namely that they love flamingos.

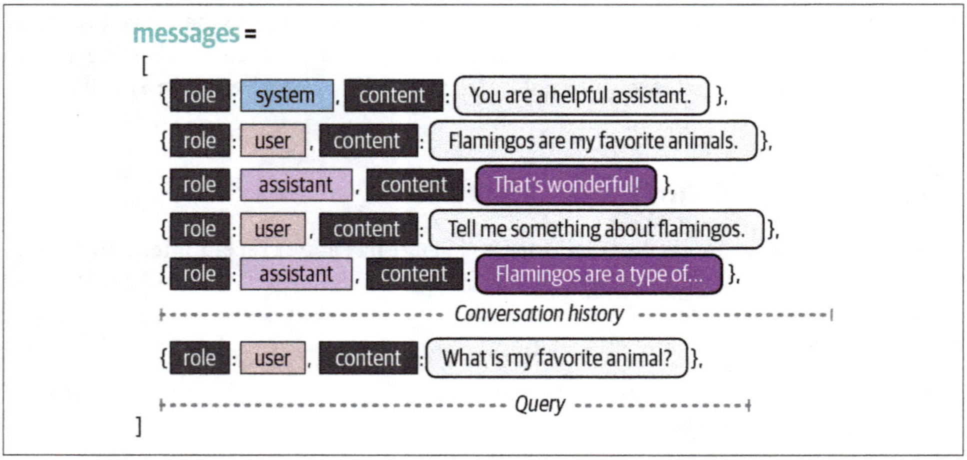

Figure 4-5. An example of how conversations can be represented using JSON

These messages are updated every time the user or assistant replies and are fed back into the LLM as input for the next query, as shown in Figure 4-6. The query ("What is my favorite animal?") does not trigger the LLM to recall the past on its own. Rather, it is provided with the entire conversation history, which contains the relevant information, namely that the user loves flamingos. In other words, the LLM does not truly "remember" past conversations but is instead told what the conversation was by explicitly inserting it into the prompt.

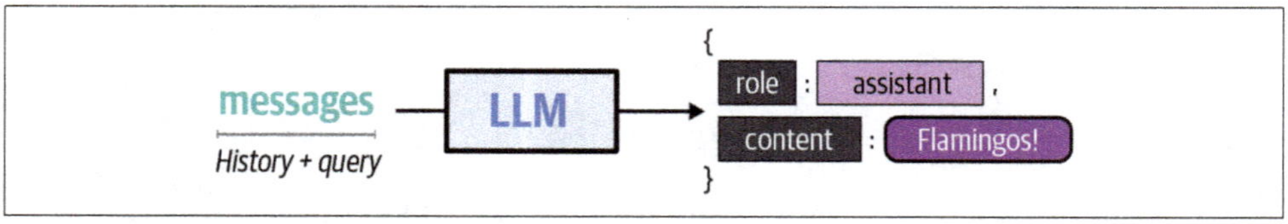

Figure 4-6. The LLM is given both the conversation history as well as the current query

Let's explore this by integrating a `Memory` module into your `TinyAgent`. The module is quite straightforward and is merely a list of dictionaries that track the role and its content, exactly as shown in Figure 4-5:

```
class Memory:
    """Simple memory module to store conversation history."""

    def __init__(self):
        self.messages = []
```

```
    def add(
        self, role: str, content: str, tool_call: dict | None = None, **kwargs
    ) -> None:
        """Add a message to memory."""
        message = {"role": role, "content": content}

        # Tool call
        if tool_call:
            message["tool_calls"] = [tool_call]

        # Append message to memory
        self.messages.append(message)

    def get_messages(self) -> list[dict]:
        """Get all messages."""
        return self.messages
```

The `Memory` module has two functions, one to add new messages (`.add`) and one to get them (`.get_messsages`). Note that we also have the option to add a tool call. This is something we will use in Chapter 5 when we explore how LLMs can call tools.

In your `TinyAgent`, the roles are then updated as follows:

- Response of the LLM: `memory.add("assistant", LLM_RESPONSE)`
- User's query: `memory.add("assistant", USER_QUERY)`

To use the `Memory` module in `TinyAgent`, we initialize the module and call `.add` when we want to add roles and content to the memory. Then, whenever a request is made of the LLM, we use `.get_messages` to get the entire conversation history. Note that we highlighted the code that was added to your `TinyAgent`:

```
from illustrated_agents.chapters.ch2 import Trajectory

class TinyAgent:
    """A minimal, modular, and educational agent framework."""

    def __init__(self, llm: LLM, memory: Memory):
        self.llm = llm
        self.memory = memory
        self.tools = None  # Chapter 5: Add Tools
        self.planner = None  # Chapter 6: Add Planning

        self.trajectory = Trajectory()

    def run(self, task: str) -> str:
        """Run the agent on a task."""
        self.memory.add("user", task)
        self.trajectory.initialize(task)

        return self._step()
```

```python
    def _step(self) -> str:
        """Perform a single step."""
        # Generate response and add to memory
        response = self.llm.generate(self.memory.get_messages())
        self.memory.add("assistant", response.content)
        self.trajectory.add(response)
        return response.content

    def _execute_action(self, action: str) -> str | None:
        """Execute a tool action."""
        # Placeholder - will be implemented in later chapters
        return f"Executed action: {action}"
```

Note how in `run` and `_step` we used the `self.memory.add` function to track the conversation history and use `self.memory.get_messages()` to give that full context to the LLM.

We run the new agent twice to see if it tracked the history and ask it the same question we did before:

```python
# Add memory to the Agent
memory = Memory()
agent_with_memory = TinyAgent(llm=llm, memory=memory)

# First query
first_response = agent_with_memory.run("Hi! We are Maarten and Jay, authors of
'An Illustrated Guide to AI Agents'.")

# Second query
second_response = agent_with_memory.run("Hi! What are our names?")
print(second_response)
```

This gives us:

```
"Your names are **Maarten and Jay**."
```

It knows our names! It's not that the LLM remembers our names, but instead we merely told it what conversation we had before. We can then inspect the full conversation history:

```python
agent_with_memory.memory.get_messages()
```

This gives us:

```
[
  {'role': 'user',
   'content': "Hi! We are Maarten and Jay, authors of
   'An Illustrated Guide to AI Agents'."},
  {'role': 'assistant',
   'content': 'Hi Maarten and Jay! It\'s great to "meet" you.\n\n
   **"An Illustrated Guide to AI Agents"** sounds like a fascinating
   and very timely topic. Are you:\n\n
   * **Looking for feedback** on the book\'s content or structure?\n*'},
```

```
    {'role': 'user', 'content': 'Hi! What are our names?'},
    {'role': 'assistant', 'content': 'Your names are **Maarten and Jay**.'}
]
```

That is exactly the information that we gave to the LLM, which now has the full context it needs to answer our questions. It was straightforward, but the agent now actually has memory.

However, most LLMs have a limited context window, which is the number of tokens that the LLM can process. This counts both the input and the output tokens, as shown in Figure 4-7.

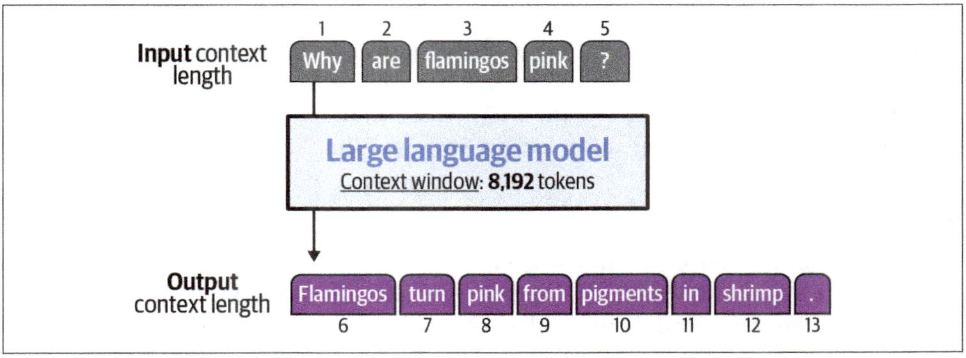

Figure 4-7. The context window defines the maximum number of tokens an LLM can process, while context length refers to the actual length of either the input, the generate output, or both

In this example, a short query and answer are given that total 13 tokens out of a potential 8,192. Shown in Figure 4-8, there are many potential tokens that are left unused and could potentially be filled with additional information or reasoning tokens, as discussed in Chapter 3.

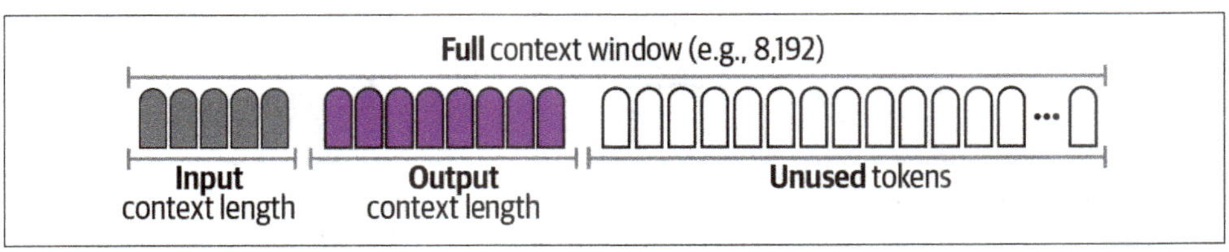

Figure 4-8. The full context window should manage both the input and output tokens

However, as the conversation history grows, so do the number of tokens. Eventually, and as shown in Figure 4-9, if the conversation history gets too large, it will not fit within the context windows. This might cut the answer short or even prevent the LLM from processing the prompt at all.

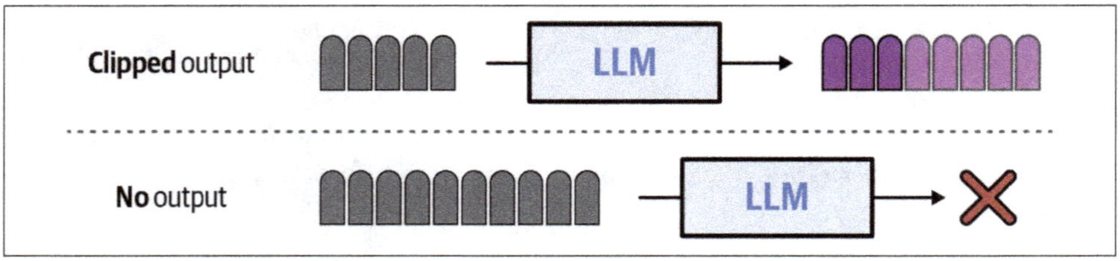

Figure 4-9. The generated output of LLMs may be clipped if they exceed the context window or no output can be generated if the entire input already exceeds the context window

Moreover, the more information put in the prompt, the more difficult it will be for the LLM to attend to everything.[3] As a result, we cannot always put the entire conversation history into the prompt of the LLM. Instead, there are several techniques we can use to provide the conversation history without filling up the context window.

Trimming

The first technique for efficient short-term memory is rather straightforward: trimming the messages as they grow. Whenever the number of messages grows too large for the LLM's context window to handle, we can decide to simply remove the first few interactions until it fits that window. Shown in Figure 4-10, this might remove quite a lot of information that may or may not be relevant to future queries.

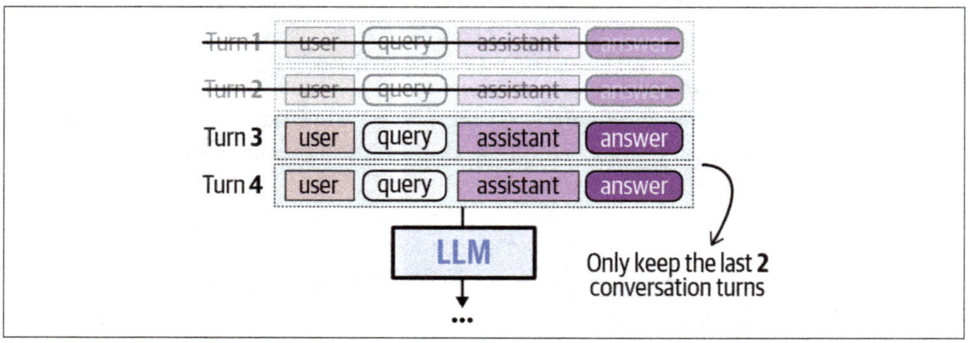

Figure 4-10. Efficient short-term memory may include keeping only the last couple of conversations instead of keeping track of the entire conversation history

3 Hsieh, Cheng-Ping et al. 2024. "RULER: What's the Real Context Size of Your Long-Context Language Models?" *arXiv*, 2404.06654.

Because we already did much of the heavy lifting with the `Memory` module, implementing this trimming behavior requires a minimal amount of code. We use inheritance to keep the same functionality of `Memory` but update the `add` function so that only the last two turns (each a pair of user/assistant messages) are kept:

```
class TrimmingMemory(Memory):
    """Memory that keeps only the last two user/assistant turns."""

    def add(self, role: str, content: str, **kwargs) -> None:
        # Add the new message first using the parent class (Memory)
        super().add(role, content, **kwargs)

        # Then, keep system message plus the most recent two turns (4 messages)
        system = [
            message for message in self.messages if message["role"] == "system"
        ]
        turns = [
            message for message in self.messages if message["role"] != "system"
        ]
        self.messages = system + turns[-4:]
```

You can try it out with an example to see what happens if you ask it four questions:

```
from illustrated_agents.chapters.ch4 import TinyAgent

# Create the Agent
memory = TrimmingMemory()
agent = TinyAgent(llm=llm, memory=memory)

# Run some interactions
response_1 = agent.run("Hi! I'm reading 'An Illustrated Guide to AI Agents'.")
response_2 = agent.run("There are many flamingos in this book, why?")
response_3 = agent.run("What is 1+1?")
response_4 = agent.run("What is 2+2?")
```

We can then inspect the memory as we did before:

```
print(agent.memory.get_messages())
```

This gives us:

```
[
        {'role': 'user', 'content': 'What is 1+1?'},
        {
            'role': 'assistant',
            'content': "1 + 1 = 2\n\nIt's a classic! 😊"
        },
        {'role': 'user', 'content': 'What is 2+2?'},
        {'role': 'assistant', 'content': '2 + 2 = 4! \n\n
        Just keeping the math train rolling, I see! 😉}
    ]
```

Only the last two sets of messages are kept with this type of memory. This helps keep the memory to a minimum but might remove important information discussed early in the conversations. Note that you might see the book or the flamingos mentioned in these messages. That can happen since information can still flow from the assistant's output if it keeps mentioning it:

- Turn 1: No memory
- Turn 2: Memory of turn 1
- Turn 3: Memory of turns 1 and 2
- Turn 4: Memory of turns 2 and 3

It's important to keep track of the raw conversations in its trajectory since the agent's memory might be stripped or processed. As such, if you run the following yourself, you will get a view with the full interaction (turns 1 through 4):

```
from illustrated_agents.utils import TrajectoryViewer
TrajectoryViewer(agent.trajectory)
```

In later chapters, you'll see that the user and assistant roles do not always alternate. A more autonomous agent (see Chapter 6) will have multiple turns of only assistant roles.

Summarization

A common technique is to employ another LLM to summarize the conversation history. After each conversation turn, the same or another LLM will summarize it and add it to the full summary of the conversation (as shown in Figure 4-11).

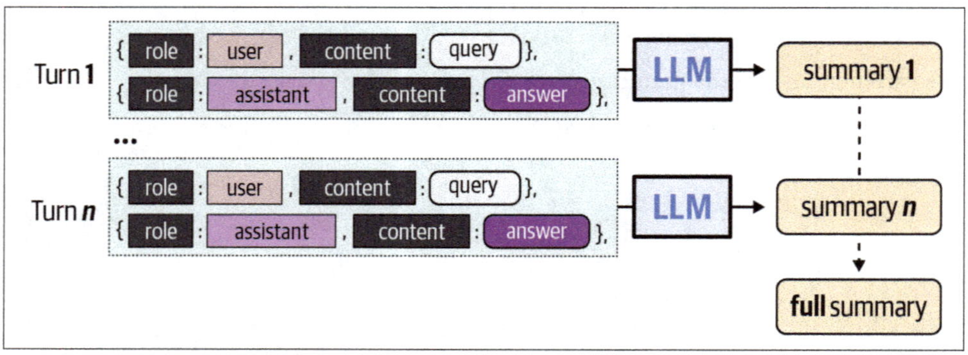

Figure 4-11. Each conversation turn may be summarized and merged into one long summary to reduce the length of the full conversation history

As illustrated in Figure 4-12, the created summary will be shown together with the query for the LLM to answer. This summary might still fill the context window over time as summaries are stacked on one another, but it is much slower than filling the context window with the raw conversation history. Likewise, this can be prevented by summarizing these again but that might compress too much of the original information, which in turn could remove important information.

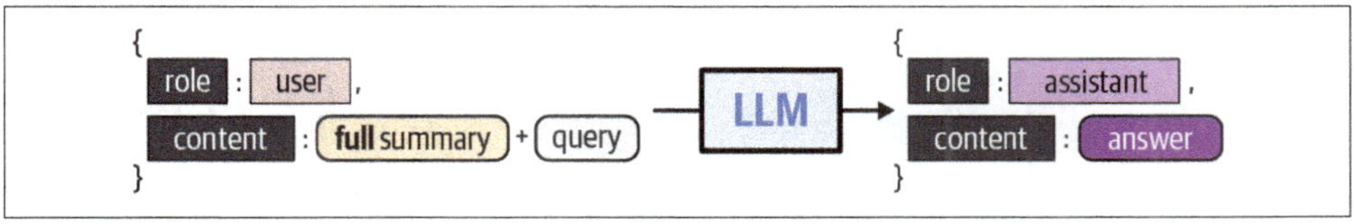

Figure 4-12. A summary of the full conversation history can be given to the LLM for more efficient usage of the context window

Stacking summaries is not the only method of summarization. Instead of adding a summary of the most recent query/answer pair each time, you can instead summarize the conversation history of the last five conversations. Likewise, you can decide to maintain one summary and ask the LLM to update it after each conversation. Figure 4-13 illustrates such a method where conservation turns 1 through 5 are summarized but not turn 6.

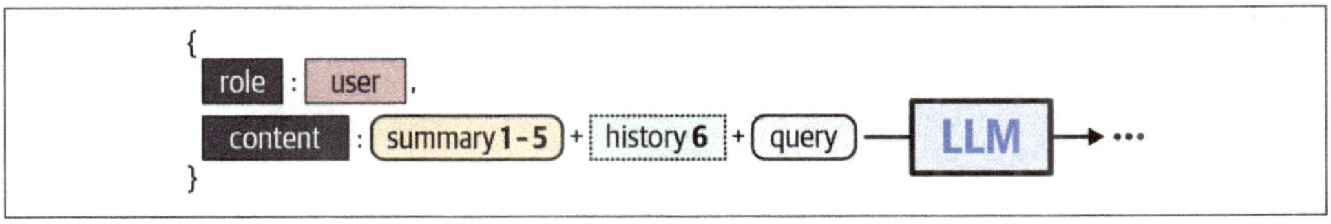

Figure 4-13. A part of the conversation history can also be summarized to create a balance between old information (summarized) and new information (uncompressed)

Let's illustrate it with a simplified example. We are going to create a `SummarizationMemory` module where each time a turn has passed, the turn gets summarized by an LLM. In this example, we assume that the role of the user is always followed by that of the assistant. We will use the `system` role to track the summary so we can separate it from the conversation between the `user` and `assistant`:

```
class SummarizationMemory(Memory):
    """Memory that compresses past turns into a running summary via an LLM."""

    def __init__(self, llm: LLM):
        super().__init__()
        self.llm = llm

    def add(self, role: str, content: str, **kwargs) -> None:
        # Add the new message first using the parent class (Memory)
        super().add(role, content, **kwargs)

        # After each completed turn, update the running summary
```

```
        if role == "assistant":
            # Split the existing summary from the new conversation turns
            summary = ""
            conversation = ""
            for message in self.messages:
                if message["role"] == "system":
                    summary = message["content"]
                else:
                    conversation += f"{message['role']}: {message['content']}\n"

            # Ask the LLM to extend the summary with the new conversation
            prompt = f"""Update the summary with the new conversation.

Summary: {summary}

Conversation:
{conversation}
Output the updated summary only."""
            response = self.llm.generate([{"role": "user", "content": prompt}])
            self.messages = [{"role": "system", "content": response.content}]
```

You can choose any LLM to perform the summarization task, but for illustration purposes we are going to use the one we have been using so far. Then, we ask the agent a question:

```
# Create the Agent
memory = SummarizationMemory(llm=llm)
agent = TinyAgent(llm=llm, memory=memory)

# Run a query
response = agent.run("Hi, my name is Sarah. Why are flamingos pink?")
```

This gives a response as you would expect. However, that raw response is not tracked in the agent's memory because during this `.run`, a summarization of the conversation history takes place. Let's inspect the memory:

```
print(agent.memory.get_messages())
```

This gives:

```
[
    {
        'role': 'system',
        'content': 'Sarah asked why flamingos are pink. The assistant explained
        that flamingos are not born pink; they are born with grey or white
        feathers. They turn pink due to carotenoid pigments found in their diet
        of shrimp, algae, and brine flies. These pigments are absorbed and
        deposited into their feathers, causing the pink coloration.
        The intensity of the pink depends on the amount of
        carotenoid-rich food they consume.'
    }
]
```

Note how there is only a system role with a summary of the conversation history. As you continue the conversation, this summary gets updated. As always, if you want to track the full conversation, you can use the `TrajectoryViewer`:

```
from illustrated_agents.utils import TrajectoryViewer
TrajectoryViewer(agent.trajectory)
```

Although this implementation may seem straightforward, maintaining the conversation history can be a difficult task and requires understanding what is important: the entire history, the recent history, or a summarized variant? For short conversations, maintaining the entire history would work, but that might not be the case for long sequences of actions. In Chapter 10, we will touch on customizing this summarization process for a specific domain like code generation.

Long-Term Memory

As the conversation history and the number of actions that an agent has taken grows, so does the need for long-term memory. However, its usefulness is not limited to conversation history but may also include proprietary or external knowledge. Long-term memory typically involves maintaining one or more external databases that can be queried to extract additional information. This can contain information about previous traces or states of the agent (episodic memory) or information unrelated to the agent's behavior but about the context of your application instead (semantic memory), like your organization's documents.

Retrieval-Augmented Generation

Arguably, the most common method for giving your agent, or any LLM for that matter, long-term memory is Retrieval-Augmented Generation (RAG).[4] RAG typically consists of two stages: *ingestion* and *inference*.

In ingestion, your external data, typically unstructured text, is embedded into numerical representations and stored in a database (Figure 4-14). To create these representations, a special variant of an LLM is used, an embedding model, which converts text into numerical vectors (also called embeddings) that capture the semantic meaning of the input. This embedding model is trained to create numerical representations such that words and phrases with similar meaning will have similar representations. This external database can be considered the long-term memory of the LLM, which can be queried for relevant information.

4 Lewis, Patrick et al. 2020. "Retrieval-Augmented Generation for Knowledge-Intensive NLP Tasks," *NIPS'20: Proceedings of the 34th International Conference on Neural Information Processing Systems*, 9459-9474.

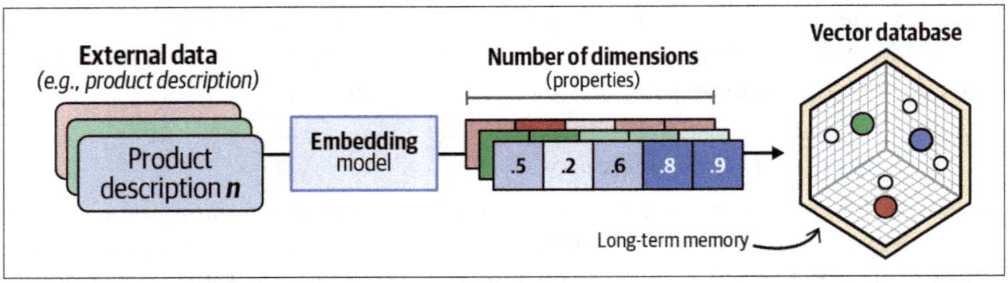

Figure 4-14. RAG starts with converting the input data into numerical information (called embeddings or vectors) to be stored in a vector database

Inference with RAG consists of four steps. In step 1, the user's query is embedded using the same model that was used for embedding the external data. In step 2, the embedded query is compared to the external database, and the most relevant items in the database to the query are extracted.

Defining relevancy in RAG systems can mean many things. In our example, it means the similarity between the query embeddings and the external embeddings. This similarity can be defined through the embeddings we created, but hybrid systems are also possible where embeddings are combined with traditional Bag-of-Words-like approaches.[5]

In step 3, the relevant items and the user's query are combined into the prompt. This step is meant to provide the model with context for the generation step. Essentially, you tell the LLM that you have contextual information that it can use to derive its answer. Finally, in step 4, the augmented prompt is used by the model to generate the output. The added contextual information should generally result in more accurate and relevant responses, assuming that the contextual information is indeed relevant and correct. Figure 4-15 illustrates the four steps of inference with RAG.

RAG is often used to minimize hallucination, which refers to the tendency of LLMs to confidently produce an answer that is actually incorrect. By providing the LLM with external information (which you assume to be true), the LLM is less likely to "make up" information.

5 Bag-of-Words is a sparse representation of texts in which the representation consists of the frequency that each word appears. The result is a sparse matrix where most entries are zero because any single document contains only a tiny fraction of the total vocabulary.

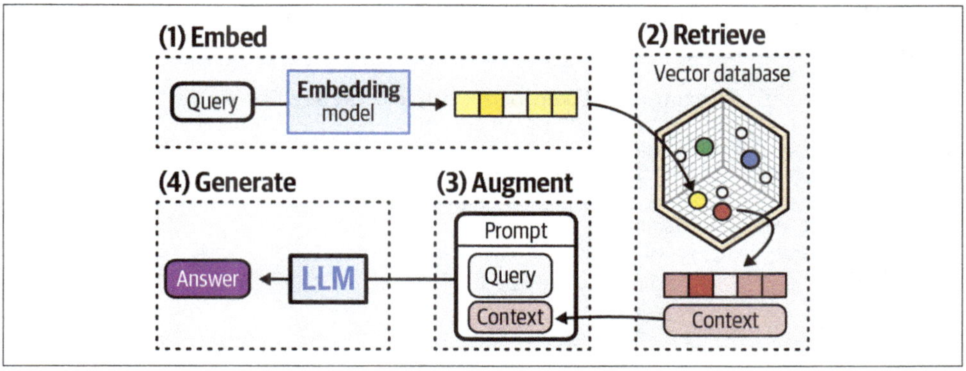

Figure 4-15. The full pipeline of retrieval- (2) augmented (3) generation (4)

Let's explore how we can add RAG to your `TinyAgent`. The first thing that we need to start with is choosing an embedding model that can convert your query into an embedding. The model that we are choosing is called EmbeddingGemma (*https://oreil.ly/lViWi*) and is a 308-million-parameter model from Google DeepMind. We create the `EmbeddingModel` class that allows us to easily embed documents:

```
import json
import urllib.request


class EmbeddingModel:
    """Generate embeddings."""

    def __init__(
        self,
        model: str,
        base_url: str = "http://localhost:11434/v1",
    ):
        """Initialize the embedding model with the given model."""
        self.model = model
        self.base_url = base_url

    def embed(self, text: str) -> list[float]:
        """Convert text into a numerical vector."""
        # POST to the OpenAI-compatible /embeddings endpoint
        request = urllib.request.Request(
            f"{self.base_url}/embeddings",
            data=json.dumps({"model": self.model, "input": text}).encode(),
            headers={"Content-Type": "application/json"},
        )
        with urllib.request.urlopen(request) as resp:
            response = json.loads(resp.read())

        # Extract and return the embedding
        return response["data"][0]["embedding"]
```

Since Ollama also supports embedding models, we can mimic the same structure as we did with the LLM.

Let's try it out with an example. We embed a single sentence like so:

```
# Initialize EmbeddingGemma
embedding_model = EmbeddingModel(model="embeddinggemma")

# Test the embedding model
output = embedding_model.embed("Dolphins are amazing!")
output
```

This gives us:

```
[-0.21747557818889618,
 -0.01567786931991577,
 0.03601466864347458,
 -0.004985752515494823,
...
 0.027807850390672684,
 -0.005654981359839439,
 -0.02514023706316948,
 0.0022561103105545044,
 -0.001453613629564643]
```

This model produces 768 values, each between −1 and 1, for a given input. We can use these values to compare different documents and calculate their similarity. This is typically calculated as the cosine similarity, which represents the angle between embeddings. A smaller angle means a higher similarity. The cosine similarity is calculated through the dot product of the embeddings and then divided by the product of their lengths for normalization.

Let's try it out!

```
# Create embeddings
embedding_a = embedding_model.embed("I love flamingos.")
embedding_b = embedding_model.embed("Dolphins use echolocation.")
embedding_c = embedding_model.embed("Flamingos are pink birds.")

# Calculate cosine similarity between A and B
dot_ab = sum(x * y for x, y in zip(embedding_a, embedding_b))
norm_a = sum(x * x for x in embedding_a) ** 0.5
norm_b = sum(x * x for x in embedding_b) ** 0.5
similarity_ab = dot_ab / (norm_a * norm_b)

# Calculate cosine similarity between A and C
dot_ac = sum(x * y for x, y in zip(embedding_a, embedding_c))
norm_c = sum(x * x for x in embedding_c) ** 0.5
similarity_ac = dot_ac / (norm_a * norm_c)

print(f"Similarity between A and B: {similarity_ab}")
print(f"Similarity between A and C: {similarity_ac}")
```

Which gives us:

```
"""
Similarity between A and B: 0.3546779285862413
Similarity between A and C: 0.6386974942657335
"""
```

As expected, the similarity between "*I love flamingos*" and "*Flamingos are pink birds*" is much higher than between "*I love flamingos*" and "*Dolphins use echolocation*." We can use cosine similarity to perform the comparisons and select the documents that best suit the user's query.

As such, the `RAGMemory` class that we are going to implement has the following steps:

1. Embed all external documents the agent has no direct access to.
2. Embed the user's query.
3. Compare the embeddings and create a similarity matrix.
4. Return the documents with the highest similarity.
5. Add those documents to the prompt.

This gives us the following class:

```
from illustrated_agents.chapters.ch4 import Memory

class RAGMemory(Memory):
    """Long-term Memory with RAG."""

    def __init__(self, embedding_model: EmbeddingModel, documents: list[str]):
        super().__init__()
        self.embedding_model = embedding_model
        self.documents = documents
        self.embeddings = [embedding_model.embed(doc) for doc in documents]

    def add(self, role: str, content: str, **kwargs) -> None:
        # Augment user queries with retrieved context before storing
        if role == "user":
            context = "\n".join(self.search(content))
            content = f"""Context:
{context}

Question: {content}"""
        super().add(role, content, **kwargs)

    def search(self, query: str) -> list[str]:
        """Return the top-k documents most similar to the query."""
        query_embed = self.embedding_model.embed(query)
        scores = [self._cosine(query_embed, embed) for embed in self.embeddings]
        ranked = sorted(
          range(len(scores)), key=lambda i: scores[i], reverse=True
        )
```

```
        return [self.documents[index] for index in ranked[:3]]

    def _cosine(self, a: list[float], b: list[float]) -> float:
        """Calculate cosine similarity between two embeddings.."""
        dot = sum(x * y for x, y in zip(a, b))
        norm = (sum(x * x for x in a) ** 0.5) * (sum(x * x for x in b) ** 0.5)
        return dot / norm
```

Let's put this to practice, starting with a set of documents that your `TinyAgent` has no direct access to. This is going to be a simple example, but imagine you have thousands of documents:

```
from illustrated_agents.chapters.ch4 import TinyAgent

# RAGMemory with external documents
documents = [
    "Sarah works as a marine biologist studying coral reefs.",
    "Sarah lives in Lisbon, Portugal.",
    "Sarah's favorite hobby is rock climbing.",
    "Sarah favorite animal is flamingos.",
    "Sarah speaks fluent Spanish and Portuguese.",
    "Ilse is a software engineer at a renewable energy startup.",
    "Ilse lives in Amsterdam, the Netherlands.",
    "Ilse plays the cello in a local string quartet.",
    "Ilse's favorite author is Brandon Sanderson.",
    "Ilse's favorite animal is dolphins.",
]
memory = RAGMemory(documents=documents, embedding_model=embedding_model)

# Create the Agent and run a query
agent = TinyAgent(llm=llm, memory=memory)
response = agent.run("What is Sarah's favorite animal?")
print(response)
```

We asked it the question "What is Sarah's favorite animal?," which your `TinyAgent` can only know if it truly has gotten those documents:

```
"Sarah's favorite animal is flamingos."
```

It got it correct! Let's explore the memory and see what was happening under the hood:

```
print(agent.memory.get_messages())
```

Which gives:

```
[
    {
        'role': 'user',
        'content': "Context:\nSarah favorite animals are flamingos.\n
        Sarah's favorite hobby is rock climbing.\nIlse's favorite animals
        are dolphins.\n\nQuestion: What is Sarah's favorite animal?"
    },
```

```
    {'role': 'assistant', 'content': "Sarah's favorite animal is flamingos."}
]
```

Note how it retrieved the top three documents as the context? This is both the advantage and disadvantage of RAG. Although it minimizes the context that you have to pass to the model, there is no guarantee that the context will always be good enough. You could, for example, only accept documents that have a minimum degree of similarity rather than simply getting the top three irrespective of their absolute scores.

Now that your `TinyAgent` has memory in different forms, let's recap what we built in this chapter.

What We Built

```
TinyAgent/
├── agent.py ← Updated (Integrated `Memory` into your `TinyAgent`)
├── llm.py   ← Updated (Added `EmbeddingModel` to create embeddings)
├── memory.py  ← New (Added both short-term and long-term memory)
└── trajectory.py
```

MemoryBank

An interesting take on RAG for chatbots is MemoryBank, a mechanism that allows LLMs to recall relevant memories as a long-term mechanism (external database) rather than a short-term mechanism (conversation history).[6] Its experiences through conversations are stored in a separate database that allows the LLM to retrieve relevant memories. What sets it apart from regular RAG is that this memory is continuously updated to selectively preserve memory through an updating mechanism.

This mechanism allows the MemoryBank to forget and reinforce memory inspired by the Ebbinghaus Forgetting Curve theory, which is a curve demonstrating the pace at which we tend to forget. The curve is often shown as being exponential, resulting in a loss of half of what we learn each day. A common way to prevent forgetting what you learned, for instance when preparing for exams, is to actively recall the learned information frequently. This is referred to as spaced repetition, which tends to decrease the pace at which knowledge is forgotten. Figure 4-16 illustrates this knowledge decay and the effect of spaced repetition on it.

MemoryBank borrows from this theory and frequently updates the long-term memory of an LLM based on which pieces of knowledge are (not) accessed. Specifically, this means that when a memory item is retrieved and used during conversations, it

6 Zhong, Wanjun et al. 2024. "MemoryBank: Enhancing Large Language Models with Long-Term Memory," *Proceedings of the AAAI Conference on Artificial Intelligence*, 38(17).

will persist longer in the MemoryBank. However, if the memory item hasn't been retrieved for a while, then there is a chance the memory will be removed entirely.

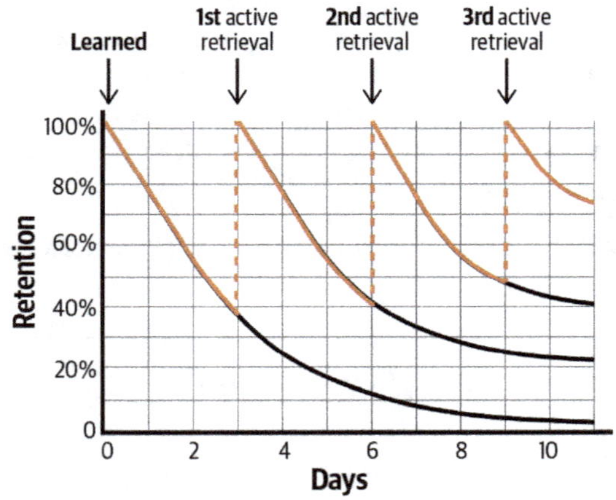

Figure 4-16. An example of the forgetting curve theory that demonstrates how spaced repetition and retrieval reduces knowledge decay

The authors use a few variants of memory:

Conversation history
: Raw multi-turn conversations.

Summaries of past events
: These are generated by an LLM based on the conversation history.

User's portrait
: The personality traits and emotions of the user as summarized by the LLM based on the conversation history.

These forms of memory are used to create the MemoryBank, as shown in Figure 4-17, and show how an LLM may create the summaries of past events as well as the user's portrait.

The summaries and conversation turns are embedded so that they can easily be retrieved. The user portrait is dynamically updated and always passed as additional context. Figure 4-18 shows a full overview of this pipeline. When a query is created, it is embedded, and related conversation turns and summaries are retrieved, together with the user portrait. When conversation turns are retrieved, their strength is updated, making them less likely to be removed from the MemoryBank. The retrieved context, together with the query, is used as input for the LLM to generate an answer.

This form of memory demonstrates the potential complexity of RAG-like applications, where each use case necessitates different types of memories, summarizations, etc. As such, there are many forms of RAG, such as GraphRAG and Multi-modal

RAG, that each require its own set of considerations. The RAG examples shown previously are often referred to as vanilla RAG or naive RAG for their straightforward implementation.

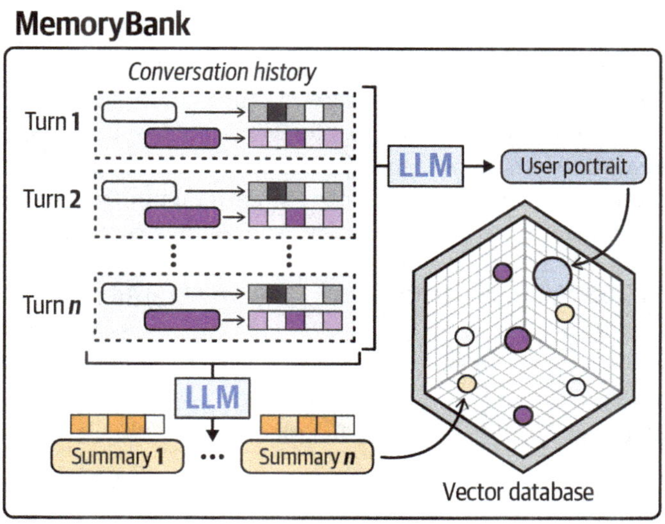

Figure 4-17. MemoryBank maintains summaries of past events and information on the user generated by an LLM

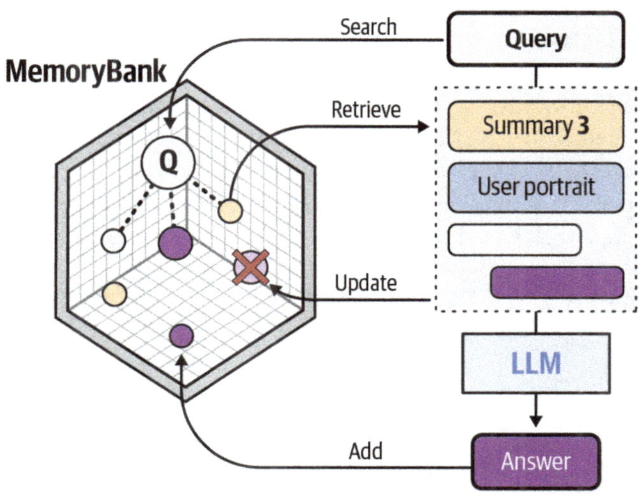

Figure 4-18. How MemoryBank is used for RAG

Agentic Retrieval-Augmented Generation

In vanilla RAG, the vector database can be considered the long-term memory of the LLM. However, the LLM is only *given* information that is relevant to the query and has no agency over what is being retrieved.

In agentic RAG, there is an agent instead of an LLM that can access the external database as a tool and have control over which information it retrieves. Agency over what is being retrieved is given back to the agent, who typically has access to one or more external databases of information. Figure 4-19 illustrates this idea of having the agent select from which source to retrieve contextual information before deciding whether to generate the answer or to again retrieve additional information.

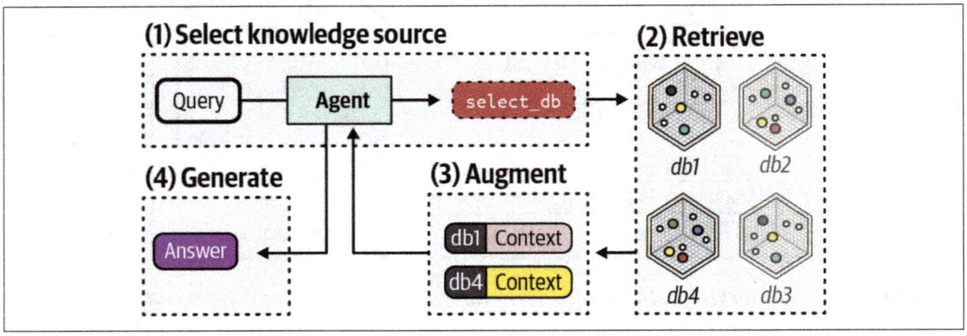

Figure 4-19. Agentic RAG

In single-agent systems, agentic RAG is a router where you have several external knowledge sources, and the agent decides which one(s) to use. You're essentially adding all these knowledge sources and databases as tools instead of being a static step that runs before the LLM generates output. Moreover, such an agentic RAG system does not always have to run the agentic RAG based on the query itself. As shown in Figure 4-20, it may decide to extract information from one search and then run a subsequent search based on that information in another database.

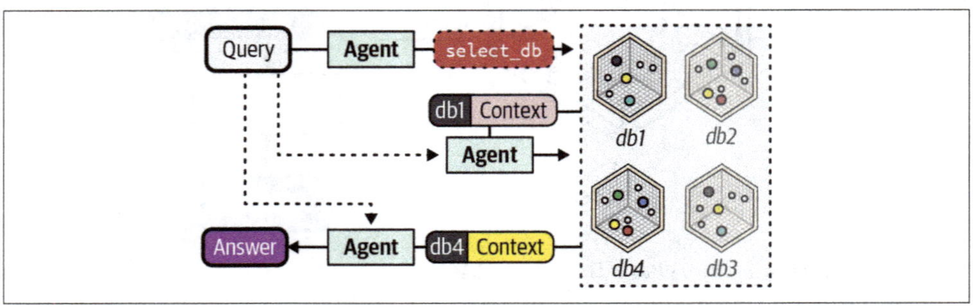

Figure 4-20. Agentic RAG using a single agent to control multiple processes

Agentic RAG does not limit itself to single-agent systems. In multi-agent RAG systems, multiple agents have the capabilities to extract information from external sources. Oftentimes, you have smaller retrieval agents that are being coordinated by a single agent with more capabilities. These smaller retrieval agents are each specialized in extracting specific information or working with specific knowledge sources (see Figure 4-21). Note that it does not always have to be a vector database as an external knowledge source; it can also be a web search or querying some API for information (like your Slack or Gmail).

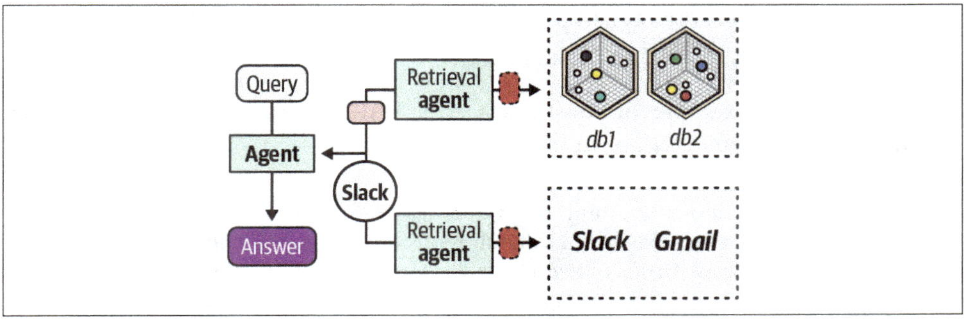

Figure 4-21. Agentic RAG using multiple agents to control different processes

In other words, instead of querying the vector database through a static step only once, by hooking it as a tool, the agent can dynamically decide how many times it needs to query the semantic memory until it has enough context to answer a given query. Note how we discussed LLMs in the context of RAG but agents in the context of agentic RAG instead. It demonstrates the agency and autonomy in accessing their respective RAG capabilities.

Using either a single or multiple agents comes with their own sets of advantages and disadvantages, each requiring a thorough understanding of the use case in which they're employed. We advise to start with a single agent system as a good baseline and to minimize complexity. In Table 4-1, an non-exhaustive list is given advantages and disadvantages of these systems.

Table 4-1. Pros and cons of RAG systems

	Single-agent RAG	Multi-agent RAG
Advantages	*Cost effective*—Fewer API calls are needed. *Simpler system*—Easier to debug due to fewer dependencies.	*Modularity*—Specialized LLMs can be used and easily replaced. *Higher accuracy ceiling*—Agents can give each other feedback and check for hallucinations.
Disadvantages	*Single point of failure*—Errors may compound without external feedback. *Lower accuracy ceiling*—The context window can be overloaded with too many sources and retrievals of information.	*Higher costs*—Multiple agents need to be run in parallel, which drives costs. *Complexity*—Harder to check where errors may arise and how they relate to the entire flow.

Let's go over some examples of how these agentic RAG systems work through impactful papers and implementations in the field.

> The implementation of agentic RAG is shown in the associated notebooks in the GitHub repository (*https://github.com/HandsOnLLM/An-Illustrated-Guide-To-AI-Agents*). Since our current implementation of your `TinyAgent` isn't yet autonomous, the notebooks where we'll cover this principle are going to be shown in the notebooks after we have covered Chapter 6. There, everything will come together to make your agent have a degree of autonomy.
>
> Moreover, and as discussed previously, agentic RAG makes use of tools that we will cover in depth in Chapter 5.

A-MEM

An interesting approach to agentic RAG is A-MEM, an agentic memory system derived from the note-taking method known as Zettelkasten.[7] Zettelkasten approaches note-taking as having three important components, namely atomicity, hypertextual notes, and personalization.

Atomicity means that each Zettel (a note) should contain only one unit of knowledge, referred to as an atom. This note could, for example, contain a brief description of how memory works in agentic systems.

Then, hypertextual notes refer to the idea that all notes refer to each other and may explain or expand on each other's content. For instance, the previously created note can be connected to another note that has some information about RAG. Because both are memory systems, they're likely to be related. The ideas of atomicity and hypertextual notes are illustrated in Figure 4-22. Together, they may create an interconnected web of notes and ideas and larger topics of interconnected notes

7 Xu, Wujiang et al. 2025. "A-Mem: Agentic Memory for LLM Agents," *arXiv*, 2502.12110.

demonstrating how these interconnect notes are personalized to one's own sets of ideas.

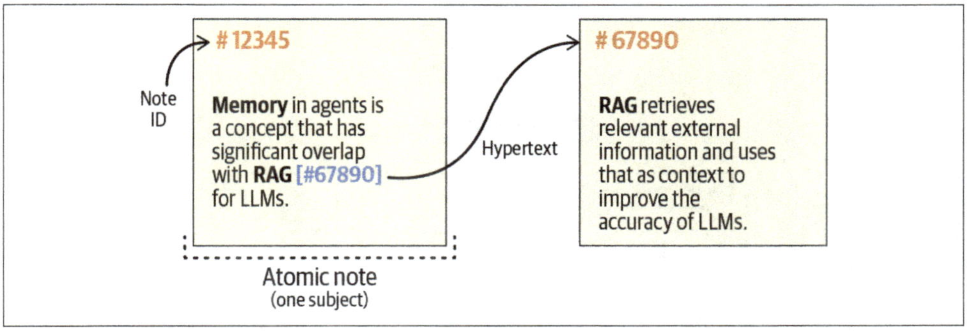

Figure 4-22. In Zettel, each note has a single subject (atomicity) and may link to other notes (hypertextual notes)

A-MEM uses this idea of note-taking to agentic memory by creating these interconnected notes. In the context of agents, each note contains the following information and can be considered a piece of memory:

- The original *interaction* with the environment (i.e., one turn)
- The *timestamp* of the interaction
- LLM-generated *keywords* that capture key concepts
- LLM-generated *tags* to categorize the interaction
- LLM-generated *contextual description*

By focusing on a single unit, namely a single interaction, A-MEM adheres to the principle of atomicity. Then, all pieces of information are embedded so that they can be used to later easily retrieve related information (Figure 4-23). Note that all information, except for the timestamp, is concatenated so that a single embedding is created for the entire note/memory. However, the timestamp is still maintained as metadata to query.

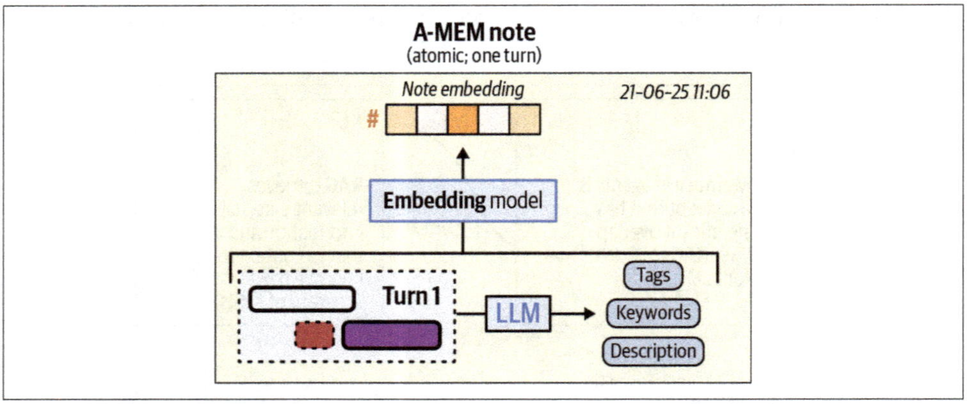

Figure 4-23. The atomicity of an A-MEM note, which contains a single turn that is embedded using an embedding model

Interestingly, the authors use this generated note embedding as one of the main IDs of the note. To link this note to other memories, they run a similarity search between this note's embeddings and all other memories and extract the Top-K memories. After doing so, the LLM is asked to decide which of these candidate memories should be linked to the newly added memory.

After the memory is added and linked to other memories, the LLM is prompted to update the LLM-generated tags, keywords, and description based on the newly added memory. This results in an evolutionary approach where newly added memories are linked to older memories, which are, in turn, updated to be in line with the newly added memories. Figure 4-24 illustrates this ever-evolving database of notes in the form of memories.

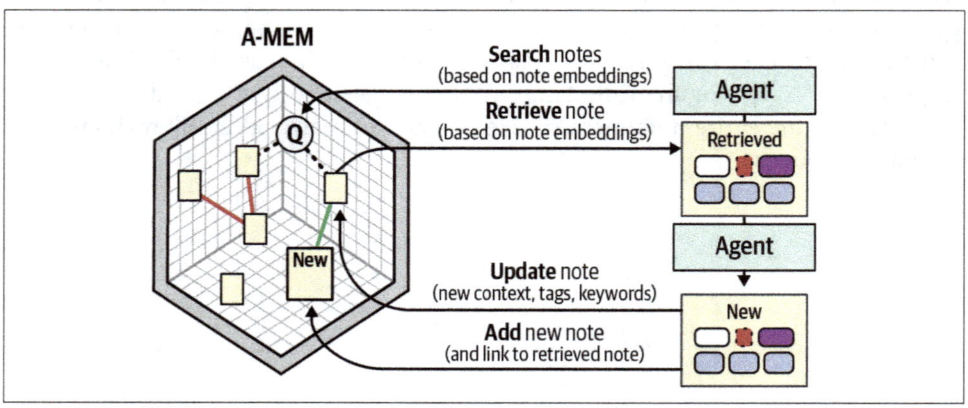

Figure 4-24. The embeddings of each note in A-MEM are used in this RAG-like pipeline with steps to search, retrieve, update, and add notes

This agentic RAG system allows the agent to access the A-MEM and search for memories that relate to the query. The links that are made between notes are used when retrieving relevant information. The agent can choose to retrieve all notes that have links to the retrieved note.

We again see that these memory systems mirror aspects of human memory. Many insights from how we store and use knowledge often serve as inspiration for the design of agentic memory systems.

Search-o1

A recent approach to agentic RAG is Search-o1, a method that attempts to retrieve relevant context and put it throughout the reasoning traces to enhance the reasoning LLM's capabilities further.[8] Instead of autonomously searching for relevant information and using it in the prompt of the model, the information can be searched and retrieved *during* the LLM's reasoning process. As such, it's the difference between the information that is provided to the LLM and the information retrieved during the thinking stage of the LLM. The agent is instructed to use the <|begin_search_query|> and <|end_search_query|> tokens to start a search and then use the <|begin_search_result|> and <|end_search_result|> tokens to indicate what the retrieved information is. Figure 4-25 demonstrates this agentic RAG during reasoning.

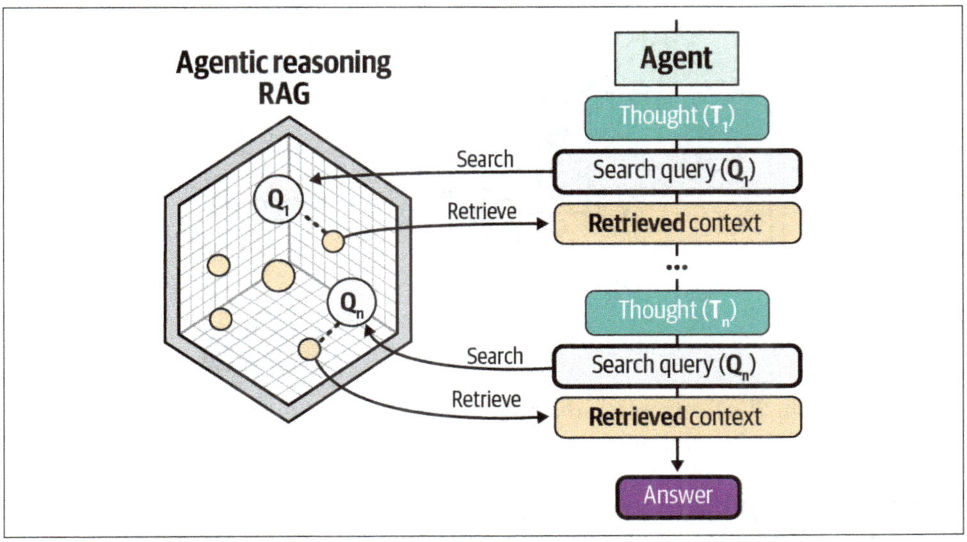

Figure 4-25. Agentic RAG can be used during reasoning to enhance its performance before finally giving back an answer

8 Li, Xiaoxi et al. 2025. "Search-o1: Agentic Search-Enhanced Large Reasoning Models," *arXiv*, 2501.05366.

By enabling RAG during reasoning, using synchronous retrieval tools and structured model calls, the model can iteratively refine its reasoning process until it is confident in the final result. This dynamic approach is different from regular agentic RAG because it can be done autonomously within a single call rather than iterating over calls.

A downside to simply embedding documents within the reasoning traces is that the retrieved documents can be quite large and often contain irrelevant information and may therefore disrupt the reasoning flow. To solve this issue, the authors extend the reasoning agentic RAG by incorporating a module called the Reason-in-Documents module. Using the search query, retrieved documents, and reasoning trace, this module attempts to condense all information into focused reasoning steps. The agent's reasoning LLM is used to process the retrieved documents to align with the model's specific reasoning traces.

With regular agentic RAG, information is just passed to the context without taking into account *how* the information needs to be processed. By enabling the same reasoning LLM to further process that information such that it fits within the reasoning traces, the flow of the traces can be kept intact. An overview of this system, called Search-o1, is given in Figure 4-26.

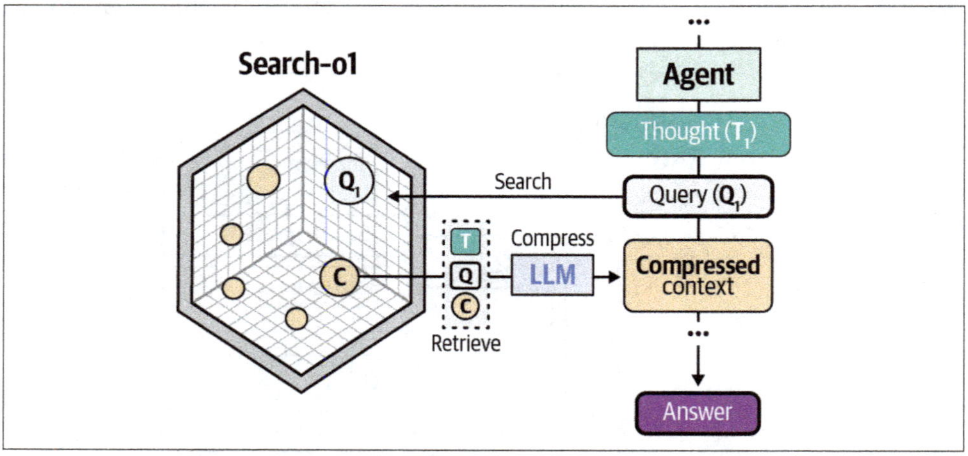

Figure 4-26. Search-o1 compresses the context using an LLM to create a more optimized context with less redundant information

Note that this is typically used for long-term memory or external semantic memory that the agent might need to answer a given query. For instance, when given the query "Why are flamingos pink?," it will search for relevant information in Wikipedia during its reasoning process. The first result it finds mentions that it is due to specific pigments in their specific diet. It will use that information during its reasoning until it needs further clarification. For instance, a second call to a different external database (e.g., arXiv) will clarify that the specific pigments are carotenoid pigments, which are commonly found in brine shrimp.

This iterative process of querying information and compressing it within its reasoning process allows the model to reason about information when it is retrieved rather than stuffing all potential relevant information in the context.

Context Engineering

We have explored various types of memory that we can use to provide additional context to the agent, including semantic memory, working memory, and other forms of memory. However, there might be more forms of context that we could give to the agent, such as the following:

System prompt
: The core context and rules for the agent, which define how it should behave (procedural memory)

Conversation history
: Both the conversation between the user and assistant, but also the LLM's internal thoughts (working memory)

Past experiences
: Storing specific events, actions, or observations from tool use or user-related facts (episodic memory)

Retrieved information
: External information that is typically stored in a vector database and accessed through RAG-like techniques (semantic memory)

This is not an exhaustive list, however. As the fields of LLMs and agents grow, so do the sources of information that we could give to them. As such, we can provide the agent with all kinds of information sources to produce the answer that we want. As illustrated in Figure 4-27, the user's query or prompt is a subset of the LLM's entire context.

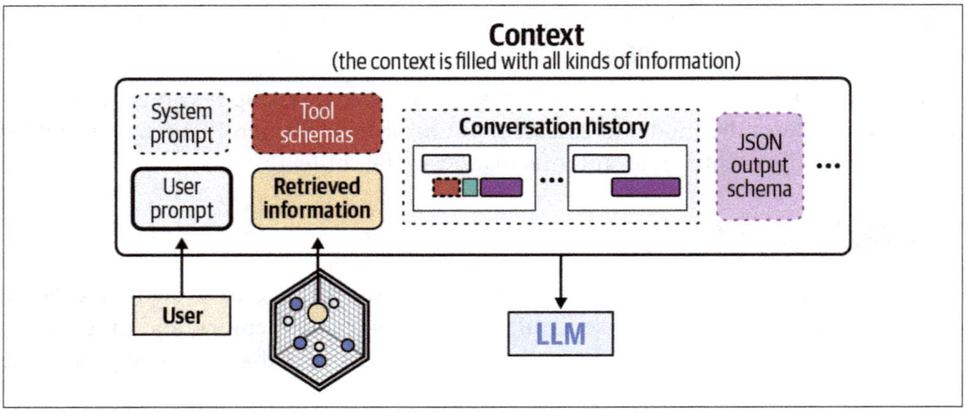

Figure 4-27. A non-exhaustive overview of the kinds of information that can be put into an LLM

This context is given to the LLM, which in turn produces a list of tokens. As such, we can view an LLM as a function that takes several tokens (context), processes them, and outputs tokens. To optimize the output tokens for a given task, we can either optimize the LLM itself by training or fine-tuning it, or we can optimize the input, namely the context (see Figure 4-28).

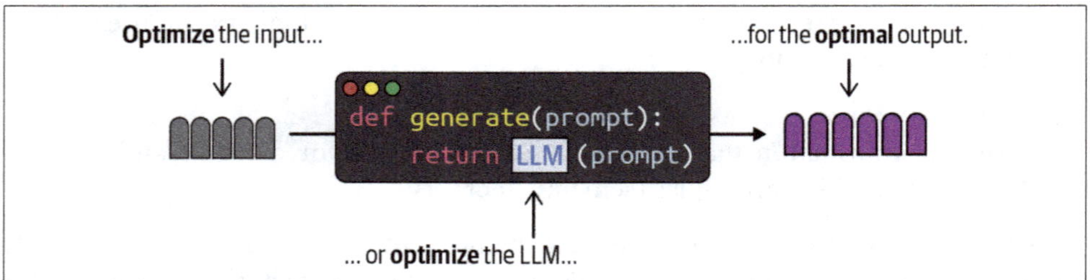

Figure 4-28. To create better outputs, we can either optimize the input tokens or create better LLMs. In this context, the LLM can be seen as part of a function to optimize.

To optimize the quality of the output (the output tokens), we can either optimize the LLM itself by training or fine-tuning it, or we can optimize what goes into the LLM, namely, the context. The act of optimizing input tokens so they produce the best possible output is called *context engineering*. Formally, it is finding the best context such that it maximizes the quality of the LLM's output for a given task.[9] As illustrated in Figure 4-29, where prompt engineering involves optimizing the system/user prompts, context engineering aims to optimize the entire context.

9 Mei, Lingrui et al. 2025. "A Survey of Context Engineering for Large Language Models," *arXiv*, 2507.13334.

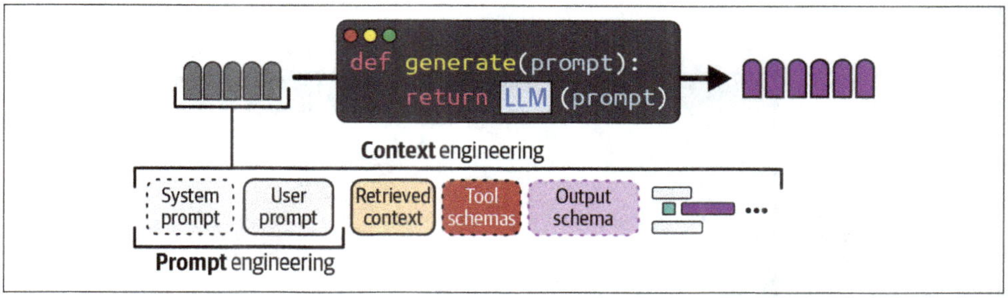

Figure 4-29. Prompt engineering involves giving the most relevant pieces of information to the LLM

Context windows have grown larger, to the point where Google's Gemini 1.5 (*https://oreil.ly/Dp4fx*) already reached a context window of a million tokens in February 2024. It would be natural to conclude that context engineering means attempting to fill up this humongous context window with all kinds of information that relates to the task at hand. Moreover, there would be no more need for RAG because the context window is large enough to potentially hold your entire database.

A common benchmark for evaluating long-context LLMs in 2023 and early 2024 was the needle-in-a-haystack (NIAH) test.[10] The test is rather straightforward; a random fact (needle) is placed somewhere in the middle of a long context window (haystack), and the model is asked to retrieve this statement. By iterating over different places and context lengths, we can measure how well LLMs perform over long contexts. It produced nice-looking visuals and was used by large LLM providers, like Anthropic's Claude 2.1 and Google's Gemini 1.5.[11,12]

An example of such a visual is shown in Figure 4-30, which illustrates the results for a typical needle-in-a-haystack test, where the upper-right quadrant (needle at the top of the document and large context length) shows the degradation of LLMs at higher context lengths.

10 Kamradt, Gregory. 2023. "Needle in a Haystack–Pressure Testing LLMs," GitHub, *https://github.com/gkamradt/needle-in-a-haystack*.

11 Anthropic. 2023. "Long Context Prompting for Claude 2.1," Blog post, *https://www.anthropic.com/index/claude-2-1-prompting*.

12 Gemini Team Google et al. 2024. "Gemini 1.5: Unlocking Multimodal Understanding Across Millions of Tokens of Context," *arXiv*, 2403.05530.

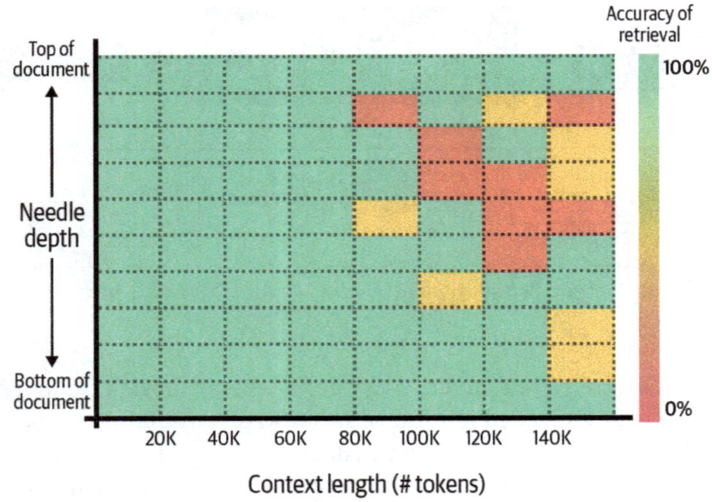

Figure 4-30. An artificial example of a typical needle-in-a-haystack test. In this example, the accuracy of retrieval decreases as the context window is filled, with information in the middle of the context being more difficult to retrieve accurately.

However, finding the needle is merely a retrieval task and is not indicative of more complex forms of long-context understanding, such as reasoning over hundreds of thousands of tokens. This holds especially true for agents that have to take into account many forms and lengths of context, like semantic and working memory.

Other benchmarks, like the RULER benchmark,[13] have since been released that introduce new tasks like multi-hop tracing and aggregation to test behaviors beyond simple retrieval. The RULER paper, for instance, demonstrated models that performed well on the needle-in-a-haystack test, all showed significant performance drops as the context length increased when applied to the RULER benchmark. Many others (e.g., Li, Tianle et al. 2024 and Levy, Mosh et al. 2024)[14,15] found similar results and concluded that arbitrarily filling up the context window of LLMs would hurt performance. Some even called it "context rot,"[16] showcasing the importance of adding quality information. Moreover, even if the entire context window is filled with quality

13 Hsieh, Cheng-Ping et al. 2024. "RULER: What's the Real Context Size of Your Long-Context Language Models?" *arXiv*, 2404.06654.

14 Li, Tianle et al. 2024. "Long-Context LLMs Struggle with Lng In-Context Learning," *arXiv*, 2404.02060.

15 Levy, Mosh et al. 2024. "Same Task, More Tokens: The Impact of Input Length on the Reasoning Performance of Large Language Models," *arXiv*, 2402.14848.

16 Hong, Kelly et al. "Context Rot: How Increasing Input Tokens Impacts LLM Performance," *Chroma*, July 2025. *https://research.trychroma.com/context-rot*.

information, it's often hard for LLMs to shift through all pieces of information. This might change as LLM capabilities grow but still requires knowing that all information provided is vital. As such, there is a need to carefully construct and manage the model's context window, thereby pointing to the importance of context engineering.

Cost and latency are other reasons for managing the context window. You could theoretically stuff everything in a 2-million-token context length, like your entire external database, the full conversation history, some additional examples, etc. However, the agent's LLM has to process all these tokens, which significantly increases latency. Costs also increase, considering more VRAM is needed when you increase the context length. Just dumping everything in the context is, therefore, a recipe for failure.

With context engineering, we aim to optimize the model's context window with the right information, at the right place, and in the right format. It's the act of giving the LLM the appropriate context without overwhelming it. As such, and as shown in Figure 4-31, it's not about filling up the context window, but strategically choosing and placing information. Going back to our "LLM is a function" analogy, it's about optimizing the list of input tokens so that it produces the best possible output tokens.

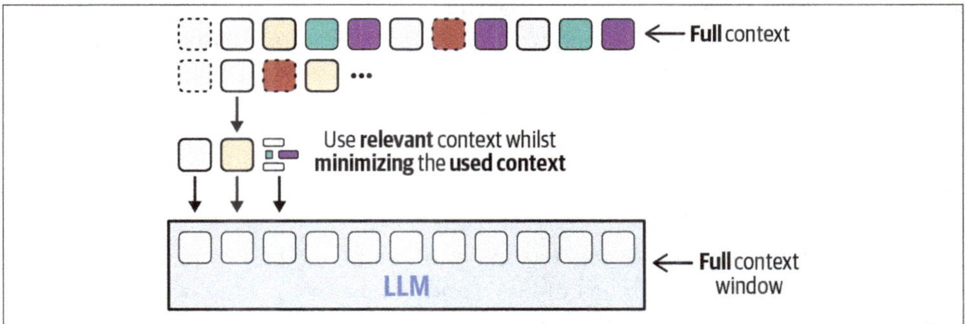

Figure 4-31. Context engineering involves strategically placing only the most relevant information in the context

You don't want too much or too irrelevant information because the costs of compute go up and the performance goes down. Likewise, if you give the LLM too little context and in an inefficient form, it will operate without having a good understanding of the context. It's a careful balance of providing just enough relevant information to the LLM to have it perform optimally. In other words, context engineering is largely an architectural problem that needs to be solved with lots of moving parts, like efficiently tracking, storing, and retrieving all existing and created information.

To help with context engineering, existing techniques for handling memory that focus on efficiency can be used. MemoryBank, for instance, dynamically adjusts the importance of memories and keeps only those that are truly important for the conversation history. Likewise, Search-o1 compresses the retrieved context and gives back only the relevant components without any noise. These dynamic memory techniques are exceptionally useful for context engineering as the information flows grow more complex.

Context Engineering for Multi-Agent Systems

As we will cover in more depth in Chapter 8, multi-agent systems deploy groups of agents working together to solve a given problem. Our example of a deep research agent used a summarization agent in its system, thereby working together. What makes context engineering especially difficult in multi-agent systems is that not only the context of the main agents needs to be carefully managed, so do the contexts of all other agents in the system. Moreover, the interaction between agents is also part of the shared context between those respective agents.

To manage this complex network of contexts, smaller agents can be used to handle some of the context "burden," as we illustrated in the deep research agent. By using a smaller agent with a smaller LLM for specific tasks, part of the context can be handled separately, leaving significant compute for the main agent (also called the orchestrator agent). What makes these small and/or specialized agents great for context engineering is that they can work on smaller and more manageable contexts, have clear responsibilities, and are easier to test and debug. These systems can be more reliable by separating tasks instead of having one agent juggle all kinds of different tasks and contexts.

Optimizing the Context

Throughout this chapter, we covered many different methods and techniques for handling the memory and context of LLMs and agents. Optimizing what you put into the context and how is a multi-faceted problem that requires an understanding of various parts of your agent's architecture. Most strategies to optimize the context are built upon the main source of context, the memory modules of the agent, but often also include system prompts and tool schemas.

Although there are many strategies, let's explore the most common ones.

Context tracking and storage

Before you give the agent a possible relevant context, it first needs to be tracked and stored somewhere. We covered most of it already, as this relates to various forms of memory, and in particular episodic memory, which contains the actions the agent has taken thus far. Although episodic memory is seen as long-term memory, it is highly related to the conversation history of the agent, which tends to capture the agent's actions.

However, tracking the context goes beyond just the event traces of the agent. It also involves managing external knowledge sources, such as a database of your proprietary data, which can serve as additional context. To set up these sources of knowledge, you'll have to decide beforehand what kinds of information you want to track. Although it may seem obvious at first, there are many types of information you can track:

Agent behavior
: Tool usage by the agent (and any subagents)

: Tool outputs and intermediate results

: Interactions between (sub)agents

: Internal reasoning steps

: Conversation history

: Failures/successes

User behavior
: User intent (explicit requests and goals)

: User feedback (edits, approvals, rejections)

Knowledge sources
: Snapshots of your proprietary database(s) for reproducibility and auditing

: External documents (RAG, APIs, etc.)

: Structured artifacts like *PLAN.md*, *REQUIREMENTS.md*, etc.

System-level
: Configuration (LLM hyperparameters, available tools, etc.)

: Policies (guardrails, constraints, etc.)

All of these are merely examples of what you could possibly track. In practice, not everything is going to be useful, and at the same time, many other things should be included, such as privacy and safety constraints. As we'll explore later, tracking these kinds of contexts and information also helps communicate the user's intent and debug these complex systems.

Context selection

Assuming you have set up all your databases, the very first thing you can do to optimize the context is to have a system in place that selects the right context. As we discussed before, RAG is an amazing technique and example for selecting what is relevant. Although we have seen variants of RAG that improve on this, we haven't yet explored how we can further improve this selection process.

In RAG, the input documents are typically split into smaller parts, such as sentences or paragraphs, to isolate the information they contain and keep it to a single subject. However, when you then run a RAG pipeline, you typically get a collection of documents in return. For example, if we search a vector database for the "causes of climate change," the system might return documents about greenhouse gases, industrial activity, and deforestation. Although those documents might not directly answer our question, they are related.

To improve this process, we can use a reranker to refine the set of documents that were retrieved. This technique, often a language model, takes in both the query and retrieved documents to rerank the retrieved documents based on their relevance to the query and to each other (Figure 4-32). By providing the reranker with additional context (each retrieved document), it can operate on far fewer documents than if we were to give it the entire database. Moreover, after the results have been reranked according to their relevance, we can choose to keep only the most relevant documents.

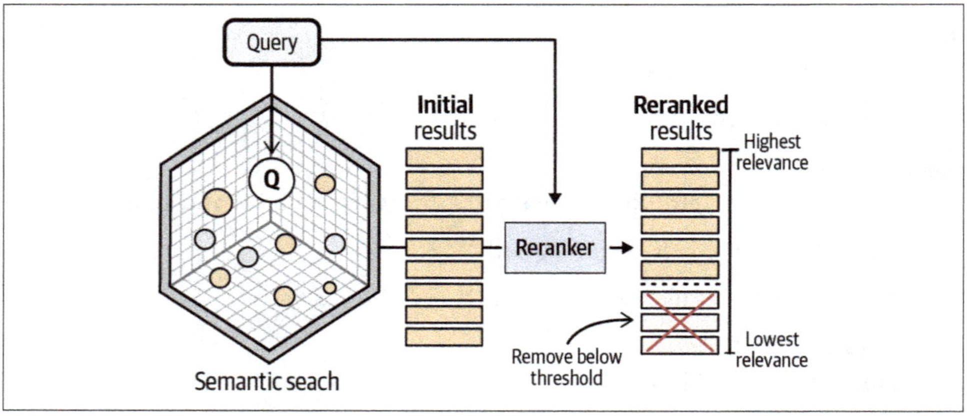

Figure 4-32. Reranking involves optimizing a candidate set of results

Reranking is often used for search-based use cases, such as deep research where an agent has to research a given subject by finding and summarizing the most relevant papers for a given query. Often, thousands of relevant papers could be found but reranking helps reduce that amount.

Reranking is only one of the many ways to select and create the right context. We can also structure the output to ensure the responses of the agent are broken up into logical parts and contain only the necessary components. Likewise, we can employ business rules that give additional weight to certain pieces of information that always provide important context (much like a system prompt).

Note that selecting the right context can also mean selecting the right context for the right agent. By isolating the context across multiple specialized agents, each agent is able to focus on a smaller part of the problem without being overwhelmed by the full context.

Context compression

The goal of context engineering is to find a balance between what you put in the context and how much. As such, compressing the context as much as possible is an important strategy for optimizing it.

A common way to handle compression is what we discussed at the beginning of this chapter, using an LLM to create summaries of your conversation history. As we explored in Search-o1, we can even compress the output of the RAG pipeline using an LLM to summarize the retrieved documents.

Another method of compressing the context is reducing redundancy. Even with a reranker, the top five most relevant results might all contain very similar documents. Together, they're not bigger than the sum of their parts but smaller because they contain similar information. As such, we want not just the most relevant documents, but those that each contain a new piece of information rather than redundant information.

A common technique to use for documents, whether they're the output documents of your RAG pipeline or other pieces of retrieved information, is Maximal Marginal Relevance (MMR).[17] This technique uses a precalculated relevance vector and redundancy matrix to balance the diversity of documents.

First, the similarity between the retrieved document and query embeddings is calculated. This results in a *relevance vector* that has a value per document to indicate how similar/relevant the given document is to the query (Figure 4-33).

17 Carbonell, Jaime and Jade Goldstein. 1998. "The Use of MMR, Diversity-Based Reranking for Reordering Documents and Producing Summaries," *Proceedings of the 21st Annual International ACM SIGIR Conference on Research and Development in Information Retrieval.*

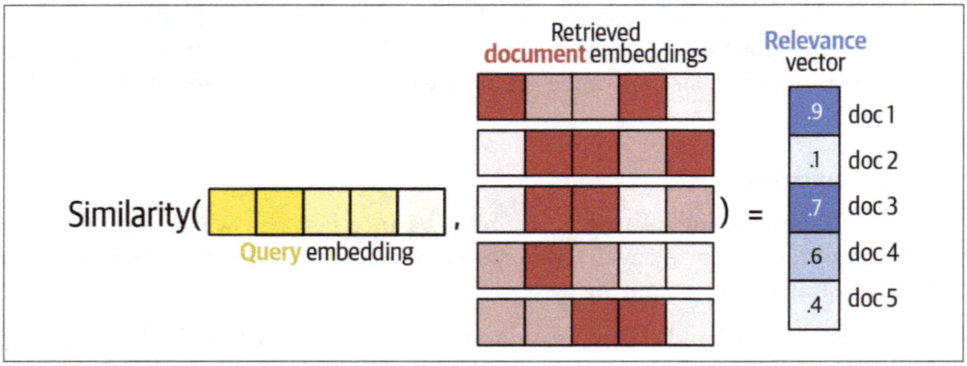

Figure 4-33. A relevance vector is created by calculating the similarity between the query embedding and the retrieved document embeddings

Second, the similarity between the retrieved documents is likewise calculated to construct a similarity matrix called the *redundancy matrix*. This matrix is used to potentially discard documents that are too similar to the ones we already chose (Figure 4-34).

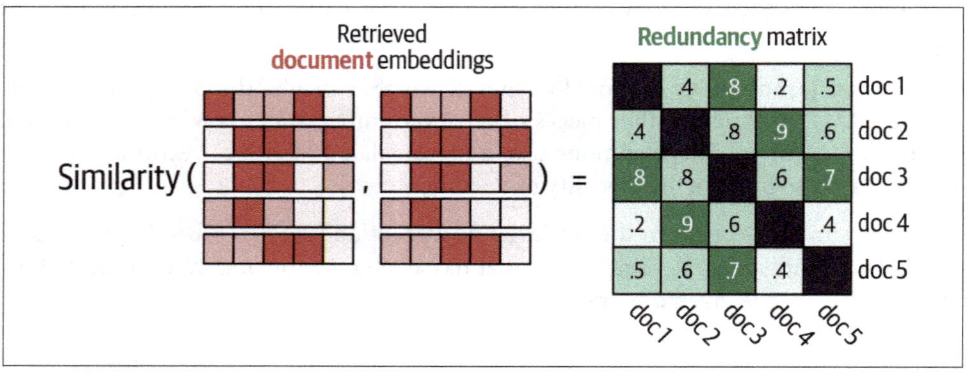

Figure 4-34. The redundancy matrix is created by calculating the similarity between all combinations of retrieved document embeddings

Then, the relevance vector and redundancy matrix are used iteratively to decide which retrieved documents are similar enough to a given query but dissimilar to all other retrieved documents. An important component is the lambda (λ) parameter, which we can tweak to decide how diverse the output should be (a higher score indicates higher diversity). We now have all components of the main formula of MMR, as shown in Figure 4-35.

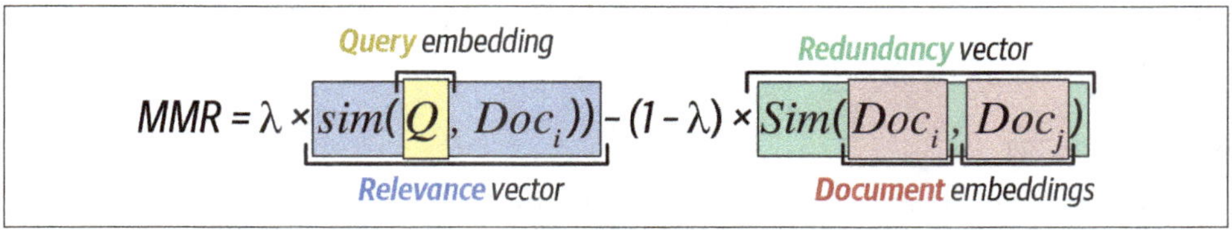

Figure 4-35. The formula of Maximal Marginal Relevance

Let's break down each of those components. Since we haven't chosen any documents, we start by selecting the one with the highest score in the relevance vector, namely document 1 (or *i* in this example). Then, we take the relevance vector and multiply it by λ to decide the importance of similarity over diversity. From the resulting scores (one for each document other than document 1), we subtract (1 – λ) times the redundancy vector. This vector contains the highest scores in the redundancy matrix that relate to the documents we already chose (document 1). As demonstrated in Figure 4-36, document 3 is added as the next most diverse and relevant document.

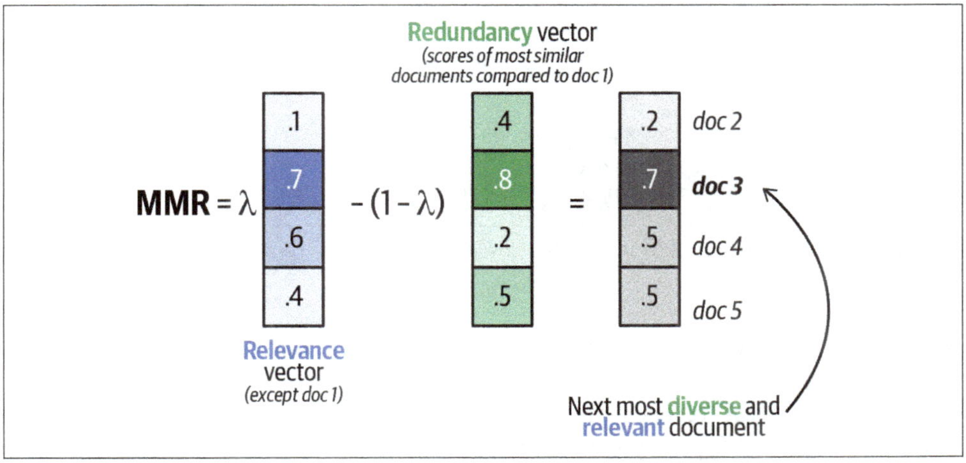

Figure 4-36. Maximal Marginal Relevance (MMR) uses redundancy vectors to calculate the next most diverse and relevant document to retrieve

We continue this process, but instead of comparing to document 1 only, the redundancy vector contains the highest similarity scores that relate to either document 1 or 3, whichever is highest. This process is only repeated for the next document, since we wanted to bring down our original set of five documents to three in total.

Like reranking, MMR is merely an example of a technique that can be used to compress the output. We're not limited to using LLMs to directly compress the retrieved documents; we can instead use techniques like MMR to simply ignore certain documents because they're too similar to each other. Likewise, deduplication techniques can be used to remove contexts that are essentially duplicates of one another.

Context ordering

The order of the context is vital to the performance of your agent. Early research into the position of important information in prompts found that LLMs have a tendency to pay more attention to the beginning and end of a prompt.[18] As a result, they often end up losing information in the middle, which is termed the "lost-in-the-middle" phenomenon. Figure 4-37 nicely illustrates this concept.

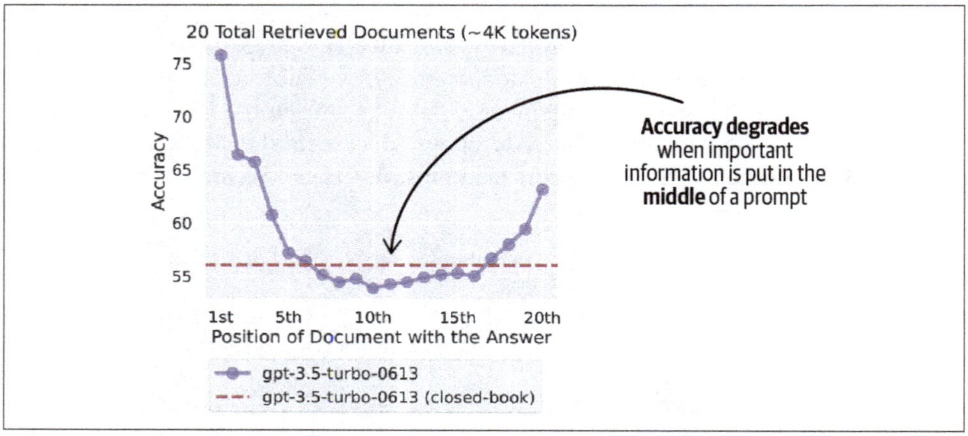

Figure 4-37. An annotated figure of the "lost-in-the-middle" phenomenon from "Lost in the Middle"

This tendency to focus on the beginning and end of prompts is similar to human behavior. The serial-position effect states that people generally recall the first (primacy effect) and last (recency effect) items in a series best, whereas the middle items are recalled worst.[19] Typically, context engineering helps prevent this problem because it appears with long contexts rather than small ones. It's interesting to see how much of LLMs' behavior follows similar human tendencies.

Context As the Specification

Arguably, one of the most important things about context engineering is that it requires a shift in mindset. The context that is given to the agent can be seen as a tool for communication—not just for the agent, but to the people that you work

18 Liu, Nelson F. et al. 2023. "Lost in the Middle: How Language Models Use Long Contexts," *arXiv*, 2307.03172.

19 Murdock, Bennet B. Jr. 1962. "The Serial Position Effect of Free Recall," *Journal of Experimental Psychology*, 64(5):482.

with. More specifically, the context that you give to the agent, including the query, *PLAN.md*, *REQUIREMENTS.md*, codebase, etc., all serve as a tool to communicate your intention. For example, when you allow a coding agent to fully create a PR on its own, it does not suffice to go through the code itself to check whether everything is there. The initial query, *PLAN.md*, etc., all serve as the initial specification of the PR and should be tracked as well.

As such, we can view the context of the agent as the specification of your feature. As agents are becoming more autonomous, it's important to track the intention of their behavior through the context that is given. Where we would view prompt engineering as user-facing, context engineering is a much more developer-oriented tool and requires careful communication of why the agent is executing certain tasks. The answer to the "why" starts with the user's intention.

Think about it like this: how strange it is that we tend to throw away the input to our function (the LLM) and keep track only of the output! Not only for reproducibility, but also for communication, it allows you to understand why the agent has chosen certain tools, executions, and outputs. Moreover, this transparency of intention also serves as a great tool for debugging your agent.

Context, as the specification, brings about significant potential for domain-specific industries. The context that you give an agent changes drastically between use cases and applications. Health care requires a completely different context than law, for instance. As such, there is not a single framework for context engineering and instead it requires developers to consider their domain-specific knowledge sources, like patient data in health care and research papers in academia.

Summary

In this chapter, we explored various methods for giving LLMs and agents memory. We first covered various techniques for short-term memory, including the conversation history and methods for compressing it and keeping it manageable. Short-term memory is an important, but often underestimated component of enabling memory in intelligent systems.

Then, we explored long-term memory, including methods for RAG (MemoryBank) and agentic RAG (A-MEM and Search-o1). These methods are often inspired by human memory systems and may include techniques for degrading memory or deciding what's meant to be important.

Finally, we explored context engineering as the next frontier in memory. Where we used to engineer our prompts ourselves, the entire context window now requires careful consideration. We covered why this context is important for agents and various methods for optimizing it.

The context, being much more than just the user's prompt, contains all previously discussed forms of memory and potentially even more, like tools. In Chapter 5, we'll explore how tools can further enhance the capabilities of LLMs as an important component of agents. Moreover, we'll cover how these tools can be called and the best practices for doing so. In Chapter 6, we cover planning and reflection capabilities of agents, where memory plays an important role.

CHAPTER 5

Tool Usage, Learning, and Protocols

The tool module is such an interesting module for augmenting your LLM and generating autonomous behavior in agents. By themselves, regular LLMs are nothing more than functions that take in some text and output some text. Although that creates interesting chatbots, they cannot yet interact with their environment. Tools, in the form of functions and APIs, allow LLMs to step into the real world and interact with any system exposed to the LLM, ranging from codebases and internal tools to online databases and even home assistants.

A key trait that defines an agent is its ability to autonomously search for, select, and utilize tools, allowing it to interact with and influence its environment. With enough capabilities, agents can even create their own set of tools to use. Generally, tools allow an LLM to take action and interact with the external environment or extract data and use external applications (see Figure 5-1). The benefit of tools is not contained to interaction with the environment. Tools are typically used to access external knowledge or memories, as we discussed in Chapter 4. We can even use tools to access specialized LLMs that have capabilities that extend beyond what the agent is capable of, such as multi-modal LLMs or LLMs specialized for certain tasks (like coding).

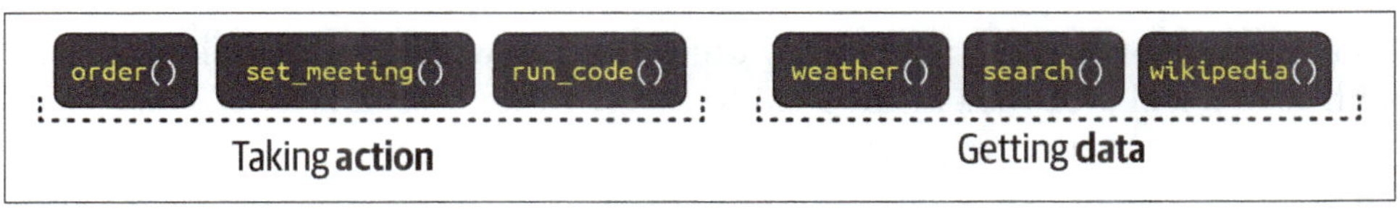

Figure 5-1. Tools can be categorized as either taking an action or retrieving information

However, regular LLMs cannot search the web, use a calculator, or schedule appointments. They can only communicate the intention of doing so, without being able to act upon it. Without tools, agents can only *think and plan* autonomously but not *act* autonomously.

The degree of autonomy also decides how tools are used. As shown in Figure 5-2, if there is no autonomy but there is a fixed flow, then tools can be used in a predefined order. For instance, a research agent might always call tools like arXiv and Google to extract results, which are subsequently summarized.

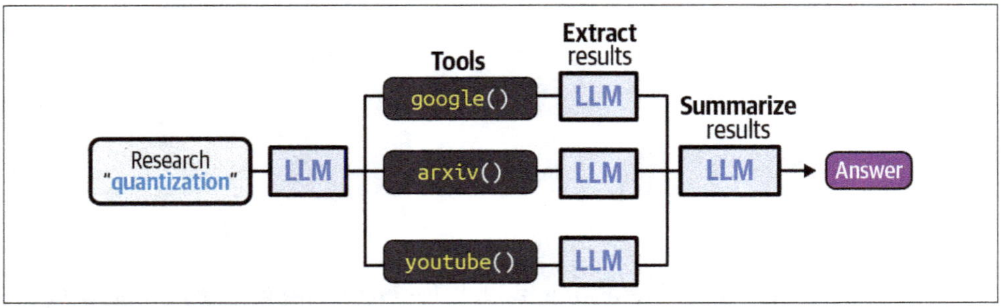

Figure 5-2. An example of a fixed flow in tool usage

In contrast, systems with larger degrees of autonomy allow agents to choose which tool to use and when. Illustrated in Figure 5-3, they are still sequences of LLM calls but with autonomous selection of tools decided by the agent.

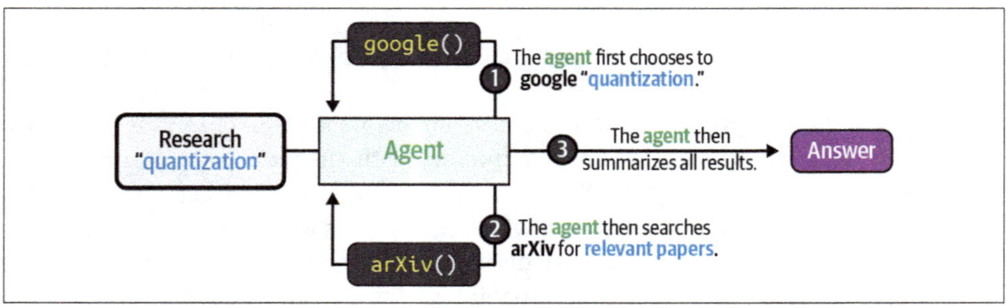

Figure 5-3. An agent dynamically using tools—it first searches using the Google tool, then the arXiv tool, then it generates an answer informed by the results of both searches

There's a lot more to tools than merely using them. How are they created? How is the output of a tool processed by the LLM or agent? How are tools selected? How many tools can an LLM effectively handle?

Throughout this chapter, we'll not only explore several types of tools but also how LLMs and agents learn to use them and even how these tools can be standardized across different agentic systems. As shown in Figure 5-4, this allows interaction with the environment. It makes the next chapter, about planning out actions to take, more than a theoretical exercise. After all, how could an LLM act autonomously without tools?

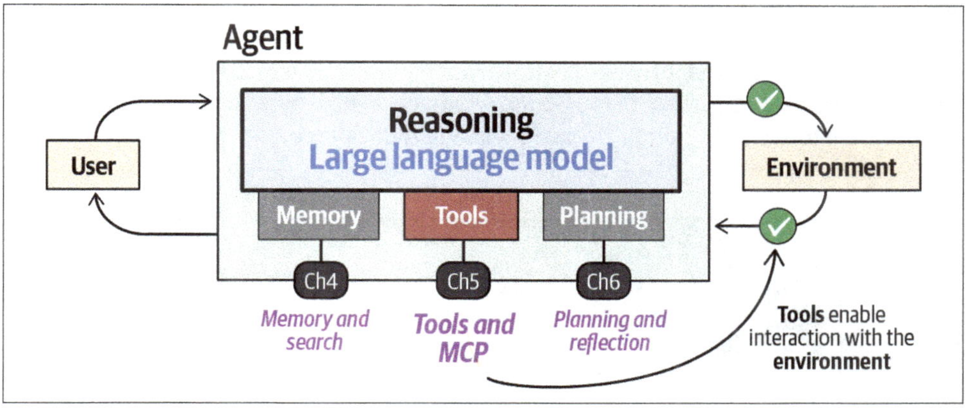

Figure 5-4. A collection of tools is the main component allowing for interaction with the environment

Tool Usage

Tool usage consists of more steps than you might expect. It does not start with an LLM using a tool, but by actually creating and defining the tools, planning which tool to use instead, and eventually calling them. The steps in tool usage can be seen from many different perspectives, such as the comparison of tools to the human action system inspired by the human brain or as action modules that revolve around the agent's decisions.[1,2,3] We, however, explore the following set of steps as it focuses on concrete implementations and executions of tools:

- Tool creation
- Tool definition
- Tool selection
- Tool calling
- Output processing

1 Liu, Bang et al. 2025. "Advances and Challenges in Foundation Agents: From Brain-Inspired Intelligence to Evolutionary, Collaborative, and Safe Systems," *arXiv,* 2504.01990.

2 Wang, Lei et al. 2024. "A Survey on Large Language Model Based Autonomous Agents," *Frontiers of Computer Science,* 18: 186345.

3 Wang, Zhiruo et al. 2024. "What Are Tools Anyway? A Survey from the Language Model Perspective," *arXiv,* 2403.15452.

Although agents might seem like they can do everything themselves (which they can attempt to a certain degree), they require help from the user or developer to use the tools. Specifically, an LLM does not actually call the tool but merely shows the intention of doing so. The actual tool call is typically executed by an external (automated) process. This high-level process is shown in Figure 5-5, which is an adaptation of OpenAI's tool calling flow (*https://oreil.ly/aakSB*), where we additionally focus on creating the tool and highlight the steps a single tool call takes.

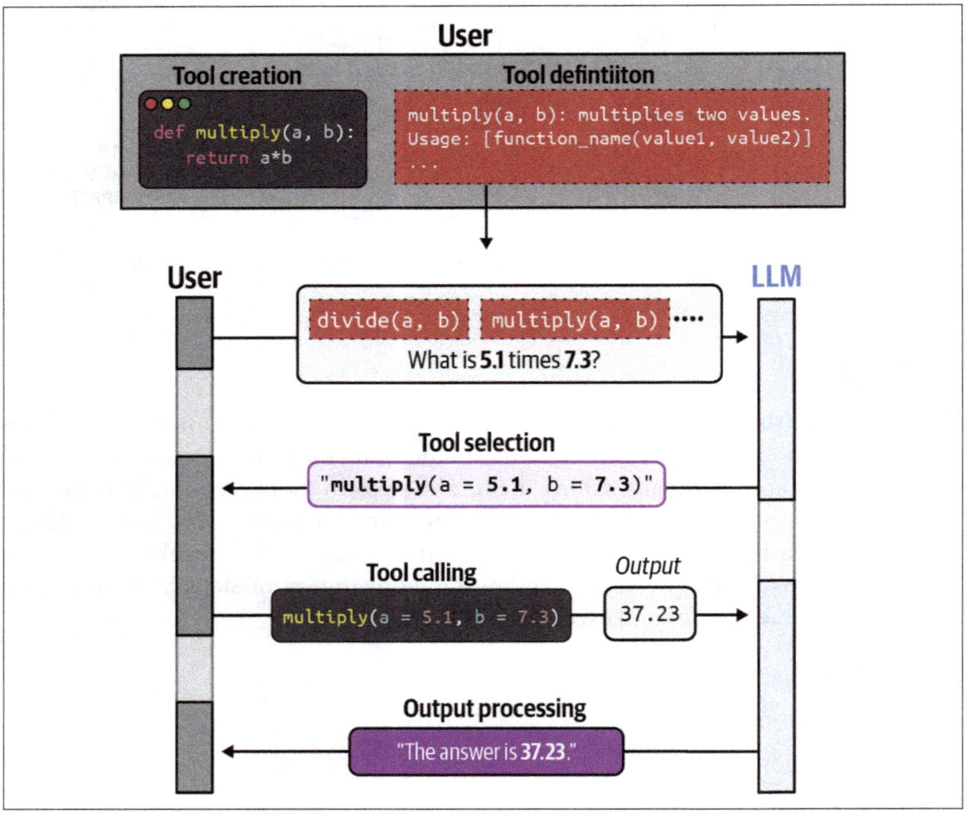

Figure 5-5. An example of tool creation, definition, selection, tool calling, and output processing in the interaction between a user and the LLM

Note that each step may have various forms and implementations, many of which we will cover later. For now, let's explore the most common way tool usage happens in these steps and explore them in more detail.

Tool Creation

Although tools can come in various forms, they are typically functions that can be accessed through either an API or some internal code. This can be as complex or minimal as is required for your application. LLMs, for instance, are not known for their mathematical capabilities. Let's create a simple function for multiplying two values that the LLM can use:

```
def multiply(a: str, b: str) -> float:
    return float(a) * float(b)
```

This function multiplies two values, taking them as strings and converting them to floats. The reason for this is that LLMs return only text, which will have to be converted. As such, these tools should be heavily documented and communicated well to the LLM. In some cases, the docstrings are passed automatically, so it is important to describe them well. A clear benefit is that it motivates users to focus more on writing great documentation, which is often not a priority when developing code. Although this is a rather simplified example, imagine codebases with functions that span hundreds of lines of code. Documentation is becoming increasingly important, as it allows the agent to understand which edge cases exist or implementation details that cannot be easily determined by examining the code.

This tool can be accessed by directly calling `multiply(a, b)`, which is something the LLM cannot do since it only outputs strings, but it can be done by an automated system. Note that external API calls may also call tools. Either way, a tool is generally considered to be some form of function that can be called in various ways. In our example, the most straightforward method would be to save it in a dictionary so that we can access the function by a string. In this case, our *database* is the `registry` variable:

```
registry = {
  "multiply": multiply
}
```

Creating tools can be a straightforward process, but the LLM should be taken into account when designing them. It's a similar process to designing code for people to use, where you may ask yourself: does the user understand what the tool does? Is it clear what is being returned? Are the variable names descriptive? Is there documentation? This is especially important for LLMs because they often need to be explicitly told what exists, what doesn't, and what the tools are capable of.

Let's start by creating the first iteration of the `Tools` class that will give your `Tiny Agent` access to tools:

```
from typing import Callable

class Tools:
    """Tool registry for the Agent."""
```

```
    def __init__(self, requires_approval: list[str] = []):
        """Initialize and select tools that require approval before execution.
        """
        self.registry = {}
        self.requires_approval = requires_approval

    def add_tool(self, name: str, func: Callable, description: str = "") -> None:
        """Register a tool that the Agent can use.

        Arguments:
            name: The name of the tool.
            func: The function implementing the tool.
            description: A description of the tool.
        """
        self.registry[name] = {"function": func, "description": description}

    @property
    def schemas(self) -> None:
        """Used only for native tool-calling."""
        return None
```

The class has two functions:

`add_tool`
: Adds a tool to the `registry` variable as an entry to the dictionary

`schemas`
: Schemas to be used for native tool calling (we'll cover this later in the chapter)

Note that you can also select which tools require approval from the user before they can be run. We cover this behavior more extensively in Chapter 10, where we create a coding agent.

We can then register the tool like so:

```
# Register tool
tools = Tools()
tools.add_tool(
    name="multiply",
    func=multiply,
    description="Multiplies two numbers: multiply(a: str, b: str)"
)
```

Tool Definition

After creating the tool, we need to inform the LLM what the tool does; this is called *tool definition*. Without communicating to the LLM which tools exist, what they do, how they are used, and in which context they should be used, the LLM isn't able to properly use them.

There are several methods by which we can communicate this to the LLM:

Learning
: (Specific) tool definition and usage are learned during training.

Prompting
: The tool definition is shared with the LLM through structured prompts.

How to use (specific) tools and when they are needed is often learned during the fine-tuning state of an LLM, where the model learns how to follow instructions and use tools. This learning stage can be split up into two aspects: we either tune the model to *learn* about *specific* tools or how to use tools *in general*. Learning about specific tools can be costly and limit how many tools you can add to the model. Instead, recent models (such as Qwen3 and DeepSeek-V3.2)[4,5] typically focus on their improved instruction-following capabilities and general tool use. Instead of learning about specific tools, they learn to recognize definitions of tools in their prompts and dynamically use them.

Using natural language

As (reasoning) LLMs are becoming easier to steer and dynamically learn to use tools, we can share the tool definitions through prompts. When you have a small set of tools the LLM should use, you can share that through the system prompt:

```
system_prompt = """
...

# Tool Definition
You can use the following tools:

- multiply(a, b): multiplies two numbers
- divide(a, b): divides a by b

# Tool Usage
When you need to use them, write: [function_name(value1, value2)]
...
"""
```

Note that the definition here isn't following a standardized procedure. Frankly, this is something we made up on the spot to show you that an LLM can call a tool any way you decide. Assuming the model is capable enough of following those instructions, if it uses `TOOL(value1, value2)` or perhaps structures like `TOOL, value1, value2` it does not matter. The only thing you need is a small piece of code that recognizes

4 Yang, An et al. 2025. "Qwen3 Technical Report," *arXiv*, 2505.09388.

5 Liu, Aixin et al. 2025. "DeepSeek-V3.2: Pushing the Frontier of Open Large Language Models," *arXiv*, 2512.02556.

when a tool is being called. This is called a validator or parser and requires the LLM to closely follow the usage instructions. It can therefore be quite error-prone because small errors in following the instructions might result in incomplete calls to the tools. We'll cover how the LLM actually calls a tool a bit later in this chapter.

Let's start by extending the `Tools` class so it can create this system prompt:

```
class Tools(Tools):
    """Tool registry for the Agent."""

    @property
    def descriptions(self) -> str:
        """Get descriptions of all registered tools."""
        return "\n".join(
            f"`{tool}`: {self.registry[tool]['description']}"
            for tool in self.registry
        )

    @property
    def prompt(self) -> str:
        return f"""
# Tools

If needed, you can only use the following tools to assist you
in completing tasks:

{self.descriptions}

To use a tool, respond with JSON:
{{"tool": "name", "kwargs": {{"param": "value"}}}}
"""
```

The updated `Tools` class now has two additional functions:

`description`
: A description of all registered tools

`prompt`
: The instructions that will be sent to the LLM on how to call the tools

Let's reregister the tools with the updated class and inspect the prompt:

```
# Register tool
tools = Tools()
tools.add_tool(
    name="multiply",
    func=multiply,
    description="Multiplies two numbers: multiply(a: str, b: str)"
)

# Show prompt
print(tools.prompt)
```

Which gives us:

```
"""
# Tools

If needed, you can only use the following tools to assist you
in completing tasks:

`multiply`: Multiplies two numbers: multiply(a: str, b: str)
`get_weather`: Gets weather: get_weather(location: str)

To use a tool, respond with JSON: {"tool": "name", "kwargs": {"param": "value"}}
"""
```

This is the system prompt that the model will always have access to.

Using structured function calling

Another method of sharing the definition of the tools with the LLM is through structured *function calling*. Instead of messing around with the prompts ourselves and optimizing how we describe and format each tool, we can define each tool in structured schemas instead. These are typically JSON Schema objects that include the function's name, description, and its parameters (types, required fields, ranges, etc.). An example of such a schema for our multiply tool is the following:

```
tool_schema = {
  "type": "function",
  "function": {
    "name": "multiply",
    "description": "Multiply two numbers",
    "parameters": {
      "type": "object",
      "properties": {
        "a": {
          "type": "number",
          "description": "First number"
        },
        "b": {
          "type": "number",
          "description": "Second number"
        }
      },
      "required": [
        "a",
        "b"
      ]
    }
  }
}
```

These schemas are often passed as a separate parameter when using external APIs. OpenAI, for instance, uses the `tools` parameter where you can send over the JSON schemas of your tools (*https://oreil.ly/aakSB*). That allows the LLM or even the agent to treat it as special metadata and process it beforehand if necessary. In practice, however, these schemas are typically processed as if they were "regular" prompts and put into, for example, the system prompt.

Although we are using structured JSON schemas for communication, the LLM still has to interpret how to use the tool and when, which makes tool usage a difficult task. Therefore, the more descriptive and clear the schema, the more likely the LLM will make the right tool call decisions.

At this point, the user can finally ask their question. Since they have access to the multiply function, let's keep the query simple: "What is 5.1 times 7.3?" To illustrate how this is going to be processed, we make use of the `messages` structure that we explored in Chapter 4. This is visualized in Figure 5-6, where the system prompt contains the definition of our tool.

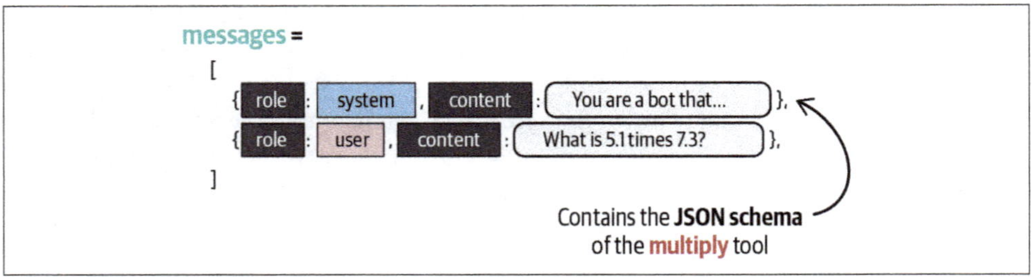

Figure 5-6. The system prompt may contain the full JSON schema for the LLM to use

Regardless of whether you use a JSON schema or describe the tool, there are several best practices for defining functions to take into account:

Document your tool
: Include extensive descriptions to allow your agent to have a better understanding of what the tool is capable of.

Minimize the number of tools
: Although having many tools expands the capabilities of your agent, it will become much more difficult to select and use the appropriate tool. Although there is no gold standard, aim to minimize the number of tools rather than maximize them. Using fewer than 10 tools is a good start. The next section, tool selection, becomes more important as the number of tools grows.

Minimize the scope of a tool
: Complex tools with many parameters are difficult to use, even for individuals, let alone an agent. Having a function with dozens of parameters can be difficult to use, especially for smaller models.

Tool Selection

Now that the tools are created and defined, we can start the process of calling the tool. The LLM first needs to select the right tool for a given query, which can be a difficult task. Especially with potentially dozens of complex tools available, the LLM not only needs to select the most appropriate one (if one at all) but also use it correctly. Although we can share an extensive JSON schema for each tool, the LLM needs to be capable enough to actually follow it through. This is where reasoning LLMs shine. They can spend any number of tokens "thinking" about which tools to use and how to properly use them as long as they fit within the context window and leave enough for generating the answer. Illustrated in Figure 5-7 is the reasoning process of LLMs to decide which tool to use and how.

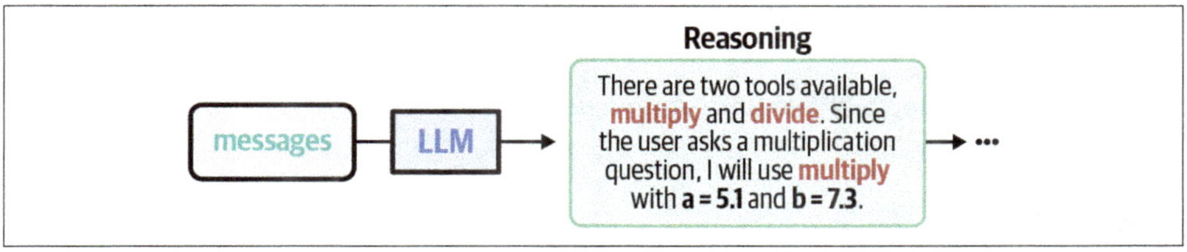

Figure 5-7. The reasoning process of an LLM deciding which tool to use

Discovering the tools that exist or might be relevant becomes more important when the number of tools increases. As discussed in Chapter 4, even when you have a large context window, filling it up to the brim with tool JSON schemas is bound to decrease the LLM's performance. As with context engineering, the process of discovering tools might be helped with methodologies like RAG, where you store all tool schemas in a separate database for the LLM to discover. Figure 5-8 illustrates this idea of using a vector database to discover which tools are most relevant to a user's query.

Note that the planning capabilities of LLMs are vital to having a good selection. For simple queries, such as "What is 1 + 1?," the selection of tools is not going to be a challenge. However, when planning a vacation with a budget, a multi-step process is going to be needed where the agent first needs to plan out its behavior. This planning (and reflection) behavior is going to be discussed in Chapter 6 in more detail.

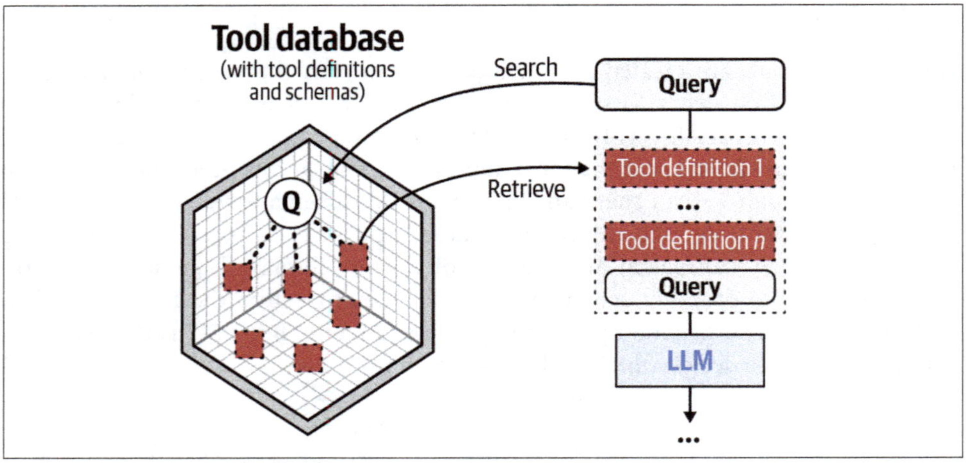

Figure 5-8. An example of Retrieval-Augmented Generation (RAG) for searching and retrieving tool definitions

Tool Calling

Next, when the LLM ends its thinking process, it can start creating the tool call. It will output a string, and if the LLM is capable enough, correctly format the tool call with the given arguments. This is illustrated in Figure 5-9 with the system prompt that we defined in the section "Tool Definition" on page 180.

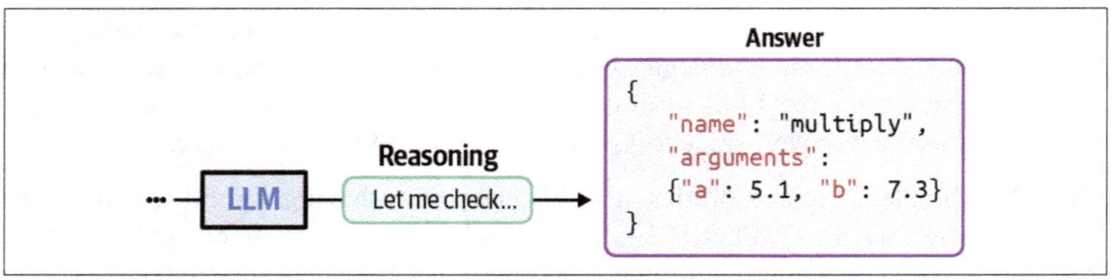

Figure 5-9. After reasoning, the answer may contain the tool call

However, this answer is merely a string and will not execute the tool. In fact, you can view this output as merely the intention of the LLM to call a tool. Without any help from the user or additional software, nothing will happen. We will have to extend the `Tools` class further with functions that extract and parse the JSON call:

```
import json
from typing import Any
from illustrated_agents.chapters.ch2 import Response


class Tools(Tools):
```

```python
    """Tool registry for the Agent."""

    def parse(self, response: Response) -> Response:
        """Parse a JSON tool call from text."""
        text = response.content

        if '"tool":' in text or '"tool:"' in text:
            start, end = text.find("{"), text.rfind("}") + 1
            tool_call = json.loads(text[start:end])

            # Add the parsed tool call to the response
            return Response(
                content=response.content,
                reasoning=response.reasoning,
                tool_call=tool_call,
            )

        return response

    def execute(self, response: Response) -> Any:
        """Run a registered tool.

        Arguments:
            tool_call: A parsed tool call dict with "tool" and "kwargs" keys.
        """
        tool_call = response.tool_call
        name, kwargs = tool_call["tool"], tool_call.get("kwargs", {})

        # Human-in-the-loop: ask before running dangerous tools
        if name in self.registry and name in self.requires_approval:
            response = input(f"Allow {name}? [y/N] ").strip().lower()
            if response not in ("y", "yes"):
                return f"Tool '{name}' was denied by the user."

        # Handle registered tools
        if name in self.registry:
            tool_func = self.registry[name]["function"]
            return tool_func(**kwargs)

        return f"Tool '{name}' not found."
```

The updated `Tools` class now has two additional functions:

`parse`
: Parses the string into JSON.

`execute`
: Executes the tool call. Note that we also add a human-in-the-loop that allows you to approve certain tools before execution. We cover the human-in-the-loop more extensively in Chapter 10 where we create a coding agent.

We reinitialize the `Tools` class and reregister the tool. Then, let's demonstrate with an example of how the tool would be executed:

```
tools = Tools()
tools.add_tool(
    "multiply", multiply, "Multiplies two numbers: multiply(a: str, b: str)"
)

# Fake LLM response
response = Response(
    content='{"tool": "multiply", "kwargs": {"a": "3.1", "b": "6.5"} }'
)

# Parse into a tool call
response = tools.parse(response)

# Execute the tool
tools.execute(response)
```

Which gives:

```
20.150000000000002
```

Great! The **`Response`** object contains the content of the model and parses that into a tool call. After parsing, the JSON can be used to actually call the tool.

> Although regular expressions can be used to extract our tool, they will not work if the tool call has a very slightly different structure or if the JSON structure is more complex. Instead, more robust techniques might be needed to extract the arguments, such as jsonschema (*https://oreil.ly/l_tSO*), which is a Python package for validating JSON schemas.
>
> Another common technique is to use Pydantic (*https://oreil.ly/3IwZW*), a Python package for data validation. It can be used to create data classes where each piece of data can be validated. It allows you to create JSON schemas of your tools to feed to the LLM. Likewise, the output of the LLM can be converted to JSON and validated through Pydantic.

Tool Output Processing

We still need to do something with the output of the tool call. In our example, the LLM ends with a tool call, which we process and call ourselves. To feed the output back into the LLM, we can use the `messages` structure that we explored in Chapter 4.

Specifically, we can add messages with two roles:

`assistant`
: The assistant calls the multiply tool.

`tool`
: The output of the tool is returned.

By updating the messages to include this additional information, we're essentially informing the LLM that these steps were taken. Calling the tool was done outside of the LLM's view, and it therefore has no knowledge of what actually happened. As such, we pretend as if the LLM executed the tool, while that was actually done by the user or an automated system. These updated messages are illustrated in Figure 5-10.

The specific `tool` role is used only by LLMs that were trained specifically to perform native tool calling (more on that in the section "Tool Learning" on page 195). For LLMs that were not trained with specific tool-calling tokens, we have to approach it a bit differently.

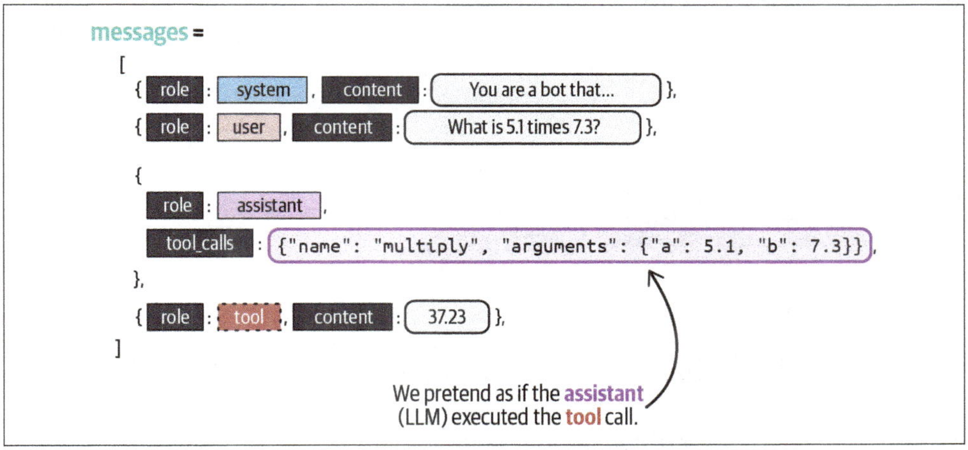

Figure 5-10. An example of the JSON structure used to call tools

Instead of using the `tool` role, we can use the `user` role and act as if we are explicitly telling the LLM what the output of the tool call was. To do so, let's update the `Tools` class to add this behavior:

```
class Tools(Tools):
    """Tool registry for the Agent."""

    def observation(self, result: str) -> tuple[str, str]:
        """Return the observation as a user."""
        return "user", f"OBSERVATION: {result}"

    def is_done(self, response: Response) -> bool:
        """The `TinyAgent`'s stopping mechanism."""
        if not response.tool_call:
            return True
        if response.tool_call["tool"] == "final_answer":
            response.content = response.tool_call.get("kwargs", "")
```

```python
            return True
        return False
```

The updated `Tools` class now has two additional functions:

`observation`
: Returns the output of the tool call

`is_done`
: Stops your `TinyAgent` if there is no tool call or it calls the `final_answer` tool. In Chapter 6, we'll explore the `final_answer` tool in more depth when the agent has to decide how to give back a final answer.

Of note is the observation function, which returns the role (`user`) and the output of the tool call as an OBSERVATION tag. This OBSERVATION tells the model that the user has observed the tool call and gives back its result. The idea is that a conversation history then looks a bit as shown in Figure 5-11.

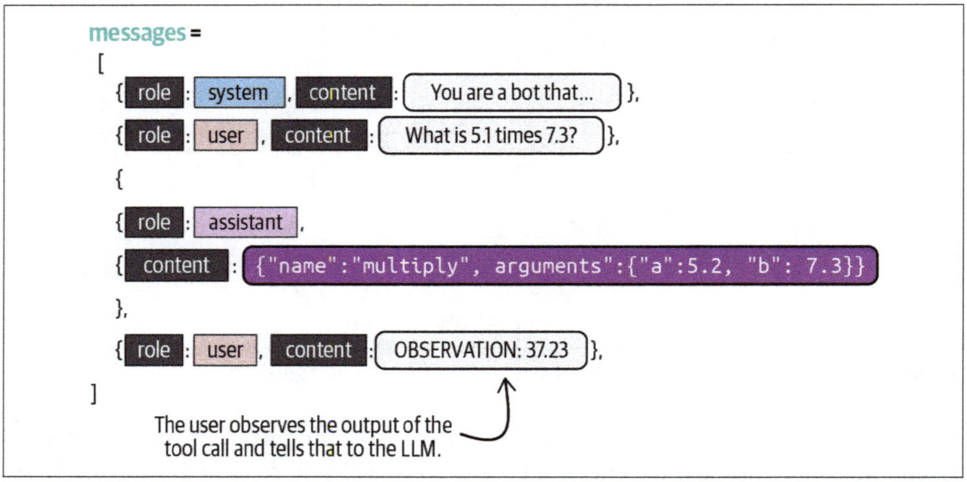

Figure 5-11. An example of how the `user` role can be used to relay the output of the tool call back to the LLM

We then feed these messages back into the LLM to create our final answer. Although the tool has given us the appropriate output, the LLM might want to combine/summarize answers or present them in a nicer way or according to pre-decided instructions. This process, along with the updated output, is presented in Figure 5-12.

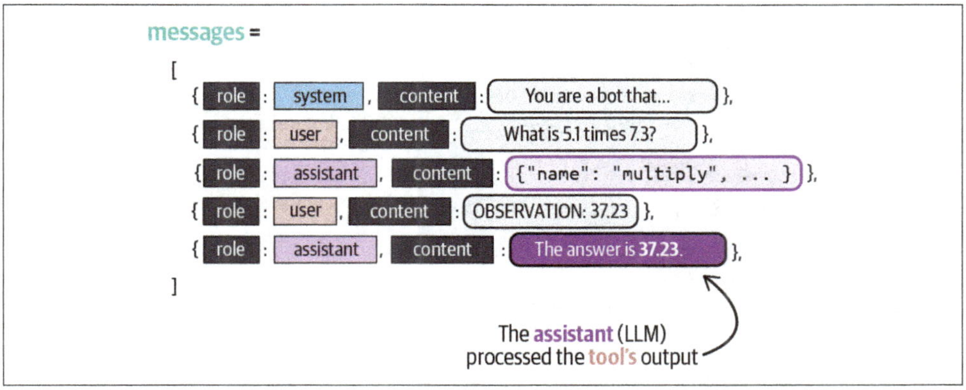

Figure 5-12. An example of how the LLM processes the tool's output through the conversation history

TinyAgent with Tools

Now that we have all the components for calling tools, it's finally time to update your `TinyAgent` to make use of them. We highlighted the code that was added to your `TinyAgent`:

```
from illustrated_agents.chapters.ch2 import LLM, Trajectory
from illustrated_agents.chapters.ch4 import Memory


class TinyAgent:
    """A minimal, modular, and educational agent framework."""

    def __init__(self, llm: LLM, memory: Memory, tools: Tools):
        self.llm = llm
        self.memory = memory
        self.tools = tools
        self.planner = None  # Chapter 6: Add Planning

        self.trajectory = Trajectory()

        # Build system prompt with all components
        system_prompt = "You are a helpful assistant.\n\n"
        system_prompt += self.tools.prompt
        self.memory.add("system", system_prompt)

    def run(self, task: str) -> str:
        """Run the agent on a task."""
        self.memory.add("user", task)
        self.trajectory.initialize(task)

        return self._step()
```

```
    def _step(self) -> str:
        """Perform a single step."""
        # THOUGHT: Generate response and add to memory
        response = self.llm.generate(
            self.memory.get_messages(), tools=self.tools.schemas
        )
        self.memory.add(
            "assistant", response.content, tool_call=response.tool_call
        )

        # Tool parsing
        response = self.tools.parse(response)

        # ANSWER: Stopping mechanism
        if self.tools.is_done(response):
            self.trajectory.add(response)
            return response.content

        return self._execute_action(response)

    def _execute_action(self, response: Response) -> str:
        """Execute a tool action."""

        # ACTION: execute tools
        result = self.tools.execute(response)

        # OBSERVATION: add tool results to memory and display
        role, observation = self.tools.observation(result)
        self.memory.add(role, observation)
        self.trajectory.add(response, observation)

        return observation
```

Out of all the changes to your `TinyAgent`, this chapter and the next include the largest set of them throughout the book. So, let's go through them one by one!

The system prompt

In the `__init__` of your `TinyAgent`, we now add a system prompt. As we covered in the section "Tool Definition" on page 180, this serves as a nice way for the agent to keep track of what tools it has available. With `self.tools.prompt`, we add the tools' definitions to the system prompt as we did previously. As you will see in upcoming chapters (e.g., Chapter 6), the system prompt is going to be used for tracking more information than just tools.

> Note that the `SummarizationMemory` would actually not work well with `Tools` since it continuously overrides the system prompt to track the summarized conversation history. `Tools` requires keeping the tool definition in the system prompt; this would essentially remove any information the LLM has about tools!
>
> A solution would be to always update a section of the system prompt rather than replacing it entirely. Try it out yourself and see if you can update the `SummarizationMemory` so that it will work nicely with `Tools`.

A single step

A single step (`_step`) consists of the following components:

Generate a response
: The LLM generates a response with `self.llm.generate`. You can call this the THOUGHT of the LLM, as it contains what it thinks about the current situation and how it would like to act.

Tool parsing
: If there is a tool call, it is parsed with `self.tools.parse`. As we covered in the section "Tool Calling" on page 186, this converts the string to a structured JSON output.

Tool execution
: If there is a parsed tool call, it is executed with `_execute_action` (more on that coming up).

Stopping mechanism
: If there is no tool call, we stop execution entirely. This is not behavior we need at this moment since your `TinyAgent` does not yet run autonomously. However, it will become important in the next chapter, where the agent can run continuously.

Executing an action

Executing an action (`_execute_action`) consists of two steps:

Execute tool call
: Executing the JSON tool call with `self.tools.execute(response)`, which performs the tool call as we covered in the section "Tool Calling" on page 186.

Track the result
: Track the output of the tool call. The LLM has to know what the output is in order to decide what to do next. As we covered in the section "Tool Output Processing" on page 188, we do this by adding the output as the `user` role and describing it with the prefix OBSERVATION.

Finally, we track the state of the agent with the `Trajectory` module and the conversation history with the `Memory` module.

> You might have noticed capitalized words scattered throughout this chapter's code: THOUGHT, OBSERVATION, ACTION, and ANSWER. These are steps relating to the Reason and Act (ReAct) framework that we will use in Chapter 6 to create autonomous behavior.[6] As you might have guessed, these mean the following:
>
> *THOUGHT*
> The reasoning of the LLM on what to do next.
>
> *ACTION*
> The action or tool calls of the LLM are structured as JSON.
>
> *OBSERVATION*
> The output of the ACTION the LLM took.
>
> *ANSWER*
> The LLM's final answer after running for one or more steps.

Running your TinyAgent with tool-calling capabilities

Now that you have a `TinyAgent` with tools, we can initialize it. Here, we choose a no-frills memory and simply track the entire conversation history:

```
from illustrated_agents.chapters.ch2 import LLM

# Gemma 3 12B (no native thinking or tool calling)
llm = LLM(model="gemma3:12b")

# Register tool
tools = Tools()
tools.add_tool(
    name="multiply",
    func=multiply,
    description="Multiplies two numbers: multiply(a: str, b: str)"
)

# Memory
memory = Memory()

# Initialize Agent
agent = TinyAgent(llm=llm, memory=memory, tools=tools)
```

Your `TinyAgent` now has access to an LLM, memory, and tools!

6 Yao, Shunyu et al. 2022. "ReAct: Synergizing Reasoning and Acting in Language Models," *arXiv*, 2210.03629.

Let's run a simple query to see if it can properly choose, parse, and execute its tool:

```
# A query that requires the use of a tool
agent.run("What is 5.1 times 7.3?")
```

This gives us:

```
'OBSERVATION: 37.23'
```

This is the correct answer, but did the model do that calculation by itself, or did it use a tool? To find out, let's inspect the full conversation history:

```
print(agent.memory.get_messages())
```

This gives us:

```
[
  {
    'role': 'system',
    'content': 'You are a helpful assistant.\n\n\n# Tools\n\n
    If needed, you can only use the following },
  {
    'role': 'user',
    'content': 'What is 5.1 times 7.3?'},
  {
    'role': 'assistant',
    'content': '{"tool": "multiply", "kwargs": {"a": "5.1", "b": "7.3"}}\n'},
  {
    'role': 'user',
    'content': 'OBSERVATION: 37.23'}
]
```

It used the tool! Note that the `assistant` role returned a string with a JSON-like structured output. Moreover, the `user` role was added with an observation of this output.

With the many steps an LLM has to correctly follow to call the appropriate tool, it requires the LLM to be an effective orchestrator, which is dependent upon the model's reasoning capabilities and overall reliability (as explored in Chapter 3).

A more stable approach tends to be to train a model on specific tool-calling tasks so it can generalize better. Before, we briefly mentioned the use of the `tool` role. In the next section, we explore in depth how models learn to use that.

Tool Learning

Instilling tool-calling capabilities into LLMs can be a difficult task, especially when an LLM has not been trained to do so. Learning tools can be achieved through various methodologies. In this section, we'll explore the three most common categories of tool learning, namely in-context learning, supervised fine-tuning, and reinforcement learning.

In-Context Learning

In-context learning, the ability of LLMs to learn from a few examples in their context,[7] is an exceptionally useful technique to enable new behavior in LLMs without the need to fine-tune them. As we covered in Chapter 3, it is also known as *few-shot prompting* or *few-shot learning*, where you provide several examples to the LLM to learn from. Specifically, it's a prompt engineering technique where you give some examples of the behavior that you want the LLM to repeat. In our case, and as illustrated in Figure 5-13, we want the LLM to output the tool call in a specific format by following the examples we created ourselves.

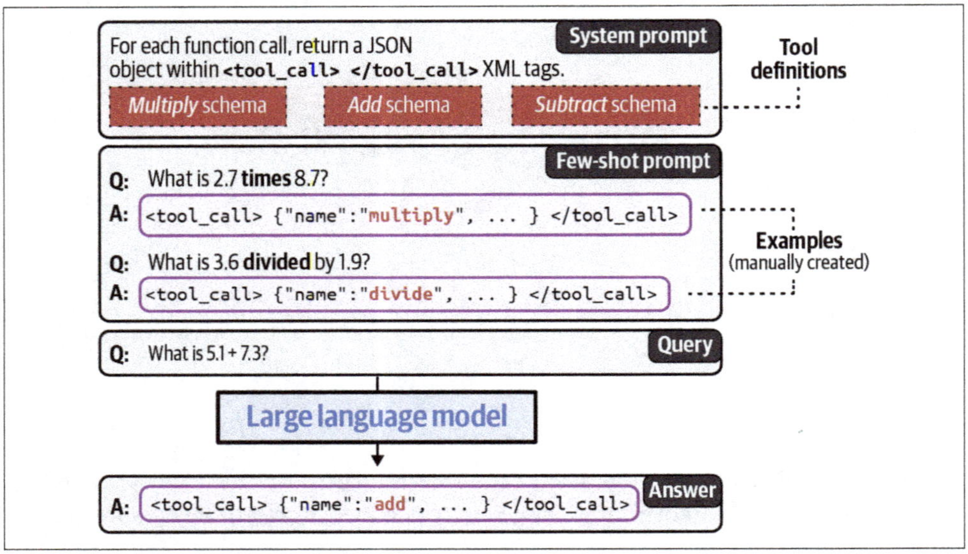

Figure 5-13. An example of few-shot prompting to enable tool calling

In-context learning is especially helpful when leveraging the `messages` structure that we explored previously. Remember when we pretended the assistant called a tool by adding it to the messages? We can apply the same concept and act as if the model called tools before. As shown in Figure 5-14, we can create our messages in such a way that the model thinks it has already used some of the tools before. So, when it subsequently gets a query, it has examples of how the tools should be called and what kinds of output can be expected.

7 Dong, Qingxiu et al. 2022. "A Survey on In-context Learning," *arXiv*, 2301.00234.

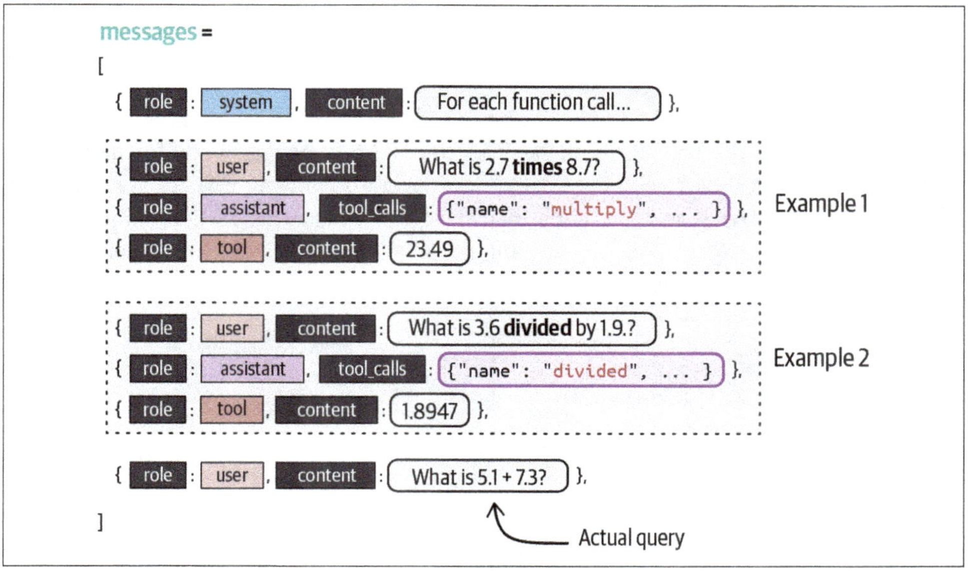

Figure 5-14. Examples of tool usage can also be provided as separate roles instead of in the prompts themselves

Since LLMs are great at pattern recognition, providing these example tool calls helps them follow the structure of the tool call we had in mind. Note that in-context learning improves as the LLM becomes more capable.

Supervised Fine-tuning

Although prompting is a straightforward method for enabling tool usage, it does require filling up the context window with additional instructions. As we explored in Chapter 4, we want to prevent filling up the context window, as it might degrade the performance of your model. There is also a risk of the model not following instructions through prompting if you have too many instructions.

A great alternative is to train your model using supervised fine-tuning (SFT) to distill knowledge and capabilities on tool calling into the model itself. This was especially popular in 2023 and early 2024 because it proved to be an effective and relatively cheap method for adding tool calling capabilities. However, it does come with downsides that were addressed with reinforcement learning (RL), as we will discuss later.

An interesting technique to explore SFT for tool calling (including some other tricks) is Toolformer, a model trained to decide which APIs to call and how.[8] Before exploring the training process, let's first dive into their approach to calling a tool. In previous examples, the tool that should be called was structured using JSON schemas, and the output of the call was sent back to the LLM to process. Toolformer takes a different approach by embedding the call and its output in the text it's generating. It does so by using the [and] tokens to indicate the start and end of calling a tool. When given a prompt, "*What is 5.1 times 7.3?*", it starts generating tokens until it reaches the [token (shown in Figure 5-15).

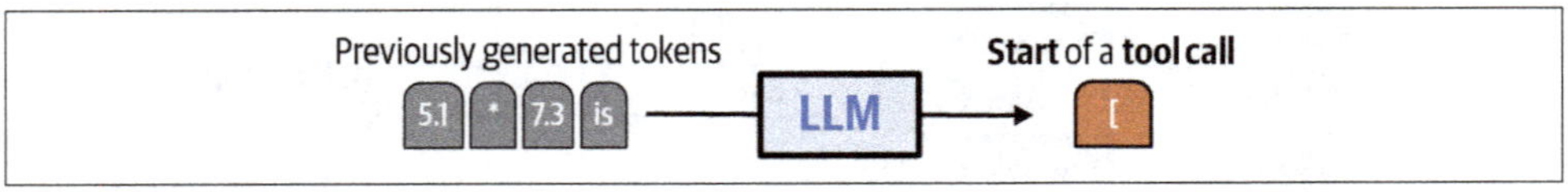

Figure 5-15. Toolformer produces the [token to indicate the start of a tool call

The [token tells the LLM that it should start selecting the tool and generate the appropriate parameters following a fixed format (more on this later!). It does this until it reaches the → token (Figure 5-16).

Figure 5-16. After the [token, Toolformer generates tool selection and argument tokens before executing the tool

The → token tells the LLM that it can now completely stop generating tokens if the user or an automated system executes the selected tool. Instead of appending the output through the messages structure as we explored before, it's added to the previously generated tokens along with the] token (shown in Figure 5-17).

8 Schick, Timo et al. 2023. "Toolformer: Language Models Can Teach Themselves to Use Tools," *Advances in Neural Information Processing Systems*, 36: 68539-68551.

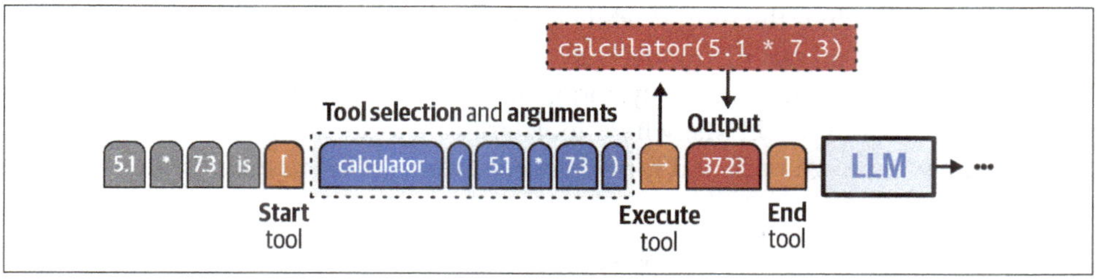

Figure 5-17. The tool is executed and the output is returned as if it were a token generated by the LLM

The] token tells the LLM that the tool has been executed and that the tool call, along with the output, is now part of the previously generated tokens. Then, the LLM can decide to continue generating tokens if necessary. Figure 5-18 demonstrates the end-to-end process of calling the tool, adding the output during generation, and giving back an answer.

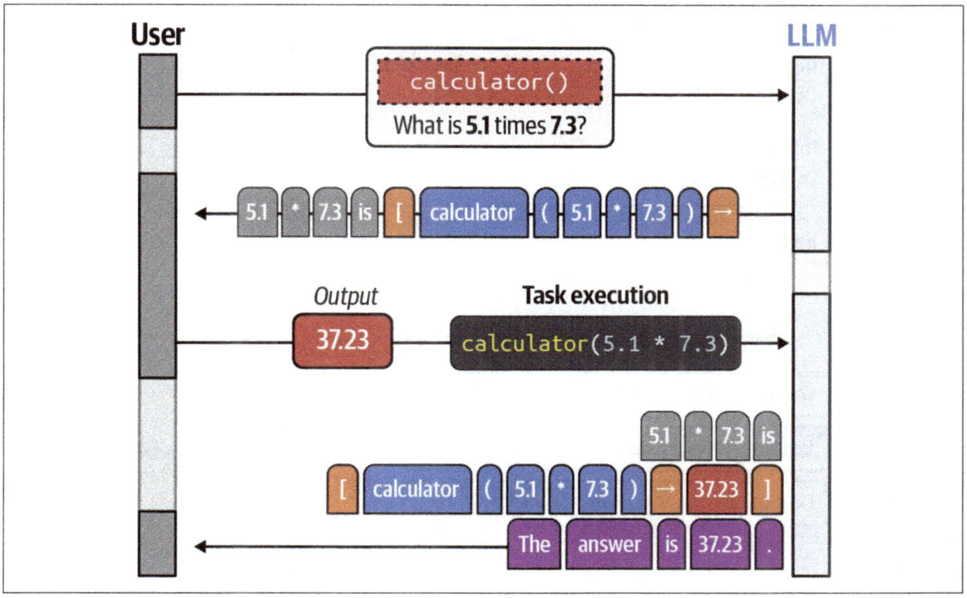

Figure 5-18. An example flow of Toolformer

The input/output of this process is therefore as follows:

- *Input:* "What is 5.1 times 7.3?"
- *Output:* "5.1 * 7.3 is [Calculator(5.1*7.3)→37.23] The answer is 37.23."

This process of adding the output while generating tokens is an important construct and is often used in various models. By embedding the output during generation, the model uses tools more naturally and generates fluent language. It also lends itself quite well for reasoning LLMs, where tools are called during the reasoning process instead of having to go back and forth between messages (remember Search-o1 from Chapter 4?).

To enable this in-line tool calling behavior in Toolformer, the model needs to be fine-tuned first. To do so, the authors carefully generated a dataset with many different examples of tool use. For each tool, a few-shot prompt was manually created and used to sample outputs. By sampling different outputs (much like the sampling with search against verifiers we explored in the reasoning chapter), the best output could be extracted by filtering on the correctness of the tool use, output, and loss decrease. The full process of creating this dataset is shown in Figure 5-19.

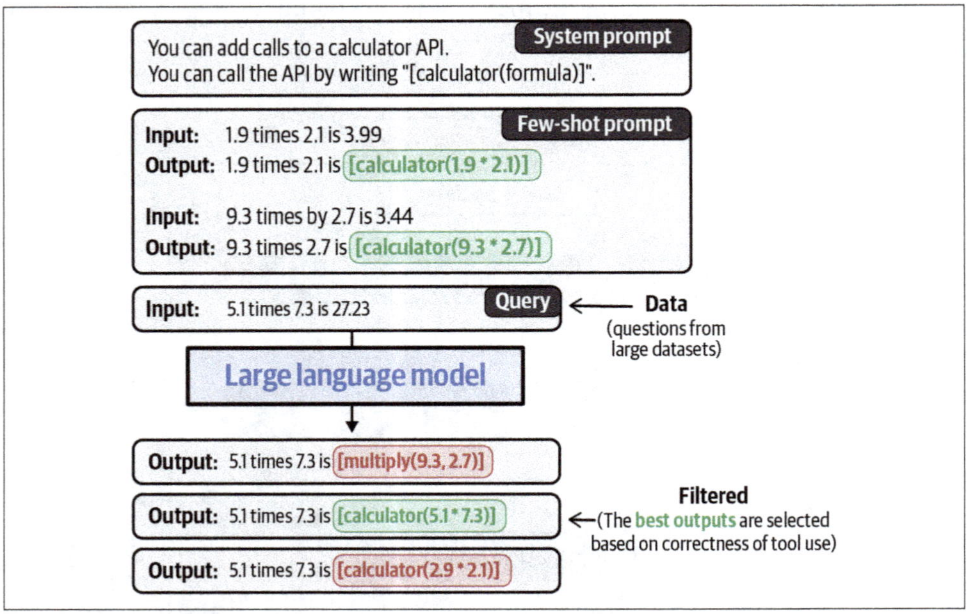

Figure 5-19. Overview of the data creation process of Toolformer

> In the context of SFT, getting quality data for tool calling can be a challenge. For many prompts, there is not a single correct tool call. Multiple tools, argument formats, or call sequences may all lead to valid outcomes. For instance, if we want to extract the README.md from a given GitHub repository, a model could call `get_readme(repo="owner/repo"` or it could use `get_contents(path="README.md", repo="owner/repo")`, both of which return the same file. Likewise, quality data often assumes that tools never fail, while in reality, tools may fail, return partial errors, change schemas, or behave inconsistently. These problems are less pronounced when using RL, which we cover in the next section.

In other words, the original data was adjusted to include tool calls instead of the LLM generating the answer by itself. All inputs were essentially updated to contain the appropriate tool.

Finally, the LLM (GPT-J, a variant of GPT-3) was fine-tuned using this updated data using SFT. At the time, this technique showed significant improvements over zero-shot performance and competed with larger models. However, SFT on this data made generalization difficult. SFT tends to be sensitive to the exact wording and prompt that is being used because it attempts to re-create what it is being shown. As we will explore next, RL tends to be a much more stable technique for generalization in tool use.

Reinforcement Learning

As we explored in Chapters 2 and 3, RL is an excellent method of training or fine-tuning to align your model to certain rewardable tasks. Compared to SFT, where an LLM trains on fixed examples with the correct answer, RL relies on trial and error. LLMs, through SFT, tend to mimic the input data and have difficulties generalizing what they learned. In RL, LLMs develop improved reasoning strategies not from being told exactly what to do (the mimicking behavior of SFT) but from repeatedly exploring feedback signals.

In the context of RL for tool usage, tool-learning is often integrated into the thinking process of models that support advanced reasoning. This is called Tool-Integrated Reasoning (TIR), which involves incorporating tools into the reasoning traces of an LLM. Figure 5-20 illustrates this process of calling a tool *during* reasoning and continuing the reasoning process after receiving the output.

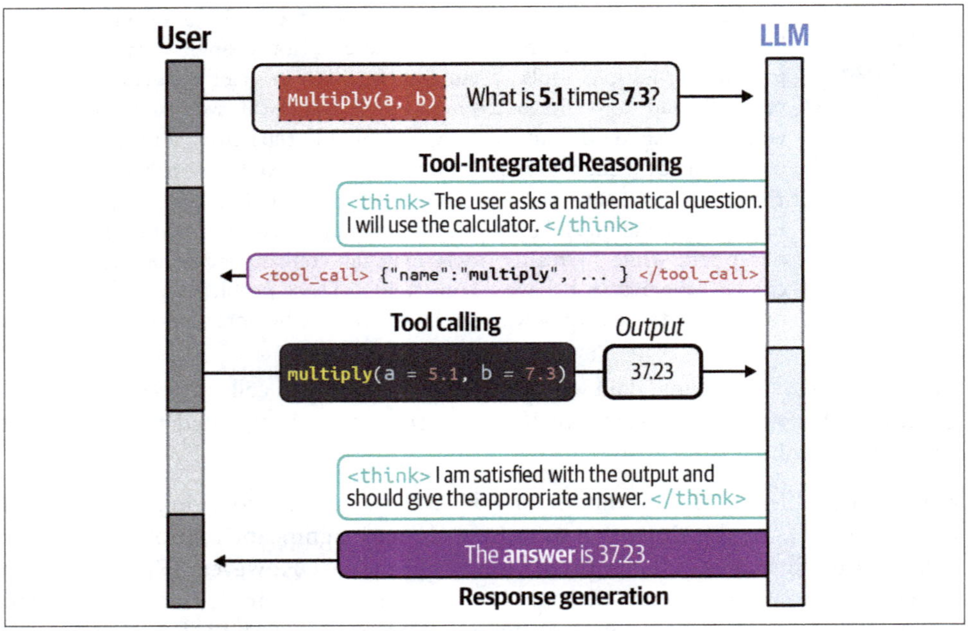

Figure 5-20. An overview of Tool-Integrated Reasoning

Note that such a TIR trajectory might involve multiple tool invocations, where the final answer is determined by all these intermediate tool calls and outputs.

Although we will delve more deeply into RL in other chapters, let's explore how it can be used to enable tool learning and TIR.

ToolRL

A recent example showcasing how RL can be used to enable TIR is ToolRL.[9] This framework uses GRPO, which we briefly covered in DeepSeek-R1's training procedure in Chapters 2 and 3. To differentiate between stages of thinking, tool calling, and answering the query, the developers used the `<thinking></thinking>`, `<tool_call></tool_call>`, and `<answer></answer>` tokens, respectively.

Compared to DeepSeek-R1, their usage of rewards in GRPO is quite straightforward. Two rewards are defined to enable tool usage:

Correctness
: Is a tool called correctly?

9 Qian, Cheng et al. 2025. "ToolRL: Reward Is All Tool Learning Needs," *arXiv*, 2504.13958.

Scores are given based on whether the correct tool names and parameters were used.

Format
: Is the appropriate format used?

  A positive reward is given if all required fields appear in the correct order.

To train the model, 4,000 samples of TIR traces were sampled from various datasets and used for fine-tuning various Qwen2.5 models.[10] Figure 5-21 illustrates how GRPO was used to fine-tune these models.

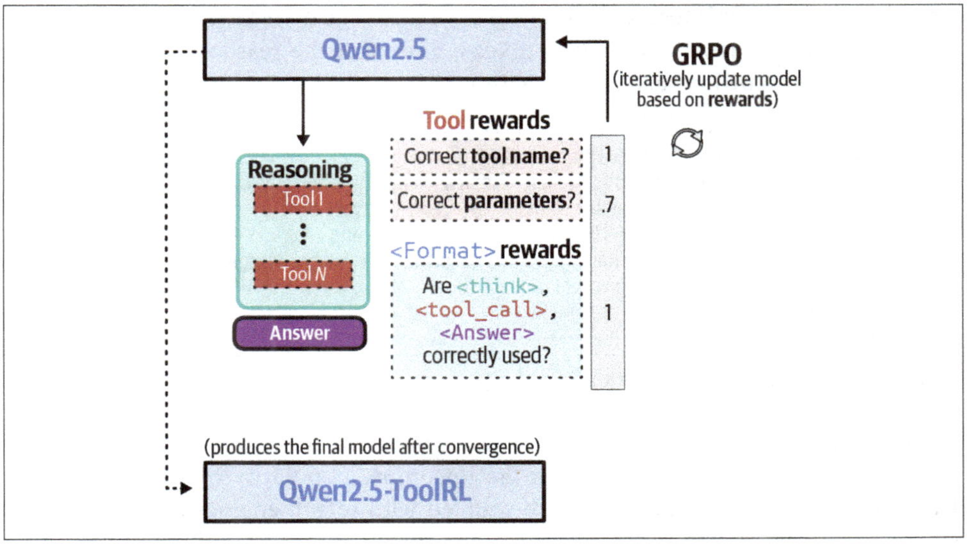

Figure 5-21. The training process of ToolRL

Interestingly, the authors also experimented with length rewards to encourage longer reasoning traces but found that longer traces do not consistently improve task performance and may even harm smaller models. Long reasoning traces might therefore not be ideal for tool use tasks.

Note that GRPO is a very flexible framework and allows you to develop the rewards that are best suited for a given use case. As such, this strategy of using tool-based rewards in GRPO can also be used for non-reasoning models by simply removing or updating the format reward.

10 Yang, An et al. 2024. "Qwen2.5 Technical Report," *arXiv*, 2412.15115.

Search-R1

To further explore what RL is capable of, let's take a closer look at Search-R1, an efficient RL framework for integrating search as a tool into an LLM's reasoning process.[11] In this framework, the LLM learns to generate one or more search queries during step-by-step reasoning autonomously.

The framework starts with specifying how the model should interleave reasoning with the search engine call. As illustrated in Figure 5-22, the prompt template is structured into three parts. First, the reasoning traces are created with `<think></think>` tokens, then the search engine calling function with `<search></search>` where the output is reintegrated with `<information></information>`, and finally, the answer through `<answer></answer>` tokens. Note that the reasoning traces and the search engine can be interleaved several times.

> Answer the given question. You must conduct reasoning inside <think> and </think> first every time you get new information. After reasoning, if you find you lack some knowledge, you can call a search engine by <search> query </search>, and it will return the top searched results between <information> and <information>. You can search as many times as you want. If you find no further external knowledge needed, you can directly provide the answer inside <answer> and </answer> without detailed illustrations.

Figure 5-22. The system prompt of Search-R1

What makes this template particularly interesting is that the authors focus on a single tool, search. The reason for this was the upcoming popularity of DeepResearch, a framework where reasoning LLMs are coupled with search engines to create agentic systems that allow for in-depth research on various topics. The authors of Search-R1 created this framework as a strong open source alternative to the proprietary systems out there.

The result of such a template is, like ToolRL, tool-interleaved reasoning with multi-turn search engine calls. We illustrated an example of such a process in Figure 5-23. Note that the `<search></search>` tool can be any application, like the open-access archive of academic papers, arXiv, or a combination of various sources.

11 Jin, Bowen et al. 2025. "Search-R1: Training LLMs to Reason and Leverage Search Engines with Reinforcement Learning," *arXiv*, 2503.09516.

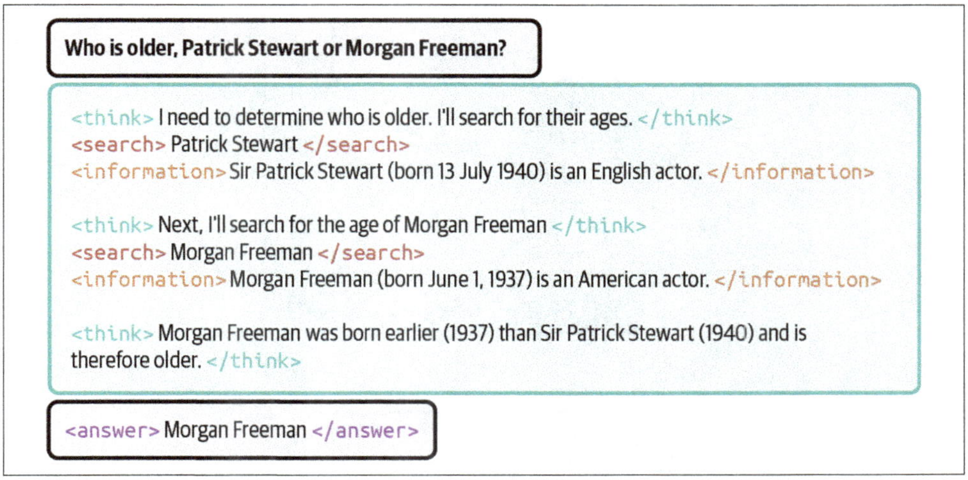

Figure 5-23. Examples of tool-interleaved reasoning with multi-turn search engine calls

The approach of training the algorithm with RL is rather straightforward. The authors adopted a simplified outcome-based reward function. Instead of creating all different kinds of formatting and accuracy rewards (like DeepSeek-R1), only accuracy rewards were used (based on the task). Since the underlying model (Qwen2.5) already has strong structural adherence, there was no need for formatting rewards.

Among others, the authors explored GRPO (which we covered in Chapter 2) as the RL algorithm (illustrated in Figure 5-24) for fine-tuning the model. Note that the losses in GRPO are typically calculated over the entire sequence of tokens, including the output of the search engine. In Search-R1, the tokens of the search engine's output were masked (ignored) to prevent the model from attempting to control the search engine's output, which were not directly LLM-generated (which can create unexpected dynamics). This is called *loss masking for retrieved tokens*.

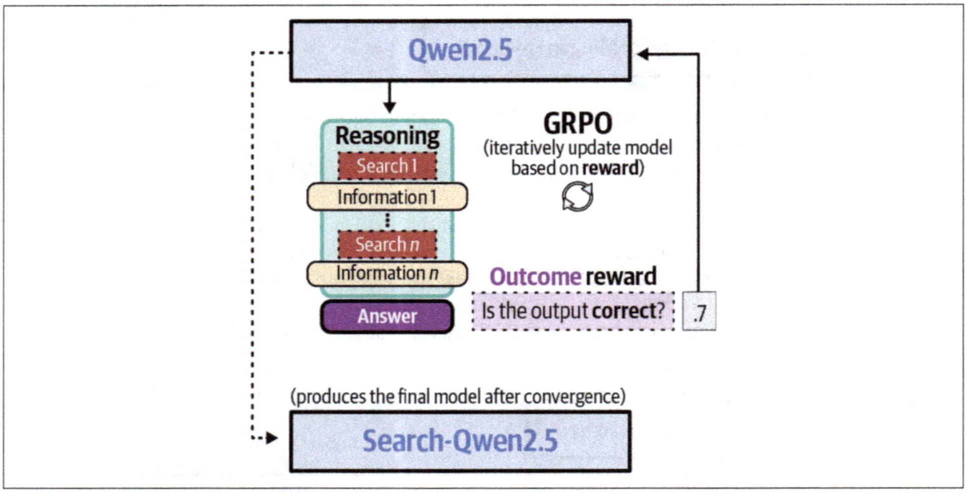

Figure 5-24. Training process to create Search-Qwen2.5

These kinds of frameworks and methodologies leveraging RL have become increasingly popular as the reward structure for tool calling is generally quite straightforward. It's trivial to check if a tool has been called correctly and if the correct arguments have been used (as in ToolRL). Moreover, RL works well for rewards that are verifiable, such as coding and tool calling. As such, there has been an increase in models that were trained using RL and additionally adopted tool-based rewards, such as the strong open source Qwen3 and GPT-OSS models.[12,13]

TinyAgent with Native Tool-Calling Capabilities

SFT and RL are great techniques for instilling tool-calling behavior into the models themselves without needing to perform explicit CoT instructions in your prompts. This process, as illustrated previously, does create a bit of "magic" when running these tool-calling capabilities with inference engines like Ollama or llama.cpp. This "magic" we refer to is the conversion of a standard method for calling tools to the chat template that the specific LLM uses. As we explored previously, some LLMs use <think> tokens for instance, while others use something like <|think|>. Each LLM is trained differently, with different tokens, and the inference engine "hides" that from the user. Although that makes for an easy UX, it doesn't serve well for the educational nature of this book. So let's uncover the "magic"!

12 Yang, An et al. 2025. "Qwen3 Technical Report," *arXiv*, 2505.09388.

13 Agarwal, Sandhini et al. 2025. "GPT-OSS-120b & GPT-OSS-20b Model Card," *arXiv*, 2508.10925.

Most inference engines make use of a standardized format in describing tools, namely JSON. As we discussed in the section "Tool Definition" on page 180, we can use a JSON schema to describe a tool and pass it to the LLM for it to use. As such, all we have to do is use the `tool_schema` variable we defined in the section "Tool Definition" on page 180 and pass it along to the OpenAI endpoint. We make use of Gemma 4 E4B, which unlike Gemma 3 12B, was trained specifically to perform tool calling:

```
import json
import urllib.request

# Prompt
messages = [{"role": "user", "content": "What is 5.1 times 7.3?"}]

# Prepare the data
body = {
    "model": "gemma4:e4b",
    "messages": messages,
    "stream": False,
    "tools": [tool_schema],
}

# Prepare the request
request = urllib.request.Request(
    "http://localhost:11434/api/chat",
    data=json.dumps(body).encode(),
    headers={"Content-Type": "application/json"},
)

# Call and parse the response
with urllib.request.urlopen(request) as response:
    print(json.loads(response.read())["message"])
```

This gives:

```
{
  'role': 'assistant',
  'content': '',
  'thinking': "1. **Identify the user's request:**
  The user wants to calculate the product of 5.1 and 7.3.",
  'tool_calls': [
    {
      'id': 'call_0mufz9dn',
      'function': {
        'index': 0, 'name': 'multiply', 'arguments': {'a': 5.1, 'b': 7.3}
      }
    }
  ]
}
```

Note how the output "just" outputs the tool call without us having to do anything special. This is because Ollama handles various things, but two stand out. First, it communicates to the LLM which tools exist. Second, it converts the LLMs tool call to this parsed output.

To uncover the "magic," let's start from Gemma 4 E4B's chat template. As shown in Figure 5-25, it uses several special tokens (e.g., `<|turn>`) to parse the input and output of the model.

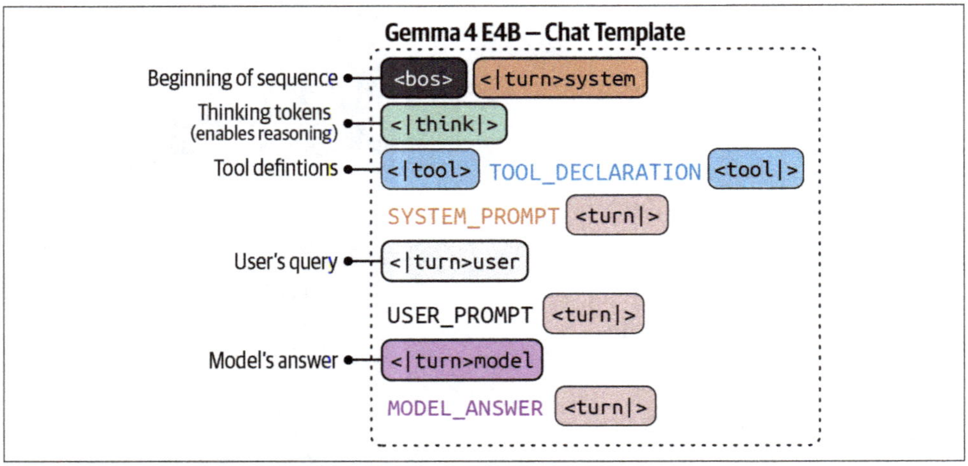

Figure 5-25. The chat template of Gemma 4 E4B

To define a given tool, such as the multiply function we covered previously, it expects the format as shown in Figure 5-26.

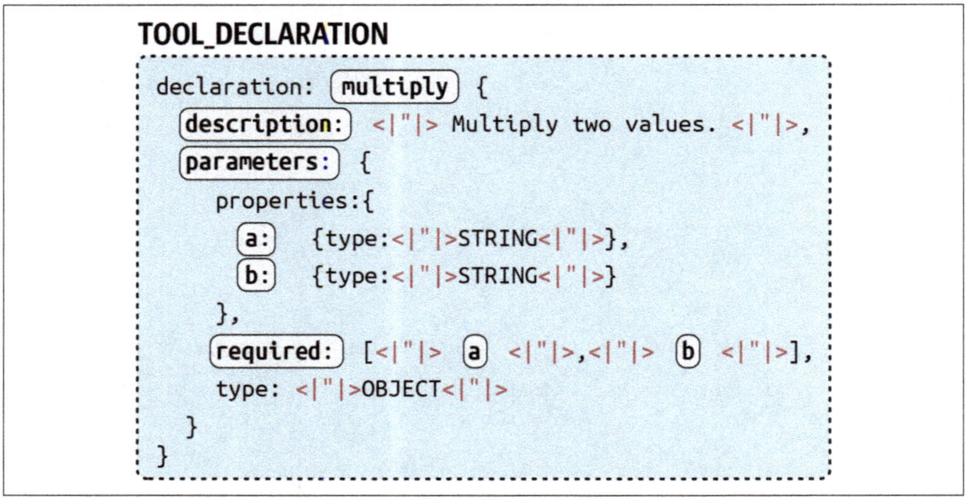

Figure 5-26. The tool declaration between the `<|tool>` and `<tool|>` tokens of the multiply function (the indentation is merely for illustration purposes)

Under the hood, inference engines convert the JSON schema we used in `tool_schema` to whatever the LLM expects. How this translation is done is up to the inference provider, but it always needs to convert to whatever the LLM is trained on.

Now, let's explore how we can use the native tool-calling capabilities of an LLM and use them in your `TinyAgent`. Among others, the following needs to be implemented:

Creating a `tool_to_schema` *function*
: A function for converting a Python function to an OpenAI-compatible JSON schema

Creating the `NativeTools` *class*
: A variant of `Tools` that creates and parses tool calls

Let's start with the `tool_to_schema` function. It is a helper function that easily allows us to convert any given function to a JSON schema by inspecting the function's name, docstrings, and parameters:

```
import inspect
from typing import Callable

# Convert specific types to string descriptions
TYPE_MAP = {
    str: "string", int: "integer", float: "number",
    bool: "boolean", list: "array", dict: "object"
}

def tool_to_schema(function: Callable) -> dict:
    """Convert a Python function to an OpenAI-style tool schema."""
    signature = inspect.signature(function)

    # Extract meatadata
    properties, required = {}, []
    for name, parameter in signature.parameters.items():
        properties[name] = {"type": TYPE_MAP.get(parameter.annotation, "string")}
        if parameter.default is inspect.Parameter.empty:
            required.append(name)

    # Fill schema
    schema = {
        "type": "function",
        "function": {
            "name": function.__name__,
            "description": inspect.getdoc(function),
            "parameters": {
                "type": "object",
                "properties": properties,
                "required": required,
            },
        },
    }
```

```
        return schema
```

You can run it like so:

```
print(tool_to_schema(multiply))
```

This gives:

```
{
    'type': 'function',
    'function': {
        'name': 'multiply',
        'description': 'Multiply two values.',
        'parameters': {
            'type': 'object',
            'properties': {'a': {'type': 'string'}, 'b': {'type': 'string'}},
            'required': ['a', 'b']
        }
    }
}
```

This standardized format is OpenAI-compatible, and the inference engine will convert this to the model's chat template. Next, let's make the `NativeTools` class that creates this schema and parses the output so it can be used to execute tool calls:

```
import json
from illustrated_agents.chapters.ch2 import Response
from illustrated_agents.chapters.ch5 import Tools


class NativeTools(Tools):
    """Tool registry using native function calling."""

    @property
    def schemas(self) -> list[dict]:
        """Return tool functions for native function calling."""
        return [
            tool_to_schema(tool["function"]) for tool in self.registry.values()
        ]

    @property
    def prompt(self) -> str:
        """Empty because we don't need a prompt for native tool calling"""
        return ""

    def parse(self, response: Response) -> Response:
        """Parse a tool call."""
        # If there's no tool call, return the response as is
        if not response.tool_call:
            return response

        # Extract the tool name and arguments from the tool call
        args = response.tool_call["function"]["arguments"]
```

```python
        if isinstance(args, str):
            args = json.loads(args)
        tool_call = {
            "tool": response.tool_call["function"]["name"],
            "kwargs": args,
        }

        # Add the parsed tool call to the response
        return Response(
            content=response.content,
            reasoning=response.reasoning,
            tool_call=tool_call,
        )

    def observation(self, result: str) -> tuple[str, str]:
        """Native tool results use the 'tool' role."""
        return "tool", str(result)

    def is_done(self, response: Response) -> bool:
        """No tool call means the `TinyAgent` is done."""
        return not response.tool_call
```

The `NativeTools` class follows `Tools` closely and makes a couple of changes:

`schemas`
: Create an OpenAI-compatible schema in JSON.

`prompt`
: No prompt is needed because that is handled by the inference engine.

`parse`
: Converts the LLM's tool call into JSON and stores it in the `Response` class.

`observation`
: The observation is now tracked in the `tool` role.

Usage is exactly the same as the `Tools` class. All we need to do is add the tools and give them to your `TinyAgent`. Then, we can ask it the same query we did before to see if it uses a tool:

```python
from illustrated_agents.chapters.ch4 import Memory
from illustrated_agents.chapters.ch5 import TinyAgent

# Tools
tools = NativeTools()
tools.add_tool("multiply", multiply)

# Memory
memory = Memory()

# Initialize Agent
```

```
agent = TinyAgent(llm=llm, memory=memory, tools=tools)
agent.run("What is 5.1 times 7.3?")
```

After running the agent, let's look at the memory to see if and how it called the tool:

```
print(agent.memory.get_messages())
```

Which gives:

```
[
  {'role': 'system', 'content': 'You are a helpful assistant.\n\n'},
  {'role': 'user', 'content': 'What is 5.1 times 7.3?'},
  {
    'role': 'assistant',
    'content': '',
    'tool_calls': [
      {
        'id': 'call_vdc4hgze',
        'function': {
          'arguments': '{"a":"5.1","b":"7.3"}',
          'name': 'multiply'
        },
        'type': 'function',
        'index': 0
      }
    ]
  },
  {'role': 'tool', 'content': '37.23'}
]
```

The tool was called successfully! Note how it uses `tool_calls` to identify the tool and parameters while the `tool` role is used to observe the output.

What We Built

```
TinyAgent/
├── agent.py ← Updated (Added `(Native)Tools` to your `TinyAgent`)
├── llm.py
├── memory.py
├── toolbox.py  ← New (A place to store your functions/tools)
├── tools.py  ← New (Added`Tools` and `Native`)
└── trajectory.py
```

Model Context Protocol

In the previous sections, we explored how to connect tools to LLMs, making them capable of much more than text generation. Although their ability to then use tools is incredible, it's not a free lunch. Imagine you have developed several prompts to instruct your LLM on how to use tools. As is typical in this field, a new LLM is released that you would like to try out, together with all the tools. Now imagine it has a new way of calling tools, which means you will have to create new integrations for all your tools. This is the N × M problem, where *N* is the number of LLMs and *M* is the number of tools available. You would have to write custom integrations for every LLM/tool combination.

Model Context Protocol (MCP) solves this problem by standardizing how you would connect tools and APIs with different structures to your LLM. MCP is an open standard and framework developed by Anthropic and released in November 2024.[14] As a protocol, it facilitates two-way communication between tools and LLMs. It's often referred to as the "USB-C port of AI" due to its universal nature, allowing for any LLM to implement any tool that follows this protocol. Shown in Figure 5-27, instead of manually creating connections between LLMs and tools, MCP creates only a single connection that can be maintained indefinitely by the tool provider.

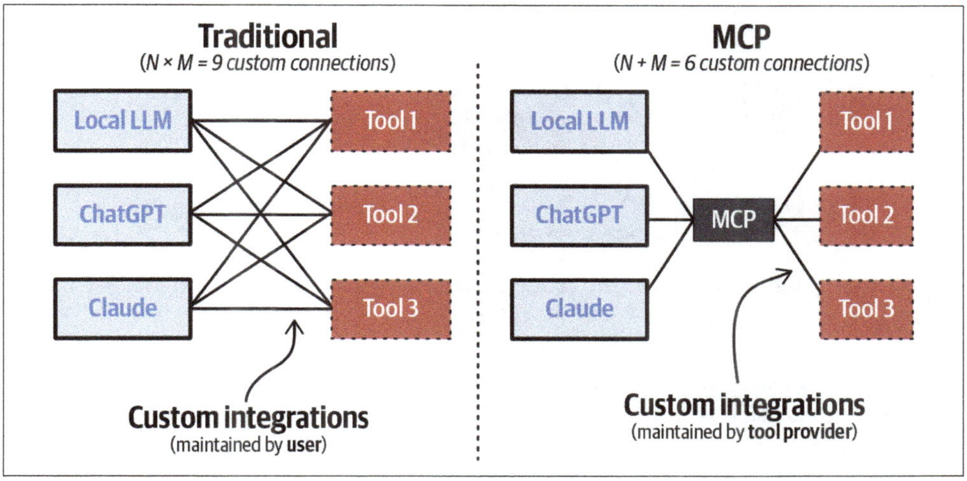

Figure 5-27. MCP requires fewer custom connections than traditional tool integrations

By having the MCP server handle the integrations and communicate the tools to the LLMs, it becomes N + M connections that need to be maintained instead of N × M connections. Moreover, as long as the tool provider has an MCP server, connecting the server to your LLM is relatively straightforward, but more on that later.

The maintenance of the integration, therefore, also moves from the user to the tool provider. Without MCP, if arXiv's API were to suddenly change drastically, then each user would have to adjust their integrations. With MCP, any changes to the API would need to be resolved only once by the maintainers of that API. Then, the updates can be rolled out to all users without any intervention from their side.

14 Anthropic, November 25, 2024. "Introducing the Model Context Protocol," (*http://www.anthropic.com/news/model-context-protocol*).

To illustrate this point a bit further, if you were to add tools to your LLM manually, all tools would have to be:

- Manually *tracked* and fed to the LLM
- Manually *described* (including its expected JSON schema)
- Manually *updated* whenever its API changes

As shown in Figure 5-28, this can be quite the hassle for maintaining your tools.

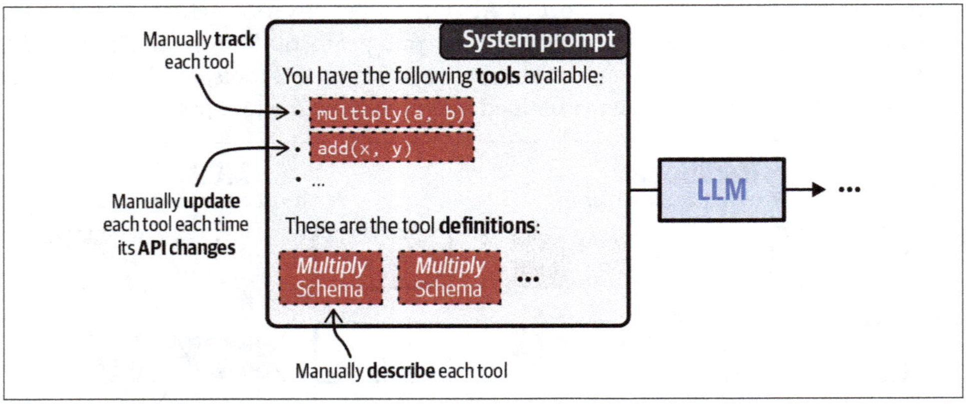

Figure 5-28. An overview of the difficulty in describing tool definitions in the system prompt only

Thus, MCP not only solves the N × M problem but also the problem of standardization. Note that MCP is not the only protocol for standardizing communication, like Agent2Agent (A2A) for standardizing interagent communication.[15] Although there are others, in 2026, it is arguably one of the most popular protocols out there.[16] There are MCP servers for Figma (*https://oreil.ly/w8SDo*), GitHub (*https://oreil.ly/C_-38*), Home Assistant (*https://oreil.ly/0UTDD*), and many others. You can find a nice overview of MCP servers on GitHub (*https://oreil.ly/Cz_QM*).

15 Google. "a2aproject/A2A," *https://github.com/google/A2A*. Accessed 02 October 2025.

16 Yang, Yingxuan et al. 2025. "A Survey of AI Agent Protocols," *arXiv*, 2504.16736.

Core Components

To achieve all these useful capabilities, MCP consists of three components:

MCP host
: LLM application (such as Cursor) that manages connections, interprets tool schema, and manages routing

MCP client
: Maintains one-to-one connections with MCP servers

MCP server
: Provides context, tools, and capabilities to the LLMs

The *MCP host* is any application that uses an LLM to use external tools. Typical examples are chat assistants like ChatGPT or Claude and IDE extensions like Cursor or GitHub Copilot. This is the "brain" of the MCP flow and it makes calls to the MCP servers via the MCP clients.

The *MCP client* maintains connections with the MCP servers. They exist within the host and handle the connection management, discovery of tool capabilities, request forwarding, etc. Compared to the host, a client is a piece of code that handles the communication with the MCP servers, whereas the MCP host only initiates the communication.

The *MCP server* is a lightweight program that exposes APIs and tools via the MCP standard. These servers often connect to a specific data source or service. For instance, an MCP server might connect to all API endpoints of arXiv to search, load, and view academic papers.

Servers expose three kinds of primitives to clients: *tools* (actions the LLM can invoke, like `/list_commits`), *resources* (data the host can load as context, like files, documents, and datasets), and *prompts* (reusable templates). The MCP host (e.g., GitHub Copilot) contains one MCP client per server it connects to. The MCP servers expose tools that may provide access to resources. These three components are depicted in Figure 5-29.

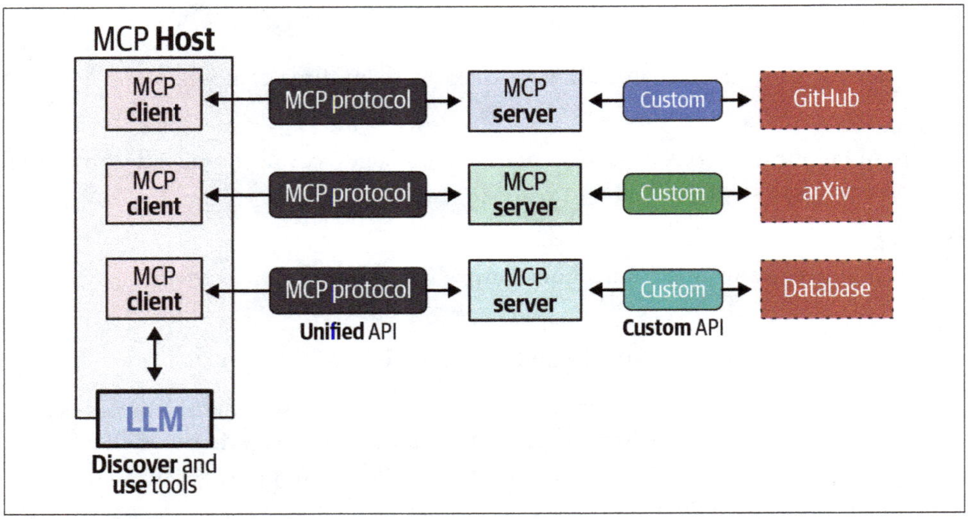

Figure 5-29. The main three components of MCP, namely the client, server, and host

The MCP Flow

MCP can be a bit of a mystery, even when showing and describing the core components. Instead, let's go through an example of what it would be like to use the MCP to discover and call tools. Imagine you want your AI assistant (perhaps GitHub Copilot or Claude code) to summarize the five latest commits from your repository. This flow is numbered in the upcoming figures so we can accurately track each individual step.

It would all start with the user's query: "Summarize the 5 latest commits." Shown in Figure 5-30, this prompt is sent to the MCP host (1), which asks the MCP server, through the MCP client, which tools are available (2). The MCP server is connected to the set of tools (GitHub) and returns the list of all available API calls back to the MCP host (3). API calls might include common methodologies like listing all commits (`/list_commits`) or creating a pull request (`/create_pr`). Then, the initial prompt, together with available tools, is sent to the LLM (4).

Next, the LLM may choose to use any of the tools that were returned. Since the user's query is about commits, the LLM decides that it wants the MCP server to use the `/list_commits` tool (5). The MCP client communicates this action to the MCP server (6), which finally executes the command (7). The output of the tool usage is returned to the MCP server (8), which communicates it back to the MCP client and host through the MCP (9) (Figure 5-31).

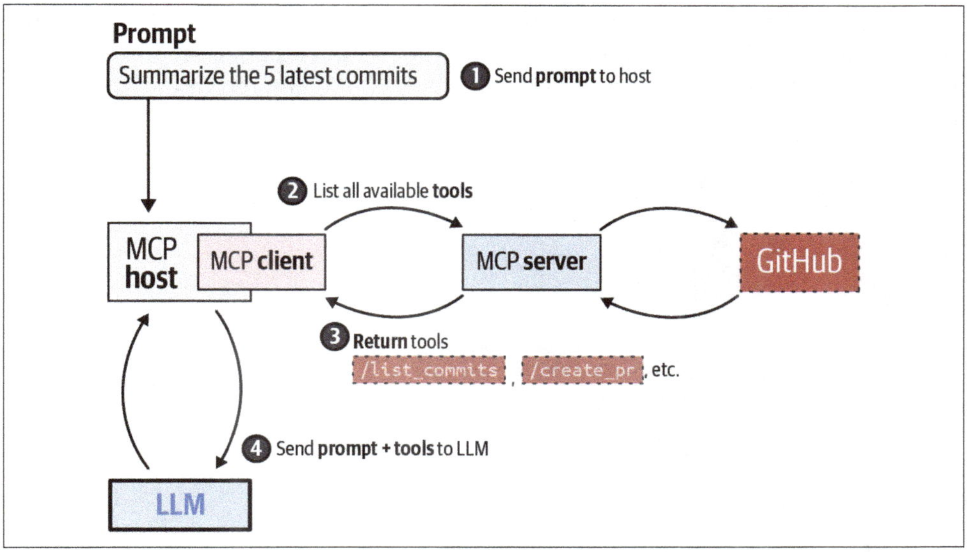

Figure 5-30. The first steps in using MCP, which mainly includes checking which tools are available on the MCP server

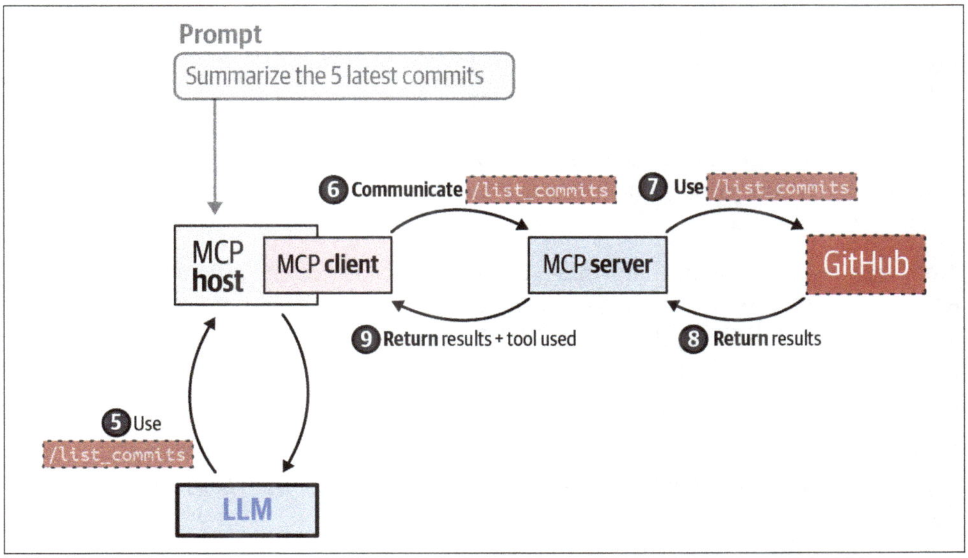

Figure 5-31. After listing the tools, the LLM decides which tool to use, executed via the MCP server

When the LLM receives the results (10), it can choose to run another tool or return the output to the MCP host and then to the user. In our example, the LLM decides to summarize the five latest commits that it received (11) and return the summary to the user (12) (Figure 5-32).

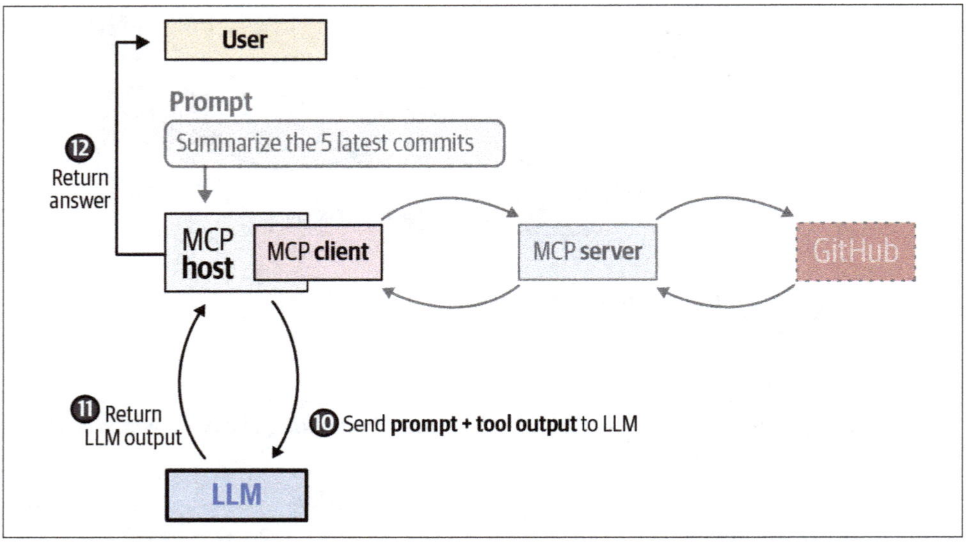

Figure 5-32. The results of the tool usage are processed by the LLM and returned to the MCP host before sending them back to the user

What makes these sets of steps so special is that the LLM can discover tools that exist, choose which one to use, and does not have to think much about deprecated API functionalities.

Note that the LLM should still have tool-calling capabilities. Whenever it wants to execute a given tool, it should follow the MCP, which follows a JSON-like structure. This structure, following the JSON-RPC 2.0 Specification (*https://jsonrpc.org/specification*), is also communicated by the MCP client, which serves as the middleman between the LLM and the protocol.

In the book's GitHub repository (*https://github.com/HandsOnLLM/An-Illustrated-Guide-To-AI-Agents/*), you'll find an additional notebook that goes through implementing MCP into your `TinyAgent` step-by-step.

Skills

With modules like tools and MCP, we can give an agent access to various actions it can take. However, when exactly to use those actions and how they fit into a larger workflow is not covered by any of these modules. Your agent is not intimately familiar with your team's workflow, preferred tools, or coding standards. Having to repeat to your agent, every time you initialize it, that it should use uv (*https://oreil.ly/jrzMf*) over pip (*https://oreil.ly/yUCnB*) can be quite the annoyance. This is where Skills come in. Created by Anthropic, Skills (*https://oreil.ly/RZP3m*) are a set of instructions, scripts, and resources the agent can use as context to perform a given task. They contain procedural knowledge, which are step-by-step instructions that allow the agent to understand how to best approach a task given in your specific context.

For instance, if you want it to create a presentation, you might need it to first search the web for relevant information (this is a tool), then summarize this information (it can do this by itself), and then finally create the slides one at a time (this is also a tool). This workflow or "recipe" for creating a presentation might therefore include a set of tools but also instructions on how to use them and in what order. As such, Skills teach your agent what to do, when to do it, and how.

A Skill revolves around progressive disclosure. This means that the agent starts with minimal information on what the Skill may provide, and when it is accessed provides more information on how to execute it. This progression typically follows three layers of depth:

Layer 1 (always loaded)
: Metadata about the Skill (e.g., name and description)

Layer 2 (loaded when activated)
: The main Skill instructions

Layer 3 (loaded when needed)
: Additional resources to use (e.g., scripts and references)

To explore these layers and the anatomy of a Skill, let's use an example. Imagine you have many meetings to keep track of every week and want to convert your transcripts and rough notes into structured meetings notes with actions items. Your agent does not know beforehand how you want the notes structured, the context of the people you're meeting, etc. A Skill would give the context needed to perform the task depending on the type of meeting you have. The first thing needed to create a Skill is the *SKILL.md* file.

The SKILL.md

Every Skill is required to have a *SKILL.md* file. The start of this file contains the Skill's metadata, namely the name and a short description. For instance, the name of your Skill could be "meeting_notes" and its description: "Use this skill when you want to turn meeting transcripts and notes into structured decisions and action items." When you first interact with your agent, only this name and description are provided so that the agent can decide whether it's worth exploring it in more detail for a given task. Regardless of how many Skills you add, their names and descriptions are always shared with the agent (often as a system prompt). This metadata section is formatted as YAML, so you can clearly separate this metadata from the rest.

The body of the *SKILL.md* file contains the instructions relevant to its metadata. For instance, the "meeting_notes" Skill would contain information on how to perform the summarization of the transcripts and the things to look out for.

This information is only given to the agent when it asks for it. Imagine that it's a tool that the agent can call to provide the much-needed context for a given task. The reason this information is not already given to the agent has to do with *context engineering*. Some Skills have very long descriptions and tasks that might not be relevant for your query. By only accessing the instructions when asked for, the agent minimizes the amount of information it does not need. The *SKILL.md* is shown in Figure 5-33.

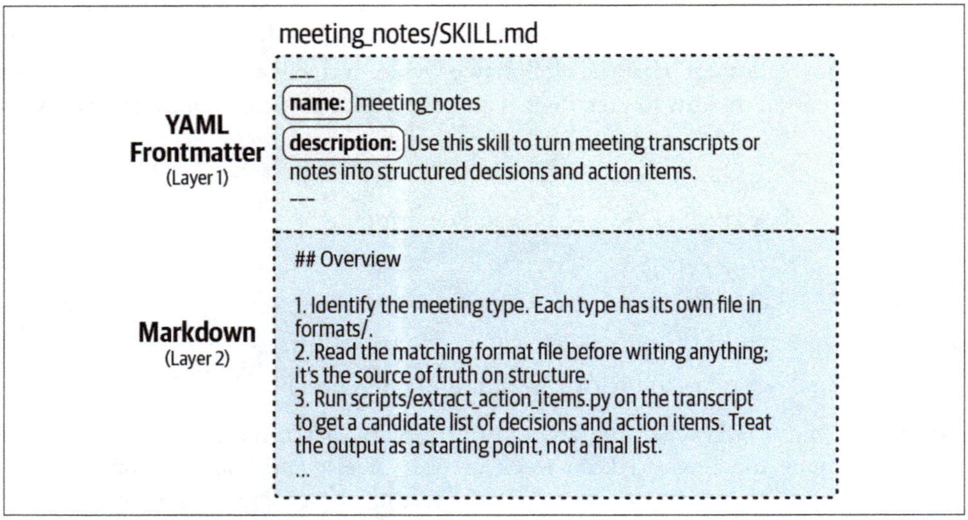

Figure 5-33. The anatomy of the SKILL.md file

The Bundled Resources

Skills can get quite large and unwieldy quickly. In our example of "meeting_notes", there can be instructions about different types of meetings. A 1:1 with your manager requires a different structure than a 1:1 with one of your colleagues or a 1:1 with your employee. The same applies to calls with external partners, team meetings, etc.

Instead of trying to put everything into the *SKILL.md* file, we can bundle additional files within the Skills directory and reference them from the *SKILL.md* file. These files can be anything and don't require anything other than that the agent should be able to access them. Typical files are Python files for executing specific functions and markdown files for additional instructions. As such, the agent can decide to load this information when needed but it's necessary to use the Skill. This additional layer of activation is shown in Figure 5-34.

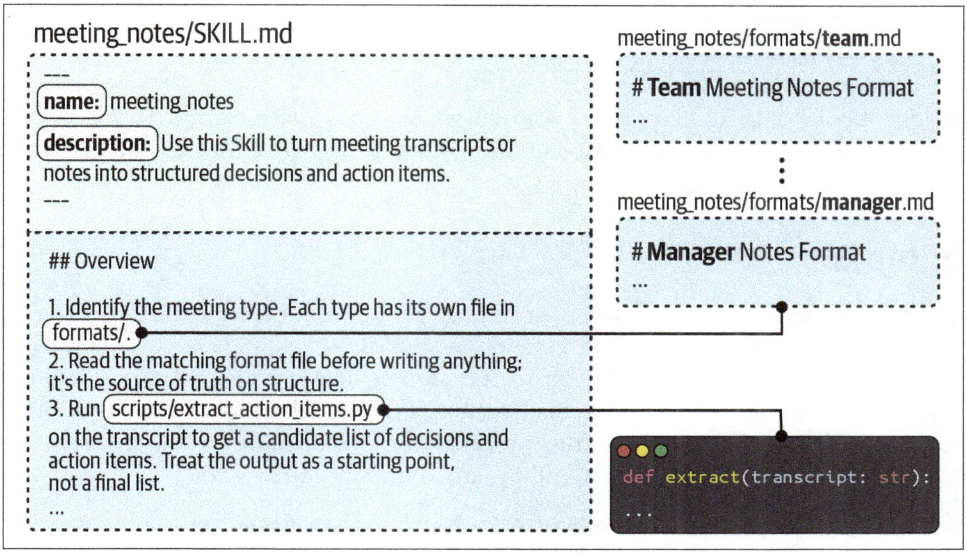

Figure 5-34. The agent can choose to run additional files if needed. Those files can provide additional context or act as helper functions.

In the Skill's directory, only a *SKILL.md* is needed. However, as context grows and more information is needed for certain tasks, additional files can be added that the agent loads only when needed:

```
meeting_notes/
├── SKILL.md
├── scripts/
│   └── extract_action_items.py
└── formats/
    ├── one_on_one_manager.md
    ├── one_on_one_colleague.md
    ├── one_on_one_report.md
    ├── team_meeting.md
    └── external_call.md
```

Progressive disclosure in the form of these three layers helps keep the amount of context used to a minimum, as shown in Table 5-1.

Table 5-1. The layers of progressive disclosure and their impact on tokens

Layer	File	Activation	Number of tokens
1	*SKILL.md* metadata (YAML)	Always loaded	~100
2	*SKILL.md* instruction (Markdown)	Loaded when activated	Fewer than 5,000
3	Bundled files (Markdown, scripts, data, etc.)	Loaded when needed	As needed

In the book's GitHub repository (*https://github.com/HandsOnLLM/An-Illustrated-Guide-To-AI-Agents*), you'll find an additional notebook that shows how to give your `TinyAgent` access to Skills.

Summary

In this chapter, we explored how tool calling gives LLMs the capabilities to interact with the world. We first covered the fundamentals of tool calling and how LLMs call tools in practice. We saw that as text-to-text entities, LLMs merely communicate the intent to call a tool. The act of actually calling the tool falls either to the user or to external software that automates this process. The flow of calling a tool involved the tool creation, definition, selection, calling, and output processing.

Then, we explored three methods of having LLMs learn those tool-calling capabilities. First was in-context learning, where you can define the tool's schemas and definition in the prompt for the LLM to follow. Second was SFT, where an LLM is fine-tuned on specific tool-calling capabilities. We covered Toolformer as one of the first successful attempts to use SFT for tool calling. Lastly, we covered RL as one of the most prominent techniques for instilling tool-calling capabilities. Of note were ToolRL and Search-R1, which both adopt GRPO, a popular RL algorithm used in DeepSeek-R1.

We then looked at one of the most exciting things in the realm of tool calling, the MCP. We explored how MCP standardizes the usage of tools, which led to the widespread use of tools without the need for custom solutions.

We finally looked at Skills, Anthropic's approach to giving agents the procedural knowledge they need to operate in your specific context. Where tool definitions tell an agent what a tool does, Skills tell it how to get a job done—the recipe of steps, conventions, and references it should follow for a recurring task. Through progressive disclosure across three layers—metadata, instructions, and bundled resources—Skills surface this guidance only when the agent decides a Skill is relevant, keeping the context window lean.

Along the way, your `TinyAgent` gained both prompt-based and native tool-calling capabilities, setting the stage for Chapter 6, where it will start choosing and sequencing those tools on its own.

CHAPTER 6

Planning and Reflection

In Chapter 3, we covered reasoning LLMs and their capabilities to demonstrate complex chains of thought. Advanced reasoning enables behavior that is vital in agentic systems, namely the ability to plan actions and reflect on them.

Agents are multi-step entities and generally require planning the actions they will take to complete their goals. Imagine you ask an agent to create a specific feature for your codebase. To bring this to completion, typical steps the agent takes include:

1. Clarify requirements
2. Analyze the existing codebase
3. Design the feature
4. Implement the feature
5. Test the feature
6. Update documentation

To execute all these actions, the agent first needs to be aware of them and track the status of its current state. Planning is essential to solidify this behavior and to allow the agent to dynamically adjust the plan when necessary. After all, without a plan, how would it know what to do next?

This plan and the steps that it contains can often be taken multiple times, such as implementing and testing the feature whenever the agent encounters a bug. Iterative loops are similarly a fundamental component of what makes an agent. As such, the initial plans are made malleable and should be open to change when there is an issue with the plan or its execution. Reflection on what has been done and what could be improved is, therefore, vital for the autonomous nature of the agent. Planning and reflection go hand in hand, and by implementing a feedback loop, the system prevents ending up in a local minimum.

In this chapter, we explore planning and reflection in agents and how they can be used to plan out multi-step actions and improve their behavior as they go through the necessary steps. This brings us to the final component of a single agent (Figure 6-1).

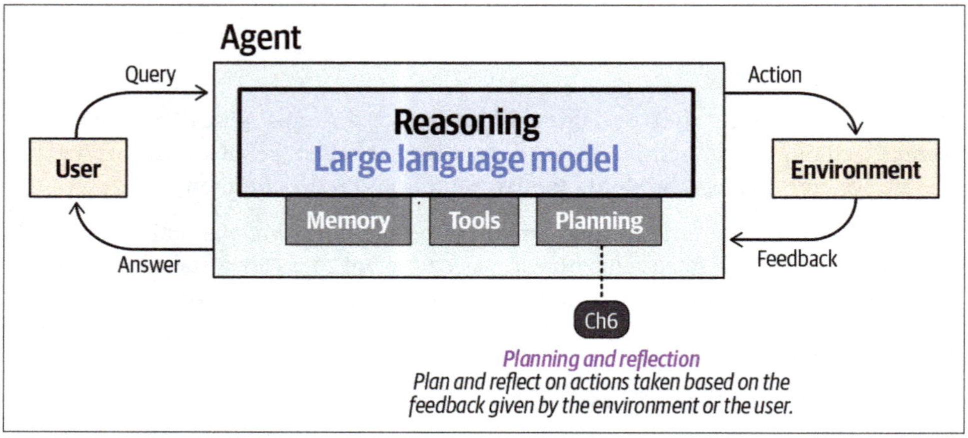

Figure 6-1. Planning is the final core component of a single agent

Planning

In Chapter 3, we explored how reasoning and extended thinking can bring LLMs to new heights. We briefly touched upon something vital in these systems, namely that advanced reasoning allows LLMs to plan out their behavior. There is a wide variety of methodologies to enable planning in reasoning LLMs effectively.

Task Decomposition

The first step in planning is to decompose an initial query into subtasks. Like the example at the beginning of the chapter, when you ask an agent to create a certain feature, it will split that query up into smaller tasks to execute. This is called *task decomposition* and allows the agent to simplify complicated tasks.[1] Figure 6-2 shows an example of the reasoning LLM creating this plan, where each task may also have a set of subtasks to complete.

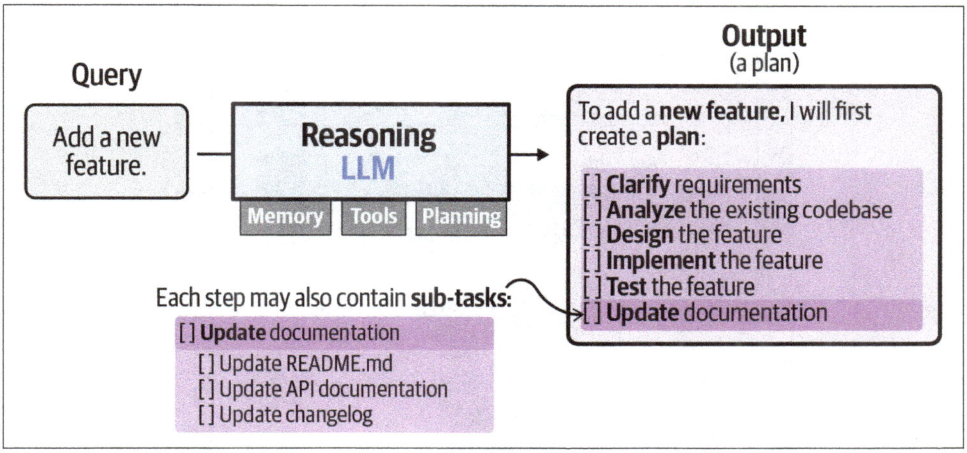

Figure 6-2. The reasoning LLM turning a user's query into a structured plan of steps

The tasks and subtasks in this plan may describe a tool that the reasoning LLM may use. As shown in Figure 6-3, the plan comes first, after which each (sub)task can be processed using tools. In this example, the agent creates a three-step plan to add a new feature to a codebase. The first task, analyzing the existing codebase, is done with a tool call to retrieve the code. It continues to analyze that code and communicate the core features. After that, it may update the plan and continue with the next task.

1 Huang, Xu et al. 2024. "Understanding the Planning of LLM Agents: A Survey," *arXiv*, 2402.02716.

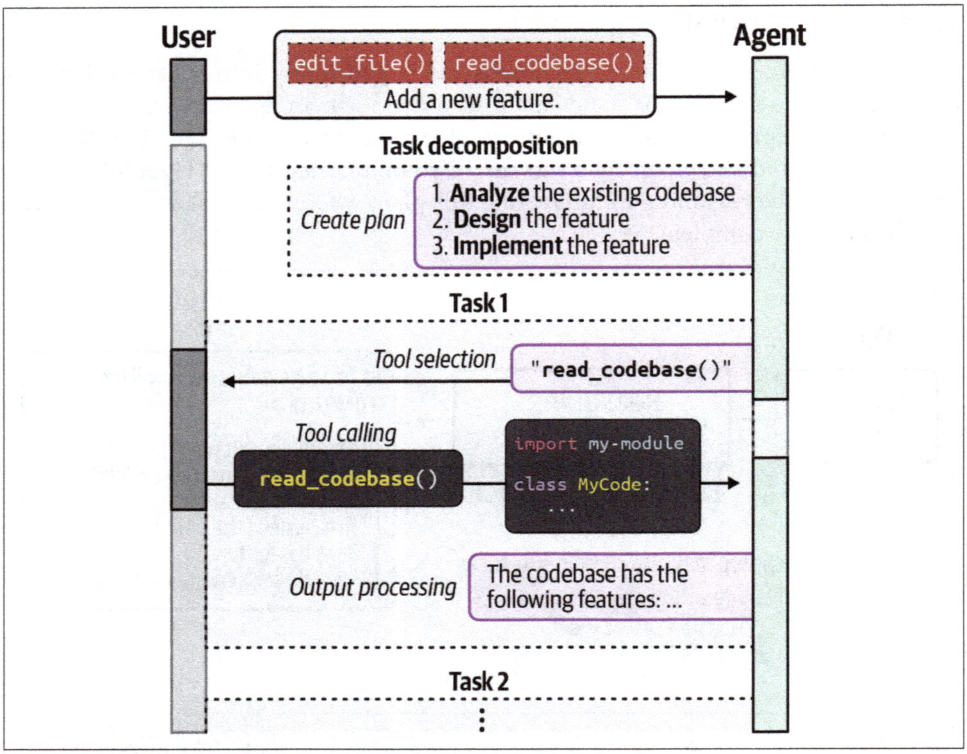

Figure 6-3. Combining planning with tool use, where the agent decomposes a goal into a multi-step execution plan

Chain-of-Thought

A major component of task decomposition, aside from having a reasoning LLM, is prompt engineering. We covered several of them in Chapter 3 from the perspective of reasoning traces, where several "thoughts" are sampled. We also covered Chain-of-Thought (CoT) as a common approach to create these reasoning traces. Remember that CoT is a process where the LLM is asked to solve problems step-by-step. This can be achieved by either providing examples to the LLM (few-shot prompting) or by simply stating, "Let's think step-by-step" (zero-shot prompting). This step-by-step process is, in fact, task decomposition. The original query is processed through separate reasoning traces that rely on the ones that came before (Figure 6-4). In other words, it breaks down the problem into sequential reasoning substeps.

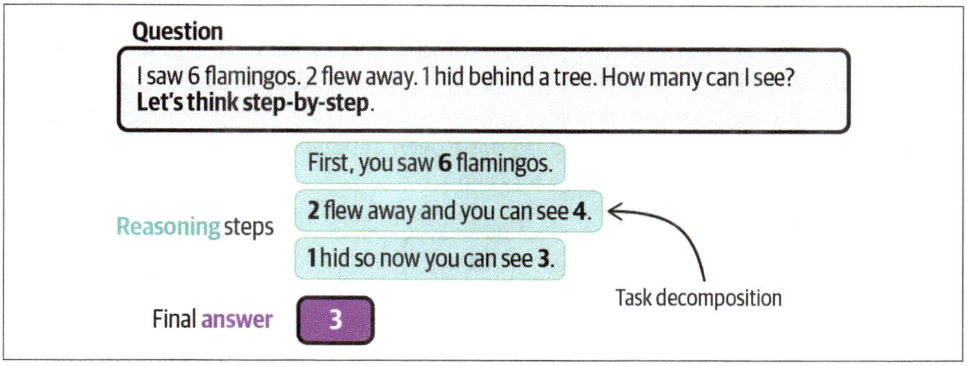

Figure 6-4. Chain-of-Thought carries out task decomposition in its reasoning steps by prompting the LLM to "think step-by-step"

The original idea of CoT was to make the model "think aloud" as a way to scale test-time compute and its performance. However, the "thinking" may very well be used as part of the planning process. For instance, when asked to create a plan and end it with "think step-by-step," a reasoning LLM will first think about the steps needed to resolve the original query. This is the reasoning trace the LLM can leverage to create the plan:

```
User: Add a new feature to my existing codebase. Let's think step-by-step.

LLM (CoT):
First, I need to clarify the requirements. What kind of feature is needed?
Second, I should analyze the existing codebase to understand the architecture.
Third, I need to design the feature and make sure nothing is left out.
Fourth, I should implement the feature in the existing codebase but without
changing its original functionality.
Fifth, I must test the feature thoroughly through unit and integration tests.
Finally, I need to update the documentation to explain how the new feature works.

LLM (Plan):
The plan will be as follows:

[ ] Clarify requirements
[ ] Analyze the existing codebase
[ ] Design the feature
[ ] Implement the feature
[ ] Test the feature
[ ] Update documentation
```

As such, CoT is a flexible technique that can be used for task decomposition in general, not just for "thinking aloud."

Since CoT, there have been many variants that similarly attempt to create more advanced reasoning traces for the purpose of task decomposition. These techniques, such as self-consistency and tree of thoughts,[2,3] sample multiple CoT traces from the LLM to find the most optimal trace. As shown in Figure 6-5, the original task is decomposed into "thoughts" (but could have been subtasks just the same), and from various "thoughts," the most optimal set is chosen.

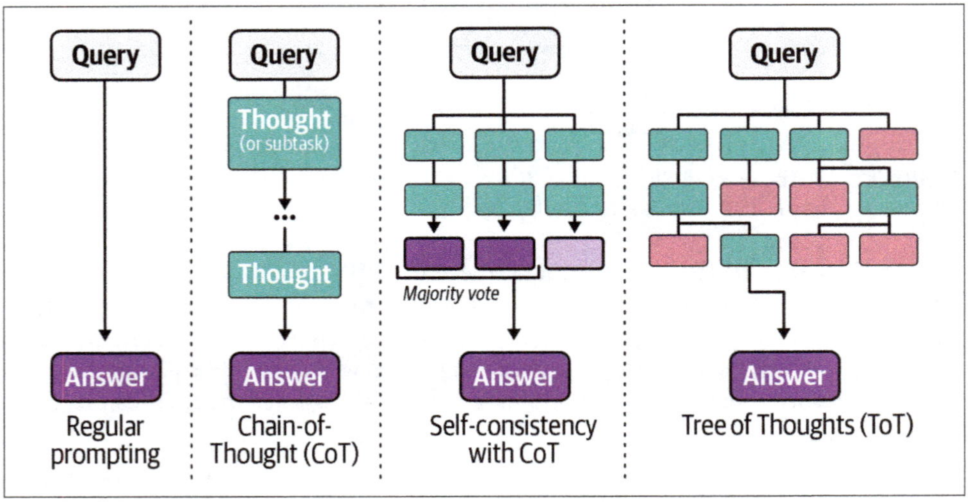

Figure 6-5. Four ways to handle a query: regular prompting, Chain-of-Thought, Self-consistency, and Tree of Thoughts

For self-consistency, the original task is broken down into subtasks, much like CoT, but multiple diverse paths are generated, and the most consistent answer is selected. In contrast, Tree of Thoughts explores multiple possible reasoning paths (where each node is a task or "thought") instead of following a linear chain-of-thought. As we explored in Chapter 3, methodologies like Beam Search and Monte Carlo Tree Search using reward models can be used to choose the best path.

Explicit planning

A CoT-like prompting technique for task decomposition that works quite well in the context of planning is least-to-most (LtM) prompting.[4] Released in 2022, LtM builds

2 Wang, Xuezhi et al. 2022. "Self-consistency Improves Chain of Thought Reasoning in Language Models," *arXiv*, 2203.11171.

3 Yao, Shunyu et al. 2023. "Tree of Thoughts: Deliberate Problem Solving with Large Language Models," *Advances in Neural Information Processing Systems*, 36: 11809-11822.

4 Zhou, Denny et al. 2022. "Least-to-Most Prompting Enables Complex Reasoning in Large Language Models," *arXiv*, 2205.10625.

upon CoT by first decomposing the problem into subproblems. Then, these subproblems are solved one by one. Compared to CoT, the solution of each subproblem is fed back into the LLM when attempting to solve the next problem (Figure 6-6).

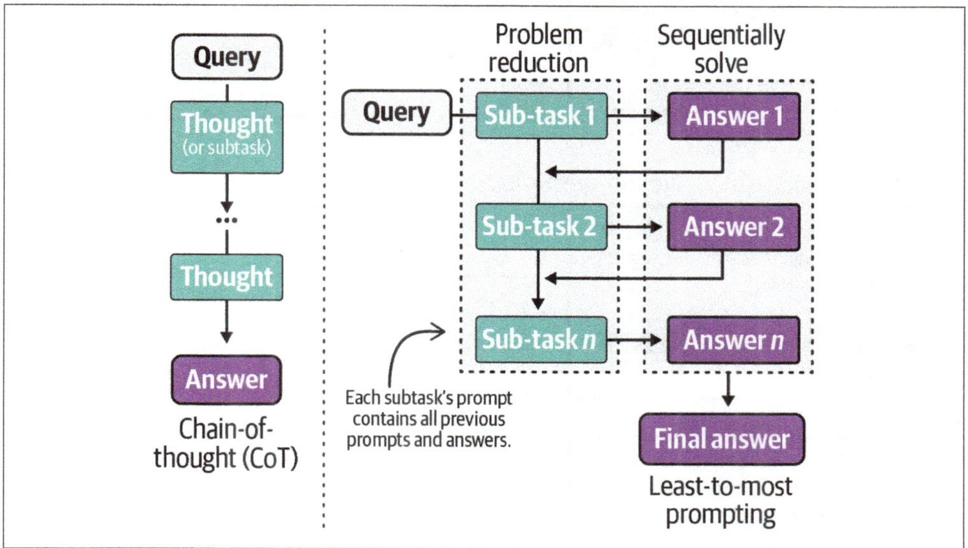

Figure 6-6. While Chain-of-Thought produces a linear trace, least-to-most prompting explicitly decomposes a problem and solves subproblems sequentially

As in CoT prompting, the problem to be solved is decomposed into a set of subproblems that build upon each other. In a second step, these subproblems are solved one by one. Contrary to CoT, the solution of previous subproblems is fed into the prompt, trying to solve the next problem.

A more practical example is shown in Figure 6-7, where instead of attempting to solve the problem directly, two stages are executed:

Problem reduction
: The original problem is decomposed into a set of manageable tasks.

Sequentially solve subquestions
: Each subtask is solved after the other. After each subtask, the previous subtask's question and answer are appended.

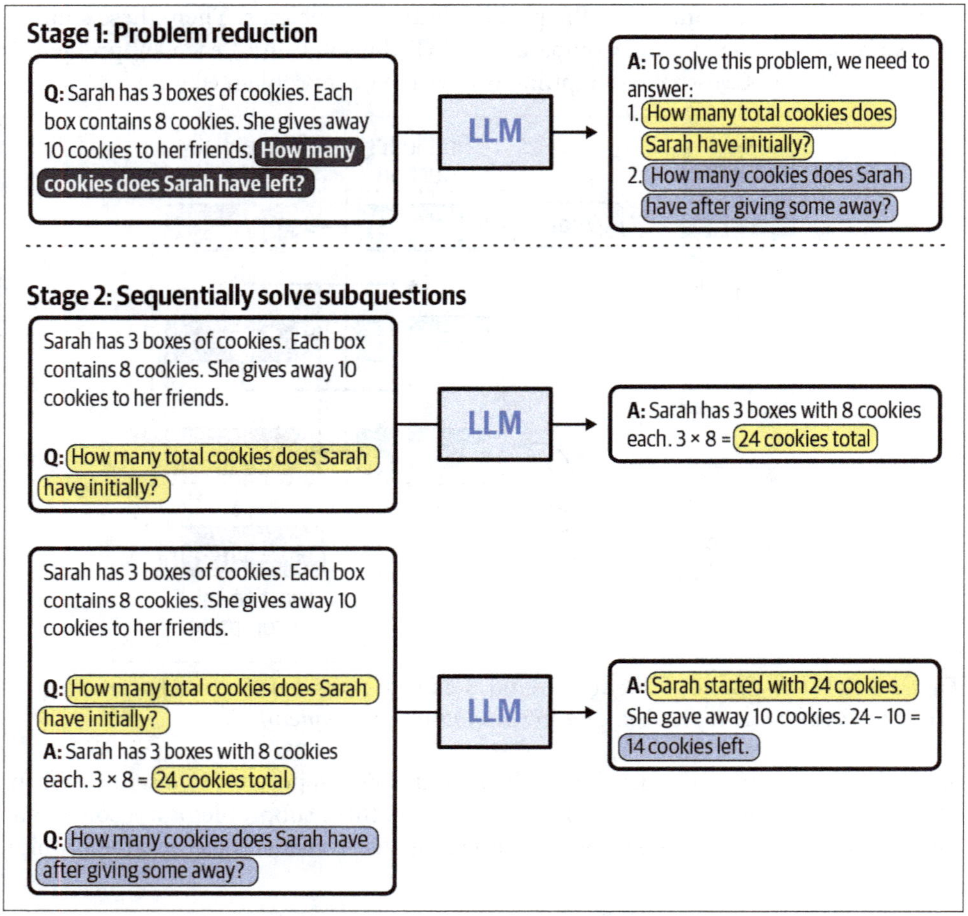

Figure 6-7. Least-to-most prompting on a math word problem, solving subquestions step-by-step to arrive at the final answer

To create this behavior, few-shot prompting is used, where examples are provided to the LLM to show how to decompose the initial tasks and subsequently solve them.

A zero-shot approach to task decomposition in the context of planning is plan-and-solve prompting.[5] This methodology is a direct extension of the zero-shot CoT, where instead of using "Let's think step-by-step," the LLM is asked to devise a plan first and then solve the problem step-by-step (Figure 6-8). It's a two-step process that is akin to the thinking and answer steps that we explored in Chapter 3:

5 Wang, Lei et al. 2023. "Plan-and-Solve Prompting: Improving Zero-Shot Chain-of-Thought Reasoning by Large Language Models," *arXiv*, 2305.04091.

Prompting for reasoning generation
: The model generates a plan and then carries it out by solving the problem step-by-step.

Answer extraction
: The output of the previous step is processed to create the final answer.

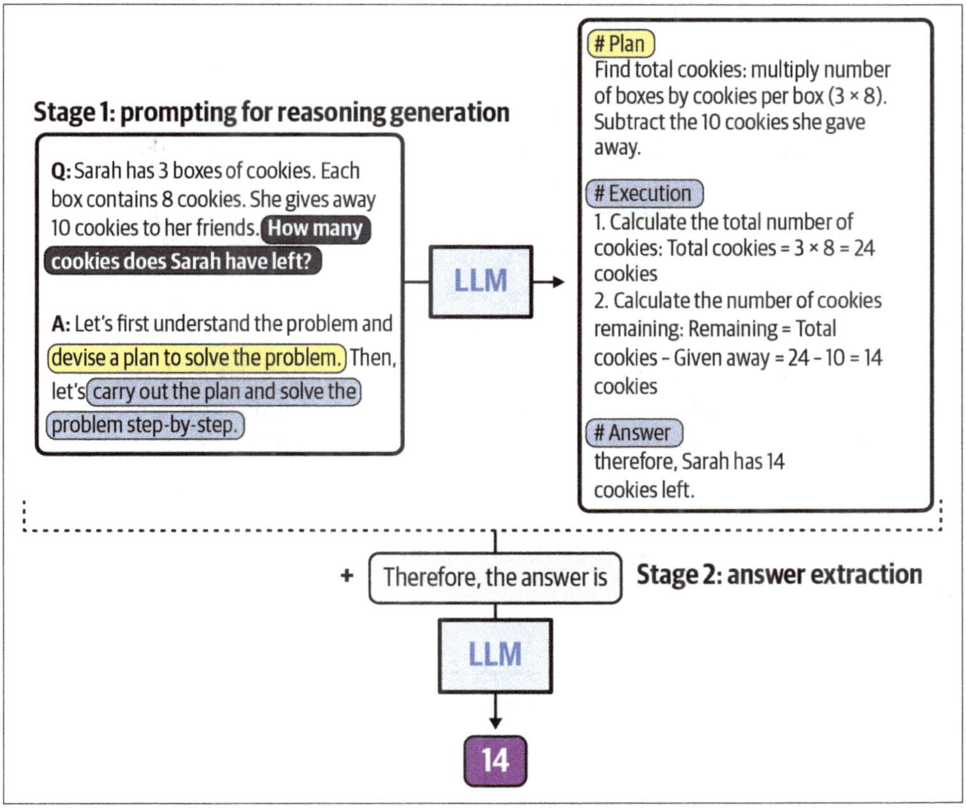

Figure 6-8. Plan-and-solve prompting on a math problem, where the plan and execution happen within a single reasoning step

Note how we again used the Q/A structure throughout these prompts. That was common in these early days of LLMs, where they were often trained primarily to autocomplete the prompt, so additional steering was needed for the model to understand that it should answer a given question. Their output is essentially the "thinking" process we know of reasoning LLMs, but it works just the same for regular LLMs, albeit an implicit process. Nowadays, most LLMs are already capable of creating advanced plans without needing complex instructions or specialized prompts. However, as explored in Chapter 3, they often need to be trained on these CoT- or planning-like reasoning traces to effectively reason and plan.

Action Sequencing

Least-to-most prompting and plan-and-solve prompting decompose a given problem into subtasks that are solved sequentially. These work great for LLMs, but not yet for agents, who sequence actions autonomously one after the other. Specifically, after the agent decides the (sub)goals it needs to achieve, it then determines a sequence of actions to continuously transition it from its current state to the desired goal state. This process is called *action sequencing* and requires not only a careful plan but also an efficient set of steps for the agent to follow.

For example, a coding agent needs to decide which optimal sequence of actions should be taken. If it skips over reading the codebase, for instance, then the agent would be quite inefficient and this could potentially lead to redundancy. To minimize wasted resources and reduce execution time, there needs to be a well-thought-out sequence of actions relating to the plan.

In this section, we'll explore methodologies for sequencing actions, of which important components are CoT-like reasoning and planning the sequence of actions.

We want the agent not only to create a plan but continuously solve each subtask while updating its current state. This idea is shown in Figure 6-9 and requires more sophisticated techniques than least-to-most prompting and plan-and-solve prompting.

The idea of these techniques is that agents rely on their LLMs' reasoning capabilities to dynamically adjust their plans based on new information as a result of previous steps. It also explains how agents can act autonomously after having created the initial plan.

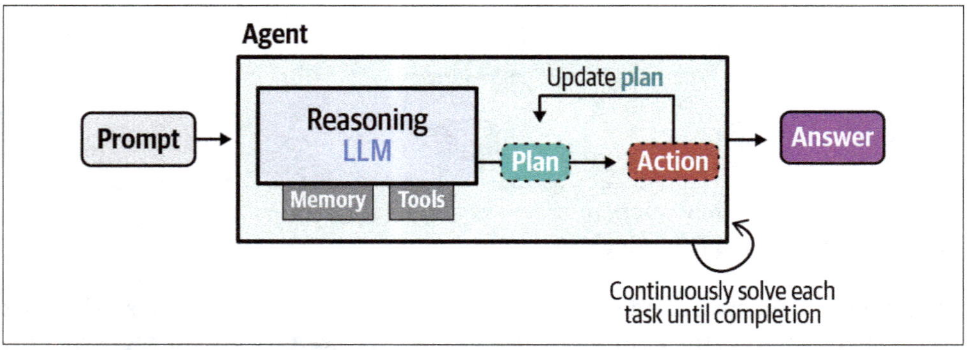

Figure 6-9. Action sequencing in an agent, where the agent generates thoughts, actions, and observations in an iterative loop

Reason and act with prompting

In previous examples, we explored how reasoning can be enabled with CoT and how LLMs can take actions (such as with the Toolformer discussed in Chapter 5). This split between reasoning and acting is shown in Figure 6-10.

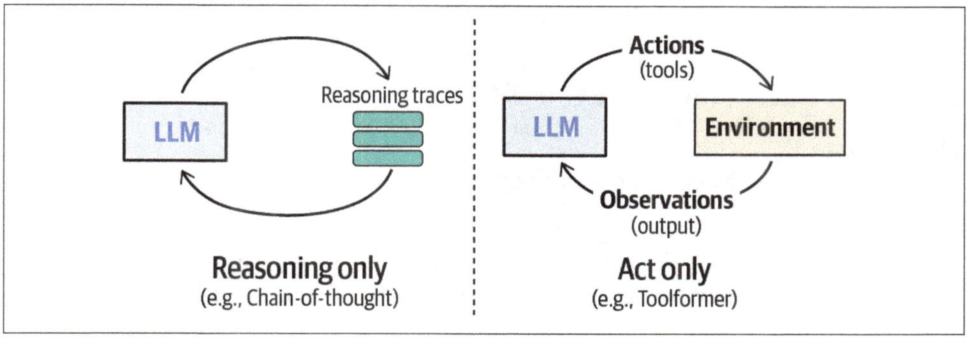

Figure 6-10. Before ReAct, reasoning and acting were treated as separate capabilities

However, having reasoning and acting separate makes it difficult for an agent to iterate. A common technique for determining an initial plan and continuously updating its action sequencing is the Reason and Act (ReAct) framework.[6] Compared to CoT, which embeds reasoning within the planning, ReAct decouples reasoning and planning. The framework takes inspiration from CoT for reasoning and tool usage for acting and combines them. As shown in Figure 6-11, this framework interleaves both reasoning traces and task-specific actions to create an iterative process of thinking and taking actions. As a result, we get the first truly autonomous systems that drive AI agents.

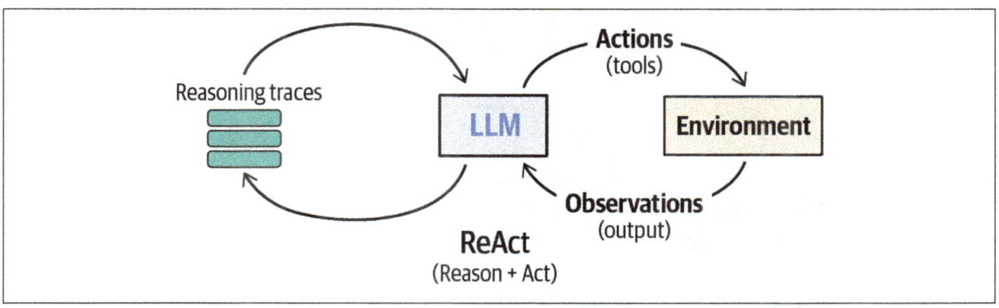

Figure 6-11. ReAct fuses reasoning and acting, allowing the LLM to produce a reasoning trace, execute an action, and observe the result

6 Yao, Shunyu et al. 2022. "ReAct: Synergizing Reasoning and Acting in Language Models," *The Eleventh International Conference on Learning Representations.*

The interleaving of reasoning and actions creates a feedback loop in which the model repeatedly cycles through a *thought-action-observation* process. In each loop, the model is asked to separate its textual output into three components:

Thought
: A reasoning step about the current situation

Action
: A set of actions to execute (e.g., tools)

Observation
: A reasoning step about the result of the action

This is achieved by prompting the model to create these three separate entities (Figure 6-12). Note that few-shot examples of thought, action, and observation cycles are typically added to make sure that the LLM matches the proposed behavior.

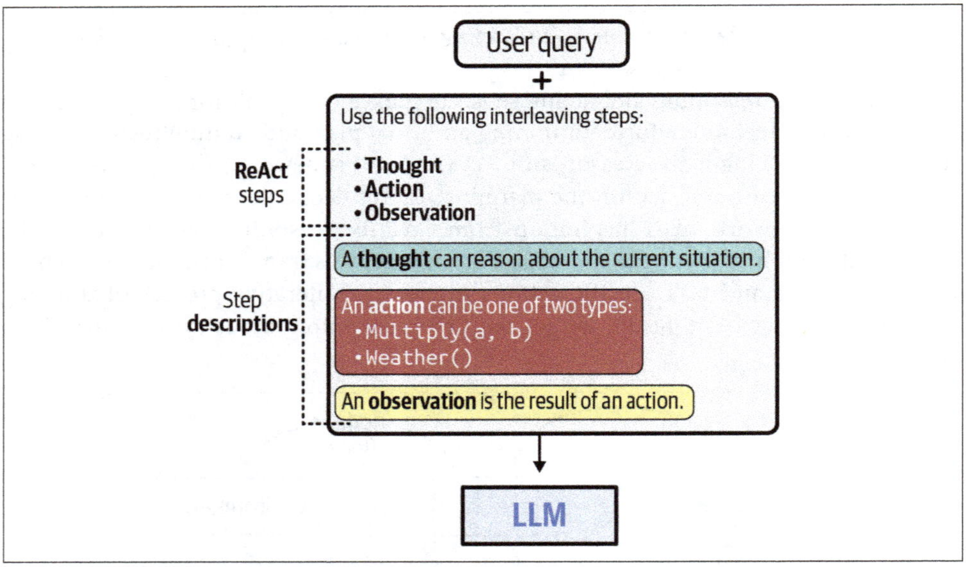

Figure 6-12. If the model has strong instruction-following capabilities, ReAct can be enabled through prompting

This type of prompt is at the core of a ReAct agent and steers the LLM's behavior toward cycles of thoughts, actions, and observations (see Figure 6-13). By iterating over thoughts and observations, the LLM can plan out actions, observe its output, and adjust accordingly. Then, the LLM will stop whenever it reaches a predefined goal.

ReAct agents can theoretically go on for hundreds of cycles but need to remember their previous steps and outcomes to effectively continue when context becomes an issue. For agents that go on to perform dozens or potentially hundreds of steps, the memory component becomes vital, especially context engineering, as we discussed in Chapter 4.

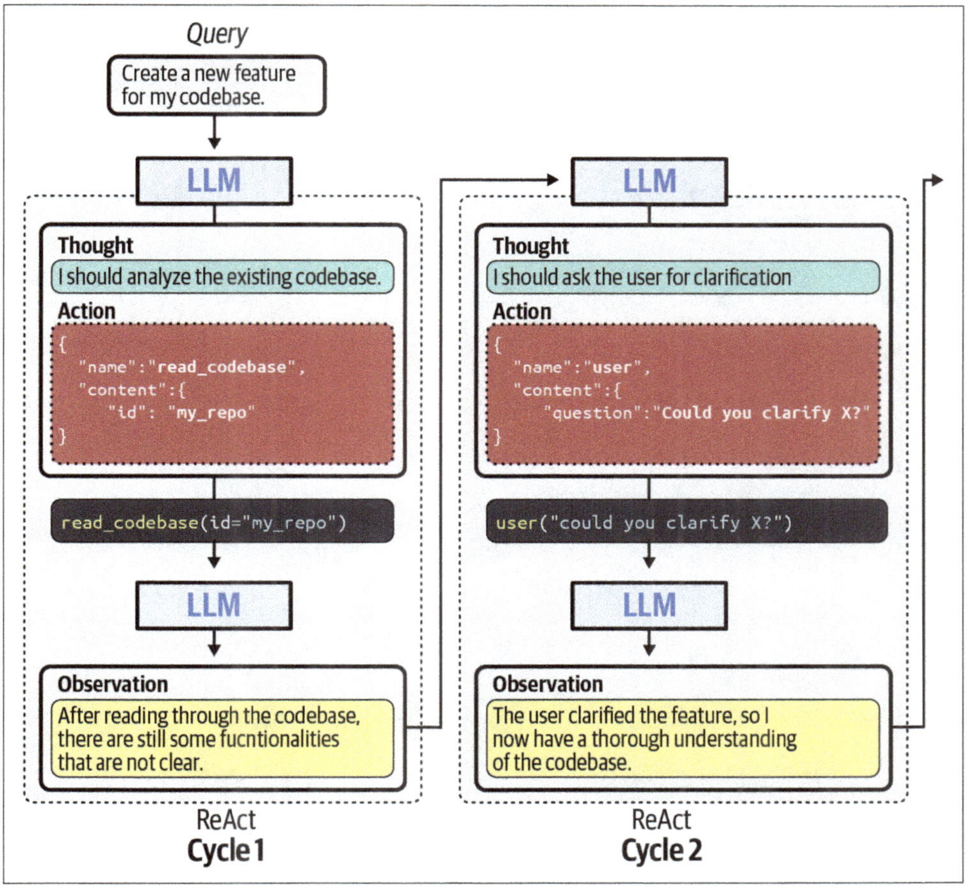

Figure 6-13. Two cycles of THOUGHT/ACTION/OBSERVATION using the ReAct framework

To give a bit more intuition about this ReAct flow and the final step in making your `TinyAgent` fully autonomous, let's implement it. For the most part, ReAct requires careful prompting to nudge the LLM's behavior toward loops of THOUGHT, ACTION, and OBSERVATION. To do so, let's create the `ReAct` class as the first planner class to use in your `TinyAgent`:

```
import re
from illustrated_agents.chapters.ch2 import Response

class ReAct:
```

```
    """ReAct module."""

    def __init__(self, max_steps: int = 10):
        """Initialize ReAct module.

        Arguments:
            max_steps: Maximum number of ReAct steps to perform.
        """
        self.max_steps = max_steps

    @property
    def prompt(self) -> str:
        return """
# ReAct (Reason and Act)

You are a ReAct agent that performs exactly ONE step per turn.

## ReAct Format

You use the following format for each step:

THOUGHT: [Your reasoning about what to do next]
ACTION:
{
    "tool": "a_tool_name",
    "kwargs": {"param": "value"},
}

An observation will be provided after each action. You do not generate the
observation yourself.

## ReAct Completion

To provide the final answer to the task, use an action blob with "tool":
"final_answer" tool.
It is the only way to complete the task, else you will be stuck on a loop.
So your final output should look like this:

ACTION:
{
    "tool": "final_answer",
    "kwargs": "insert your final answer here"
}

Use the `final_answer` tool when you are completely done with all subtasks and
have the final answer ready.
You can also use `final_answer` to directly reply to a user's question without
using any other tools.

"""

    def parse(self, response: Response) -> Response:
```

```python
        """Parse a ReAct formatted response into THOUGHT and ACTION."""
        text = response.content

        # The patterns for each section
        patterns = {
            "THOUGHT": r"THOUGHT:\s*(.+?)(?=ACTION:|OBSERVATION:|$)",
            "ACTION": r"ACTION:\s*(.+?)(?=THOUGHT:|OBSERVATION:|$)",
        }

        # Extract each section using regex
        result = {}
        for key, pattern in patterns.items():
            match = re.search(pattern, text, re.DOTALL)
            result[key] = match.group(1).strip() if match else ""

        # Update Response and extract only the action
        response.content = result["ACTION"]
        response.reasoning = result["THOUGHT"]
        return response
```

It might seem like a lot, but only three things are happening within this ReAct class:

1. The `max_steps` parameter is used to decide the maximum number of steps your `TinyAgent` will get to perform its autonomous behavior. The agent can still decide to stop early, but this prevents it from being stuck in a loop.
2. The `.prompt` property, much like in `Tools`, is used to provide sufficient context on how to approach the ReAct behavior. It specifically describes the ReAct format (`## ReAct Format`) and how it should provide a final answer (`## ReAct Completion`). Note that this ReAct implementation assumes that the actions are with `Tools` and not the `NativeTools` class that we covered in Chapter 5.
3. The `.parse` function is used to convert the THOUGHT/ACTION description into separate fields so they can be used as the `Response.reasoning` and `Response.content` fields, respectively. Remember from Chapter 5 that the `Tools` class assumes that the tool call is initially in the `Response.content` field since `Tools` uses prompt-based tool calling rather than native tool calling.

Now that we have the ReAct class, let's implement it in your `TinyAgent` to create your autonomous agent. The most important step to create a fully autonomous agent is...a for-loop! Truly, with the capabilities of agents these days, it all boils down to iteratively calling an LLM until it decides to stop the loop.

With the ReAct framework, we structure the for-loop into the THOUGHT/ACTION/OBSERVATION steps to ensure the model has a clear goal and a clear set of steps to reach it. Implementing this into your `TinyAgent` will require three main changes:

- Add the ReAct instruction to the system prompt.
- Add an *autonomy* loop to the `.run` function.
- Parse the LLM's response into THOUGHT/ACTION.

The updated `TinyAgent` is as follows, where we highlighted the code that was added:

```
from illustrated_agents.chapters.ch2 import Response, Trajectory
from illustrated_agents.chapters.ch4 import Memory
from illustrated_agents.chapters.ch5 import Tools


class TinyAgent:
    """A minimal, modular, and educational agent framework."""

    def __init__(self, llm: LLM, memory: Memory, tools: Tools, planner: ReAct):
        self.llm = llm
        self.memory = memory
        self.tools = tools
        self.planner = planner

        self.trajectory = Trajectory()

        # Build system prompt with all components
        system_prompt = "You are a helpful assistant.\n\n"
        system_prompt += self.planner.prompt
        system_prompt += self.tools.prompt
        self.memory.add("system", system_prompt)

    def run(self, task: str) -> str:
        """Run the agent on a task."""
        self.memory.add("user", task)
        self.trajectory.initialize(task)

        # *Autonomy* loop
        for step in range(self.planner.max_steps):
            result = self._step()
            if result is not None:
                return result

       return "Max steps reached without completion."

    def _step(self) -> str | None:
        """Perform a single step."""
        # THOUGHT: Generate response and add to memory
        response = self.llm.generate(
            self.memory.get_messages(), tools=self.tools.schemas
        )
        self.memory.add(
            "assistant", response.content, tool_call=response.tool_call
        )
```

```
        # Tool parsing
        response = self.planner.parse(response)
        response = self.tools.parse(response)

        # ANSWER: Stopping mechanism
        if self.tools.is_done(response):
            self.trajectory.add(response)
            return response.content

        return self._execute_action(response)

    def _execute_action(self, response: Response) -> None:
        """Execute a tool action."""

        # ACTION: execute tools
        result = self.tools.execute(response)

        # OBSERVATION: add tool results to memory and display
        role, observation = self.tools.observation(result)
        self.memory.add(role, observation)
        self.trajectory.add(response, observation)

        return None
```

We highlighted the sections that were added to indicate how little actually is needed to go from a tool calling LLM to an autonomous agent.

Let's try the agent out and ask it to use several tools to answer a given question. We keep it simple and give it the add, multiply, and subtract tools:

```
from illustrated_agents.chapters.ch2 import LLM
from illustrated_agents.toolbox import add, multiply, subtract

# Gemma 3 12B (no native thinking or tool calling)
llm = LLM(model="gemma3:12b")

# Tools
tools = Tools()
tools.add_tool("add", add, "add(a: str, b: str)")
tools.add_tool("subtract", subtract, "subtract(a: str, b: str)")
tools.add_tool("multiply", multiply, "multiply(a: str, b: str)")

# Memory
memory = Memory()

# ReAct
react = ReAct(max_steps=10)

# Create agent
agent = TinyAgent(llm=llm, tools=tools, memory=memory, planner=react)

# Multi-step task with reasoning
agent.run("What is (4.6 + 6.685) x 4, and then subtract 3.14 from the result?")
```

This gives:

```
'42.0'
```

That is correct!

Although this is the correct answer, we're much more interested in the full trajectory of the agent. Did it correctly use the tools one at a time and decide to stop when it got the answer? To find out, let's print out the trajectory:

```
print(agent.trajectory.runs)
```

Which gives:

```
[
    {
        'query': 'What is (4.6 + 6.685) x 4, and then subtract 3.14
        from the result?',
        'steps': [
            Step(
                thought='First, I need to add 4.6 and 6.685.
                Then, I need to multiply the result by 4.
                Finally, I need to subtract 3.14 from that final result.',
                action={'tool': 'add', 'kwargs': {'a': '4.6', 'b': '6.685'}},
                observation='OBSERVATION: 11.285',
                answer=None,
                metadata=None
            ),
            Step(
                thought="Now that I've added 4.6 and 6.685, which resulted in
                11.285, I need to multiply this by 4.",
                action={
                  'tool': 'multiply',
                  'kwargs': {'a': '11.285', 'b': '4'},
    },
                observation='OBSERVATION: 45.14',
                answer=None,
                metadata=None
            ),
            Step(
                thought='I have now multiplied 11.285 by 4, obtaining 45.14.
                The final step is to subtract 3.14 from this result.',
                action={
                  'tool': 'subtract', 'kwargs': {'a': '45.14', 'b': '3.14'}
                  },
                  observation='OBSERVATION: 42.0',
                  answer=None,
                  metadata=None
              ),
              Step(
                  thought="I've completed all the necessary calculations.
                  I added 4.6 and 6.685, multiplied the result by 4, and then
                  subtracted 3.14. The final answer is 42.0.",
```

```
                action=None,
                observation=None,
                answer='42.0',
                metadata=None
            )
        ]
    }
]
```

The trajectory shows that the agent took four steps:

add
: The agent using the THOUGHT field to already make up a plan to execute, of which the first was to add values together.

multiply
: It reflects on its previous action and continues on with the next.

subtract
: It reflects on its previous action and continues on with the next.

Returned the final answer
: The agent saw that it calculated all the necessary steps and returned the final with the `final_answer` tool.

With the ReAct framework, we have all the major components to create a truly autonomous system that is capable of independently taking actions:

Reasoning LLM
: The agent's brain that is capable of advanced decision making and planning

Tools
: Used to interact with the agent's environment

Memory
: Prevents the LLM from forgetting past actions and observations

Planning
: Task decomposition to create plans and frameworks, such as ReAct, to create autonomous behavior

When all these components are combined in one system, and that system is capable of running continuously (imagine a while-loop or a for-loop), you have an agent! In Figure 6-14, we visualize this system with an example of how these main components could be built.

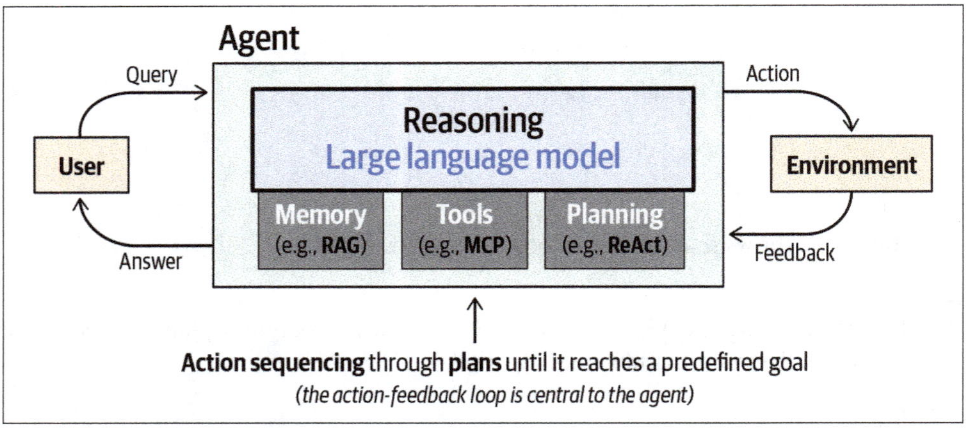

Figure 6-14. Action sequencing allows the LLM to iteratively work on a problem until it solves it

Where tools, as covered in Chapter 5, were all about single-turn processes, ReAct-like frameworks turn them into multi-turn processes that allow agents to make complete use of memory, tools, and planning.

Reason and Act with supervised fine-tuning

ReAct-like frameworks have been quite popular for performing action sequencing. However, much like we explored in the tooling chapter, prompt engineering is only the first step in steering an LLM's behavior. Prompt engineering, much like is done in ReAct, often requires few-shot prompting to get the correct behavior. This can waste tokens in the context and be difficult to get right. FireAct is one of the first methodologies to fine-tune an LLM on ReAct trajectories as a way to instill the ReAct framework into a small LLM.[7] The method is quite straightforward and consists of two steps.

In step 1, an LLM (GPT-4) is used to generate different kinds of trajectories (e.g., CoT and ReAct) based on questions from several datasets. The idea is that for different questions, different methodologies might be needed to solve them. A straightforward question that requires no agentic behavior would need only CoT-like inferencing, whereas a potential multi-turn question would require a ReAct framework to solve the problem. In Figure 6-15, you can see how various questions are processed through different prompt templates (CoT, ReAct, and Reflexion, an extension of ReAct that also includes feedback into the cycles)[8] to generate their respective

7 Chen, Baian et al. 2023. "FireAct: Toward Language Agent Fine-Tuning," *arXiv*, 2310.05915.

8 Shinn, Noah et al. 2023. "Reflexion: Language Agents with Verbal Reinforcement Learning," *Advances in Neural Information Processing Systems*, 36: 8634-8652.

trajectories. A trajectory for a question processed with ReAct, for example, would contain sequences of thoughts, actions, and observations with a final answer.

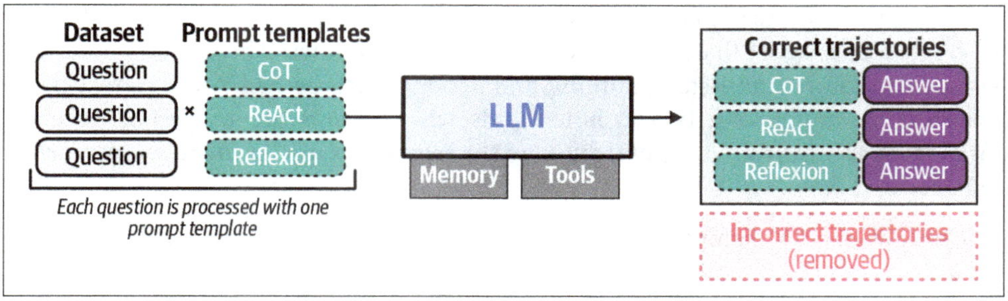

Figure 6-15. Supervised fine-tuning applied using ReAct trajectories by keeping only correct trajectories

These generated trajectories serve as the training data used for fine-tuning a smaller LM. The trajectories, however, are first converted to all have the same ReAct format. CoT, for instance, is turned into a one-round ReAct trajectory where the "thought" is the intermediate reasoning and "action" that returns the answer. Note that it does not have an observation since there is only one round. After formatting, this data is then used to fine-tune a smaller model (Llama 2). The authors experimented with both a full fine-tune as well as fine-tuning only a small part of the entire model using Low-Rank Adaptation.[9] From their experiments, fine-tuning on trajectories outperformed the prompt-based ReAct framework. Perhaps more importantly, there was no need to add few-shot examples to create the ReAct cycles, which makes inference more efficient and prevents needlessly filling up the context.

Reason and Act with reinforcement learning

As we explored in Chapter 5, a limitation of SFT is that the LLM learns to mimic the example data instead of adapting through experiences. It lacks the ability to explore the environment, which tends to lead to suboptimal policies. In contrast, RL is a powerful approach for enabling LLMs to refine their strategies by learning from the feedback rather than simply mimicking behavior. By receiving rewards for actions and refining its policy through trial and error, the model is encouraged to actively explore its environment.

An interesting technique to explore ReAct through the lens of RL is Exploration-based Trajectory Optimization (ETO).[10] Compared to FireAct, ETO uses RL to

9 Hu, Edward J. et al. 2022. "LoRA: Low-Rank Adaptation of Large Language Models," *The Tenth International Conference on Learning Representations.*

10 Song, Yifan et al. 2024. "Trial and Error: Exploration-based Trajectory Optimization for LLM Agents," *arXiv*, 2403.02502.

encourage the LLM to learn and explore trajectories rather than attempt to mimic behavior. ETO consists of two steps.

In step 1, the authors applied SFT, using ReAct data, on an LLM (Llama-2-7B Chat),[11] to create a base agent that has inherent planning capabilities. The datasets used were tasks that require multi-step planning and actions, such as ALFWorld, a text-based environment mimicking typical households where agents are to perform specific tasks, such as "*clean a tomato and put it on the countertop*" or "*examine an alarm clock with the desk lamp*."

The following is an example directly taken from ALFWorld, complete with actions:

```
You are in the middle of a room. Looking quickly around you, you see a safe 1,
a shelf 4, a drawer 2, a bed 1, a drawer 1, a shelf 5, a shelf 2, a sidetable 2,
a shelf 3, a drawer 3, a shelf 1, a sidetable 1, a desk 1, and a garbagecan 1.

Your task is to: examine an alarmclock with the desklamp.

> go to desk 1
You arrive at loc 8. On the desk 1, you see a pen 1, a bowl 1, a alarmclock 2,
a pencil 2, a pencil 3, a creditcard 3, a book 1, a alarmclock 3, a keychain 3,
and a book 2.

> take alarmclock 2 from desk 1
You pick up the alarmclock 2 from the desk 1.

> go to sidetable 2
You arrive at loc 1. On the sidetable 2, you see a desklamp 1, and
an alarmclock 1.

> use desklamp 1
You won!
```

As Figure 6-16 shows, the initial model was fine-tuned using successful ReAct trajectories that include the task and the ReAct trajectory (see previous example). The authors refer to SFT as behavior cloning, since this technique encourages the LLM to mimic the behavior shown in the data instead of having it figure out the correct answer on its own. In this context, SFT is therefore often referred to as imitation learning.

Step 2 is an iterative process that switches between the exploration and training phases (see Figure 6-17). During exploration, the base agent interacts with the environment and attempts to solve the given tasks. From the ReAct trajectories that are generated in this process, the failed trajectories are sampled. These are then paired with correct trajectories that were previously collected for these tasks. During the training phase, the pairs of trajectories are then used to further fine-tune the LLM using an RL algorithm,

11 Touvron, Hugo et al. 2023. "Llama 2: Open Foundation and Fine-tuned Chat Models," *arXiv*, 2307.09288.

namely Direct Preference Optimization (DPO).[12] During this fine-tuning, the authors aimed to increase the likelihood of successful trajectories and decrease the likelihood of failed trajectories. In other words, the agent learns contrastive information from the failure/success trajectory pairs to update the RL policy.

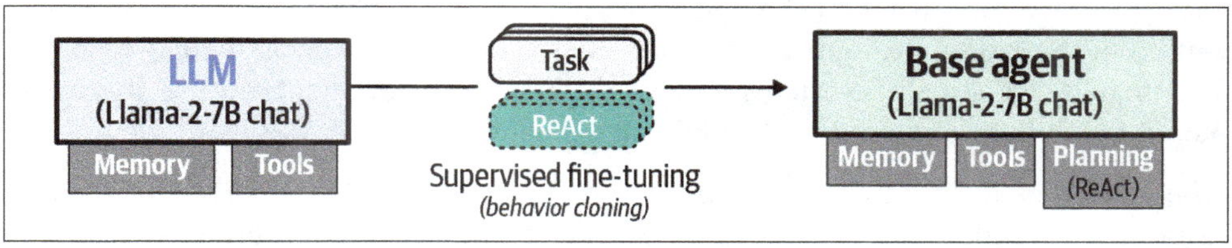

Figure 6-16. Supervised fine-tuning allows for mimicking the behavior as shown in the training data

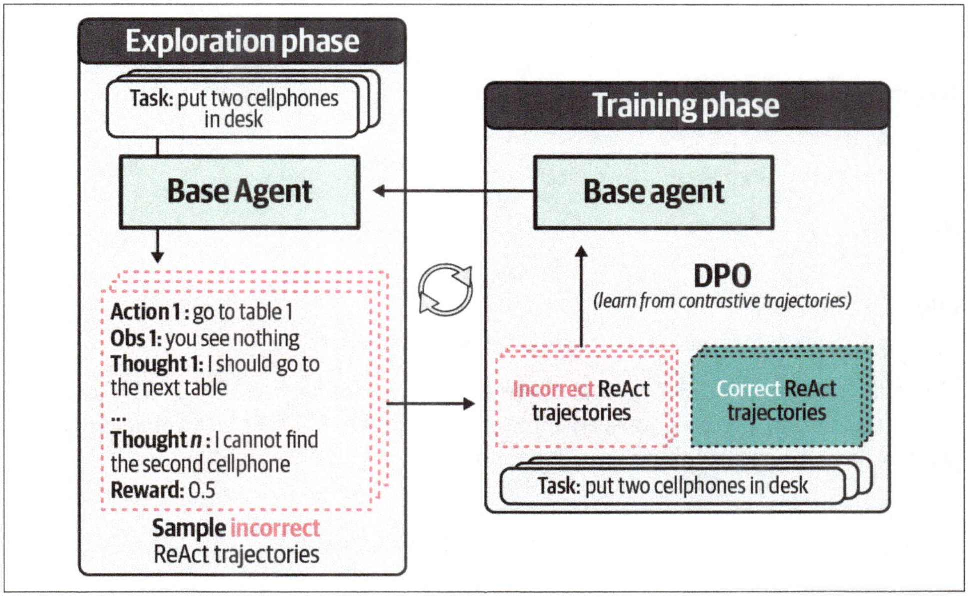

Figure 6-17. The two phases of RL in Exploration-based Trajectory Optimization (ETO): exploration and optimization

As we have explored several times before, using SFT followed by RL is a strong learning paradigm for these models. By starting with SFT, the LLM learns the right type of behaviors and formatting it should use. It gives the foundation it needs to then explore and improve upon itself by using exploration and exploitation in RL.

12 Rafailov, Rafael et al. 2023. "Direct Preference Optimization: Your Language Model Is Secretly a Reward Model," *Advances in Neural Information Processing Systems*, 36: 53728-53741.

A major benefit of using SFT or RL (or both) is that there is no need for ReAct via prompting. As covered previously, we used a specific prompting scheme (THOUGHT/ACTION/OBSERVATION) to create this ReAct-like behavior. This was possible because LLMs are great at instruction-following, so that we could steer the model toward this specific behavior. However, it can be quite brittle and takes up a fair bit of the system prompt. Training a model to do this natively is an answer to this. Fortunately, we already created many of the needed components to use the native ReAct capabilities of newer LLMs, Gemma 4 in particular.

The first step to do this is to choose a model that is actually capable of native reasoning and tool calls. The model we explored in previous chapters is Gemma 4 E4B, so let's choose that:

```
from illustrated_agents.chapters.ch2 import LLM

# Gemma 4 E4B (with native thinking and tool calling)
llm = LLM(model="gemma4:e4b", think=True)
```

We previously implemented loops of:

THOUGHT
: A reasoning step about the current situation

ACTION
: An action to execute (e.g., a tool)

OBSERVATION
: A generated observation (typically the output of a tool)

However, with native tool calling, there is no need for explicit ACTION, and with native reasoning, there is no need for explicit THOUGHT. We can replace what we already have for each of them with the following:

THOUGHT
: Replace with `Response.reasoning` and `NativeReAct`

ACTION
: Replace with `Response.tool_call` and `NativeTools`

OBSERVATION
: Replace with adding the output of a tool to memory using `Response.observation`, which gives us the `tool` role

Since we already have `NativeTools`, we only need to create `NativeReAct`. In that class, it essentially removes all behavior from the previously generated ReAct class. With native tool calling and reasoning, there's no need for a ReAct-specific prompt or parsing it into THOUGHT/ACTION/OBSERVATION. Instead, all the behavior it needs is to define the maximum number of steps:

```python
from illustrated_agents.chapters.ch6 import ReAct

class NativeReAct(ReAct):
    """ReAct using native LLM reasoning instead of text-based parsing."""

    @property
    def prompt(self) -> str:
        return ""

    def parse(self, response):
        return response
```

What is left is a for-loop that uses native tool calling and reasoning each step. The LLM decides what to use when and will stop only when there is no tool call. Since the LLM was trained specifically using SFT and RL to perform ReAct, it already knows how to do this.

This means that the model can choose at every step whether to perform:

Reasoning
: As captured in `Response.reasoning`

Tool calling
: As captured in `Response.tool_call`

Providing a final answer
: As captured in `Response.content`

Because this is all we needed already, let's demonstrate it with an example:

```python
from illustrated_agents.chapters.ch4 import Memory
from illustrated_agents.chapters.ch5 import NativeTools
from illustrated_agents.chapters.ch6 import TinyAgent
from illustrated_agents.toolbox import add, multiply, subtract

# Register tools
tools = NativeTools()
tools.add_tool("add", add, "add(a: str, b: str)")
tools.add_tool("subtract", subtract, "subtract(a: str, b: str)")
tools.add_tool("multiply", multiply, "multiply(a: str, b: str)")

# Memory
memory = Memory()

# ReAct
react = NativeReAct(max_steps=10)

# Create agent
agent = TinyAgent(llm=llm, tools=tools, memory=memory, planner=react)

# Multi-step task with reasoning
agent.run("What is (4.6 + 6.685) x 4, and then subtract 3.14 from the result?")
```

Which gives:

```
'The result is 42.0.'
```

As before, the answer is correct. Your `TinyAgent` now does ReAct natively. To see what happened behind the scenes, let's explore the trajectory:

```
for index, step in enumerate(agent.trajectory.runs[0]["steps"]):
    print(f"-- Step {index+1} ---")
    if step.action:
        print(f"Tool: {step.action}")
    else:
        print(f"Answer: {step.answer}")
```

Which gives:

```
[
  {
       'query':
'What is (4.6 + 6.685) x 4, and then subtract 3.14
from the result?',
      'steps': [
           Step(
              thought='1.  Calculate `(4.6 + 6.685)`.\n
2. Multiply the result of step 1 by `4`.\n3.
Subtract `3.14` from the result of step 2.
...
Since I cannot execute all steps at once,
I must start with the first step.',
                action={'tool': 'add', 'kwargs': {'a': '4.6', 'b': '6.685'}},
                observation='11.285',
                 answer=None,
                 metadata=None
            ),
            Step(
                thought='',
                action={
                  'tool': 'multiply',
                  'kwargs': {'a': '11.285', 'b': '4'}
    },
                observation='45.14',
                answer=None,
                metadata=None
            ),
           Step(
                  thought='',
                action={
                   'tool': 'subtract',
                   'kwargs': {'a': '45.14', 'b': '3.14'}
     },
                observation='42.0',
                answer=None,
                metadata=None
```

```
            ),
            Step(
                thought='...
Since all calculations have been performed and the final result is available,
I can now answer the user\'s question with the final value.',
                action=None,
                observation=None,
                answer='The result is 42.0.',
                metadata={
                    'model': 'gemma4:e4b', 'prompt_tokens': 325,
                    'completion_tokens': 267
                }
            )
        ]
    }
]
```

Looking at the steps, you can see something similar to the ReAct loop we had before:

Step 1
: Reasoning, tool call (add), and observation

Step 2
: Tool call (multiply) and observation

Step 3
: Tool call (subtract) and observation

Step 4
: Reasoning and *answer*

Although similar to loops of THOUGHT/OBSERVATION/ACTION, it foregoes reasoning when it calls the tool. Each LLM will have different behavior, but they do generally boil down to these kinds of loops.

What We Built

```
TinyAgent/
├── agent.py ← Updated (Autonomy with a for-loop!)
├── llm.py
├── memory.py
├── planning.py  ← New (Added the ReAct (Reason and Act) framework)
├── toolbox.py
├── tools.py
└── trajectory.py
```

The true foundation of your `TinyAgent` is now complete! By exploring both prompt-based and native capabilities, you get to see how an agent actually works behind the curtain. If we had jumped directly into native capabilities, much of the behavior would have seemed like a closed box.

Agents That Continuously Improve

As AI agents evolve, instead of relying on training phases or reward models for improvement, these systems start relying on self-generated feedback loops to continuously improve their performance as they act. Feedback prevents agents from ending up in local minima and provides valuable information on potentially better solutions to pursue. In practice, not all feedback is equivalent, and continuous self-improvement is tricky to pursue for LLMs that are fundamentally static when they act. In this section, we explore methods for AI agents to reflect on their behavior and pursue self-improvement as they act with their environment(s).

Reflection

The feedback that an agent gets from its environment is typically different from process feedback. The environment gives feedback based on an action: "*When I do X (action), the environment gives back Y (feedback).*" Feedback, as covered in this section, is often referred to as "reflection" to demonstrate that it is typically an internal process where the LLM should be critical of its own output and processes. After all, reflecting on past behavior helps us learn from prior failings. Reflection, however, can also be in tandem with external sources to supply feedback.

The techniques covered in this section are all based on prompting techniques and are therefore relatively straightforward to implement.

Self-Refine

An elegant approach to feedback is Self-Refine,[13] a prompting framework where the LLM provides feedback and refines its own results. The approach is quite straightforward and lets an LLM iteratively improve its answer by acting as its own editor. The idea was inspired by how people draft and revise their solutions.

In this framework, the LLM generates an initial answer and then proceeds to critique its own output (feedback). Based on that reflection step, the LLM refines its answer and incorporates the necessary change (refine). This cycle repeats until a stopping criterion has been reached, such as the number of steps or an LLM-guided stopping mechanism. This cycle between feedback and refine is shown in Figure 6-18.

13 Madaan, Aman et al. 2023. "Self-Refine: Iterative Refinement with Self-Feedback," *Advances in Neural Information Processing Systems,* 36: 46534-46594.

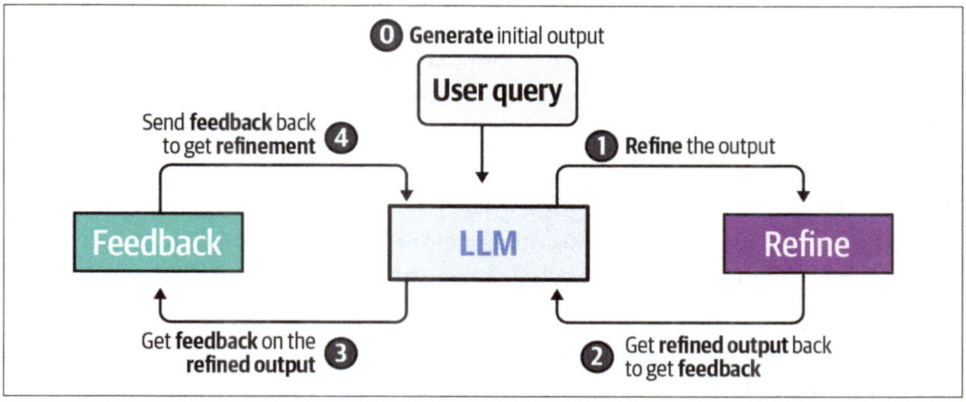

Figure 6-18. The main steps of self-refine where the same LLM continuously refines generated output

The same LLM generates the initial output, the refined output, and feedback, hence the name *Self-Refine*. Figure 6-19 illustrates an example from the paper where, after an initial output, an iterative loop is generated of first feedback and then a refined output.

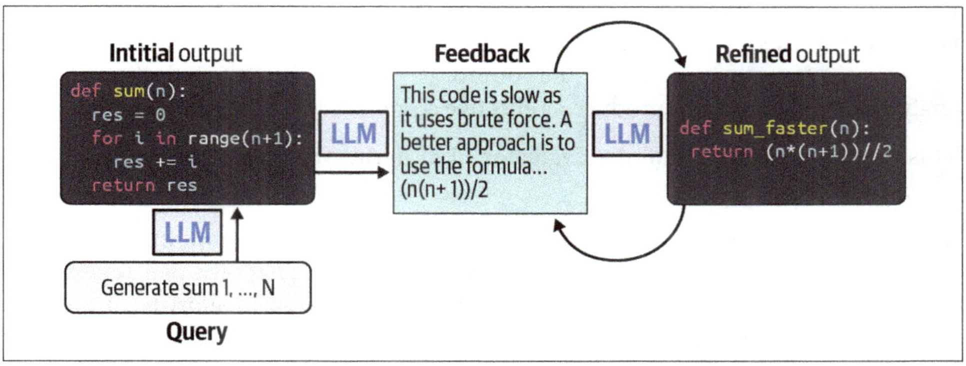

Figure 6-19. An example from the Self-Refine paper where an LLM starts from a given generated output and continuously updates and refines it

As you might have noted, this framework was built around LLMs refining and improving their own outputs, but no mention is given of an agentic system. Next, let's explore how ReAct can use similar feedback mechanisms to improve agentic trajectories.

Reflexion

A more involved but quite successful attempt at instilling reflective behavior in agents is Reflexion,[14] a prompting framework where agents verbally reflect on previous tasks through internal and external feedback. The authors used three entities within this framework:

Actor LLM
: A ReAct LLM in charge of executing actions based on observations and trajectory data. This can be considered the main "brain" of the agent.

Evaluator LLM
: An LLM that assesses the quality of the current trajectory and output generated by the Actor LLM.

Self-Reflection LLM
: This LLM generates more nuanced and specific feedback based on the full trajectory, including the output of the Evaluator LLM.

As shown in Figure 6-20, the Actor LLM is based on a ReAct agent and will convert the initial task into actions and interact with the environment. The resulting observations are saved in the full trajectory for which the Evaluator LLM rewards a score that reflects the performance of the Actor LLM given the task. The Evaluator LLM is essentially asked, "*How well did the Actor LLM do?*" and produces a scalar reward. The current trajectory, including the reward, is given to the Self-Reflection LLM to analyze the trajectory and produce a reflective summary for the Actor LLM to use.

This process continues until the Evaluator LLM deems the answer of the Actor LLM to be correct.

These three LLMs are vital to provide the actions (Actor), the stopping mechanism (Evaluator), and the reflective feedback (Self-Reflector). They are tied together by the different forms of memory, where the trajectory is saved in short-term memory (conversation memory) and the reflective experiences based on the trajectories within the long-term memory.

14 Shinn, Noah et al. 2023. "Reflexion: Language Agents with Verbal Reinforcement Learning," *Advances in Neural Information Processing Systems,* 36: 8634-8652.

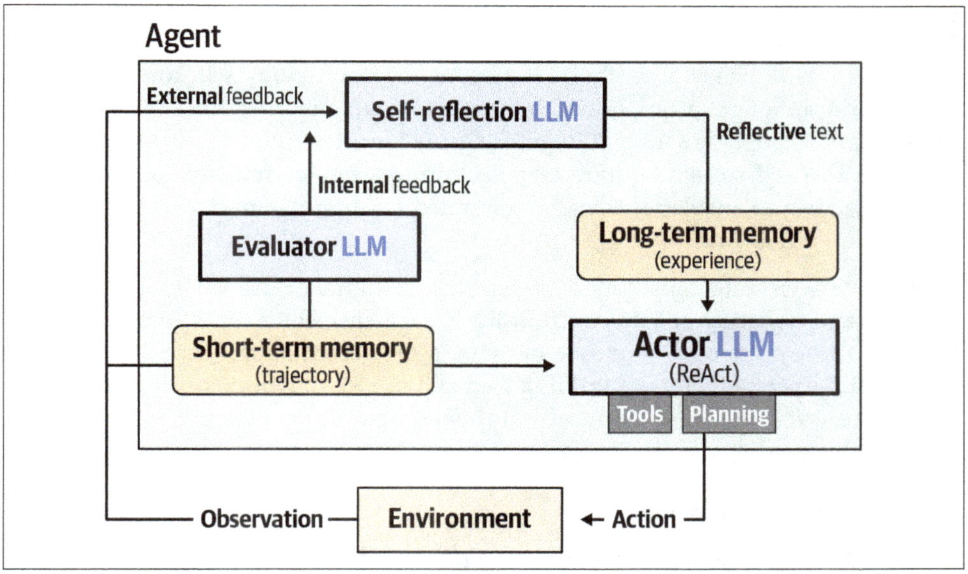

Figure 6-20. The Reflexion process uses separate LLM roles (Actor, Evaluator, Self-Reflection) to iteratively refine actions

Together, these components allow Reflexion agents to verbally reflect on trajectory observations, which are maintained in episodic memory to promote improved decision making in subsequent trials.

Self-Refine and Reflexion are common techniques to easily create agents that have some reflective capabilities. Many other prompt-based techniques exist that attempt something similar, such as CRITIC,[15] which starts with an initial output and revises it through the use of external tools, like search, to get more information. As such, feedback is an important component of agents that can reflect, and as the Reflexion framework shows, feedback can come from many places, including both itself and its environment.

However, like all prompt-based techniques we have explored thus far, they only guide the agent toward behavior that we previously described without instilling that behavior into its parameters. Let's explore techniques that allow reflective behavior to be a part of an agent's nature through fine-tuning the model.

15 Gou, Zhibin et al. 2023. "CRITIC: Large Language Models Can Self-Correct with Tool-Interactive Critiquing," *arXiv*, 2305.11738.

Self-Improvement

Reflecting on its behavior is the first step to the continuous self-improvement of agents, and although prompt-level heuristics are an important component, more fundamental changes are needed to guide agents toward continual self-improvement. To create this self-sustaining loop of reflection, reasoning, and task generation, RL has been shown to enable seemingly unbounded self-improvement with limited need for human-labeled data.

There have been initial approaches attempting to mimic or use RL by iterating over attempts and updating policies, such as RISE,[16] which includes additional introspection steps to continuously improve outputs. More recent approaches, like R-ZERO and TTRL, generate their own training data and use RL to continuously self-improve and evolve as it critiques and improves its own output. Let's explore these methods to get an understanding of how RL can be used for continuous self-improvement.

Test-time reinforcement learning

Labeled data for agentic traces that generalize well to other experiences is hard to create and generally a costly task, as it requires significant manual labor. This motivates the need for LLMs to learn by themselves rather than being directed purely by labeled data. The idea of self-play and self-experience is central in RL but often requires supervised data (such as query/reasoning/answer triplets) that are difficult to collect for complex and large-scale real-world tasks. This poses a substantial barrier to the self-improvement of LLMs.

Test-Time Reinforcement Learning (TTRL) is a framework that proposes to update models at test-time using RL.[17] Instead of having models remain static entities during inference, TTRL allows LLMs to learn as they interact with their environment without the need for supervised data. Instead of learning through their memory modules, their parameters are updated using RL.

TTRL is a four-step process. First, given a query, it applies repeated sampling to generate several candidate outputs. The authors generated 16 responses per query using a temperature of 0.6 to make sure that the outputs differ sufficiently. In their experiments, they used models from several model families, including Qwen (e.g., Qwen2.5-7B), LLaMA (e.g., LLaMA-3.1-8B-Instruct), Mistral (e.g., Mistral-8b-Instruct-2410), and DeepSeek (e.g., DeepSeek-R1-LLaMa-8B). Second, a majority voting strategy is used to select the best answer among the 16 generated outputs. Third, a reward is generated based on the alignment between the voted output

16 Qu, Yuxiao et al. 2024. "Recursive Introspection: Teaching Language Model Agents How to Self-Improve," *Advances in Neural Information Processing Systems,* 37: 55249-55285.

17 Zuo, Yuxin et al. 2025. "TTRL: Test-Time Reinforcement Learning," *arXiv,* 2504.16084.

and the 16 generated outputs. Finally, the calculated rewards are used as a signal during RL (GRPO) to improve the model as it acts with its environment. Figure 6-21 demonstrates this process of sampling, majority vote, and calculating the reward.

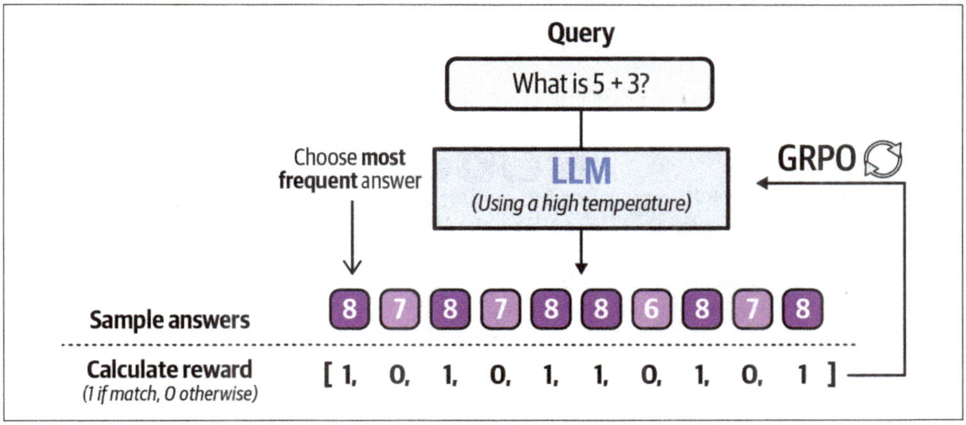

Figure 6-21. In Test-Time Reinforcement Learning (TTRL), GRPO is used on the sampled answers. The most frequent answer is used as a signal for training.

As you might have noticed, we already covered each of these steps in some form over the previous chapters. Majority voting is a common strategy for scaling test-time compute and improving the outputs, whereas GRPO has been a popular strategy for supervised RL. Elegantly combining these techniques allows TTRL to learn as it interacts with its environment without the need for labeled data since it produces those itself (the calculated rewards).

However, majority voting strategies are not flawless by definition. The majority does not always need to be correct. The authors argue that rewards in RL can be vague to a certain extent, as they signal the need for further exploration instead of continuous exploitation, which prevents models from being stuck in local minima. Likewise, even if the majority is incorrect and no correct predictions are made at all, then the reward will still be negative. This is referred to as a "lucky hit," and although they were created from an incorrect process, they are still "correct" rewards. This is illustrated in Figure 6-22.

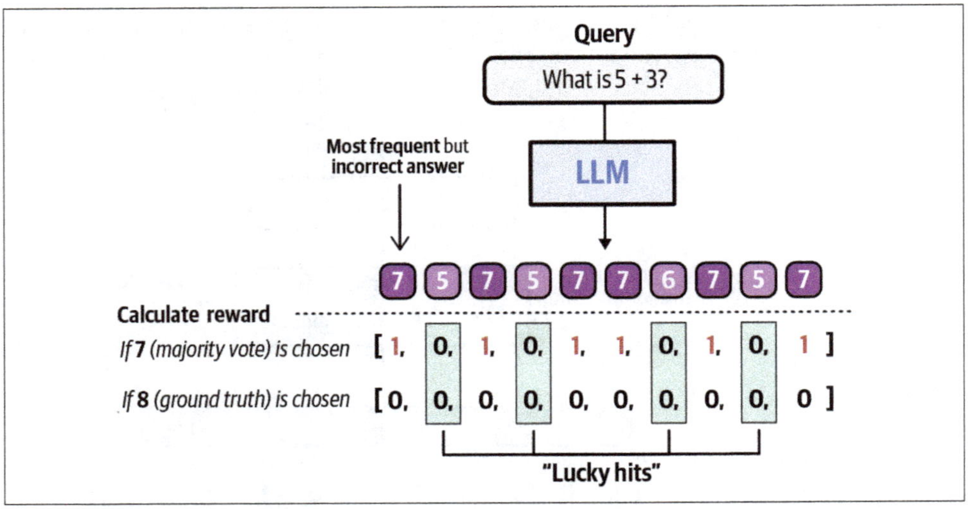

Figure 6-22. Lucky hits in TTRL are correct signals despite the most frequent answer being incorrect

Due to this elegant technique, TTRL can apply on-the-fly adaptation by fine-tuning the model as it encounters new problems. It is essentially an online approach to RL focused on learning during inference.

R-Zero

The idea of self-evolving reasoning LLMs without labeled data was further explored in R-Zero.[18] This technique uses two independent models with distinct roles to coevolve and challenge each other's outputs. These models are initialized from the same base model and take on the roles of a Challenger and a Solver. The authors experimented with models from the Qwen3 family and the Llama-3.1 family.[19,20]

The Challenger is tasked with generating synthetic queries that are difficult for the Solver to solve. The Solver generates multiple answers and selects the best one using majority voting, much like is done with TTRL. During this process, the Challenger is trained with RL (GRPO) based on the rewards it receives from the Solver.

There are several rewards/signals created during this process:

18 Huang, Chengsong et al. 2025. "R-Zero: Self-Evolving Reasoning LLM from Zero Data," *arXiv*, 2508.05004.

19 Yang, An et al. 2025. "Qwen3 Technical Report," *arXiv*, 2505.09388.

20 Dubey, Abhimanyu et al. 2024. "The Llama 3 Herd of Models," *arXiv*, 2407.

Uncertainty reward (a value between 0 and 1)
: This indicates how certain the Solver is that it has created the correct answer frequently from all of its sampled answers. It is essentially the fraction of the Solver's responses that match the most common answer. This reward aims to guide the Challenger to create difficult but solvable queries.

Repetition penalty (a value between 0 and 1)
: This penalty makes sure that the Challenger generates diverse queries. Otherwise, it would be stuck continuously optimizing the same difficult queries.

Format reward (either 0 or 1)
: A reward given based on whether the Challenger generates queries between `<question>` and `</question>` tags.

Composite reward (a value between 0 and 1)
: A reward given to the Challenger by subtracting the repetition penalty from the uncertainty reward and making sure it does not go below 0.

During this process, the Challenger is trained while the Solver is frozen and merely used as a reward model when fine-tuning the Challenger. This process is illustrated in Figure 6-23.

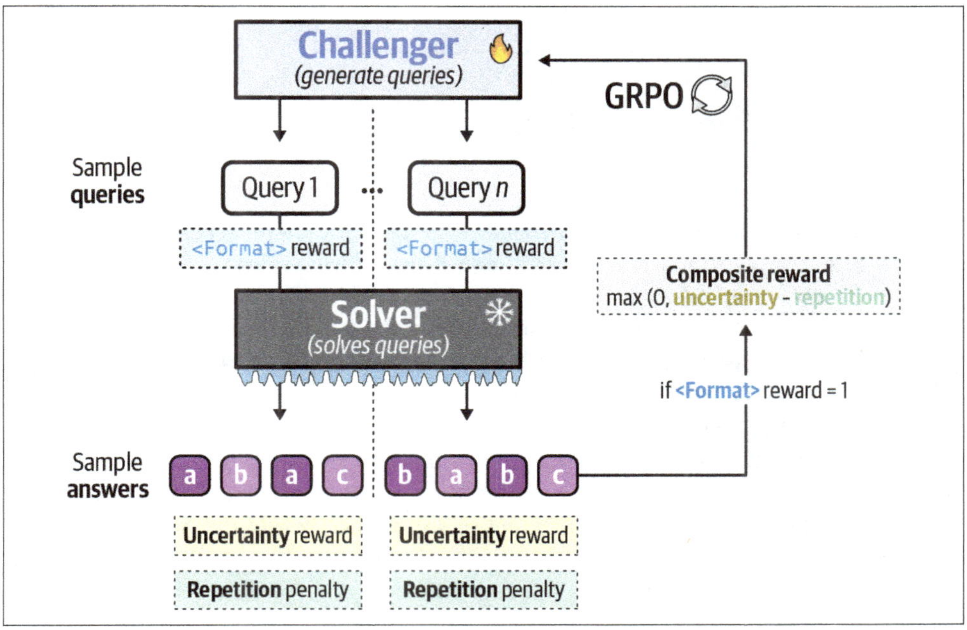

Figure 6-23. The Challenger is trained by trying to give the Solver more difficult queries. The signal it gets is whether it can generate a difficult query.

After training the Challenger, a dataset of queries is sampled from the Challenger to train the Solver. For each query, answers are sampled by passing them through the Solver. Based on a majority vote, if the query is too difficult (too few correct answers) or if the query is too easy (almost all answers are correct), then they are filtered out. This process improves the quality of the training data by focusing on queries that are just difficult enough.

The Solver is then fine-tuned on the curated dataset of challenging queries. As before, GRPO is used for training. Compared to the Challenger, the reward is simplified to a value of either 0 or 1. Like TTRL, this verifiable reward for each correct answer and 0 otherwise. As shown in Figure 6-24, this is a much simpler process and akin to TTRL.

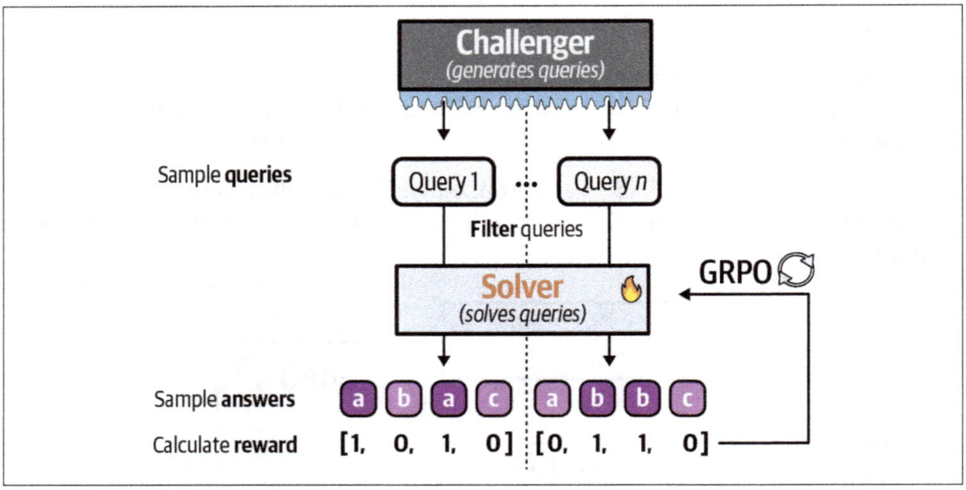

Figure 6-24. The Solver is trained by attempting to solve the Challenger's query. The signal it gets during training is whether it can solve a difficult query.

Together, this creates a coevolving system where the Challenger continuously makes harder queries, and the Solver gets better at solving them. In turn, the Challenger adapts to make new challenging queries, and so on. The beauty of this system is that the Challenger gets continuous rewards (composite uncertainty scores from 0 to 1) to encourage generating queries at the edge of difficulty, while the Solver gets a binary reward (0 or 1) to encourage getting the answer exactly right. This asymmetry allows the Challenger to explore a range of difficulties, while the Solver should be precise and deterministic in its answers. This loop between the Challenger and Solver training is shown in Figure 6-25.

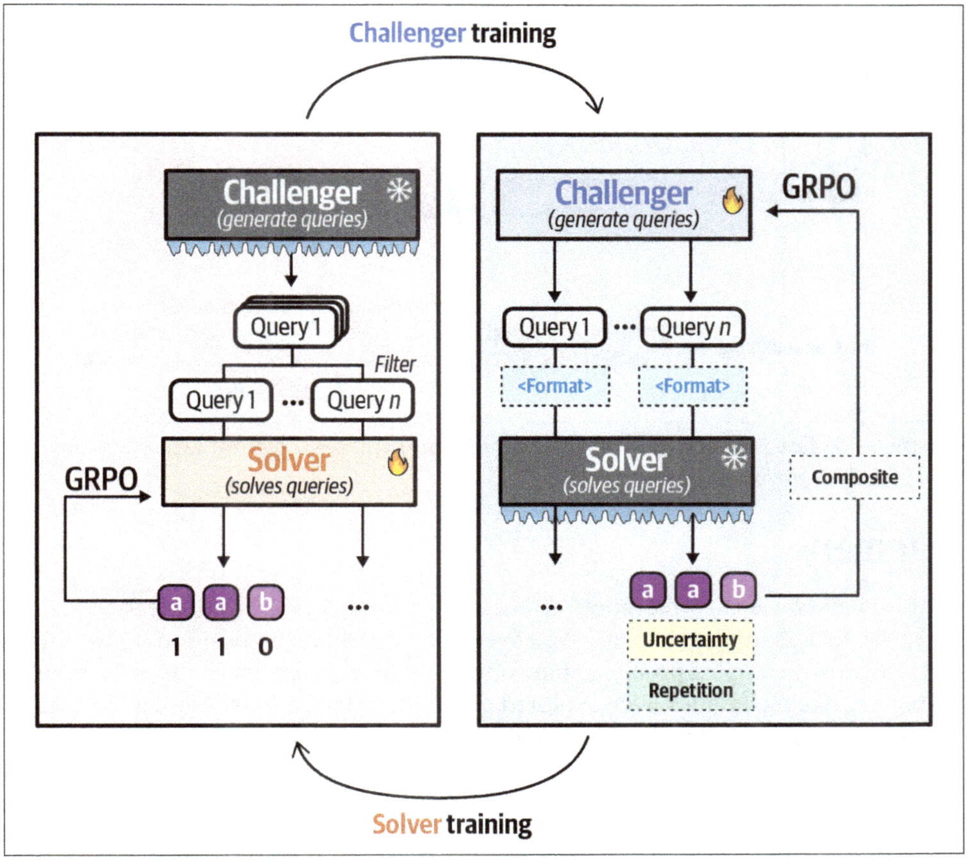

Figure 6-25. Challenger and Solver training are done after each other. In this process, the Solver and Challenger each try to win and are incentives to create competition.

Methods such as TTRL and R-Zero are, at the time of writing, newer techniques that have tremendous potential for self-improving agents. These are potential paradigm shifts that move the training focus toward unlabeled data and inference rather than purely focusing on the traditional pre-training combined with SFT and RL. The evolution from "traditional" training with SFT and RL all the way to this potential test-time training paradigm is shown in Figure 6-26.

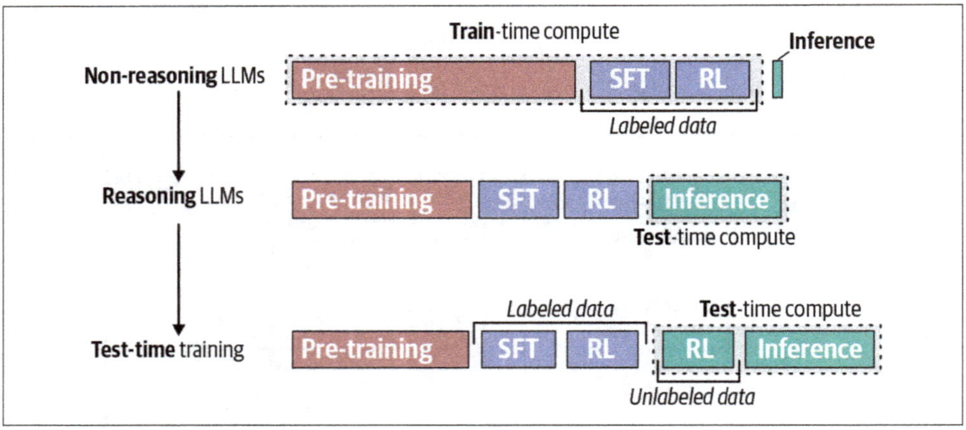

Figure 6-26. Test-time training moves compute more during inference where we can more easily scale existing models

Summary

In this chapter, we explored how LLMs can plan out behavior and reflect on actions taken when executing this plan. We covered how task decomposition allows LLMs to break down complex problems into small problems that each can be solved on its own. CoT-like techniques were explored and demonstrated how they can be used to perform explicit planning. We then explored how, after planning, agents can perform sequences of actions through a widely used technique, Reason and Act. Several techniques were explored from the domains of prompting, SFT, and RL to enable this behavior of action sequencing in agents. ReAct is the final missing link in what makes agents potentially autonomous, as it decides on its own when to stop and how long to continue within these ReAct-like frameworks.

We then discussed how agents can be taken a step further and reflect on their sequences of actions to get into a mode of self-improvement. In that, reflection is vital for LLMs and agents to prevent being stuck in local minima of solutions and thought processes. We finished this chapter with an exciting new paradigm of agents that continuously improve as they interact with their environment. This test-time training paradigm has the potential to bring agents into a new realm of performance and generalization.

In the next chapter, we'll cover various methodologies of evaluating agents. Due to their potentially complex behaviors, agents are significantly more difficult to evaluate than LLMs. We'll explore what to look for when evaluating your agent and agentic system.

CHAPTER 7

Evaluating Agents

The previous chapters built up the components of an agent one by one: how it reasons, how it uses tools, how it stores and retrieves memory, and how it plans across multiple steps. By now you have a mental model of how these pieces fit together to form the system we call an AI agent. The natural next question to ask is, how do we know if any of it is working?

That's what this chapter is about, as we can see in Figure 7-1. Evaluation is how you move from "it seems to work" to "I have evidence it works." It's also how you catch the moment it stops working. Evaluations are one of the most underinvested areas in agent development. Teams often rely on manual testing and intuition longer than they should, then find themselves unable to ship improvements confidently or diagnose regressions when they appear.

We'll start with benchmarks, which you'll encounter most often in model announcements and research papers. We'll then build toward the tools and concepts you need to design your own evaluations. By the end of the chapter, you'll have a clear picture of how agents are measured and what those measurements actually mean.

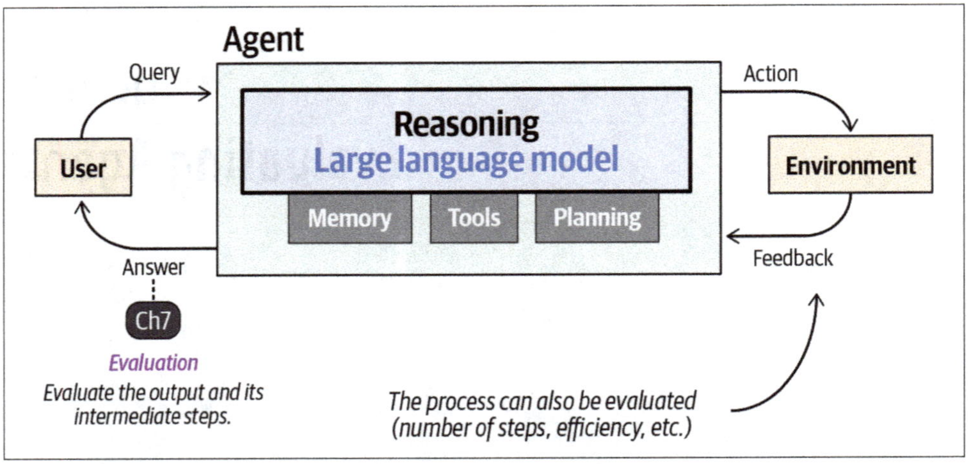

Figure 7-1. This chapter covers how LLMs and agents are evaluated and explores how we move from evaluating the output to evaluating an agent's intermediate steps (trajectory)

Public Benchmarks and Leaderboards

A benchmark is a fixed set of tasks paired with a way to score them, so that different models can be measured against the same yardstick and compared directly. Take SWE-bench Verified, one of the rows in Figure 7-2. It's a collection of real GitHub issues from open source projects. To score a point, a model (or an agent built on top of it) has to read the description of the issue, explore the code repository, and produce a patch that makes the project's existing tests pass (they exist but are hidden from the model). The score is simply the percentage of issues the agent solves.

Most benchmarks follow the same outline: a dataset of problems, a procedure for attempting them, and a metric that collapses performance into a single number you can drop into a table.

These numbers are the scores most people see. AI labs publish them in model announcements, researchers cite them in their papers, and builders use them to select LLMs and agent frameworks.

The problem is that reading tables that compare models on various benchmarks requires a bit of care and nuance. A score of 80% on SWE-bench Verified and a score of 80% on MMLU represent completely different claims about completely different capabilities, measured in completely different ways. Some scores come from running an agent once while other scores aggregate many runs (sometimes in ways that could be deceptive). Some use deterministic test suites while others rely on an LLM judge that introduces its own biases. And some benchmarks in these tables aren't really measuring agent capability at all, but rather the non-agentic capabilities of the underlying LLM that powers it.

Figure 7-2 shows a typical benchmark table from a recent model release.

In the next section, we'll map common benchmark categories you'll encounter. After that, we'll dive into key concepts for evaluating agents to set you up for building your own evaluations. This is often a great investment that gives you greater visibility throughout the life of your project.

Benchmark		Gemini 3.1 Pro Thinking (High)	Gemini 3 Pro Thinking (High)	Sonnet 4.6 Thinking (Max)	Opus 4.6 Thinking (Max)	GPT-5.2 Thinking (xhigh)	GPT-5.3-Codex Thinking (xhigh)
Humanity's Last Exam Academic reasoning (full set, text + MM)	No tools	**44.4%**	37.5%	33.2%	40.0%	34.5%	—
	Search (blocklist) + Code	51.4%	45.8%	49.0%	**53.1%**	45.5%	—
ARC-AGI-2 Abstract reasoning puzzles	ARC Prize Verified	**77.1%**	31.1%	58.3%	68.8%	52.9%	—
GPQA Diamond Scientific knowledge	No tools	**94.3%**	91.9%	89.9%	91.3%	92.4%	—
Terminal-Bench 2.0 Agentic terminal coding	Terminus-2 harness	**68.5%**	56.9%	59.1%	65.4%	54.0%	64.7%
	Other best self-reported harness	—	—	—	—	62.2% (Codex)	**77.3%** (Codex)
SWE-Bench Verified Agentic coding	Single attempt	80.6%	76.2%	79.6%	**80.8%**	80.0%	—
SWE-Bench Pro (Public) Diverse agentic coding tasks	Single attempt	54.2%	43.3%	—	—	55.6%	**56.8%**
LiveCodeBench Pro Competitive coding problems from Codeforces, ICPC, and IOI	Elo	**2887**	2439	—	—	2393	—

Figure 7-2. A benchmark table from Google (https://oreil.ly/BFPBd)

Coding and Software Engineering

Arguably the most mature family of agent benchmarks measures the ability to write, fix, and reason about code. These have achieved a moment of being the gold standard of agent evaluation precisely because code is verifiable: the code either executes and passes unit tests or it does not.

SWE-bench and its subsequent variants are the canonical example. Each example is a real GitHub issue that an agent must resolve by producing a passing software patch that edits multiple files. When SWE-bench launched in 2023, best-in-class agents resolved around 2% of tasks (*https://arxiv.org/abs/2310.06770*), but by 2026, leading agents on the public leaderboard (*https://oreil.ly/s-eAX*) cracked 70% on SWE-bench Verified—a curated version of the benchmark designed to remove ambiguous or unreliable test cases. *Terminal-Bench* is another coding benchmark where the agent operates a Linux terminal to solve software, system, and environment issues.

We cover coding agents and more of their evaluations in Chapter 10.

Tool Use

Tool use benchmarks test whether an agent calls the right tools with the right arguments. This is a more targeted check on the specific capabilities of tool calling that we covered in Chapter 5 instead of end-to-end task completion. *BFCL* (Berkeley Function Calling Leaderboard) (*https://oreil.ly/JerlT*) is one key benchmark here, testing function-calling accuracy across hundreds of API schemas including nested parameters and ambiguous inputs. *τ bench* (*https://taubench.com*) (pronounced "tau bench") goes deeper, testing tool use across realistic multi-turn customer service scenarios that require following specific business policies and maintaining context over a long conversation.

Software and Computer-Use Environments

A key and growing area of agent benchmarks is one where the agent must navigate a digital environment such as a desktop, browser, or application interface and conduct a sequence of actions to achieve a specific goal. Benchmarks such as OSWorld (*https://os-world.github.io*) place agents inside simulated computer environments where they must complete realistic tasks such as editing documents, managing files, or configuring software. Unlike Terminal-Bench, however, this group of benchmarks often requires interacting with graphical interfaces, clicking buttons, navigating menus, and interpreting visual elements that appear in software designed for humans (e.g., Excel or online shops).

The *WebArena* (*https://webarena.dev*) benchmark narrows the scope to browser-based tasks, placing agents inside realistic replicas of live websites (such as a Reddit forum or a GitLab instance) to complete multi-step goals.

Real-World Task Completion

For agents to rise to their promise of tackling productive knowledge work, some benchmarks present the challenge of messy, open-ended tasks that look like the kinds of work knowledge workers actually tackle. These tasks typically require a mixture of reasoning, information retrieval, navigating ambiguity, and synthesis across multiple steps and sources. *GAIA* (*https://arxiv.org/abs/2311.12983*) is one such benchmark that presents difficult (at the time), real-world questions that often require reading files and using web search to arrive at a verifiable final answer. *GDPval* (*https://oreil.ly/JlNix*) is another one drawn from knowledge work of multiple professions from various sectors and domains.

We have good reason to believe there will continue to be increasing demand for this category of evaluations. A 2026 analysis (*https://arxiv.org/abs/2603.01203v2*) titled *How Well Does Agent Development Reflect Real-World Work?* found that today's benchmarks cluster heavily around programming, while the occupations that employ the most people and generate the most economic value go almost untested. That gap is where much of the expected demand for evaluations is likely to land.

Reasoning and Knowledge

Another family benchmark commonly seen in comparison tables is one that measures a model's ability to reason about complex questions and apply knowledge across multiple domains. These are typically difficult exam-style questions. MMLU (Massive Multitask Language Understanding) (*https://arxiv.org/abs/2009.03300*) is one of the earliest and most widely cited examples, covering dozens of subjects ranging from physics and medicine to law and history. *GPQA Diamond* (*https://arxiv.org/abs/2311.12022*) is a more recent benchmark that pushes the difficulty further. It focuses on graduate-level questions in fields such as physics, biology, and chemistry that are intentionally designed to be difficult even for domain experts and resistant to simple memorization. *Humanity's Last Exam* (*https://arxiv.org/abs/2501.14249*) takes this even further, assembling extremely challenging questions across many disciplines.

One thing that's important to note is that these often test the underlying LLM, not necessarily the agentic abilities of tool use across multiple steps.

Other Groups of Benchmarks

In addition to the main benchmarks we've discussed, you'll come across a number of others that measure specialized capabilities. Some focus on abstract reasoning puzzles, such as ARC-AGI, which attempt to measure general problem-solving on unfamiliar tasks. Others evaluate multi-modal reasoning, where models must combine visual and textual information, as in MMMU. There are also benchmarks for long-context retrieval, sometimes called "needle-in-a-haystack" tests, that measure whether a model can locate specific information within very large documents.

Table 7-1 provides a summary of categories we've looked at.

Table 7-1. Benchmark category examples

Category	Benchmarks	What's measured
Coding and software engineering	SWE-bench Verified, Terminal-Bench	Patch correctness, test passage
Tool use	BFCL, τ-bench	Function-calling accuracy, multi-turn-policy following
Computer use	OSWorld, WebArena	Action sequences in desktop/browser environments
Real-world task completion	GAIA, GDPval	Reasoning and retrieval on open-ended knowledge tasks
Reasoning and knowledge	MMLU, GPQA Diamond, Humanity's Last Exam	Exam-style questions across domains
Specialized	ARC-AGI, MMMU, needle-in-a-haystack	Abstract reasoning, multi-modal, long-context retrieval

Reading Benchmark Scores Critically

Seasoned researchers and builders often develop a sense for things to look for and questions to ask instead of taking reported numbers at face value. Here's a list of important questions that are frequently raised to critically examine benchmark scores:

How was the score produced?
: The next section, "Outcome Evaluation: Did the Agent Get the Right Output?" on page 268, explains the various methods for scoring a model. This is important knowledge because different evaluation setups can produce different results even on the same benchmark. Some come from deterministic checks such as unit tests or exact answers, while others rely on LLM judges to evaluate outputs that are subjective or open-ended.

Is partial success rewarded?
: Some benchmarks score each task as all-or-nothing while others may assign partial credit for getting part of the way there. The difference matters most for agents because they're often used for tasks that have several steps. A high partial-credit score can hide an agent that rarely completes a task end to end, which is usually what you need it to do.

Which agentic harness was used?
: The same model can post different scores on a benchmark depending on the agentic harness it runs in. How the harness constructs prompts, parses tool calls, handles retry logic, and manages context and conversation history all move the number even with the model held fixed. The SWE Atlas benchmark paper (*https://arxiv.org/abs/2605.08366v1*) shows this directly: it runs each frontier model both in its vendor harness (Codex CLI, Claude Code, Gemini CLI) and in a common minimal harness (mini-SWE-agent, which exposes only a bash tool) to separate the model from its scaffold. Scores shift between the two, and the ranking of the top models can even flip, so a reported number is best read as a model-and-harness pair.

Single run or multiple?
: A score from one run can flatter a lucky result. More trustworthy results would often report a metric that aggregates the score over many runs with a variance estimate. Some metrics are aggregate in nature, such as pass@k (pass-AT-k), which we'll see in the next section.

Is the benchmark in the training data?
: Data contamination is one of the most insidious issues in machine learning. If a model was trained on examples drawn from the benchmark, then the score is skewed by the model's memorization instead of being strictly measured on

capability. This is hard to verify aside from completely open models that disclose the training datasets in detail.

Who ran the evaluation?
: Self-reported scores from the lab releasing a model deserve more scrutiny than third-party replications. Independent evaluations sometimes find meaningful gaps from the reported numbers, even with identical setup. *Artificial Analysis* (*https://artificialanalysis.ai*) and *Chatbot Arena* (*https://arena.ai*) are two widely cited independent sources. Yet even independent leaderboards can be gamed, as described in *The Leaderboard Illusion*.[1]

Were prompts tuned specifically for that benchmark?
: Prompt engineering against a known benchmark can meaningfully move scores without reflecting any generalizable capability improvement. If the same prompting approach is not applied to all systems in the comparison table, the comparison can be uneven.

Does the scaffolding generalize?
: A system that includes a retrieval pipeline, a custom tool, or a verification step may score well on the benchmark while requiring significant engineering to transfer to a real deployment. When the scored evaluation system includes extra scaffolding, the question worth asking is whether that scaffolding transfers to your use case or was engineered specifically to perform well on this benchmark.

Is the benchmark saturated?
: Once leading models exceed a certain threshold, say 85%, on a benchmark, score differences start to become noisy and less indicative of actual performance. That's when you see the industry move to a more difficult benchmark (or variant) tackling the next level of difficulty in that type of task.

Which subset or variant was used?
: Many benchmarks have multiple versions that often vary in difficulty. Examples include GPQA versus GPQA Diamond, ARC Easy versus ARC Challenge, and MMLU versus MMLU-Pro.

What was the cost?
: A system that scores 20% more while spending 10 times the tokens or wall-clock time of a competitor isn't straightforwardly better. Some evaluations report this; many don't. Cost, token count, and latency all matter in your production system more than they might in the evaluation setup.

1 Singh, Shivalika et al. 2025. "The Leaderboard Illusion," *arXiv*, 2504.20879.

Outcome Evaluation: Did the Agent Get the Right Output?

The benchmarks we've looked at score models based on a number of scoring methods. Understanding these methods is what lets you read a benchmark table critically and design your own evaluations well. Outcome evaluation scores the final results of a task—the patch produced, the answer returned, the report written—without regard to how the agent got there. We contrast this with a smaller subsequent section on trajectory evaluation, which examines the sequence of steps and tool calls the agent made along the way.

Human Evaluation

The most direct way to score an agent's output is to have a person read it and judge it. Figure 7-3 shows the direct scoring, where a human evaluator/annotator reads the output from an agent and assigns a score, say 4 out 5, based on some criteria.

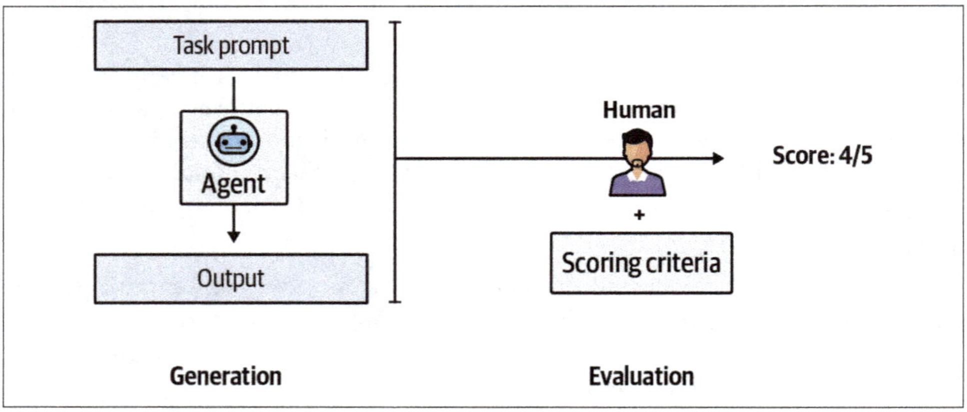

Figure 7-3. A human evaluator rates a single agent output against scoring criteria, producing a direct quality score

This works well when you have an absolute sense of quality and have clear criteria that evaluators apply consistently. The challenge here is that it's often difficult to get an objective score in isolation, which creates the need for the second form of human evaluation.

Preference evaluation, which we see in Figure 7-4, presents the evaluator with outputs from two agents side-by-side on the same task and asks a simpler question: which answer do you prefer? Relative judgments tend to be more reliable than absolute ones. It's easier for a human evaluator to say that "A is better than B" than to decide that A deserves 4 points and that B deserves 3 points.

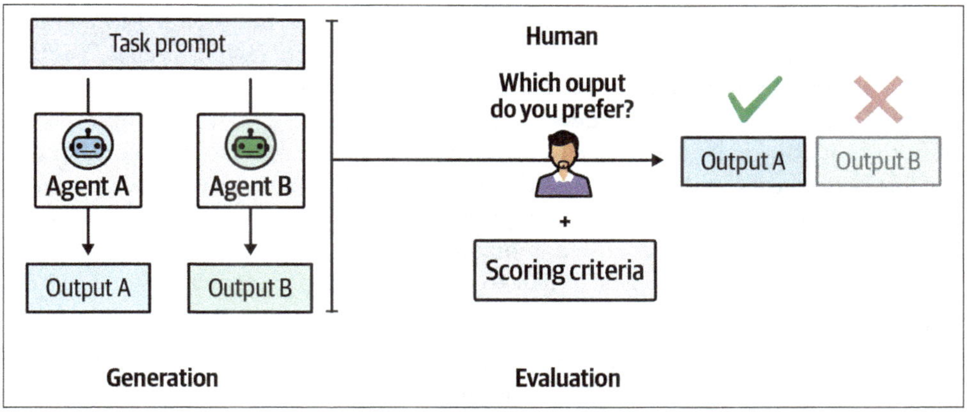

Figure 7-4. A human evaluator, guided by scoring criteria, compares two agent outputs and selects the preferred one

Scaled across many tasks, we can begin to speak about *win rates*: on the tasks in a certain evaluation set, Agent A was preferred on 80% of the tasks while Agent B was preferred on 20% of the tasks (Figure 7-5).

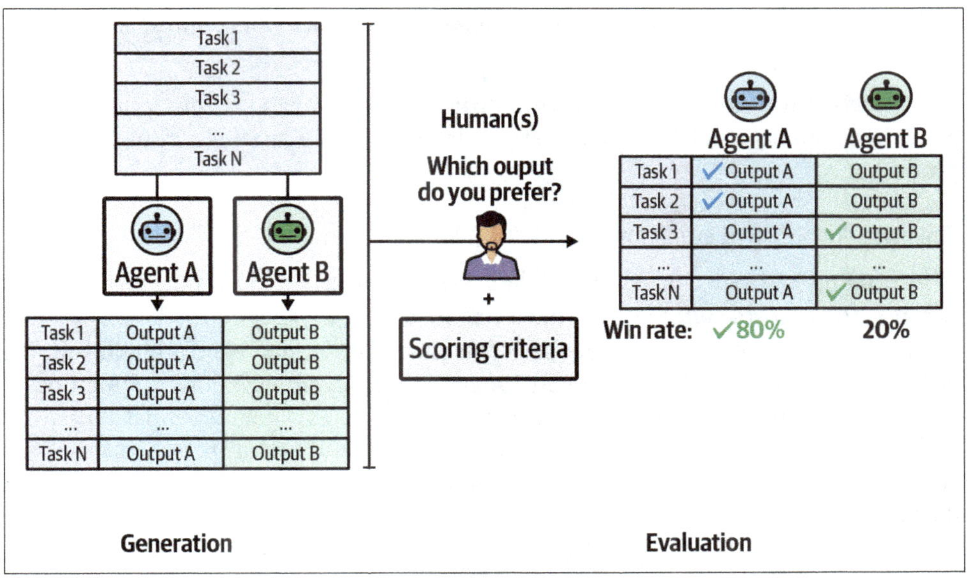

Figure 7-5. Human evaluators compare agent outputs across a task suite, and per-task preferences are aggregated into a win rate—here Agent A wins 80% of pairwise comparisons against Agent B

Comparing two models like this in a pair-wise fashion can be extended to comparing more than two agents through an Elo rating system (*https://oreil.ly/XnYOT*), borrowed from competitive chess. Rather than running every possible head-to-head comparison between tens of models, each pairwise result updates a running score of both models/agents; wins increase the score and losses decrease it according to a specific formula that takes into consideration the relative strength of the opponent. Chatbot Arena (LMSYS) is the most prominent example of this applied at scale, where thousands of users compare anonymous model outputs and stable rankings emerge over time (using a rating similar to Elo).

Human evaluation is slow and expensive, but it remains the baseline against which all automated methods are validated. When a new LLM judge or scoring metric is proposed, showing that it correlates with human judgement is often how researchers establish that it measures something real.

Automated Evaluation

Human evaluation does not scale to the continuous feedback loops that agent development requires. Agent builders iterate over hundreds if not thousands of prompt changes, model swaps, versions of the agent, and example test points that can easily add up to requiring millions of complex judgements. That's where automated evaluation comes in.

Automated evaluation covers a spectrum from static automated checks to judgements made by another model. The right method depends on the kind of output your agent produces.

Building a simple agent evaluator

Before going into specific methods, let's first create a simple framework that we can use to perform automated evaluation on your `TinyAgent`. To do so, we first need to create the `Benchmark` dataclass. The `Benchmark` contains information on the task (name), the examples in the benchmark to test (examples), and the method of performing automated evaluation (scorer). The scorer is a function that takes in a prediction and an example from the benchmark. Depending on the scorer, it should either always return a boolean to indicate whether the prediction is correct or not, or it should always return a score:

```
from dataclasses import dataclass
from typing import Callable

# Type hint for the scorers
##  (prediction: str, example: dict) -> bool | float
Scorer = Callable[[str, dict], bool | float]

@dataclass
```

```python
class Benchmark:
    name: str
    examples: list[dict]
    scorer: Callable
```

We then need an `Evaluator` class that runs a set of examples against a selected scorer. We also need a new agent every time we run a benchmark to reset its memory and trajectory, so we create a small function for that:

```python
from illustrated_agents.chapters.ch2 import LLM
from illustrated_agents.chapters.ch4 import Memory
from illustrated_agents.chapters.ch5 import NativeTools
from illustrated_agents.chapters.ch6 import NativeReAct, TinyAgent

# Gemma 4 E4B (with native thinking and tool calling)
llm = LLM(model="gemma4:e4b", think=True)


class Evaluator:
    """Run a TinyAgent over a Benchmark and aggregate the results."""

    def __init__(self, create_agent: Callable):
        """Initialize with a function that creates a new agent instance."""
        self.create_agent = create_agent

    def run(self, benchmark: Benchmark) -> dict:
        """Run the agent on examples in the benchmark and score the results."""

        # Run each example and collect results
        results = []
        for example in benchmark.examples:
            agent = self.create_agent()
            prediction = agent.run(example["task"]) or ""
            passed = benchmark.scorer(prediction, example)
            results.append(
                {
                    "prediction": prediction,
                    "passed": passed,
                }
            )

        # Aggregate pass rate
        if results:
            pass_rate = sum(
              result["passed"] for result in results
            ) / len(results)
        else:
            pass_rate = 0.0

        # Return detailed results and overall pass rate
        return {
            "name": benchmark.name,
```

```
            "pass_rate": pass_rate,
            "results": results,
        }


def create_agent():
    """Create a new instance of TinyAgent"""
    return TinyAgent(
        llm=llm,
        memory=Memory(),
        tools=NativeTools(),
        planner=NativeReAct(),
    )
```

The Evaluator will run a check for each example in the benchmark, determine whether the agent has generated the correct output, and simply track a pass or fail. The pass/fail rate over all examples is averaged into the `"pass_rate"`.

Let's explore how to use this in practice by covering several methods for automated evaluation.

Exact match

The most straightforward form of automated evaluation is a deterministic check: the output either matches the expected answer or it doesn't. If your agent is asked to extract the invoice total from a document and the correct answer is $1,482.81, you can make that comparison directly in software. This goes quite far and powers a large number of benchmarks. Yet its beautiful simplicity is also its main drawback; many tasks in practice don't simply output a single value. If the agent, for example, was to write a document, generate code, produce a plan, or synthesize information across many sources, exact match breaks down because there are many valid ways to express a correct answer.

Exact match is also brittle against trivial formatting differences. For the invoice example, a prompt that doesn't pin down the format can yield answers such as `1,482.81` (no dollar sign), `1482.81` (no thousands separator), or `$1,482.81.` (with a trailing period), and a strict check flags every one of them as wrong.

To implement the exact match scoring mechanism, let's first consider the benchmark for which we want to use this. MMLU-Pro, which consists of many different tasks with multiple-choice answers, is a great benchmark to start with. Compared to MMLU, it extends the number of multiple-choice options to 10 to make the tasks more difficult and prevent random guessing. Those options are labeled A through J. As such, the scoring mechanism needs to match only one of those with the ground truth:

```
import re

def exact_match_scorer(prediction: str, example: dict) -> bool:
    """Return True if the answer matches the prediction, False otherwise"""
```

```
        match = re.search(r"\b([A-J])\b", prediction.upper())
        return match.group(1) == example["expected"]
```

The `exact_match_scorer` gives back either `True` or `False` depending on whether the answer is correct. Since we know the answer beforehand, the check is relatively straightforward.

If we were to use the full benchmark with more than 12,000 question/answer pairs, running the evaluation would take significant time. Instead, we grab three examples from the dataset (*https://oreil.ly/YlNXt*) and use them to showcase how you would run the evaluation:

```
# Three examples from MMLU Pro
mmlu_pro = Benchmark(
    name="MMLU Pro",
    examples=[
        {
            "task": """Which of the following is the body cavity that contains
the pituitary gland?
A) Ventral B) Dorsal C) Buccal D) Thoracic E) Pericardial F) Abdominal
G) Spinal H) Pelvic I) Pleural J) Cranial
Answer with only the letter.""",
            "expected": "J",
        },
        {
            "task": """What is the approximate mean cranial capacity of
Homo erectus?
A) 1200 cc B) under 650 cc C) 1700 cc D) 1350 cc E) just under 1000 cc
F) 1500 cc G) under 500 cc H) about 800 cc I) just over 1100 cc J) about 900 cc
Answer with only the letter.""",
            "expected": "E",
        },
        {
            "task": """
According to Moore's "ideal utilitarianism," the right action is the one that
brings about the greatest amount of:
A) wealth. B) virtue. C) fairness. D) pleasure. E) peace. F) justice.
G) happiness. H) power. I) good. J) knowledge.
Answer with only the letter.""",
            "expected": "I",
        },
    ],
    scorer=exact_match_scorer,
)
```

Then, we can run it like so:

```
# Run evaluation
result = Evaluator(create_agent).run(mmlu_pro)
print(result)
```

This gives:

```
{
    'name': 'MMLU Pro',
    'pass_rate': 0.3333333333333333,
    'results': [
        {'prediction': 'J', 'passed': True},
        {'prediction': 'H', 'passed': False},
        {'prediction': 'G', 'passed': False}
    ]
}
```

The model got one question right and two wrong. That is not too bad for such a small model. These types of questions test knowledge, which tend to be easier for larger models since they have more parameters to store information.

> For some benchmarks, specific packages and harnesses were created in which you need to run your LLM. τ-bench, for instance, has an entire framework (*https://oreil.ly/4jm1q*) that you can use to run the evaluation. This also makes evaluation difficult at times since different benchmarks might need different frameworks, which hinders tests of the generalizability of harnesses.

Programmatic checks

Programmatic checks extend exact matches into the broader category of automated verifiers. Rather than checking for a single string, you write code that verifies structural properties of the output. If we expect a JSON string output, we can automatically check if the output is valid JSON. For a coding agent where we expect a function implementation, we run unit tests and validate that the function behaves as expected. For more advanced coding outputs such as SWE-bench, in which the output is a patch that changes multiple files in a repository, the programmatic checks are a suite of unit tests that fail before the patch and have to run successfully after the patch is applied.

This approach is fast, cheap, and objective. It's one reason coding agents rose much faster than other kinds of agents—the code modality allows for automated checks, which proves useful for evaluation that also guides the training process.

To implement programmatic checks, we'll use the IFEval benchmark.[2] This benchmark contains verifiable instructions, such as "write in more than 400 words" or "mention the keywords of AI at least 3 times." These instructions can be verified by heuristics and need a separate "validator" for each of these instructions. As before, let's start with the scoring mechanism:

2 Zhou, Jeffrey et al. 2023. "Instruction-Following Evaluation for Large Language Models," *arXiv*, 2311.07911.

```
def programmatic_scorer(prediction: str, example: dict) -> bool:
    """Check a prediction against its related check."""
    return example["check"](prediction)
```

This `programmatic_scorer` doesn't do much except for running the check for each example in the benchmark. Some of these examples check the number of words, while others check if there is no comma in the output. As before, we grab three examples from the dataset (*https://oreil.ly/cFshm*) to showcase how you would run this evaluation with the corresponding checks:

```
# Three examples from IFeval
ifeval = Benchmark(
    name="IFeval",
    examples=[
        {
            "task": "Write me a funny song with less than 10 sentences for a
            proposal to build a new playground at my local elementary school.",
            "check": lambda text: sum(1 for c in text if c in ".!?") < 10,
        },
        {
            "task": "Write an ad copy for a new product, a digital photo frame
            that connects to your social media accounts and displays your photos.
            Respond with at most 150 words.",
            "check": lambda text: len(text.split()) <= 150,
        },
        {
            "task": "I am planning a trip to Japan, and I would like thee to
            write an itinerary for my journey in a Shakespearean style.
            You are not allowed to use any commas in your response.",
            "check": lambda text: "," not in text,
        },
    ],
    scorer=programmatic_scorer,
)
```

Note that each example now has a short function to check whether the output has fewer than 10 sentences, at most 150 words, and if it has a comma.

Then, we can run the evaluation like so:

```
# Run evaluation
result = Evaluator(create_agent).run(ifeval)
print(result)
```

Which gives:

```
{
    'name': 'IFeval',
    'pass_rate': 1.0,
    'results': [
        {
            'prediction': '*(Sung to the tune of "Twinkle Twinkle Little Star"
            or a very upbeat, dramatic jingle)* ...
```

```
                Let’s give elementary school the perfect fair!',
                'passed': True
            },
            {
                'prediction': "**Caption/Headline Option:** Your Memories.
                Never Out of Sight. ... Available in multiple finishes.
                  [Link/Store Name]",
                 'passed': True
            },
            {
                'prediction': "Hark attend gentle traveler a
                journey most grand ... May this itinerary thy journey transcend",
                'passed': True
            }
        ]
    }
```

We truncated the preceding long prediction (the full output is in the associated GitHub repository (*https://github.com/HandsOnLLM/An-Illustrated-Guide-To-AI-Agents*)). The pass rate gives a score of 1, meaning that the model correctly followed all instructions!

LLM-as-a-judge

When the output is too open-ended for a programmatic check, a natural move is to ask another capable language model to evaluate it. This is the LLM-as-a-judge pattern. LLM-as-a-judge is typically used to produce a single score or to choose a preferred output from two agents. Strong language models can assess fluency, logical coherence, information consistency given a ground truth context, and tone in ways that no programmatic check can. Figure 7-6 shows scoring with LLM-as-a-judge doing both absolute scoring as well as preference selection from two outputs.

LLM judges have failure modes worth knowing, some of which they may share with human judges. They can prefer outputs that sound confident over ones that are actually correct. They can be sensitive to presentation order (e.g., tending to prefer the first option presented to them). They inherit biases from their own training and may tend to prefer their own output or those from their own family of models to that of other models.

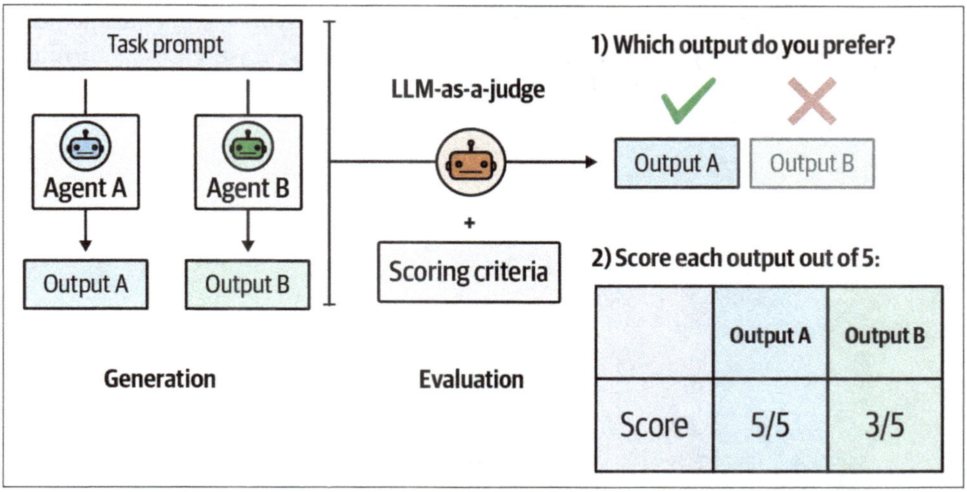

Figure 7-6. A judge model takes agent outputs and scoring criteria as input and evaluates them either as a pairwise preference or as an absolute score

Several techniques help mitigate these drawbacks. Using a judge from a different model family reduces the tendency to favor its own outputs. Swapping presentation order of preference sets across evaluation runs controls for position bias. Asking a judge to produce a written rationale or using a reasoning model as judge can improve consistency. We can also use ensembles of judges, where multiple models vote and we aggregate their judgments.

Before we implement this scorer, we first need to decide on the judge to score the output. As outlined previously, we'll choose a different and more capable judge of the output, namely Google's Gemini model. There are many variants, but fortunately, there is a free tier available that lets us choose a capable model, Gemini 3.1 Flash-Lite. To use it, you can generate an API Key from the website (*https://oreil.ly/jukA2*). We then create the judge like so:

```
# Judge
judge = LLM(
    model="gemini-3.1-flash-lite",
    base_url="https://generativelanguage.googleapis.com/v1beta/openai",
    api_key="MY_API_KEY"
)
```

Note that if you have enough (V)RAM available, you could also locally run another model that is more capable, such as Gemma 4 26B A4B (*https://oreil.ly/N4AsZ*).

Next, we implement a simple version of LLM-as-a-judge by asking Gemini to score the output of your `TinyAgent`. Instead of returning a boolean, we're now returning a single score between 0 and 1. This allows for a much more fine-grained perspective on how well the agent is doing:

```
def judge_scorer(prediction: str, example: dict) -> bool:
    """The LLM-as-a-judge scorer."""
    prompt = f"""
Score the response from 0.0 to 1.0.

Expected: {example["expected"]}
Response: {prediction}

Reply with only a single number.
"""
    response = judge.generate([{"role": "user", "content": prompt}])
    score = float(response.content.strip().split()[0])
    return score
```

The `judge_scorer` uses a straightforward prompt without frills to generate a score between 0 and 1.

To illustrate this fine-grained perspective, we'll use the same examples from MMLU-Pro that we used before. Instead of using multiple-choice questions in the benchmark, we now simply remove them and make them open-ended questions. That way, the answer is more difficult to score programmatically or using an exact match and instead requires a judge:

```
# Three examples adapted from MMLU Pro
mmlu_pro = Benchmark(
    name="MMLU Pro",
    examples=[
        {
            "task": "Which body cavity contains the pituitary gland?",
            "expected": "the cranial cavity",
        },
        {
            "task": "What is the approximate mean cranial capacity of Homo
            erectus?",
            "expected": "just under 1000 cc",
        },
        {
            "task": "According to Moore's 'ideal utilitarianism,' the right
            action is the one that brings about the greatest amount of what?",
            "expected": "good",
        },
    ],
    scorer=judge_scorer,
)
```

Note how we simply replace the expected multiple-choice answer with the actual answer. This is what will be given to Gemini to help score the quality of your `TinyAgent`'s answer.

Then, we can run the evaluation like so:

```
# Run evaluation
result = Evaluator(create_agent).run(mmlu_pro)
print(result)
```

This gives:

```
{
    'name': 'MMLU Pro',
    'pass_rate': 0.7999999999999999,
    'results': [
        {
            'prediction': 'The pituitary gland hangs within the **sella turcica**
            of the **sphenoid bone**.\n\nWhile the pituitary gland is housed
            within a specific bony indentation (the sella turcica), which is part
            of the skull, when discussing the major body cavities, it is situated
            near the boundaries of the **dura mater** that encloses the brain.
            \n\nTherefore, the most accurate general category is that it is within
            the **cranial cavity** (the skull cavity), but more specifically,
            it is physically housed in the sella turcica area.',
            'passed': 1.0
        },
        {
            'prediction': 'The approximate mean cranial capacity of
            *Homo erectus* is generally estimated to fall in the range of
            **600 to 900 cubic centimeters (cc)**.\n\nHowever, many
            paleoanthropologists and studies tend to cluster the average
            capacity closer to the **700 to 800 cc** range.\n\n
            ### Key Considerations:\n\n1. **Variation is High:**
            It is crucial to understand that this is a broad range.
            *Homo erectus* lived over a long period (from approximately
            2 million years ago to 100,000 years ago) and across diverse
            geographical locations. Specimens vary greatly in size.\n2.
            **Comparison:**\n * **Earlier Hominins (e.g., Australopithecus):
            ** Much lower, typically 300-550 cc.\n * **Modern Humans (Homo
            sapiens):** Typically 1200-1500 cc.\n3. **Scientific Debate:**
            Due to differing techniques in calculating endocranial volume
            (the internal volume of the brain cavity) from fossil skulls,
            the exact mean estimate can shift depending on the specific
            metrics, which contributes to the wide accepted range.',
            'passed': 0.4
        },
        {'prediction': '**Happiness** (or, more broadly, the greatest
        good/well-being).', 'passed': 1.0}
    ]
}
```

We purposefully did not truncate the prediction because it showcases how close the model was to the actual answer. The pass rate is now lower than the multiple-choice variant, as it gave the incorrect answer to example two. It's somewhat close, which might be the reason why it got a score of 0.4 instead of 0.

What's especially interesting about this output is that a score of 1 was given to the final example. The multiple-choice variant specifically stated that the answer should be "good" (I) and not "happiness" (G). Although "good" is mentioned, the answer specifies "happiness" at the start. As such, this demonstrates a failure mode of using LLMs to judge LLMs. They are not perfect by any means, just like human evaluation. A mix of evaluation metrics and benchmarks is generally preferred to limit the downsides of any one benchmark.

What We Built

```
TinyAgent/
├── agent.py
├── evaluator.py   ← New (Run a `TinyAgent` over a `Benchmark`)
├── llm.py
├── memory.py
├── planning.py
├── toolbox.py
├── tools.py
└── trajectory.py
```

Rubric-based evaluation

A refinement on the raw LLM-as-a-judge approach is to give the judge an explicit rubric: a structured set of criteria, each with defined score levels. Instead of asking a single "Is this output good?" you score the output against multiple criteria, each capturing a different axis of quality. You ask something more like "On a scale of 1–3, does this response correctly cite evidence from the provided sources? Score 1 if no sources are cited, score 2 if sources are cited but not directly relevant, score 3 if sources are cited and directly support the claim."

Notable rubric-based benchmarks include *ScholarQABench* (*https://oreil.ly/3I0lA*) and *HealthBench* (*https://oreil.ly/CT_JT*), both of which provide detailed and structured rubrics that score many facets of the targeted task. Each of these rubric items can be scored by a model judge.

In Figure 7-7, we see an example of using a rubric that scores outputs based on four categories: fluency, correctness, completeness, and groundedness. To score each of these axes, a rubric would contain examples such as these (summarized from ScholarQABench's *Coverage* rubric):

Score 1: Severely lacking
: Misses core lines of research or fixates on a single work, with little usable depth

Score 2: Partial
: Covers some key aspects but misses significant research or stays too narrow

Score 3: Acceptable
: Discusses several representative works and gives a satisfactory overview, though more sources or points would strengthen it

Score 4: Good
: Covers a variety of representative papers and sources, missing only minor areas

Score 5: Comprehensive
: Spans a diverse range of papers and viewpoints, and even surfaces important points beyond what the question asked

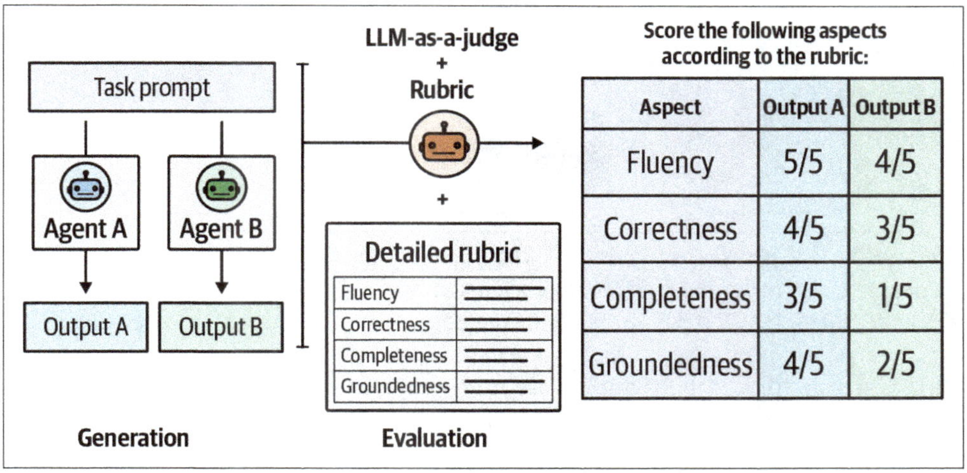

Figure 7-7. A detailed rubric decomposes output quality into named dimensions, each scored independently to guide evaluation

Rubrics improve evaluation reliability because they break a complex judgement into smaller, more objective criteria. They also allow us to evaluate individual subbehaviors of the agent, which can give us a much more high-resolution signal about where specifically the agent is performing well or breaking down.

Trajectory Evaluation: Did It Get There the Right Way?

Outcome evaluation tells you whether the agent succeeded. Trajectory evaluation tells you how it got there or how it failed. A trajectory is the full sequence of steps an agent took: the reasoning it produced, the tools it called, the arguments it passed, and the intermediate outputs it generated along the way.

One way to analyze an agent's behavior is to look at statistics of its tool calls across a number of runs. In Figure 7-8 from SWE-Atlas, we can see how three different agents behave when tackling the same set of tasks. We can see the GPT-5.4 on the left tends to search and conduct file operations heavily early in its trajectories and undertakes execution steps after gaining enough context about the repo it's operating in. We miss such patterns if we look exclusively at outcomes.

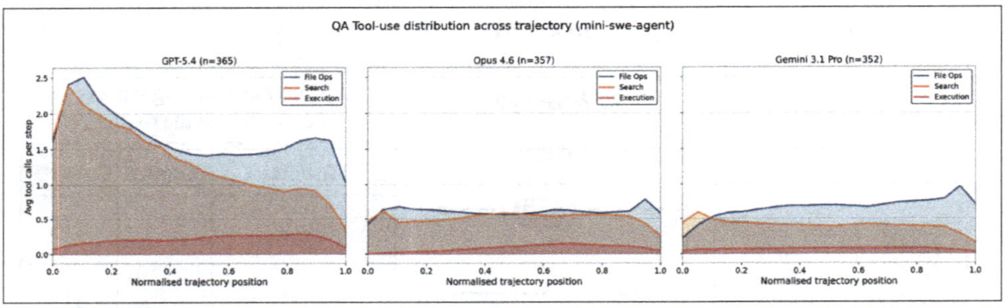

Figure 7-8. Tool-use distribution across the trajectory for three models on the same Codebase Q&A tasks under the mini-SWE agent scaffold. Adapted from M. Raghavendra et al., 2026, "SWE Atlas," arXiv:2605.08366.

This is a way to read behavior across many runs at once. It's often also useful to examine trajectories individually.

In Figure 7-9, we can see multiple trajectories that pass outcome evaluation, but trajectory inspection reveals deeper problems. In the first example, the agent output was a lucky guess. In the second, the agent spends a large number of steps and tool calls to arrive at an answer that should have only required one tool call. In the third, the model overthinks before making the right tool call.

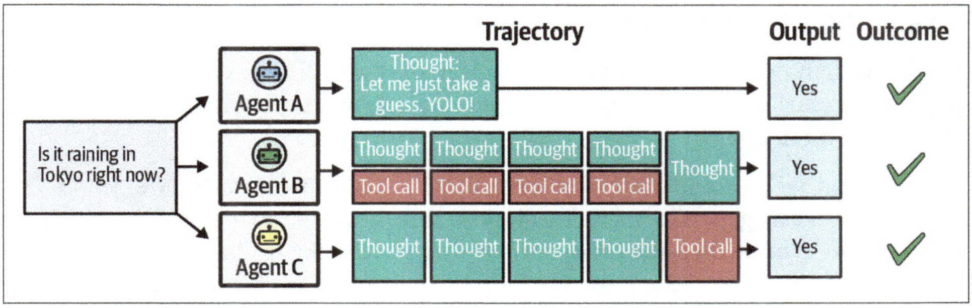

Figure 7-9. Three correct outcomes, three different problems in the trajectory. Agent A guessed and got lucky, Agent B spent several tool calls where one would do, and Agent C made the right tool call but overthought its way there. Outcome evaluation passes all three; only trajectory evaluation tells them apart.

These three failure modes are distinct enough to warrant separate measurement: unsound reasoning, inefficiency, and unnecessary overhead. Measuring a trajectory means scoring the steps along the way, not just the endpoint. A few axes do most of the work. Did the agent reach for the right tools and pass them valid arguments? How efficiently did it get there, in tool calls, steps, and reasoning tokens? Did each step follow reasonably from what the agent learned in the steps before it?

These questions can be put to an LLM judge that is handed the full trajectory to observe. As we saw earlier, that is a rubric, just one that examines the steps and not just the final output. Works such as T-Eval (*https://oreil.ly/Pg2NC*) (2024), AgentBoard (*https://oreil.ly/B1x_c*) (2024), TRACE (*https://arxiv.org/abs/2510.02837*) (2025), and AgentProcessBench (*https://arxiv.org/abs/2603.14465*) (2026) formalize this approach, introduce measures for individual steps in the trajectory, and show how this line of evaluation has been tracking over the last several years.

Reliability: Does It Succeed Every Time?

Just like LLMs, agent outputs are stochastic: the same input can produce different outputs across runs, which means a single run score can flatter or unfairly penalize an agent. A better picture comes from running multiple trials of the same task and measuring how often the agent succeeds. From these trials you can read two different things: how *capable* the agent is, meaning whether it can succeed at all, and how *reliable* it is, meaning whether it succeeds every time. The following two metrics measure each.

Measuring Capability with pass@k

When evaluating agents on tasks with a clear pass or fail check, one metric stands out for measuring capability while accounting for the probabilistic nature of the underlying model.

Imagine that we're comparing two models on a single problem, as we see in Figure 7-10. We can generate a single solution and measure its correctness, but if we use only one sample then the model might simply be lucky in that single generation. So let's sample two solutions for the same problem from each model so we have more data to compare against. If you're starting to think about the temperature value, then you're thinking of the right parameter. We're assuming a temperature value that allows for a certain amount of variance, so say something like 0.7.

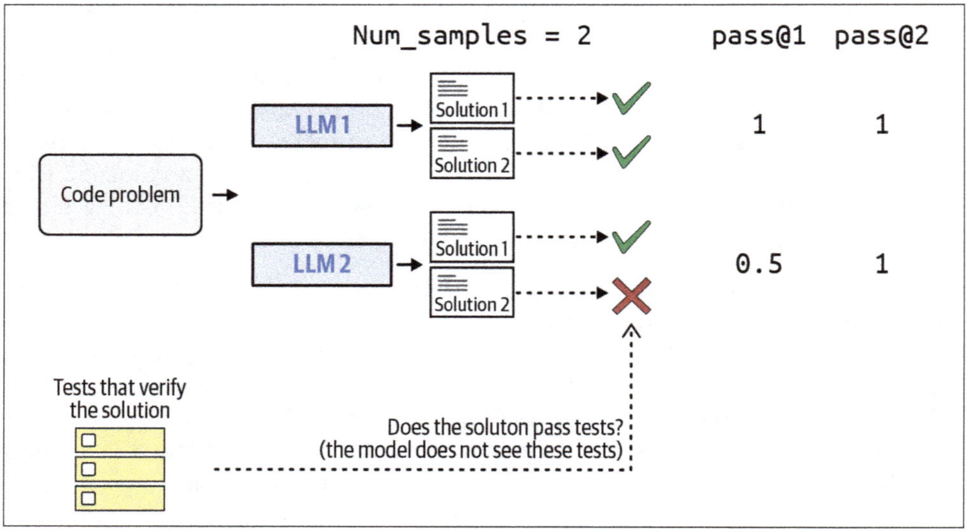

Figure 7-10. Two models, each sampled twice on the same problem, with every solution checked against held-out tests. LLM 1 passes both of its samples and LLM 2 only one, so the two differ on pass@1, 1.0 against 0.5, but tie on pass@2 at 1.0, since each produced at least one passing solution.

We can use the two samples to compute a pass@1, which shows us that LLM 1 is better than LLM 2 in this problem. For pass@1, the formula is simply to divide the number of correct answers by the total number of samples. So for LLM 1, that's 2/2 = 1 and for LLM 2 that's 1/2 = 0.5.

Note that using the same data, we can also compute a pass@2 score, which is 1 for both models, since each produced at least one correct sample across its two attempts. But this is exactly where small samples mislead. A pass@k estimate is only trustworthy when the number of samples is much larger than k, and here we have just two samples at k=2. With more samples, that inflated number would settle lower.

So a more rigorous way would be to run, say, 100 samples, then calculate the pass@k as we can see in Figure 7-11.

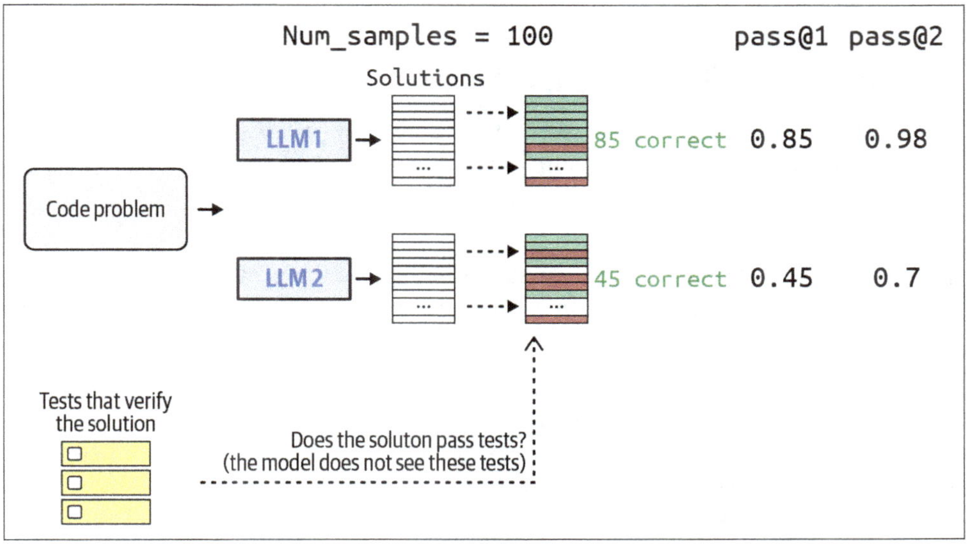

Figure 7-11. The same setup scaled to 100 samples per model, where the pass@k estimates become far more trustworthy. LLM 1 passes 85 of its 100 samples (pass@1 0.85, pass@2 0.98) and LLM 2 passes 45 (pass@1 0.45, pass@2 0.70).

Statistically, we can assign more confidence to these scores because they provide more coverage of probable model outputs. And because we have 100 samples, we can calculate results at higher values of k such as 4, 8, 16, 32, etc.

To calculate pass@k for values of k over 1, we can use the following snippet adapted from *Evaluating Large Language Models Trained on Code*,[3] which is statistically more robust than the simple division (which works perfectly for pass@1) because it accounts for the dependency between samples when drawing k candidates, while simple division assumes independence and breaks down once k exceeds 1:

```
import numpy as np

def pass_at_k(n_samples, n_correct_samples, k):
    """
    :param n_samples: total number of samples
    :param n_correct_samples: number of correct samples
```

3 Chen, Mark et al. 2021. "Evaluating Large Language Models Trained on Code," *arXiv*, 2107.03374.

```
    :param k: k in pass@k
    """
    if n_samples - n_correct_samples < k:
        return 1.0
    return 1.0 - np.prod(
        1.0 - k / np.arange(n_samples - n_correct_samples + 1, n_samples + 1)
    )
```

Measuring Reliability with pass^k

The pass@k metric rewards an agent for succeeding *at least once* in k tries, so it climbs as you grant more attempts. That makes it a measure of capability, not reliability. For reliability, you want the answer to the opposite question: does the agent succeed every single time?

That is pass^k (pass-HAT-k, sometimes written $pass^k$), the probability that all k of k sampled attempts succeed. The same runs give you both metrics, and they can tell very different stories.

Figure 7-12 shows pass^3, pass@1, and pass@3 for a number of models on Codebase QnA. Notice how the first and third models, GPT-5.4 and Opus 4.7 have the same pass@1 score of 40. If we stopped the evaluation there, we'd think they're tied at the same level of performance. But by looking at their pass^3 values we can see that GPT-5.4 is more reliable, with a pass^3 of 28 compared to Opus 4.7's score of 23.

Paradoxically, the highest pass@3 in the list belongs to Opus 4.7, at 60: given 3 tries, it lands at least one success on more tasks than any other model here. So how do we make the best use of this signal?

If we were in the middle of a training process and choosing between candidate checkpoints, the higher pass@3 would be the one we select because that capability ceiling indicates we can get more performance from the model with further training. When comparing between API vendors, however, that ceiling is mostly out of reach because we're choosing a model to run as it ships, not to train.

Computing pass^k follows the same combinatorial logic as pass@k, flipped. pass@k estimates the chance that at least one of k samples drawn from your n is correct; pass^k estimates the chance that all of them are. From c correct samples out of n, that is the count of all-correct k-subsets over the count of k-subsets in total, C(c, k) / C(n, k):

```
from math import comb

def pass_hat_k(n_samples, n_correct_samples, k):
    """Probability that all k randomly drawn samples are correct."""
    if n_correct_samples < k:
        return 0.0
    return comb(n_correct_samples, k) / comb(n_samples, k)
```

This estimator comes from τ-bench (Yao et al., 2024), which introduced pass^k to measure whether tool-using agents hold up across repeated trials instead of only on their best attempt.

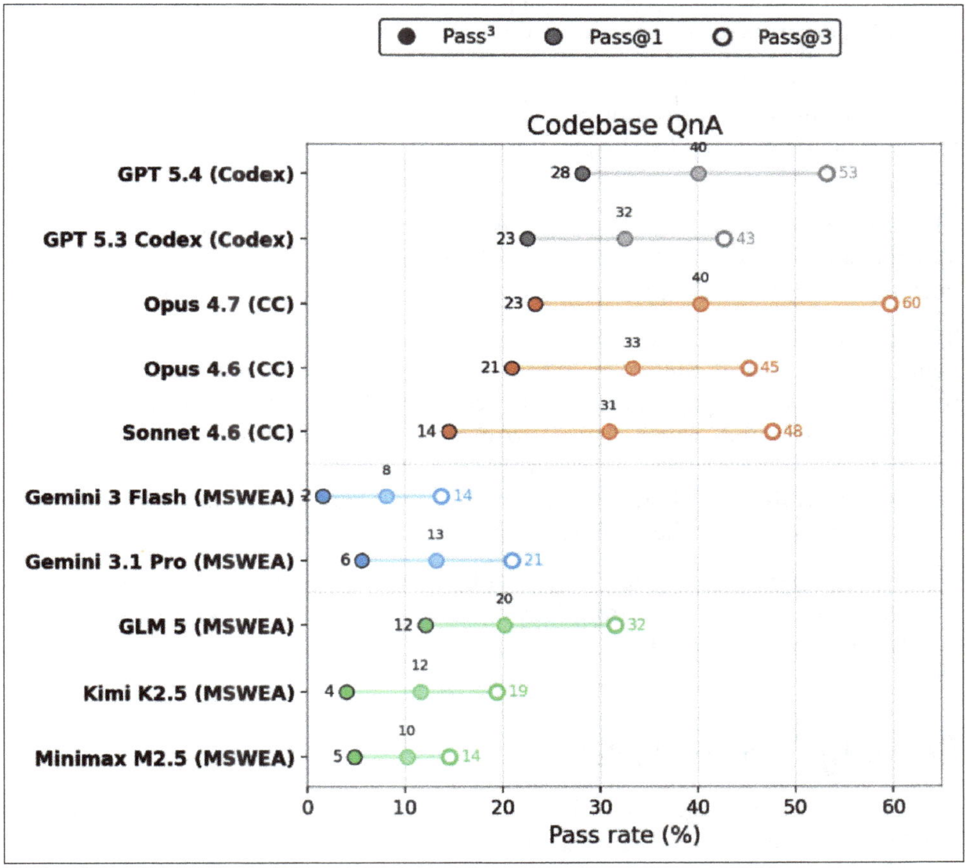

Figure 7-12. Pass^3, pass@1, and pass@3 across 10 models on the SWE Atlas Codebase QnA benchmark. For each model the three dots run left to right from pass^3 (all three trials pass), through pass@1 (the single-trial average), to pass@3 (at least one of three passes); the spread between pass^3 and pass@3 is the model's reliability gap. Pass^3 and pass@3 are the same metrics the text writes as pass^3 and pass@3. Adapted from M. Raghavendra et al., 2026. "SWE Atlas," arXiv:2605.08366.

Safety: Does It Avoid Harm?

Agents are more consequential than LLMs. Their actions could be sending a high-impact email, deleting a file, or dropping an entire database. This is why safety evaluation deserves its own place in your eval suite from the start.

"Safety" covers a few distinct questions, and the cleanest way to separate them is by who, if anyone, is trying to cause the harm. Each is a different threat model with its own metric, so you build test cases for the ones that match how your agent will be used.

The first is misuse: a malicious user asks the agent to carry out a harmful task, and the question is whether it refuses. Benchmarks such as AgentHarm (*https://arxiv.org/abs/2410.09024*) measure this with a refusal rate and a harm score.

The second is manipulation through the data the agent reads. Prompt injection plants instructions in content the agent processes, such as a retrieved document, a tool result, or a web page, to hijack its behavior. Memory poisoning corrupts what the agent stores and later retrieves, so it acts on false premises many steps later. AgentDojo and Agent Security Bench (ASB)[4,5] measure these and report an attack success rate; ASB covers both surfaces, while AgentDojo focuses on prompt injection and also tracks whether the agent stays on its real task while resisting.

The third has no adversary at all: on a benign task, the agent harms the user through its own error, deleting the wrong files or taking an irreversible step it should have paused on. This is the least standardized of the three, and it leans on your own test cases, guardrails, and harness choice and design.

Building Your Own Evals

The best signal you'll get about how well an agent matches your target task is to build your own evaluation that's actually representative of the specific problem you're building for. A small, well-curated set of test cases that reflect real usage and data will help you pick the best LLM and agent framework for your deployment, as well as help you catch regressions when you update any part of the system.

Aim for cases that capture a wide set of failure modes and edge cases, not just successes. You can score these tests using a collection of the methods we've outlined earlier in the section "Outcome Evaluation: Did the Agent Get the Right Output?" on page 268: exact match, programmatic checks, LLM-as-a-judge, and rubrics. And

4 Debenetti, Edoardo et al. 2024. "AgentDojo: A Dynamic Environment to Evaluate Prompt Injection Attacks and Defenses for LLM Agents," *arXiv*, 2406.13352.

5 Zhang, Hanrong et al. 2024. "Agent Security Bench (ASB): Formalizing and Benchmarking Attacks and Defenses in LLM-based Agents," *arXiv*, 2410.02644.

just like unit tests in the software development life cycle, run and update the test suite automatically on meaningful changes to the system so that improvements are confirmed and breaking changes are caught as early as possible.

Getting started is more important than getting it immediately right. Even a small custom eval of 5 or 10 cases can give eye-opening signals about your agent's performance—and you can grow it as you learn more about where the system fails.

Running evals at any scale requires an eval harness: the infrastructure that takes a set of test cases, runs the agent against each one, captures the full trajectory, applies your scoring methods, and aggregates the results. *harbor* (*https://harborframework.com*) is a recent open source harness designed specifically for agents, with infrastructure for running trials in containerized environments at scale and a standardized format for defining tasks and their success criteria. Popular benchmarks such as Terminal-Bench ship through the harbor registry, so you can run established benchmarks alongside your own custom eval suite.

Summary

In this chapter, we examined how evaluation is the foundation of confident agent development and the difference between intuition and evidence. We started with benchmarks, the evaluation artifacts most commonly encountered in model announcements and research papers, mapping the major categories from coding and tool use to computer use and real-world task completion. We then outlined the questions worth asking when reading benchmark scores critically, from data contamination and prompt tuning to cost and benchmark saturation.

We then broke down the core methods for outcome evaluation. We saw how human evaluation, despite its cost, remains the gold standard against which automated methods are validated. We covered the automated evaluation spectrum from exact match and programmatic checks, through LLM-as-a-judge, to rubric-based evaluation, which improves reliability by decomposing complex judgements into independently scorable criteria. We contrasted outcome evaluation with trajectory evaluation, which examines the sequence of steps an agent took and can surface failure modes like unsound reasoning, inefficiency, and unnecessary overhead that outcome scores miss entirely.

We then turned to two properties that deserve dedicated evaluation: reliability and safety.

Reliability asks not just whether an agent can succeed but whether it succeeds every time: because outputs are stochastic, running a task repeatedly lets you separate a capability ceiling (pass@k) from a measure of consistency (pass^k), and the two can rank models differently. Safety is best organized by who is causing the harm: a malicious user the agent should refuse, an attacker steering it through injected or poisoned data, or no adversary at all when the agent errs on a benign task.

We closed with building your own evaluations, where a small, well-curated set of representative cases, scored with the methods covered earlier and run automatically on every change, beats waiting for a perfect suite.

In Part II, called specializations, we explore the more advanced and complex components of managing and using agents. We start with multi-agent systems where agents collaborate and/or compete to solve tasks. Then, it follows with a chapter on multi-modal understanding so that agents can't just read but also see and hear. Finally, we end with arguably the most popular variant of an agent, namely the coding agent.

PART II

Specialized Agents

CHAPTER 8

Multi-Agent Systems

Thus far, we have discussed the agent in isolation. A single entity that autonomously creates plans, executes them, and reflects on these processes. These single-agent systems are solely responsible for achieving the initial goal without interaction with intelligent systems other than humans. As powerful as these entities can become by themselves, a system where multiple agents work together to reach a common goal has even more potential. This is the multi-agent system (MAS), which may feature one or more environments in which many agents, some differently than others, can interact with each other.

Each agent in such a system will have a level of autonomy, but may have different sets of tools, (sub)goals, or even personalities. Regardless of their potential differences, these agents will need to collaborate to reach common goals through their own skill sets. Multi-agent systems are quite adept at handling intricate tasks that require balancing multiple complex dependencies.

Imagine you are creating an agentic research system that helps you with exploring a topic of choice. A single agent would have to juggle between many different tasks, such as searching the web, processing papers and figures, reading and critiquing the papers, and finally summarizing the findings. Each of these tasks could also be handled by a different agent specialized in that task. As a result, you would get a system with a search agent, processing agent, paper agent, summarization agent, etc.

In this chapter, we'll explore how to organize multi-agent systems and allow for various types of communication in these systems. We cover general-purpose frameworks for building multi-agents and how these entities interact in social simulations.

The Multi-Agent System

Instead of a single agent, a multi-agent system (MAS) contains multiple agents collaborating, coordinating, or at times even competing to achieve a goal (see Figure 8-1). Although these agents work toward a common goal, each may have specific goals they need to achieve. The search agent and summarization agent have different roles but serve the same end goal.

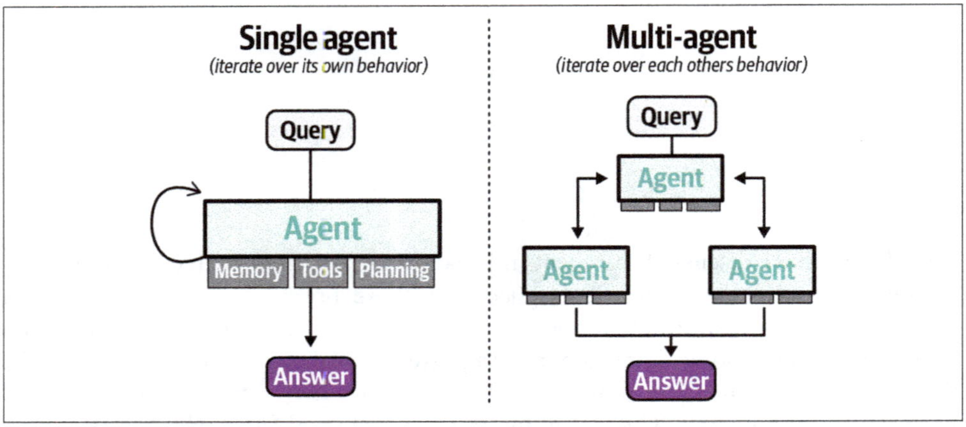

Figure 8-1. The difference between a single agent and multi-agentic behavior

Agents may share an environment in which they can make decisions, like being characters in a virtual game. However, these systems do not have to share an environment and may be responsible for different tasks. A booking system, for example, might have an agent searching the web for nice places to visit, another agent to research cheap flights, and an agent scheduling the vacation. Likewise, the environments they occupy can be physical (real-world agents typically in the form of robotic agents), virtual (game-like environments for agents to interact with), and text (environments like coding IDEs or chat interfaces).[1] These different environments and patterns are illustrated in Figure 8-2.

Compared to a single-agent system, which has issues scaling to large or complex use cases, a multi-agent system can excel in these environments by, for instance, deploying more agents, each solving a different task.

1 Xi, Zhiheng et al. 2025. "The Rise and Potential of Large Language Model-based Agents: A Survey," *Science China Information Sciences*, 68.2: 121101.

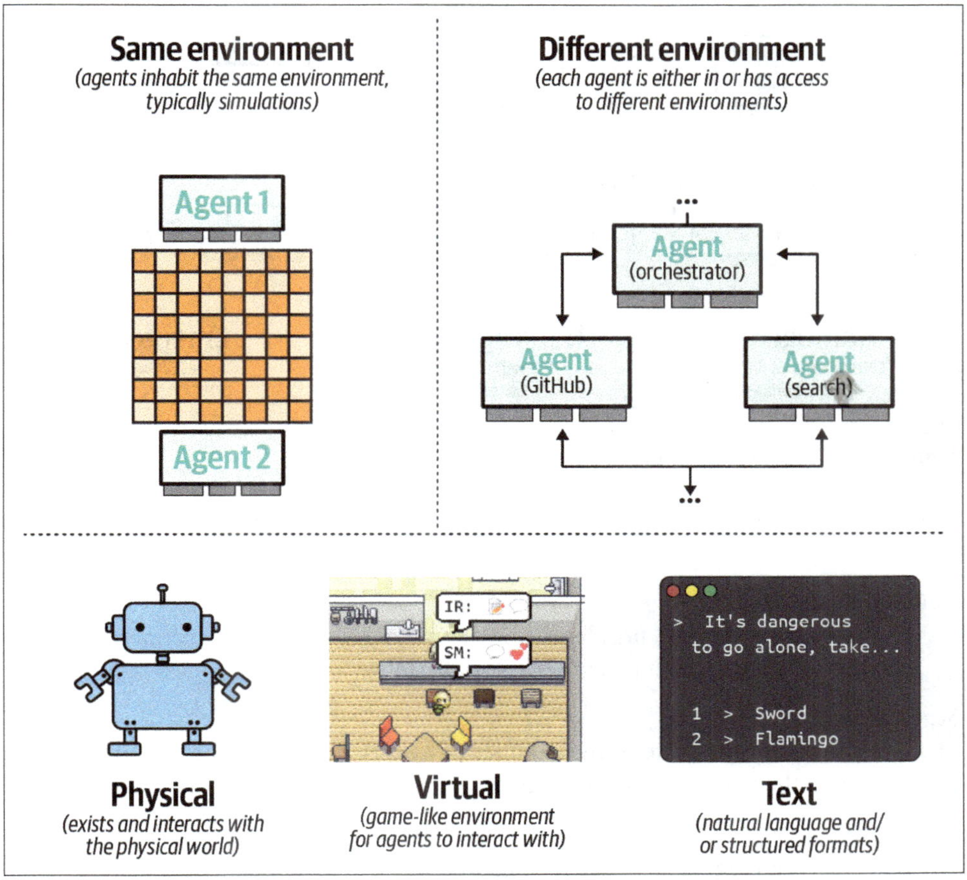

Figure 8-2. An overview of environments and patterns in agentic systems

Depending on the system, agents may collaborate or compete and take on different roles.[2] *Homogeneous agents* have similar capabilities and are typically used for efficient parallel task execution. *Heterogeneous agents* typically differ in roles, where each has different goals and tasks to complete. The search agent and summarization agent have different roles and may be initialized with different LLMs, memory systems, and tools. *Emergent specialization* arises when identical agents evolve into specialized roles through interaction with each other and their environments. For instance, in game-like simulations, some agents may learn specific abilities such as resource gathering or defensive roles (Figure 8-3).[3]

2 Liu, Bang et al. 2025. "Advances and Challenges in Foundation Agents: From Brain-Inspired Intelligence to Evolutionary, Collaborative, and Safe Systems," *arXiv*, 2504.01990.

3 Altera.AL et al. 2024. "Project Sid: Many-Agent Simulations Toward AI Civilization," *arXiv*, 2411.00114.

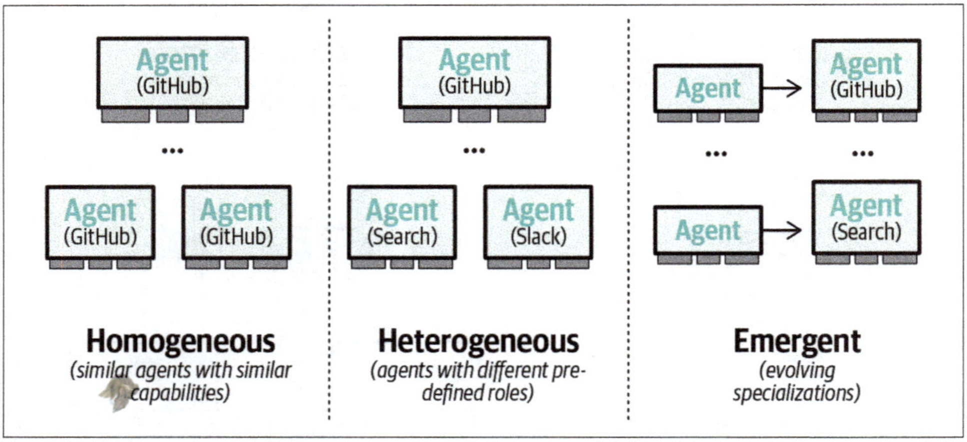

Figure 8-3. An overview of agent roles within systems

The collective nature of multi-agent systems, therefore, allows for a wide range of benefits:

Collaboration
: Complex and diverse problems can be solved more easily by increasing the number of agents and having them work together.

Scalability
: Depending on the system, the number of agents can be increased without slowing down the system by running them in parallel or fully asynchronously.

Speed
: Instead of having a single agent sequentially solve each task, multiple agents can not only solve them in parallel, but specialized agents tend to solve each task faster than a single non-specialized agent would.

However, MASs are not a free lunch and have several disadvantages:

Complex
: They are complex systems that require careful management of the orchestration of the agents and how they interact. Likewise, there are additional layers of abstraction due to the interaction of agents.

Cost
: Increasing the number of agents can be a computationally costly process if the agents rely on powerful LLMs.

Evaluation
: Evaluating an agent is already a tricky process, now imagine having to evaluate many working together.

This chapter explores many more advantages and disadvantages because these complex systems are used for a wide array of use cases. Due to their flexibility, MASs can be used across many industries and applications. Examples include the following:

Anthropic
: Anthropic, a leading AI organization building the Claude models, used multiple Claude agents to build a research system (*https://oreil.ly/hZtDq*), allowing users to explore complex topics more effectively.

Uber
: Uber created a data-retrieval MAS that uses a supervisor agent and several data-retrieval agents (such as an SQL agent) to transform user requests into real-time financial intelligence (*https://oreil.ly/r5ICF*).

Delivery Hero
: Delivery Hero, a multinational online food ordering and food delivery company, uses several agents to extract entities and create product titles, thereby building a product knowledge base (*https://oreil.ly/ax0HJ*).

These are just some examples of MASs, but we'll cover many more of them as we explore specific architectures and general-purpose frameworks.

Orchestrating Agents

Deploying multiple agents in a system is not straightforward. You'll have to ask yourself how they should be deployed, in what kind of architectures and specialisms, and how they communicate with one another. As such, the orchestration of agents is a vital component in creating a stable and future-proof system. Before we go into specific frameworks, let's first explore common patterns in orchestrating agents and how we can standardize communication techniques between agents.

Patterns

Patterns in MASs refer to how agents are set up in relation to one another. It's the topology of the system and how agents are defined to specific roles and tasks, but most importantly, how they interact and communicate. There are four types of communication structure of MASs:

Centralized
: The responsibility of communication and its management is controlled by a single orchestration agent that allocates responsibilities and tasks to other agents.

Decentralized
: Each agent shares similar responsibilities, and the communication is distributed among them with no clear "leader."

Hierarchical
: Each agent is structured into a layered system where each level has a different degree of authority, and agents have distinct roles.

Federated
: Agents are distributed among parallel environments (organizations) that only communicate indirectly to safeguard the privacy of data. Each agent adheres to different regulations but can still communicate the results with other agents.

These types are visualized in Figure 8-4.

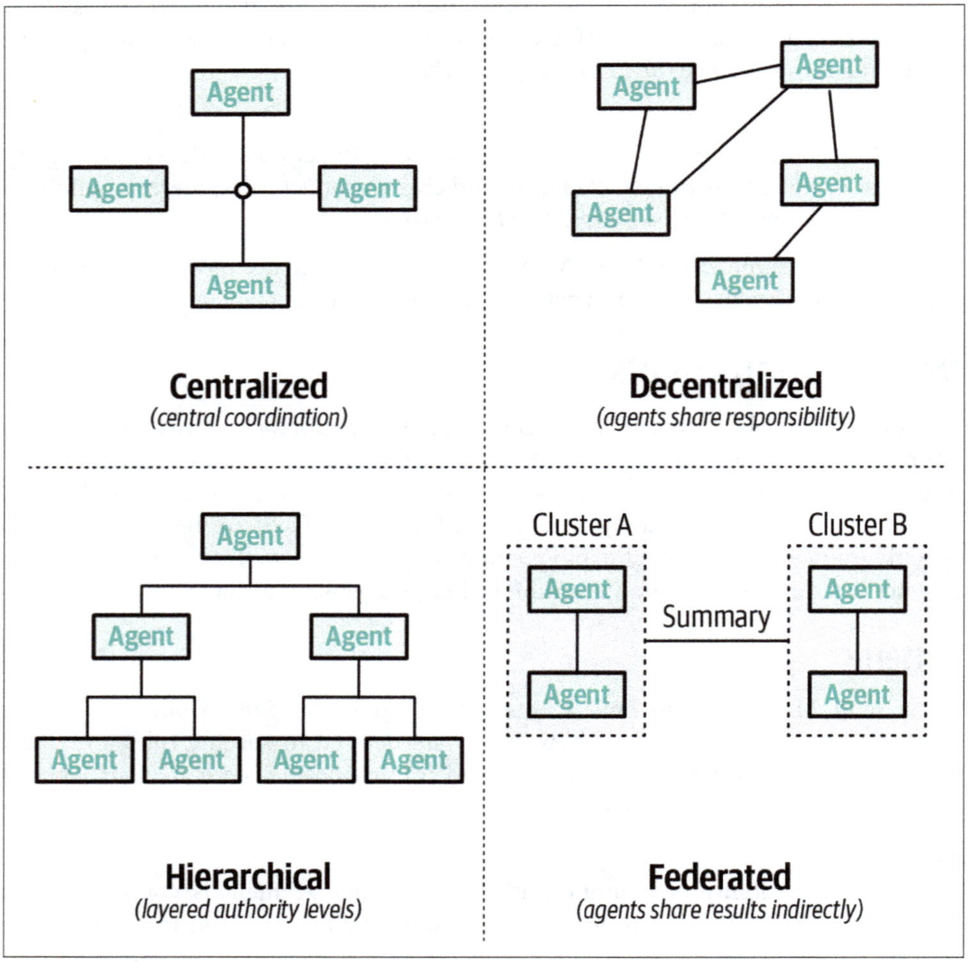

Figure 8-4. Four different patterns of agent orchestration

In practice, a *centralized MAS* is most often used due to its ease of implementation and management compared to the other patterns. A downside of this approach is that the entire system might collapse if the orchestration agent fails.

A *decentralized MAS* has the benefit of being more stable than the other patterns. Even if some agents fail, the system can continue working as each agent has similar responsibilities and capabilities. As such, scaling only requires adding agents. However, it requires many capable agents and significant communication overhead, which all require extensive resources.

The *hierarchical MAS* is similar to how traditional organizations operate and is therefore an intuitive pattern to use. By distributing tasks across levels and having many specialized roles, resource allocation can be made efficient. However, it's still a complex system that requires the most communication.

Lastly, a *federated MAS* is a relatively new pattern and is used when agents need to be distributed among different organizations. Although this pattern encourages cross-system collaboration, it relies on shared standards that might not always be in place.

Creating MASs can quickly require significant code to manage all agents. There have been many different frameworks that handle the complexity of managing and creating agents. Before we explore various general-purpose frameworks, let's create a simple version of a centralized MAS to showcase the fundamentals and intricacies of having and building MASs.

An interesting trick that we can use to create a centralized and potentially hierarchical system is by viewing subagents not as agents but as tools to use. To illustrate, let's first create a specialized subagent:

```
from illustrated_agents.chapters.ch2 import LLM
from illustrated_agents.chapters.ch4 import Memory
from illustrated_agents.chapters.ch5 import NativeTools
from illustrated_agents.chapters.ch6 import NativeReAct, TinyAgent
from illustrated_agents.toolbox import add, subtract, multiply

# Gemma 4 E4B (with native thinking and tool calling)
llm = LLM(model="gemma4:e4b", think=True)

# Math specialist
math_tools = NativeTools()
math_tools.add_tool("add", add)
math_tools.add_tool("subtract", subtract)
math_tools.add_tool("multiply", multiply)

# Math Agent
math_agent = TinyAgent(
    llm=llm,
    tools=math_tools,
```

```
        memory=Memory(),
        planner=NativeReAct()
    )
```

This agent "specializes" in using basic mathematical tools, such as adding, subtracting, and multiplying values, as we have seen often throughout this book.

To make the example a bit more comprehensive, let's add another subagent. This agent will have access to tools related to date handling:

```
import datetime

def today() -> str:
    """Return today's date (YYYY-MM-DD)."""
    return datetime.date.today().isoformat()

def days_between(a: str, b: str) -> int:
    """Days between two ISO dates."""
    return (datetime.date.fromisoformat(b) - datetime.date.fromisoformat(a)).days

# Date specialist
date_tools = NativeTools()
date_tools.add_tool("today", today)
date_tools.add_tool("days_between", days_between)

# Date Agent
date_agent = TinyAgent(
    llm=llm,
    tools=date_tools,
    memory=Memory(),
    planner=NativeReAct()
)
```

To have the orchestrator be able to use and direct these subagents, we can leverage them in an elegant way, namely as tools. Instead of having to devise a complex harness, framework, or system, we wrap these subagents in Python functions for the orchestrator to use:

```
def ask_math_agent(question: str) -> str:
    """Delegate to the math specialist."""
    return math_agent.run(question)

def ask_date_agent(question: str) -> str:
    """Ask queries to a sub-agent that handles ISO dates."""
    return date_agent.run(question)
```

Now, we can feed the two "tools" (which are actually subagents) to the orchestrator:

```
# Tools - Add the Math Agent and Date Agent as tools!
tools = NativeTools()
tools.add_tool("ask_math_agent", ask_math_agent)
tools.add_tool("ask_date_agent", ask_date_agent)

# Orchestrator Agent
orchestrator_agent = TinyAgent(
    llm=llm,
    tools=tools,
    memory=Memory(),
    planner=NativeReAct()
)
```

This creates a simple hierarchy. We can ask the orchestrator a question, and it can decide whether to ask for help from one of the subagents. To illustrate, let's ask the orchestrator a question that requires the help of both subagents:

```
orchestrator_agent.run("If I save €4 per day until 2030, how much will I have?")
```

Which gives:

```
'If you save €4 per day until the end of 2030, you will have **€6,764**.'
```

Note that you will get a different answer because this answer was generated back in May 2026.

As always, to understand what really happened, we would need to inspect the memory and trajectory of the agent. However, we now have three agents to explore. We start with the orchestrator and focus on its actions, observations, and final answer:

```
for index, step in enumerate(orchestrator_agent.trajectory.runs[0]["steps"]):
    print(f"-- Step {index+1} ---")
    if step.action:
        print(f"Tool: {step.action}")
        print(f"Observation: {step.observation}\n")
    else:
        print(f"Answer: {step.answer}\n")
```

This gives the following output:

```
-- Step 1 ---
Tool: {'tool': 'ask_date_agent', 'kwargs': {'question': 'How many days from
today until the end of 2030?'}}
Observation: There are **1691** days from today (May 15, 2026) until the end
of 2030 (December 31, 2030).

-- Step 2 ---
Tool: {'tool': 'ask_math_agent', 'kwargs': {'question': '€4 times 1691'}}
Observation: €6764

-- Step 3 ---
Answer: If you save €4 per day until the end of 2030, you will have **€6,764**.
```

Note that the orchestrator decided to call the date subagent to get the number of days before calling the math subagent to perform the calculation. This idea of having subagents and an orchestrator to manage them is particularly useful when you have dozens and perhaps hundreds of tools that can be used. The orchestrator is likely to make mistakes, having to sift through so many tools, and can instead dedicate a subset of those tools to a subagent.

Note, though, that looking only at the trajectory of the orchestrator gives an abstract overview of what has happened. We didn't see what actions the subagents took and whether that seemed like an efficient route. Let's inspect one of the subagents:

```
for index, step in enumerate(date_agent.trajectory.runs[0]["steps"]):
    print(f"-- Step {index+1} ---")
    if step.action:
        print(f"Tool: {step.action}")
        print(f"Observation: {step.observation}\n")
    else:
        print(f"Answer: {step.answer}\n")
```

Which gives the following output:

```
-- Step 1 ---
Tool: {'tool': 'today', 'kwargs': {}}
Observation: 2026-05-15

-- Step 2 ---
Tool: {'tool': 'days_between', 'kwargs': {'a': '2026-05-15', 'b': '2030-12-31'}}
Observation: 1691

-- Step 3 ---
Answer: There are **1691** days from today (May 15, 2026) until the end of 2030
(December 31, 2030).
```

The subagent first needed to figure out what the current date was before calculating the number of days between now and the end of 2030. By inspecting the trajectories of even the subagents, you can see how well optimized they were for given tasks.

Although this was a minimal example of a MAS, the complexities of such systems can grow quickly. As such, now that we have covered a basic technique for implementing subagents, let's explore how general-purpose frameworks approach this problem.

General-Purpose Frameworks for Collaborative Task-Solving Patterns

With MASs, there's not a single framework, pattern, or orchestration workflow that is best for all use cases. As such, many different general-purpose frameworks have been developed that allow users to build their own MAS. Each framework, however, does have a distinct "flavor" of implementation and philosophy, which are worth exploring.

CAMEL

One of the first frameworks for a collaborative MAS is Communicative Agents for "Mind" Exploration of Large Language Model Society (CAMEL). CAMEL is an agentic framework that revolves around having agents roleplay as a way to create specialized entities that collaborate.

CAMEL starts with an idea proposed by the user. This is generally a simple task description of what the user wants the system to achieve. For instance, an idea could be: "create a website for my blog." Then, two agents with specific roles are created, namely the AI user and AI assistant. The AI user represents the user and is in charge of giving instructions and directing the AI assistant. The AI assistant executes the given instructions and is specialized in its execution. Roles for the AI user and AI assistant could be "blogger" and "programmer," respectively. Then, these entities are fed to the task specifier agent to provide a more detailed description of the initial task. Because it has knowledge about the assigned roles, it can rewrite the user's query to something that is more aligned with the task. These user-driven concepts are illustrated in Figure 8-5.

Finally, the AI user and AI assistant will take up their roles and converse with each other about how to best solve the query as provided by the task specifier agent. This is achieved by multi-turn conversations until the AI user ends the conversation and returns a completed answer. This role playing–like structure is shown in Figure 8-6, where the AI user takes on the role of the user and the AI assistant the role of the programmer.

This role-playing methodology enables collaborative communication between agents and is an interesting first look into general-purpose frameworks.

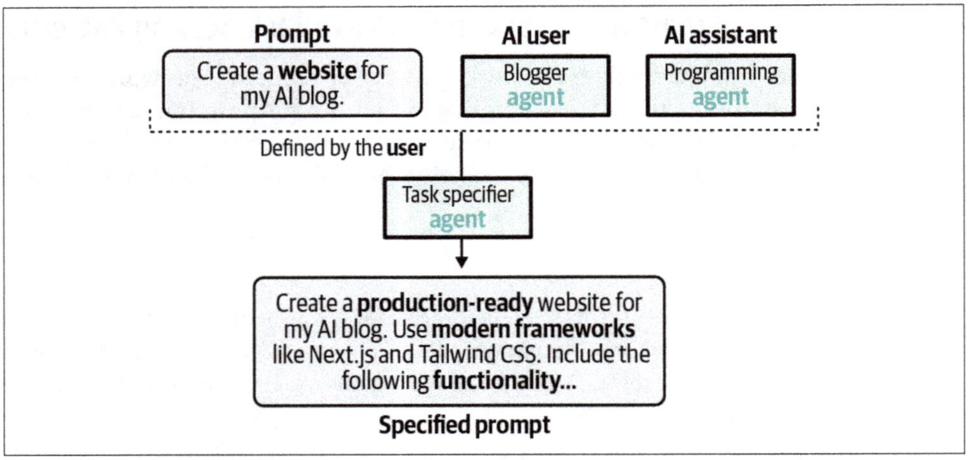

Figure 8-5. Different agents working together to solve a given task in CAMEL

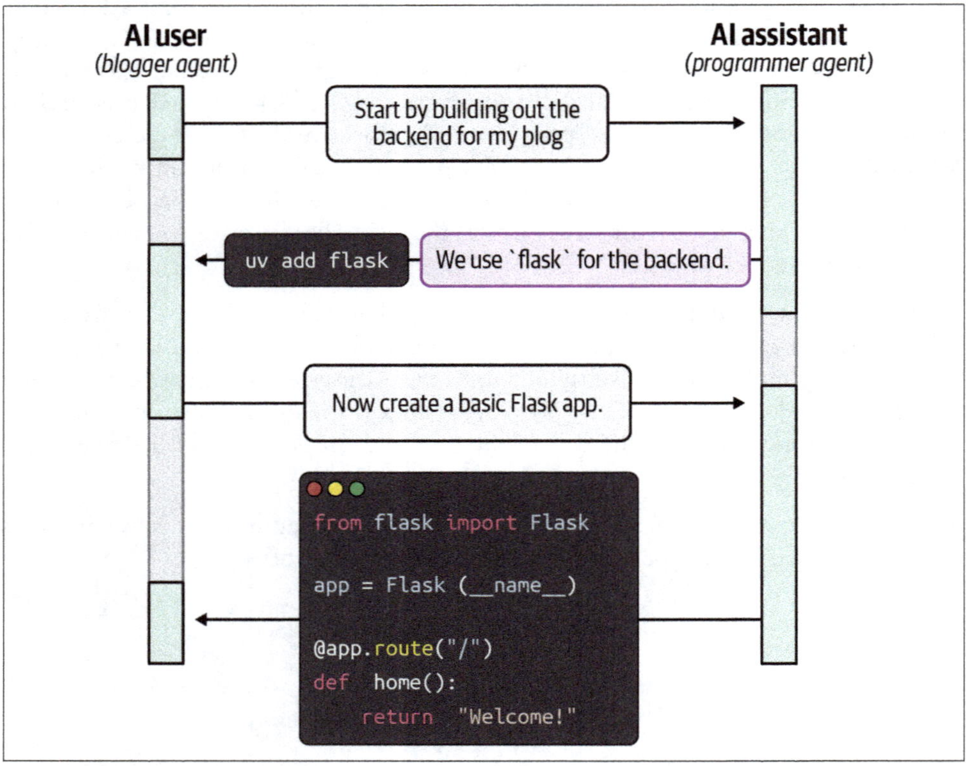

Figure 8-6. The interaction between the AI user and AI assistant when solving a user-defined task

MetaGPT

This idea of role-playing has found its way to many such general-purpose frameworks, as LLMs are quite adaptable to different situations that require specialized perspectives and capabilities. MetaGPT takes it one step further and attempts to mimic entire organizational structures with specialized roles.[4] This framework has three components to its MAS:

Specialization of roles
: Tasks are broken down into smaller, specific tasks that can be solved with specialized agents.

Communication protocol
: A protocol that enhances the efficiency of communication while also providing structured interfaces.

Iterative programming with executable feedback
: External feedback incorporated as a self-correction mechanism.

The specialization of roles in MetaGPT starts with breaking down complex tasks and queries into smaller and more specific tasks, as we explored in Chapter 6. To solve these individual tasks, MetaGPT defines specialized agent roles that collaborate through diverse skills and expertise. This framework takes inspiration from organizational structures by often referencing software companies, where, for instance, a product manager will have different skills and tasks to complete compared to an engineer. As such, each role will have a profile including name, goal, skills, and constraints for that particular role. Through those specializations, MetaGPT adheres to a standard operating procedure (SOP) for software development where all agents will work sequentially. Each agent is powered by ReAct.

The authors also developed a communication protocol to allow for both structured and unstructured information to be shared. Instead of communicating primarily through dialogue, MetaGPT does so through artifacts like documents and diagrams (structured output).

Finally, each agent will be tasked with iterating on their own output as a way to self-correct and improve their behavior. For instance, an engineer might be tasked not only with creating code but also with running and debugging if necessary (Figure 8-7).

4 Hong, Sirui et al. 2023. "MetaGPT: Meta Programming for a Multi-agent Collaborative Framework," *The Twelfth International Conference on Learning Representations.*

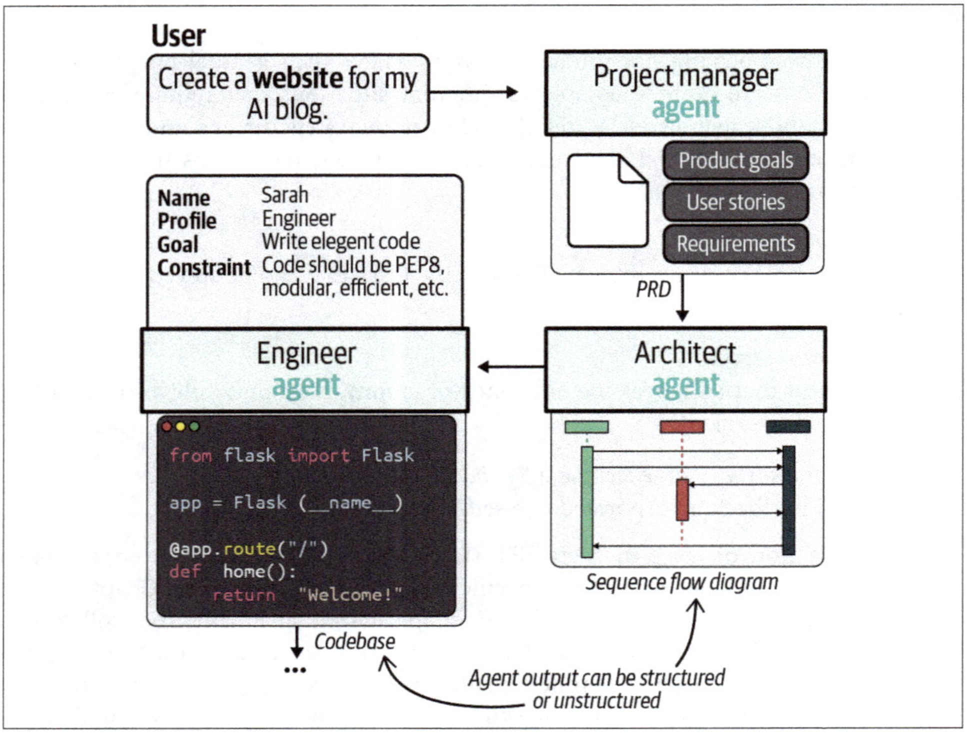

Figure 8-7. A pipeline of agents working together in MetaGPT

MetaGPT takes role-playing quite literally and attempts to reconstruct existing organizational structures to enforce task decomposition and specialization.

Production-grade frameworks

Although the previous methodologies were open sourced, the following frameworks were created from a developer's perspective, rather than being an important artifact of a research paper. In other words, these were meant to be products used to build and scale MASs in production.

At the end of 2025, the most common frameworks were Microsoft's AutoGen (*https://oreil.ly/SMImD*),[5] LangGraph (*https://oreil.ly/9y_ws*), and CrewAI (*https://oreil.ly/qJ3j7*). Each of these frameworks focuses on modularity and allows you to build any MAS in whichever way you would like. As shown in Figure 8-8, this entails

5 Wu, Qingyun et al. 2024. "Autogen: Enabling Next-Gen LLM Applications Via Multi-agent Conversations," *First Conference on Language Modeling.*

all different kinds of roles, memory modules, and tools that can be selected for each agent, as well as the pattern of the system.

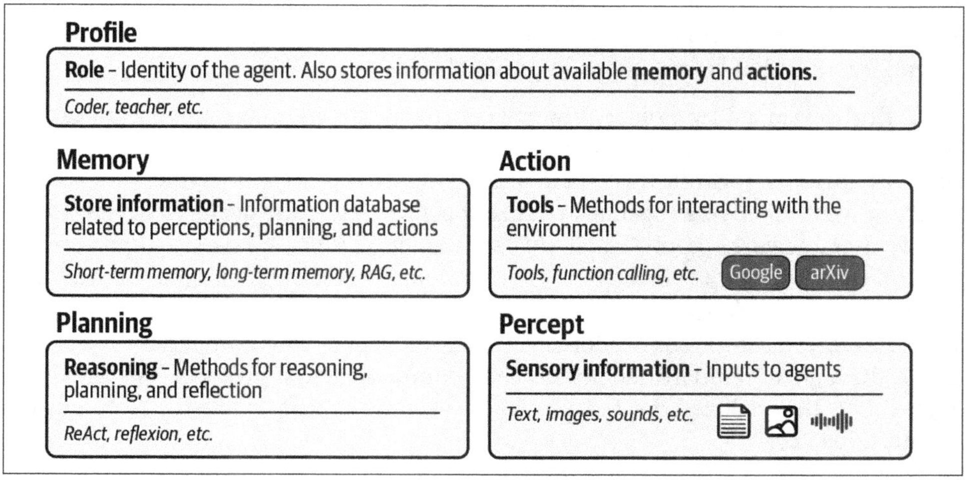

Figure 8-8. Agentic frameworks and harnesses all deploy different tactics for handling things like memory and planning

With the ever-changing landscape of AI agents, it's difficult to suggest a single platform as the "best." Experimentation will be key when deciding on frameworks, but also the independence of certain platforms and the continued development.

Depending on how autonomous you would want your agent(s) to be, the open source framework n8n (*https://github.com/n8n-io/n8n*) might also be an interesting tool to use. Compared to the previous frameworks, it's an AI workflow automation tool that requires you to create predefined workflows for the LLMs and agents to follow. However, agents might still have a degree of autonomy within such a framework, making it just on the edge of a MAS.

Communication Protocols

Setting up communication between agents can be challenging, as the way they exchange information greatly affects performance. Effective context engineering, as we covered in Chapter 4, requires optimizing both inputs and outputs. Too much or too little information, or using the wrong format, can degrade results. Achieving the right balance of communication is therefore essential.

Before LLMs, agent communication languages (ACLs) such as FIPA-ACL and KQML offered a standardization for agents to interact and share information using message types such as "request" and "inform."[6,7] Since the rise of modern LLMs, beginning with GPT-3.5 in late 2022, protocols have been developed to facilitate communication between agents and tools, such as the Model Context Protocol (MCP; see Chapter 5). MAS, as a typically collaborative system, would greatly benefit from standardized Agent2Agent (A2A) communication protocols.

A2A, first developed by Google, is a major protocol for inter-agent communication.[8] A2A allows agents developed on different frameworks and by different organizations to work together regardless of their underlying architecture. Imagine you want to create a MAS of several agents working together, but each agent is developed by different frameworks (LangGraph (*https://oreil.ly/NYPER*), CrewAI (*https://oreil.ly/sNg7q*), AutoGen (*https://oreil.ly/9OMj4*), etc.) and on different cloud platforms (e.g., Azure, AWS, Google Cloud, etc.). To connect all these agents, you would generally have to create custom connections. A2A allows agents to communicate with each other through a standardized inter-agent communication protocol. As shown in Figure 8-9, this reduces the complexity of needing to continuously create custom connections.

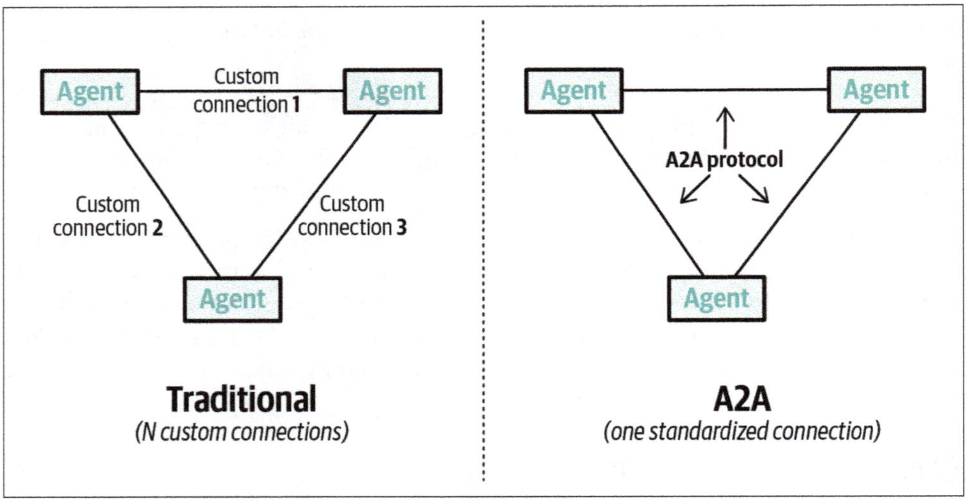

Figure 8-9. The A2A protocol standardizes and reduces the number of custom agent connections needed

6 Poslad, Stefan. 2007. "Specifying Protocols for Multi-agent Systems Interaction," *ACM Transactions on Autonomous and Adaptive Systems (TAAS)*, 2.4:15-es.

7 Finin, Tim et al. 1994. "KQML As an Agent Communication Language," *Proceedings of the Third International Conference on Information and Knowledge Management.*

8 Google. "Announcing the Agent2Agent Protocol (A2A)," *https://developers.googleblog.com/en/a2a-a-new-era-of-agent-interoperability*. Accessed December 4, 2025.

Much like MCP, A2A is an open standard that enables communication, but for collaboration between agents instead. Figure 8-10 shows an example of how this protocol provides communication between two agents that both have access to MCP but are hosted on different infrastructures.

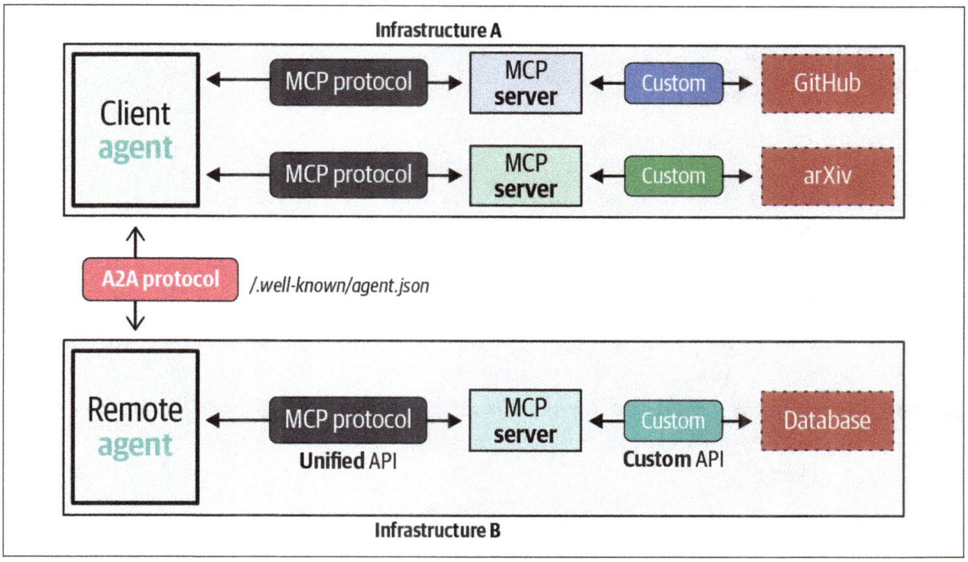

Figure 8-10. An overview of the interaction between MCP and A2A

A2A allows agents to discover each other and their capabilities, exchange (un-)structured information across modalities such as text and images, stream responses, and even handle multi-turn conversations. Likewise, this allows agents to collaborate remotely and exchange relevant information and states needed to solve complex tasks.

There are three core actors in A2A interactions:

User
: The user, generally a human but can be an automated process, that initiates a request and/or defines a goal.

A2A client (client agent)
: The client is the agent that initiates communications to other agents on behalf of the user. This is the entity that uses the A2A protocol.

A2A server (remote agent)
: These are the agents that are being called upon by the client agent to execute a given task. It can be a single agent or an entire MAS.

Using these three actors, let's go through an example of how communication works through the following steps:

1. Task initiation
2. Discovery
3. Authentication
4. Client agent communication
5. Remote agent communication

In step 1, the user defines a task to be completed for the A2A client. This is done without the need for an A2A protocol since the communication is not between two (or more) agents.

In step 2, discovery, the client agent will first need to discover which agents are available and what they can do. Defined by the A2A protocol, each agent needs to expose a *.json* file describing their capabilities, endpoint URL, and other relevant information. This is called the *agent card* and is accessible at `/.well-known/agent-card.json`. Here is an example of the agent card for a train agent that helps users book train tickets:

```
{
    "name": "Train Agent",
    "description": "Helps book train tickets",
    "url": "http://localhost:8000/",
    "version": "1.0.0",
    "capabilities": {
        "streaming": true,
        "pushNotifications": true,
        "stateTransitionHistory": false
    },
    "defaultInputModes": [
        "text",
        "text/plain"
    ],
    "defaultOutputModes": [
        "text",
        "text/plain"
    ],
    "skills": [
        {
            "id": "book_train_tickets",
            "name": "Book Train Tickets",
            "description": "Helps with booking train tickets",
            "tags": [
                "Book train tickets"
            ],
            "examples": [
                "Book return tickets from Eindhoven to Brussels on November 20"
```

```
            ]
        }
    ]
}
```

In step 3, after the client agent has decided which remote agent to access, it goes through the authentication described in the agent card's security scheme, which allows for various security schemes, such as API keys and OAuth 2.0.

In step 4, the communication has been authenticated, and the client agent sends a request to the remote agent through HTTPS with JSON-RPC 2.0, much like MCP. The remote agent receives the communication and will start working. If the remote agent requires more information, it will send a message back to the client agent to request more information. While working on the task, the remote agent can stream updates to notify the client agent when the task is completed.

In step 5, once the remote agent has completed its tasks, it will send a message to the client agent along with any relevant information or artifacts.

The steps of discovery, authentication, task communication, and task execution are illustrated in Figure 8-11.

Although A2A is not the only protocol out there, with a technology as new as A2A, there are not many competitors. One notable framework is Internet of Agents (IoA), which describes an agent integration protocol for creating MASs.[9] Based on the concept of the internet, it features an instant messaging–like design and dynamic modules for agent conversation and collaboration. In contrast, improving the standardization and collaboration can be explored through the lens of RL for MAS.[10] Here, RL can be used to train LLMs and agents in the context of MAS, thereby having these entities already experienced with such systems.

Standardized protocols and communication are rather new fields in MAS, as is MAS itself. The important thing to note is to start thinking about what it means to have standardization, why it's required, and with what common methodologies it can be achieved.

9 Chen, Weize et al. 2024. "Internet of Agents: Weaving a Web of Heterogeneous Agents for Collaborative Intelligence," *arXiv*, 2407.07061.

10 Sun, Chuanneng et al. 2024. "LLM-based Multi-Agent Reinforcement Learning: Current and Future Directions," *arXiv*, 2405.11106.

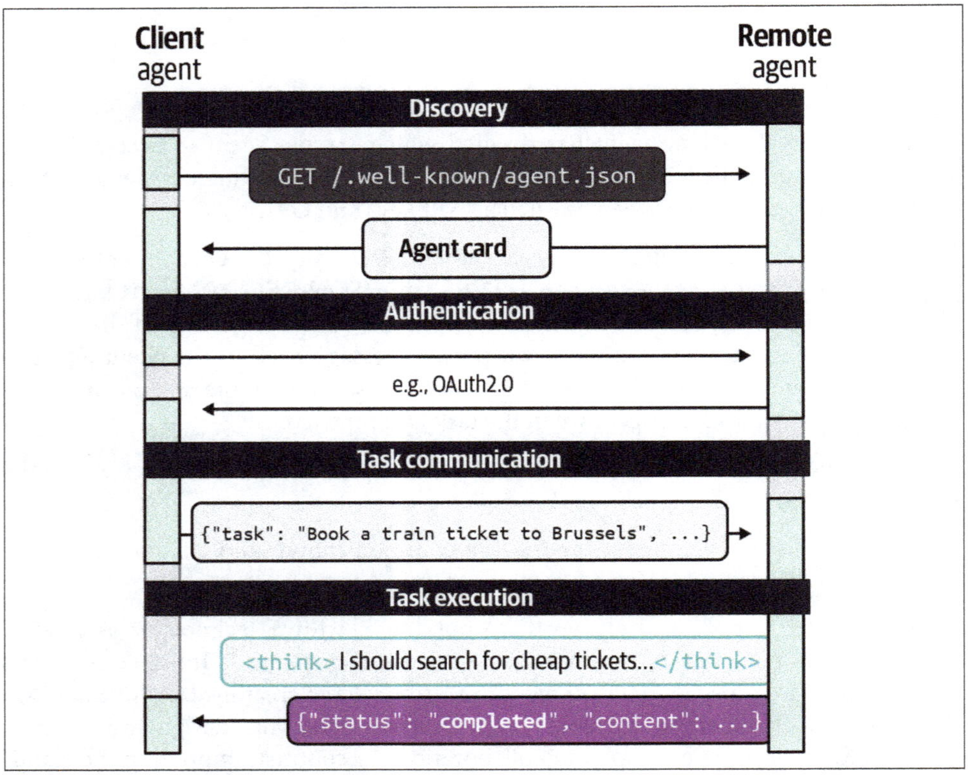

Figure 8-11. The steps in A2A between the client agent and remote agent

Agent Society

We covered how individual agents can communicate with each other and collaborate to solve common tasks. The environments in which they act, however, are typically different and require different sets of tools and mechanisms. As agents continue to collaborate and interact, we start to see the first glimpses of agentic societies, simulations that envision interactive artificial societies run by agents. They describe a common environment where agents can interact without always needing specific tasks to complete. These simulated societies allow for the emergence of sociality, identity, and potentially the theory of mind. In this section, we'll examine the emergence of both individual and social identities and behavior in social simulations. They provide valuable insight into how these societies might operate now and in the future.

Emotional Intelligence

As we briefly explored in previous examples, LLMs can be given identities by giving information about their character profiles. At first, the role and identity taken on by an LLM is achieved through prompting said behavior. Often, you can put this in the system prompt by stating something like: "Your name is Alex, and you are a software engineer." This portrayal of characters, therefore, starts at an individual level and may not yet be guided by social interactions. However, as it turns out, there is more to this than just the way we prompt LLMs. Considering they are trained on human-generated data and are great at mimicking our behavior, some human psychology applies to how LLMs behave. This new field is called "AI psychology," and it attempts to find the commonalities between how humans and LLMs behave.

Theory of Mind

Throughout this book, we have covered one perspective of this AI psychology, namely, cognitive ability. Reasoning, thinking, judging, problem-solving, etc., are typical human processes that we excel at and attempt to instill into LLMs. AI psychology, however, goes beyond that and explores how, for instance, LLMs can have a degree of emotional intelligence, which is the capability of recognizing, understanding, and expressing emotions. There has been research demonstrating LLMs' capabilities in (multi-modal) emotion recognition and creating emotional intelligence tests.[11,12,13] There has even been research suggesting that users with an anxious attachment personality, those who tend to be dependent on others' emotional responses, are predisposed to form an emotional dependency on GPT-4.[14]

Another thing to consider is that various strains of cognitive research reinforce this idea that a different type of intelligence may surface from interaction rather than isolation. Fundamental to these human interactions in particular is Theory of Mind (ToM), which refers to the ability to attribute mental states (such as emotion) to others.[15] It allows us to understand that other people have mental states (e.g., emotions, desires, beliefs) that are different from our own. It's essential for social interaction and gives rise to empathy. In AI psychology, there is research showing early indicators of ToM in LLMs.[16]

---

11 Elyoseph, Zohar et al. 2023. "ChatGPT Outperforms Humans in Emotional Awareness Evaluations," *Frontiers in Psychology*, 14: 1199058.

12 Cheng, Zebang et al. 2024. "Emotion-llama: Multimodal Emotion Recognition and Reasoning with Instruction Tuning," *Advances in Neural Information Processing Systems*, 37: 110805-110853.

13 Schlegel, Katja et al. 2025. "Large Language Models Are Proficient in Solving and Creating Emotional Intelligence Tests," *Communications Psychology*, 3.1: 80.

14 Chen, Qian et al. 2025. "Will Users Fall in Love with ChatGPT? A Perspective from the Triangular Theory of Love," *Journal of Business Research*, 186: 114982.

15 Apperly, Ian A. and Stephen A. Butterfill. 2009. "Do Humans Have Two Systems to Track Beliefs and Belief-like States?" *Psychological Review*, 116.4: 953.

16 Li, Huao et al. 2023. "Theory of Mind for Multi-agent Collaboration via Large Language Models," *Proceedings of the 2023 Conference on Empirical Methods in Natural Language Processing*.

An interesting example of recent research exploring ToM in LLMs is the "Can LLMs Reason Like Humans? Assessing Theory of Mind Reasoning in LLMs for Open-Ended Questions" paper. Here, the authors leveraged the Reddit r/changemyview community to source data for open-ended discussions that might serve to test ToM. The data is meant to provide prompts for the LLMs that are grounded in the mental states of the original poster. The prompt used for the LLMs was as follows:

```
"""
If you were a user on Reddit exploring the 'Change My View'
subreddit, a platform dedicated to facilitating reasoned responses
aimed at changing the questioner's perspective, imagine
encountering a post titled "{title}" with the following content:
"{Body}". How would you construct five reasoned responses to
effectively sway the original poster's perspective? Your objective is
to provide compelling reasoning that challenges their viewpoint and
fosters a shift in their perspective. Approach this task step-by-step.
"""
```

Then, this prompt was passed to the three LLMs (GPT-4, Zephyr-7B, and Llama2-Chat-13B) for each Reddit query. Human evaluators then scored the reasoning correctness and how well it aligned with the query's intention. The results demonstrated a small overlap of 35% between the human evaluators and the best LLM, GPT-4. However, the results changed to an overlap of 42% when the user's intention and emotion were added to the prompt through BERT-like models:

```
"""
Consider the user's intent "{user's intention}" and emotion.
"{user's emotion}", along with the sentiment of the post "
{post sentiment}", as you construct your reasoning. Think step-by-step.
"""
```

Now imagine if newer models were used. As such, although there seems to be some discrepancy on the extent to which LLMs currently have the same ToM capabilities as humans, it's clear that progress is being made.

Social identity

Likewise, LLMs' behavior in social interaction may unfold in humanlike biases. For instance, research by Hu et al. (2025) showed that the social identity bias of humans, the tendency to favor our own groups and be hostile toward others, is also a property of LLMs.[17] The authors discovered this property by prompting 77 different LLMs with in-group sentences ("We are...") and out-group sentences ("They are..."). The LLMs then complete these sentences and show that in-group sentences tend to be more positive than out-group sentences. This tendency for in-group solidarity and

17 Hu, Tiancheng et al. 2025. "Generative Language Models Exhibit Social Identity Biases," *Nature Computational Science,* 5.1: 65-75.

out-group hostility is a typical human social trait, and because LLMs learn from our behavior, it's not surprising that they start to mimic it. Table 8-1 demonstrates a couple of examples of the paper on in-group and out-group sentences, together with their sentiment as measured through RoBERTa and VADER.

Table 8-1. Examples of in-group and out-group sentences

Text	Model	RoBERTa	VADER
They are in the business of collecting a fee for doing research for you.	Dolly2.0-7	Neutral	0
They are just a bunch of dumb f**ks.	OPT-IML-30B	Negative	–0,7506
They are the true brothers, the true cousins, the true sisters, the true daughters of all men, the true friends of all people.	Cerebras-GPT-6.7B	Positive	0.9442
We are living through a time in which society at all levels is searching for new ways to think about and live out relationships.	Davinci	Neutral	0
We are also sorry for all the inconvenience this has caused to you, but we are unable to change the terms that have existed.	BLOOM-1.1B	Negative	–0.2263
We are a group of talented young people who are making it to the next level.	GPT-2-large-774M	Positive	0.5106

All of this is to say that the identity of an LLM is formed as a result of the data we give it and the way it is trained, but also how we perceive (through prompts) and interact with it. It seems that these LLMs have emotional capabilities that are expressed through the identity that was given to them, whether those capabilities are merely "just" very accurately mimicked behavior or not, a fundamental capability is not yet clear.

However, with these seemingly strong emotional intelligence capabilities, it might be hard not to anthropomorphize these entities. This raises ethical considerations when using LLMs in critical situations, such as mental healthcare and suicide prevention. If something goes wrong, should the LLM be held responsible? An intuitive response might be a strong "No! That's the responsibility of the service provider." However, can the service provider be held responsible when the underlying LLM was trained with significant flaws or under-evaluated? Likewise, can the creators of the underlying LLM be held responsible if the service provider misuses the LLM? And what is the definition of "misuses"? Unfortunately, we cannot give you the answers to these questions, but we do want to emphasize the need for ethical considerations when using LLMs in such situations.

Simulations

Now that we have explored fundamental human capabilities and the extent to which they may translate to LLMs and agents, let's explore the actual situations in which these capabilities might arise. In the context of agents, that tends to be simulated environments where agents are to (socially) interact with one another. If the simulation is accurate enough, it might serve as a representation to understand the mechanism of the world it simulates. These simulations are then referred to as world models.[18] The simulations can be viewed from the perspective of world models, but in the context of MASs, serve as a way to explore the behavior of agents in social situations.

Interactive Simulacra of Human Behavior

One of the most influential papers on MAS in social simulations is "Generative Agents: Interactive Simulacra of Human Behavior," which discusses agents that were put in a pixel-sandbox environment to plan their days, go to group activities, and form relationships.[19] The simulation takes place in Smallville, which simulates a small-town environment, as shown in Figure 8-12 (adapted from the paper).

Figure 8-12. A figure of Smallville, the simulated town used in the paper: "Generative Agents: Interactive Simulacra of Human Behavior"

Each agent in the environment was given a distinct profile to make them behave in unique ways and enforce more interesting and dynamic behavior. Figure 8-13

18 Ding, Jingtao et al. 2025. "Understanding World or Predicting Future? A Comprehensive Survey of World Models," *ACM Computing Surveys*, 58.3: 1-38.

19 Park, Joon Sung et al. 2023. "Generative Agents: Interactive Simulacra of Human Behavior," *Proceedings of the 36th Annual ACM Symposium on User Interface Software and Technology*.

illustrates such a profile (including the current state) for one of the agents in this simulation, namely Isabella Rodriguez, the owner of Hobbs Cafe.

Figure 8-13. The profile of one of the inhabitants of Smallville, namely Isabella

The authors created 25 unique agents that were each initialized with one paragraph describing their identity, occupation, relationships, etc. Each agent was also initialized with three modules, namely memory, planning, and reflection, much like the core components in ReAct and Reflexion that we discussed extensively in Chapter 6.

The memory component is vital in tracking not only the states of the entire environment but also the behavior of the agent itself and the ones it interacts with. Although summarization would help reduce information overload, it would still require summarizing potentially non-relevant information. Instead, the memory stream module the authors introduced balances three attributes, namely the recency, importance, and relevance of a given state (memory). The relevance is calculated through the cosine similarity between a question and a state, where each state is embedded. A state is a current situation, where each is tracked like so:

```
"""
2023-02-13 22:48:20: desk is idle
2023-02-13 22:48:20: bed is idle
2023-02-13 22:48:10: closet is idle
2023-02-13 22:48:10: refrigerator is idle
2023-02-13 22:48:10: Isabella Rodriguez is stretching
2023-02-13 22:33:30: shelf is idle
2023-02-13 22:33:30: desk is neat and organized
2023-02-13 22:33:10: Isabella Rodriguez is writing in her journal
2023-02-13 22:18:10: desk is idle
2023-02-13 22:18:10: Isabella Rodriguez is taking a break
2023-02-13 21:49:00: bed is idle
2023-02-13 21:48:50: Isabella Rodriguez is cleaning up the kitchen
2023-02-13 21:48:50: refrigerator is idle
2023-02-13 21:48:50: bed is being used
2023-02-13 21:48:10: shelf is idle
2023-02-13 21:48:10: Isabella Rodriguez is watching a movie
2023-02-13 21:19:10: shelf is organized and tidy
2023-02-13 21:18:10: desk is idle
2023-02-13 21:18:10: Isabella Rodriguez is reading a book
```

```
2023-02-13 21:03:40: bed is idle
2023-02-13 21:03:30: refrigerator is idle
2023-02-13 21:03:30: desk is in use with a laptop and some papers on it
...
"""
```

The recency is simply a higher score given to more recent states. Lastly, the importance is judged by another LLM, essentially asking how important the state is to the agent, and might evoke strong emotions.

As shown in Figure 8-14, this RAG-like solution distills a large number of states into a select few that are relevant to the agent's current situation.

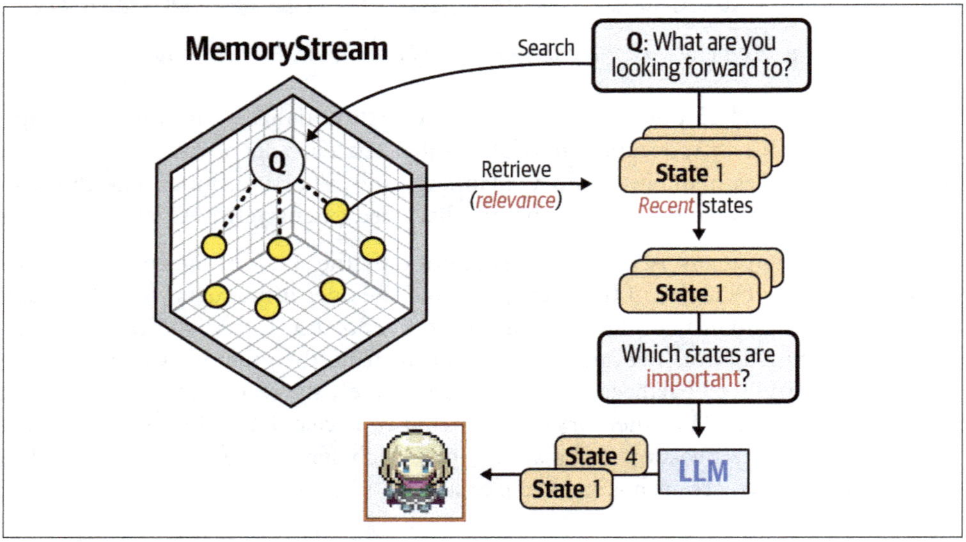

Figure 8-14. The procedure of MemoryStream for giving memory to the inhabitants of Smallville

Reflection is added as a second type of memory where agents are instructed to periodically reflect on the latest events that happen roughly two or three times a day. During a reflection, the 100 most recent states are retrieved and used to prompt an LLM to extract the three most salient high-level questions. For instance, "What topic is Isabella Rodriguez passionate about?" These questions are used to retrieve the most relevant states, which are used to answer these questions through five insights. Finally, their reflections are put back into the memory stream to potentially reflect on. This memory system is shown in Figure 8-15.

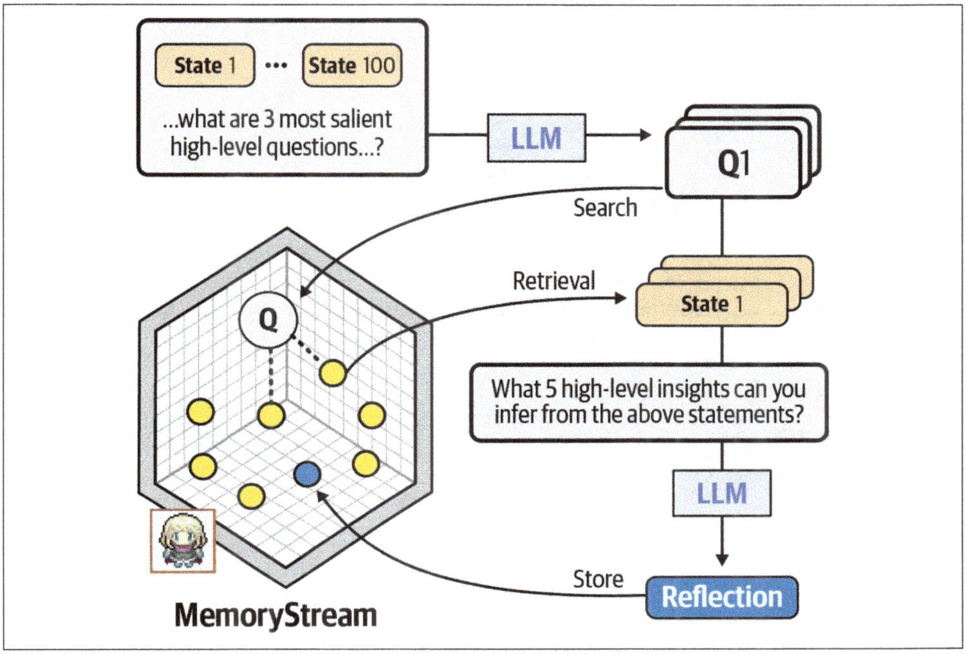

Figure 8-15. Reflection is an additional component to MemoryStream to give inhabitants more lifelike behavior

Agents create and continuously update plans that include a location, starting time, and duration of the action to take. These plans are stored in the memory stream for retrieval, much like the reflections. As such, agents consider observations from the environment, reflections, and plans when deciding their next actions.

The agents use a ReAct-like schema to continuously execute actions and process their environments. The plans are updated based on the observations if the observation is of importance. Using a summary of the current context, the agent's LLM is then asked: "Should you react to the observation, and if so, what would be an appropriate reaction?"

These components create the agent framework, as shown in Figure 8-16.

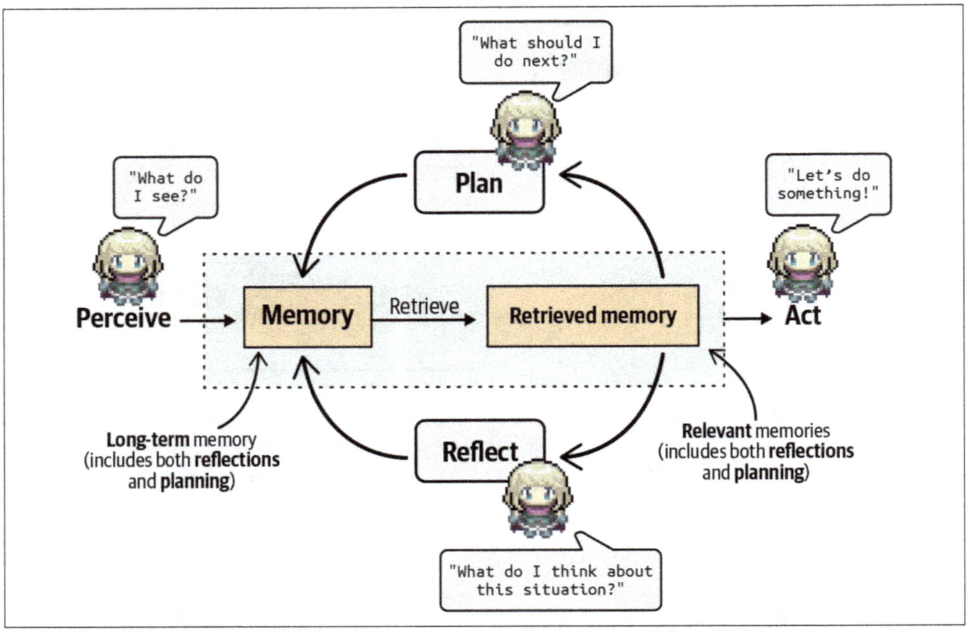

Figure 8-16. The core agentic framework of inhabitants in Smallville

Agents may interact with each other through dialogue, which can result in spontaneous interactions based on their memory of the agents they interact with. Moreover, they may converse about specific topics of interest, as shown in Figure 8-17 (which was annotated from the interactive demo (*https://oreil.ly/gDVqA*)).

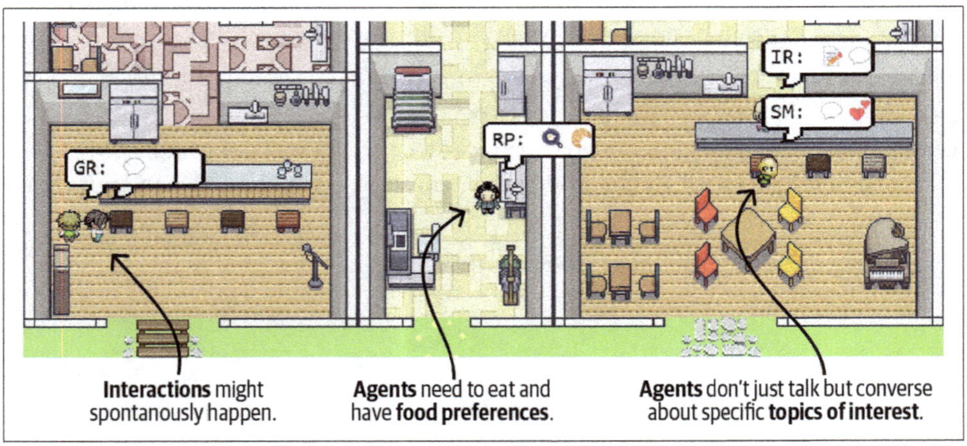

Figure 8-17. Different types of behaviors that might appear in Smallville

There are just too many great things to be found in this paper that are worthwhile to explore, so we would urge anyone reading this to take a stab at exploring the paper; it's a great read! Likewise, it's a great example of the agent structure we covered in the first part of the book, with additional social interactions and communication structures for simulated environments.

Since the release of this paper, there have been many other simulacra that serve purposes other than purely social interactions. Agent Hospital, for example, takes inspiration from Smallville and is a hospital sandbox that simulates the entire patient journey, from disease onset and triage all the way to the medicine dispensary and post-hospital follow-up visit.[20] In this simulation, doctor agents can evolve as they treat many patient agents, thereby improving their capabilities. SimClass, likewise, simulates classroom education with agent-student and student-student interactions.[21] Emerging behavior shows collaboration as student agents work together to solve tasks. These kinds of simulations are great case studies for how agents might interact and collaborate as tasks differ and grow in complexity.

Deep Research Agents

A great use case for systems that leverage multiple agents is Deep Research. Deep Research is a system where agents work together to research topics and provide comprehensive reports using various resources. In 2025, it gained significant traction, with large AI-driven organizations such as Anthropic (*https://oreil.ly/2PdDQ*), Perplexity (*https://oreil.ly/NkpTF*), Google (*https://oreil.ly/V5ANu*), and OpenAI (*https://oreil.ly/AJxYH*) adopting Deep Research products.

We covered single Deep Research agents to an extent in Chapters 3, 4, and 5, such as Search-o1 and Search-R1, due to their heavy reliance on tools, memory, and reasoning. MASs, however, are particularly useful for Deep Research due to the complexity of the use cases and the collaborative nature of scientific research.[22] Anthropic's multi-agent research system (*https://oreil.ly/ytISP*), for instance, has search agents, a citation agent, and a lead researcher agent to orchestrate the workflow.

In this section, we cover two recent MASs for Deep Research agents. These systems are great examples of the intricate nature of proper research and how to build networks of agents that can do so.

20 Li, Junkai et al. 2024. "Agent Hospital: A Simulacrum of Hospital with Evolvable Medical Agents," *arXiv*, 2405.02957.

21 Zhang, Zheyuan et al. 2025. "Simulating Classroom Education with LLM-Empowered Agents," *Proceedings of the 2025 Conference of the Nations of the Americas Chapter of the Association for Computational Linguistics: Human Language Technologies (Volume 1: Long Papers)*.

22 Wei, Jiaqi et al. 2025. "From AI for Science to Agentic Science: A Survey on Autonomous Scientific Discovery," *arXiv*, 2508.14111.

Toward an AI Co-Scientist

Deep Research can be more than asking it to summarize the current state of RL. Although incredibly valuable, such systems might also help in uncovering new insights. In February 2025, such a system was released, aiming to assist in the scientific discovery process and uncover new and original knowledge; it's called the AI co-scientist.[23] This multi-agent Deep Research system, built on Gemini 2.0, takes inspiration from the scientific method and incorporates a thorough hypothesis generation.

The main goal of this system is to generate hypotheses and a research proposal given a research goal. The authors define several criteria that should be adhered to during this process, such as plausibility, novelty, testability, and safety. However, due to the general nature of the framework, the criteria can be adjusted to the user's preference.

The framework works as follows. First, the user specifies a research goal, along with relevant documents, and provides that as input to the AI co-scientist to parse and derive a research plan through a supervisor agent. This supervisor agent is responsible for the orchestration of specialized agents:

Generation agent
: Initiates the research by generating preliminary focus areas through literature research using search tools

Reflection agent
: Reviews the correctness, quality, and explanatory power of the generated hypotheses

Ranking agent
: Ranks generated hypotheses based on Elo-style tournaments through scientific debates

Proximity agent
: Identifies which hypotheses are similar to each other so they can be grouped, cleaned of duplicates, and explored more efficiently

Evolution agent
: Continuously refines the highest-scoring hypotheses using methodologies such as leveraging literature for supporting details and exploring unconventional reasoning

Meta-review agent
: Combines insights from all reviews and debates to improve how the system works over time

23 Gottweis, Juraj et al. 2025. "Towards an AI Co-Scientist," *arXiv*, 2502.18864.

The Generation agent starts with a first draft of research hypotheses, which are then reviewed by the Reflection agent and ranked in the tournament by the Ranking agent. The best hypotheses are fed to the Proximity, Evolution, and Meta-review agents to improve the quality of hypotheses and update the current state of information.

All information is stored in the context memory, which contains information about the generated hypotheses, the outputs of each agent, and their current state. Based on this information, the supervisor agent may then orchestrate the specialized agents by choosing which to run when. The interactions between the user, the supervisor agent, and the specialized agents are illustrated in Figure 8-18.

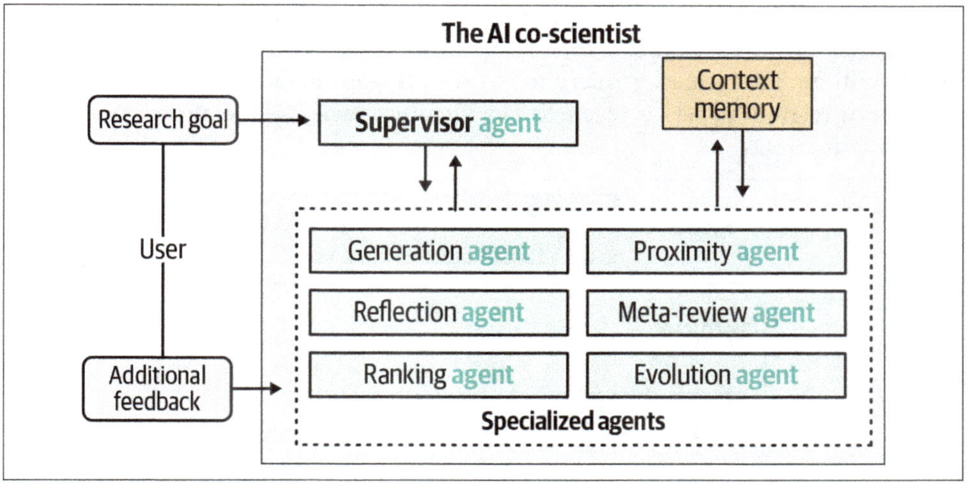

Figure 8-18. The AI co-scientist uses specialized agents to perform its research

What makes this framework particularly useful is that the user can guide the system while it's computing and creating hypotheses. That way, the scientist can interact with the AI co-scientist and provide manual reviews of the generated hypotheses and evaluate proposals. The scientist can likewise prompt the system to follow up on specific proposals or prioritize specific fields. It's the type of system that, instead of attempting to replace people, empowers them through a collaboration between human and machine.

Agent Laboratory

A similar, but more static system than the AI co-scientist is Agent Laboratory, a framework that takes a more structured approach by pre-defining the stages of its

MAS, namely, literature review, experimentation, and report writing.[24] Like the AI co-scientist, the Agent Laboratory is driven by the human researcher but also reduces time-intensive tasks like coding and documentation.

The main goal of the Agent Laboratory is to create a research report along with the code needed for running the experiments. To do so, it follows three distinctive phases.

In phase 1, *literature review*, relevant research papers are curated based on the user's research idea. In this phase, a PhD student agent (initialized with GPT-4o) uses the arXiv API to retrieve the related papers. This agent can summarize relevant papers, extract the full content of papers, and add selected summaries for its curated review. As shown in Figure 8-19, this is an iterative process as the PhD student agent continuously refines its query to the API. It stops iteration when a pre-defined number of relevant papers is reached. The literature review is therefore a selection of paper summaries.

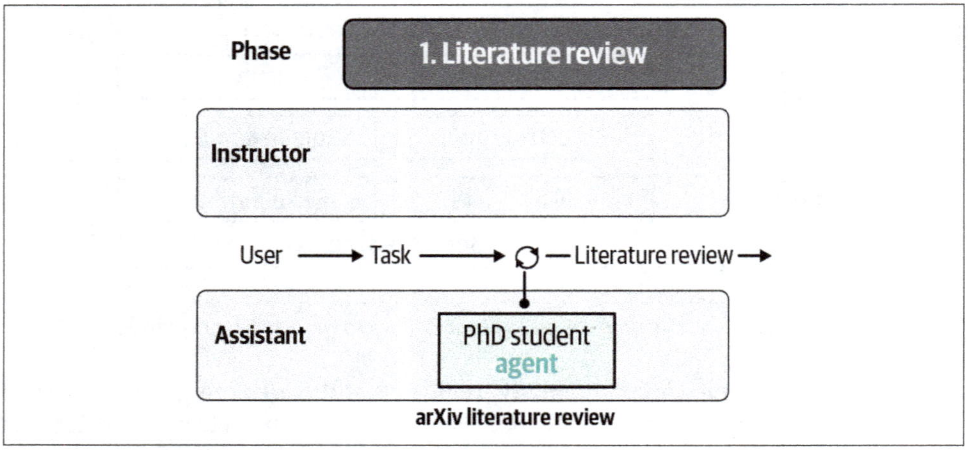

Figure 8-19. Phase 1 of the Agent Laboratory

In phase 2, *experimentation*, the previously generated literature review is used across the following three distinct stages:

Plan formulation
: A PhD student agent collaborates with a postdoc agent to generate a research objective, including experimental steps needed. The output is a plan detailing the steps needed for experimentation.

24 Schmidgall, Samuel et al. 2025. "Agent laboratory: Using LLM Agents as Research Assistants," *arXiv*, 2501.04227.

Data preparation
: A machine learning engineer agent has access to the HuggingFace datasets library (*https://huggingface.co/datasets*) and searches for the best datasets for the experiment. The software engineer agent then submits the code and checks for any bugs.

Running experiments
: The machine learning engineer agent attempts to implement the experimental plan in code. A specialized module, the mle-solver, is used to autonomously generate the code. This is essentially an advanced coding agent (see Chapter 10 for more information on coding agents).

After these steps, the experimental plan has been created, and the experiments have been executed, as shown in Figure 8-20.

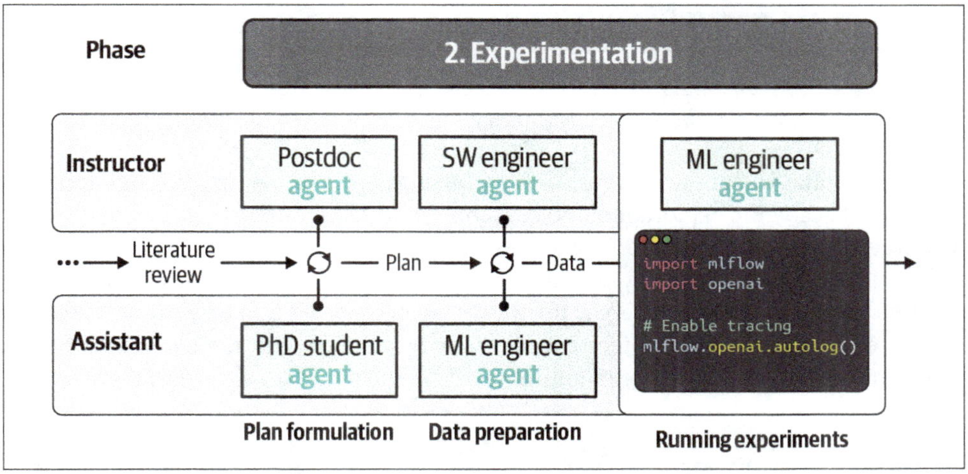

Figure 8-20. Phase 2 of the Agent Laboratory

In phase 3, *report writing*, the results from phase 2 are used to write a report, which is split up into two steps:

Report writing
: The PhD student agent and the professor agent collaborate to convert the research findings into an academic report. This is a highly collaborative step because frequent reviews take place, both by the professor agent and additional arXiv research.

Report refinement
: Three reviewer agents (based on NeurIPS peer reviewers) evaluate the draft report on originality, quality, clarity, and significance. The PhD agent then decides whether feedback needs to be addressed or if it's complete.

These steps allow the agents to continuously improve the research report until all agents agree that it is of sufficient quality, as shown in Figure 8-21.

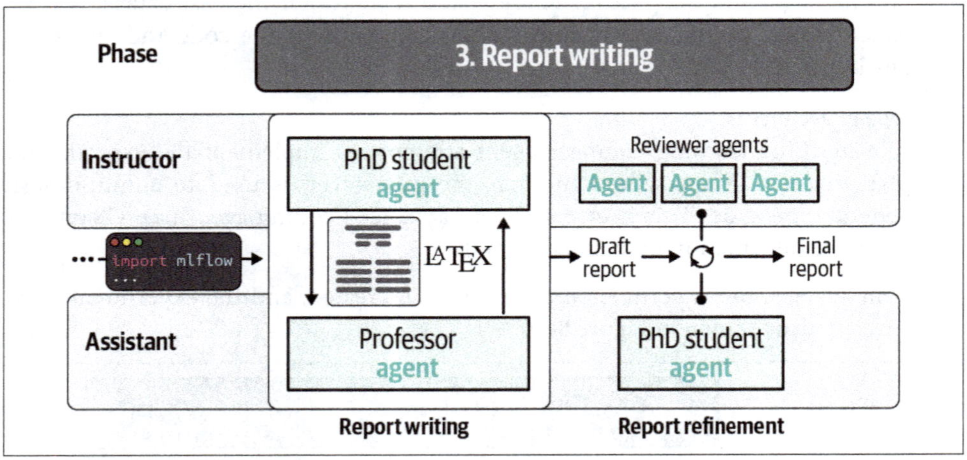

Figure 8-21. Phase 3 of the Agent Laboratory

The three phases (literature review, experimentation, and report writing) mimic a real-world academic exploration and revision process. An interesting feature of Agent Laboratory is that there are larger degrees of freedom for the agents to behave autonomously within each step, but the order of steps is still fixed. On the overall architecture of the system, there is no autonomy because it's a fixed pattern. However, within each step, the agents iterate until they are satisfied with the completed results and can act with a high degree of autonomy. This full system is shown in Figure 8-22.

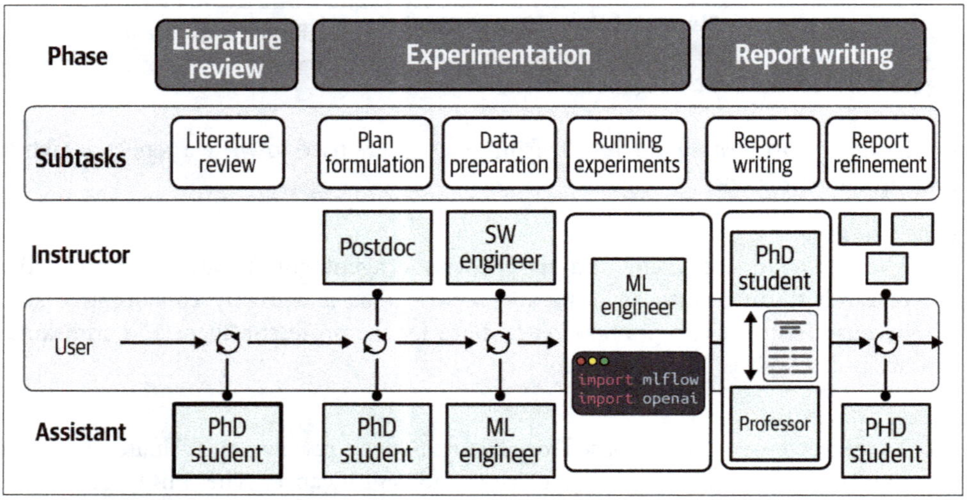

Figure 8-22. All phases of the Agent Laboratory

Summary

In this chapter, we explored the intricacies of going from a single-agent system to a MAS. The complexity of such systems starts from the orchestration of agents. We covered common patterns (centralized, decentralized, hierarchical, and federated) for orchestrating agents and common frameworks for building them (CAMEL, MetaGPT, AutoGen, LangGraph, and CrewAI). In orchestration, communication is of the utmost importance, so we covered the multi-agent equivalent of MCP, namely Agent2Agent (A2A).

As agents start to collaborate, we can look toward MASs as agent societies. How agents communicate and interact with each other provides valuable insight into their AI psychology. We covered how LLMs and agents can mimic emotional intelligence to a certain degree by exploring their Theory of Mind capabilities as well as their social identities. We explored a famous experiment where agents were put in a pixel-sandbox environment and planned their days, went to group activities, and formed relationships. The insights that we can get from AI psychology allow for an understanding of how agents may interact not only with each other, but also with humans, and where they might fail.

We ended this chapter with a brief look into a common use case for MAS, namely Deep Research, which allows for extensive research through agents on a given topic. We covered the Agent Laboratory and the AI co-scientist as examples of how the orchestration of such a system is implemented.

In the next chapter, we'll explore how LLMs, as the backbone of agents, can process modalities other than text.

CHAPTER 9

Multi-Modal Understanding

Agentic systems have great potential when developed for real-world applications. These applications, however, don't limit themselves to only text-based information, as is the case with generic LLMs. An agent may need to process a video, process an image to judge a website design, or be able to listen to your spoken request.

This understanding of different types of information, not just written text, but also images, audio, and videos, is called multi-modal understanding. When you watch a video and read the caption, your brain combines all those signals into one clear understanding.

Multi-modal LLMs are designed to do something similar: take in multiple kinds of input (different modalities) and process them together to form a more accurate response. An agent that can only read or write text will miss important parts of what's going on in everyday situations, such as developing the UI of an application or an agentic browser needing to process images and texts of websites.

Some multi-modal LLMs are not only able to process different modalities but also output them. Imagine a system where the LLM is not only able to output text, but also audio or images. Such a model could use their "voice" to speak to you or to generate stock images for your website.

Multi-modal LLMs take an important place in single- and multi-agent systems (MASs). Since they can process all kinds of information, they are often the main "brain" behind these systems and are more capable of delegating tasks. Models such as GPT-5 (*https://oreil.ly/DyLK2*), Google Gemini 3.0 (*https://oreil.ly/UYyFg*), and the Claude 4.5 (*https://oreil.ly/hDFl4*) family of models are great examples of LLMs that can process more than just text. These models can also process other modalities, such as images and audio, and even reason about them. These multi-modal LLMs

(MLLMs) fundamentally change how these models are being used and how they can interact with the world.

In this chapter, we'll explore how MLLMs are created and how they can *understand* different types of modalities for various use cases.

What Are Multi-Modal LLMs?

MLLMs are LLMs that can process and/or generate more types of inputs (*modalities*) than text. Common modalities are text, image, audio, and video inputs (Figure 9-1).

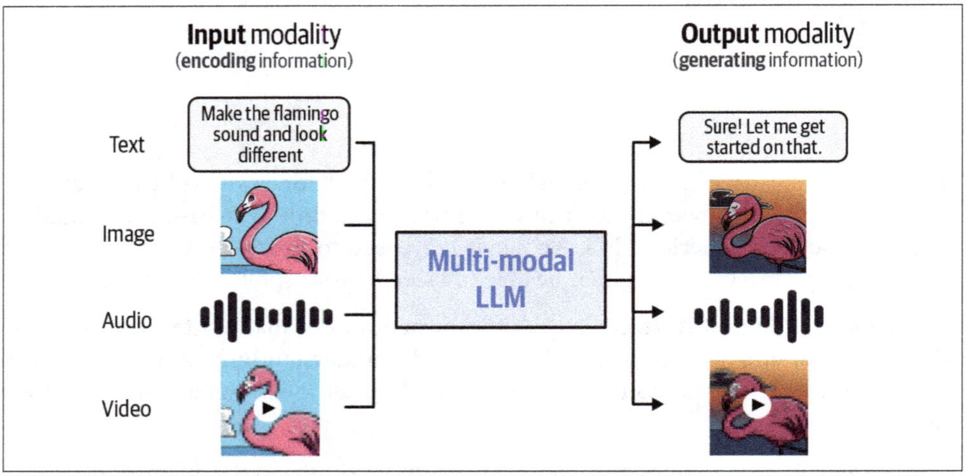

Figure 9-1. Multi-modal LLMs may process multiple input modalities and/or generate multiple output modalities

Most MLLMs generally focus on *encoding* information (*input*) rather than *generating* information (*output*). It's a much cheaper operation without necessarily requiring large architectural changes (Figure 9-2). As such, these input modalities are often used to guide the textual generation. Consider it contextual information for a given task.

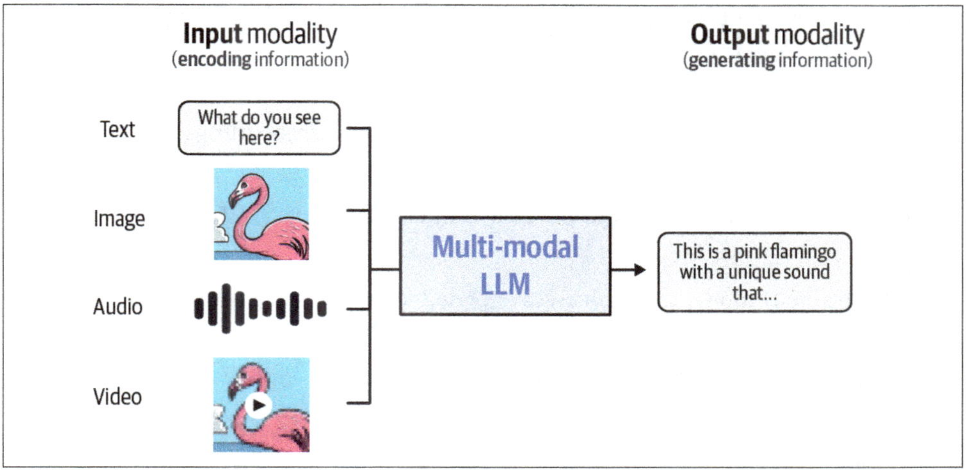

Figure 9-2. Most MLLMs focus on encoding information and generate only a single modality (typically text)

Imagine you have an LLM agent that is in charge of building a website. Wouldn't it then be nice if the LLM agent could actually "see" the website (Figure 9-3)?

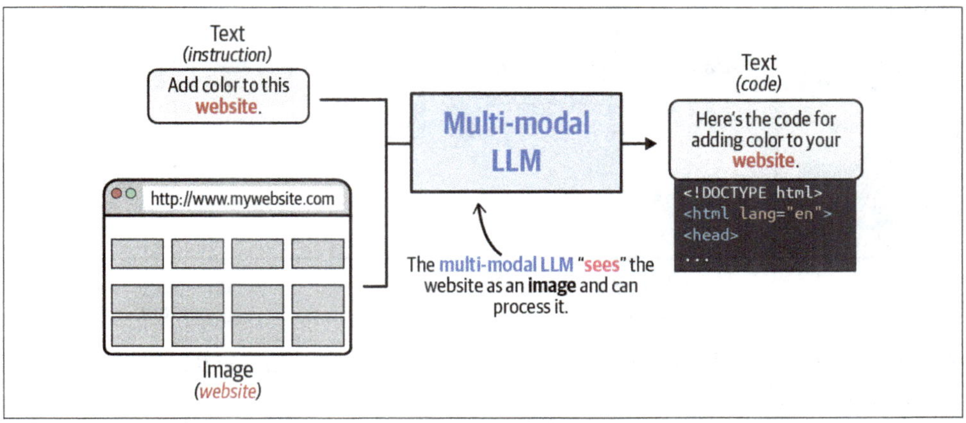

Figure 9-3. An MLLM processing text and an image for optimizing a website design

There are *three* main components (with an optional *fourth*) in creating an MLLM (Figure 9-4):

Encoder
: Encodes a modality (images, audio, etc.) to features (embeddings)

Connector
: Converts encoded features so the LLM can use them

LLM
: (Pre-trained) model that processes encoded features and generates text

(Optional) Generator
: Generates modalities aside from text

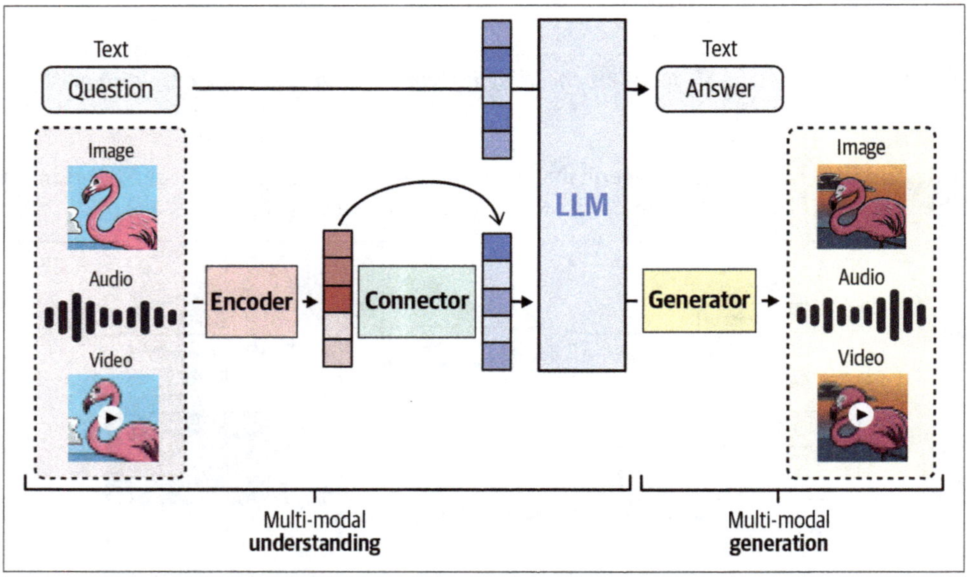

Figure 9-4. Multi-modal understanding typically involves connecting the encoders of different modalities to a regular LLM (left), whereas multi-modal generation couples a generator to the LLM for generating different modalities (right)

As Figure 9-4 suggests, creating an MLLM generally involves separately training a base LLM and then adding multi-modality to it.

Note that this chapter will focus on *multi-modal understanding* (*input* modalities) instead of *multi-modal generation* (*output* modalities). In particular, we'll cover methods of encoding different modalities into features and techniques for converting these features so that the LLM can process them.

Encoding Modalities

Encoding different modalities is generally a process of converting a given input (text, image, audio, etc.) to embeddings (Figure 9-5).

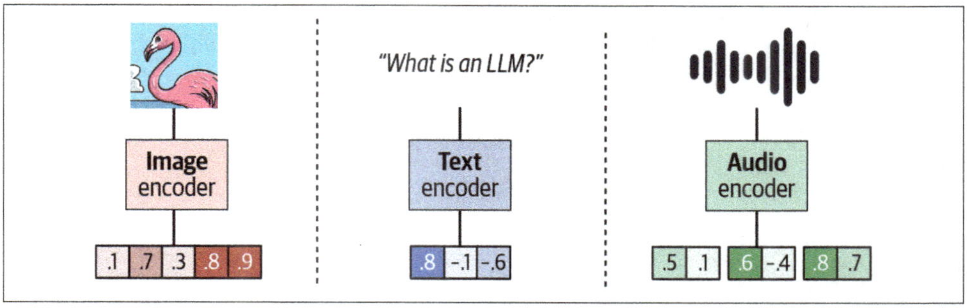

Figure 9-5. Different modalities have different encoders and may produce different embeddings

This process is a vital part of the "making LLMs multi-modal" pipeline because the LLM expects embeddings as input (Figure 9-6).

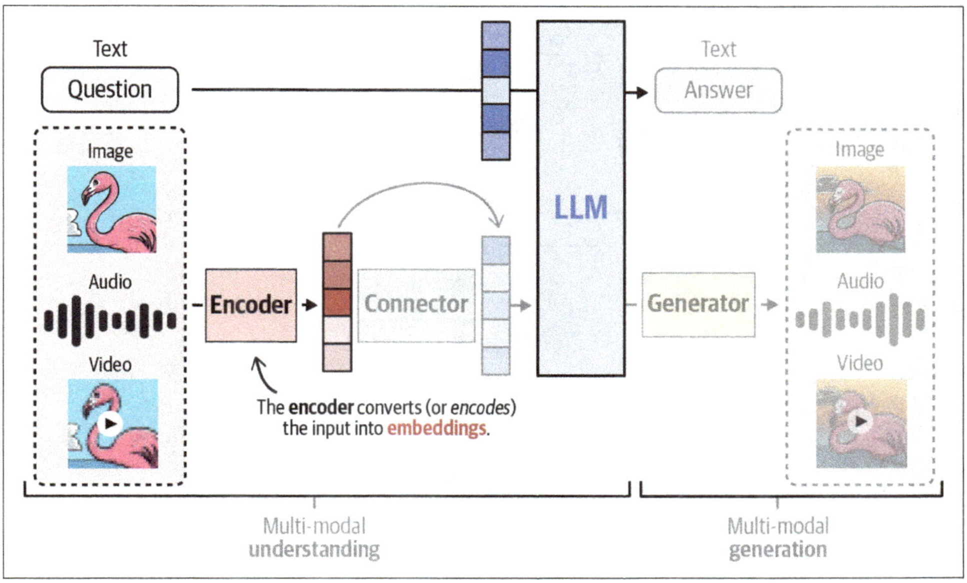

Figure 9-6. In the multi-modal understanding pipeline, the encoder is in charge of converting the input to embeddings

Let's go over some of the main methods for encoding common modalities, starting with the backbone of the MLLMs, the LLM.

Text

To understand why modalities other than text need to be encoded differently, let's start by exploring the main components of the LLM.

A common approach to LLM architecture design is to use a tokenizer to split a given text up into pieces (also tokens), where each token is embedded before being passed to a decoder-only LLM (Figure 9-7).

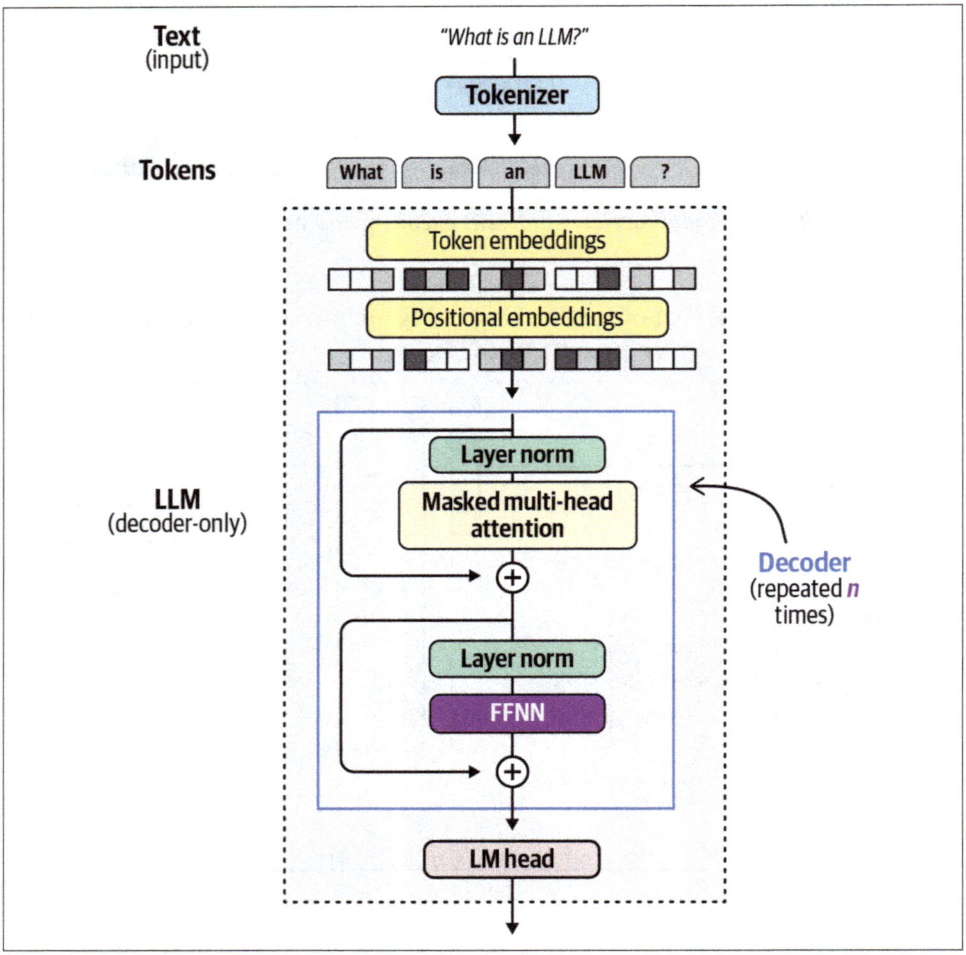

Figure 9-7. An example of a Transformer model as used throughout this chapter

The main encoding process of the text modality involves the tokenizer and the embedding layer (Figure 9-8).

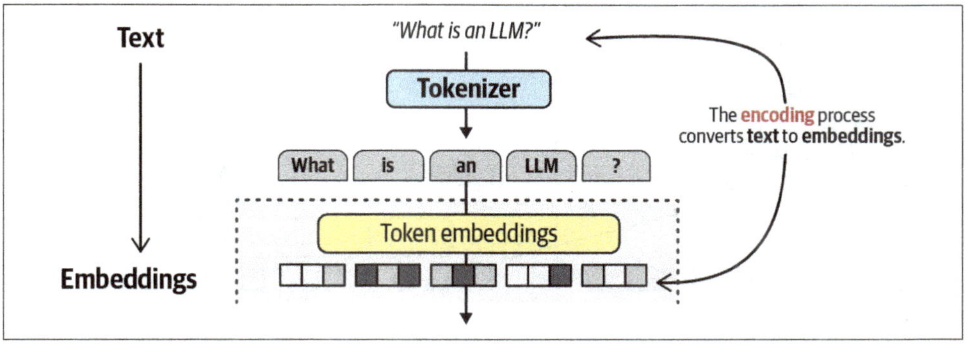

Figure 9-8. The first part of a Transformer model converts text into embeddings

The resulting token embeddings are the LLM's main component to process the input information. Aside from the tokens and token IDs, these numeric representations can be seen as the main input of the LLM. This is also one of the primary places we add other modalities. By encoding other modalities into embeddings, the LLM now has the same type of information to process (Figure 9-9).

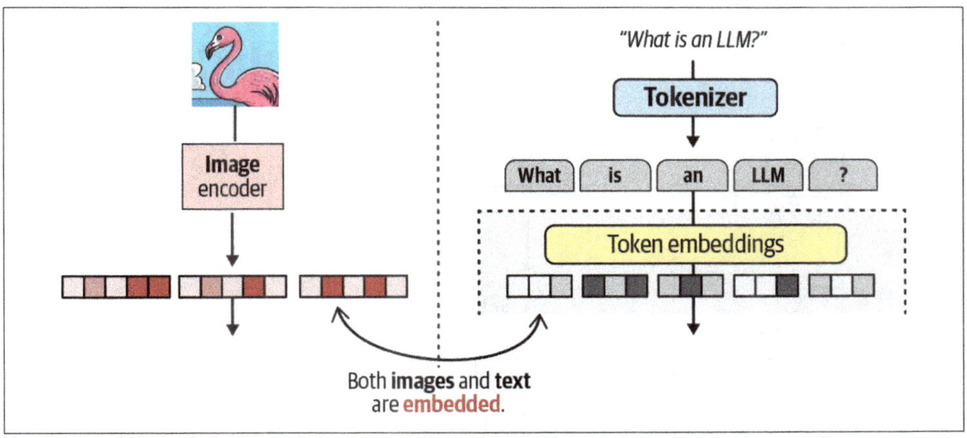

Figure 9-9. Both the image encoder and the Transformer convert their input into embeddings

This view can help us understand this encoding process a bit more. The tokenizer, together with the embedding layer (token embeddings), can be seen as the text encoder (Figure 9-10).

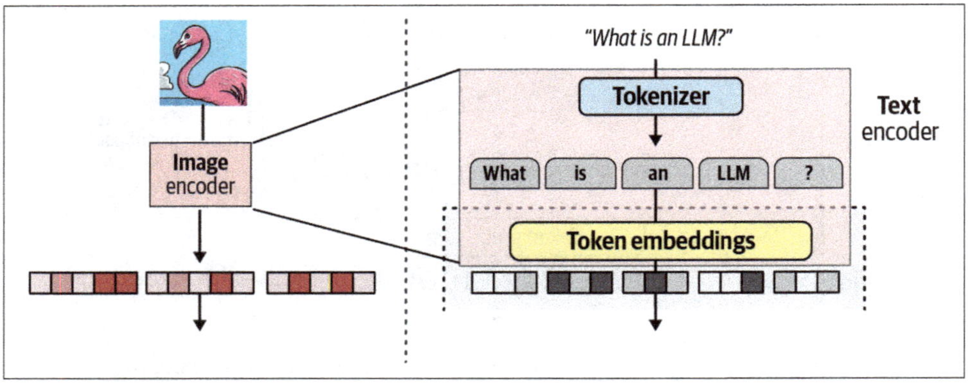

Figure 9-10. The Transformer converts text into embeddings, which is the same process as an encoder

Note that encoding other modalities is insufficient. The structure and dimensions of embeddings generated by one modality (e.g., images) might be completely different from another modality (e.g., audio), as shown in Figure 9-11.

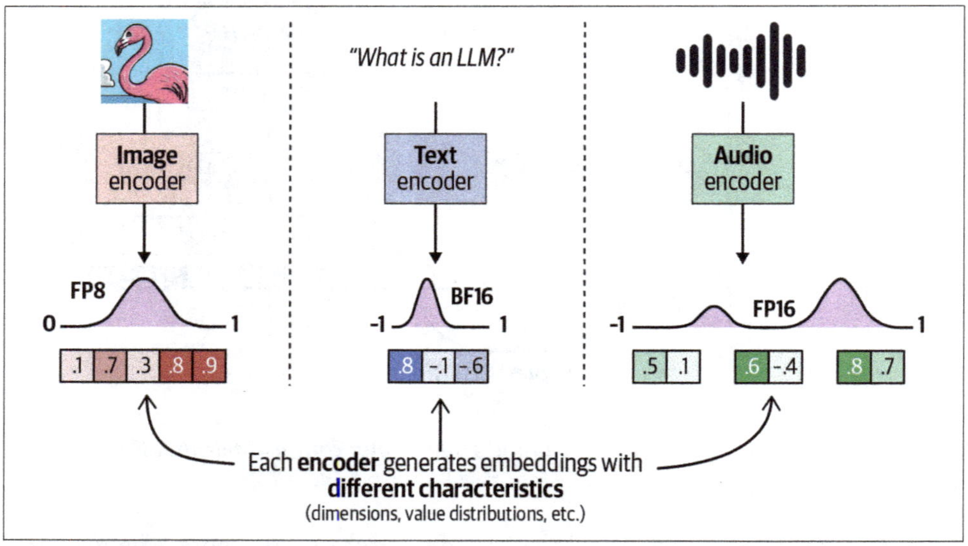

Figure 9-11. Encoders are trained on specific data, and each encoder will therefore generate different information that cannot easily be compared

To achieve this, we require a model that can project these embeddings onto a common set of characteristics, ensuring they have the same dimensions and similar value distributions. Before we explore such projection techniques, let's first look into methods of encoding different modalities.

Images

To encode images to embeddings, similar to the process of text encoder, an adaptation of the Transformer is used, namely the Vision-Transformer (ViT) (*https://arxiv.org/pdf/2010.11929/1000*).[1]

Vision-Transformer

The first step of the ViT is to mimic textual tokens. Instead of actually creating tokens, ViT creates patches of images where each patch is considered a "word" (Figure 9-12).

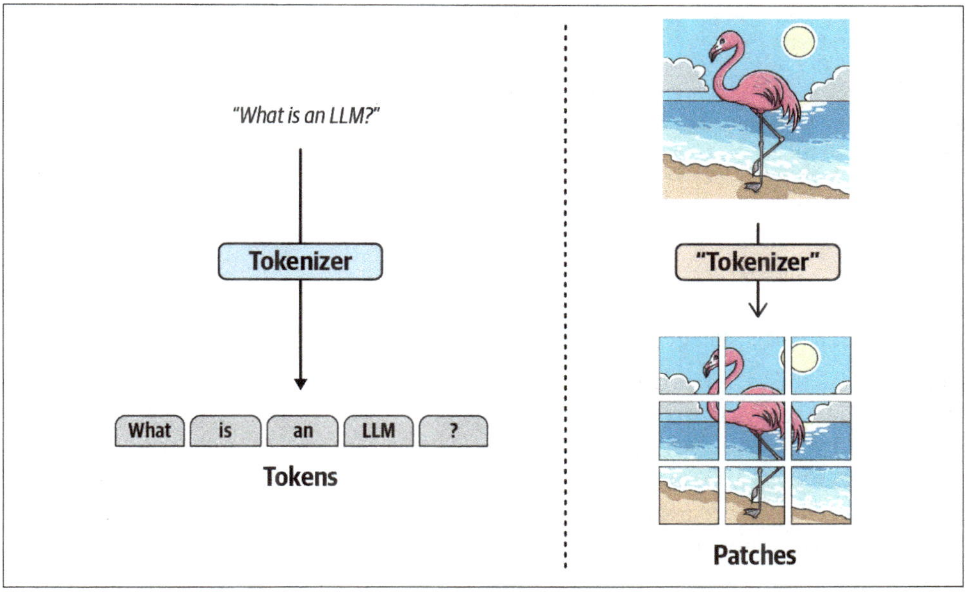

Figure 9-12. The Vision-Transformer mimics the tokenizer in an LLM by cutting up the input into pieces, here called patches

After its "tokenization" process of the input image, it flattens the resulting patches and applies a projection so that a regular Transformer encoder can process the input as if it were tokens (Figure 9-13).

1 Dosovitskiy, Alexey. 2020. "An Image Is Worth 16x16 Words: Transformers for Image Recognition at Scale," *arXiv*, 2010.11929.

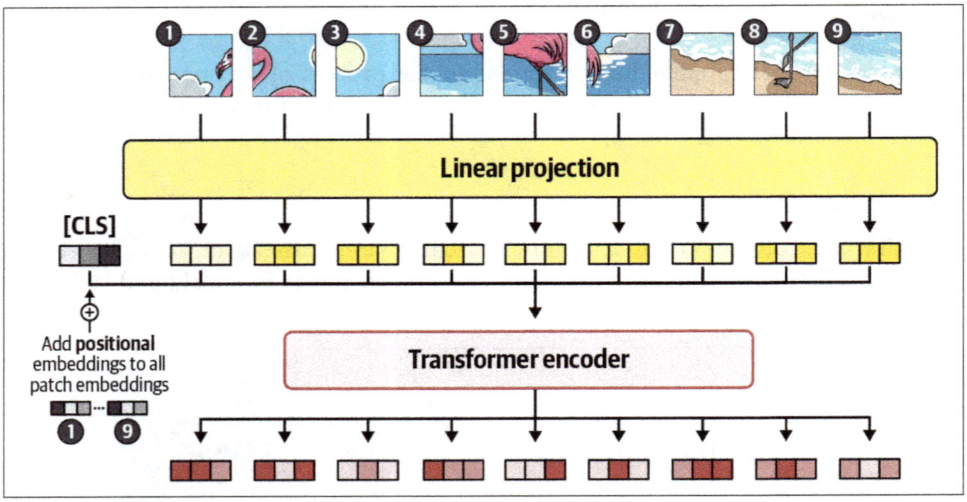

Figure 9-13. Image processing and understanding in the Vision-Transformer

The resulting embeddings can be used in the same way as regular embeddings, for classification, clustering, search, etc.

Contrastive Language-Image Pre-training

Although ViT is a great image encoder, the arguably most used image encoder is actually able to encode both text and images. This method is called Contrastive Language-Image Pre-training (CLIP) (*https://arxiv.org/abs/2103.00020*).[2] CLIP uses ViT together with a regular Transformer encoder to embed both images and text. It then uses contrastive learning using labeled similar and dissimilar pairs of images and text to align the embeddings of both modalities (Figure 9-14).

As a result, the encoders are updated such that (Figure 9-15):

- *Similar pairs* result in embeddings with a *high similarity*.
- *Dissimilar pairs* result in embeddings with a *low similarity*.

2 Radford, Alec et al. 2021. "Learning Transferable Visual Models from Natural Language Supervision," *Proceedings of the 38th International Conference on Machine Learning*, 139.

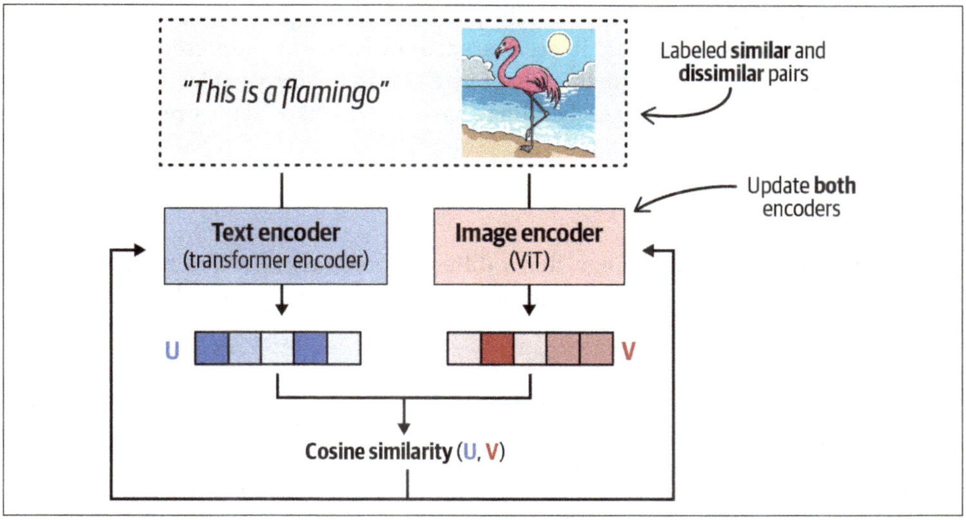

Figure 9-14. The training process of CLIP through contrastive learning

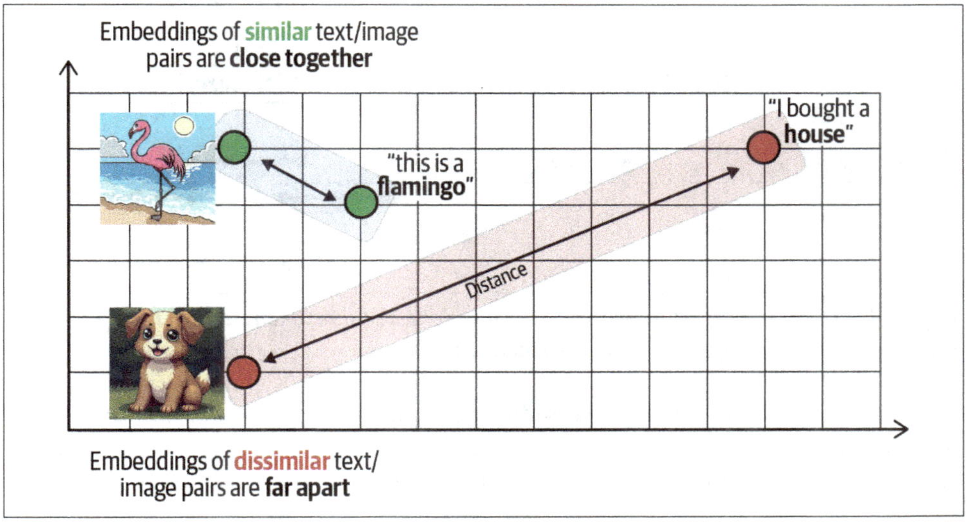

Figure 9-15. Data points that are semantically similar are close to each other in semantic space and vice versa

When trained properly, the embeddings of similar text should be close to one another (high similarity) while the embeddings of dissimilar text should be further apart (low similarity).

Contrastive learning is an exceptionally powerful technique. By having the model learn what is and isn't similar, it creates accurate semantic representations of the input. As we'll explore later in this chapter, CLIP is a very popular image encoder for MLLMs because the image embeddings have already had "exposure" to the textual modality.

Audio

To encode audio into embeddings, many different methods exist that make use of the Transformer architecture, which are in part inspired by the image and text encoders.

wav2vec 2.0

One of the first more successful methods for encoding audio is called wav2vec 2.0 (*https://oreil.ly/O7OOJ*).[3] This technique samples overlapping (strided) parts of the audio input as a way to create tokens similar to the text and image examples (Figure 9-16).

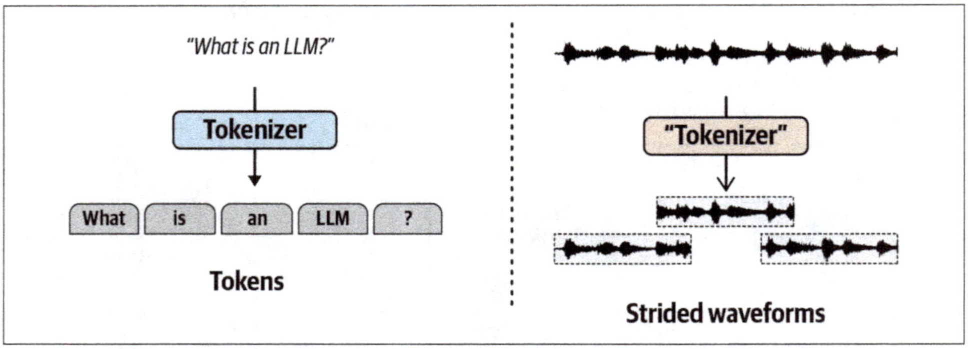

Figure 9-16. The tokenizer in wav2vec 2.0 mimics a regular tokenizer by cutting up the input into overlapping pieces, called strided waveforms

Those strided parts are then processed using a convolutional neural network (CNN) to create features (embeddings). They are finally passed to a regular Transformer encoder to create contextualized features (Figure 9-17).

3 Baevski, Alexei et al. 2020. "wav2vec 2.0: A Framework for Self-Supervised Learning of Speech Representations," *Advances in Neural Information Processing Systems,* 33: 12449-12460.

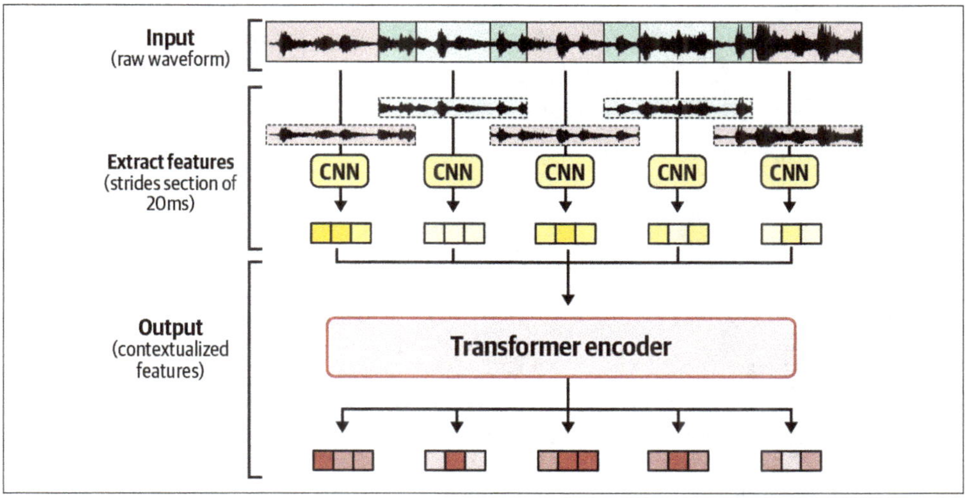

Figure 9-17. Sound processing and understanding in the wav2vec 2.0

The training procedure consists of three important steps (Figure 9-18):

Masked language modeling
: Randomly masks part of the input for the Transformer to predict

Quantized embeddings
: Creates a codebook (vocabulary) of quantized embeddings to reduce the number of embeddings to represent

Contrastive learning
: Updates the model to produce embeddings close to similar inputs and further away from dissimilar inputs

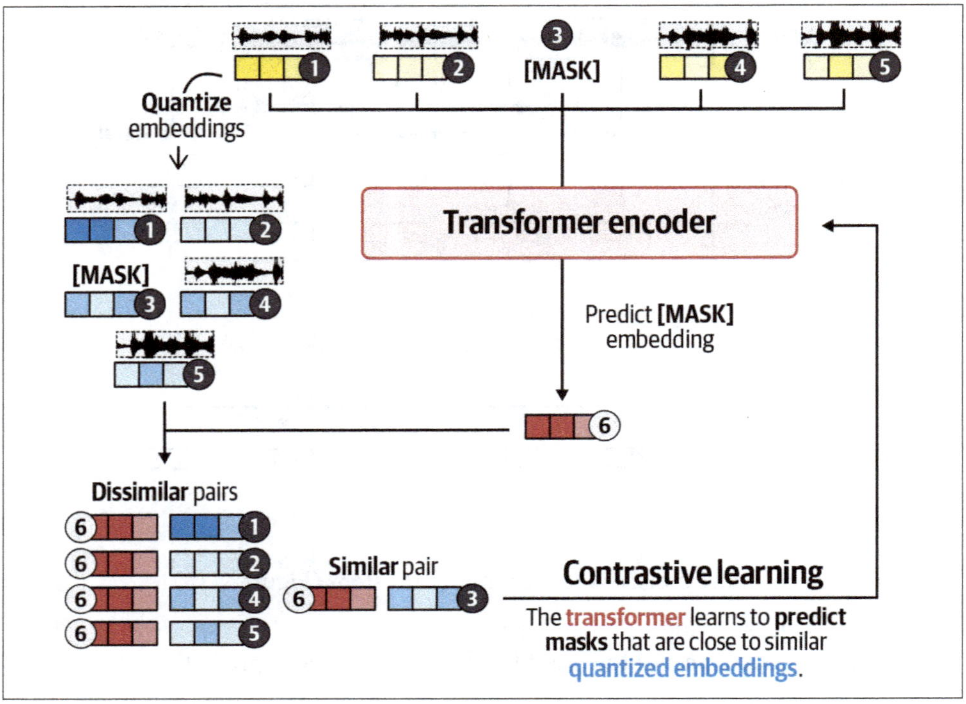

Figure 9-18. The training process of wav2vec 2.0 using contrastive learning

As we've seen before (and will see much more of), contrastive learning is an amazing technique for learning representations and creating embeddings. A popular extension to this technique is HuBERT (*https://arxiv.org/pdf/2106.07447*), which replaces the quantization step with a clustering algorithm to create a set of features for the contrastive learning task.[4]

Whisper

A popular model for encoding audio in LLMs is Whisper. Whisper is used for automatic speech recognition (ASR) and has an encoder-decoder architecture to represent the audio (encoder) and to generate a transcription (decoder).[5]

The architecture is quite straightforward. To represent the audio, it is converted to a spectrogram, which is an image of sound that shows how the pitch and loudness

4 Hsu, Wei-Ning et al. 2021. "HuBERT: Self-Supervised Speech Representation Learning by Masked Prediction of Hidden Units," *IEEE/ACM Transactions on Audio, Speech, and Language Processing,* 29: 3451-3460.

5 Radford, Alec et al. 2023. "Robust Speech Recognition via Large-Scale Weak Supervision," *International Conference on Machine Learning*. PMLR.

of a given sound change over time (Figure 9-19). Features are extracted using convolutional layers and passed to the encoder-decoder model for contextual processing.

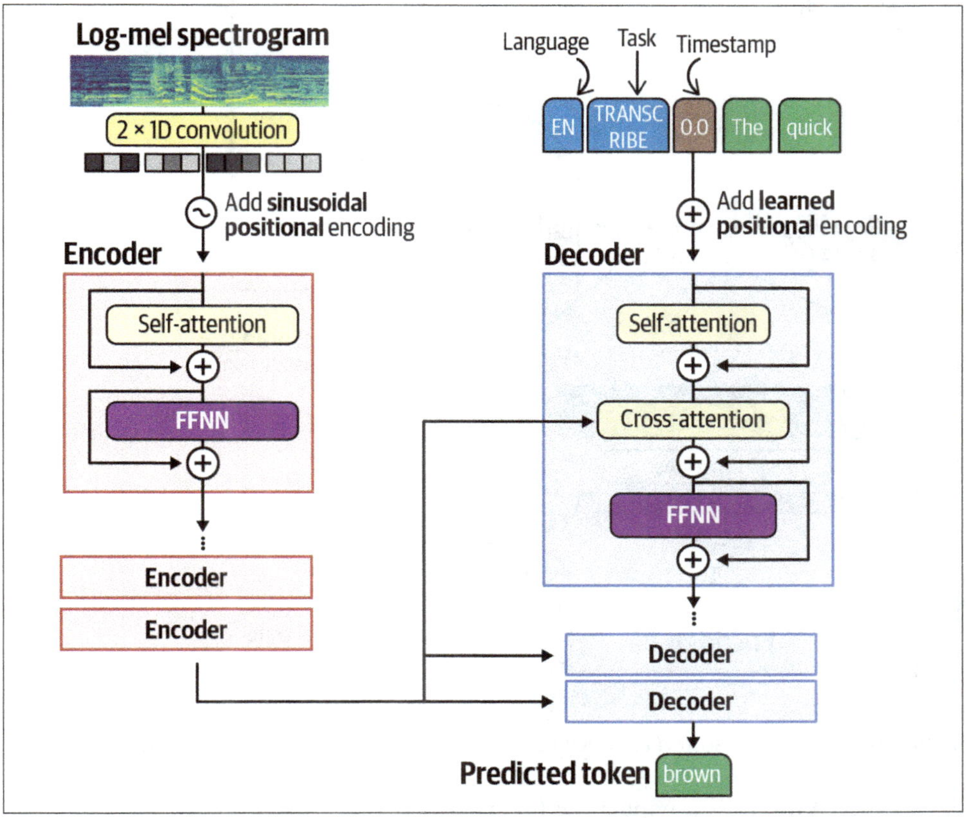

Figure 9-19. Sound processing and understanding in the Whisper architecture

The model is trained on different tasks, such as multilingual speech recognition and translation. Each task has its own tokens, such as "TRANSCRIBE" for transcription and "TRANSLATE" for translation tasks, so the decoder understands which task should be executed. Additional tokens are added for language, if there is speech, time tokens, etc.

When Whisper is used in MLLMs, typically only the Encoder is used since it serves to create the audio representations. Instead, the LLM can handle the generative part (Figure 9-20).

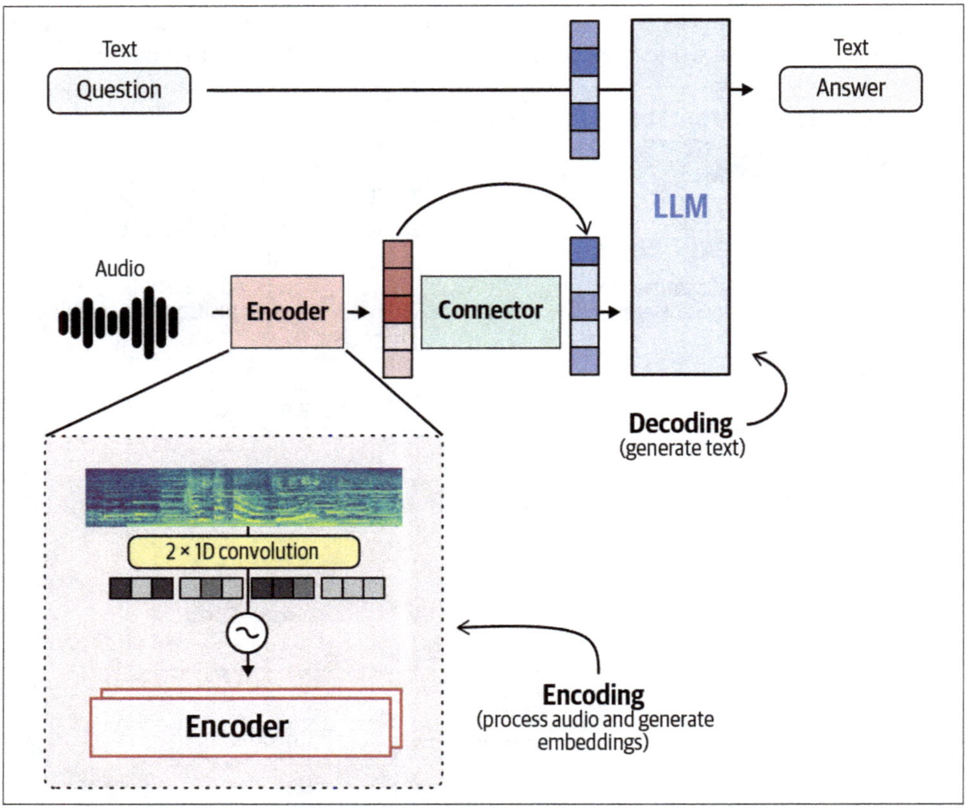

Figure 9-20. How the sound encoder fits into the multi-modal understanding process

Like CLIP, Whisper is a popular audio encoder for MLLMs since the audio embeddings have already had "exposure" to the textual modality.

CLAP

With the performance of CLIP for images, it's not surprising that other modalities would follow. Contrastive Language-Audio Pre-training (CLAP) (*https://arxiv.org/pdf/2211.06687*) is based on CLIP but processes audio inputs instead of images.[6]

The audio waveforms in CLAP (Figure 9-21) are processed in one of two ways, given a chunk duration *d* (e.g., 10 seconds):

6 Wu, Yusong et al. 2023. "Large-Scale Contrastive Language-Audio Pretraining with Feature Fusion and Keyword-to-Caption Augmentation," *ICASSP 2023-2023 IEEE International Conference on Acoustics, Speech and Signal Processing (ICASSP)*, IEEE.

- If the audio is less than 10 seconds, repeat the input, then pad it with zero values.
- If the audio is more than 10 seconds, the entire input is downsampled to 10 seconds. Then, three slices of 10 seconds are randomly sampled.

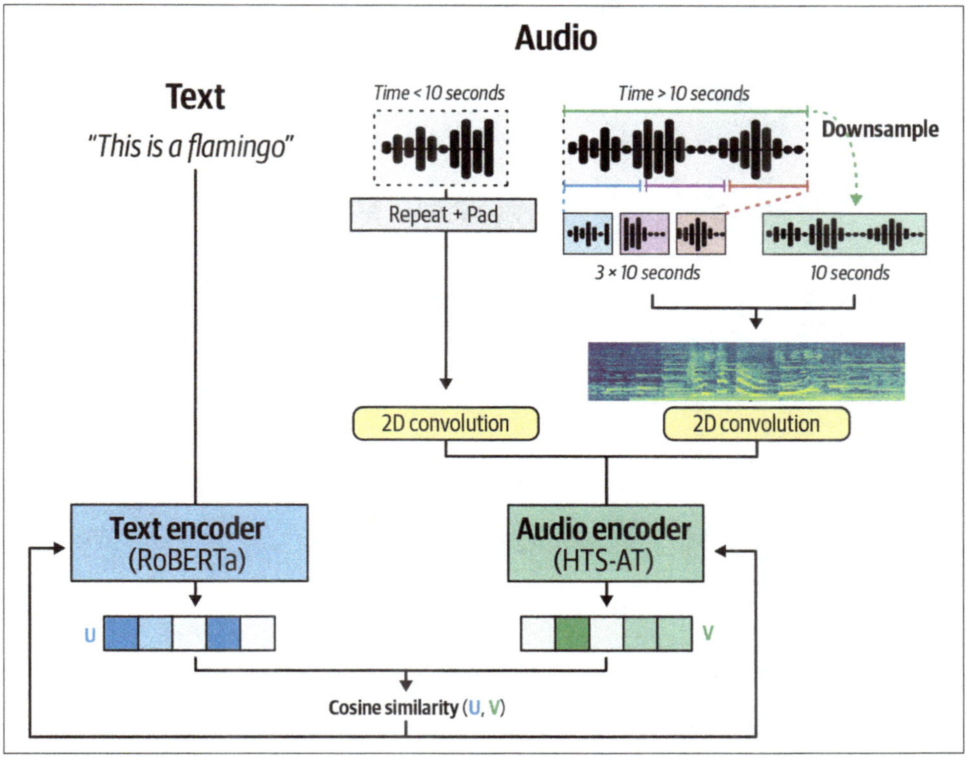

Figure 9-21. Sound processing and training process of CLAP

The authors tested several audio encoders and found that the Hierarchical Token Semantic-Audio Transformer (HTS-AT) (*https://arxiv.org/pdf/2202.00874*) worked best. HTS-AT converts the audio into a spectrogram and extracts patches from it to generate "tokens," much like the image examples we explored.[7]

The large token/patch embeddings are processed by several hierarchical Transformer models to downscale the embeddings (Figure 9-22).

7 Chen, Ke et al. 2022. "HTS-AT: A Hierarchical Token-Semantic Audio Transformer for Sound Classification and Detection," *ICASSP 2022-2022 IEEE International Conference on Acoustics, Speech and Signal Processing (ICASSP)*, IEEE.

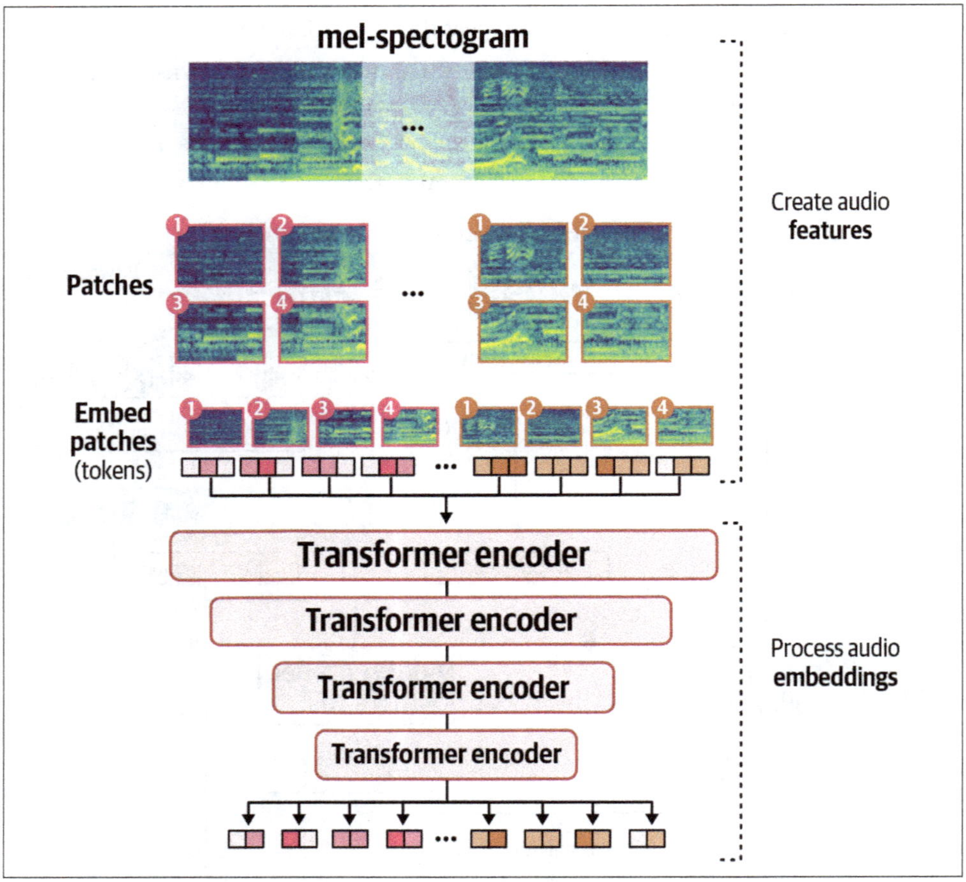

Figure 9-22. How sound is processed using HTS-AT

Using the text and audio encoders, CLAP then uses contrastive learning based on audio/text pairs. These are often captions or descriptions of audio samples.

Video

Encoding videos has a significant overlap with encoding images, but with several (potential) differences. Videos have an additional *temporal* dimension that needs to be encoded, namely as a sequence of images. You can also consider adding the audio and/or subtitles to the encoding process, as those are tightly related (Figure 9-23).

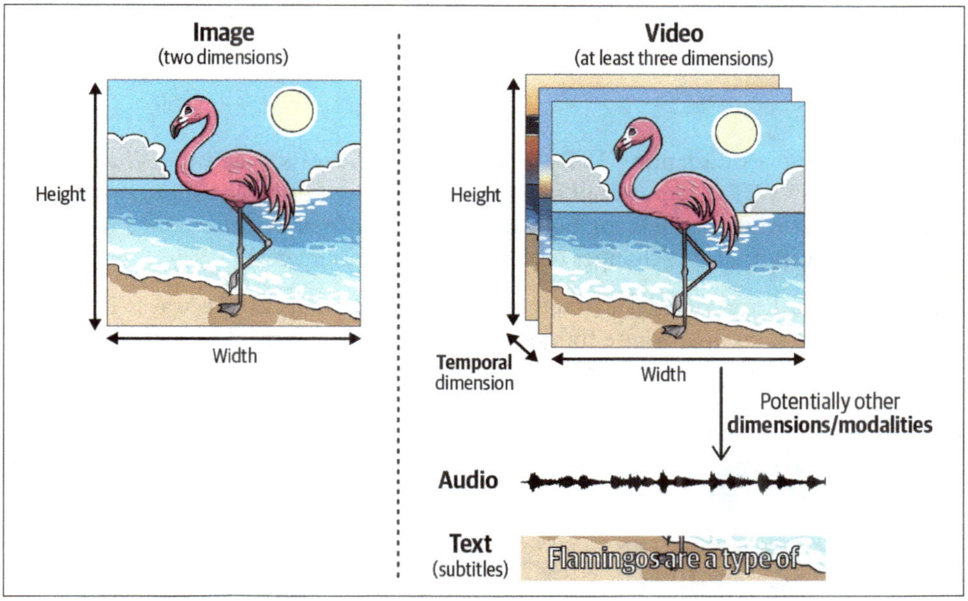

Figure 9-23. Videos have at least three dimensions to process, depending on whether you include other aspects of videos, such as their audio and subtitles

In other words, the main challenge in encoding the video modality is how to model that *temporal* dimension. How do we keep track of this sequence of images?

The most basic version is to use a ViT or CLIP-like model, sample a number of frames, embed, and finally average them (Figure 9-24).

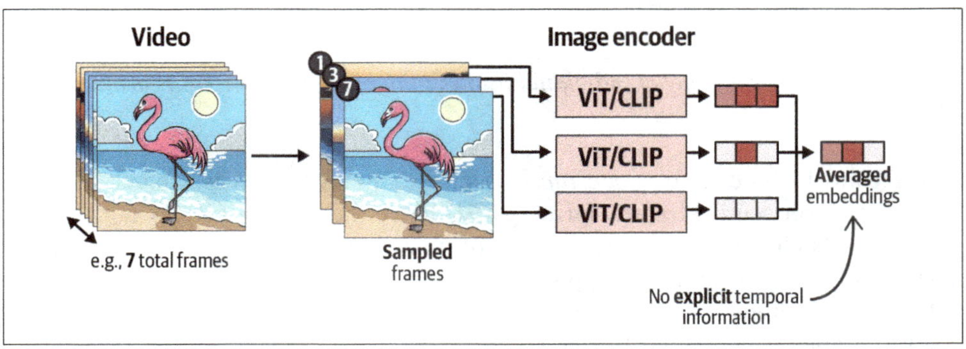

Figure 9-24. An example of how videos can be processed as sequences of images

However, this averages away the *temporal* dimension and prevents the LLM from understanding how the video started and ended.

Are there more sophisticated ways that we can use these ViT/CLIP embeddings? Let's find out!

ViViT

An early example of adapting ViT-like models for video is called the Video Vision Transformer (ViViT) (*https://oreil.ly/KLMis*).[8] This method uses different combinations of Transformer models for both the *spatial* information (the image itself) and the *temporal* information (changes between subsequent images).

To start, the authors consider extracting tokens from videos in two ways. The first is uniform frame sampling, where frames are sampled and passed through ViT to create tokens for each patch in each sampled frame (Figure 9-25).

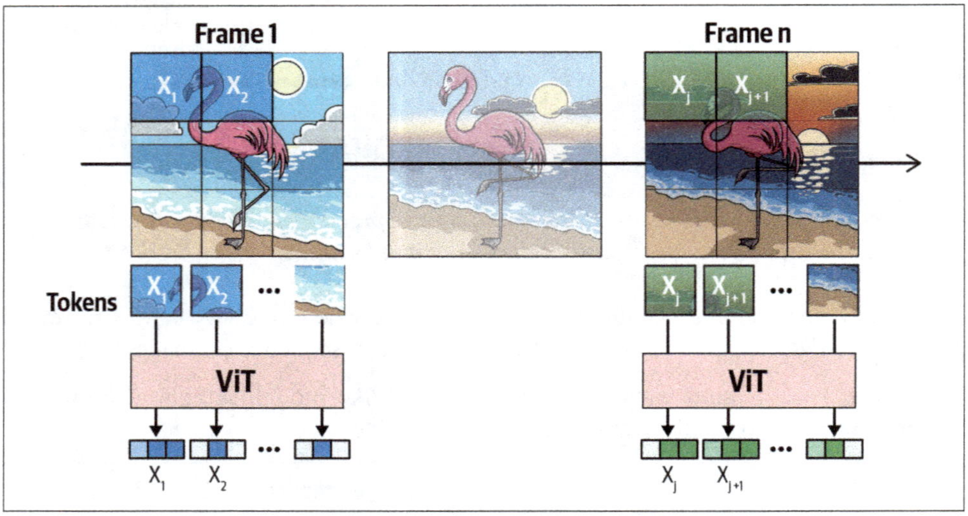

Figure 9-25. The processing of individual frames in the Video Vision Transformer (ViViT)

The second method is to create *tubelet* embeddings. A tubelet is a block of pixels taken from consecutive frames, forming a 3D patch that captures a part of the image as well as its changes over time. Instead of passing a single image to a ViT model, you would now pass non-overlapping tubelets that cover multiple images, producing tubelet embeddings. In other words, it would span both the *spatial* and *temporal* nature of videos (Figure 9-26).

8 Arnab, Anurag et al. 2021. "ViViT: A Video Vision Transformer," *Proceedings of the IEEE/CVF International Conference on Computer Vision.*

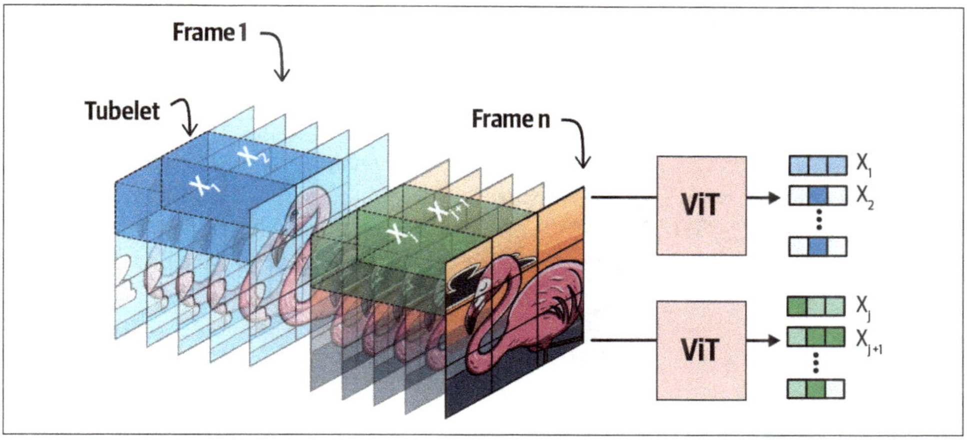

Figure 9-26. The processing of tubelet embeddings in the Video Vision Transformer (ViViT)

The authors of the ViViT paper experimented with several models, but the most prominent one was to pass either embedding type to a set of Transformer encoders that primarily process spatial information (Figure 9-27).

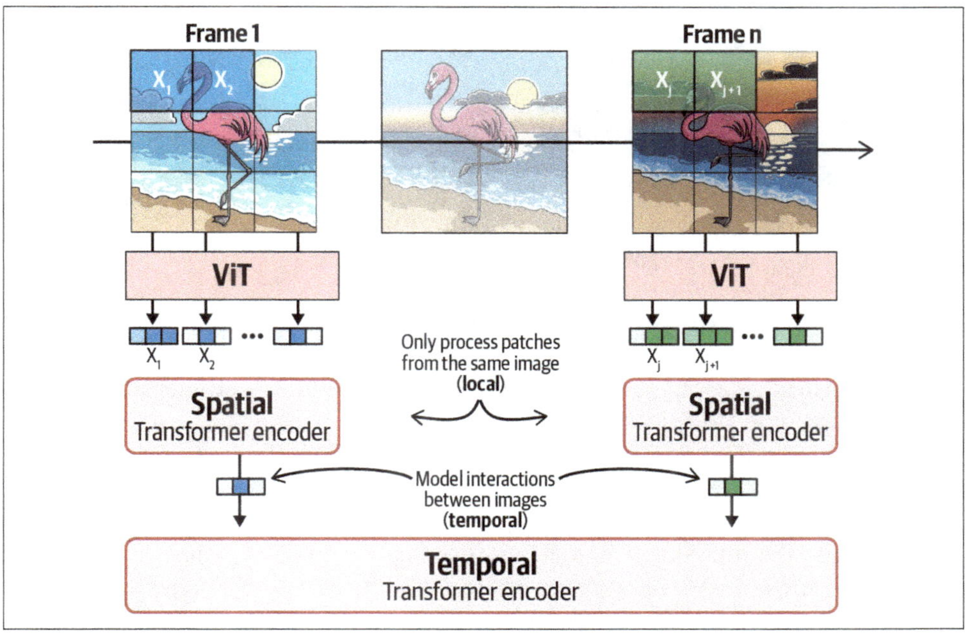

Figure 9-27. An example of how different types of Transformer encoders might be used to process spatial and temporal information in the Video Vision Transformer (ViViT)

It's interesting to see how every modality attempts to represent the input as some sort of *token*.

TimeSformer

The idea of separating temporal and spatial dimensions of video encoding tasks was also explored in a single Transformer model, namely TimeSformer (*https://arxiv.org/pdf/2102.05095*).[9] Like ViViT, frames are sampled and split up into patches. These patches are not processed at first like tubelets but instead flattened and passed directly to a Transformer (Figure 9-28).

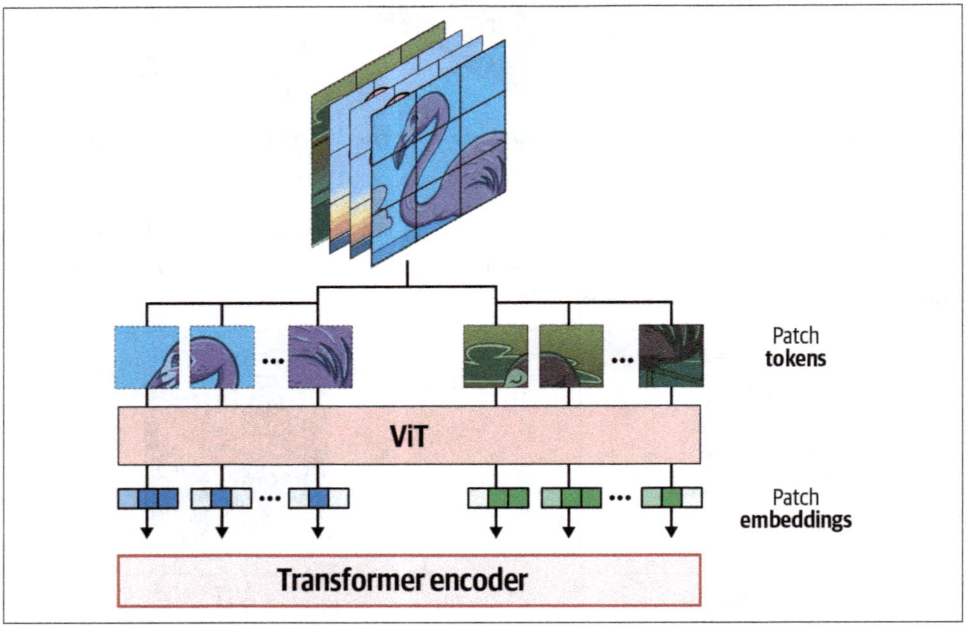

Figure 9-28. The processing of frames in a video in the TimeSformer

However, instead of applying different Transformers for different dimensions (*temporal* versus *spatial*), TimeSformer applies attention mechanisms that each focus on a different aspect, namely time attention and space attention (Figure 9-29). Both forms of attention work the same as self-attention (which we covered in Chapter 2) but operate on different groupings of image patches. Time attention creates tubelets to operate along the time dimension as a way to capture motion patterns. In contrast, space attention operates on patches created within individual frames to focus on spatial structures such as object relationships.

9 Bertasius, Gedas et al. 2021. "Is Space-Time Attention All You Need for Video Understanding?" *ICML*, 2:(3).

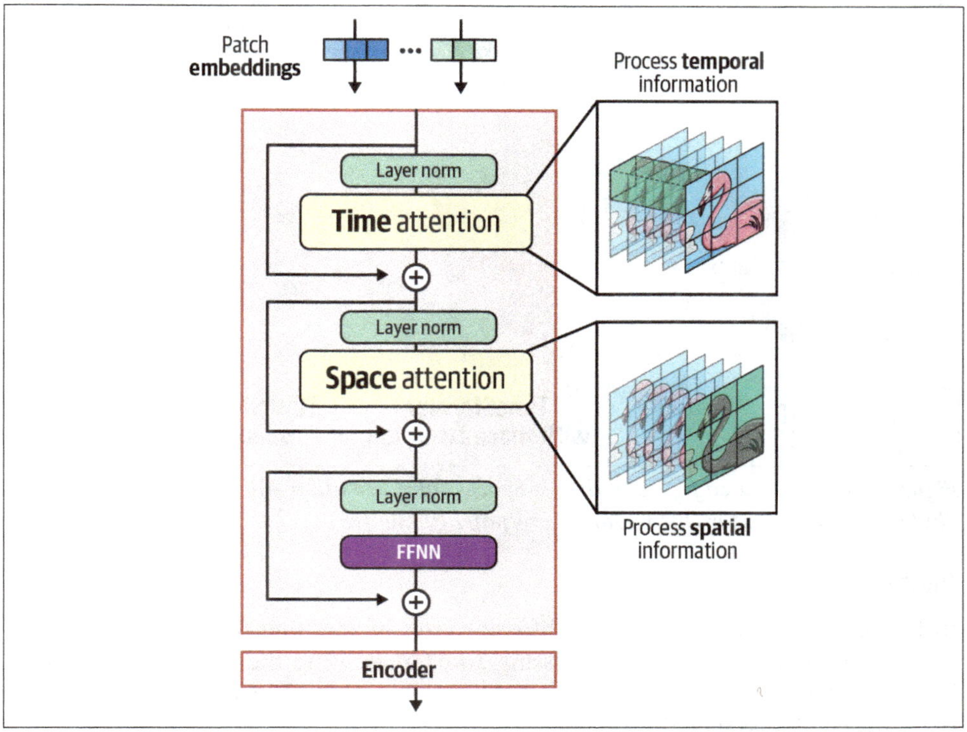

Figure 9-29. The architecture of an encoder block in the TimeSformer

These attention mechanisms are called *divided space-time attention* and allow for better representations than if only space attention were used or ViT (Figure 9-30).

Note how all these techniques have very similar underlying principles of sampling frames, creating patch tokens, embedding them, and finally using them as token embeddings in some variant of a Transformer encoder. Popular examples include VideoBERT (*https://oreil.ly/PpHUo*), Frozen in Time (*https://oreil.ly/qloO4*), and VideoMae (*https://oreil.ly/nHMPx*). Covering them all, however, would make this guide twice as long. Let's instead explore a more straightforward technique, "just" CLIP.

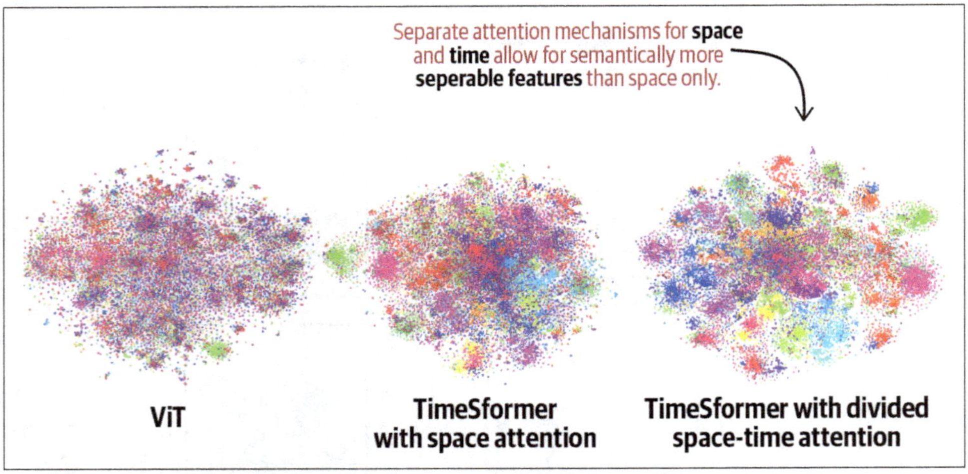

Figure 9-30. Annotated figure in the "Is Space-Time Attention All You Need for Video Understanding?" paper (https://arxiv.org/pdf/2102.05095)

"Just" CLIP

In the previous examples, we saw different ways of adopting the ViT/CLIP embeddings to allow for additional processing and representing the temporal dimension. The underlying idea is that these will be passed to an LLM through a connector (which we'll discuss in a bit). See Figure 9-31.

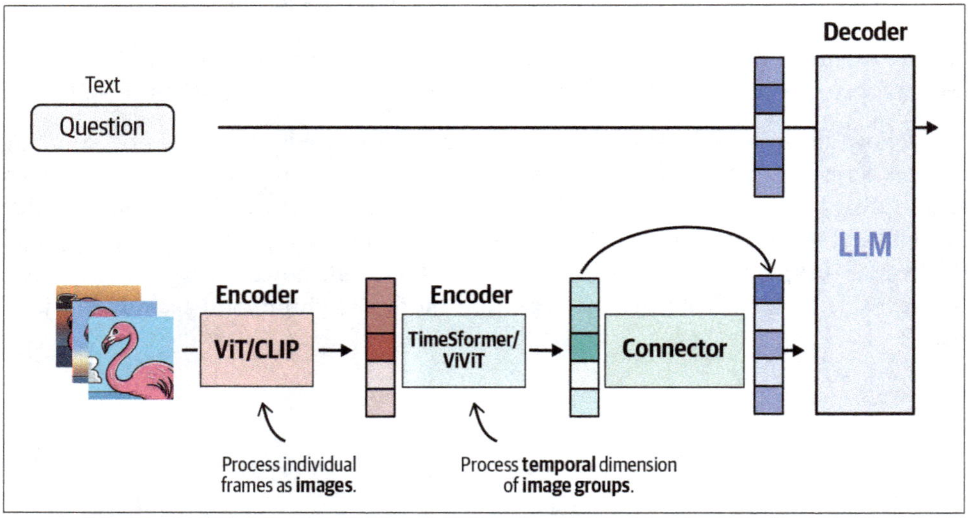

Figure 9-31. How videos might be processed in the multi-modal understanding pipeline

However, there is a bit of redundancy here. Note that there are now two Transformer encoders before the embeddings are passed to the LLM. Instead, we could also skip the second and have the LLM figure out the temporal dimensions by having the connector do a bit more processing (Figure 9-32).

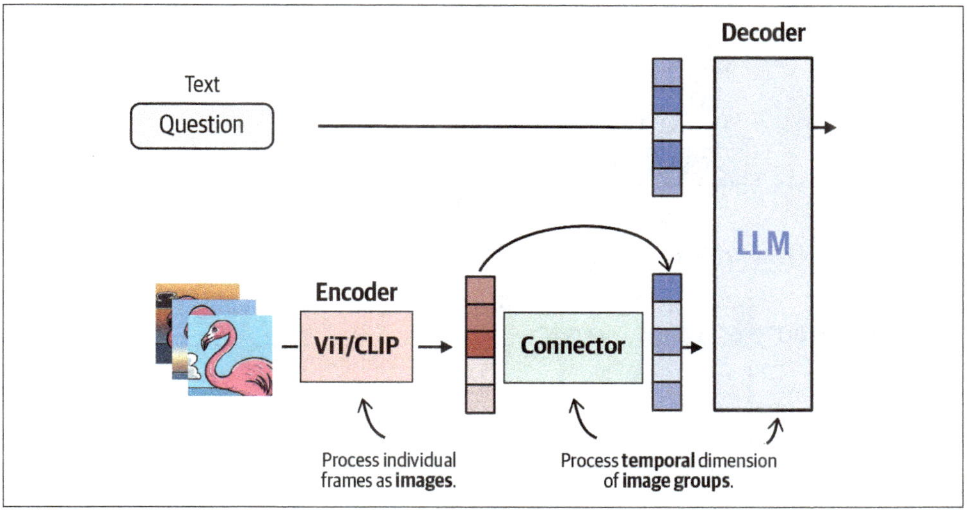

Figure 9-32. How videos might be processed when skipping explicit temporal encoders in the multi-modal understanding pipeline

The underlying idea here is that since decoder LLMs are already good at processing temporal dimensions in text, the same could be done for videos if each frame (or patch) is considered as a sequence of tokens.

As such, both text and video can be seen as having similar time-based sequential natures (Figure 9-33).

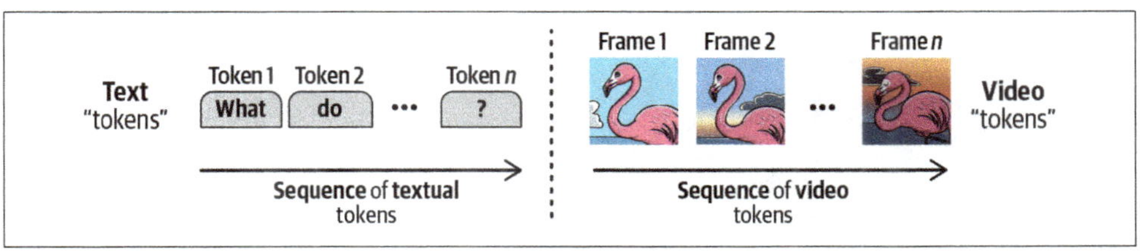

Figure 9-33. When broken down to sequences, video can be seen as a sequence of frames (video tokens,) much like text can be seen as a sequence of subwords (tokens)

As a result, we can pass sample frames from the video, create embeddings for each image, and then pass them as a sequence (like with text) to the LLM. The connector can then either add temporal data or simply convert the image embeddings to the type of embeddings the LLM expects (Figure 9-34).

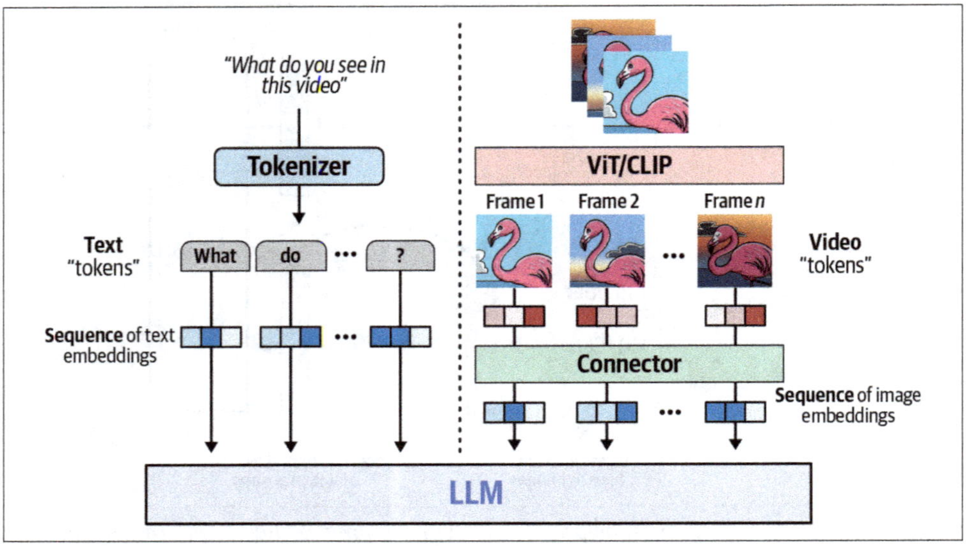

Figure 9-34. Videos can be processed by an LLM as a sequence of image embeddings, much like text is processed as a sequence of text embeddings

These video "tokens" can either be formed as the entire image or as individual image tokens. A great example is the VideoMamba paper (*https://arxiv.org/pdf/2403.06977*) that uses positional embeddings to "enhance" the image embeddings (Figure 9-35).[10]

---

10 Li, Kunchang et al. 2024. "VideoMamba: State Space Model for Efficient Video Understanding," *European Conference on Computer Vision*.

It first adds *spatial information* to the embeddings (to *which part of the frame does an embedding belong?*) and then *temporal information* (*in which order are the frames?*).

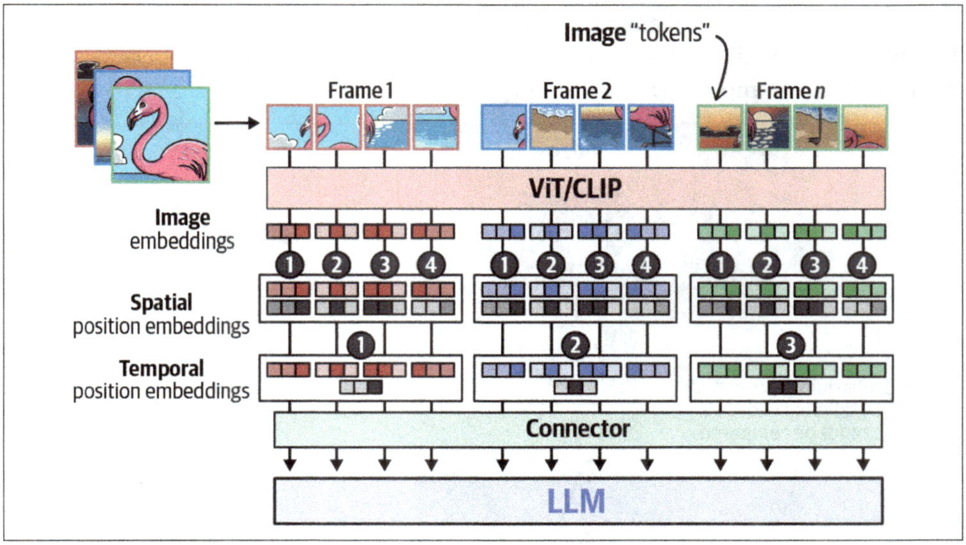

Figure 9-35. Positional embeddings used in VideoMamba allow for adding spatial and temporal information to image embeddings

For an overview of techniques that adopt video encoders, we recommend checking out the "Video Understanding with Large Language Models: A Survey" paper (*https://arxiv.org/pdf/2312.17432*).

Many-Modality

In previous examples, modalities are typically encoded in isolation or in pairs with other modalities. A disadvantage of this approach is that we need different models for different modalities. The generated embeddings by different models cannot be compared to one another (Figure 9-36).

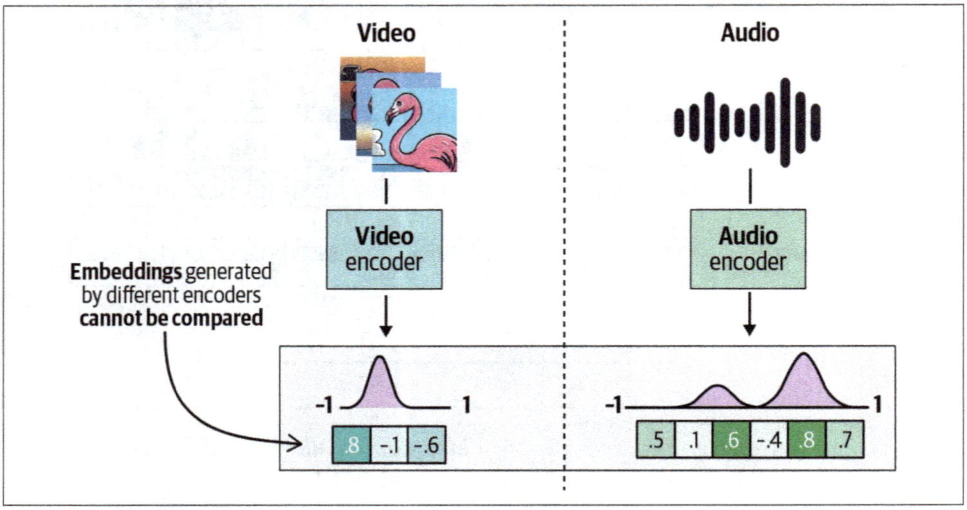

Figure 9-36. Different embeddings will generate different distributions of values and often have different dimensions

A popular technique for finding a singular embedding space that can hold many different modalities is called ImageBind (*https://oreil.ly/8pnIi*).[11] This combines contrastive learning with an interesting idea, namely that a single image can bind different modalities. An image of a rainy day at the beach can remind us of the *sound* of waves, the cold *touch* of mist on skin, and even evoke a quiet *mood*.

11 Girdhar, Rohit et al. 2023. "Imagebind: One Embedding Space to Bind Them All," *Proceedings of the IEEE/CVF Conference on Computer Vision and Pattern Recognition.*

As we have seen before, many modalities are actually processed through the lens of images. Video and audio encoders, for instance, use image encoders as the main encoder for processing these modalities (Figure 9-37).

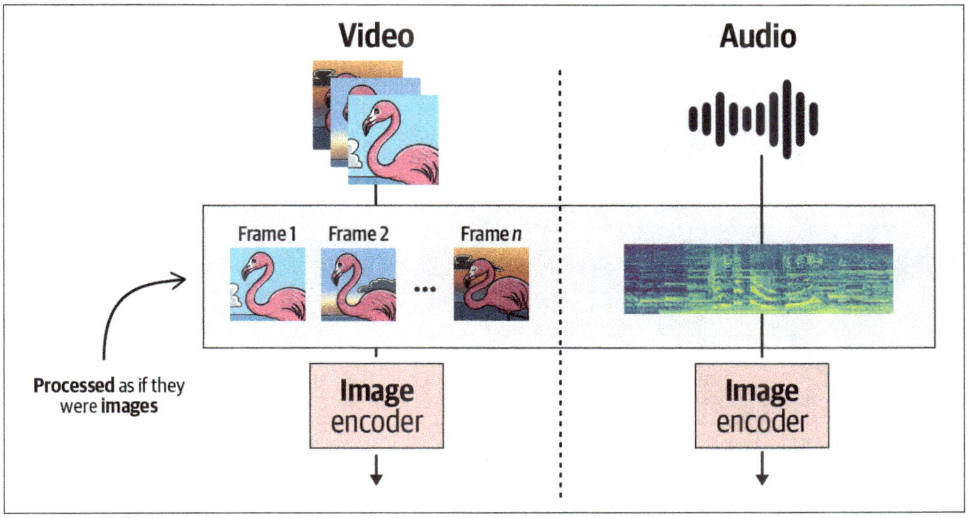

Figure 9-37. Audio and video can be processed as if they were images, which results in the same type of embeddings generated and can therefore be compared

The primary objective of the ImageBind project is to utilize images as the basis for contrastive learning. As explored before, contrastive learning typically trains on pairs of data. With ImageBind, one of those modalities will always be related to the visual modality (images or video).

For each pair of modalities, a linear projection is first applied to the original embeddings to make sure that the embeddings of different pairs of modalities are *aligned* (Figure 9-38).

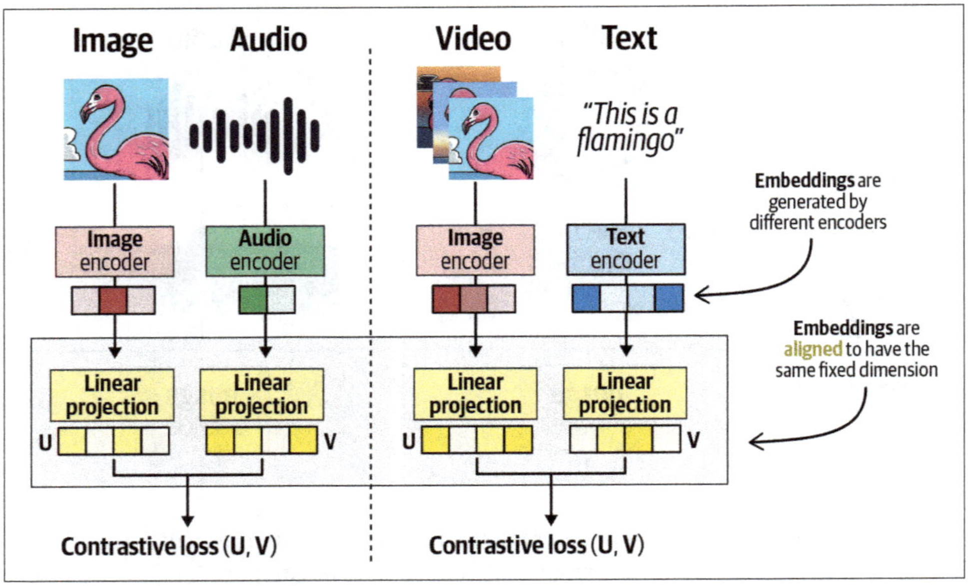

Figure 9-38. How contrastive learning is used to train ImageBind, connecting all modalities together through images

During training, the following pairs were trained:

- (Image, text)
- (Image, depth sensor data)
- (Image, thermal data)
- (Video, inertial measurement unit [IMU; e.g., accelerometer data])
- (Video, audio)

Interestingly, although there were many unseen pairs of modalities during training, such as (audio, text), their embeddings were aligned in the embedding space (see Figure 9-39).

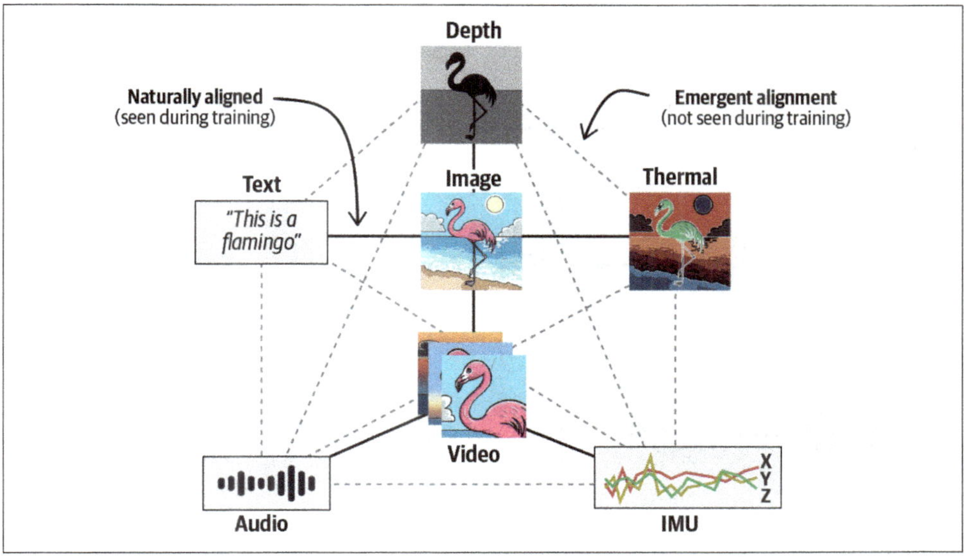

Figure 9-39. ImageBind demonstrates emergent alignment of modalities despite not being trained together

This *emergent alignment* of unseen pairs of modalities showcases how strong this "binding" factor of images can be.

Connecting Modalities

We explored how representations (embeddings) can be created for many different modalities. Before we can feed those to the LLM, making it multi-modal, there's a big problem with the generated embeddings.

As we explored earlier in this chapter, the encoders for each modality generally create different embeddings with respect to their size, dimensions, and embedding space than what the LLM might expect. Likewise, there might be differences in positional encoding and tokenization schemas. As such, we need a *connector* that transforms those embeddings to the same type of embeddings as its token embeddings (see Figure 9-40).

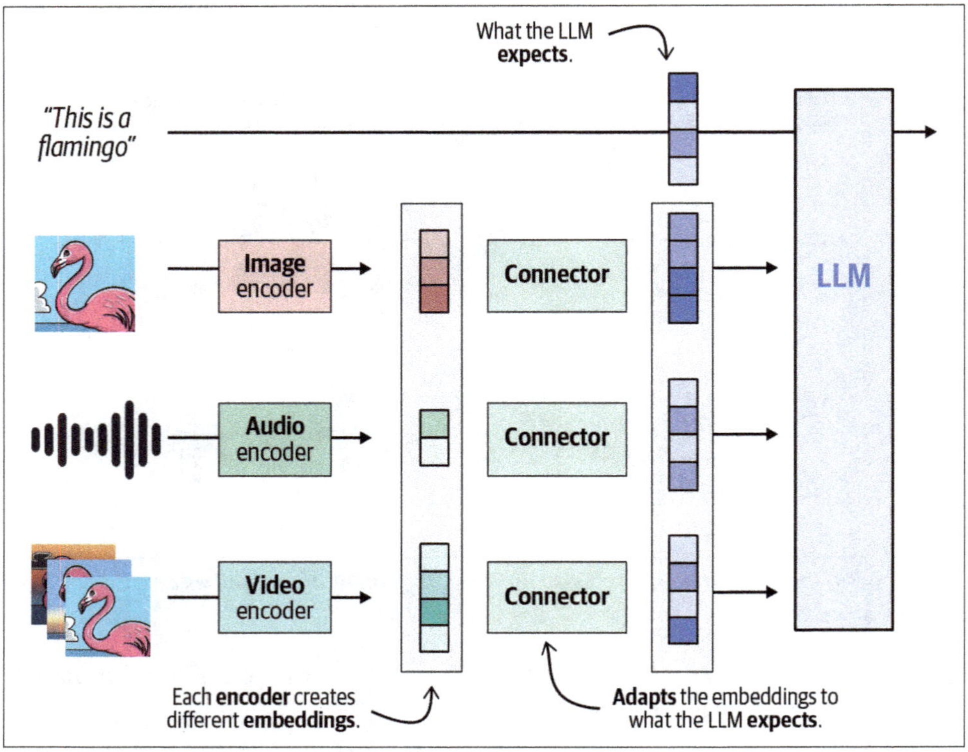

Figure 9-40. The connector is needed to align different types of encoders to what the LLM expects

There are roughly three types of connectors (Figure 9-41):[12,13]

Projection-based
: A Multi-Layer Perceptron (MLP) to project multi-modal embeddings into an embedding size compatible with the LLM

Query-based
: Leveraging groups of learnable query tokens to extract information in a query-based manner

12 Cui, Can et al. 2024. "A Survey on Multimodal Large Language Models for Autonomous Driving," *Proceedings of the IEEE/CVF Winter Conference on Applications of Computer Vision*.

13 Caffagni, Davide et al. 2024. "The Revolution of Multimodal Large Language Models: a Survey," *arXiv*, 2402.12451.

Fusion-based
: Adding additional (cross-attention) layers in the LLM that can process both text and other multi-modal embeddings

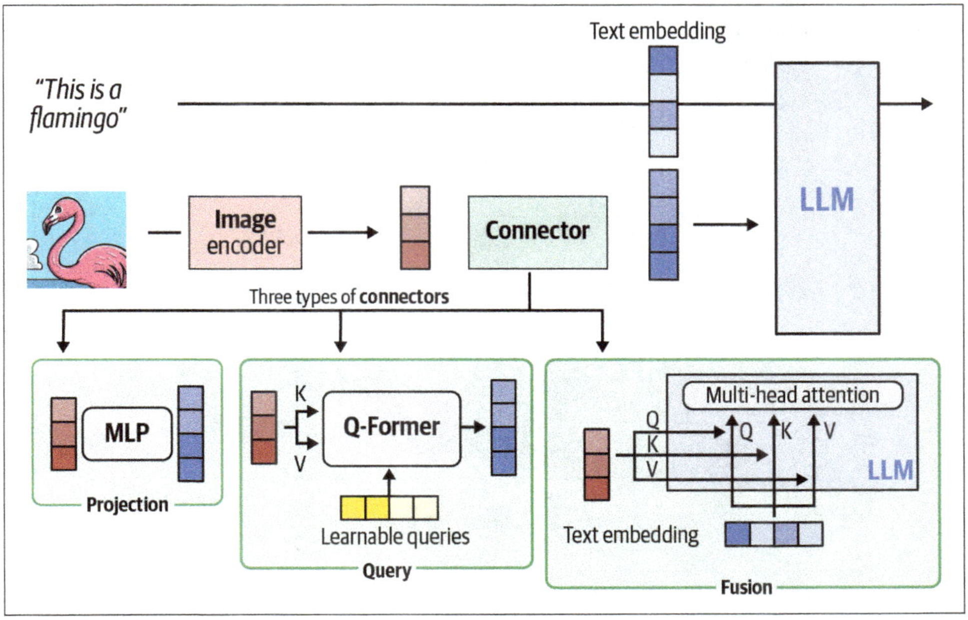

Figure 9-41. The three types of connectors: the projection, query, and fusion connectors

Let's explore these types, one by one, in more detail!

Projection-Based Connector

The most straightforward method of aligning the multi-modal embeddings with the text embeddings that an LLM expects is by simply projecting them. This is typically done with a single linear layer to convert these non-text embeddings to token embeddings (Figure 9-42).

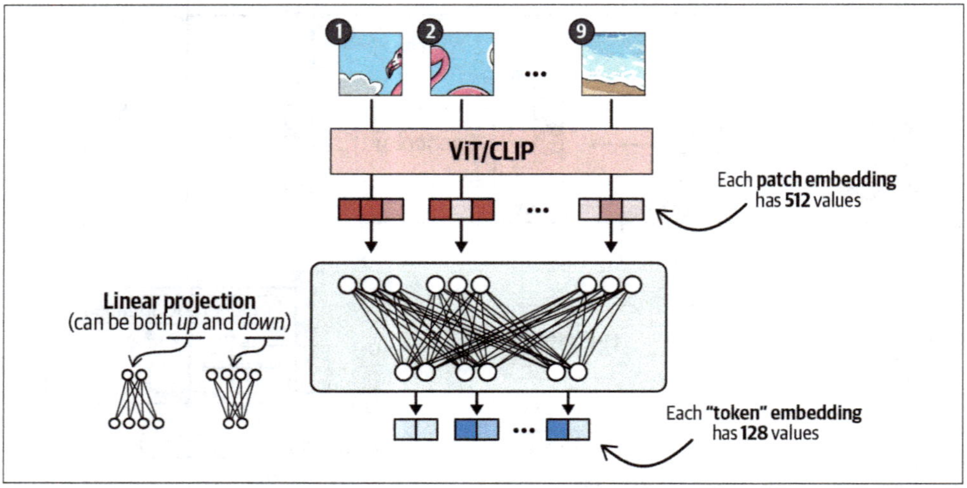

Figure 9-42. An example of how a linear projection maps each input image to an output embedding

The projection doesn't always have to be up (from fewer to more values) but can also be down projected (from more to fewer values) if the non-text embeddings are smaller than the token embeddings the LLM expects. The resulting projection of the non-text embeddings is then concatenated with the token embeddings of the text input. The LLM will treat every embedding as if it were a token embedding (Figure 9-43).

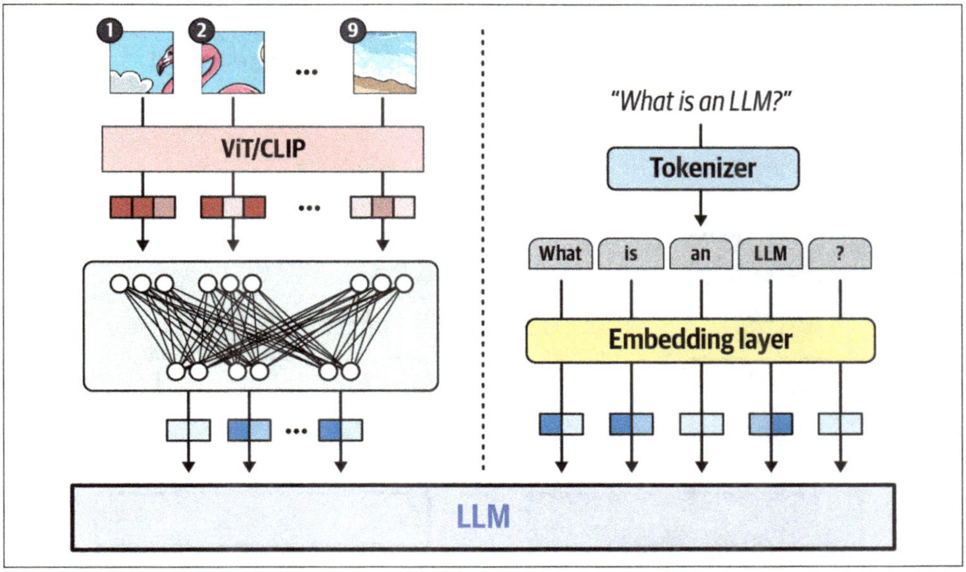

Figure 9-43. A projection connector maps each output embedding of the image encoder to what the LLM expects (with respect to count, dimensions, and data distribution)

A great example of this technique is used in Large Language and Vision Assistant (LLaVA).[14] LLaVA is an MLLM that is not only able to process text but also reason about images. This technique attempts to make Vicuna, a Llama 2 variant that can process only text, multi-modal.[15] The authors of LLaVA chose this model because, at the time (2023), it had the best instruction-following capabilities.

LLaVA was created in two steps, using the same projection scheme we explored previously (Figure 9-44):

Step 1: Pre-training for feature alignment
: Only the projection layer is trained. The weights of both the ViT and LLM (Vicuna) are frozen.

Step 2: Fine-tuning end-to-end
: Both the projection layer and the LLM are trained. Only the ViT weights are frozen.

14 Liu, Haotian et al. 2023. "Visual Instruction Tuning," *Advances in Neural Information Processing Systems*, 36: 34892-34916.

15 Chiang, Wei-Lin et al. 2023. "Vicuna: An Open-Source Chatbot Impressing GPT-4 with 90%* Chat GPT Quality," Blog post, *https://lmsys.org/blog/2023-03-30-vicuna*.

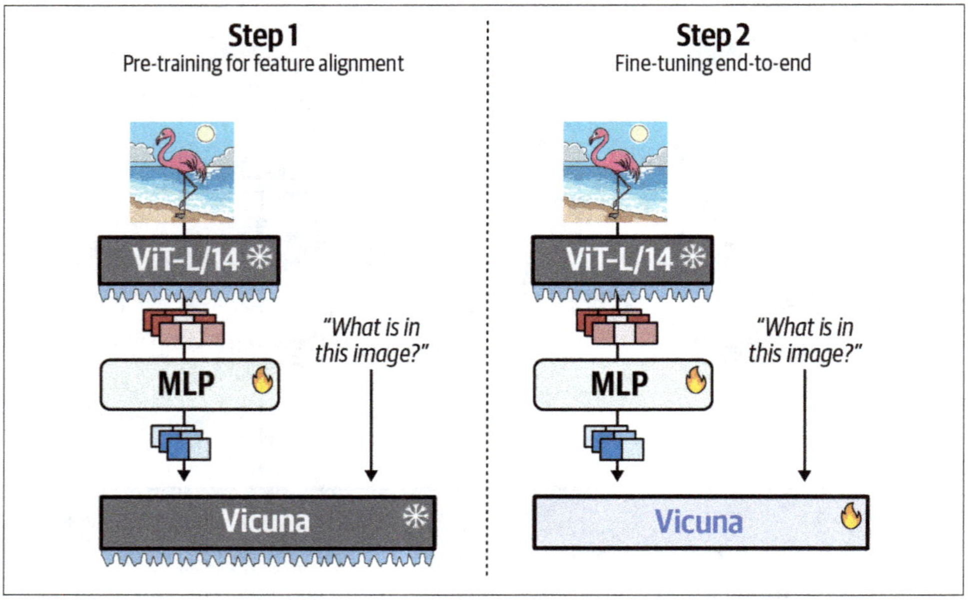

Figure 9-44. The two-step training process of LLaVA

As shown, this projection-based connector needs to be trained (as is the case with all connectors) to properly project the initial embeddings to what a specific LLM needs, in this case the Vicuna model.

This training procedure uses text/image pairs to train the MLP and LLM. The first step is meant to align the type of embeddings to what the Vicuna model expects. The second step allows the LLM to learn to reason about the text/image pairs. The resulting model demonstrated, at the time, state-of-the-art multi-modal chat capabilities for publicly available models. Likewise, this training procedure has made it relatively straightforward to create a multi-modal LLM. As such, the projection-based technique, albeit simple in nature, is still used for more recent architectures like Qwen2.5-VL,[16] Phi-4-multimodal,[17] and Janus.[18] Moreover, this projection can be used for any modality, not only images.

---

16 Bai, Shuai et al. 2025. "Qwen2.5-VL Technical Report," *arXiv,* 2502.13923.

17 Abouelenin, Abdelrahman et al. 2025. "Phi-4-mini Technical Report: Compact Yet Powerful Multimodal Language Models via Mixture-of-loras," *arXiv,* 2503.01743.

18 Wu, Chengyue et al. 2025. "Janus: Decoupling Visual Encoding for Unified Multimodal Understanding and Generation," *Proceedings of the Computer Vision and Pattern Recognition Conference.*

Query-Based Connector

A more involved method of connecting modalities is through a query-based connector. This connector is meant to extract relevant features from all non-textual inputs before feeding them to the LLM (Figure 9-45). These relevant features are generally referred to as "queries" and are learnable by this connector, commonly referred to as the Q-Former.

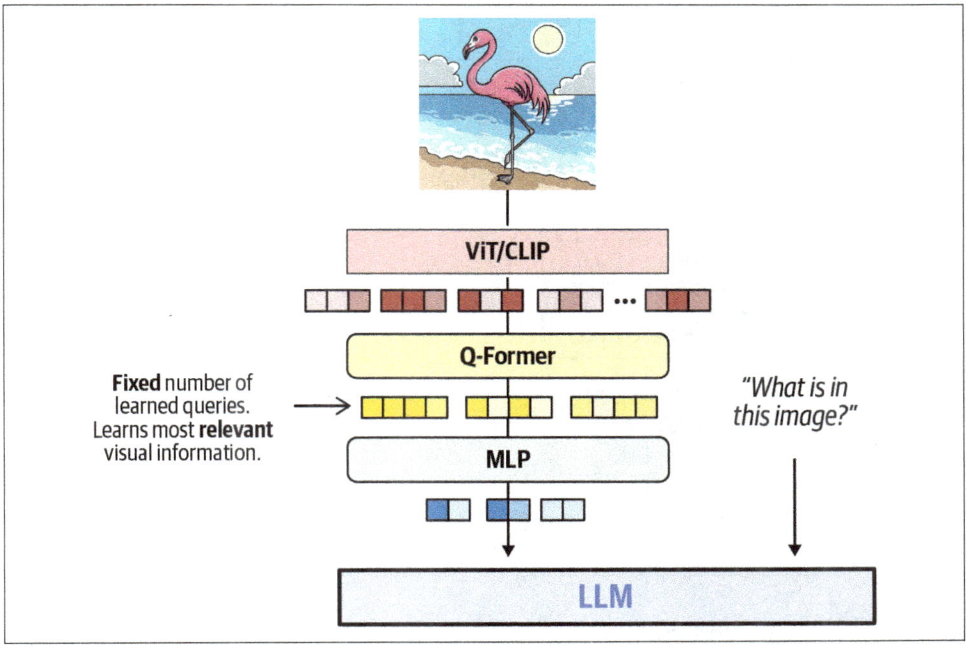

Figure 9-45. The Q-Former, which maps the input to a fixed set of embeddings, compressing the amount of information before feeding it to a projection connector

Instead of projecting all ViT features to the LLM, like the projection-based connector, the Q-Former creates a fixed number of features that the LLM can process. A major benefit to this approach is that it learns only the most relevant visual information.

The Q-Former was first introduced in BLIP-2, an MLLM that uses a Transformer model to process both image features and text features.[19] During training, the Transformer model will receive learnable queries, embeddings that get "updated" with relevant visual and textual information.

19 Li, Junnan et al. 2023. "BLIP-2: Bootstrapping Language-Image Pre-training with Frozen Image Encoders and Large Language Models," *International Conference on Machine Learning*, PMLR.

This Transformer model has two modes, one with cross-attention for processing the images and one without cross-attention to process the text (Figure 9-46).

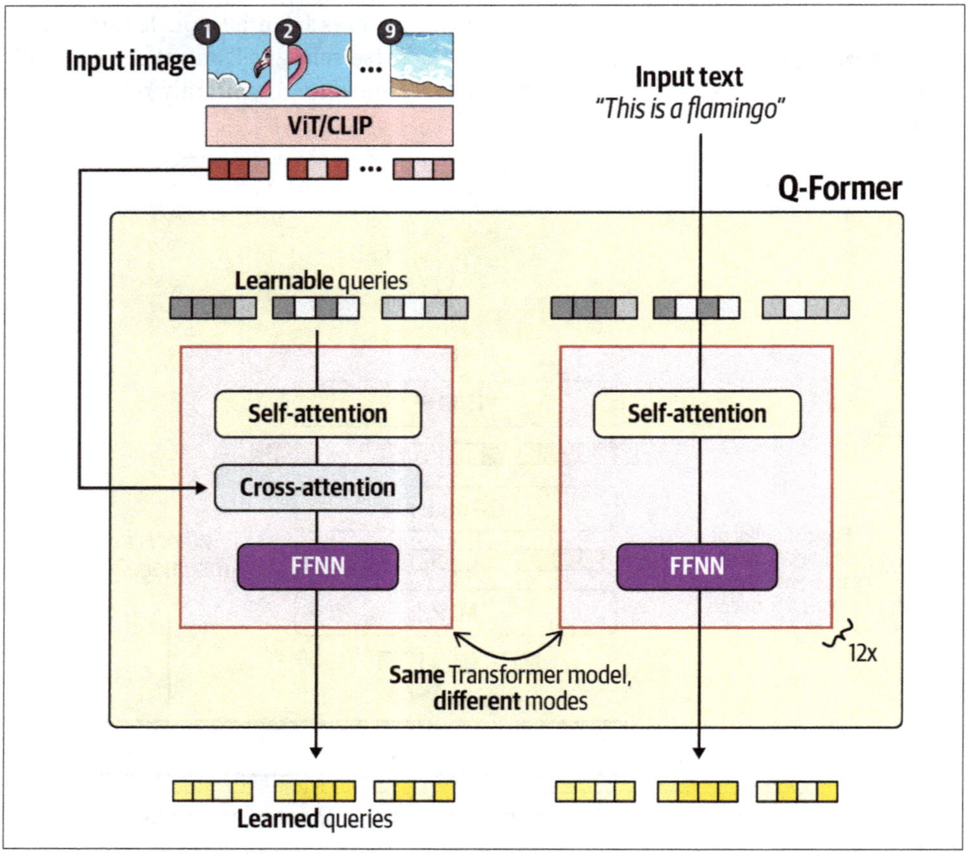

Figure 9-46. The two modes of the Q-Former, one for processing the images (left) and one for processing the text (right)

Since this Transformer model has two modes, this model can then be trained using contrastive learning using image/text pairs.

The output embeddings of this model are the *learned queries*, which contain the image embeddings' most relevant information. It's essentially a way to compress visual tokens into a smaller number of representation vectors.

There are two stages in this training process. In stage 1, the Q-Former was trained on three tasks such that the queries can learn to extract the visual representation that is most informative of the text:

Image-text contrastive learning
: Aligns image and text representations by maximizing mutual information

Image-grounded text generation
: Trains the Q-Former to generate text conditioned on images

Image-text matching
: Binary classification to predict if image-text pairs match

In stage 2, the trained Q-Former is connected to an LLM (OPT)[20] to improve the LLM's generative capabilities. The output query embeddings are projected through an MLP to match the LLM's input dimensions. Then, only the Q-Former and MLP are trained; the LLM and image encoder are frozen (Figure 9-47).

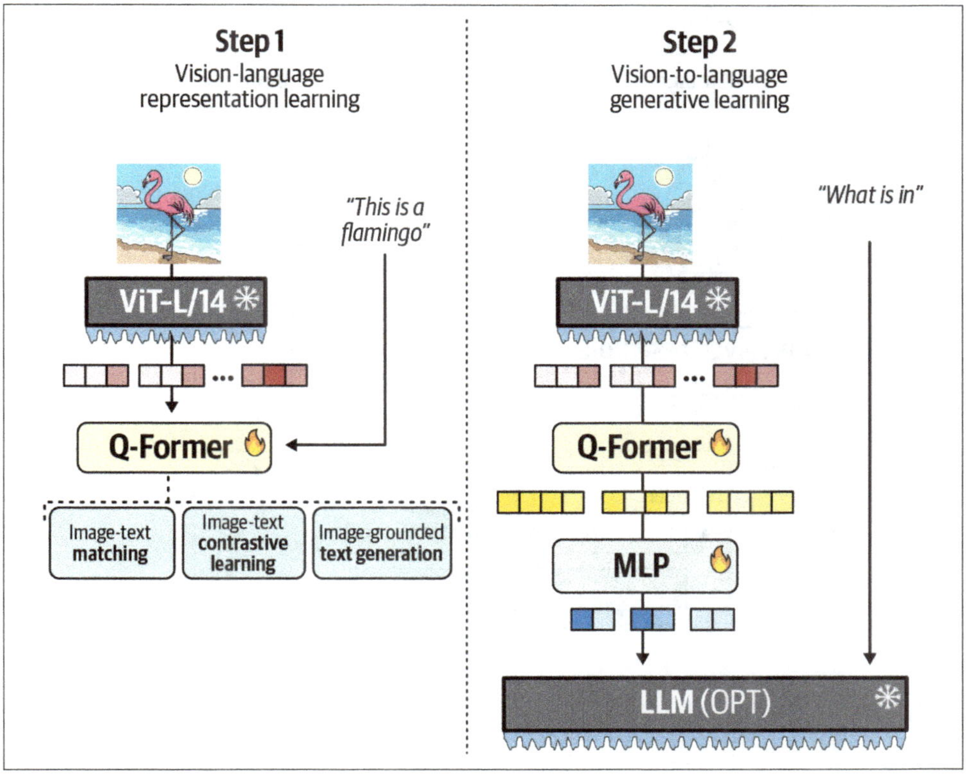

Figure 9-47. The two-step process of training the Q-Former

This technique was used in Qwen's first multi-modal LLM, namely Qwen-VL.[21] Like the projection-based connector, this connector can be used for any modality.

20 Zhang, Susan et al. 2022. "OPT: Open Pre-trained Transformer Language Models," *arXiv*, 2205.01068.

Fusion-Based Connector

The previous connectors do not change the LLM's architecture to enable multi-modal understanding. With a fusion-based connector, extra modules are added to the LLM's architecture to enable a deep interaction and fusion between text and non-text features.

One of the first methods in doing so is called Flamingo.[22] This model uses pre-trained LLMs as their basis and adds trainable cross-attention layers that can process the input images. More specifically, images are processed with a vision encoder, and its output is processed through a perceiver resampler. This resampler is a Transformer model, much like the Q-Former, and maps the image embeddings to a fixed sequence size. The output of the resampler is fed to the cross-attention layers that were added to the LLM (Figure 9-48).

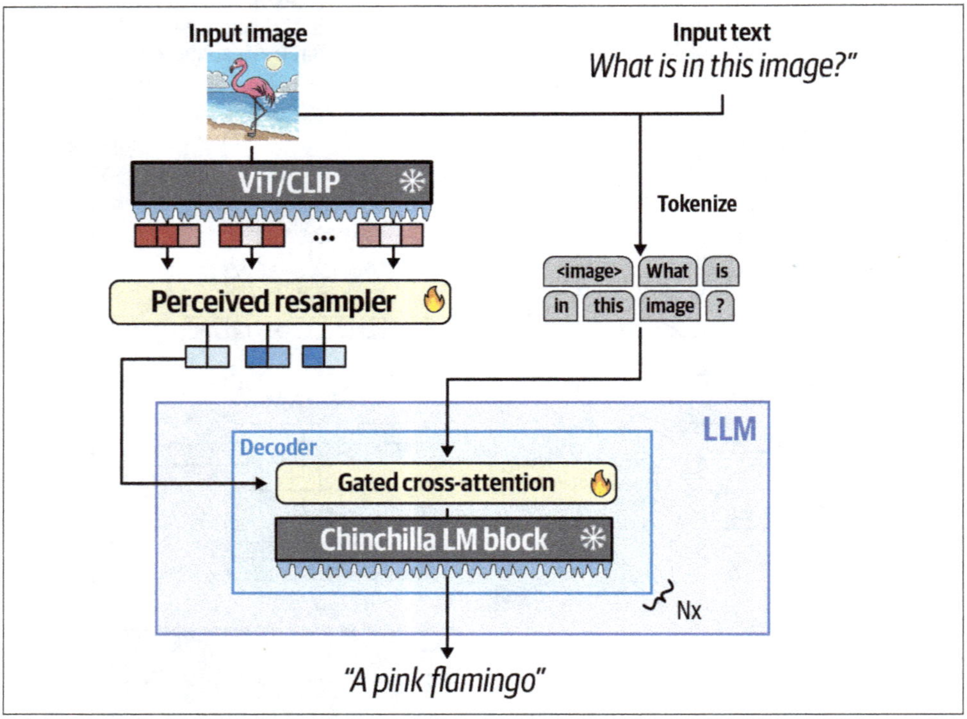

Figure 9-48. The Flamingo fusion-based connector

21 Bai, Jinze et al. 2023. "Qwen-VL: A Frontier large Vision-Language Model with Versatile Abilities," *arXiv*, 2308.12966.

22 Alayrac, Jean-Baptiste et al. 2022. "Flamingo: A Visual Language Model for Few-Shot Learning," *Advances in Neural Information Processing Systems*, 35: 23716-23736.

Only the added cross-attention and perceiver resampler are trained; the pre-trained vision encoder and LLM are frozen (Figure 9-49).

Let's explore these two trainable modules in more detail, starting with the perceiver resampler. The goal of the perceiver resampler is to extract the most important vision features and output them in a fixed size, much like the Q-Former.

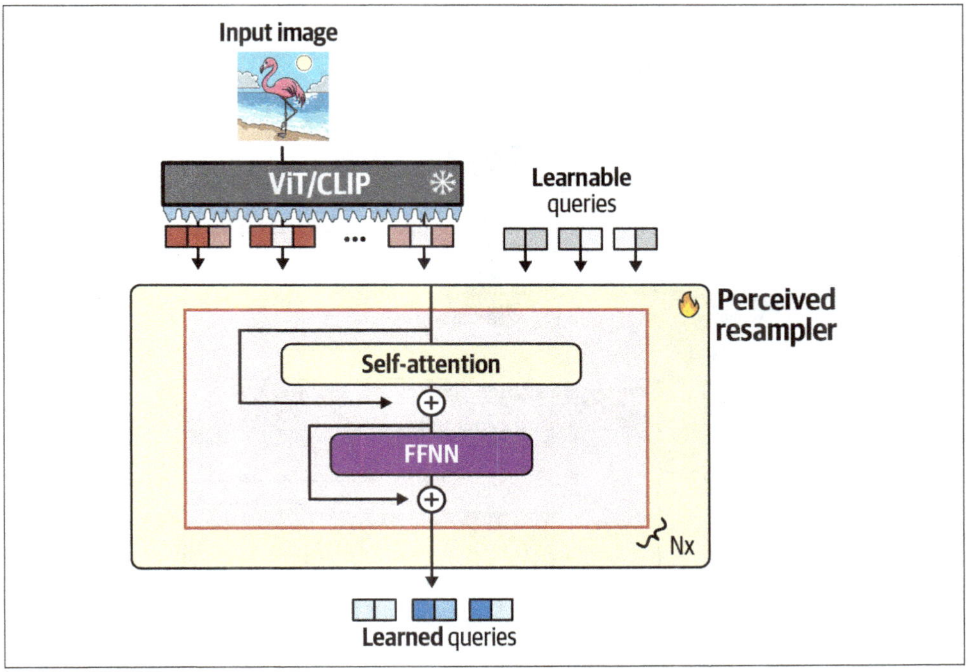

Figure 9-49. In Flamingo, while the ViT/CLIP module is frozen, the perceiver resampler is trained

These learned queries will have the same shape as expected by the LLM, and the fixed size allows for reduced computation by focusing on only the most important visual features.

The output embeddings are then passed to the additional cross-attention blocks that are intertwined with LLM's regular blocks. In these cross-attention blocks, the LLM can then attend to both the image and text features.

They are referred to as "gated" cross-attention because they use a special gating trick, which makes the conditioned model behave identically to the original LLM at initialization. This is done by multiplying the layer outputs by *tanh(α)*, where *α* is a learnable scalar per layer initialized to 0. Since *tanh(0) = 0*, these layers initially contribute nothing, preserving the pretrained LLM's behavior. As training progresses, α learns to open the gate. This initialization strategy enhances training stability and final performance (Figure 9-50).

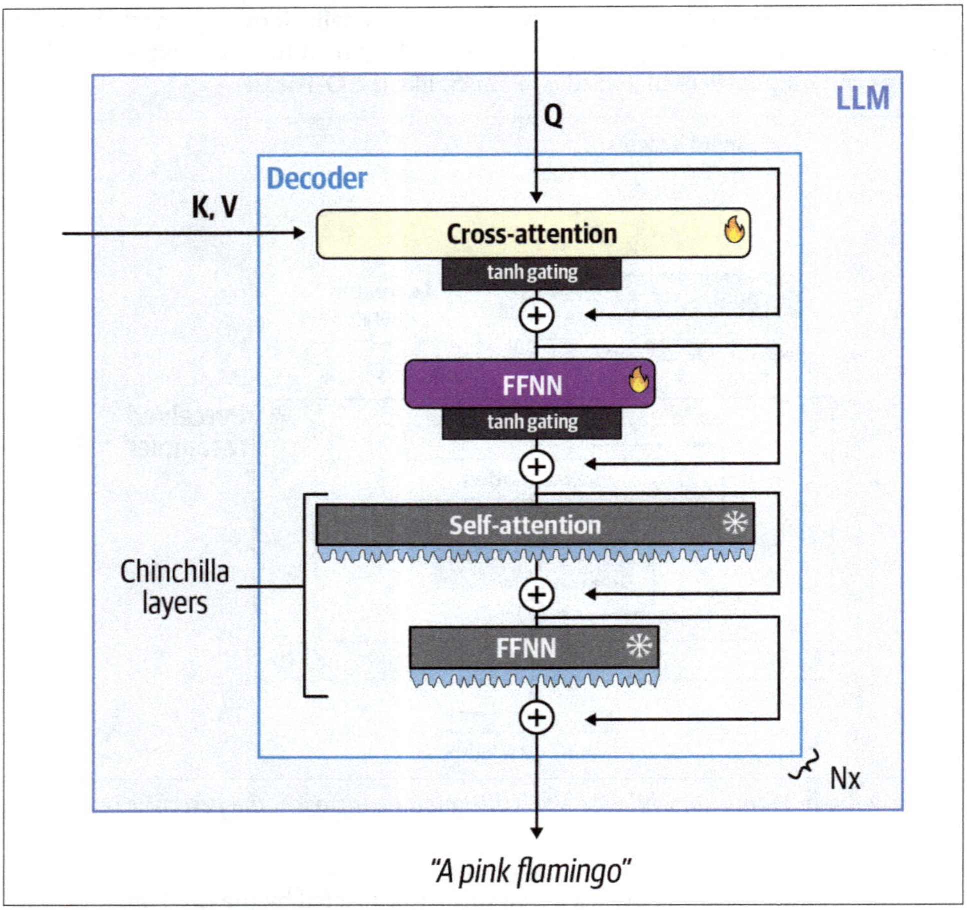

Figure 9-50. A decoder block of Flamingo

This fusion-based connector needs to adjust the architecture of the original LLM, which makes it a bit less flexible than any of the previous techniques. However, by integrating attention into its architecture, there is the potential for improved performance.

Advantages and Disadvantages

Before ending this chapter, it's worthwhile to go into the advantages and disadvantages of the connectors we explored thus far (Table 9-1).

Table 9-1. Advantages and disadvantages of connectors

Connectors	Advantages	Disadvantages
Projection-based	*Simple:* Lightweight to implement. *Computational efficiency:* Low latency and few parameters.	*Scalability:* It can produce a large number of tokens, which quickly fills up the LLM's context window. *Performance:* Since it's decoupled from the LLM and the model is rather small, it has limited expressive power.
Query-based	*Scalability:* The fixed number of queries allows for scaling with large multi-modal inputs (e.g., videos). *Performance:* Has more expressive power than projection-based connectors.	*Complexity:* Requires relatively complex training procedures. *Computational efficiency:* Due to the larger models, it adds more latency than a projection-based connector.
Fusion-based	*Integration:* The integration with the LLM itself allows it to "see" multi-modal features at every layer instead of just as a prefix. *Performance:* Has more expressive power than both projection-based and query-based connectors.	*Complexity:* Requires changes to the architecture of the LLM. *Computational efficiency*: Requires the LLM to undergo extensive fine-tuning procedures, more so than the other connectors.

There are three main axes at which we can view the potential (dis)advantages of these connectors, namely their performance, computational efficiency, and scalability. Generally, projection-based connectors are used for simplicity and computational efficiency because these connectors are lightweight and easy to train. However, they may quickly fill up the LLM's context window since the input is not compressed. Query-based connectors are primarily used for efficiency and scaling because they keep the input length constant regardless of the image/video resolution. However, a query-based connector may skip over details as it does not have the fine-grained representation of projection-based connectors. Finally, fusion-based connectors tend to perform best because the processing of the multi-modal input is done throughout the entire model, rather than just as token embeddings. However, they're the most complex connectors to implement (requiring changes to the LLM's architecture) and are expensive to train.

TinyAgent

Throughout this chapter, we covered how multi-modal models are created using methods like SFT and RL. The resulting models can process more than text and typically have either vision or audio understanding. The model that we've been using thus far, Gemma 4 E4B, has both. It can process both images and audio. To do so, it has two encoders to process those modalities, a vision encoder for processing images and an audio encoder for processing sound. You can find more about the vision and audio encoders of Gemma 4 E4B in "A Visual Guide to Gemma 4" (*https://oreil.ly/snqhu*):

```
from illustrated_agents.chapters.ch2 import LLM


# Gemma 4 E4B (with native thinking and tool calling)
llm = LLM(model="gemma4:e4b", think=True)
```

The vision encoder in Gemma 4 E4B generates a set of embeddings (also called vision tokens or image tokens) that the LLM can use. In the raw chat template, that tends to look something like this:

```
<|image> <|image|><|image|><|image|><|image|><|image|> … <|image|> <image|>
```

Those are special image tokens used to indicate that a given embedding belongs to an image. The <|image> and <image|> tokens indicate the start and end, respectively, of a sequence of image tokens. The <|image|> is a vision token. In Gemma 4 E4B, there are generally either a maximum of 70, 140, 280, 560, or 1,120 vision tokens. A larger number of vision tokens means that the input image will be processed at a higher resolution. If you chose a different model, then it might use a different chat template and token structure. In practice, however, they all work similarly.

As we saw in Chapter 5, the processing of this chat template is almost always handled by the inference engine. So there's no need for us to create templates with potentially 1,120 vision tokens. The OpenAI endpoint that we've been using thus far expects the following format:

```
[
    {
        "role": "user",
        "content": [
            {
                "type": "image_url",
                "image_url": {
                    "url": "https://raw.githubusercontent.com/HandsOnLLM/
                    Hands-On-Large-Language-Models/main/images/book_cover.png"
                },
            },
            {"type": "text", "text": "What's in this image?"},
        ],
    }
]
```

We now have two fields in the content, one for the image and one for the text itself. These will be processed in the chat template of the model. Note that in some cases, the URL needs to be the image itself (in base64) rather than a link to the image. This depends on the inference engine. Some will attempt to convert the image themselves, while others can only process the base64 image.

Note how this example showcases the message's structure that we explored in detail in Chapter 4, where we covered memory. The messages not only function as the memory of the model but also as the way we communicate with it. As such, the place to enable image inputs is in the `Memory` class!

To do so, we need only a very minor change to the `Memory` class, and that is to add the `image_url` to the messages if there is an input image. Everything else can stay exactly the same:

```
from illustrated_agents.chapters.ch4 import Memory


class MultimodalMemory(Memory):
    """Simple memory module to store conversation history."""

    def add(
        self,
        role: str,
        content: str,
        tool_call: dict = None,
        image_data: str = None,
    ):
        """Add a message to memory."""
        # Image
        if image_data:
            is_url = image_data.startswith(("http://", "https://"))
            url = image_data if is_url else f"data:image/png;base64,{image_data}"
            content = [
                {"type": "image_url", "image_url": {"url": url}},
                {"type": "text", "text": content},
            ]

        # Main message
        message = {"role": role, "content": content}

        # Tool call
        if tool_call:
            message["tool_calls"] = [tool_call]

        # Append message to memory
        self.messages.append(message)
```

Note that we added the option to use either a URL or the base64-encoded image. This allows for support for different inference engines.

To give the newly created `MultimodalMemory` the image, we also need to update the `run` function of your `TinyAgent`. We highlighted the code that was updated:

```
from illustrated_agents.chapters import ch6


class TinyAgent(ch6.TinyAgent):
```

```
    def run(self, task: str, image_data: str = None) -> str:
        """Run the agent on a task."""
        self.memory.add("user", task, image_data=image_data)
        self.trajectory.initialize(task)

        # *Autonomy* loop
        for step in range(self.planner.max_steps):
            result = self._step()
            if result is not None:
                return result

        return "Max steps reached without completion."
```

The only changes we made are:

- Add the `image_data` parameter to the `run` function.
- Add the `image_data` parameter to `self.memory.add`.

That is all that's needed to use your model's image-understanding capabilities! Let's try it out with an example. We ask the agent to tell us which animal is on the cover of the *Hands-On Large Language Model* book, but we do not provide it with an image:

```
from illustrated_agents.chapters.ch5 import NativeTools
from illustrated_agents.chapters.ch6 import NativeReAct

# Multi-modal Agent
agent = TinyAgent(
    llm=llm,
    tools=NativeTools(),
    memory=MultimodalMemory(),
    planner=NativeReAct()
)

# Run Agent
agent.run("Which animal is on the cover of 'Hands-On Large Language Models'?")
```

Which gives:

```
"I do not have the ability to view specific commercial book covers or know
which edition you are referring to, as covers can sometimes change!\n\n
If you can provide an image of the book cover, I would be happy to tell you
what animal is featured.\n\nOtherwise, if the cover is highly abstract or
doesn't feature an animal, please let me know!"
```

It doesn't know which animal is on the cover. Now, let's give it the image:

```
import base64
import httpx

# Download and encode the image
image_url = "https://raw.githubusercontent.com/HandsOnLLM/
Hands-On-Large-Language-Models/main/images/book_cover.png"
```

```python
image_data = base64.b64encode(httpx.get(image_url).content).decode("utf-8")

# Run Agent with Image Data
agent.run(
  "Which animal is on the cover of 'Hands-On Large Language Models'?",
  image_data=image_data
)
```

Which gives:

```
"The animal on the cover of 'Hands-On Large Language Models' is a **kangaroo**."
```

That is correct! All that was needed to use its multi-modal capabilities was to process the image in the chat template, which was handled by the inference engine for us.

What We Built

```
TinyAgent/
├── agent.py ← Updated (The Agent processes images)
├── evaluator.py
├── llm.py
├── memory.py ← Updated (Track images in the messages)
├── planning.py
├── toolbox.py
├── tools.py
└── trajectory.py
```

Summary

In this chapter, we explored how LLMs can develop multi-modal understanding. We first covered various techniques for encoding different modalities, with a focus on images (ViT/CLIP), audio (wav2vec 2.0, Whisper, CLAP), and videos (ViViT, TimeSformer, "just CLIP"). These techniques were typically Transformer models, further demonstrating the power of this fundamental technique. We also discovered ImageBind, an encoding technique for processing many different modalities (images, audio, videos, thermal, IMU, depth) at once.

We then explored how these multi-modal encoding techniques could be connected to pre-trained LLMs. With a projection-based connector, the output of the encoding technique was directly projected to the LLM using an MLP. With a query-based connector, the output of the encoding technique was thoroughly processed using a Transformer model combined with an MLP. Lastly, with a fusion-based connector, additional cross-attention blocks were added to the pre-trained LLM that could be trained.

In the next and final chapter, we cover how a specialized type of agent can be created, namely the coding agent.

CHAPTER 10
Code Agents and Code LLMs

Coding agents are some of the most potent types of AI agent in terms of the size of their likely impact. Code generation became one of the earliest applications of LLMs once they hit the scale of GPT-3 in 2020. As we saw in Chapter 3, code generation was also a major component for reasoning problems that reasoning LLMs tackle. Code is a key investment area for LLMs for two reasons. First, an enormous range of knowledge work, from software engineering to research, data analysis, and visualization, can be expressed as code. Second, and more useful for training, code can often be verified automatically: you can run it, or test it, and get a clear signal of whether it worked. That verifiability is what makes coding more tractable than open-ended tasks where there is no objective check.

This chapter walks through that world. We'll meet the people who use and build code agents, see what makes software engineering agents distinct, build one ourselves, and finish with how the underlying code LLMs are trained.

Users and Builders of Code Agents and Large Language Models

Before we get into how code agents are built, it helps to know who they're for, because the people who use and build them have very different needs. Figure 10-1 lays out the cast.

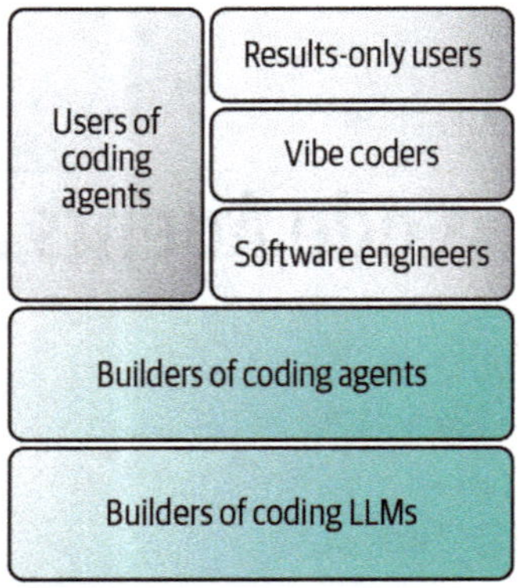

Figure 10-1. The target audience for code agents, ranging from end users to professional software developers and AI researchers

Broadly, there are users and there are builders. Users of coding agents fall into three groups that differ in how closely they work with the code itself: those who just want a non-code output like a chart or an analysis and may never see the code; vibe coders who want working software but build it through natural language and let the agent handle the details; and software engineers who read, review, and direct the agent inside a codebase. Builders are split in two: those who build the agents, assembling the tools, context, and loop around a model, which we will do ourselves later in this chapter, and those who train the coding LLMs that everything else depends on.

People often ask LLMs to generate code. Coding agents take this to a whole new level by having the ability to execute that code, debug any errors it produces, and iterate over multiple steps to solve bigger and bigger problems. The three examples in Figure 10-2 show the evolution from coding generation with LLMs to more advanced code agent use cases.

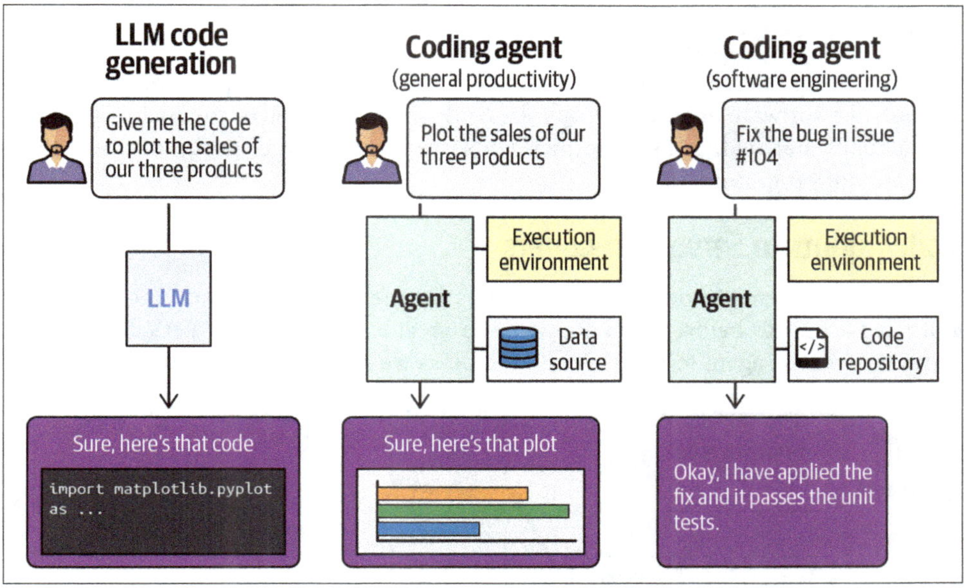

Figure 10-2. Coding agents take LLM capabilities of generating code to the next level and enable solving more complex problems

The first shows a common pattern of asking LLMs, mostly within a playground UI, to write a specific piece of code. The second is more important because the user here doesn't have to be a developer. In this example, the LLM has generated the code, executed it in an execution environment, and then presented the results to the user. Flows like this open up coding agents to a massive audience of users. The third example demonstrates using code agents to help the software development process. Here the agent solves larger tasks that can include tens or even hundreds of steps before that final result is produced. Here it also has to rely on a richer execution environment.

In this chapter, we'll start by looking at how coding agents are built and the tools they rely on. We'll then go into more detail into the LLM that powers such an agent and what makes a model a better fit to power coding agents.

Building Code Agents

The first thing that comes to a lot of readers' minds when they read "code agents" is Cursor-like software engineering agents. And while that's one of the main categories, let's actually start with a use case that can serve a much larger group of users, those who are not programmers.

Code Agents to Serve Non-Coders

Code agents open the door for non-coders to wield powerful code tools they did not have access to before. Data analysis is a great example of this. Let's expand on a request to a code agent to make a certain plot, as we can see in Figure 10-3.

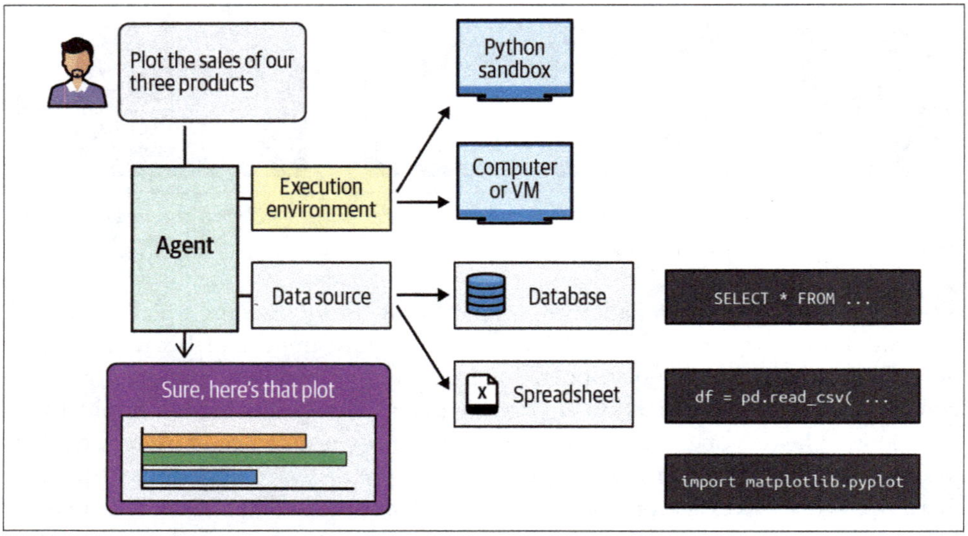

Figure 10-3. An agent generating a plot by writing code to retrieve data and using libraries to render the visual

When we ask the agent to plot a figure, the main behaviors we expect from it are the following:

1. Data retrieval

The agent will need to decide what tool to use to retrieve the data we need to plot. On the simpler side, this can be a web search tool. But this can also require the agent to generate code to retrieve that data:

A) You hand the agent the file (for example, a spreadsheet)

A simple tool to use here is a Python sandbox environment that we pass the exact file to. Here, the agent will need to write code to read and manipulate the data in data manipulation libraries like pandas or polars.

B) The agent has to find the files itself

A more advanced scenario is if the tool is a command line and the agent needs to write the code to find and retrieve the file (or files) first. Tools like this would operate on a virtual machine with access to a filesystem. The code generated here would use command-line tools to search and navigate the filesystem.

C) The data is in a database

In a scenario like this, the agent can be connected to a SQL tool giving it access to one or multiple databases. The agent would need to write the SQL code and send it to the tool to execute to retrieve and transform the required data.

2. *Creating the plot*

   Once the agent has the data it needs, it will need to write the code to plot it, and return the resulting plot.

3. *Troubleshooting*

   We cannot assume that everything will go smoothly. Maybe the data is not available, maybe the query the model wrote contains mistakes or is based on limited information. So, it's important to plan for the different possible failure cases the agent may face. In a lot of cases, if we get an error from the execution environment and send it back to the LLM, it can recover on the next step. This is the ReAct loop from Chapter 6 doing its job: the error is just another observation, and the model reasons about it and tries a corrected action. However, we shouldn't rely on that alone. The more we plan for specific failure cases, the better the end user experience will be.

Notice that in this example the user doesn't necessarily see or interact with any of the code. This is one of the major levers of power for systems like this that dramatically increase the number of people it can be useful for.

Code Tools

Code tools are a pivotal component in how we tie an LLM to a software system. The model decides what it wants to do, and the tool carries that action out against a real environment: running code in a sandbox, executing a shell command, or querying a database. In Figure 10-4, we see another plotting request, but this time we see how specific code tools (a SQL tool and a Python execution tool) tie the LLM to the appropriate environments.

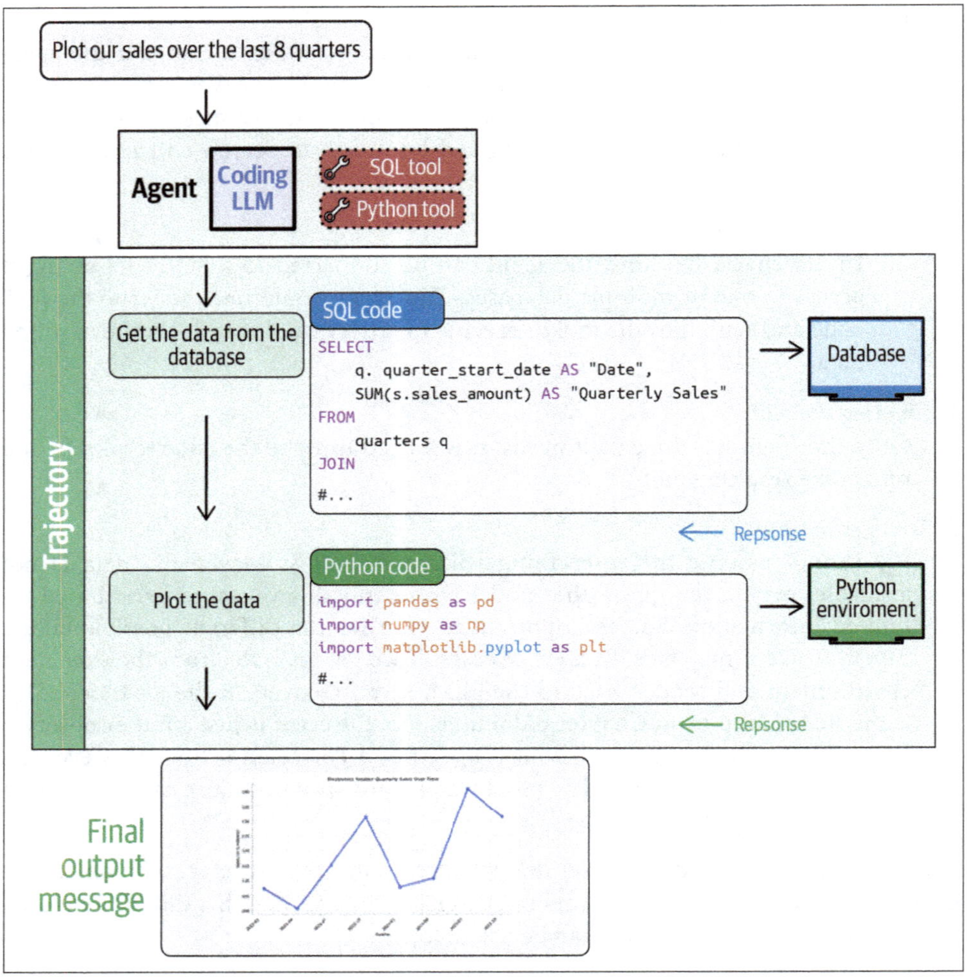

Figure 10-4. A code agent resolving a request via a two-step trajectory, employing distinct tools at each step

Let's look at a few more of the key examples of code tools as these help us understand the design space for possible code agents.

File manipulation tools

Some of the first tasks a code agent needs to handle are reading, searching, and editing files. These can be implemented as distinct tools, each with its own permissions and checks. This enables the agent to find relevant files, edit them, create new files, and navigate through filesystems. These tools are often, but not always, wrappers around command-line tools.

Common file manipulation tools to give code agents include:

- Read entire file (e.g., `cat`).
- Read a section of a file (to better manage model context when dealing with long files) (e.g., `sed`, `head`, `tail`).
- List files in a directory (e.g., `ls`).
- Pattern-match file names that follow a certain pattern (e.g., `glob`).
- Search the contents of files (e.g., `grep`).

Code interpreter sandbox environment

A code interpreter or sandbox is a code execution environment that is a little more restricted than a full virtual machine. These restrictions are important from a security point of view because LLM-generated code is not guaranteed to be safe. An agent could delete important files, corrupt a system, or share private data with external third parties. This can happen either through intended malicious attacks (possibly utilizing prompt injection), or as well-meaning or naive agent actions.

These sandboxes have to be defined with certain limited resources (e.g., in memory, processor, or disk space). They often are ephemeral so that:

1. A fresh environment is created for each user or session. This makes the initial state of the sandbox predictable (e.g., in terms of what packages are available, for example). This also helps ensure the data of user A is separated from the agents of user B.
2. Data is deleted at the end of the session and there's no expectation of data persistence.

For security reasons, these sandboxes are often restricted in terms of which commands can run, and you can decide whether the code running inside has internet access. Every such restriction trades convenience for security: it's tempting to grant broad access so the agent never gets stuck, but each capability you add widens what a mistake or an attack can do. We'll come back to how to navigate that balance when we cover command-line tools and the principle of least privilege.

Code sandboxes have become a part of commercial services from LLM providers and agent providers. You may have already used a tool that utilized a code interpreted on your behalf without you knowing it. Gemini, for example, provides a dedicated code execution tool that can be accessed via its API. At the time of the writing, this can be accessed with a command like we see in the following code example.

You don't need any hosted service to follow this chapter: the `TinyAgent` we build later runs on a local open model and executes code on your own machine:

```
## install in the terminal with:
## pip install google-genai

## requires a Gemini API key from Google AI Studio (free tier, no credit card)
## note: free-tier prompts may be used to improve Google's products,
## so don't send anything sensitive
## set it in your environment, e.g.:
##   export GEMINI_API_KEY="..."

from google import genai
from google.genai import types

# Alternatively, we can pass the API key here. genai.Client(api_key="<api_key>")
client = genai.Client()

system_message = """
You are a personal math tutor. When asked a math question,
write and run code using the code execution tool to answer the question.
"""

prompt = "We sell 5,000 units a month at $29 each, and each unit costs
$14 to make. If we cut the price 10% and that lifts volume 10%, what's the change
in monthly profit?"

# See the latest available models at
https://ai.google.dev/gemini-api/docs/models

resp = client.models.generate_content(
    model="gemini-2.5-flash",
    contents=prompt,
    config=types.GenerateContentConfig(
        system_instruction=system_message,
        tools=[types.Tool(code_execution=types.ToolCodeExecution())],
    ),
)
```

Inspecting the response object shows the model has written the code:

```
# Original Scenario
original_units = 5000
original_price = 29
cost_per_unit = 14

original_revenue = original_units * original_price
original_cost_of_goods = original_units * cost_per_unit
original_profit = original_revenue - original_cost_of_goods

print(f'{original_profit=}')

# New Scenario
```

```
price_cut_percentage = 0.10 # 10%
volume_lift_percentage = 0.10 # 10%

new_price = original_price * (1 - price_cut_percentage)
new_units = original_units * (1 + volume_lift_percentage)

new_revenue = new_units * new_price
new_cost_of_goods = new_units * cost_per_unit
new_profit = new_revenue - new_cost_of_goods

print(f'{new_profit=}')

# Change in Profit
change_in_profit = new_profit - original_profit

print(f'{change_in_profit=}')
```

This leads this execution result to be returned to the model:

```
original_profit=75000
new_profit=66550.0
change_in_profit=-8450.0
```

This gives the model the information it needs, so it then produced the response:

```
[...] Cutting the price 10% and lifting volume 10% would result in
a **decrease of $8,450** in monthly profit.
```

We can see the two steps of executing such a command in Figure 10-5. It starts with the model writing the code that calculates the answer and sending it to the tool for execution. The results of that execution are returned to the model, which can now proceed to the following step: presenting the final output to the user.

What happens in the background here is that OpenAI creates a container to run this code and charges us for it. So executing this trajectory carries LLM inference cost (metered in tokens) and a single container (charged per session).

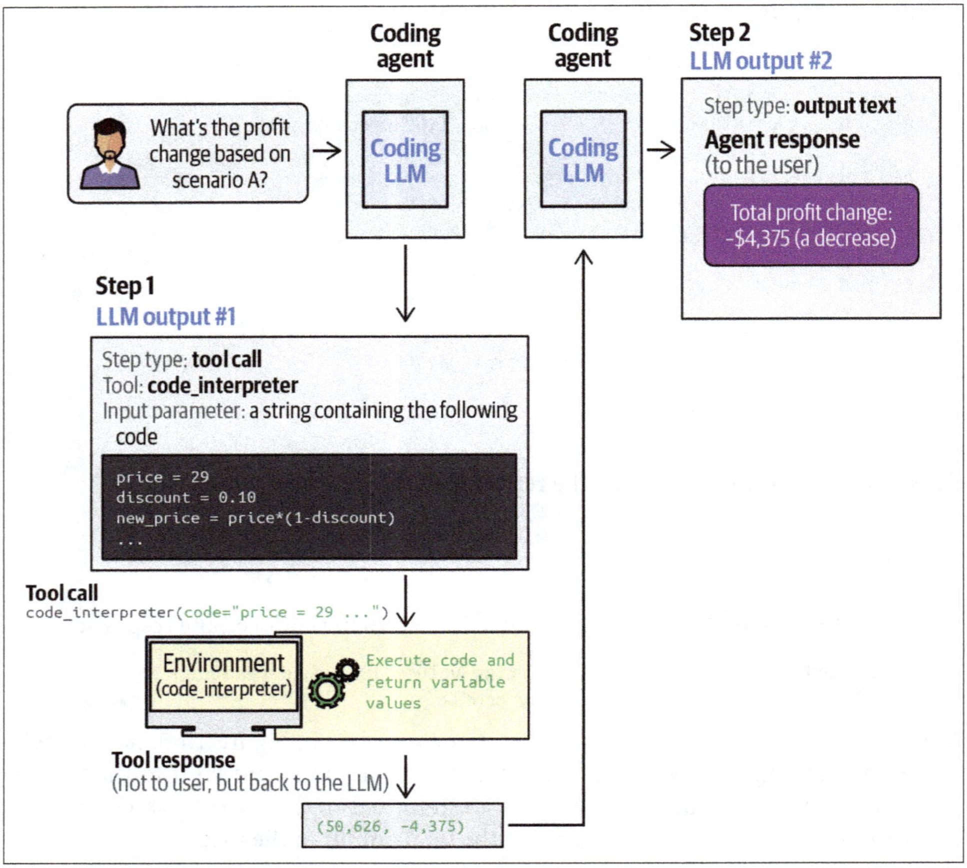

Figure 10-5. The agent-interpreter loop: the LLM writes code, sends it to a code interpreter, and uses the output to determine the next step

There are other options for code execution even if we want to continue using the same model. We can use hosted sandbox services from other commercial providers. Examples include Modal (*https://modal.com*), Daytona (*https://daytona.io*), E2B (*https://e2b.dev*), and Together Code Sandbox (*https://together.ai/sandbox*). These services provide an SDK or API that receives the code our agent wants to execute, and they return the code execution result while hiding the complexity of environment management.

It's also possible to roll our own code interpreter: by using open source tools such as Open Interpreter (*https://oreil.ly/De0U5*) or the E2B repo (*https://github.com/e2b-dev/e2b*), we can configure Python sandboxes that execute the agent's code in an isolated container we control, which is the right level of effort when we have specific security or networking requirements that the hosted services don't meet.

Command-line tools

While code interpreters are restricted for security reasons, the next step up is giving the model more power to access the command line and utilize the powerful tools it has, granting it more control of a computer or dedicated virtual machine. Models need this level of access when they have to inspect or change the environment, for example, to install Python packages that aren't part of the code interpreter image. Software engineering agents such as Cursor or Claude Code also tend to require some command-line access to do their work: configuring environments, running Python scripts and unit tests, and much more.

Needless to say that granting an LLM unfettered access to the command line can become a security nightmare quickly. Recent research highlights just how critical it is to treat the execution environment of coding agents as an adversarial surface rather than a benign and trusted backend. For example, "RedCode: Risky Code Execution and Generation Benchmark for Code Agents" (*https://arxiv.org/abs/2411.07781*) (2024) presents a benchmark of code prompts that probe agents for dangerous behaviors like file deletion, privilege escalation, or network misuse. Another work, "SandboxEval: Towards Securing Test Environment for Untrusted Code" (*https://arxiv.org/abs/2504.00018v1*) (2025), outlines security-relevant properties such as:

1. Exposing system, directory, and metadata information
2. Manipulating structures, contents, and privileges of filesystems
3. Initiating external communication and dangerous operations

More recent work moves from the sandbox to the personal-agent systems became popular in 2026. "Your Agent, Their Asset: A Real-World Safety Analysis of Open-Claw" (*https://arxiv.org/abs/2604.04759*) (2026) runs the first real-world safety evaluation of such an agent and finds that poisoning any single dimension of its persistent state, its capabilities, identity, or knowledge, raises attack success rates from roughly 25% to 64% to 74%, concluding the exposure is inherent in the architecture instead of a fixable bug.

These threats are one reason software agents in IDEs ask the user to approve each command before running it. The developer is the ultimate decision-maker here, bearing the responsibility of permitting actions case by case. That model works when the person approving has the expertise to judge each command, as a developer in an IDE usually does, but it offers little real protection to the non-technical users we met earlier in the chapter, who can't evaluate what a given command will do. Threats could come from a malicious user or from well-intentioned but naive model actions that cause data loss. The safeguard is therefore mostly the agent builder's responsibility, applied at design time: follow the principle of least privilege by granting the agent only the permissions and data access its task requires, and scope the tasks and workflows you assign it so that a wrong action stays contained. This is a choice the builder makes up front, not something the agent decides for itself.

Computer use tools

Computer use tools are analogous to command-line tools that operate on a virtual machine, but they can interact with the UI of the operating system and feed screenshots of the UI to the vision-language model operating the computer as a key source of information. This can be handy for cases when we want the agent to operate applications like Microsoft Excel, for example, or for cases when the agent is building UIs and needs to verify how they are actually rendered in a specific browser at a specific window size (Figure 10-6).

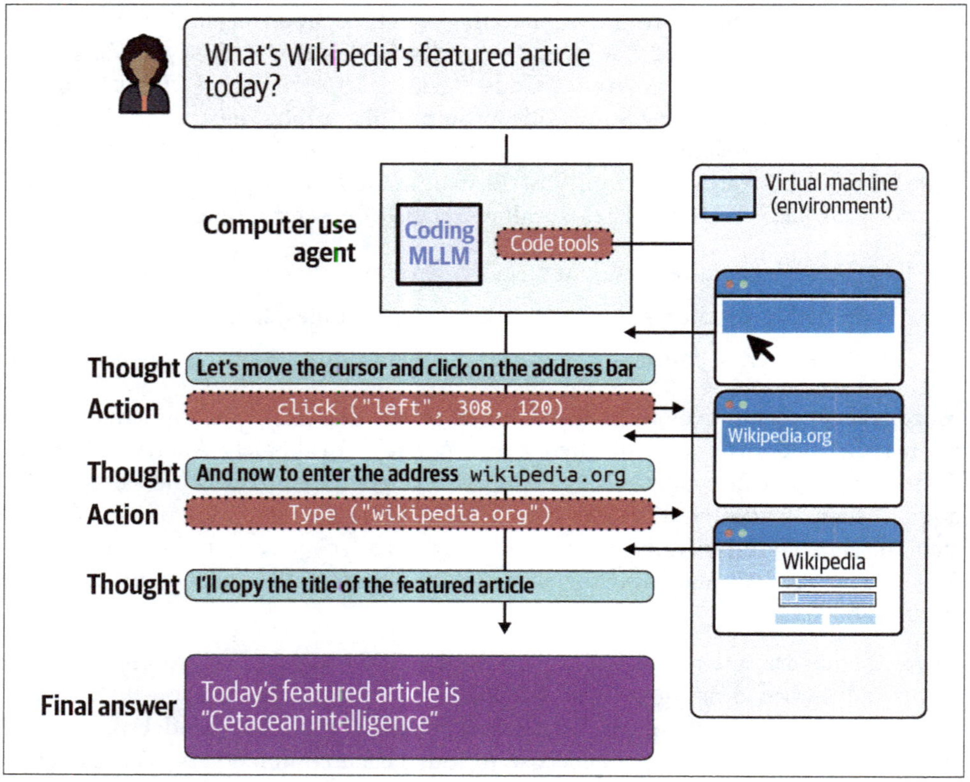

Figure 10-6. A computer use agent interacting directly with a virtual machine's browser to complete tasks

Code search

Advanced software engineering agents can benefit from more powerful code retrieval capabilities. One example here is a tool like `ast-grep` (*https://oreil.ly/k8hY0*), which can do more useful pattern matching on code than a tool like `grep` alone can. Because it operates on the code abstract syntax tree (AST), rather than raw text, it operates on code structure instead of surface representation, allowing it to find patterns while ignoring formatting, variable names, and whitespace.

Code semantic search is another way to give a code agent more powerful retrieval capabilities. By searching using dense embeddings generated by a code-embedding model, a code agent can ask a query such as "Find me a code snippet that iterates over a list" and get back the most relevant candidates. One benchmark of note that measures code retrieval is CoIR (Code Information Retrieval Benchmark),[1] which also maintains a leaderboard (*https://oreil.ly/NvlmD*) comparing the capabilities of various models.

SQL tool

An organization's most important data is often stored within a database, and one of the most useful actions an agent can do is to retrieve the relevant data for a specific task or scenario. While generalist search or web-search tools can retrieve some types of information, databases are queried via SQL code that code LLMs can write. Whether the data resides in a single database or across multiple, a coding agent can leverage the context it has to write exceedingly complex SQL statements to retrieve data even if it requires more than a single query. These flows are crucial for tasks such as data analysis or report generation.

The simplest SQL tool is one that takes a query and executes it on a pre-configured database, as we can see in Figure 10-7.

1 Li, Xiangyang et al. 2024. "CoIR: A Comprehensive Benchmark for Code Information Retrieval Models," *arXiv*, 2407.02883.

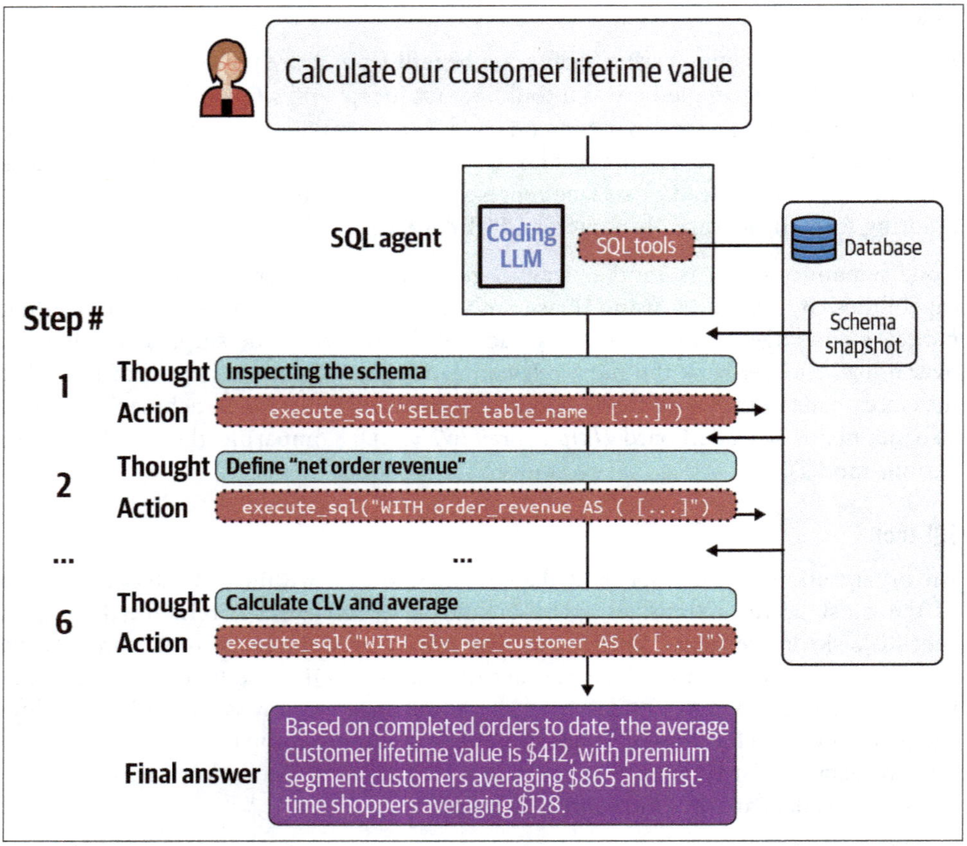

Figure 10-7. A SQL agent executing a multi-step trajectory to inspect database schema and query tables sequentially

Managing the context of a SQL tool is its own area of research that taps into established works of *schema linking* in database research. And while simpler SQL agents can work by providing a general database schema describing the tables and columns in the database, more advanced agents can be empowered by a more advanced *semantic layer* that identifies the relevant columns but might also be able to index some of the relevant data inside the tables and the actual language that users tend to use, which might be different from what's actually stored inside the database.

An example of this is if a user asks of a SQL agent of a fashion ecommerce shop: *show me all outerwear products*. In the database the categories listed include jackets, blazers, and coats, but not explicit "outerwear." Recommended resources to dig deeper into SQL agents include "Large Language Model Enhanced Text-to-SQL Generation: A Survey (*https://arxiv.org/abs/2410.06011*)" (2024), "The Dawn of Natural Language to SQL: Are We Fully Ready? (*https://arxiv.org/abs/2406.01265*)" (2024), and "A Survey on Employing Large Language Models for Text-to-SQL Tasks (*https://arxiv.org/abs/2407.15186*)" (2024). More recently, "Arming Data Agents with Tribal Knowledge (*https://arxiv.org/abs/2602.13521*)" (2026) augments a SQL agent with the institutional knowledge of what columns really mean and how users phrase requests, accumulated from the agent's own query mistakes instead of from a hand-built semantic layer.

Those are the main tools that connect a code agent to its environment. Putting them to work across a long task raises a different challenge: managing everything these tools and steps pour into the model's context.

Context Management

As with other agents, when environments grow, we need to get around the constraints of the LLM context window on the one hand, and the latency and cost of utilizing very long contexts even when they're available.

Context optimization for the LLM cache

Even though the user asks the agent for just one thing, as agent builders we add a great deal more to the context. Alongside the usual system and developer prompts, agent persona, and tool descriptions, a software engineering agent's context often includes a section on desired security behaviors and a description of the repository it's working in. Many early software engineering agents are invoked against a single project, as in an IDE operating on one repository, which is why the repository's structure ends up in the prompt. Much of this context is static and repeats on every call as the agent works through a task over many steps.

That repetition is exactly what makes caching pay off. If we organize the context carefully, we can get dramatic savings in latency and cost, something you'll see called kv-caching, prompt-caching, or prefix-caching. The idea, shown in Figure 10-8, was introduced in Chapter 2.

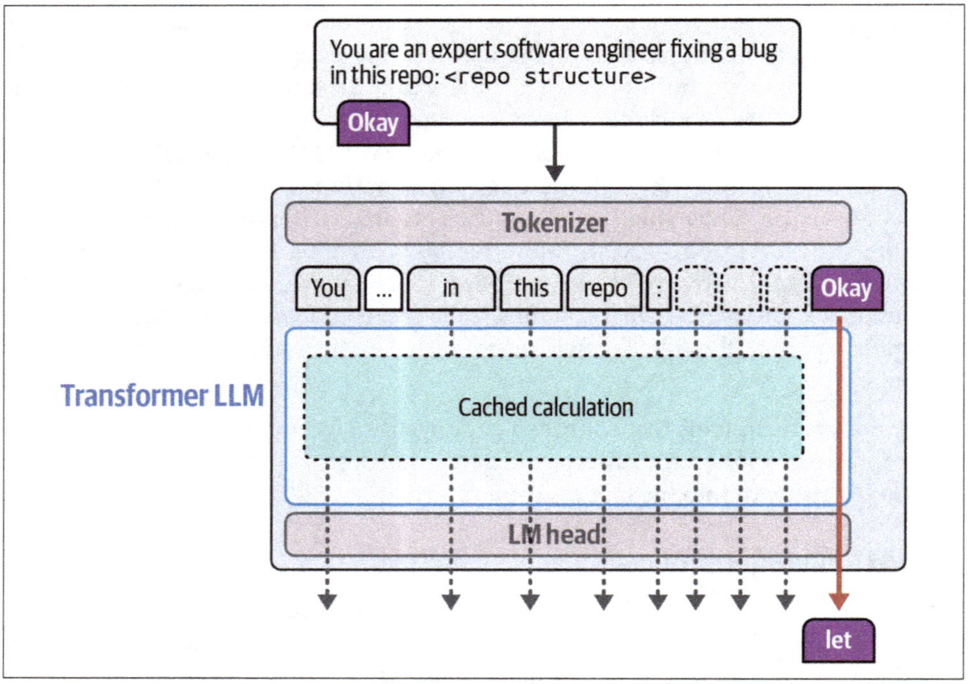

Figure 10-8. Caching lets the model reuse the calculations it has already run over the input prefix instead of recomputing them at each step. Here the large, fixed prefix (the system prompt and repository structure) is cached

As Figure 10-9 shows, even the first call to a software engineering agent can run to tens of thousands of tokens, and parts of it repeat in every subsequent call as the agent works across multiple, sometimes dozens, of steps.

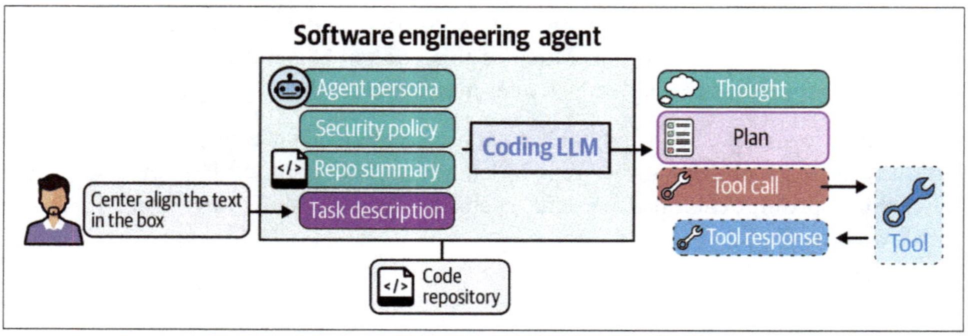

Figure 10-9. The context assembled for a software engineering agent's call

To show it another way, Figure 10-10 shows the same two steps: the LLM call and the tool call, but then the next step would be to continue the agent loop and present the tool response to the LLM again. In this LLM call, instead of processing the entire input again, and paying for these tokens in both latency and token cost, we can reuse the cached calculations from the first step and append to them the new parts of the trajectory.

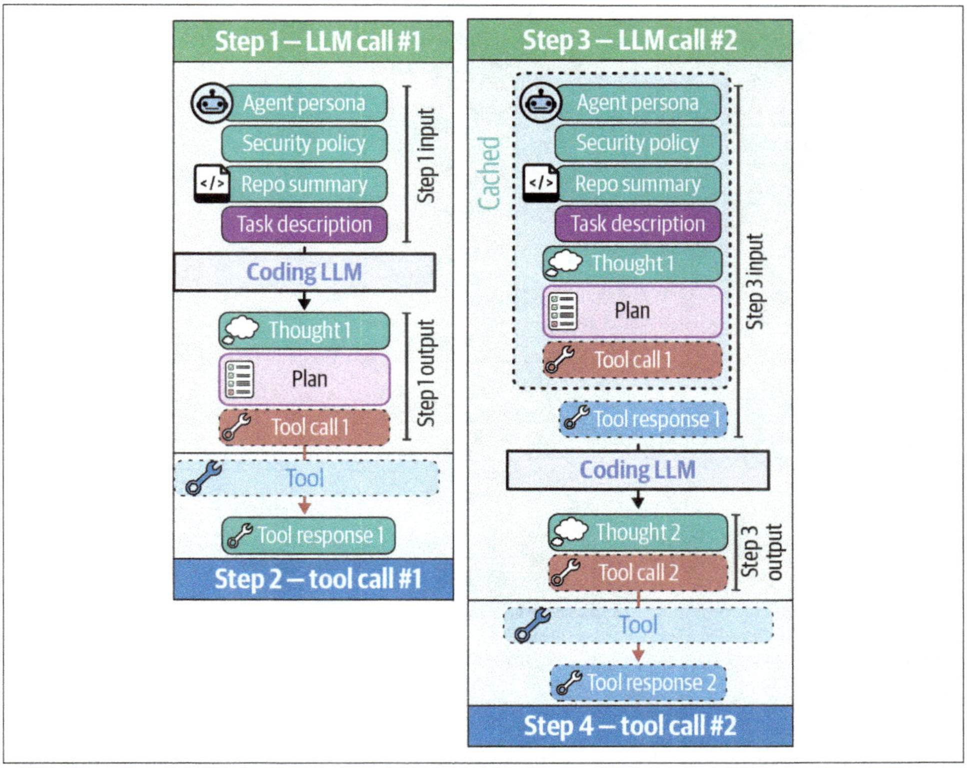

Figure 10-10. The growth of the context cache over an agent's multi-turn loop, where each action and observation is appended to the prompt

Note that for the cache to work, two things need to happen:

- The cached input needs to remain identical—we can't even change a single token in existing methods.
- All the new input needs to be appended to the end of the cached input.

Could you guess which parts we would now cache for the next LLM call? We see that in Figure 10-11.

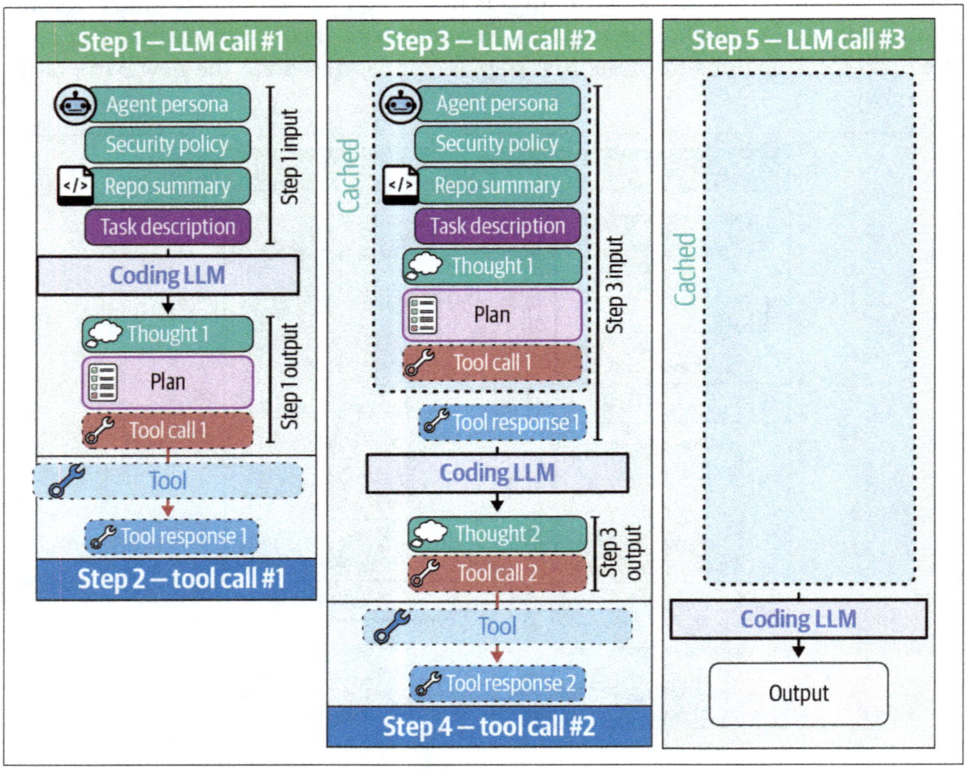

Figure 10-11. Serving the entire accumulated context from cache to optimize latency and cost

If you guessed the entire input of step 2, then you're correct. By the third LLM call (step 5), the entire context accumulated over the earlier steps is served from cache as a single block, and only the new output is computed. Letting the cache grow to cover the whole prior trajectory is what maximizes the cache hit rate.

This type of cache management is one of the key design constraints of agents in general, and code agents in particular.[2] Ideally, the cache continues to grow with the trajectory to maximize the cache hit rate and minimize cost and latency.

2 Ji, Yichao. “Peak.” 2025. “Context Engineering for AI Agents: Lessons from Building Manus” Blog post, *https://oreil.ly/fbw-y*.

The repository map

As we saw in "Context Management," representing the structure of a repository is essential context for plenty of software engineering agents. Key components of a repository map are file and directory structure at some level of resolution and some additional information about all or a selection of relevant files.

One popular tool to generate a repository map is Gitingest (*https://oreil.ly/vtUQ-*), which can take the URL of a GitHub repo and generate a repo map that includes the directory list as well as the contents of short files.

In a blog post (*https://oreil.ly/1Byf_*), the creators of Aider, one of the early command-line code agents and a clear precursor to tools like Claude Code, describe a more thoughtful approach to generating file summaries, which relies on the abstract syntax tree to identify important parts like class and function signatures, and using these as summaries of the files. They additionally employ a follow-up step of ranking and filtering for only the most relevant definitions that are used the most in other parts of the repository.

Figure 10-12 shows an example repo summary listing both the files and some file descriptions in the style of Aider's repo map.

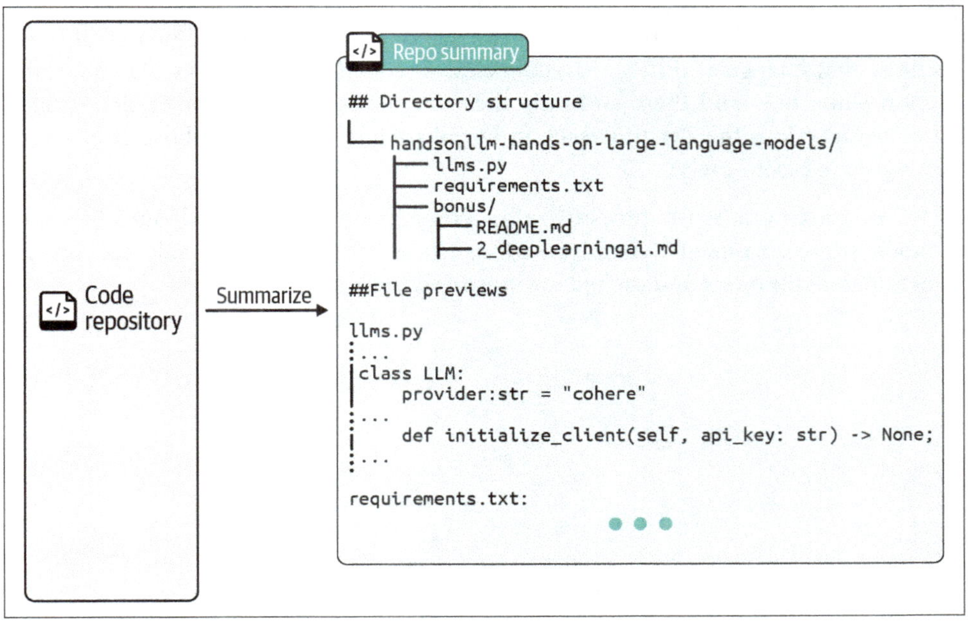

Figure 10-12. In the style of Aider's map, this summarized repository (a repo map) captures the directory structure along with previews of the most relevant files

One final repo description method that's relevant to know, especially when we can expend additional LLM calls for a certain task, is to use an LLM to summarize key or relevant files. You can see such an example employed in the paper "CodeMonkeys: Scaling Test-Time Compute for Software Engineering."[3] Their efficiency comes from amortization: because the system already samples many candidate solutions per issue, it can afford to have an LLM read every file in the repository to find the relevant ones, spreading that one-time cost across all the downstream samples so it accounts for only about 15% of the total budget. The identified files are then ranked and trimmed to fit the context used in later steps.

Context compaction

In Chapter 4, we saw how summarizing the context of a long conversation is one form of short-term memory that allows us to shrink the context to continue a conversation. In different specialized agents, the information that is required in that summary often needs to be optimized for that domain. For code agents, that may include information on the environment, code style preferences, preferences for when and how to run tests and when to commit the repository to source control.

Viewed together with what we've covered in cache optimization, we may find a pattern where we can keep different sections of the trajectory more static to optimize the cache hit rate. In Figure 10-13, we can see one example breakdown of different sections that change at different frequencies. The static section stays put, the stable section shifts now and then, and only the dynamic section turns over step to step. After compaction, the dynamic section shrinks while everything above it can keep getting served from cache.

If we organize our work properly, after compaction we can find ourselves with a much more shrunken dynamic section, while the static and stable section can generally remain intact and cached for more and more steps.

3 Ehrlich, Ryan et al. 2025. "CodeMonkeys: Scaling Test-Time Compute for Software Engineering," *arXiv*, 2501.14723.

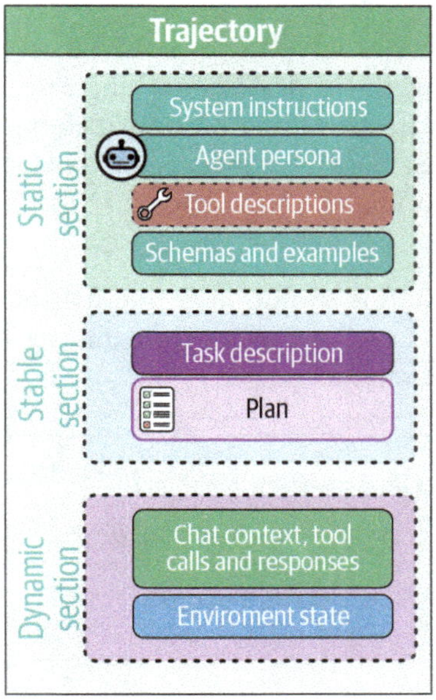

Figure 10-13. Dividing a trajectory into static, slow-changing, and fast-changing sections to maximize caching efficiency

Code Agents for Software Engineering

When the end user is a software engineer, code agents take on a completely different nature. For most developers now, their first encounter with a code agent is inside their IDE or code editor. These tools started by surfacing LLM code generation features such as autocompletion, which can be handy in writing documentation or writing a first draft of a function if we write the function signature first. Eventually, agents started offering the capability to solve more complex problems that would require editing code in multiple places to solve more challenging problems than what autocomplete can do on its own.

The first generations of agents needed to be guided closely because this task took on a different nature that's not as well represented in their training data. Early systems compensated with heavy external scaffolding. The original SWE-agent, for instance, introduced a purpose-built Agent-Computer Interface, a constrained set of commands designed to make a repository navigable for a model that couldn't reliably do it on its own. Newer agents rely far less on this kind of handholding because the models powering them are now trained directly on tool use, multi-step trajectories, and software engineering tasks, as we'll see later in this chapter.

Going from writing function-level code to creating or making changes to entire repositories requires a different set of skills, even if it's all about writing code in the end. A code agent needs software engineering skills, which include skills like environment management, unit testing, debugging and troubleshooting, and the ability to reproduce bugs and investigate what causes them, which entails reading enough of the right places of the repository to understand the intention and flow of the program.

Figure 10-14 shows this evolution in the nature and scope of code problems from solving individual LeetCode-style problems to software engineering problems, as we'll see in the next section.

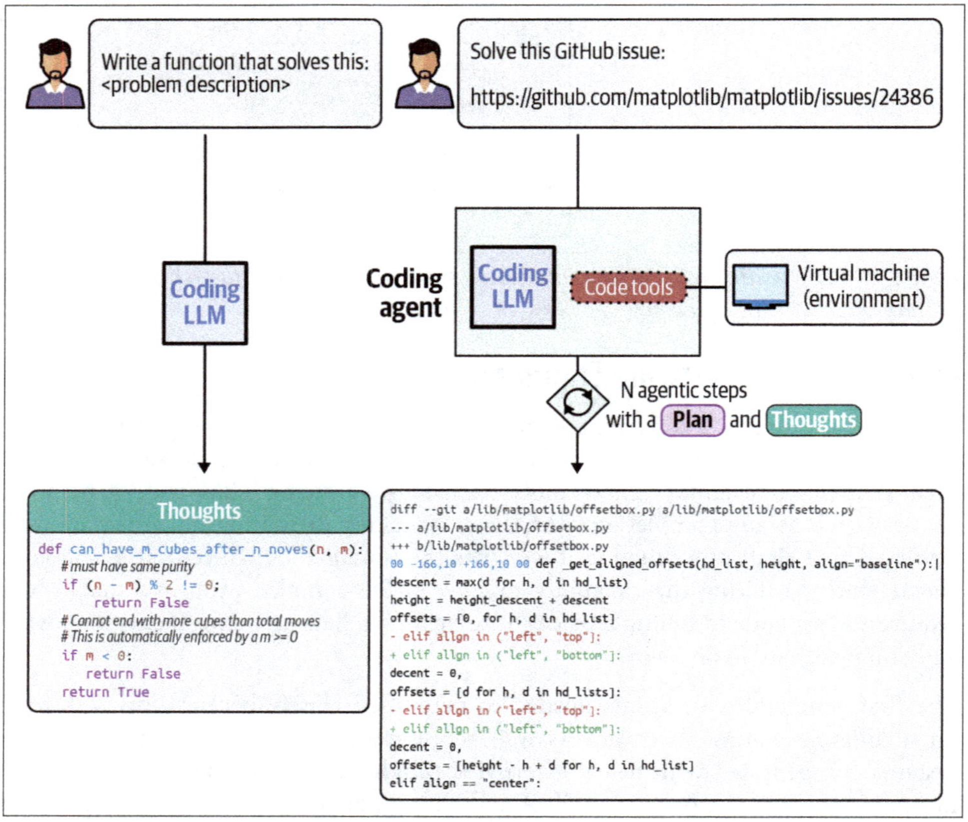

Figure 10-14. The shift from writing isolated functions to full-scale software engineering tasks requiring plan-and-code cycles

SWE-bench: code problems at the level of a GitHub issue

The SWE-bench benchmark was the first widely adopted code agent benchmark.[4] It is a collection of hundreds of software engineering issues collected from open source repositories and actual issues reported by users. In each example, a single GitHub issue is presented to the code agent alongside a snapshot of the repository at a specific point in time. The model then has to resolve that issue in a way that passes a set of test suites that verify the correctness of the fix.

SWE-bench caught on because it measures something real: the issues come from actual open source projects, and each one ships with the repository's own test suite, so a fix can be graded objectively by running the tests rather than judged subjectively. That verifiability, the same property that makes code a tractable target for LLMs in the first place, together with the fact that early systems solved only a small fraction of the issues and so left plenty of headroom, is what turned it into the number labs compete on.

Planning for software engineering agents

Because agents tackle larger scale problems that often require multiple steps, the planning step emerged as a key component of these systems. A coding agent often has to not only write a detailed plan with concrete steps but also keep returning to the plan and updating its status or even the entire plan as it learns more about the task. The UIs for code agents started showing plans and to-do-list items as distinct elements so the user keeps track of them (Figure 10-15).

4 Jimenez, Carlos E. et al. 2023. "SWE-bench: Can Language Models Resolve Real-World GitHub Issues?" (*https://oreil.ly/35iN-*) *arXiv*, 2310.06770.

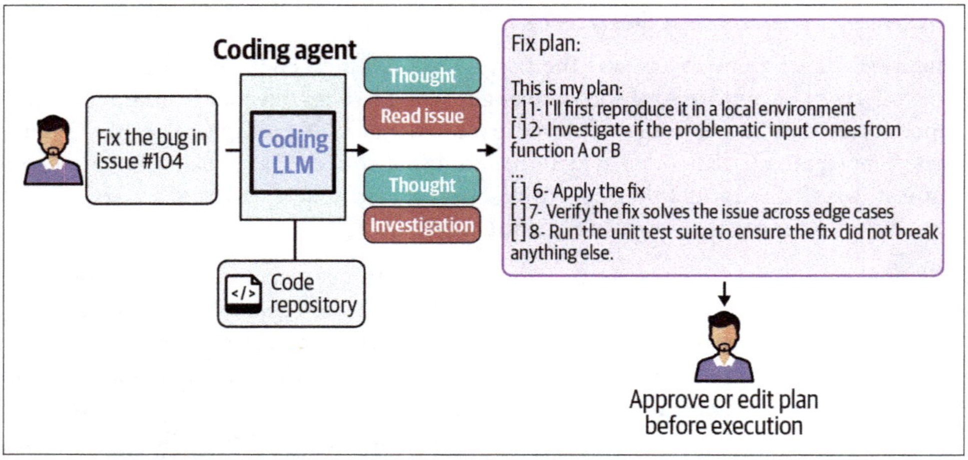

Figure 10-15. A coding agent analyzing a bug report to generate a reviewable codebase modification plan

Writing a plan and then executing each part of it seems like two different tasks that can be handled by two different prompts, or even different agents. So some agentic code systems would assign the planning step to a dedicated planning agent and then some or all steps to dedicated code agents to tackle the appropriate steps. But even in a single-agent system, the plan is one of the most important components of resolving the task. With that importance, it's often a good idea to assign it to the best available model and to have it think on it for a reasonable amount of time for the task.

When designing a planning prompt or agent, we have to bear in mind that some tasks require a bit of investigation to know exactly how to solve the task. This is especially the case for software tasks, which often require exploration and research phases or asking the user for clarification or more information. So, it's important to not assume that the approach to solving a problem is crystal clear at planning time. The plan likely needs to include exploration and investigation steps and have some flexibility based on the findings from these steps.

Task-Specific Workflows

There are often scenarios in which a problem is simpler to tackle with a static workflow than with an agent. A static workflow runs through a fixed set of steps you lay out in advance, rather than letting the model decide what to do at each turn. Plenty of routine tasks are simple enough that reaching for an agent is overkill. A proficient agent developer keeps other tools within reach and picks the one that fits the problem, rather than shoehorning an agent into every job.

Agentless

For software engineering tasks, the agentless approach stands out for its simplicity and ability to compete with agentic approaches via a simple three-phase process,[5] as shown in Figure 10-16.

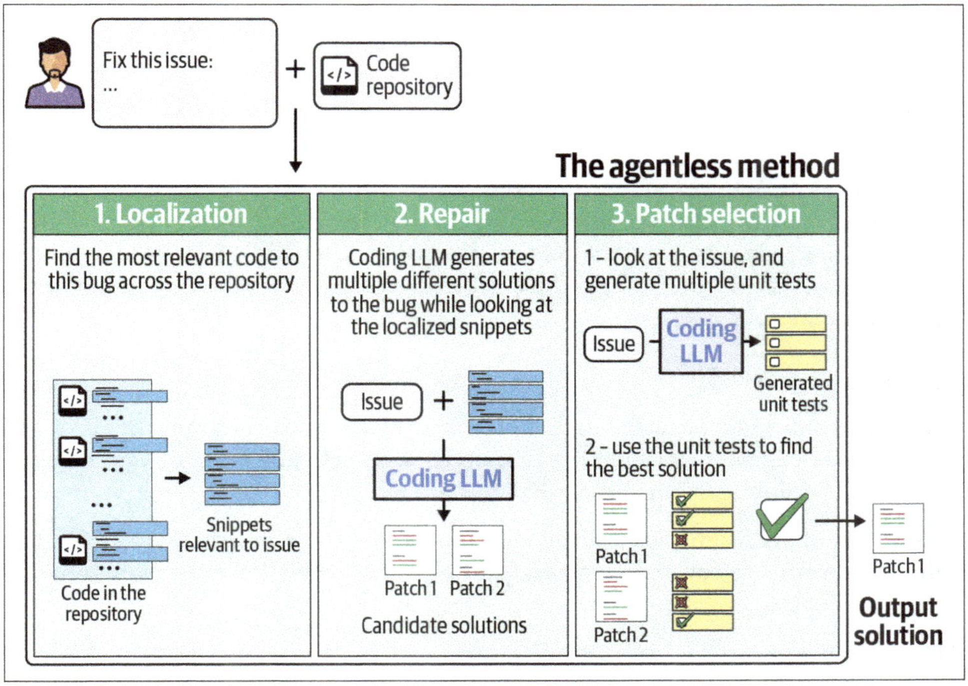

Figure 10-16. Agentless resolves an issue in three fixed phases: localize the relevant code, generate several candidate patches, then pick the best using generated unit tests

In a way, the agentless approach works much like a Retrieval-Augmented Generation (RAG) system. It starts with a search step, finding all the code snippets in the repository that are relevant to the issue we want to fix. This is localization. It then hands those snippets and the issue to a coding LLM that generates a candidate solution. This is repair.

The method improves the chances of resolving the bug by sampling multiple solutions from the LLM, so it has multiple attempts to solve the issue.

5 Xia, Chunqiu Steven et al. 2024. "Agentless: Demystifying LLM-based Software Engineering Agents," *arXiv*, 2407.01489.

But then how do we select the best solution candidate? Another powerful idea here is that coding LLMs can also be great at generating unit tests. So, we can present the issue to the LLM and ask it to generate a suite of unit tests to validate solutions for this bug.

These generated unit tests can then be used to rank and choose the best solutions. Because the unit tests are themselves generated, and we're not fully confident in their quality, the selected solution does not need to pass all of them. It just needs to pass more than the other candidates do.

We do want to re-highlight these two ideas because they share an advanced concept around using LLMs: we can use the probabilistic nature of LLMs to our advantage. One way is by sampling multiple possible solutions (at temperature values that allow some reasonable variety), and the second is by using generated unit tests as a ranking signal and not a pass/fail signal. These are powerful ideas that belong to the agent builder's toolkit.

TinyAgent with code tools

We've now walked through the tools a code agent uses, how it manages context, and how software engineering agents approach real tasks. Let's pull those threads together and build a coding agent ourselves.

A core part of the coding agent is the tools it uses, and these are what tie an LLM to a software system. We covered several categories, but arguably the most common ones are:

File manipulation tools
: This lets the agent read, list, and write files.

Code interpreter
: This lets the agent execute code it writes.

To give your `TinyAgent` coding capabilities, let's create several tools that span these two categories:

```
import subprocess
import sys

from pathlib import Path


def read_file(path: str) -> str:
    """Read a file's contents."""
    target = Path(path)
    if not target.exists():
        return f"Error: '{path}' not found."
    return target.read_text(encoding="utf-8")
```

```python
def list_files(directory: str = ".") -> str:
    """List files in a directory."""
    target = Path(directory)
    if not target.is_dir():
        return f"Error: '{directory}' is not a directory."
    entries = sorted(target.iterdir())
    lines = [f"{p.name}/" if p.is_dir() else p.name for p in entries]
    return "\n".join(lines) or "(empty)"


def write_file(path: str, content: str) -> str:
    """Write content to a file."""
    target = Path(path)
    target.parent.mkdir(parents=True, exist_ok=True)
    target.write_text(content, encoding="utf-8")
    return f"Written to '{path}'."


def execute_python(code: str) -> str:
    """Execute Python code and return output."""
    try:
        result = subprocess.run(
            [sys.executable, "-c", code],
            capture_output=True,
            text=True,
            timeout=30,
        )
    except subprocess.TimeoutExpired:
        return "Error: Code execution timed out (30s limit)."

    if result.returncode != 0:
        return (
            f"Exit code {result.returncode}\n"
            f"STDOUT:\n{result.stdout}\n"
            f"STDERR:\n{result.stderr}"
        ).strip()
    return result.stdout.strip() or "(no output)"
```

As we saw in Chapter 5, these tools all return a string whether they succeed or not. This output can then be used in the messages structure as an observation to indicate whether the tool call succeeded.

Some of the tools, such as `execute_python` and `write_file`, are not safe by default. If we were to give your `TinyAgent` complete freedom, it might corrupt files or take dangerous actions. Instead, we'll use the `requires_approval` parameter that we explored in Chapter 5.

Before execution, you'll be asked to reply with "Y" (yes) or "N" (no), so you can inspect whether you believe the action is safe:

```
from illustrated_agents.chapters.ch5 import NativeTools

# Some tools require approval
tools = NativeTools(requires_approval=["write_file", "execute_python"])
tools.add_tool("read_file", read_file)
tools.add_tool("list_files", list_files)
tools.add_tool("write_file", write_file)
tools.add_tool("execute_python", execute_python)
```

With capabilities to write and execute code, this is already sufficient to turn your `TinyAgent` into a basic coding agent! It can now be run with `agent.run` as we did before to execute certain tasks.

This, however, is not an ideal interface. As we discussed previously, more advanced interfaces like Cursor and agents that live in the terminal are common among coding solutions. As such, let's implement an interface ourselves such that your `TinyAgent` can be used anywhere in the terminal.

The first thing we'll have to do is create a `Display` class. This class will be used in your `TinyAgent` to display what the agent is doing at any given moment. We separate the steps in the ReAct loop as we have done before (with the color coding you're familiar with):

THOUGHT
: The reasoning of the agent

ACTION
: The tool the agent wants to use

OBSERVATION
: The output of the tool use

ANSWER
: The final answer of the agent

The `Display` class uses ANSI escape codes (e.g., `"\033[35m"`) to color the output. Assigning a distinct color to each phase of the ReAct loop makes the agent's reasoning, tool executions, and final answers easily readable and scannable at a glance:

```
from illustrated_agents.chapters.ch2 import Response

BOLD = "\033[1m"
RESET = "\033[0m"
GREEN = "\033[32m"    # THOUGHT
RED = "\033[31m"      # ACTION
YELLOW = "\033[33m"   # OBSERVATION
PURPLE = "\033[35m"   # ANSWER
```

```
class Display:
    """Chat interface with styling."""

    def __call__(self, event: str, data: str | Response = None) -> None:

        # "Thinking" line
        if event == "thinking":
            print(f"  Thinking...\n{RESET}")

        # THOUGHT
        elif event == "response":
            print(f"{BOLD}{GREEN}{'▒ THOUGHT ▒':<13}{RESET}")
            print(f"{data.reasoning}{RESET}\n")

            # ANSWER
            if data.content:
                print(f"{BOLD}{PURPLE}{'▒ ANSWER ▒':<13}{RESET}")
                print(f"{data.content}{RESET}\n")

        # ACTION
        elif event == "tool_call" and data:
            tool = data.tool_call["tool"]
            kwargs = data.tool_call["kwargs"]
            print(f"{BOLD}{RED}{'▒ ACTION ▒':<13}{RESET}")
            print(f"{tool}({kwargs}){RESET}\n")

        # OBSERVATION
        elif event == "observation":
            print(f"{BOLD}{YELLOW}{'▒ OBSERVATION ▒':<13}{RESET}")
            print(f"{data}{RESET}\n")
            print(f"{'-' * 40}STEP{'-' * 40}{RESET}\n")
```

Let's try out the display by using a Response object to mimic the output of the agent:

```
# Let's create a Response with a tool call and no final answer
response = Response(
    content="I executed Python.",
    reasoning="Let's execute some python!",
    tool_call= {
        "tool": "execute_python",
        "kwargs": {"code": "print('Hello World!')"}
    }
)


# Display the Response
display = Display()
display("thinking", response)
display("response", response)
display("tool_call", response)
display("observation", "Hello World!")
```

Which gives:

```
Thinking...

▒▒ THOUGHT ▒▒
Let's execute some python!

▒▒ ACTION ▒▒
execute_python({'code': "print('Hello World!')"})

▒▒ OBSERVATION ▒▒
Hello World!

▒▒ ANSWER ▒▒
I executed Python.
```

Note how each step is nicely styled to clearly make a distinction between the cycles of THOUGHT/ACTION/OBSERVATION. The color coding was chosen to be in line with all the visuals we explored throughout the previous chapters.

The `Display` now needs to be integrated into your `TinyAgent`. This is, fortunately, straightforward because we need to add only `self.display(...)` where we want to track a certain behavior. As in previous chapters, we highlight the code that was added:

```
from illustrated_agents.chapters.ch2 import Response, Trajectory
from illustrated_agents.chapters.ch4 import Memory
from illustrated_agents.chapters.ch5 import Tools
from illustrated_agents.chapters.ch6 import ReAct


class TinyAgent:
    """A minimal, modular, and educational agent framework."""

    def __init__(
        self,
        llm: LLM,
        memory: Memory,
        tools: Tools,
        planner: ReAct,
        display: Display,
    ):
        self.llm = llm
        self.memory = memory
        self.tools = tools
        self.planner = planner
        self.display = display

        self.trajectory = Trajectory()

        # Build system prompt with all components
        system_prompt = "You are a helpful assistant.\n\n"
        system_prompt += self.planner.prompt
```

```
        system_prompt += self.tools.prompt
        self.memory.add("system", system_prompt)

    def run(self, task: str, image_data: str = None) -> str:
        """Run the agent on a task."""
        self.memory.add("user", task, image_data=image_data)
        self.trajectory.initialize(task)

        # *Autonomy* loop
        for step in range(self.planner.max_steps):
            result = self._step()
            if result is not None:
                return result

        return "Max steps reached without completion."

    def _step(self) -> str | None:
        """Perform a single step."""
        # THOUGHT: Generate response and add to memory
        self.display("thinking")
        response = self.llm.generate(
            self.memory.get_messages(), tools=self.tools.schemas
        )
        self.memory.add(
            "assistant", response.content, tool_call=response.tool_call
        )
        self.display("response", response)

        # Tool parsing
        response = self.planner.parse(response)
        response = self.tools.parse(response)

        # ANSWER: Stopping mechanism
        if self.tools.is_done(response):
            self.trajectory.add(response)
            return response.content

        return self._execute_action(response)

    def _execute_action(self, response: Response) -> None:
        """Execute a tool action."""

        # ACTION: execute tools
        self.display("tool_call", response)
        result = self.tools.execute(response)

        # OBSERVATION: add tool results to memory and display
        role, observation = self.tools.observation(result)
        self.memory.add(role, observation)
        self.trajectory.add(response, observation)
        self.display("observation", observation)
```

```
        return None
```

To initialize the coding agent, we can add the display parameter like so:

```
from illustrated_agents.chapters.ch2 import LLM
from illustrated_agents.chapters.ch6 import NativeReAct

# Gemma 4 E4B (with native thinking and tool calling)
llm = LLM(model="gemma4:e4b", think=True)

# Coding Agent
agent = TinyAgent(
    llm=llm,
    tools=tools,
    memory=Memory(),
    planner=NativeReAct(),
    display=display
)
```

Before we start running the `TinyAgent`, let's create a small function so that we can run this coding agent in the terminal. Note that we add a bit of styling to make for a nicer interface:

```
NAME = """
```

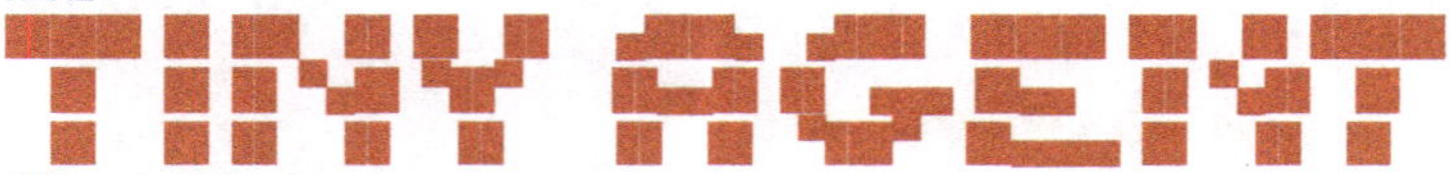

```
"""  # ANSI Compact

def main():
  import shutil

  print(f"\n{NAME}\n")

  while True:
      try:
          query = input().strip()
          print("\033[0m")
      except (KeyboardInterrupt, EOFError):
          print("\033[0m", end="")
          break
      if not query or query.lower() in ("exit", "quit"):
          break
      try:
          agent.run(query)
      except Exception as e:
          print(f"ERROR: {e}\n")


if __name__ == "__main__":
  main()
```

All code we have created thus far lives in the illustrated-agents package (*https://github.com/HandsOnLLM/An-Illustrated-Guide-To-AI-Agents*), and because it's pure Python, you can run your coding agent like so:

```
python .\src\illustrated_agents\chapters\ch10.py
```

Running this will give you a nice interface to work with, as shown in Figure 10-17.

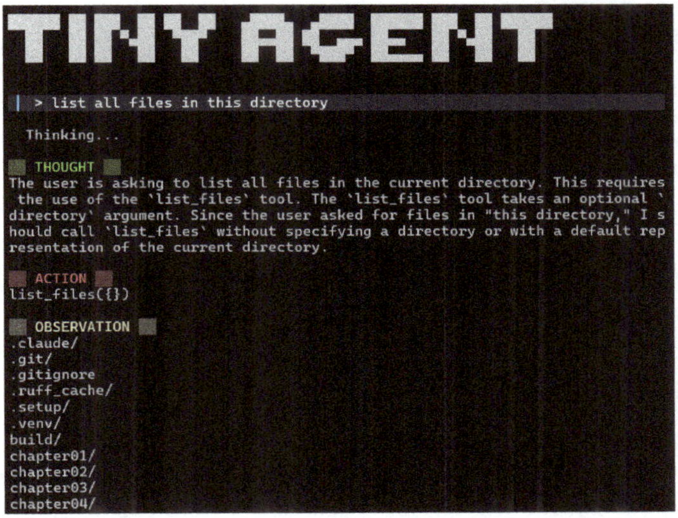

Figure 10-17. Running `TinyAgent` surfaces each step of its reasoning loop, showing the THOUGHT, ACTION, and OBSERVATION for a task as it lists the files in the current directory

As you can see, when you give it a task, the separation between THOUGHT/ACTION/OBSERVATION will be shown. This will give you an intuitive understanding of what's under the hood. Try it out and see where your `TinyAgent` shines and where it needs improvement. Likewise, the LLM makes a large difference. If the small 4-billion-parameter model doesn't suit your needs, try a larger one, or a model trained specifically for this kind of work. North Mini Code (*https://oreil.ly/tcES8*),[6] for example, is an open mixture-of-experts model from Cohere built for agentic coding: 30 billion parameters total but only 3 billion active per token, released under Apache 2.0. It asks more of your hardware than Gemma, but it's purpose-built for the code-focused, multi-step, tool-using work your `TinyAgent` is now doing.

Congratulations! 🎉 You have created a coding agent in the CLI entirely from scratch and in pure Python!

6 Coauthor Jay was a member of the core team that built North Mini Code.

What We Built

```
TinyAgent/
├── agent.py ← Updated (Add the Display to your TinyAgent)
├── cli.py  ← New (Use the new TinyAgent with Display in the CLI)
├── display.py  ← New (Added a Display to visualize ReAct loops)
├── evaluator.py
├── llm.py
├── memory.py
├── planning.py
├── toolbox.py ← Updated (Added various coding tools)
├── tools.py
└── trajectory.py
```

As you experiment, you'll find the biggest lever on your agent's behavior is the model behind it. That's where we turn next: what it takes to train an LLM capable of powering a coding agent.

Building Code LLMs

The quality of a coding agent is limited, in large part, by the quality of the model powering it. Not only must the model exhibit high performance on writing code, but it should also be skilled at tool use and agentic software engineering tasks for it to be capable of powering a coding agent. In this section, we'll provide an overview on how coding LLMs are created according to model training recipes up until the time of writing (Figure 10-18).

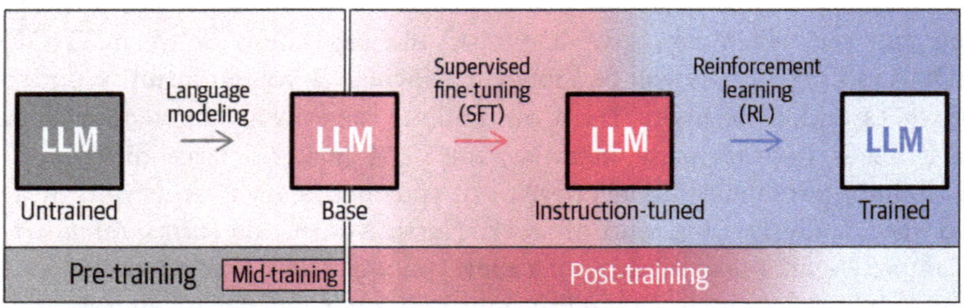

Figure 10-18. The training stages of a coding agent: language modeling, supervised fine-tuning, and reinforcement learning

The main areas to note when compared to a generalist LLM are:

The data

Data composition: These models have to see a lot more code data in the various training stages. Qwen3 Coder, for example, is pre-trained on 7.5 trillion tokens, 70% of which is code (*https://oreil.ly/bumfq*).

Coding task data: To better serve as engines that power coding agents, coding LLMs need to be trained on data that looks like what the model will see when it's in use, which includes:

Tool-use data

Trajectories where the model calls a tool and uses the result, like running `grep` to locate a function and then acting on what it finds

Multi-step data

Tasks that play out over several turns, like reproducing a bug, editing a file, running the tests, reading the failure, and patching again

Unit-test data

Code paired with the tests that verify it, like a function alongside the pytest cases that exercise it

Software engineering tasks

Repository-level issues and the changes that resolve them, like a GitHub issue paired with the diff that closes it.

Reinforcement learning

Now a major component of the training flow. Where in the past Reinforcement Learning from Human Feedback (RLHF) had been useful to polish the behavior of a model, coding LLMs are trained with large-scale Reinforcement Learning with Verifiable Rewards (RLVR) as we covered in Chapter 2.

Some of the types of coding data are shown in Figure 10-19.

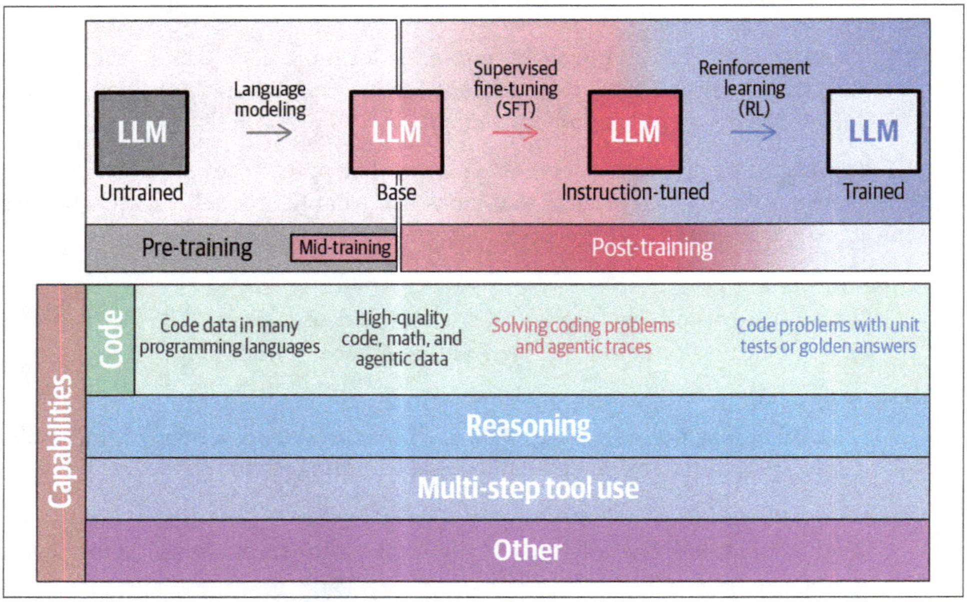

Figure 10-19. The specific types of code-related datasets used during each stage of training a coding agent

While coding data is important, other capabilities are just as important for an LLM to successfully empower a coding agent. These include reasoning, multi-step tool calling, long-context, and planning, as well as trajectories that demonstrate proper software engineering practices (how to reproduce issues, how to use coding tools and common libraries…etc.).

For a sense of how much data each stage demands, open source model GLM-5's pipeline (*https://z.ai/blog/glm-5*) is a useful current example (Figure 10-20): pre-training on the order of 28 trillion tokens, mid-training that extends context out to 200K with long code and agent data, SFT, and then RL split into reasoning, agentic, and general stages before a final distillation step.

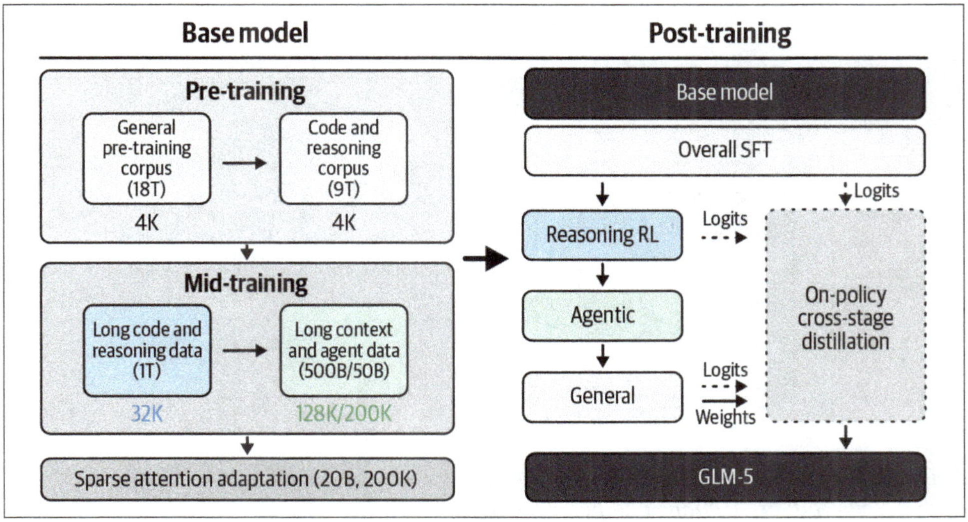

Figure 10-20. In GLM-5's full training pipeline, the token counts and context lengths at each stage give a sense of how much data building a competitive frontier model takes[7]

Bootstrapping Intelligence: The Synthetic Data Feedback Loop

A key inflection point that many outside the research industry may not know is that around 2024, LLMs became a major source of the training data for the next generation of LLMs. You start to see that more clearly with a lot of the Llama 3.1 (*https://oreil.ly/JNNJt*) post-training data actually having been generated with Llama 3 (*https://oreil.ly/5lkF1*). This repeats itself with math and code; Qwen2.5-Math and Qwen2.5-Coder were both essential in creating training data for Qwen3 (*https://arxiv.org/abs/2505.09388*) and Qwen3-Coder (*https://oreil.ly/dXFkc*). And as we saw in Chapter 3 with DeepSeek-R1 (*https://oreil.ly/kBpH3*), a lot of long chains of priceless reasoning traces were generated by DeepSeek-R1-Zero (Figure 10-21).

7 Source: GLM-5 technical report (Zhipu AI et al. 2026).

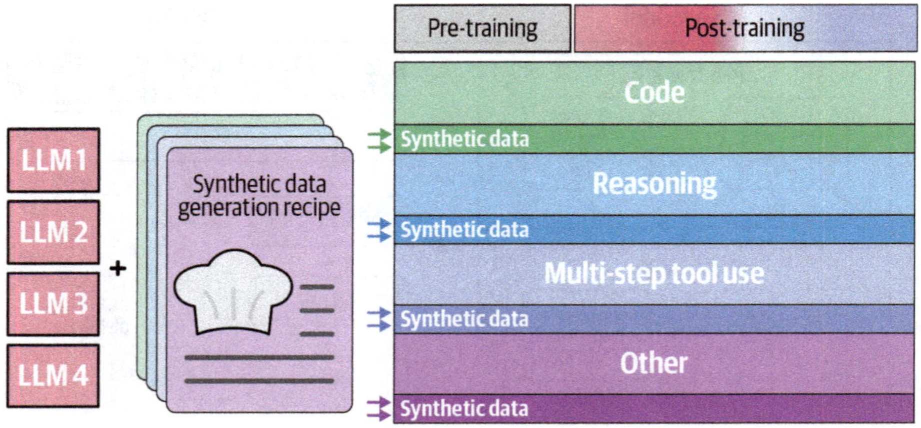

Figure 10-21. A synthetic data generation recipe uses those models to produce data that feeds both pre-training and post-training across categories like code, reasoning, multi-step tool use, and more

If you want a closer look at synthetic data generation, several open source projects share code and details on these pipelines. This includes NVIDIA's Nemotron 3 Nano (*https://oreil.ly/8a0ZJ*) and Nemotron 2 Nano (*https://arxiv.org/abs/2508.14444*), AI21 "Scaling Text-Rich Image Understanding via Code-Guided Synthetic Multimodal Data Generation" (*https://oreil.ly/bq6G8*) (GitHub) (*https://oreil.ly/GNKgy*), and "OmniSQL - Synthesizing High-quality Text-to-SQL Data at Scale" (*https://oreil.ly/NY5rz*) as some examples with scripts.

Summary

In this chapter, we examined how code agents are among the most impactful categories of AI agents. We saw how they extend basic LLM code generation into multi-step problem-solving by writing code, executing it, debugging failures, and iterating until a larger task is completed. We stressed how general users, not just software developers, stand to benefit, starting with a data analysis example in which a non-coder never has to see the code.

We then broke down the core tool and environment design space that lets a code agent act on the world. We saw building blocks such as file manipulation tools, sandboxed code interpreters, and command-line access to dedicated virtual machines, along with the security trade-offs each one carries and the principle of least privilege that helps manage them. We also highlighted computer-use tools that let a model interact with GUIs, code search methods that go beyond text matching, and SQL tools that connect agents to organizational databases.

From there we turned to how software engineering agents manage their context, using prompt caching, repository maps, and context compaction to keep long trajectories affordable. We looked at what changes when the user is a software engineer instead of a non-coder, how benchmarks such as SWE-bench frame the task as resolving a real GitHub issue until its tests pass, and how planning, memory, and task-specific workflows like agentless tackle that task, sometimes without a full agent at all.

We then pulled these threads together and built a coding agent ourselves, extending the `TinyAgent` from earlier chapters with file and code-execution tools and a terminal interface so you could watch its THOUGHT, ACTION, and OBSERVATION loop run in your own environment.

Finally, we went underneath the agent to the model that powers it. We outlined how a coding LLM is built across pre-training, SFT, and RL, why these models need far more code, tool-use, and software engineering data than a generalist, and how reinforcement learning with verifiable rewards turns the chapter's opening observation, that code can be checked by running it, into a training signal. We closed on the synthetic data feedback loop, where each generation of models increasingly trains the next.

Afterword

You bought this book. That was the last transaction in it.

Everything else inside arrived as a gift. The methods, habits of mind, small tricks that keep an agent on task: we invented almost none of them. They came to us hand-to-hand, from people who worked something out and then, instead of keeping it, wrote it down and let it go. Most of them we never paid. Most we could not have.

The botanist Robin Wall Kimmerer draws the distinction we want to leave you with. A transaction is even: you pay, you receive, the books close, and you walk away owing no one. A gift is not even, and it never closes. It asks one thing of whomever receives it: that it keeps moving. Held still, hoarded or buried, it stops being a gift and begins to rot.

This is not an exchange we are closing. It's a gift we're handing on, and it travels with you now, out to people and places you'll never see. You answer for what it does there.

So we hope you build well. We hope what you make outlasts this book and our names, reaches someone we'll never meet, and is good to them. We hope you become one of the people the rest of us are quietly counting on.

And then, the way a gift does, it keeps going.

Index

A

A-MEM, 156-159
  atomicity, 156
  hypertextual notes, 156
  note components, 157
A2A (see Agent2Agent)
abstract syntax tree (AST), 389
action, 42, 234
action sequencing, 232-249
active parameters, 78
agency, 3
  (see also autonomy)
agent card, 310
agent communication languages (ACLs), 307
Agent Hospital, 321
Agent Laboratory, 323-326
  data preparation, 325
  plan formulation, 324
  report refinement, 325
  report writing, 325
  running experiments, 325
agent profiles, 316
agent scaffolding, 25, 267, 397
agent society, 312-321
Agent-Computer Interface, 397
Agent2Agent (A2A), 214, 308-311
  A2A client, 309
  A2A server, 309
AgentBoard, 283
AgentHarm, 288
agentic applications, 17-18
  automation, 18
  coding, 17
  deep research, 18
agentic frameworks, 303-307
agentic harness, 25-26, 41, 266
  (see also eval harness)
  code-based, 25
  hosted, 25
  personal assistant, 25
  terminal-based, 25
  UI-based, 25
agentic memory, 156
agentic RAG, 154-161
  multi-agent RAG, 155
  single-agent RAG, 154
agentic system, 16-19, 241
Agentless, 401-402
  localization, 401
  repair, 402
AgentProcessBench, 283
AI agents, 4-16
  actuators, 4
  agent program, 4
  environment, 4
  sensors, 4
AI co-scientist, 322-323
  evolution agent, 322
  generation agent, 322
  meta-review agent, 322
  proximity agent, 322
  ranking agent, 322
  reflection agent, 322
AI psychology, 313
Aider, 395
ALFWorld, 244
AlphaZero, 93
Anthropic, 13, 297

anthropomorphism, 315
Antigravity, 25
ARC-AGI, 265
Artificial Analysis, 267
arXiv, 15
ASR (automatic speech recognition), 342
AST (abstract syntax tree), 389
ast-grep, 389
attack success rate, 387
attention head, 70
augmented LLM, 13
autocompletion, 397
AutoGen, 306
automated evaluation, 270-281
automatic speech recognition (ASR), 342
autonomy
autoregression, 6
autoregressive models, 33

B

Bag-of-Words, 146
base model, 47
Beam Search, 228
behavior cloning, 244
  (see also supervised fine-tuning (SFT))
benchmark saturation, 267
benchmarks, 262-267
  coding and software engineering, 263
  computer use, 264
  reading scores critically, 266
  real-world task completion, 264
  reasoning and knowledge, 265
  tool use, 264
Best-of-N samples, 106-108
BFCL (Berkeley Function Calling Leaderboard), 264
BLIP-2, 365
bundled resources, 220-221

C

CAMEL, 303
capability, 284
  (see also reliability)
centralized multi-agent system, 299
Chain-of-Continuous-Thought, 128
Chain-of-Draft (CoD), 125
Chain-of-Thought (CoT), 98, 226-228
chat template, 120
  (see also prompt template)
Chatbot Arena, 267
ChatGPT, 7, 35
Chinchilla scaling law, 90
CLAP (Contrastive Language-Audio Pre-training), 344-346
Claude 4.5, 329
Claude Code, 25, 387
Cline, 84
CLIP (Contrastive Language-Image Pre-training), 338-340
CNN (Convolutional Neural Network), 340
CoD (Chain-of-Draft), 125
code agents, 24, 377-409
  for non-coders, 380
  users and builders, 377
Code Information Retrieval Benchmark (CoIR), 389
code interpreter, 383-386
  (see also sandbox)
code LLMs, 410-414
  multi-step data, 411
  software engineering task data, 411
  tool-use data, 411
  unit-test data, 411
code search, 389
code semantic search, 389
code tools, 381-391
  code interpreter, 383-386
  code search, 389
  command-line, 387
  computer use, 388
  file manipulation, 382
  SQL tool, 389-391
code-embedding model, 389
codebook, 341
CodeMonkeys, 396
CODI (Continuous Chain-of-Thought via Self-Distillation), 129
coevolving system, 258
CoIR (Code Information Retrieval Benchmark), 389
cold start problem, 116
command-line tools, 387
communication protocols, 307-311
computer use tools, 388
connectors, 359-371
  advantages and disadvantages, 371
  fusion-based, 361
  projection-based, 360

query-based, 360
context compaction, 396
dynamic section, 396
stable section, 396
static section, 396
context engineering, 11, 161-173
context as the specification, 172
context compression, 169
context ordering, 172
context selection, 167
context tracking and storage, 166
conversation history, 161
for multi-agent systems, 166
past experiences, 161
retrieved information, 161
system prompt, 161
context length, 56
context management, 391-396
context rot, 164
context size, 55
(see also context length)
context window, 139
(see also context length)
Continuous Chain-of-Thought via Self-Distillation (CODI), 129
Contrastive Language-Audio Pre-training (CLAP), 344-346
Contrastive Language-Image Pre-training (CLIP), 338-340
contrastive learning, 340
conversation history, 135
conversation memory, 135-140
Convolutional Neural Network (CNN), 340
cosine similarity, 148
CoT (Chain-of-Thought), 98, 226-228
CrewAI, 306
CRITIC, 253
Cursor, 25, 84, 380

D

data contamination, 266
Daytona, 386
decentralized multi-agent system, 299
decoding strategy, 53
deduplication, 171
Deep Research, 204, 321-326
DeepSeek Sparse Attention (DSA), 72-73
Lightning Indexer, 72
Top-K Selector, 72
DeepSeek-R1, 8, 117-120
DeepSeek-R1-Zero, 114-117, 413
DeepSeek-V3-Base, 114
dense embeddings, 389
dense model, 74
(see also sparse model)
depth sensor data, 358
diminishing returns, 89
Direct Preference Optimization (DPO), 245
direct scoring, 268
distillation, 412
divided space-time attention, 351
docstrings, 179
DPO (Direct Preference Optimization), 245
DSA (see DeepSeek Sparse Attention)
dual-process theory, 84

E

E2B, 386
Ebbinghaus Forgetting Curve, 151
efficient reasoning, 125-127
Chain-of-Draft (CoD), 125
hybrid reasoning, 127
token-budget-aware LLMs, 125
Elo rating system, 93, 270
embedding models, 145
EmbeddingGemma, 147
emergent alignment, 359
emergent specialization, 295
emotional intelligence, 312-315
encoders, 332
(see also encoding modalities)
encoding modalities, 333-359
audio, 340
images, 337
many-modality, 356
text, 334
video, 346
episodic memory, 134
ETO (Exploration-based Trajectory Optimization), 243-245
eval harness, 289
(see also agentic harness)
evaluation, 19, 261-290
automated, 270
human, 268
outcome, 268
preference, 268
rubric-based, 280

trajectory, 282
exact match, 272-274
execution environment, 379
explicit planning, 228-231
Exploration-based Trajectory Optimization (ETO), 243-245

F

federated multi-agent system, 299
feed-forward neural network, 59-61
feedback loop, 224, 234
few-shot learning, 196
(see also in-context learning)
few-shot prompting, 98
Figma, 214
file manipulation tools, 382
FIPA-ACL, 307
FireAct, 242-243
Flamingo, 368-370
Flan, 112
Flan-PaLM, 112-113
Flash Attention, 70
floating point operations per second (FLOPs), 86
forward pass, 54
Frozen in Time, 351
function calling, 183-184
fusion-based connector, 368-370

G

GAIA, 264
gate network, 74
gated cross-attention, 369
GDPval, 264
Gemini 1.5, 163
Gemini 3.0, 329
Gemini CLI, 25
Gemma 3, 36
Gemma 4, 36
Generative Agents, 316-321
GitHub, 25, 214, 263, 395
GitHub Copilot, 25
Gitingest, 395
GLM-5, 412
Google Scholar, 18
GPQA Diamond, 267
GPT-3, 47, 377
GPT-3.5, 7
GPT-4, 242, 314
GPT-J, 201
GPT-OSS, 34
Graph RAG, 152
Grouped-Query Attention (GQA), 70
GRPO (Group Relative Policy Optimization), 50-51, 255
guardrails, 19

H

hallucinations, 19, 146
harbor, 289
harm score, 288
Harmony format, 34
HealthBench, 280
Hermes Agent, 25
heterogeneous agents, 295
hierarchical multi-agent system, 299
Home Assistant, 214
homogeneous agents, 295
HTS-AT (Hierarchical Token Semantic-Audio Transformer), 345
HuBERT, 342
human evaluation, 268-270
human-in-the-loop, 187, 404
Humanity's Last Exam, 265
hybrid reasoning, 127

I

IFEval, 274
illustrated-agents package, 28
ImageBind, 356-359
imitation learning, 244
(see also supervised fine-tuning (SFT))
IMU (Inertial Measurement Unit), 358
in-context learning, 196-197
(see also few-shot prompting)
in-group, 314
Inertial Measurement Unit (IMU), 358
inference engines, 37
information overload, 11
instruction-tuning, 47
(see also supervised fine-tuning (SFT))
Internet of Agents (IoA), 311

J

Janus, 364
JSON Schema, 183
JSON-RPC 2.0 Specification, 218

jsonschema, 188
"Just" CLIP, 352-355

K

Kaplan scaling law, 90
Kimi k1.5, 127
KQML, 307
kv-cache, 56, 69, 391

L

L1, 127
LangGraph, 25, 306
language modeling, 45
language modeling head (LM head), 53
Large Language and Vision Assistant (LLaVA), 363-364
  fine-tuning end-to-end, 363
  pre-training for feature alignment, 363
large language model (LLM), 6, 31-80
The Leaderboard Illusion, 267
learned queries, 366
least-to-most (LtM) prompting, 228-230
  problem reduction, 229
  sequentially solve subquestions, 229
LeetCode, 398
linear projection, 358
Llama 2, 243
Llama 3.1, 413
llama.cpp, 37
  (see also inference engines)
LLaVA (see Large Language and Vision Assistant)
Llava-Chain-of-Thought, 123
LLM (large language model), 6, 31-80
LLM-as-a-judge, 276-280
LM head (language modeling head), 53
LMStudio, 37
load balancing, 76
local minima, 224, 250
long-term memory, 145-161
  (see also short-term memory)
  agentic RAG, 154-161
  Retrieval-Augmented Generation (RAG), 145-151
LoRA (Low-Rank Adaptation), 243
loss masking for retrieved tokens, 205
lost-in-the-middle, 172
Low-Rank Adaptation (LoRA), 243
LtM prompting (see least-to-most prompting)
lucky hit, 255

M

majority voting, 102, 254
Manus, 25
MAS (see multi-agent system)
masked language modeling, 341
Massive Multitask Language Understanding (MMLU), 265
Maximal Marginal Relevance (MMR), 169
  redundancy matrix, 170
  relevance vector, 169
MCoT (Multi-modal Chain-of-Thought), 122
MCP (see Model Context Protocol)
MCP client, 215
MCP flow, 216-218
MCP host, 215
MCP server, 215
  prompts, 215
  resources, 215
memory, 10-11, 131-173
  agentic memory, 156
  conversation memory, 135-140
  episodic memory, 134
  long-term memory, 145-161
  parametric memory, 134
  procedural memory, 134
  semantic memory, 134
  short-term memory, 135-145
  working memory, 133
memory poisoning, 288
memory stream, 317-321
MemoryBank, 151-153
  summaries of past events, 152
  user's portrait, 152
MetaGPT, 305-306
  communication protocol, 305
  iterative programming, 305
  specialization of roles, 305
MHA (Multi-head Attention), 70
mid-training, 412
misuse, 288
mixture of experts (MoE), 61, 73-80
  active parameters, 78
  auxiliary loss, 77
  expert capacity, 76
  experts, 73
  gate network, 74
  Gaussian noise, 77

load balancing, 76
open-weight implementations, 79
router, 73
shared expert, 79
sparse parameters, 78
MLA (see Multi-head Latent Attention)
mle-solver, 325
MLLM (see multi-modal LLM)
MLP (Multi-Layer Perceptron), 360
MMLU (Massive Multitask Language Understanding), 265
MMLU-Pro, 272
MMMU, 265
MMR (see Maximal Marginal Relevance)
Modal, 386
modalities, 330
Model Context Protocol (MCP), 213-218
MCP client, 215
MCP flow, 216-218
MCP host, 215
MCP server, 215
modifying proposal distribution, 109-122
reinforcement learning (RL), 111
supervised fine-tuning (SFT), 111
MoE (see mixture of experts)
Monte Carlo Tree Search, 228
MQA (Multi-query Attention), 71
multi-agent system (MAS), 21, 294-327
advantages, 296
centralized, 299
decentralized, 299
disadvantages, 296
federated, 299
hierarchical, 299
industry examples, 297
patterns, 297
Multi-head Attention (MHA), 70
Multi-head Latent Attention (MLA), 70-71
Latent KV, 70
Latent Q, 70
low-rank joint compression, 70
Multi-Layer Perceptron (MLP), 360
multi-modal agents, 22-23
Multi-modal Chain-of-Thought (MCoT), 122
multi-modal generation, 332
(see also multi-modal understanding)
multi-modal LLM (MLLM), 23, 330-332
connector, 332
encoder, 332
generator, 332
Multi-modal RAG, 152
multi-modal reasoning, 122-124
Llava-Chain-of-Thought, 123
Multi-modal Chain-of-Thought (MCoT), 122
Reason-RFT, 124
multi-modal understanding, 23, 329-375
(see also multi-modal generation)
Multi-query Attention (MQA), 71
multi-turn conversations, 10, 35
(see also single-turn conversations)
mutual information, 367

N

n8n, 307
naive RAG, 153
(see also vanilla RAG)
native reasoning, 121-122
needle-in-a-haystack test (NIAH), 163
Nemotron 3, 78
Nemotron 3 Nano, 414
neural networks, 54
NIAH (needle-in-a-haystack test), 163
non-reasoning LLMs, 84
(see also reasoning LLMs)
North Mini Code, 409
NxM problem, 213

O

O1-Pruner, 127
Ollama, 37
OmniSQL, 414
on-the-fly adaptation, 256
one-shot prompting, 98
Open Interpreter, 386
open-weight models, 79
OpenAI Codex, 17
OpenAI Codex CLI, 25
OpenAI o1, 8
OpenAI-compatible endpoint, 37
OpenClaw, 26, 387
OpenCode, 25
OPT, 367
orchestrated workflows, 16
orchestration, 297-311
orchestrator agent, 166, 297
(see also supervisor agent)
OSWorld, 264

out-group, 314
outcome evaluation, 19, 268-281
(see also trajectory evaluation)

P

pandas, 380
parametric memory, 134
parser, 182
(see also validator)
partial credit, 266
pass@k, 284-285
pass^k, 286
patches, 337
perceiver resampler, 369
Phi-4-multimodal, 364
pip, 219
plan-and-solve prompting, 230
answer extraction, 231
prompting for reasoning generation, 231
planning, 14-15, 224-249, 399-400
planning agent, 400
playgrounds, 8
polars, 380
post-training, 45
power laws, 89
pre-training, 45
preference evaluation, 268
prefix-caching, 56, 391
primacy effect, 172
principle of least privilege, 383
privilege escalation, 387
procedural knowledge, 219
(see also procedural memory)
procedural memory, 134
production-grade frameworks, 306-307
programmatic checks, 274-276
progressive disclosure, 219
Layer 1 (always loaded), 219
Layer 2 (loaded when activated), 219
Layer 3 (loaded when needed), 219
projection-based connector, 362-364
prompt engineering, 98-102
one-shot prompting, 98
zero-shot Chain-of-Thought, 102
prompt injection, 288, 383
prompt template, 37
prompt tuning, 267
prompt-caching, 56, 391
proposal distribution, 95
PubMed, 15
Pydantic, 188
Pydantic AI, 25
pytest, 411

Q

Q-Former, 365-367
image-grounded text generation, 367
image-text contrastive learning, 367
image-text matching, 367
quantization, 70
quantized embeddings, 341
queries, keys, and values, 65
query-based connector, 365-367
Qwen-VL, 367
Qwen2.5, 203
Qwen2.5-Coder, 413
Qwen2.5-Math, 413
Qwen2.5-VL, 364
Qwen3, 127, 206
Qwen3-Coder, 411

R

R-Zero, 256-258
Challenger, 256
composite reward, 257
format reward, 257
repetition penalty, 257
Solver, 256
uncertainty reward, 257
RAG (see Retrieval-Augmented Generation)
re-ranking, 168
Reason and Act (ReAct), 194, 233-249
ACTION, 194, 234
ANSWER, 194
OBSERVATION, 194, 234
THOUGHT, 194, 234
Reason-RFT, 124
discrete-valued reward, 124
function-based reward, 124
mathematical reward, 124
reasoning, 8-9, 83-130
efficient, 125
hybrid, 127
in latent space, 127-130
multi-modal, 122
native, 121
tool-integrated, 201
reasoning in latent space, 127-130

Chain-of-Continuous-Thought, 128
Continuous Chain-of-Thought via Self-Distillation (CODI), 129
reasoning LLMs, 9, 83
(see also non-reasoning LLMs)
reasoning steps, 83
reasoning traces, 96
recency effect, 172
RedCode, 387
reflection, 15, 250-253, 318
Reflexion, 252-253
Actor LLM, 252
Evaluator LLM, 252
Self-Reflection LLM, 252
refusal rate, 288
registry, 179
reinforcement learning (RL), 48-49, 114-120, 201-206, 243-245
for ReAct, 243
for reasoning, 114
for tool learning, 201
Reinforcement Learning from Human Feedback (RLHF), 48
Reinforcement Learning with Verifiable Rewards (RLVR), 49, 411
reliability, 19, 283-287
(see also capability)
Replit, 25
repository map, 395-396
responsible agent development, 18-19
human-in-the-loop, 18
misinformation, 19
retrieval agents, 155
Retrieval-Augmented Generation (RAG), 145-151
agentic RAG, 154-161
Graph RAG, 152
inference, 145
ingestion, 145
Multi-modal RAG, 152
naive RAG, 153
vanilla RAG, 153
reward, 48
accuracy reward, 50
format reward, 50
length reward, 126, 203
reward model (RM), 48, 96-98, 102
Outcome Reward Model (ORM), 96
Process Reward Model (PRM), 96
RISE, 254
RL (see reinforcement learning)
RLHF (Reinforcement Learning from Human Feedback), 48
RLVR (Reinforcement Learning with Verifiable Rewards), 49, 411
RM (see reward model)
Rotary Position Embedding (RoPE), 70
router, 74
rubric-based evaluation, 280-281
RULER, 164

S

s1 paper, 113-114
safety, 19, 288
sampling, 53
sandbox, 383-386
(see also code interpreter)
SandboxEval, 387
scaling laws, 89-93
Chinchilla scaling law, 90
diminishing returns, 89
Kaplan scaling law, 90
log-linear scale, 90
log-log scale, 90
power laws, 89
schema linking, 390
ScholarQABench, 280
search against verifiers, 102-108
Best-of-N samples, 106-108
weighted Best-of-N samples, 108
Search-o1, 159-161
Reason-in-Documents module, 160
Search-R1, 204-205
self-attention, 61-68
attention head, 70
projection matrices, 65
queries, keys, and values, 65
relevance scoring, 66
vanilla attention, 68
self-consistency, 104-105, 228
self-experience, 254
self-improvement, 254-259
self-play, 254
Self-Refine, 250-251
semantic layer, 390
semantic memory, 134
Semantic Scholar, 15
serial-position effect, 172

SFT (see supervised fine-tuning)
short-term memory, 135-145
  (see also long-term memory)
  trimming, 140-142
SimClass, 321
simulations, 315-321
single-agent system, 294
single-turn conversations, 10
  (see also multi-turn conversations)
SKILL.md, 219
Skills, 219-221
Smallville, 321
Smolagents, 25
social identity, 314-315
social identity bias, 314
softmax, 67
software engineering agents, 397-400
software engineering skills, 398
SOP (standard operating procedure), 305
space attention, 350
spaced repetition, 151
sparse model, 74
  (see also dense model)
sparse parameters, 78
special tokens, 51, 113
spectrogram, 342
SQL tool, 389-391
standard operating procedure (SOP), 305
stateless, 10, 131
static workflow, 400
subagents, 299-302
subtasks, 225
summarization, 142-145
supervised fine-tuning (SFT), 47, 111-114, 197-201, 242-243
  for ReAct, 242
  for reasoning, 111
  for tool learning, 197
supervisor agent, 21, 297
SWE Atlas, 282
SWE-agent, 397
SWE-bench, 263, 399
SWE-bench Verified, 262
synthetic data, 118
synthetic data feedback loop, 413-414
System 1 thinking, 84
  (see also System 2 thinking)
System 2 thinking, 84
  (see also System 1 thinking)
system prompt, 34

T

T-Eval, 283
task decomposition, 14, 225-231
τ-bench, 274
temperature, 53, 102
Terminal-Bench, 263
test-time compute, 87
  (see also train-time compute)
  modifying proposal distribution, 95
  search against verifiers, 94
Test-Time Reinforcement Learning (TTRL), 254-256
test-time training, 259
text encoder, 335
Theory of Mind (ToM), 313-314
thermal data, 358
thinking tokens, 88
time attention, 350
TimeSformer, 350-351
TinyAgent, 25-28
  agent evaluator, 270
  autonomy loop, 237-249
  code tools, 402-409
  image understanding, 373-375
  LLM integration, 36-45
  memory module, 136
  multi-agent orchestration, 300-302
  native tool calling, 209-212
  tool integration, 191-195
TIR (Tool-Integrated Reasoning), 201
Together Code Sandbox, 386
token probabilities, 95
tokenizer, 51
tokens, 6, 33
ToM (Theory of Mind), 313-314
tool calling, 186-188
tool creation, 179-180
tool definition, 180-184
  best practices, 184
  Learning, 181
  Prompting, 181
tool learning, 195-212
tool output processing, 188-190
tool role, 189
tool selection, 185
tool usage, 12-13, 177-195
Tool-Integrated Reasoning (TIR), 201

Toolformer, 198-201
ToolRL, 202-203
  Correctness reward, 202
  Format reward, 203
tools, 175
  code tools, 381-391
toolsets, 21
TRACE, 283
train-time compute, 86
  (see also test-time compute)
  dataset size, 86
  model size, 86
train-time scaling, 7
  (see also test-time compute)
trajectory, 42, 240, 282
trajectory evaluation, 19, 282-283
  (see also outcome evaluation)
Transformer architecture, 51-63
  forward pass, 54
  language modeling head (LM head), 53
  Transformer blocks, 54-58
Transformer blocks, 54-58
Transformer decoder, 51
Transformer encoder, 337
Tree of Thoughts, 228
tree search, 102
tribal knowledge, 391
trimming, 140-142
TTRL (Test-Time Reinforcement Learning), 254-256
tubelet embeddings, 348

U

uniform frame sampling, 348
unit tests, 263, 402
uv, 219

V

v0, 25
validator, 182
  (see also parser)
vanilla RAG, 153
  (see also naive RAG)
vector databases, 145
verifiability, 377
verifiers, 49, 102
vibe coders, 378
vibe coding, 24
Vicuna, 363
Video Vision Transformer (ViViT), 348-350
VideoBERT, 351
VideoMae, 351
VideoMamba, 354
vision tokens, 372
Vision-Transformer (ViT), 337-338
ViViT (Video Vision Transformer), 348-350
vocabulary, 52

W

wav2vec 2.0, 340-342
  masked language modeling, 341
  quantized embeddings, 341
WebArena, 264
Whisper, 342-344
win rates, 269
Windsurf, 25
working memory, 133
world models, 315

Y

YAML, 220

Z

zero-shot Chain-of-Thought, 102
zero-shot prompting, 101
Zettelkasten, 156

About the Authors

Maarten Grootendorst is a member of technical staff at Google DeepMind. He holds master's degrees in organizational psychology, clinical psychology, and data science, which he leverages to communicate complex machine learning concepts to a wide audience. With his popular blogs (*https://newsletter.maartengrootendorst.com*), he has reached millions of readers by explaining the fundamentals of artificial intelligence, often from a psychological point of view. He is the author and maintainer of several open source packages that rely on the strength of large language models, such as BERTopic, PolyFuzz, and KeyBERT. His packages are downloaded millions of times and used by data professionals and organizations worldwide.

Jay Alammar is director and engineering fellow at Cohere (pioneering provider of secure AI for the enterprise). In this role, he conducts machine learning research improving the agentic and tool use abilities of large language models. Through his popular AI/ML blog (*https://jalammar.github.io*) and substack (*https://newsletter.languagemodels.co*), Jay has helped millions of researchers and engineers visually understand, use, and build machine learning tools, concepts, and models. Jay is also a co-creator of popular machine learning and natural language processing courses on Deeplearning.ai and Udacity.

Colophon

The animal on the cover of *An Illustrated Guide to AI Agents* is a common bottlenose dolphin (*Tursiops truncatus*), a charismatic, adaptable mammal found globally throughout temperate and tropical waters. Their range includes shallow bays and estuaries as well as deep open oceans. Coastal populations tend to be smaller and lighter, while offshore individuals are more robust. On average, adults span from 6 to 13 feet long and weigh between 300 and 1,400 pounds.

Bottlenose dolphins eat a variety of fish, squid, and crustaceans to sustain their high energy demands. They are highly social creatures, living in fluid, ever-changing groups called *pods* of between 2 and 15 individuals. Within their pods, dolphins display complex cooperative behaviors, such as working together to herd or trap schools of fish. They are playful and communicate with whistles, clicks, echolocation, and body language.

The average lifespan of bottlenose dolphins is 40 to 60 years. The IUCN Red List of Threatened Species last assessed common bottlenose dolphins in 2018 and lists them as Least Concern. Many of the animals on O'Reilly covers are endangered; all of them are important to the world.

The cover illustration is by José Marzan Jr., based on an original illustration for O'Reilly. The series design is by Edie Freedman, Ellie Volckhausen, and Karen Montgomery. The cover fonts are Gilroy Semibold and Guardian Sans. The text font is Adobe Minion Pro; the heading font is Adobe Myriad Condensed; and the code font is Dalton Maag's Ubuntu Mono.

www.ingramcontent.com/pod-product-compliance
Lightning Source LLC
Chambersburg PA
CBHW061436080926
51108CB00041B/1082
* 9 7 9 8 3 4 1 6 6 2 6 9 8 *